Trade Smart: The Essential Guide to Markets, Analyses & Strategies

This book is for educational purposes only and does not constitute financial or investment advice. Always do your own research or consult a licensed advisor.

Publication Year: 2025

Cover design by Andy Hai Dinh

TABLE OF CONTENTS

Dedication 9

Foreword 10

SECTION 1: TRADING BASICS 12

Chapter 1: Trading Fundamentals 13

Lesson 1: What Is Trading? 14

Lesson 2: Trading vs Investing 21

Lesson 3: Trading Fundamentals Challenge 27

Chapter 2: How Trading Works 35

Lesson 1: How Trades Execute 36

Lesson 2: Trader's Dictionary 43

QUIZ: Trading Practice 53

Chapter 3: How To Trade 57

Lesson 1: Who Trades and Why 58

QUIZ: Trading Mechanics 66

Lesson 2: How To Make Significant Gains 71

SECTION 2: FINANCIAL MARKETS 80

Chapter 1: Financial Market Basics 81

Lesson 1: How Markets Work 82

Lesson 2: Centralized vs Decentralized 85

Chapter 2: Main Market Types 90

Lesson 1: Stock Market 91

Lesson 2: What Moves The Stock Market? 96

QUIZE: Stock Market 104

Lesson 3: Forex Market	108
Lesson 4: Commodity Market	113
Lesson 5: Cryptocurrency Market	119
Lesson 6: Meet The Players	124
QUIZ: Other Financial Markets	127
Chapter 3: Financial Instruments	132
Lesson 1: Instruments Traded in Financial Markets	133
QUIZ: Financial Instruments	136
Lesson 2: Market Trends and Cycles	140
QUIZ: Trends and Cycles	154
Lesson 3: Contracts for Difference	158
SECTION 3: FOREX TRADING	164
Chapter 1: Forex Fundamentals	165
Lesson 1: What Is Forex Trading?	166
Lesson 2: How The Forex Market Works	174
Lesson 3: Forex Brokers	184
QUIZ: Forex Fundamentals	191
Chapter 2: Forex Trading Fundamentals	195
Lesson 1: Currency Pairs	196
Lesson 2: Currency Correlations	202
Lesson 3: Pips and Lot Sizes	212
QUIZ: Forex Trading Fundamentals	221
Lesson 4: The Currency Game	225
Chapter 3: Technical Analysis	232
Lesson 1: Types of Analysis	233
Lesson 2: The Core Principles	237

Lesson 3: Trading Charts Types 242

QUIZ: Charts 252

Lesson 4: Candlestick Charts 101 256

QUIZ: Candlestick Charts 269

SECTION 4: CANDLESTICK PATTERNS, MARKET TRENDS, AND SUPPORT & RESISTANCE 273

Chapter 1: Candlestick Patterns 274

Lesson 1: Hammer and Shooting Star 275

Lesson 2: Engulfing Patterns 284

Lesson 3: Doji Patterns 294

QUIZ: Make A Decision 305

Chapter 2: Market Trends and Support & Resistance 309

Lesson 1: Identifying Trends 310

Lesson 2: Support and Resistance 324

Lesson 3: Market Ranges vs Trends 339

SECTION 5: INDICATORS 346

Chapter 1: Technical Indicators 347

Lesson 1: What Are Technical Indicators? 348

Lesson 2: Leading Indicators 355

Lesson 3: Practice Leading Indicators 370

Lesson 4: Lagging Indicators 378

Lesson 5: Practice Lagging Indicators 390

QUIZ: Indicators 397

Chapter 2: Moving Averages 401

Lesson 1: Simple Moving Averages 402

Lesson 2: Exponential Moving Average 411

Lesson 3: Crossover Strategies	419
QUIZ: Moving Averages	430
Chapter 3: RSI Insights	434
Lesson 1: RSI Basics	435
Lesson 2: Overbought and Oversold Conditions	439
Lesson 3: RSI Divergence	447
QUIZ: RSI Insights	457
Chapter 4: Pattern Recognition	461
Lesson 1: Why Price Action Matters	462
Lesson 2: Consolidation Patterns	469
Lesson 3: Continuation and Reversal Patterns	487
Lesson 4: Support and Resistance with MAs	500
QUIZ: Pattern Recognition	507
Chapter 5: MACD Mastery	511
Lesson 1: MACD Basics	512
Lesson 2: MACD Histogram & Momentum	521
Lesson 3: MACD Divergence Use	531
QUIZ: MACD Mastery	543
Chapter 6: Bollinger Band Tactic	547
Lesson 1: Bollinger Band Structure	548
Lesson 2: Squeeze Patterns & Breakouts	558
Lesson 3: Using Bollinger Bands in Different Markets	568
QUIZ: Bollinger Band Tactic	582
Chapter 7: Fibonacci Scenarios	586
Lesson 1: Key Fibonacci Levels	587
Lesson 2: Retracement vs Extension	596

Lesson 3: Confluence with Indicators	607
QUIZ: Fibonacci Scenarios	617
Chapter 8: Divergence In Action	621
Lesson 1: Divergence As A Strategic Signal	622
Lesson 2: Regular vs Hidden Divergence Review	631
Lesson 3: Risk Management with Divergence	643
QUIZ: Divergence In Action	656
SECTION 6: FUNDAMENTAL ANALYSIS	660
Chapter 1: Fundamental Analysis Basics	661
Lesson 1: Why Look Beyond Charts	662
Lesson 2: Principles of Fundamental Analysis	669
Lesson 3: Forces That Move Markets	677
QUIZ: Fundamental Analysis Basics	685
Chapter 2: Economic Indicators	689
Lesson 1: Employment and Growth Data	690
Lesson 2: Inflation and Prices	697
Lesson 3: Business and Trade Health	705
QUIZ: Economic Indicators	713
Lesson 4: Reading and Reacting to Scheduled Events	717
Lesson 5: Context Is King	723
SECTION 7: TRADING STRATEGY	732
Chapter 1: Building and Testing Your Trading Strategy	733
Lesson 1: How To Build A Strategy	734
Lesson 2: Entry and Exit Rules	742
Lesson 3: Strategy Optimization	756
Lesson 4: Backtesting	763

Lesson 5: Forward Testing 771
Lesson 6: Documenting Strategy Performance 777
QUIZ: Building and Testing Your Trading Strategy 782
Chapter 2: Mastering Risk Management 786
Lesson 1: Risk Management Fundamentals 787
Lesson 2: Position Sizing 794
Lesson 3: Stop-loss Orders 801
Lesson 4: Drawdown Management 809
Lesson 5: Risk Management Formulas 817
QUIZ: Mastering Risk Management 823
Chapter 3: Additional Must-Know Trading Insights 827
Lesson 1: Understanding Slippage 828
Lesson 2: Market Orders vs. Limit Orders 833
Lesson 3: Improving Execution Speed 841
Lesson 4: Hands-on Execution Analysis 845
Afterword 850
OTHER BOOKS BY THIS AUTHOR 852

Dedication

To my children, Audrey An H. Dinh and Neal Phong V. Dinh,

Your presence brings purpose to my work and meaning to my journey.

May this book serve as a lasting testament to the values of discipline, knowledge, and perseverance—principles I hope will guide you in all that you pursue.

Andy Hai Dinh

Foreword

When I first began my trading journey, I made every mistake in the book—and then some. I chased trends, ignored risk management, and believed success could come quickly with just a little luck. It didn't. What eventually changed everything for me wasn't just learning how to read charts or analyze news—it was developing the discipline to treat trading like a craft, not a gamble.

Trade Smart is the book I wish I had when I started. The principles you will learn in this book can be applied in trading stocks, crypto, forex, or options and any market.

This guide is the result of years of experience, trial and error, late-night learning, and hard-won lessons. I wrote it to be clear, practical, and actionable—something you can turn to whether you're just starting out or looking to level up your skills. Every section is designed to build a solid foundation and help you think critically, make informed decisions, and develop strategies that work for you.

Trading can be exciting, frustrating, and incredibly rewarding—but only if you approach it with the right mindset and tools. My hope is that this book becomes a steady companion for you on that path. Let it be your starting point, your reference guide, and your reminder that smart trading isn't about knowing everything—it's about learning continuously and trading with purpose.

Thank you for trusting me to be part of your journey.

— Andy Hai Dinh
08/2025

SECTION 1: TRADING BASICS

Chapter 1: Trading Fundamentals

Lesson 1: What Is Trading?

Your first day in trading!

Hey, I'm Andy. In this section of the book, I'll help you master the basics, understand the markets, and start thinking like a trader.

Let's start with the basics:

- Trading means **buying** and **selling**.
- You buy when the price is low.
- You sell when the price is high.

That's how you make a profit.

To do this, traders analyze charts, trends, and news to decide when to act. It's part logic, part timing, and all about managing risk. When they see a good opportunity, they act - quickly and decisively.

Let's try it out!

Here's a tech company stock trading at $150. Their new product launch is today and looks promising. Let's buy this stock and see what happens.

Take your profit

Excellent! You bought at $150. Two hours later, the price is $170. You have a $20 profit per share, but it's only on paper until you sell.

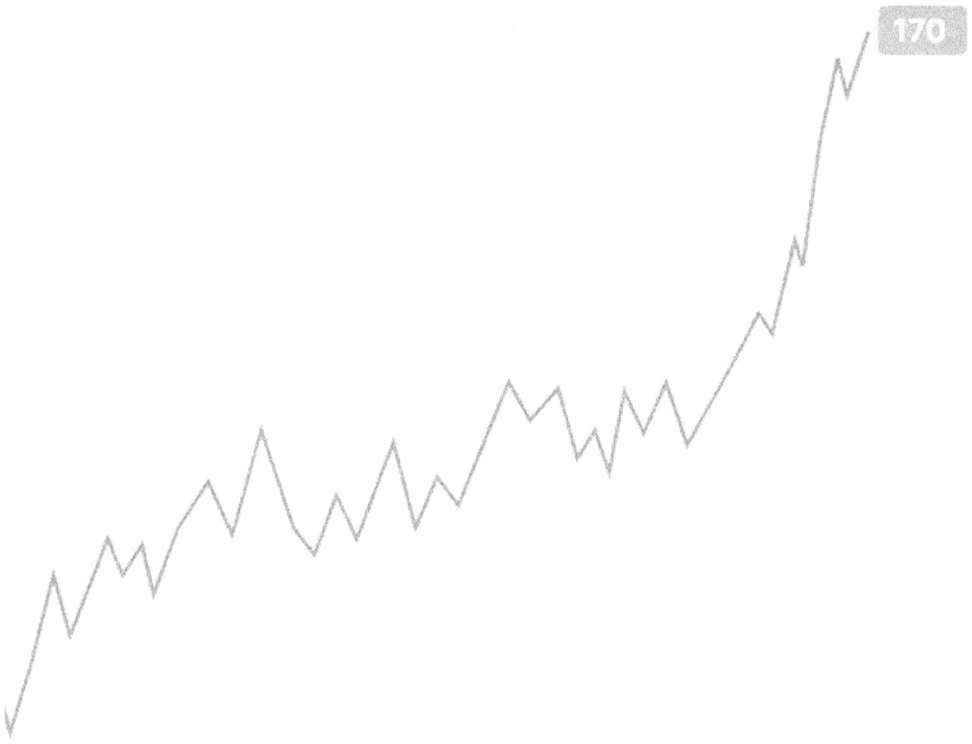

Well done! You bought at $150 and sold at $170, making a $20 profit. This is basic trading: buy low, sell high. You've completed your first successful trade.

Another opportunity

Here's an energy company stock at $50. Industry research suggests prices could rise to $75 in the coming months. Let's buy it.

New action unleashed

The stock fell to $45 but recovered slightly to $48. Many traders would sell for a small loss, but my analysts tell me that the long-term outlook remains positive. So let’s hold our position.

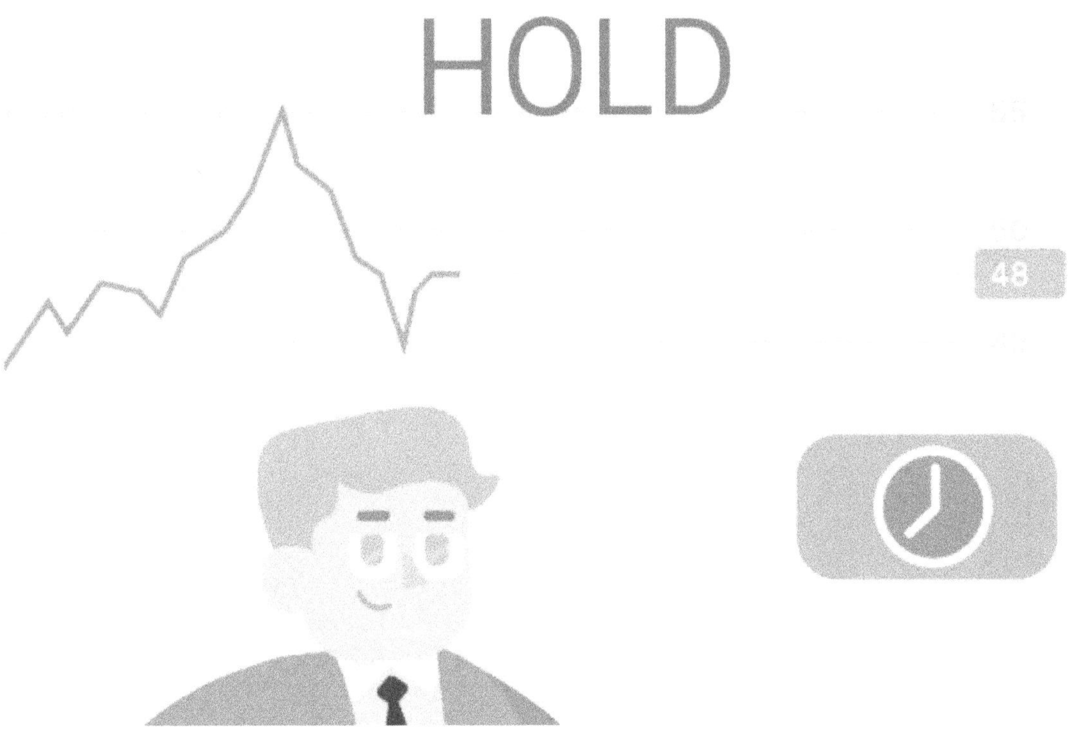

Your patience paid off! By holding through the temporary drop, the stock eventually reached $75, turning a potential loss into a $25 profit per share. This demonstrates why understanding what drives prices is essential.

Now you understand the three basic actions:

- **Buy** when research suggests prices will rise
- **Sell** to take profits or prevent losses
- **Hold** when your analysis supports longer-term growth despite short-term setbacks.

Making the right trading decisions requires knowledge about companies, markets, and economic trends. Without this knowledge, trading becomes a guessing game, and guessing rarely leads to consistent profits.

How much money do I need?

Let's move on to the most popular question. Before risking real capital, it's important to consider how you can build skills and gain experience first. How much money do you need to start learning to trade?

The answer is: Zero. Many beginners lose money because they trade with real funds before mastering the basics. There are several trading simulator apps out there where you can practice all trading decisions with virtual money.

Great job! Now, let's recap what you've learned:

- **Buy** when you think prices will rise
- **Sell** to take profits or prevent losses
- **Hold** when you believe in longer-term growth

Keep going - we're just getting started!

Lesson 2: Trading vs Investing

Trading vs investing: what's the difference?

Many confuse trading with investing. Trading is quick and active; investing is patient and steady. By the end of this course, you'll know the difference - and why it matters.

Meet Alex. He wants a stable income in retirement, so he decides to plant an apple orchard. It's not a quick process, but once the trees mature, they'll provide fruit year after year with little effort.

Meanwhile, Jane has different priorities. She needs money now and isn't willing to wait years for an orchard to grow. Instead, she plants flowers that bloom quickly and can
be sold immediately.

The apple farmer must wait years for trees to mature, but once they do, they produce fruit every season with minimal effort. This represents investing - patience leads to long-term, steady returns.

The flower grower makes money right away - within weeks of planting. But unlike the orchard, which produces apples year after year, the flower seller must constantly replant to keep earning.

Some days, the flower market is booming, and profits are high. On other days, there are too many sellers or too few buyers, resulting in losses. This represents the volatility of trading.

Both the apple farmer and flower seller deal with the concept of liquidity - how easily their assets can be bought or sold. The flower seller can quickly convert flowers to cash while selling an orchard takes time.

Let's compare investing (apple farming) and trading (flower selling):

1. Investing requires patience - the biggest returns may come after years rather than weeks. Compounding works like nature - profits are reinvested as the orchard grows larger.

2. Investors experience less daily stress - short-term price fluctuations don't matter much because the focus is on long-term growth. Even during a difficult season, a well-managed investment portfolio continues to grow.

3. Trading, like the flower business, offers the potential for fast profits but requires constant effort. Timing matters - traders need to buy and sell at the right moments, like selling flowers when demand is high.

4. Trading typically involves higher risk and higher potential reward than investing. Some trades produce substantial profits, while others result in losses. Successful traders must watch the market regularly to find opportunities.

Different ways to sell flowers

Not all florists sell their flowers the same way. Some buy fresh flowers every morning and sell everything by evening to avoid spoilage. Others are willing to store flowers overnight, hoping for better prices the next day. But waiting too long can be risky - flowers don't stay fresh forever! What might cause a florist to sell all their flowers before the day ends?

Answer: Flowers wilt quickly, and unsold stock loses value. A florist who sells all their flowers before the day ends avoids the risk of that inventory losing value overnight. This is similar to day trading, where traders close all their positions before the market closes to avoid overnight price swings. Some traders, like some florists, may choose to hold longer, but it depends on their strategy and risk tolerance.

Unlike flowers, stocks don't spoil overnight - but that doesn't mean traders always hold onto them. Some traders prefer to sell quickly to avoid unpredictable price swings, while others are willing to wait for the right opportunity, even if it means holding for days, weeks, or months. Just like in the flower business, different approaches exist depending on risk tolerance, time commitment, and strategy.

For example, day trading involves buying and selling within the same day, never holding positions overnight. This highly active style requires constant market attention and quick decision-making, as well as greater skill.

Position trading, the closest style to investing, involves holding positions for months while still actively monitoring them. This approach focuses on larger market trends rather than short-term fluctuations.

Swing trading sits between day trading and position trading as far as the expected time horizon of a position. Swing traders hold stocks for several days or weeks, aiming to profit from short- to medium-term price movements. They don't need to monitor the market all day but still require active analysis to time their trades.

Which style suits you depends on your personality, time commitment, and risk tolerance. Day trading requires constant attention, while swing and position trading allow more flexibility but still need regular monitoring.

Now, let's recap what we've learned:

- Trading vs Investing: Trading seeks short-term profits through timing; investing builds wealth over time through compounding.
- Liquidity: Important for both, but crucial for traders who need to enter and exit a market quickly.
- Trading Styles: Day trading (intraday), swing trading (days/ weeks), and position trading (months).
- Each style requires different time commitments, risk management, and personality traits.

Lesson 3: Trading Fundamentals Challenge

Your first challenge!

Hey there! I'm Andy, and this is Alex. Today, we're going to follow Alex through his first week in the markets.

Help Alex!

Your challenge is to spot good decisions from bad ones and help him improve! Ready to begin the journey?

Day 1: When to act?

Alex has been studying the basics: buy when prices are expected to rise, sell to secure profits or avoid losses, and hold when further growth is likely.

You always sell if a stock rises two days in a row. True or False?

Answer: False. A price rise doesn't always mean it's time to sell. Alex needs to know "why" the price is rising and whether it fits his plan. Sometimes it's better to hold longer; other times, quick selling makes sense. Good trading means making informed choices.

Day 2: Acting on impulse

Excited by yesterday's lessons, Alex spots XYZ stock rising for 3 straight days. Feeling the fear of missing out, he immediately buys shares without understanding the reason behind the move or setting a clear exit plan.

What is Alex missing?

Trading needs a clear plan. Correct the order of the steps which Alex should have done before buying. A good trader knows both when to enter AND exit. Which steps help protect your money and give you clear goals?

- Research why the price is moving
- Set a stop-loss point
- Define when to take profits

- Set guidelines to manage risk

Answer:

- Research why the price is moving
- Set guidelines to manage risk
- Define when to take profits
- Set a stop-loss point

Great job! Alex was just gambling, not trading strategically. He chased the price movement without any real plan. Smart traders know exactly:

- Why they're **entering a trade**
- When they'll **exit for profit**
- Where they'll **cut losses if wrong**
- How much they'll **risk on the trade**

Remember: Trading without a plan is just hoping for luck.

Day 3: Learning about liquidity

Having learned the importance of research, Alex now wants to buy 1,000 shares of a promising small tech company. When he places the order, the stock price jumps up before his purchase completes. He ends up paying much more than expected.

Liquidity problem

When there aren't enough buyers or sellers at the current price, large orders impact the stock price. Match each stock type with how the price reacts to a large order. Liquidity is how easily you can buy or sell without moving the price. Think about which markets have more buyers and sellers ready to trade.

- Small tech stock - Price moves moderately
- Mid-cap stock - Price jumps
- High-volume stock - Price barely moves

Answer:

- Small tech stock - Price jumps
- Mid-cap stock - Price moves moderately
- High-volume stock - Price barely moves

That's right! Alex ran into a liquidity problem. Large orders push prices up in stocks with few traders because there aren't enough sellers at each price level.

High liquidity = many buyers and sellers = little price impact
Low liquidity = few buyers and sellers = big price impact

This is why traders check volume and spread before placing orders, especially in smaller stocks.

Day 4: Finding a trading style

As Alex gains experience, he observes that ABC stock usually rises for 2-3 days after good earnings reports before dropping. He plans to buy right after positive earnings and sell within 48 hours.

Pick the right trading style

Based on this strategy, pick the THREE characteristics that match Alex's approach. Think about how long Alex plans to hold. Longer than a day trader, but shorter than someone following big trends.

- Trades within a day
- Focuses on fundamentals

- Holds for a few days
- Catches short moves
- Follows patterns
- Targets long trends

Answer:

- Holds for a few days
- Catches short moves
- Follows patterns

Great job! Alex is using swing trading:

- Timeframe: Holds positions for a few days (not same-day like day traders
- Setup: Trades a specific pattern (earnings announcement)
- Goal: Capture short price movements (not long-term trends)

Swing trading sits between day trading (hours) and position trading (months). It's perfect for traders who can't watch markets all day but want more action than long-term investing.

Day 5: Managing risk

After almost a week of learning, Alex decides to protect his capital by splitting money between stocks, bonds, and commodities instead of putting everything into one promising tech stock.

Complete the comparison

Finish each sentence to compare concentrated vs. diversified approaches correctly. Think about what happens if one investment performs badly. How does this affect each approach?

- Concentrated portfolios - Have more stable performance
- Diversification - Can have bigger gains or losses
- Diversified portfolios - Protect against single asset crashes

Answer:

- Concentrated portfolios - Can have bigger gains or losses
- Diversification - Protect against single asset crashes
- Diversified portfolios - Have more stable performance

You got it! Diversification is all about managing risk:

- Safety: If one investment crashes, others may still perform well
- Stability: Different assets often move in different directions
- Protection: Your portfolio won't depend on any single company or sector

Great job! You've helped Alex through his first week in the markets and used key concepts:

- Trade with clear reasons
- Plan entry. and exit points
- Check liquidity before you act
- Split orders for better fills
- Match strategy to your timeframe
- Diversify to control risk

These basics are the bedrock for everything ahead. See you next lesson!

Chapter 2: How Trading Works

Lesson 1: How Trades Execute

Behind the scenes of trading

Now that you understand what trading is, let's peek behind the curtain. Today, we visit a virtual trading floor to see how trades happen!

We step inside a bustling digital marketplace. See all these flashing numbers? This is where buyers and sellers meet. But they don't just randomly find each other - there's a system.

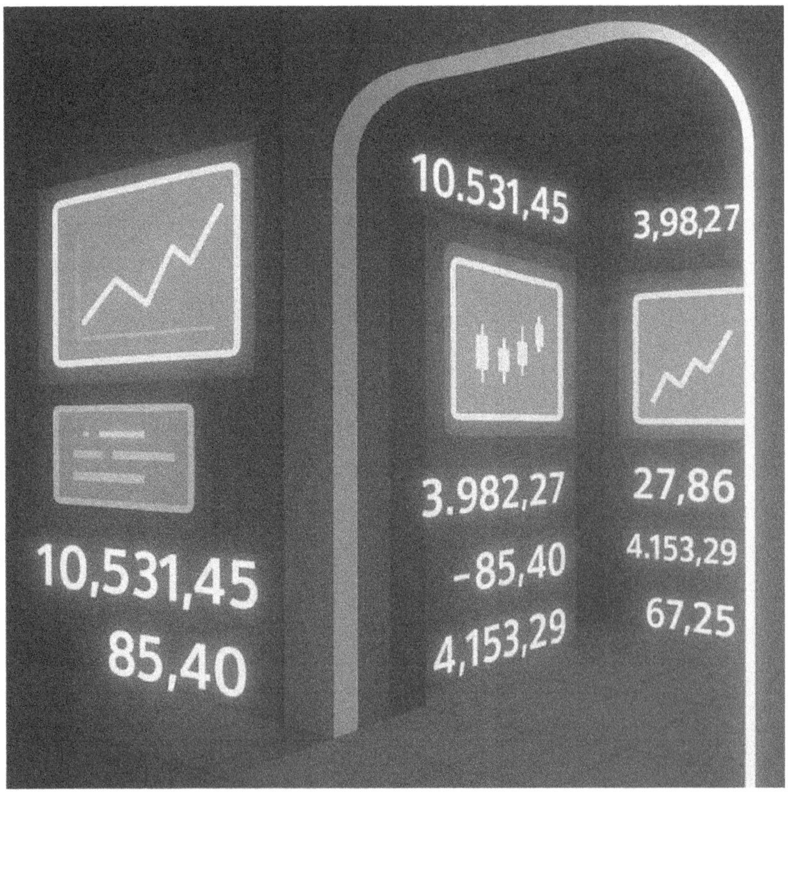

This is an order book - it's the heart of trading. When you place an order, it gets listed here. Look at the two sides - green for buyers and red for sellers.

0.85	61850.12	0.92	61852.25
1.20	61849.75	1.10	61853.10
0.45	61848.90	0.78	61854.32
2.10	61847.55	2.00	61855.75
0.95	61845.30	0.60	61858.90
3.5	61843.5	4.00	61860.15

The buy orders are called "bids" - prices people are willing to pay. The sell orders are "asks" - prices at which people are willing to sell. Notice how they're arranged by price.

This is the maximum someone will pay right now: $25.50. And this is the minimum someone will sell for: $25.55.

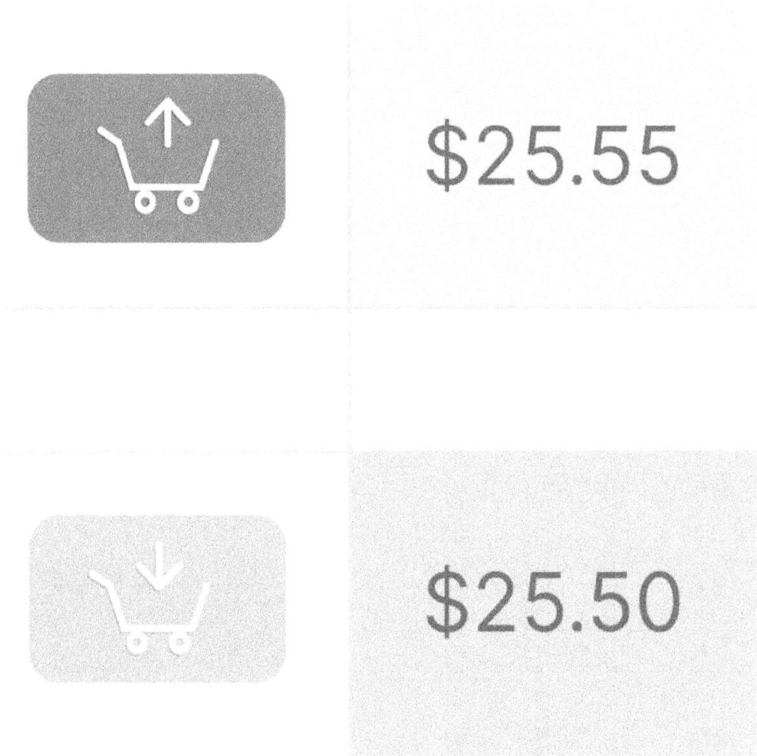

The gap between them - 5 cents - is called the "spread". It's like a bridge between buyers and sellers. A smaller spread usually means there's more activity and, therefore, higher liquidity.

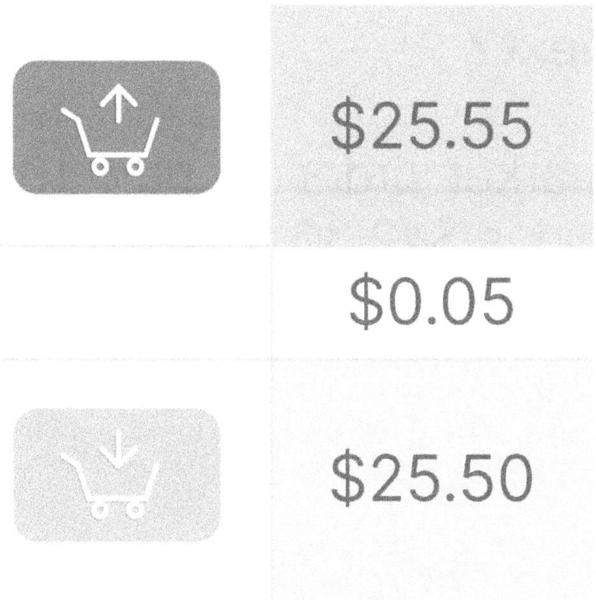

Look at this spread—it's $2 wide!
That means buyers and sellers are far apart, and there's less trading activity. This is a sign of low liquidity, which can make it harder to enter or exit trades.

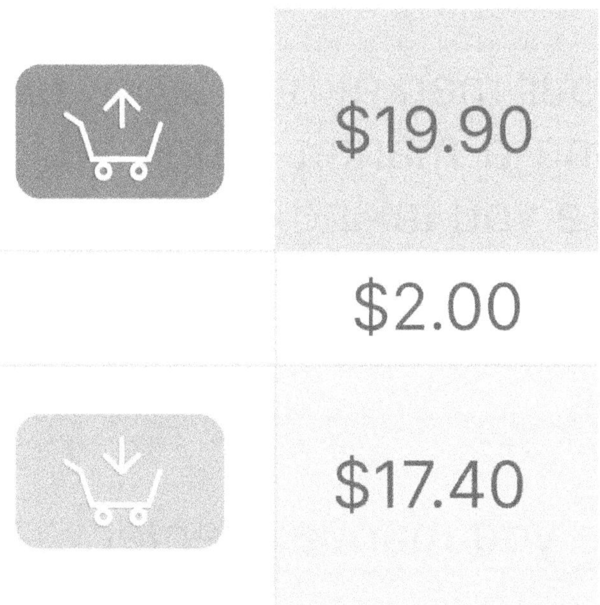

What happens next?

If you place a market order to buy 100 shares, and the highest bid is $42.30 while the lowest ask is $42.35, what price will you pay?

Shares	Price
100	$42.35
100	$42.34
100	$42.33
100	$42.32
100	$42.30

What price will your market buy order execute at? As a buyer placing a market order, which side of the order book are you taking from?

- $42.30
- Exactly $42.33
- $42.35
- Whatever price you manually enter

Answer: You'll pay $42.35 - the lowest ask price. That's the best price any seller is currently offering. Your order removes those shares from the ask side of the order book.

But what if you want to buy more shares than are available at that price? Watch what happens when someone tries to buy 1,000 shares when only 200 are available at the best price.

We watch as the large order eats through multiple price levels - first taking 200 shares at $42.35, then 300 at $42.37, and finally 500 at $42.40. This is called "walking the book".

The larger your order, the more you might move the price. It's like jumping into a small pond versus a large lake. In the pond, you make bigger waves that change the water level.

That's why big traders split their orders into smaller pieces. They're trying not to make waves that move prices against them. It's like entering the pond slowly.

As we leave the trading floor, let's recap what we learned:

- Trading happens through an order book matching buyers and sellers.
- The spread between bid and ask prices shows an asset's liquidity.
- Market orders execute immediately at the best available price, while large orders may need to "walk the book" across multiple price levels.

Lesson 2: Trader's Dictionary

The language of trading

You're making amazing progress! You've seen how trading works. But behind every trade is a world of terms - time to learn the ones that matter.

Every profession has its special language, and trading is no exception. Understanding these terms isn't just about sounding knowledgeable - it's about making better decisions and communicating effectively in the market.

Let's start with two fundamental positions you can take in the market. When you think a stock price will rise, you go "long." When you think it will fall, you go "short."

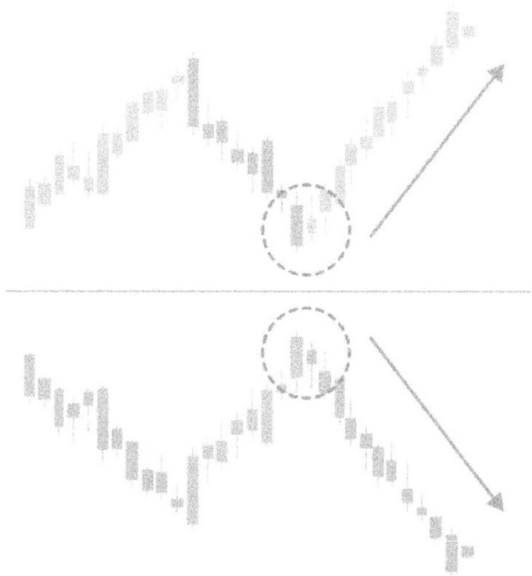

Going long is straightforward - you buy at a lower price and aim to sell at a higher price. For example, buying a stock at $10 with the goal of selling it at $20 for a profit.

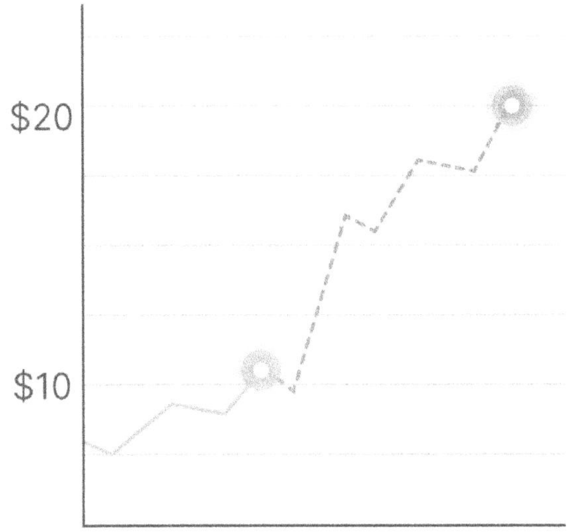

Going short is more interesting. You borrow shares from your broker, sell them at the current price, and hope to buy them back later at a lower price before returning them.

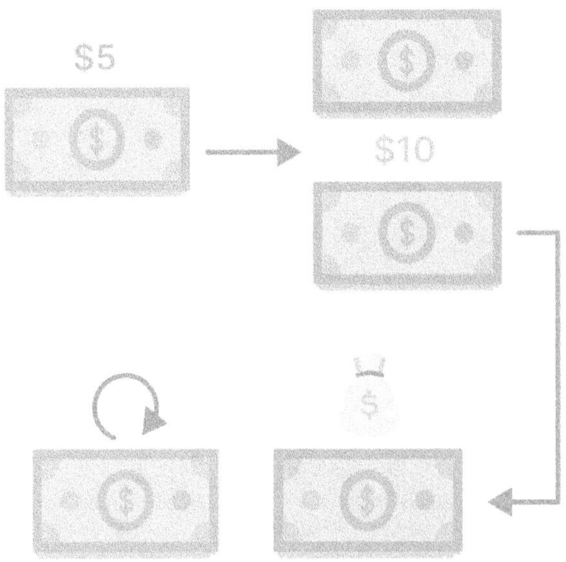

Remember our order book from the last lesson? Short-selling adds another dimension to it. When you short-sell, you're selling first and buying later - the reverse of a long position.

Short-selling steps

Short-selling follows a structured process. Order the steps into the correct sequence. Think about selling high first, then buying low later to make a profit.

- Wait for the stock price to drop
- Sell borrowed shares at the current market price
- Return the borrowed shares and keep the profit
- Buy back the shares at a lower price

Answer:

- Sell borrowed shares at the current market price
- Wait for the stock price to drop
- Buy back the shares at a lower price
- Return the borrowed shares and keep the profit

Now, let's meet two important characters in the market: bulls and bears. Bulls believe prices will rise, while bears expect them to fall.

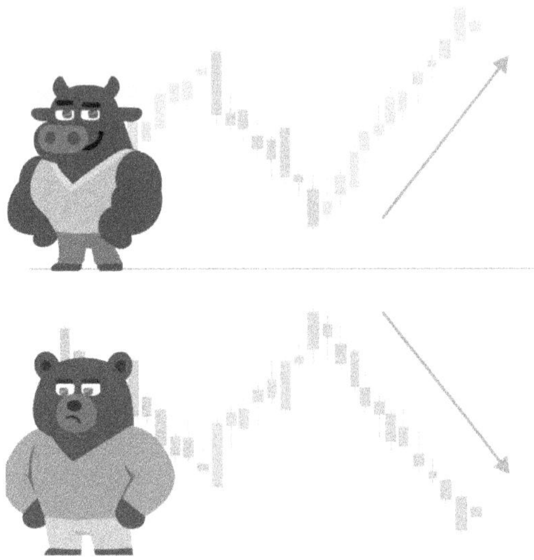

Here's an easy way to remember: bulls thrust their horns upward when they attack, while bears swipe their paws downward. When the market is rising overall, we call it a "bull market." When it's falling, it's a "bear market."

Spot the Market Trend

Drag each statement to the correct category. If prices are rising and confidence is high, it's a bull market. If prices are falling and fear is taking over, it's a bear market.

- Bear - A company reports strong earnings, and its stock price surges
- Bull - The economy is struggling, and stock prices are falling

Answer:

Bear - The economy is struggling, and stock prices are falling
Bull - A company reports strong earnings, and its stock price surges

Finally, let's explore the four essential order types that can be used to enter your trades. We've already seen market orders - they execute immediately at the current best price and continue to fill at the ask price until all shares are filled.

But sometimes, speed isn't your priority. A limit order lets you specify the exact price you're willing to accept. Want to buy a stock, but only if it falls to $40? Place a limit-buy order at $40, and it will only be executed if the price reaches your target.

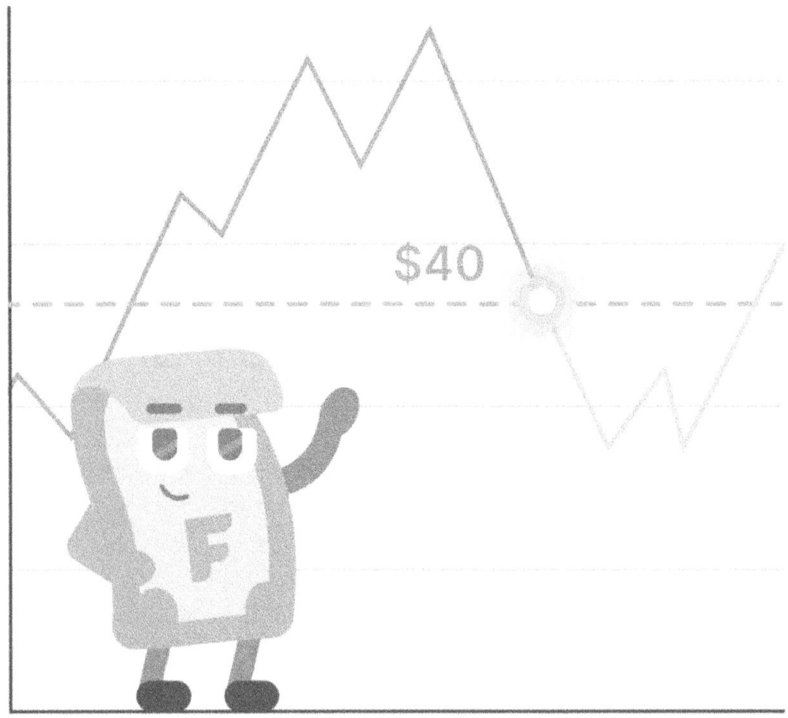

Stop orders activate when a specified price is reached, and then they become either a market order or a limit order. A stop-market order executes at the next available price once triggered. A stop-limit order gives you price control, but there's a chance it won't fill if the market moves past your limit.

For example, if a stock is at $50 and you place a buy stop at $55, your order activates only when the price rises to $55 - useful for breakout strategies.

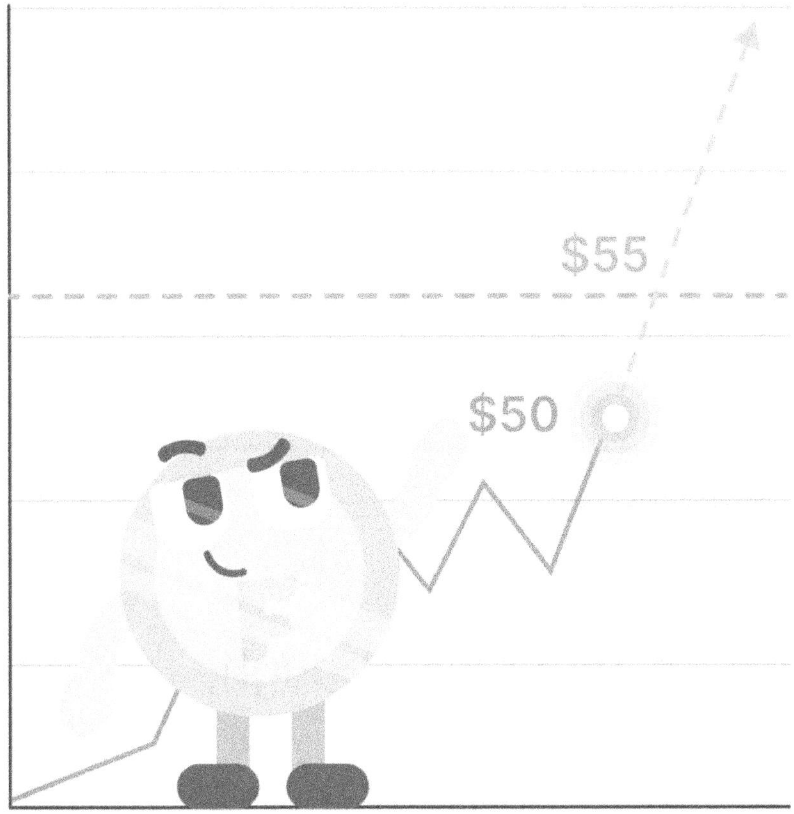

A stop-loss is a common way traders use stop-market orders to manage risk. If you buy a stock at $50 and set a stop-loss at $40, your position will automatically sell if the price drops to $40—limiting your loss to about $10 per share.

In fast-moving markets, though, the actual price you get may be slightly worse, because the market can move quickly between the time the order is triggered and when it gets filled. This is called slippage.

These order types are your tools for executing precise trading strategies. Market orders for immediate execution, limit orders for price control, stop orders for breakouts, and stop-losses for risk management.

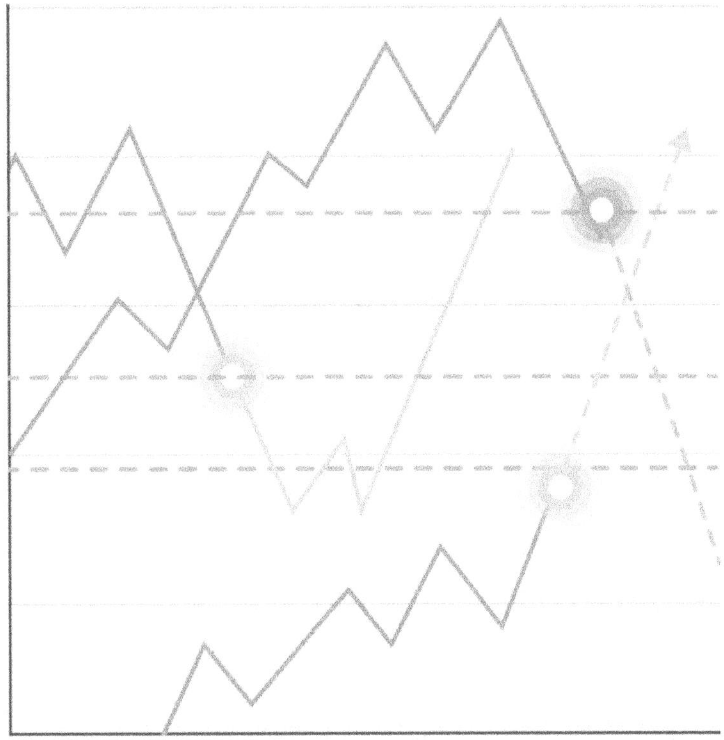

Put your knowledge to work

Let's say you believe a stock priced at $75 might drop initially but then surge higher. You want to buy only after it falls to $70 but also protect yourself if it keeps falling. Which order types would you use? Which combination of orders works best for this scenario? Which order type lets you specify the maximum price you'll pay?

- A stop buy order at $70 and a limit sell order
- A market buy order now and a stop order at $70
- A limit buy order at $70 and a stop-loss order below your entry point

- A short position now and a buy limit order at $70

Answer: A limit buy order at $70 and a stop-loss order below your entry point. A limit buy order at $70 ensures you only buy if the price falls to your target. Then, a stop-loss order protects your position if the price continues to fall after your entry instead of rebounding as you expect.

Let's recap what we've learned:

- Long positions profit from rising prices, while short positions profit from falling prices.
- Bulls expect prices to rise, and bears expect them to fall.
- And the four key order types - market, limit, stop, and stop-loss - give you control over your entries and exits.

Now, take a short quiz to test your knowledge!

QUIZ: Trading Practice

1. What is a "long position" in trading?

A. Trading with borrowed money or margin
B. Holding an asset for more than one year
C. Selling an asset with the expectation that its price will fall
D. Buying an asset with the expectation that its price will rise

2. What does it mean to "go short" or take a "short position"?

A. Holding a position for a short period of time
B. Setting a quick profit target on a trade
C. Borrowing shares to sell them, with the plan to buy them back later at a lower price
D. Buying shares with the expectation of selling them quickly

3. What does the term "bullish" mean in trading?

A. Expecting prices to rise
B. Trading with high-volume
C. Expecting prices to fall
D. Being uncertain about market direction

4. What does the term "bearish" mean in trading?

A. Expecting prices to fall
B. Expecting prices to rise
C. Trading with low-volume
D. Being uncertain about market direction

5. What is the "bid price" in trading?

A. The lowest price a seller is willing to accept
B. The last traded price
C. The highest price a buyer is willing to pay
D. The opening price for the day

6. What is the "ask price" in trading?

A. The average price over time
B. The closing price for the day
C. The highest price a buyer is willing to pay
D. The lowest price a seller is willing to accept

7. What is a "market order"?

A. An order to buy or sell immediately at the current market price
B. An order to buy or sell only at a specific price
C. An order that automatically sells if prices fall too much
D. An order that triggers a buy when prices rise to a certain level

8. What is a "limit order"?

A. An order to buy or sell immediately at any price
B. An order that executes during specific market hours
C. An order to buy or sell at a specified price or better
D. An order that automatically sells when prices fall too much

9. What is a "stop order" (can also be a stop-loss order)?

A. An order that expires after a set time period
B. An order that requires manual confirmation

C. An order that triggers a market order when a specified price is reached
D. An order to buy or sell at a specific price only

10. Which two order types would you use to enter a trade at a specific price and protect against further losses?

A. A short position and a stop buy
B. A stop-limit and a market order
C. A market buy and a limit sell
D. A limit buy and a stop-loss

Answer: 1. D; 2. C; 3. A; 4. A; 5. C; 6. D; 7. A; 8. C; 9. C; 10. D

Chapter 3: How To Trade

Lesson 1: Who Trades and Why

The players in the market

Trades don't happen in a vacuum. Behind every price move, there's someone hitting "buy" or "sell." Let's meet them.

We step into a bustling global trading marketplace. The trading world is like a vibrant marketplace with different types of participants. Some are here to buy groceries, others to sell goods, and some make sure everything runs smoothly.

Here we see retail traders - individuals like you and me - trading with our own money. Some are beginners, others are experienced, but they all make their own decisions using trading platforms.

See that? The retail traders are using the order types we learned about in our last lesson - limit orders, stop-losses, and more - but they're using smaller amounts than those big players over there.

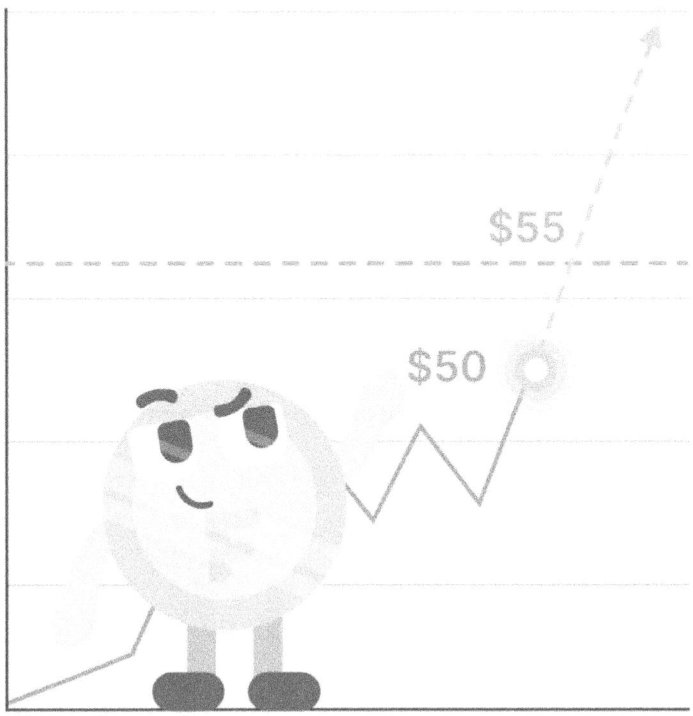

Let's move to this impressive building. Inside are institutional traders - big hedge funds, banks, and investment firms managing billions of dollars. They use advanced data and high-speed trading systems.

Institutional traders often break large orders into smaller pieces. Remember how we learned about "walking the book" in our order book lesson? This helps them avoid moving prices too much against themselves.

Now, those traders over there are doing something special - they're market makers. These firms act as financial intermediaries by constantly quoting both buy (bid) and sell (ask) prices. This ensures there's always someone to trade with, making markets more liquid and efficient.

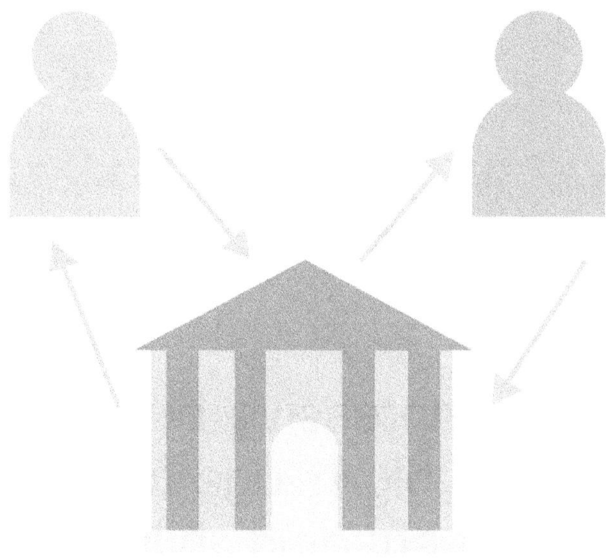

Market makers provide the liquidity that keeps the trading engine running. They help reduce friction in the market by ensuring that trades can happen smoothly. Remember the bid-ask spread we discussed earlier? That's where market makers earn their profit-buying at the bid and selling at the ask.

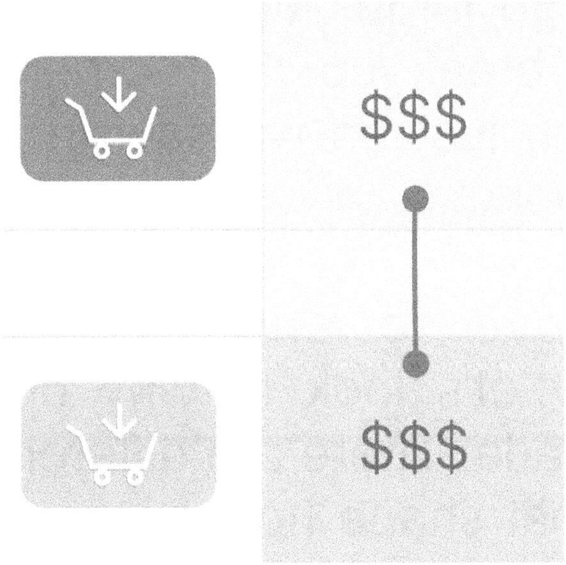

Who are these traders?

Let's test your understanding. A trader places large orders but breaks them into smaller pieces to avoid moving the market too much. They manage money for pension funds and wealthy clients. Which type of market participant is this most likely to be? Think about who manages large amounts of money for others.

- A central bank
- A retail trader
- A market maker

- An institutional trader

Answer: An institutional trader. Institutional traders manage large sums of money for others and typically break up their orders to minimize market impact, just as we saw in our lesson on how trading works.

We now move to another section of the marketplace. Let's look at why different market participants trade. There are different reasons and motivations that shape how each approaches the market.

These traders are speculators - they're trying to profit from price movements. Using strategies based on technical analysis, news, or market sentiment, they buy low and sell high (or short, sell, and buy back lower).

And there are hedgers. Unlike speculators, hedgers use the market to reduce risk, not to chase profits. They take positions that move in the opposite direction of the risk their business faces - so if the market moves against them, their trade helps cover the loss.

Finally, meet the arbitrage traders. They spot tiny price differences for the same financial asset in different markets and exploit these inefficiencies. If gold is cheaper in London than New York, they buy in London and sell in New York, for example.

Each of these traders uses the same order types and market mechanics we've learned about but with different goals. Speculators seek profit from price movement, hedgers protect against risks, and arbitrageurs exploit inefficiencies.

Why are they trading?

An airline purchases oil futures contracts whenever it needs to secure fuel prices for the next several months. Their goal isn't to profit from oil price movements but to maintain stable costs. What type of trading activity is the airline engaged in? Think about how they're using trading to manage business risks.

- Hedging
- Market making
- Arbitrage
- Speculation

Answer: Hedging. The airline isn't primarily seeking to profit from price movements or exploit price differences. It is hedging - its motivation is to reduce its exposure to the risk of rising fuel prices. This helps them maintain predictable costs even when market prices fluctuate.

Understanding these different market participants helps explain price movements. When institutional traders move large positions, they create waves. When market makers pull back, spreads widen. When hedgers rush in, certain assets may rise or fall based on underlying risks.

Let's recap!

Types of traders:

- Retail traders - Individuals trading with their own money. -
- Institutional traders - Large firms managing money for clients. -
- Market makers - Provide liquidity by always offering buy & sell prices.

Reasons for trading:

- Speculation - Profit from price movements.
- Hedging - Reduce risk in business operations.
- Arbitrage - Exploit price differences across markets.

Understanding these players and motivations helps you navigate the market landscape.

You've learned about the key players in the market and why they trade. Now, let's see how well you understand trading mechanics!

QUIZ: Trading Mechanics

1. Alex is watching a stock's order book where the highest bid is $25.30 and the lowest ask is $25.35. What is the spread for this stock?

A. $0.05
B. $25.35
C. $25.30
D. $50.65

2. Andy notices that when trading a small cryptocurrency, his order for 1000 coins filled at several different prices rather than all at one price. What trading phenomenon is Andy experiencing?

A. Market manipulation by other traders
B. Walking the book, where large orders consume multiple price levels
C. A technical glitch in the trading platform
D. Artificial price inflation

3. Alex wants to buy a stock only if it drops to $50, but not at the current price of $55. Which order type should he use?

A. Stop order at $50
B. Market buy order
C. Limit buy order at $50
D. Stop-loss order at $50

4. Andy bought shares at $75 and wants to protect himself from large losses. He wants to automatically sell if the price drops to $70. Which order type is most appropriate?

A. Market sell order
B. Buy limit order at $70
C. Stop-loss order at $70
D. Limit sell order at $70

5. Alex overhears another trader saying "I'm very bullish on this technology sector." What does the trader expect to happen with technology stocks?

A. They expect technology stock prices to fall
B. They're comparing technology companies to farming

C. They expect technology stock prices to rise
D. They plan to short sell technology stocks

6. Andy is trading oil futures not because he wants to profit from oil price movements, but because his transportation business needs to secure stable fuel prices for the coming months. What type of trading activity is Andy engaged in?

A. Hedging to manage business risk
B. Arbitrage to exploit price differences
C. Speculation for profit
D. Market making to provide liquidity

7. Alex notices a trader constantly providing both buy and sell prices for a stock, making small profits from the spread rather than from price movements. What type of market participant is this trader?

A. A market maker
B. A retail trader
C. A broker
D. An institutional trader

8. Andy wants to profit from the tiny price difference of the same stock listed on two different exchanges. He buys it on the exchange where it's cheaper and immediately sells it on the exchange where it's more expensive. What trading strategy is Andy using?

A. Market making
B. Arbitrage
C. Hedging
D. Speculation

9. Alex places a market order to sell 50 shares. The highest bid price is $42.10. At what price will his order likely execute?

A. $42.10
B. The lowest ask price
C. The average of the bid and ask prices
D. Whatever price Coin manually enters

10. Andy owns a stock currently trading at $60 and borrows 100 shares of the same stock from his broker, which he immediately sells. What position does Andy now have in this stock?

A. A short position, profiting if the price falls
B. A hedged position that's protected from price movements
C. A neutral position with no risk
D. A long position, profiting if the price rises

Answer: 1. A; 2. B; 3. C; 4. C; 5. C; 6. A; 7. A; 8. B; 9. A; 10. A

Lesson 2: How To Make Significant Gains

The path to meaningful profits

Different market players generate different scales of profit from the same percentage moves. This highlights one of the biggest challenges for retail traders like you and me.

Your potential profit is directly tied to your trading capital: with $100 in your account and a winning trade that nets 10%, you've made just $10. To earn $1,000 at that rate, you'd need to make 100 perfect trades. There must be a better way!

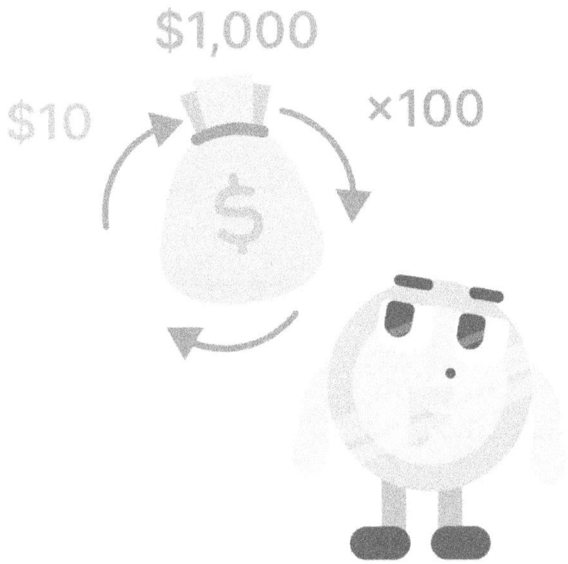

Retail traders have developed methods to bridge this gap:

1) Leveraging capital

2) Partnering with prop trading firms for increased buying power

or

3) Compounding smaller profits over time.

Each has distinct characteristics that suit different trading styles.

Let's start with leverage. Leverage allows control of more assets than your capital would normally permit, working as a multiplier. For example, with 10:1 leverage, your $1,000 can control $10,000 worth of assets. A 5% move now generates $500 instead of just $50.

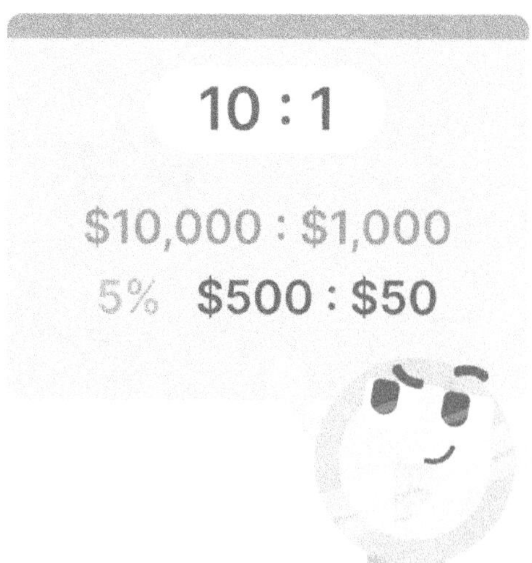

Calculate leverage impact

A trader has $2,000 and uses 10:1 leverage to control a $20,000 position. If the market moves 3% in their favor, how much profit will they make in dollars? First calculate the dollar value of the market move on the total position, not just on the initial capital. Calculate the profit:

- $60
- $6,000
- $200
- $600

Answer: $600. When calculating leveraged profits, multiply the percentage move by the total controlled position size, not just your initial capital. A 3% move on a $20,000 position equals $600 (3% of $20,000). With 10:1 leverage, that's a 30% return on the initial $2,000 capital.

When trading with leverage, both gains and losses are multiplied. A 10% market move with 5:1 leverage results in a 50% change to your account - in either direction.

Leverage is provided by your broker in exchange for a margin deposit. This margin is collateral that ensures you can cover potential losses. Different markets offer different leverage ratios - for example, the forex (foreign exchange) market might offer 50:1, while stocks might limit you to 2:1.

If your position moves against you too much, increasing your loss, you may face a margin call from your broker requiring additional funds. Without proper risk management, leverage can quickly deplete your trading account.

The second approach is joining a proprietary (prop) trading firm. These companies provide traders with much larger capital in exchange for a share of the profits. Instead of trading $1,000, you might trade $100,000 or more.

Prop firms typically require you to pass a trading evaluation first, demonstrating your strategy works and you can manage risk appropriately. They'll have specific rules about maximum drawdowns and profit targets.

Scaling up trading capital

Alex wants to significantly increase his trading profits. He's considering either using 10:1 leverage on his $1,000 account or applying to a prop firm that would let him trade with $50,000 after passing an evaluation. What's the main difference between using leverage and trading for a prop firm? Think about whose money is primarily at risk in each scenario.

- Leverage is illegal in most countries while prop trading is universally permitted
- Leverage is risk-free while prop trading always leads to losses
- Prop firms don't allow day trading, only long-term investing
- With leverage, losses affect your own capital; with a prop firm, you're risking their capital after evaluation and acceptance

Answer: With leverage, you're amplifying both gains and losses on your own capital. With a prop firm, after passing their evaluation, you're trading their capital with less personal financial risk, though you'll share the profits when successful.

The third approach is the most accessible but requires patience: compounding smaller gains over time. Instead of seeking huge, immediate returns, focus on consistent, smaller wins that build your account steadily.

Remember the power of compounding we discussed in earlier lessons? A 5% monthly return might seem small, but that's almost 80% annually when compounded! Starting with $1,000 and achieving this rate, you'd have about $1,800 after a year.

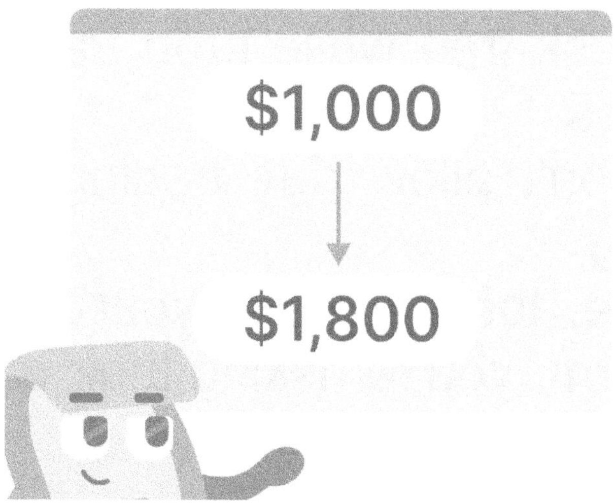

This is why many successful traders focus on consistency rather than hitting home runs. By preserving capital during drawdowns and steadily growing their account, they eventually reach a point where even average percentage returns can generate significant absolute profits.

Order the scaling approaches

Order these trading approaches from lowest to highest personal financial risk. Consider whose money is primarily at risk and the potential for losses beyond your initial investment.

- Trading personal capital without leverage
- Trading personal capital with high leverage
- Trading a prop firm's capital after evaluation
- Compounding smaller trades over time

Answer:

- Compounding smaller trades over time
- Trading a prop firm's capital after evaluation
- Trading personal capital without leverage
- Trading personal capital with high leverage

When ranking risk levels, consider both whose capital is primarily at risk and whether losses can be amplified beyond your initial investment. Compounding with careful position sizing has the lowest risk, followed by prop firm trading where you risk mainly their capital, then trading without leverage risking only your capital, and finally high leverage which can amplify losses beyond your initial investment.

Selecting your approach

Match each scaling approach with its primary requirement. Each approach has a key prerequisite that's most critical for success.

- Patience and consistency - Compounding
- Leverage - Proven profitable strategy with track record
- Prop trading - Strong risk management skills

Answer:

- Patience and consistency - Compounding
- Leverage - Strong risk management skills
- Prop trading - Proven profitable strategy with track record

You now understand how traders scale profits, manage risk, and grow their accounts using tools like leverage, prop firm capital, and compounding. Great job getting this far!

Now, let's keep the momentum going by exploring the world of financial markets and seeing how everything connects.

SECTION 2: FINANCIAL MARKETS

Chapter 1: Financial Market Basics

Lesson 1: How Markets Work

Welcome to the financial market!

You've already built a solid foundation in trading and key strategies - well done! Now, let's take the next step and explore the financial markets where all the action happens. By the end of this lesson, you'll understand how markets work, and which one suits you best.

Imagine walking through a bustling marketplace filled with different products - fresh produce, electronics, and clothing. A financial market works the same way, but instead of physical goods, people trade stocks, currencies, bonds, and commodities.

Just like a physical marketplace ensures the smooth exchange of goods, financial markets serve as intermediaries that connect buyers and sellers - often strangers who never meet directly. Financial markets provide a bridge between buyers and sellers for the smooth exchange of financial assets.

Financial markets are open to both large companies and individual traders.

These markets offer structure and speed, allowing you to capitalize on opportunities, control risk, and grow financially.

But these markets don't work alone. They depend on financial institutions and instruments to keep global trade in motion.

Financial markets depend on institutions to function smoothly. Banks, brokers, and mutual funds act as the bridge between traders and the market.

Financial institutions are organizations that manage money - like accepting deposits, giving loans, investing, or helping with financial transactions.

Here's how they work: You keep your money safely in a bank. When you decide to trade, you send funds to a broker, who helps you buy and sell assets.

If you don't want to choose investments yourself, a mutual fund does it for you by pooling money from many investors and managing it professionally.

Finally, let's talk about financial instruments - the actual assets being traded in financial markets. These include stocks, forex pairs, commodities, and cryptocurrencies. If this sounds complex, don't worry! You'll dive deeper into financial instruments soon and learn how they work in trading.

Excellent job! You've mastered the basics of financial markets, learned how institutions and instruments work, and are one step closer to becoming a smart trader. Now, it's time to dive deeper into the two key types of financial markets so you can decide which one best aligns with your trading goals. Let's keep going!

Lesson 2: Centralized vs Decentralized

What is the difference?

When trading stocks or assets, you interact with either a centralized or decentralized market. But what's the difference? Let's break it down!

Imagine a supermarket where everything is organized in one place. Shoppers can compare prices, trust the quality, and buy with confidence. The store ensures fair pricing, sets rules, and maintains order. This creates a secure and transparent shopping experience.

Similarly, in financial markets, a centralized market operates through a single, central authority. All transactions are routed through this exchange, ensuring that prices are consistent and transparent for all participants. Exchanges usually have fixed trading hours and are common for assets like stocks, futures, and options.

Now imagine a flea market where vendors set up their own booths, negotiate prices, and sell directly to buyers. There's no central organizer managing these exchanges; instead, individuals connect and negotiate terms among themselves.

Assets like forex and cryptocurrencies are typically traded this way - across a network of brokers or platforms rather than a single exchange. Decentralized markets are open 24/7 and give you more control over your trades. But with that freedom comes responsibility - you're in charge of your own security and choices.

Centralized vs decentralized markets

Let's match the key traits of centralized markets! Centralized markets are run through a central authority - think of stock exchanges with rules, schedules, and unified pricing.

- Users trade directly without intermediaries
- All trades go through one hub
- Regulated with set rules & hours
- No fixed trading hours - markets run 24/7
- Everyone trades at the same price
- Greater control, but higher risk

Answer:

- All trades go through one hub
- Regulated with set rules & hours
- Everyone trades at the same price

Which market should you trade in?

Meet Andy and Alex! They both want to start trading, but they have different needs. Let's see which financial market suits them best!

Market for Andy

Andy wants security, regulation, and stability. She prefers a user-friendly platform, high liquidity, and fixed market hours. This market must have central authority, rules, hours, regulation. Which market is best for Andy?

- Centralized market
- Decentralized market

Answer: Centralized markets offer regulation, stability, and high liquidity - just what Andy is looking for!

Market for Alex

Alex values full control, 24/7 trading, and privacy. He prefers peer-to-peer trading without middlemen and accepts higher risk for more independence. This market should have no central authority, 24/7, and high control. Which market is best for Alex?

- Centralized market
- Decentralized market

Answer: Decentralized markets offer Alex the freedom, privacy, and around-the-clock trading he values!

Andy and Alex chose markets that fit their needs. Now, it's your turn! Whether you trade in a centralized or decentralized market, understanding their benefits and risks will help you make smart decisions.

Now that you understand centralized and decentralized markets, let's recap their key differences before moving forward.

Centralized markets are regulated and secure, offering fair trading, high liquidity for easy transactions, and structured hours with customer support. However, they limit trader control due to intermediaries and aren't open 24/7.

Meanwhile, decentralized markets give traders full control with direct, peer-to-peer trades and 24/7 access. They offer more privacy and fewer restrictions, but come with higher risk due to limited regulation and lower liquidity, which can make trading slower and less predictable.

Now that you know how centralized and decentralized markets work, it's time to dive deeper into different financial markets and discover how assets like stocks, forex, commodities, and crypto are traded.

Chapter 2: Main Market Types

Lesson 1: Stock Market

Welcome to the stock market!

Noe that you have a solid understanding of financial markets, let's focus on a main type - the stock market. By the end of this lesson, you'll find out where you can buy stocks and what affects stock prices to help you trade more confidently.

You already know that a stock trade happens when a buyer's bid price matches a seller's ask price. Now, let's take a step back and really understand what you're buying and how you can make a profit.

Imagine a pie, but instead of one person owning it, it is sliced into pieces. Each slice represents a share, just like in the stock market, where company ownership is divided into shares owned by a variety of investors and traders.

Let's test your knowledge!

As you know, when a business grows, each slice of ownership (share) increases in value. If a slice costs $50 and its value rises to $75, what's your profit? Profit = the new value - the original cost.

- $35
- $125
- $25

Answer: The profit is $75 - $50 = $25.

This price increase is called capital appreciation, and as a trader, your goal is to find stocks that will grow in value over time.

Where does stock trading happen?

Stock trading happens on centralized exchanges around the world. Not all exchanges are the same - some are bigger, some are fully digital, and others specialize in certain industries.

These exchanges are fully digital and rank among the largest in the world by market cap:

- **New York Stock Exchange (NYSE) (USA):** Largest by market cap, home to giants like Coca-Cola and Microsoft.
- **NASDAQ (USA):** Tech-focused, with companies like Apple and Tesla.

These are other important exchanges around the world:

- **Euronext (Europe):** Covers multiple European countries.
- **Frankfurt Stock Exchange (FWB) (Germany):** a key European hub.
- **TSE (Japan):** Largest in Asia, home to Toyota, Sony, and Honda.

You remember how centralized markets work - these stock exchanges follow the same model! They operate with set rules, fixed hours, and intermediaries like brokers to ensure smooth and regulated trading.

However, some companies aren't big enough or choose not to list on major stock exchanges like the **NYSE** or **NASDAQ**. Such companies trade their stocks through the **Over-the-Counter (OTC)** market, which operates differently from centralized exchanges.

OTC markets are home to smaller, fast-growing companies that haven't made it to major exchanges yet. Some start here before hitting the big leagues. With lower stock prices, traders can spot early opportunities and invest in potential future giants before the rest of the market catches on. These markets can be accessed through brokers or specialized trading platforms.

OTC stocks aren't listed on major exchanges like the **NYSE** or **NASDAQ**, but trade in these key markets:

- **OTCQX:** Safest tier with strict financial and reporting rules.
- **OTCQB:** For growing companies with moderate transparency.
- **Pink Open Market (Pink Sheets):** High-risk tier with minimal requirements.

OTC markets are decentralized, offering flexibility in pricing, trade size, and terms - unlike centralized exchanges with strict rules.

Advantages of OTC markets

OTC markets have unique benefits:

- Custom trade size, no limits
- No strict rules, custom trades
- Traders set terms, no exchange rules

Despite such opportunities, **OTC** also comes with higher risks than major exchanges. With fewer regulations and lower transparency, traders need to be cautious.

Risks in OTC markets

With fewer rules and direct trading, these are challenges traders could face:

- Hard to verify company info
- One side may not follow through
- Lower bar allows risky trades

Excellent! You now know where stocks are bought and sold: from centralized exchanges to **OTC** markets. But understanding where to trade is just the start - next, we'll explore what makes stock prices rise and fall!

Lesson 2: What Moves The Stock Market?

It's time to find out why stock prices change!

Now that you know where to buy stocks, let's explore what drives their prices!

One of the biggest reasons for these price swings is volatility. Think of it like ocean waves - sometimes calm, sometimes wild. High volatility means stock prices can change quickly and unpredictably, while low volatility means stock prices are more steady.

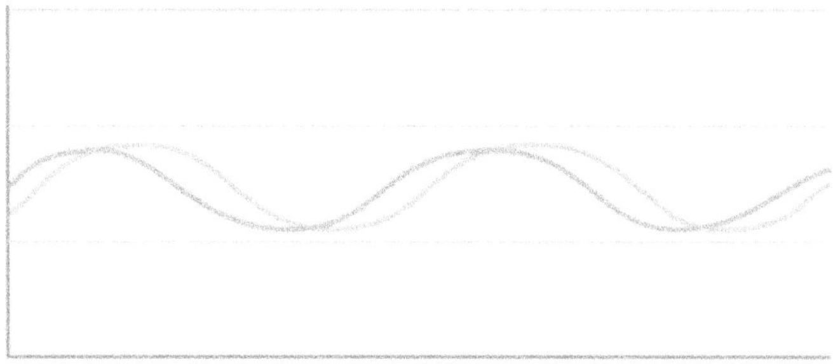

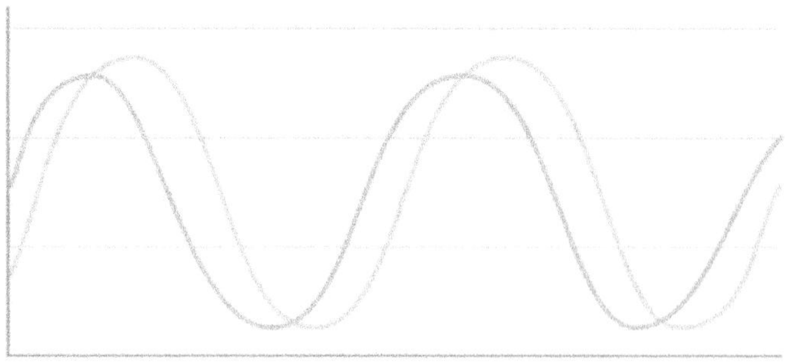

What makes stock prices go up or down? There are many reasons, but one of the biggest is how well a company is doing. If a company is making good profits and growing its business, more people usually want to buy its stock. When more people buy, the price goes up. That's because strong companies often seem like good investments.

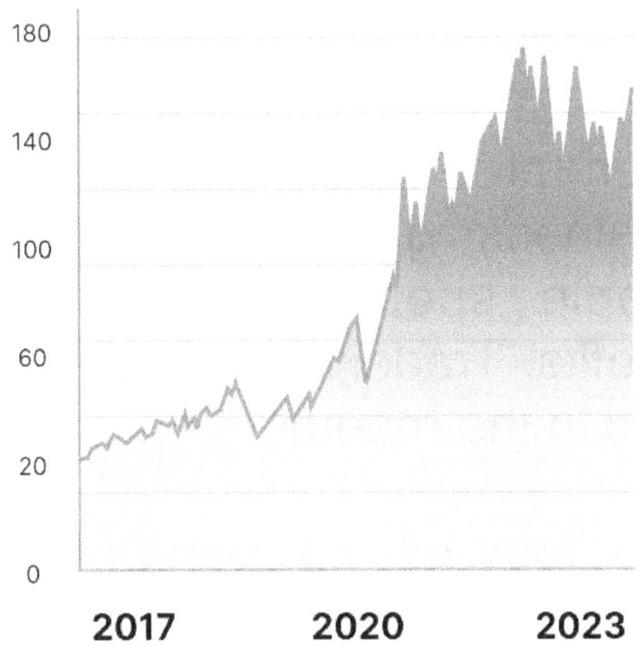

Let's see if you can predict the market!

A company just reported profits that were higher than expected. When investors hear good news, most will want to buy the stock. What do you think will happen to its stock price?

- More investors want to buy the stock, pushing the price up
- Investors lose confidence and sell their shares
- The stock price stays the same

Answer: More investors want to buy the stock, pushing the price up. Positive earnings often lead to positive price movement.

Broader influences (macroeconomic) like interest rates, inflation, and world events affect the stock market. When rates go up, borrowing gets harder, slowing business growth. Fast-rising inflation means people spend less, which can hurt company profits. Traders watch these changes to spot chances in the market.

Can you predict what happens next?

Inflation is rising - prices for goods and services are going up. How will this affect stock prices? If companies have to spend more on materials and wages, do they still earn the same amount?

- Stock prices may fall as higher costs reduce company profits

- Stock prices stay the same since inflation doesn't impact businesses
- Stock prices rise because everything becomes more expensive

Answer: Inflation often reduces company profits and investor optimism, which can lead to falling stock prices.

Apart from company performance and global events, traders also study technical factors to predict price movements.

One of the most important factors in market analysis is the understanding of price trends. Stocks don't move randomly - they follow patterns like bullish and bearish trends. Recognizing these trends helps traders decide when to buy or sell and importantly, manage risk.

Another key factor is investor behavior. The market is influenced by emotions - fear and excitement drive prices up and down. When traders panic, they sell quickly, pushing prices lower. When they feel confident, they buy more, causing upward pressure on stock prices.

Traders don't just look at what's happening in the market today - they study past price movements to identify patterns that could be repeated in the future. They look for trends, recurring price patterns, and market cycles. It might sound like a lot, but don't worry - we'll break it down step by step in the following lessons!

Finally, investor confidence also plays a huge role in stock prices. Positive news about a company, like strong earnings or a new product launch, attracts buyers and can drive prices higher. But if the economy slows down or uncertainty rises for any reason, investor confidence may fall, triggering investors to sell, and causing prices to drop.

Many traders use technical analysis to make informed trades. Instead of focusing on a company's profits, they study charts, trends, and patterns to predict where the price might go next. It's all about spotting opportunities before the market moves!

However, not all stock price movements reflect a company's real value. Sometimes, hype and speculation drive prices high, creating a bubble.

A bubble bursts when investors realize stocks are overvalued, leading to panic selling and sharp price drops. This can trigger a market crash.

Quick check!

Sometimes, stock prices rise very quickly - faster than the company's actual growth. Prices rise fast from hype, not real company value. What causes a stock market bubble?

- A stock's price slowly increases over many years
- A company announces strong profits and long-term growth
- Prices rise too high due to hype, speculation, and investor excitement

Answer: A bubble happens when investor hype drives prices far above a stock's real value.

A famous example is the Dot-com Bubble of the late 1990s. Investors rushed to invest in internet companies, expecting massive profits. But when many of these companies failed to deliver, stock prices crashed in 2000.

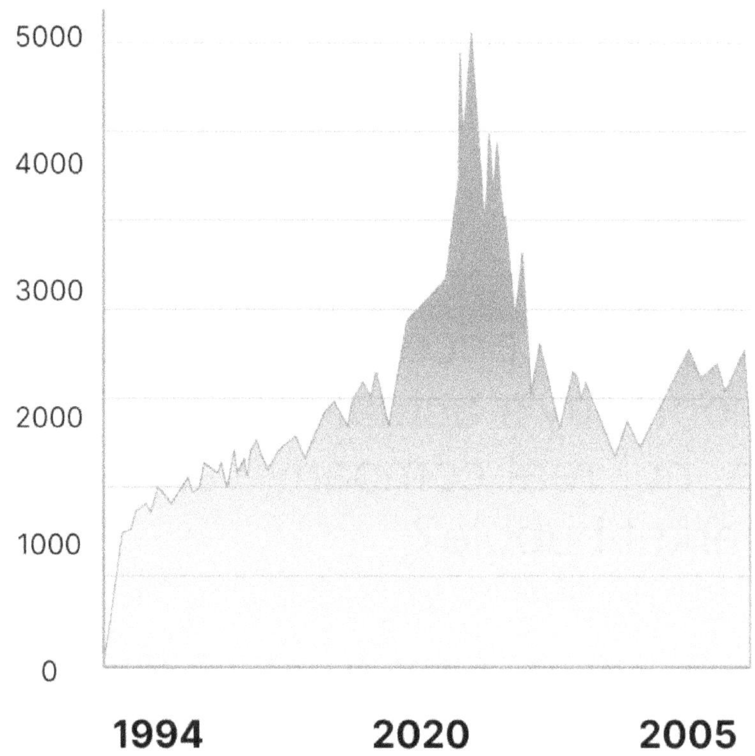

This serves as a crucial lesson for you - hype and speculation can drive markets up, but without real fundamental value behind the moves, bubbles eventually burst.

Although crashes can be painful, markets have always bounced back. Over time, investor confidence returns, and the economy stabilizes, creating new opportunities. To avoid falling into this trap, you will soon learn how to manage risk by staying informed, avoiding excessive speculation, and having a solid strategy.

Excellent! You've mastered stock trading! The stock market is a place where shares of companies are bought and sold. As you've seen, the stock market isn't random - it responds to real-world news, emotions, and patterns. Now, challenge yourself with a quiz to see how much you've learned. Let's go!

QUIZE: Stock Market

1. What is a stock?

A. A small part of a company that you can own
B. A guarantee that you will make money
C. A loan that a company gives to investors
D. A type of bank account

2. How do people buy and sell stocks?

A. By asking the government for permission
B. On stock exchanges like NYSE and NASDAQ
C. Only through private meetings
D. By going to the company's office

3. What causes stock prices to change?

A. Size of a company's office
B. The company's CEO
C. The number of employees in a company
D. Supply and demand

4. What is capital appreciation?

A. When a company makes a new product
B. When a stock's value goes up over time
C. When a stock's price stays the same
D. When a company pays its investors

5. What is an OTC market?

A. A part of a company's business
B. A market for government-approved stocks only
C. A market where stocks trade outside major exchanges
D. A place where only new companies can trade

6. What is one risk of OTC markets?

A. Some companies don't have to share much financial information
B. Stocks in **OTC** markets never lose value
C. **OTC** stocks always make higher profits
D. **OTC** markets have more rules than major exchanges

7. What happens when inflation increases?

A. Stock prices always rise when inflation is high
B. Companies make more money with inflation

C. Inflation doesn't affect stock prices
D. Stock prices may fall as costs for businesses go up

8. What is a stock market bubble?

A. When a company makes a lot of money
B. When stock prices rise too high due to hype and speculation
C. When stock prices slowly go up over many years
D. When stocks never change in value

9. What happens when a bubble bursts?

A. Stock prices go up even more
B. Stock prices drop as investors sell their shares
C. The government stops stock trading
D. Nothing changes

10. What lessons can traders learn from the Dot-com Bubble?

A. Investing in tech companies is always safe
B. Speculation has no effect on stock prices
C. Market crashes only happen in technology stocks

D. Hype can push stock prices up, but without real value, they crash

Answer: 1. A; 2. B; 3. D; 4. B; 5. C; 6. A; 7. D; 8. B; 9. B; 10. D

Lesson 3: Forex Market

Let's explore other markets!

The stock market is just one way to trade. Let's take a closer look at Forex - the biggest market of them all - and learn how things work.

Imagine you're traveling and need to exchange money for local currency - that's Forex trading! It's all about buying one currency while selling another, aiming to profit from changes in the exchange rate. Let's explore how it works!

Forex, short for FOReign EXchange, is a global market where traders buy and sell currencies. Unlike stock markets, forex has no central exchange.

How do you make money in Forex? Think of buying a currency as buying a share in a country's economy - just like buying stock in a company.

One example is, if you believe a country's economy will get stronger, you buy its currency. If the economy weakens, you sell the currency to avoid losses. The goal is to buy low and sell high for a profit.

This is how it works in action! Let's say you decide to trade Euros by selling Dollars because you believe the Euro will increase in value. You bought €1,000 when the exchange rate was 1 EUR = 1.10 USD. A few days later, the Euro rose, and the new exchange rate was 1 EUR = 1.15 USD.

Let's calculate!

You bought €1,000 when the exchange rate was 1 EUR = 1.10 USD. Now, the rate is 1 EUR = 1.15 USD and you sell your €1,000. How many US Dollars and how much profit did you make? Change €1,000 to USD, then subtract what you paid.

- $950 and $150 loss
- $1,150 and $50 profit
- $1,100 and $0 profit
- $1,200 and $100 profit

Answer: You bought €1,000 for 1.10 USD (€1,100). Selling at 1.15 USD gives you $1,150, making a $50 profit!

You're getting the hang of it! Unlike stock markets that close every evening, Forex runs 24 hours a day from Sunday at 5 p.m. ET to Friday at 5 p.m. ET. With nonstop trading, you have the freedom to trade anytime and seize opportunities around the clock! However, be aware the liquidity fluctuates throughout the day.

Why trade Forex? Forex is fast, flexible, and full of opportunities! With a constantly active market, you can buy and sell easily at any time. Since Forex operates 24/5, you have the freedom to trade whenever it suits you. You can also control larger-size trades with less money but remember - while leverage can boost profits, it also increases risk. Smart trading leads to success!

Now that you understand the basics of the Forex market, let's see how it compares to other markets! Meet Cara and Jane - two traders with different goals. Can you match them to the right market: stocks or Forex?

Market for Cara

Cara focuses on investing in major companies for the long term. She values stability, regulation, and fixed trading hours. Which market is best for Cara? Think about which market is better for long-term investing with less frequent trading.

- Forex market
- Stock market

Answer: The stock market is great for stable, long-term investments with strong regulations and set trading hours.

Market for Jane

Jane prefers fast trading and the freedom to trade anytime. She's willing to take risks, profit from price swings, and use leverage tor bigger gains. Which market is best for Jane?

Answer: The forex market operates 24/5, allowing Jane to trade anytime with high liquidity and leverage.

Great job! Now you see how different trading styles match different markets. Remember that Forex is ideal for fast-paced, high-liquidity trading with flexible hours.

Forex is just the beginning! Before going deeper, let's uncover other key markets!

Lesson 4: Commodity Market

Welcome to the commodity market!

We are about to step into the world of commodities, where traders buy and sell valuable resources! By the end of this lesson, you'll explore how commodities are traded, what affects their prices, and how traders profit from them. Let's go!

Before there was money, people bartered by trading wheat for livestock and gold for spices. That system still thrives in the commodity market, where raw materials like oil, gold, and coffee drive global trade, linking producers, traders, and businesses.

As you probably guessed, a commodity market is where natural resources and agricultural goods are traded. There are two types of commodities traded: hard and soft commodities. Hard commodities like metals and oil come from the earth. Soft commodities come from agriculture or livestock.

Hard commodities are mined or extracted like gold, silver, or oil. Soft commodities are grown or raised like coffee, wheat, or cattle. Both offer unique trading opportunities influenced by supply, demand, and global events.

You've learned about different types of commodities, but how do traders participate in this market? Some traders purchase commodities directly in the spot market for immediate delivery, while others turn to the derivatives market, using futures or options contracts to lock in prices, manage risk, or capitalize on speculative opportunities.

But what exactly are futures and options contracts? Imagine a wheat farmer who's worried that prices might drop before harvest. To avoid losing money, they lock in a good price now using a futures contract.

A futures contract is an agreement to buy or sell something - like wheat - at a set price, but at a specific time in the future. That means even if the market price changes later, the deal sticks to the price agreed upon today. On the flip side, a trader might buy that contract if they think prices will go up - and make a profit later!

An options contract gives you the right, but not the obligation, to buy or sell something - like a commodity - at a specific price before a certain date. Think of it as a "maybe" deal you can choose to use only if it benefits you.

Imagine a trader who believes the price of oil might go up. They buy an option contract that gives them the right to buy oil at $70 per barrel anytime in the next 3 months. If the price rises to $90, they can buy it at $70 and make a profit. But if the price stays below $70, they don't have to use the option - they just lose the small fee they paid to buy it.

Okay, so you've got futures and options contracts... but how do you decide when to use them?

Commodity prices shift daily due to changes in supply, demand, weather, politics, and so on. To help with that, the Global Price Index tracks the average price movement of key commodities, helping traders spot trends, manage risk, and identify opportunities.

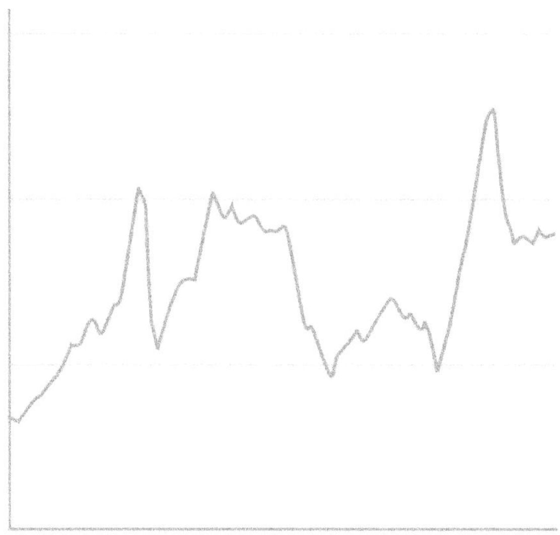

Now, let's see where traders actually participate in these markets. Commodities are bought and sold on major exchanges around the world - primarily through futures and options markets.

Key commodity exchanges include:

- **Chicago Board of Trade (CBOT)** trades corn, wheat, and gold.
- **CME Group** trades cattle, pork, and dairy.
- **NYMEX** handles oil, natural gas, and metals.
- **ICE Futures U.S.** trades coffee, cocoa, and orange juice.

Why could you consider participating in the commodity market? For individual traders, commodities can act as both a safety net and a source of opportunity. As the cost of goods rises with inflation, commodities often increase in value too. This helps protect your purchasing power over time and take advantage of price swings.

Let's see how it compares to other markets! Meet Alex and Dan - two traders with different goals. Can you match them to the right market: Forex or Commodity?

Choose the market!

Alex wants short-term trading, 24/5
market access, and uses large amounts of money to maximize profits. He focuses on short-term price movements and frequent trades. Which market suits Alex best? Which market runs 24/5 and is best for quick trades?

- Commodity market
- Forex market

Answer: Forex is ideal for short-term trading and offers high liquidity with 24/5 access.

Choose the market!

Dan wants to protect against inflation and invest in assets that gain value as prices rise. He prefers long-term trends and trading based on supply and demand. Which market suits Dan best? Which market is known as a hedge against inflation?

- Commodity market
- Forex market

Answer: Commodities hedge against inflation and follow long-term supply and demand trends.

Great job choosing the right market for Alex and Dan! Now, let's explore another fast-growing financial market. Get ready to explore how cryptocurrency works and is accessed.

Lesson 5: Cryptocurrency Market

Welcome to the crypto market!

The crypto market never sleeps, running 24/7 with endless trading opportunities. Digital assets like Bitcoin or Ethereum offer traders an alternative to traditional markets. This lesson will guide you through the fundamentals of crypto trading, market trends, and the opportunities and challenges traders face.

Cryptocurrencies like Bitcoin are decentralized digital assets, not issued or controlled by any government. Most cryptocurrencies use something called blockchain - a special kind of database that keeps transactions secure and transparent. Crypto markets never sleep, giving traders around-the-clock access.

Crypto trading works like any other market - buy low, sell high, or short-sell. Traders profit by speculating on price swings, hedging to protect against losses, and spreading investments across assets to manage risk. It's all about strategy and timing in this market.

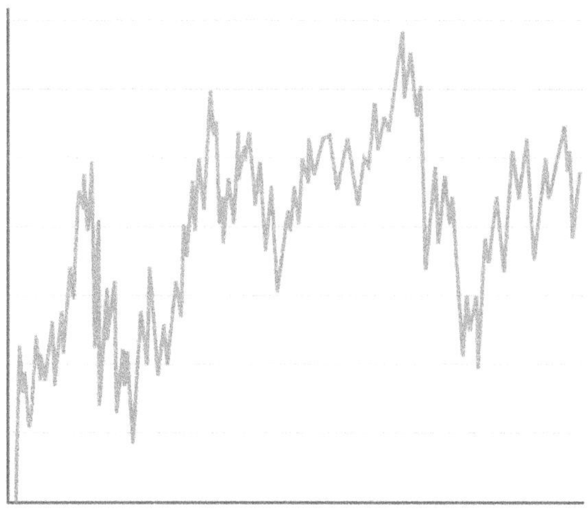

Just like in other markets, crypto prices rise and fall based on a variety of factors including changes in supply and demand, regulatory outlook, technological changes, and economic trends. Government policies, new blockchain innovations, and global events can cause big price swings as traders react to the news. So, staying informed is key to making smart trades.

Crypto's volatility can bring big wins - or big losses. With changing regulations and no safety nets, smart traders stay informed and manage risk wisely.

Let's see how it compares to other markets! These are Andy and Alex, who have goals. Can you match them to the right market: commodity or crypto?

Market for Andy

Andy prefers stability and assets with real-world value, like gold and oil. He wants to hedge against inflation and follow long-term trends. Which market suits Andy best? Which market involves physical goods and is used to protect against inflation?

- Commodity market
- Crypto market

Answer: Commodities offer a possible hedge against inflation, making them the right fit for Andy.

Market for Alex

Alex wants high-risk, high-reward opportunities with fast price swings. He's excited about digital assets and decentralized markets. Which market suits Alex best? Which market is known for digital assets and extreme volatility?

- Crypto market
- Commodity market

Answer: Crypto's volatility and fast price swings match Alex's risk-taking style. That said, keep in mind that the crypto market has been changing, and there are times when it moves more slowly and steadily.

Excellent! But where can you buy cryptocurrency? It can be traded on centralized exchanges like Coinbase or decentralized exchanges. As we discussed before, centralized exchanges offer security and ease, while decentralized ones provide full control. Each has pros and cons - you should choose what suits your trading style.

Now that you know the markets, here's a quick recap: Forex is the largest and most liquid, trading currencies 24/5. It's influenced by global events, economies, and interest rates. Commodities involve physical goods like gold or oil. Prices shift with supply and demand, weather, and geopolitics.

Crypto trades digital assets like Bitcoin 24/7. It's decentralized, volatile, and driven by tech trends, sentiment, and regulation. Each market has its own risks and rewards - traders pick based on strategy, risk level, and asset preference.

Great job! Now that you understand something about stock, Forex, commodity, and crypto markets, you're one step closer to becoming a pro trader. Next, you'll discover who participates in financial markets and how their actions impact trading.

Lesson 6: Meet The Players

Who participates in the financial markets?

Financial markets are filled with different participants, each shaping the market in unique ways. By the end of this lesson, you'll know who they are, how they impact trading activity and dynamics, and where you fit in as an individual trader.

First, let's talk about institutional traders. They are professional organizations like pension funds, mutual funds, hedge funds, and banks that manage large sums of money for clients or shareholders.

These are pension funds. They trade to ensure long-term financial security for retirees. Their goal is to generate stable returns that can provide a reliable income stream in the future. They prioritize low-risk investments to protect their clients' savings, making them less likely to engage in speculative trades.

Investment banks trade primarily to support corporate financing. While they help companies raise capital and manage mergers and acquisitions, many also engage in sales, trading, proprietary trading, and market making. By trading, they facilitate large transactions and provide liquidity to the market, helping corporations meet their financial needs and expand.

In contrast, hedge funds trade to achieve high returns through aggressive strategies. Their goal is to deliver above-average returns, even if it means facing higher risk than other asset managers.

In summary, pension funds prioritize stability, while investment banks are key players in corporate finance. Hedge funds take big risks for potentially big rewards.

Because they trade in large volumes, institutional participants' actions can move markets. To avoid disrupting prices, as we discussed before, orders are commonly broken into smaller trades over a period of time.

Now, let's meet retail traders - individual investors who trade with their own money, usually through online platforms.

Retail traders have no impact on market price because their trade size is too small. However, they have greater flexibility in how they participate and can benefit from identifying institutional behavior.

While individual retail trader activity is relatively small, their collective actions can influence stock prices in the short term.

Retail traders may not move the market alone, but as a group, they help provide activity. Unlike big institutions, retail traders can move in and out of trades quickly without causing big price swings, giving them more flexibility.

Now that you know who trades in the market, let's dive into what they trade - the financial instruments that drive the market. Let's continue!

QUIZ: Other Financial Markets

1. What is Forex?

A. A place where people trade physical goods
B. A platform for buying company shares
C. A government-controlled exchange for digital assets
D. A global market where currencies are bought and sold

2. Why do traders choose Forex?

A. It only allows large investors to trade
B. It has fixed prices that never change
C. It guarantees profits with no risk
D. It operates 24/5 and offers high liquidity

3. What is the main goal of Forex trading?

A. To invest in company stocks for long-term growth
B. To trade physical goods like oil and gold

C. To profit from changes in currency exchange rates
D. To store wealth without any market risk

4. What is a commodity?

A. A type of digital currency used in crypto markets
B. A financial loan given by banks
C. A physical good like gold, oil, or wheat that is traded
D. A stock that represents ownership in a company

5. How do traders make money in the commodity market?

A. By buying when prices are low and selling when prices rise
B. By trading only when prices are stable
C. By earning interest on stored commodities
D. By holding commodities indefinitely without selling

6. What is the difference between hard and soft commodities?

A. Hard commodities are mined or extracted; soft commodities are grown or raised
B. Soft commodities have a fixed price, while hard commodities change daily
C. Hard commodities are traded digitally, while soft commodities are physical
D. Hard commodities are used only in construction, while soft commodities are food items

7. Where are cryptocurrencies traded?

A. On the stock market alongside company shares
B. On centralized and decentralized exchanges
C. Only in physical locations like banks
D. Only on government-approved platforms

8. What is the key difference between commodities and stocks?

A. Commodities are physical assets like oil and gold, while stocks represent company ownership
B. Commodities never change in price, while stocks fluctuate daily

C. Stock trading happens 24/7, while commodities can only be traded once a week
D. Commodities are always less risky than stocks

9. Why do traders choose commodities over Forex or Crypto?

A. Commodity trading is only for long-term investors
B. Commodities have lower risk than all other markets
C. Commodities always increase in price over time
D. Commodities can provide inflation protection and real-world value

10. How does Forex trading differ from Crypto trading?

A. Forex is decentralized, while Crypto is regulated by central banks
B. Forex deals with national currencies and operates 24/5, while Crypto trades digital assets 24/7
C. Forex prices are controlled by governments, while Crypto has fixed values
D. Crypto is always more stable than Forex

Answer: 1. D; 2. D; 3. C; 4. C; 5. A; 6. A; 7. B; 8. A; 9. D; 10. B

Chapter 3: Financial Instruments

Lesson 1: Instruments Traded in Financial Markets

Let's explore financial instruments!

Stocks, shares, equities - similar words, but do they mean the same thing? By the end of this lesson, you'll know the difference and how they work!

Remember our pie analogy? When you buy stocks, you're buying a piece of a pie. But how much of the pie do you own? That's where shares come in.

Shares are the specific slices of that pie. If a company divides its ownership into 100 slices and you buy one share, you now own one slice of the pie.

To sum up, stocks refer to ownership in one or more companies, but they don't specify how many shares you own while shares specify the exact amount of that ownership.

So, now you can easily tell the difference between stocks and shares. But where do equities fit in?

In everyday conversation, "stocks" and "equities" can be used interchangeably.

However, in professional finance, "equity" refers to any ownership in a company, including both public and private companies. "Stocks" specifically refer to shares of publicly traded companies that you can buy and sell on the stock market.

Let me introduce you to another term - stock index. It is like a scoreboard for the stock market. It tracks the performance of a group of companies to give traders a big-picture view of how the market is doing. Instead of looking at individual stocks, indices help investors see overall market trends.

Each stock index includes a selection of companies, often grouped by country, industry, or market size. When these companies' stock prices rise or fall, the index moves accordingly. For example, the S&P500 tracks the 500 largest U.S. companies, while the DAX represents Germany's top firms.

As a trader, keeping an eye on stock indices helps you understand market conditions, spot trends, and make better trading decisions.

You already know about Forex, Commodities, and Crypto - all important financial instruments in global markets.

Let's have a quick recap:

- **Stocks:** Own part of companies like Apple. Earn from price growth and dividends.
- **Forex:** Trade currencies 24/5. Driven by economies and interest rates.
- **Commodities:** Trade goods like oil and gold. Prices shift with supply, demand, and global events.
- **Crypto:** Digital assets like Bitcoin, traded 24/7. Fast and volatile.

Great job! You've mastered financial instruments. Now let's test your knowledge!

QUIZ: Financial Instruments

1. What is the primary market where traders exchange currencies?

A. Crypto Market
B. Stock Market
C. Forex Market
D. Commodities Market

2. Which of the following is an example of a commodity?

A. Currency
B. Oil
C. Tesla stock
D. Bitcoin

3. What is a key feature of cryptocurrencies?

A. They are decentralized and run on blockchain technology
B. They are controlled by central banks
C. They can only be used for online gaming

D. Their value never changes

4. Which of the following is NOT a financial instrument?

A. Cryptocurrency
B. Stocks
C. Commodities
D. Real estate property

5. Why do traders buy and sell commodities?

A. To avoid inflation risks
B. To invest in technology stocks
C. To store valuable metals in bank
D. To profit from price changes in physical goods like oil, gold, and wheat

6. What makes cryptocurrency different from other financial instruments?

A. It has fixed prices set by the government
B. It is controlled by central banks
C. It is decentralized and operates on blockchain technology
D. It can only be traded during stock market hours

7. What makes Forex trading different from stock trading?

A. Forex involves trading currency, while stocks represent company ownership
B. Stocks trade 24/5, while Forex has fixed hours
C. Forex is only available to large banks, while stocks are for individuals
D. Forex is slower moving than stocks

8. Which of these is an example of a financial instrument?

A. A real estate property
B. A currency
C. A debit card
D. A savings account

9. Why do investors trade Forex?

A. To profit from changes in currency exchange rates
B. To purchase physical goods for trade
C. To buy and hold digital assets
D. To own shares in international companies

10. What do equities represent?

A. A type of government-issued bond
B. A fixed-income investment
C. Ownership in a company, including both public and private businesses
D. A contract for trading commodities

Answer: 1. C; 2. B; 3. A; 4. D; 5. D; 6. C; 7. A; 8. B; 9. A; 10. C

Lesson 2: Market Trends and Cycles

It's time to learn to analyze the market!

Remember these two? You've already met the bull and bear markets, but now it's time to go deeper. Understanding how they form and what drives them will help you anticipate market moves. By the end of this lesson, you'll know how to identify trends, recognize cycles, and use them to your advantage. Let's get started!

In a bull market, prices don't just go straight up, and in a bear market, they don't just plummet continuously. Markets move in waves - short-term ups and downs within the bigger trend.

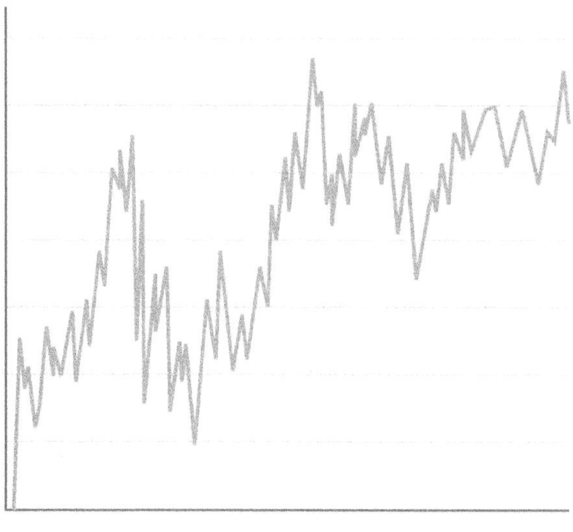

These smaller movements are called **market corrections** in **bull markets**. Think of a market correction as a quick pause to catch your breath during a climb.

In **bear markets**, these smaller movements are called **relief rallies**. They are like a temporary break in a steep downhill run before the descent continues. Recognizing this behavior that may be unfolding within a larger trend pattern manage risk and make more intelligent decisions.

A market correction is a short-term dip in a rising market. Experienced traders see it as a buying opportunity - a chance to enter the market at a lower price before the uptrend continues.

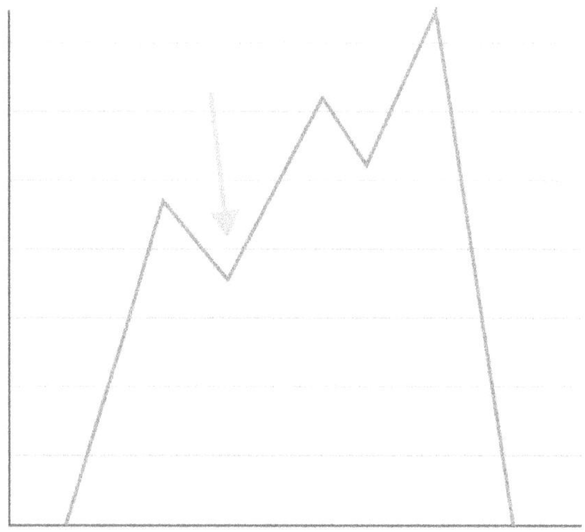

Imagine Jane, a trader, is watching ABC Corp, a stock that has been steadily rising for months. The stock recently hit $100, but then it dropped to $95 over a few days. Some traders panicked and sold, fearing a bigger drop.

But Jane recognizes this as a market correction, not a crash. She waits for signs that the stock is stabilizing, then buys at $95. A few weeks later, the uptrend resumes and the stock climbs to $110. By understanding market corrections, Jane bought low and made a profit of $15 per share.

On the other hand, a relief rally is a temporary bounce in a falling market. It can trick traders into thinking the trend is reversing, but experienced traders stay cautious, knowing that prices may continue downward.

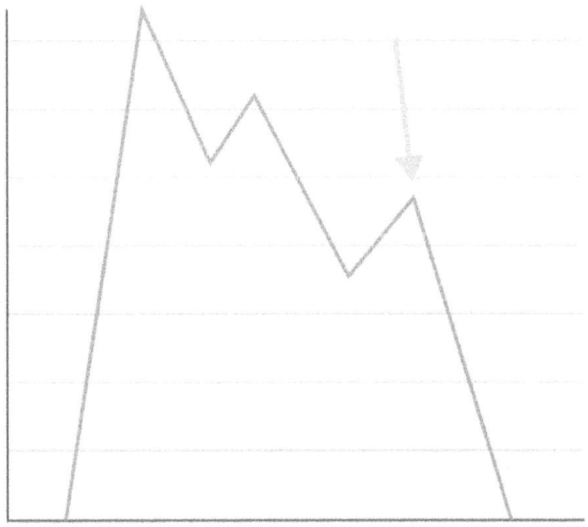

Meet Alex, a trader watching the stock of ABC Corp in a bear market. The stock has been falling for months, dropping from $80 to $50. Suddenly, it jumped to $55 in a single day. Some traders believed the trend was reversing and rushed to buy.

But Alex recognizes this as a relief rally - a short-lived bounce in a downtrend. He waited instead of buying too soon. A few days later, the stock fell to $45, confirming that the bear market was still in play. By staying cautious, he avoided a costly mistake.

Not every dip in a bull market is just a correction - sometimes it signals a deeper decline. So, how do traders tell the difference?

Here are the signs of a market correction:

- The overall trend is still upward (higher highs and higher lows).
- The decline is less than 10% and recovers within days or weeks.
- No major negative news has been reported, affecting the market in the long term.

Sometimes, a dip is more than just a correction - it could be the start of a bigger downtrend. Here's how to recognize a deeper decline:

- The trend breaks down - lower highs and lower lows appear.
- The drop exceeds 10% and lasts for a long period.
- Negative economic news or financial instability triggers fear.

Now it's time to put that knowledge into action! It might be tricky, but practice makes perfect! The more you analyze the market, the easier it becomes!

Market correction or a bigger downtrend?

Imagine you're a trader analyzing a market trend. Choose three signs of a market correction. Market corrections are usually short-term dips during an overall uptrend, often triggered by temporary events. A downtrend shows deeper, longer-lasting weakness in the market.

- Economy slows, unemployment rises

- Stocks climb, hitting 6-month highs
- No bad news, investors are optimistic
- 3% dip followed by quick recovery
- Big firms announce layoffs
- Market drops over 20% recently

Answer:

- Stocks climb, hitting 6-month highs
- No bad news, investors are optimistic
- 3% dip followed by quick recovery

Market correction or a bigger downtrend?

Now let's check if you can spot the signs of a bigger downtrend. Choose the correct signs of a decline. Look for long-term patterns and serious economic or corporate signals - not just quick dips or investor reactions. A true downtrend usually reflects deeper and lasting trouble.

- Stock drops on CEO scandal
- Stock drops after weak earnings, but bounces back
- Stock index falls 12% lately
- Retail dips on seasonal slowdown
- Market dips 3%, rebounds fast

- Crisis and inflation hit market

Answer:

- Stock drops on CEO scandal
- Stock index falls 12% lately
- Crisis and inflation hit market

Excellent! On the contrary, a relief rally can also trick traders into thinking a bear market is over. But how can you tell if it's just a temporary bounce?

- Prices jump quickly but without strong volume.
- The overall downtrend remains intact (lower highs and lower lows).
- No major improvements in the economy or company performance - things are still uncertain.

A true trend reversal signals the end of a bear market and the start of a new uptrend. Here's how to tell the difference:

- More traders are buying, increasing demand and trading activity.

- Optimism returns as the economy improves or positive news boosts confidence.

Let's practice! Don't worry if it feels challenging - every great trader improves with practice!

Relief rally or a true trend reversal?

A sudden price jump can be exciting, but don't be fooled! Can you tell if it's just a relief rally? Pick the signs that suggest the market bounce is temporary. Relief rallies are short-lived. Look for sharp price spikes without strong fundamentals, low volume, and a still bearish overall trend.

- No news, but prices still jump
- Big investors take long positions
- Leaders show confidence ahead
- Lower highs and lows continue
- 8% jump with weak trading volume
- Investor confidence is at yearly peak

Answer:

- No news, but prices still jump
- Lower highs and lows continue
- 8% jump with weak trading volume

Relief rally or a true trend reversal?

The market's moving - but is it for real? Spot the signs of a trend reversal that could mark the start of a new uptrend. A true reversal usually comes with confidence, volume, and broad participation - not just a quick bounce.

- Price pops after viral tweet
- Falling prices flip on company's earnings
- Market rises as unemployment drops
- Price breaks a long-term downtrend line
- Market rises on unconfirmed news
- Speculation fuels price rise

Answer:

- Falling prices flip on company's earnings
- Market rises as unemployment drops
- Price breaks a long-term downtrend line

Nevertheless, markets don't stay bullish or bearish forever - they move through cycles, just like the seasons. Just like spring brings growth, summer peaks, fall slows things down, and winter resets before the next cycle, markets follow a similar rhythm.

Expansion is like spring - optimism is high, businesses are growing, and stock prices are climbing. Traders look for opportunities to buy as strong profits and consumer confidence drive the market forward.

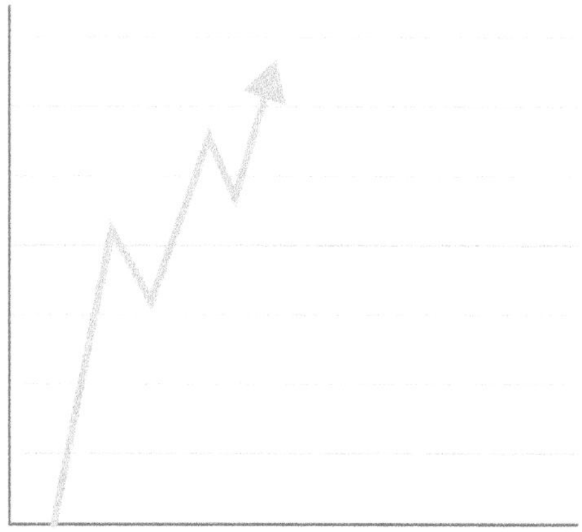

Then the market hits its peak, just like summer at its hottest. Stock prices are at record highs, and investors are overly confident. But warning signs appear - rising inflation, slowing growth, or interest rate hikes. Smart traders start taking profits before the market shifts.

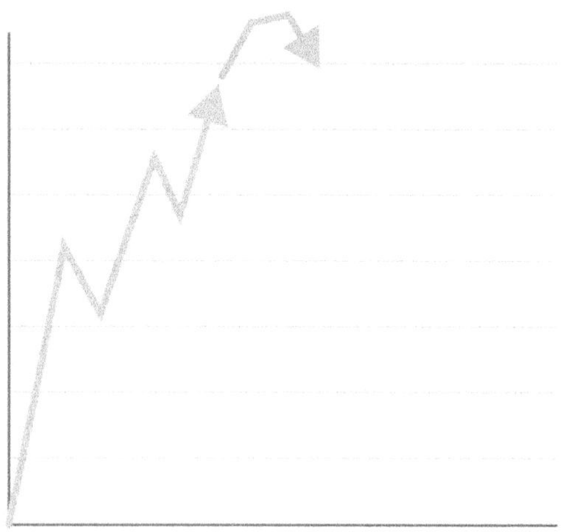

Contraction is like a fall - the market cools down, and stock prices begin to drop. Investors start selling, uncertainty rises, and businesses cut back. While some panic, experienced traders prepare for the next cycle.

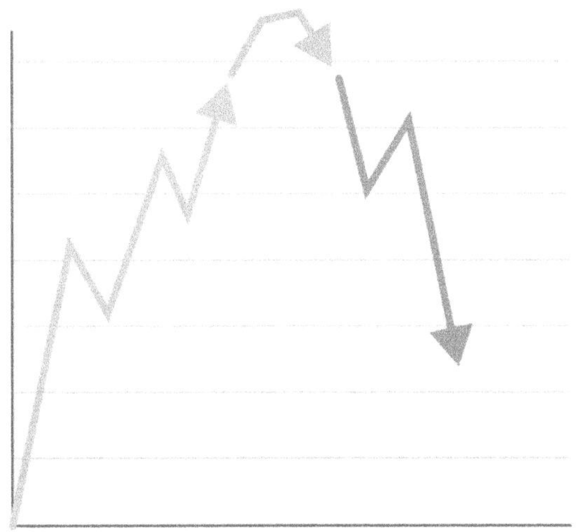

The trough is like winter - the market is at its lowest, but recovery is near. Stock prices stabilize, value investors start buying, and economic conditions slowly improve. Traders who recognize this phase position themselves for the next expansion.

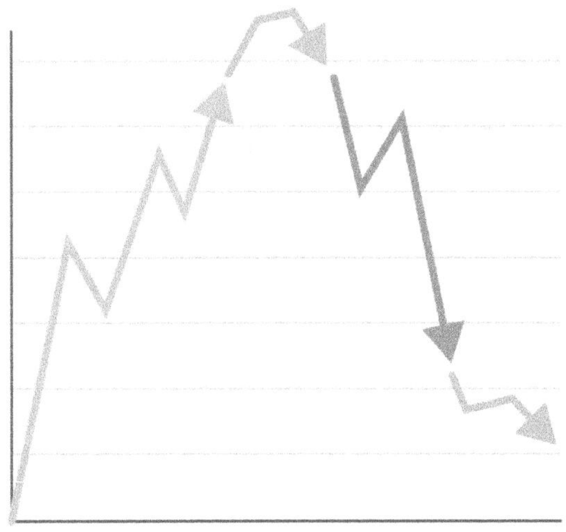

Every market goes through these cycles. Recognizing where you are helps you make better trading decisions. In expansion, traders ride the trend. At the peak, they stay cautious. During contractions, they protect their assets, and in the troughs, they look for opportunities before the next uptrend.

Market cycles

You'e learned how markets move just like the seasons - expanding like spring, peaking like summer, cooling like fall, and resetting like winter. Think like a trader and match each phase with its characteristics! In spring, everything grows. In summer, we celebrate growth. In the fall, we brace for change. In winter, we wait to bloom again. Markets move just like that.

- Contraction - Market is at its lowest, buyers step in
- Expansion - Market grows with rising optimism
- Trough - Prices peak, risks emerge.
- Peak - Drop begins amid uncertainty

Answer:

- Contraction - Drop begins amid uncertainty
- Expansion - Market grows with rising optimism
- Trough - Market is at its lowest, buyers step in
- Peak - Prices peak, risks emerge

Now you know how to spot each phase and trend and use it to make smarter trading decisions. Keep practicing, and soon you'll spot market trends like a pro! You are one step closer to beginning your trading journey, so keep up the good work!

QUIZ: Trends and Cycles

1. What is a market correction?

A. A phase where prices only go up
B. A long-term decline that signals a bear market
C. A temporary dip in an uptrend, usually less than 10%
D. A complete market crash with no recovery

2. What is a relief rally?

A. A government intervention to stop a market crash
B. The start of a long-term bull market
C. A sign that the bear market is officially over
D. A temporary bounce in a downtrend that can trick traders

3. How can traders recognize a true trend reversal?

A. Increased demand, higher volume, and positive economic signs

B. A quick increase is followed by another big drop
C. A sudden price jump with no change in fundamentals
D. Prices are rising but still making lower highs and lower lows

4. Which of these is a sign of a market correction rather than a deeper decline?

A. A bear market begins, and long-term investors exit
B. The overall trend is still upward, with higher highs and higher lows
C. Stock prices drop more than 10% and continue falling
D. Negative news or financial instability triggers fear

5. What phase of the market cycle is like spring, where optimism is high and stocks are rising?

A. Peak
B. Expansion
C. Contraction
D. Trough

6. What happens at the market peak?

A. Traders panic and sell off all assets
B. The economy completely collapses
C. Stock prices are at record highs, but warning signs appear
D. Prices continue rising indefinitely

7. What phase of the market cycle is like fall, where stocks begin to drop, and uncertainty rises?

A. Trough
B. Contraction
C. Expansion
D. Peak

8. What phase of the market cycle is like winter, where prices bottom out and smart investors start buying?

A. Peak
B. Contraction
C. Trough
D. Expansion

9. How do experienced traders use market cycles to their advantage?

A. They buy during the trough and sell during the peak
B. They sell at the bottom and buy at the top
C. They ignore cycles and make random trades
D. They only buy stocks when everyone else is buying

10. What is the best way to avoid getting caught in a relief rally?

A. Sell everything immediately at the first sign of a price bounce
B. Ignore economic conditions and focus only on price movement
C. Look for strong volume, positive fundamentals, and sustained demand before buying
D. Buy as soon as the price jumps, assuming the trend is reversing

Answer: 1. C; 2. D; 3. A; 4. B; 5. B; 6. C; 7. B; 8. C; 9. A; 10. C

Lesson 3: Contracts for Difference

Welcome to contracts for difference!

In this lesson, you'll learn how contracts for difference (CFDs) allow traders to profit from price movements without owning the actual asset. CFDs are a derivative of the underlying asset. By the end of this lesson, you'll understand how CFDs work, their advantages, and their risks.

To help explain the contract for difference, let's look at Alex. He has been watching stock prices move up and down, and he wants to profit from the changes - but he doesn't want to buy shares outright.

Instead, he trades using a contract for difference (CFD) — a financial instrument that allows him to speculate on price movements without actually owning the underlying asset.

Alex now trades using CFDs, and just like in traditional markets, he can go long or short, and he has access to leverage to amplify his positions.

If prices rise, he goes short to profit from the increase. True or false?

Answer: False. If prices rise, he goes long to profit from the increase. If prices fall, he goes short to profit from the decline.

CFDs aren't limited to one market - they can be used to trade a wide range of assets. This includes forex, commodities, indices, cryptocurrencies, and even stocks of major companies. Note that CFDs are commonly available through Forex brokers around the world, although some countries - like the U.S. - have restrictions on their use.

Unlike traditional investing, CFDs allow him to take advantage of both bullish and bearish markets.

Let's calculate the profit!

Alex expects ABC's shares to rise from $50 to $60. He goes long with a CFD at $50. The price soon reached $60. How much does Alex earn if the price of his CFD rises from $50 to $60? To calculate profit on a CFD, subtract the entry price from the exit price. Alex bought at $50 and sold at $60 - what's the difference per share?

A. $60
B. $50
C. $10
D. $20

Answer: Since Alex opened his CFD at $50 and closed it at $60, his profit is the difference of $10 per share. That's how CFDs allow traders to earn from price movements!

To sum up, a CFD is a financial contract where traders speculate on price changes without buying the actual asset. Instead, they agree to exchange the difference in price from the time they open a trade to when they close it.

Let's put your knowledge to the test! Answer the following questions to check your understanding.

With CFDs, you must own the asset represented to profit from price changes. Is it true or false?

Answer: False. CFDs let traders speculate on price movements without owning the asset. Instead, they profit (or lose) based on the difference between the buying and selling price.

As with any market, trading CFD can be profitable, but traders need to understand the accompanying risks. As CFDs use leverage, which means you can trade with more money than you put in, trading with CFDs can lead to bigger profits and also bigger losses - sometimes more than you originally invested.

If Alex expects shares of a company ABC to rise from $50 to $60 and it drops instead, he loses money. Since he doesn't own the stock, he can't wait for a recovery - his profit or loss depends on when he closes the trade.

But leverage isn't the only thing to watch out for. Widening spreads can happen when markets are volatile - this means the gap between the buying and selling price gets larger, making it more expensive to open or close a trade. Along with slippage and possible commissions, these factors can affect your results even if the price moves in your favor.

Why do traders use CFDs? CFDs offer flexibility because they let traders speculate on price movements without owning the asset. You can trade larger positions using less upfront money through leverage. You can also try to profit whether prices go up or down.

CFDs come with risks - leveraged trading can amplify both gains and losses, sometimes exceeding your initial investment. Managing risk is crucial!

Well done! You've added CFDs to your trading knowledge - an instrument that lets you profit from rising and falling markets without owning the asset. Now you know the key financial markets and what you can trade in each. Use this knowledge wisely. Keep learning and refining your skills!

SECTION 3: FOREX TRADING

Chapter 1: Forex Fundamentals

Lesson 1: What Is Forex Trading?

Pack your bags, we're going global!

Impressive progress on your trading journey! My name is Andy, and I'll guide you through the next adventure. Grab your passport - we're about to explore a market that never sleeps and spans the entire world!

We find ourselves at International Airport Terminal 3, where travelers from around the world rush to catch flights. Look at all these currency exchange kiosks! This is Forex (a.k.a. FX) in action - a $7.6 trillion daily market that's 25 times larger than global stock trading.

The screen shows today's rate: 1 EUR = 1.20 USD. I have 100 US dollars and I'm traveling to Europe. How many euros will I get?

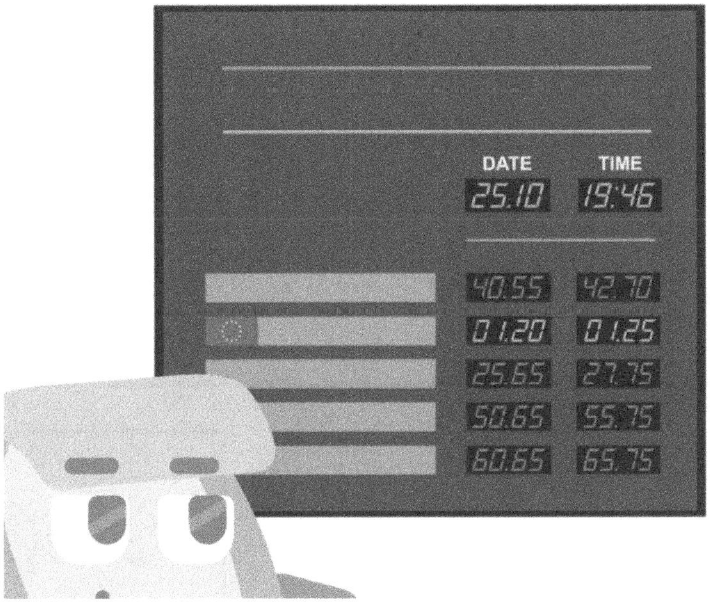

Calculate the exchange

Andy wants to know how many euros he will receive before any fees are applied. How many euros would 100 USD buy at this rate? If 1 EUR costs 1.20 USD, divide 100 by the cost per euro.

- 83.33 EUR
- 120 EUR
- 100 EUR
- 1.20 EUR

Answer: 83.33 EUR. The exchange rate tells you that 1 EUR costs 1.20 USD, so to find how many euros you can buy with 100 USD, you need to divide 100 by 1.20. That gives you 83.33 EUR, not more or less. Always pay attention to the direction of the rate.

Wait a second... I was supposed to get 83.33 euros, but my receipt says only 80. Where did the rest go?

Andy just learned the hard way - retail exchange rates come with high fees and wide spreads. That's why traders don't use airport kiosks. But don't worry; professional Forex markets offer much tighter spreads, making trading far more efficient.

Unlike stocks, where you buy a single asset, Forex always involves currency pairs - you're exchanging one currency for another. The structure of a currency pair like EUR/ USD tells us exactly what we're trading:

- The first currency (EUR) is the "base" currency
- The second currency (USD) is the "quote" currency
- The rate shows how much of the quoted currency you need to buy one unit of the base currency.

Let's see this in action with another example. If GBP/JPY shows 175.30, this means 1 British pound (base) costs 175.30 Japanese yen (quote). The base currency is always equal to 1 unit, and the quote shows how much of the second currency this equals.

Travel to Canada

Andy is now heading to Canada and needs to exchange 100 US dollars. The exchange rate for USD/ CAD is 1.35. How many CAD would 100 USD cost? In USD/CAD, USD is the base currency, and the rate tells you how many Canadian dollars one US dollar costs.

- 74.07 CAD
- 100 CAD
- 1.35 CAD
- 135 CAD

Answer: 135 CAD. Since the exchange rate is 1.35, 100 USD converts to 135 CAD. Understanding this relationship is key in Forex trading.

The order of currencies in a pair is crucial for interpretation. Let's compare:

- EUR/USD = 1.20 means €1 costs $1.20
- USD/EUR = 0.83 means $1 costs €0.83

These are the same relationship viewed from opposite sides - just like we can say "5 apples cost $10" or "each apple costs $2."

From Australia to New Zealand

You have 500 Australian dollars and need to convert them to New Zealand dollars. The exchange rate for AUD/NZD is 1.08. How many NZD would 500 AUD convert to? In AUD/NZD, the rate tells you how many New Zealand dollars one Australian dollar is worth.

- 1.08 NZD
- 500 NZD
- 540 NZD
- 463 NZD

Answer: 540 NZD. Since AUD/NZD = 1.08, this means 1 AUD is worth 1.08 NZD. So, exchanging 500 AUD gives 540 NZD. This calculation method works for any currency pair and amount once you understand the base and quote relationship.

A boarding announcement echoes through the airport. Like flights moving through time zones, Forex trading never stops during the week - it operates 24 hours a day, 5 days a week. But while the market itself doesn't open or close like stock exchanges, activity levels shift as major financial centers come online. When one region's stock markets open, Forex volume and volatility often pick up, reflecting that region's influence.

Looking at airport departure screens, we notice flights leaving for Sydney, Tokyo, London, and New York - the major Forex hubs. Each trading session has unique characteristics:

- Sydney session: 9:00 PM - 6:00 AM UTC - The first session to start each day
- Asian session (Tokyo): 12:00 AM - 9:00 AM UTC - Often quieter with slower price movements
- European session (London): 7:00 AM - 4:00 PM UTC - Highest volume and volatility
- US session (New York): 1:00 PM - 10:00 PM UTC - High liquidity, especially when both Europe and US are open

Forex markets never close during the week - they move seamlessly from one financial center to another. As one region winds down, another ramps up. This creates a continuous trading cycle that moves around the globe - from Sydney to Tokyo, to London, and finally New York.

As our flight gets called for boarding, let's recap what we've learned about Forex trading:

- Forex (FX) is the largest financial market in the world, trading over $7.6 trillion daily
- Currencies are always traded in pairs with a base and quote currency
- The exchange rate shows how much of the quote currency equals one unit of the base currency
- Forex operates 24 hours a day, 5 days a week, rotating through major global markets
- Activity levels vary throughout the day, depending on which financial centers are open
- Understanding currency pair notation is key to calculating conversions correctly

Lesson 2: How The Forex Market Works

Behind the scenes of global currency trading

Our flight has landed in London, one of the world's largest Forex trading hubs. As we step into the financial district, the towering bank buildings surround us. What actually happens inside these buildings when currencies change hands?

We approach the entrance of a major bank's trading floor. Unlike stock exchanges with central locations and trading floors, Forex has no single physical marketplace. It is a decentralized market, as you've already learned in the previous course - trading happens electronically through networks of banks, institutions, and brokers all around the world.

There's a fundamental difference in reliability. If the New York Stock Exchange, a centralized market, experienced a technical failure, stock trading could halt entirely. But in Forex, if one bank or venue goes offline, trading continues through countless other channels. The tradeoff? Less transparency - in Forex, we can't see the total market volume or order depth like in stock exchanges.

Check your memory!

Drag each statement to the correct category. Think about how stock exchanges differ from the Forex market we just described.

- Decentralized market - A single authority or exchange
- Centralized market - A network of connected participants

Answer:

- Decentralized market - A network of connected participants
- Centralized market - A single authority or exchange

Let me show you what happens when I place a Forex trade to buy 10,000 EUR/USD through my retail trading app. Unlike a stock order that goes to a specific exchange, my Forex order enters a vast network of participants (with access provided by my Forex broker). But who exactly provides the currency I'm buying?

The currency you're buying comes from liquidity providers. These are institutions that keep the Forex market running by always offering to buy and sell currencies. Primary liquidity providers include major global banks like JP Morgan, Citibank, and Deutsche Bank, who collectively handle trillions in daily volume.

That is, when I place an order:

1. My broker routes it to their liquidity providers

2. These providers compete to offer the best price

3. The trade executes with the best available rate

4. All happens electronically in milliseconds

There's no single "official" EUR/USD price - each provider may offer slightly different rates.

As we learned previously, this decentralized structure enables the 24-hour trading cycle as activity shifts between global financial centers. When London banks close, New York continues actively trading. When New York finishes, Tokyo and Sydney take over. The market never sleeps during the weekdays.

Tier 1: Interbank Market - The Core

Let's explore the key participants in this global network, starting at the very core. At the heart of Forex are the largest commercial and investment banks. They trade enormous volumes directly with each other through the interbank market - the deepest and most liquid layer with the tightest spreads.

These banks serve two key functions:

1. Market making - providing liquidity to other participants

2. Proprietary trading - seeking profit through their own trading strategies

Tier 2: Institutional Participants

Around the core circle hedge funds, asset managers, pension funds, and large corporations. These participants:

- Access the market through prime brokerage relationships with major banks
- Trade substantial volumes but not at the interbank level
- Often employ specialized Forex strategies or need currencies for business operations internally or for corporate clients.

Multinational corporations like Apple, for example, earn revenues in many currencies, but their financial reports are in USD, requiring constant currency conversion.

Tier 3: Retail Market

Finally, individual traders like us access Forex through retail brokers and dealers. As a retail trader:

- You can trade with as little as $100

- Your orders are typically aggregated with others before reaching liquidity providers
- You pay slightly wider spreads than institutional participants (transaction fee equivalent)

Follow the money

A US company needs to pay its German supplier €5 million for machinery. The company has USD and needs to convert it to EUR. Which market participants would most likely be involved in this transaction? Think about which participant has the capacity to handle large corporate transactions.

- Stock exchange brokers
- Central banks directly
- A commercial bank acting as a liquidity provider
- Individual retail traders

Answer: A commercial bank acting as a liquidity provider. Large-scale corporate transactions require deep liquidity and institutional access, which is typically provided by commercial banks. Retail traders, central banks, and stock brokers don't handle this kind of operational currency exchange.

Beyond the three tiers are central banks like the Federal Reserve, European Central Bank, and Bank of Japan. Unlike other forex market participants, they don't trade for profit but rather to implement policy and maintain price stability.

Central banks participate in Forex markets for three main reasons:

1. To implement monetary policy (raising/ lowering interest rates)

2. To stabilize their own currency when needed

3. To maintain foreign currency reserves

Their actions can create major market movements that affect all other participants.

Let's see this in action. Imagine the screens suddenly flash with breaking news: "Swiss National Bank Removes Euro Peg!"

Central bank impact

A currency peg is when a central bank fixes its currency to another at a set rate and keeps it there by stepping in to buy or sell as needed. When the Swiss National Bank removed the euro peg, it let the Swiss franc (CHF) move freely based on market supply and demand. When a currency is no longer held at a fixed rate, its value can change quickly as the market adjusts. What immediate effect would this likely have on the market?

- Trading in EUR/CHF would be temporarily suspended for 24 hours
- EUR/CHF would experience extreme volatility and likely a sharp decline
- EUR/CHF would gradually increase over several days
- EUR/CHF would remain stable as this news isn't significant

Answer: EUR/CHF would experience extreme volatility and likely a sharp decline. That's right! This actually happened in January 2015 when the Swiss National Bank (SNB) removed its peg to the euro. The EUR/CHF pair collapsed nearly 30% within minutes, creating extreme volatility.

Unexpected central bank actions can cause some of the most powerful moves in Forex markets, which is why traders closely monitor their policies.

We've explored how different market participants interact, from banks and corporations to central banks making major policy decisions. Each plays a unique role in shaping Forex price movements. Now, let's put everything to the test - can you match each participant to their role?

Match the participants

Match each Forex market participant with their primary role. Think about who actually needs foreign currency for business, who enables large transactions, and who trades mostly for personal gain in smaller amounts.

- Multinational Corporations - Large currency exchanges
- Retail Traders Participant - Trade small amounts for personal gain
- Commercial Banks - International business operations

Answer:

- Multinational Corporations - International business operations
- Retail Traders Participant - Trade small amounts for personal gain
- Commercial Banks - Large currency exchanges

That was a long journey! As our tour of the trading floor ends, let's recap what we've learned about how the Forex market works:

- Forex is a **decentralized** network with no single point of failure, unlike centralized exchanges.
- **Liquidity providers** (mainly large banks) make markets by offering currency prices & liquidity
- The market operates in **tiers**: interbank core, institutional middle layer, and retail outer layer.
- **Central banks** influence the market through policy decisions and market interventions.

Lesson 3: Forex Brokers

Choosing your market gateway

After exploring the Forex market structure, our journey takes us to London - the world's largest Forex trading hub - to learn how traders connect to the global currency market.

Every trader needs a broker to access the Forex market. Let's look at the most common methods and the industry terminology you'll encounter when opening a Forex trading account.

Brokers use different models to handle client orders - sometimes even within the same company for different clients or situations. The first model we'll explore is called "agency execution" or "A-book."

With this model, the broker acts as an intermediary, connecting you directly to the Forex market by routing your orders to liquidity providers like major banks.

When brokers use the A-book model, they typically implement systems called Electronic Communication Networks (ECNs) or Straight-Through Processing (STP) to send your orders to the market - fancy Forex lingo you might encounter in trading forums.

Think of an ECN as a highway system connecting many traders and liquidity providers around the globe. Your buy order might be matched with the best sell order from anyone in the network - it could even be from another retail trader if they offer the best price!

STP works slightly differently. Your order still goes to the market but through specific channels which the broker has established with certain liquidity providers rather than an open network.

It's like ordering food delivery through an app that works with specific restaurants. Your order goes "straight through" to the restaurant partners rather than searching every possible eatery in town.

Under the agency model, brokers typically make money by charging small commissions and/or adding a markup to the spread. Since they're passing your orders to the market, they earn this fee regardless of whether your trade is profitable.

Now, let's look at a different approach: the "principal execution" or "B-book" model. Here, the broker acts as a "market maker" by taking the opposite side of your trade instead of sending it to the external market. When using the B-book model, when you buy, they're selling to you, and when you sell, they're buying from you.

This arrangement is like how casinos operate. The casino doesn't connect players to other gamblers - it plays directly against everyone. Similarly, when using the B-book model, the broker doesn't send your order to the market - it becomes your trading counterparty.

A-Book broker characteristics

Choose 3 characteristics that apply to an A-Book broker. A-Book brokers send orders to the market and earn from volume, not client losses.

- Profits when clients lose money
- Offers variable spreads
- Takes the opposite side

- Acts as a counterparty
- Typically charges commissions
- Routes orders directly to the Forex

Answer:

- Offers variable spreads
- Typically charges commissions
- Routes orders directly to the Forex

Most brokers today use a hybrid approach, combining both models based on factors like trade size, client profile, or market conditions. They might use the B-book model for smaller trades while using the A-book model for larger positions or orders from very active traders.

One concept that differs between these execution models is "slippage." When the market moves between your order placement and execution, the difference between your expected price and actual execution price is called slippage - a term you'll need to know when trading fast-moving markets.

Slippage happens when the price you expect to trade at differs from the price your order actually gets filled at. Imagine clicking "buy" at 1.2000, but your order gets filled at 1.2010 - that 10-point difference is slippage.

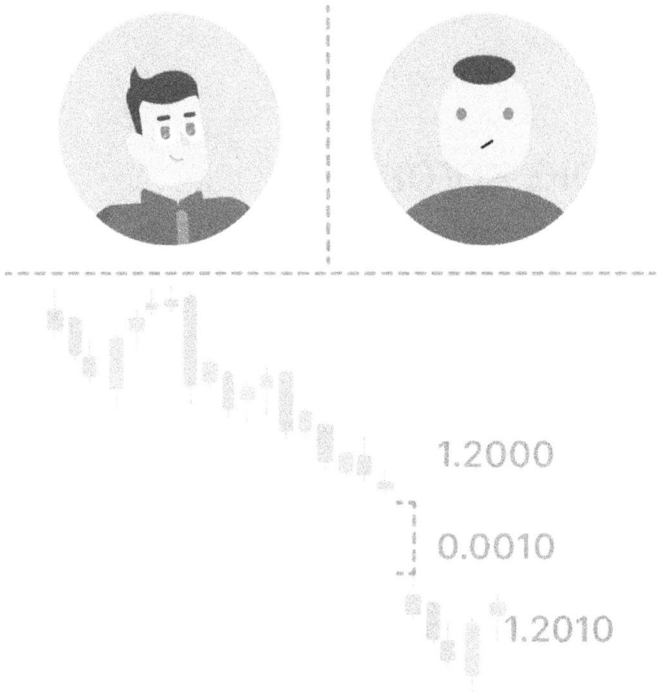

During normal market conditions, slippage is usually minimal. But when major news breaks or markets are very volatile, prices can change rapidly in the milliseconds between placing your order and its execution.

A slippage

A trader places a market order to buy EUR/USD just as a major economic report is released. With which execution model would they most likely experience significant slippage? Consider how agency execution sends orders directly to the market while principal execution handles trades internally. What happens when prices move rapidly during major news events?

- Principal execution (B-book)
- Agency execution (A-book)

Answer: Agency execution (A-book) typically shows more slippage during major news events because orders are being directed to the external market, where prices can move rapidly. Since your order takes milliseconds to reach the market, the price may change before execution.

Does this mean B-book execution is better during news events? Not necessarily. While it might result in less slippage, brokers using this model might compensate by widening spreads or restricting trading during volatility. Each model has its own set of tradeoffs.

Understanding how your broker works helps you make better trading decisions and choose the right broker for your needs. Let's recap what we've learned about Forex broker execution models:

- Brokers use different execution models: agency execution (A-book) routes orders directly to the market, while principal execution (B-book) involves the broker acting as counterparty
- Slippage occurs when orders execute at different prices than requested
- A-book execution typically shows more slippage during high-volatility news events
- B-book execution might show less slippage but may have wider spreads

Fantastic work! You've built a strong foundation on how the Forex market operates, who the key players are, and how brokers execute trades. Before we move forward, take a moment to check your understanding. Then, we'll continue exploring the next key concepts in your trading journey.

QUIZ: Forex Fundamentals

1. What is the correct interpretation of the exchange rate EUR/USD = 1.20?

A. €1 costs $1.20
B. €1 equals 120 cents
C. €1.20 costs $1
D. $1 costs €1.20

2. The Forex market trades approximately how much daily volume?

A. $7.6 trillion
B. $1 billion
C. $500 million
D. $100 trillion

3. What is slippage in Forex trading?

A. The difference between bid and ask prices
B. The minimum deposit required to open a trading account

C. The fee a broker charges for executing your trade
D. The difference between the expected trade price and the actual execution price

4. Which tier represents the core of the Forex market with the deepest liquidity?

A. Tier 2: Institutional Participants
B. Tier 1: Interbank Market
C. Tier 3: Retail Market
D. Tier 4: Central Banks

5. In a currency pair like USD/ JPY, which is the quote currency?

A. Neither currency is a quote currency
B. JPY
C. USD
D. Both currencies are quote currencies

6. Which execution model typically shows more slippage during major economic news announcements?

A. Neither model experiences slippage during news events

B. Both models show identical slippage
C. B-book (principal execution)
D. A-book (agency execution)

7. What makes the Forex market different from stock exchanges?

A. Forex is decentralized with no single physical marketplace
B. Forex has a single official price for each currency pair
C. Forex trades require physical delivery of currency
D. Forex only operates during business hours

8. If GBP/AUD = 1.85, how many Australian dollars would you receive for £500?

A. 500 AUD
B. 270.27 AUD
C. 925 AUD
D. 1.85 AUD

9. Which market participants primarily provide liquidity in the Forex market?

A. Major global banks

B. Central banks
C. Multinational corporations
D. Individual retail traders

10. How do B-book brokers typically handle client trades?

A. By taking the opposite side of the trade themselves
B. By forwarding orders to stock exchanges
C. By sending all orders directly to the interbank market
D. By matching client orders with other clients only

Answer: 1. A; 2. A; 3. D; 4. B; 5. B; 6. D; 7. A; 8. C; 9. A; 10. A

Chapter 2: Forex Trading Fundamentals

Lesson 1: Currency Pairs

The building blocks of Forex trading

We take a break at a buzzing trading cafe. Wall-to-wall screens flash with currency pairs and price movements while traders analyze charts over coffee.

Let's quickly refresh what we already know about currency pairs. In pairs like EUR/USD, the first currency (EUR) is the base currency, and the second (USD) is the quote currency. The rate shows how much of the quote you need to buy one unit of the base.

1 EUR = 1.10 USD

Test your currency knowledge

You see USD/JPY quoted at 142.50 on a trading screen. You want to convert 5,000 USD to Japanese yen. How many JPY would you get for 5,000 USD? In USD/JPY, USD is the base currency, so the rate tells you how many yen one dollar is worth.

- 142.50 JPY
- 35.09 JPY
- 35,087 JPY
- 712,500 JPY

Answer: 712,500 JPY. Since USD/JPY = 142.50 means 1 USD = 142.50 JPY, then 5,000 USD = 5,000 × 142.50 = 712,500 JPY. This is how you should apply the base/quote relationship to calculate the conversion.

Now, let's dive deeper into how these pairs are categorized and traded in the real world. Not all currency pairs are created equal - they differ in liquidity, trading volume, and behavior.

Major Pairs always include the US dollar (USD) paired with one of the other 7 major currencies:

EUR, GBP, JPY, AUD, CAD, CHF, or NZD. These pairs account for about 80% of all Forex trading volume.

The most traded pair is EUR/USD, with approximately 28% of daily Forex volume.

Minor Pairs (also called Cross Pairs) don't include USD but still pair major currencies together, like EUR/GBP or GBP/JPY. These have good liquidity but typically wider spreads than major pairs. Minor pairs are useful when you have a view on two non-USD currencies.

Exotic Pairs include one major currency paired with a currency from a developing or smaller economy, like USD/MXN (Mexican Peso) or EUR/TRY (Turkish Lira). These pairs typically have wider spreads and can be more volatile than major and minor pairs.

Match the currency pairs

Categorize each currency pair into the correct group based on what we've just learned. Remember that major pairs always include

USD, minors contain two major currencies but not USD, and exotics include currencies from smaller economies.

- USD/JPY - Exotic Pair
- EUR/GBP - Major Pair
- EUR/PLN - Minor Pair

Answer:

- USD/JPY - Major Pair
- EUR/GBP - Minor Pair
- EUR/PLN - Exotic Pair

Understanding the volatility of different currency pairs is crucial for your trading success! Major pairs like EUR/USD move less dramatically than exotic pairs - directly impacting your risk, potential profit, and how you'll set your stop losses.

Trading the volatility

The EUR/USD chart shows small, steady movements - barely 50 points in the last hour. Meanwhile, the USD/TRY chart is making wild swings of 1000+ points! A trader has $5,000 to risk across two different trades. Considering their different volatility profiles, how should they split their risk? Volatility refers to how much a currency pair moves in a given time. Higher volatility means bigger price swings, which can lead to larger gains and larger losses.

- Divide the money equally between both pairs
- Put the entire amount on EUR/ USD for maximum safety
- Put the entire amount on
- USD/TRY for maximum profit potential
- Allocate a smaller portion to USD/TRY due to its higher volatility

Answer: Allocate a smaller portion to USD/TRY due to its higher volatility Smart risk management means adjusting position sizes based on volatility. With exotic pairs like USD/TRY making much larger price swings, a smaller position helps control risk. You might allocate $1,000 to USD/ TRY and $4,000 to EUR/USD, for instance, to balance your exposure.

This difference in volatility affects your trading approach. With major pairs, you might need larger position sizes to achieve your profit targets. With exotic pairs, smaller positions may be appropriate due to their wider price swings and higher risk.

Let's recap what we've learned about currency pairs and how they're categorized:

- Currency pairs consist of a base currency (first) and a quote currency (second)
- Major pairs involve USD paired with another major currency (EUR, GBP, JPY, etc.)
- Minor/cross pairs contain two major currencies but no USD
- Exotic pairs include currencies from developing or smaller economies
- Each category offers different liquidity, spreads, volatility, and trading opportunities

Lesson 2: Currency Correlations

The hidden connections in Forex

Our Forex education continues as we visit the research department of a major trading firm in London. Analysts study how different markets influence each other through powerful statistical relationships.

Understanding correlations is essential for Forex traders. Correlation measures the statistical relationship between two variables - how closely they move together and in what direction.

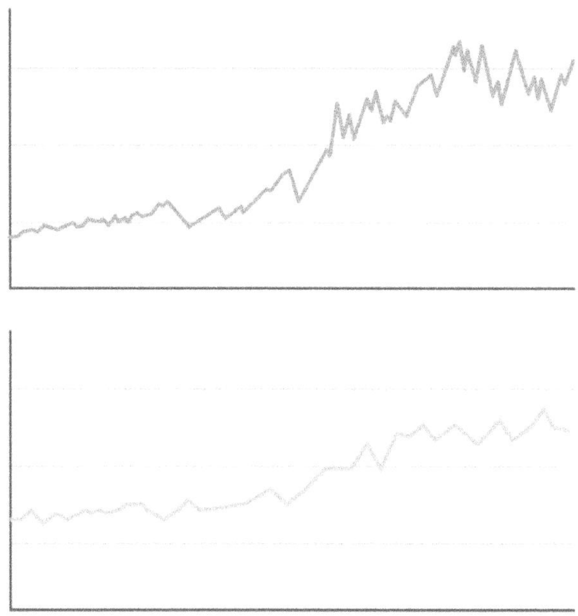

We see correlations in everyday life. Ice cream sales and temperature have a positive correlation - as temperature rises, ice cream sales typically increase in a similar pattern.

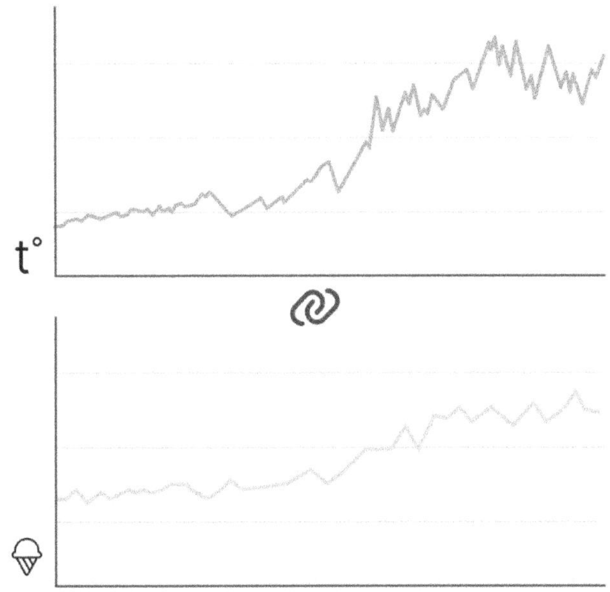

Negative correlation occurs when variables move in opposite directions. As umbrella sales increase during rainy weather, outdoor concert attendance decreases - they have a negative correlation.

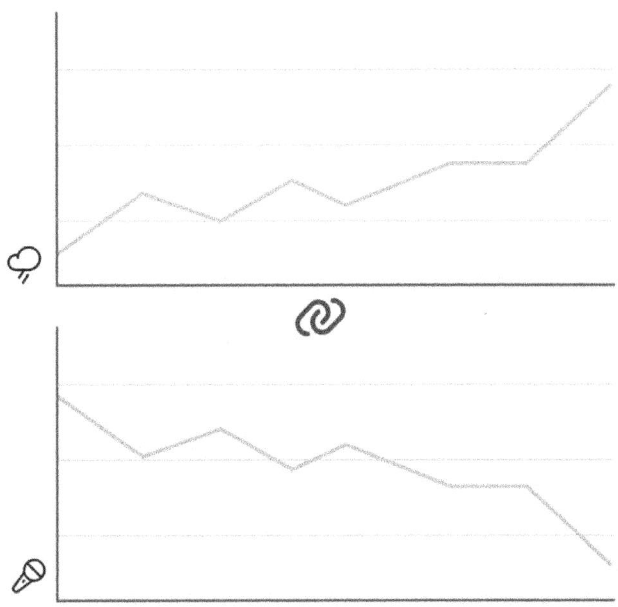

Some variables have no meaningful correlation. The number of books in your local library has virtually no relationship with daily coffee prices - they move independently of each other.

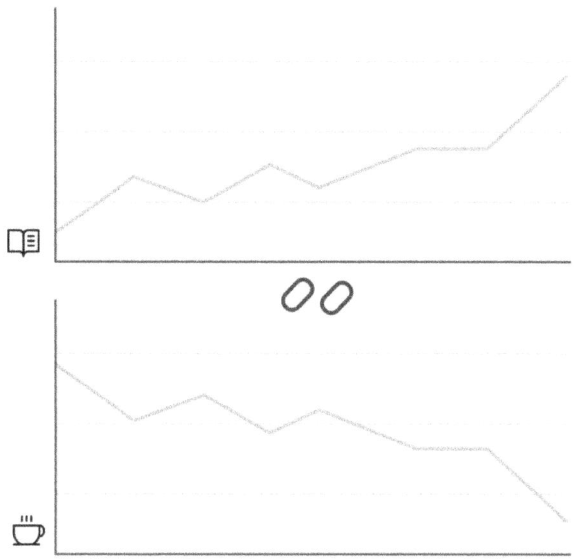

Mathematically, correlation is measured on a scale from -1 to +1:

+1: Perfect positive correlation
(move identically)
0: No correlation (move independently)
-1: Perfect negative correlation (move exactly opposite)

Most relationships fall somewhere in between.

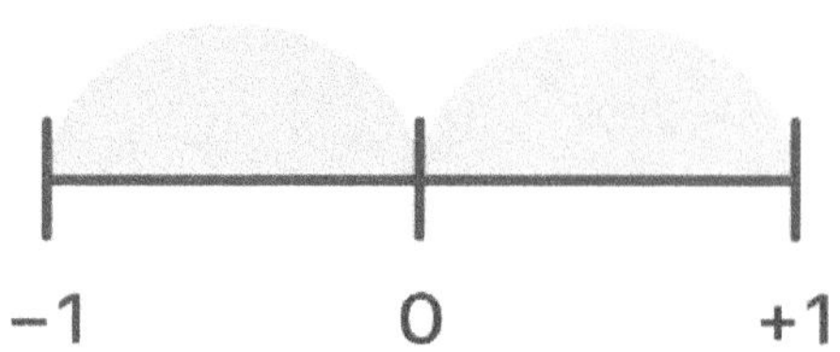

So, how does this apply to currencies? In Forex, correlation measures how closely two currency pairs move in relation to each other. These relationships arise from economic, geographic, and structural factors.

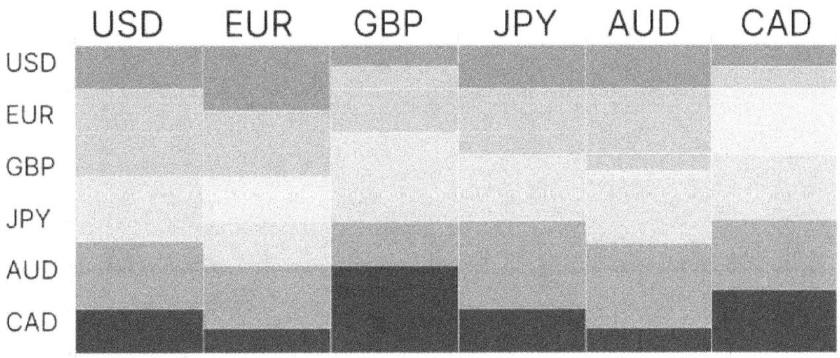

Countries with strong trade ties or similar economic structures often see their currencies move together. For example, AUD and NZD typically have a strong positive correlation.

Another reason is the dominance of certain currencies. Since USD is involved in most trades, pairs containing USD often display predictable relationships. EUR/USD and GBP/USD frequently show a positive correlation because both express value against the dollar.

Moreover, currencies can correlate strongly with commodities due to economic relationships between countries and the commodities they produce or consume. These relationships can create trading opportunities.

Oily CAD

We've already seen that the Canadian dollar (CAD) tends to move in the same direction as oil prices. Let's dig deeper. Think about how oil production affects a country's economy and currency value. Can you guess why this correlation exists?

- The Canadian government pegs CAD to oil prices
- Oil is priced exclusively in Canadian dollars
- Canada is a major oil producer and exporter
- Canadians consume more oil than other nations

Answer: Canada is a major oil producer and exporter. The Canadian dollar's correlation with oil prices isn't due to consumption patterns, currency pegs, or oil being priced in CAD. The key reason is that Canada is a major oil producer and exporter - so when oil prices rise, the Canadian economy benefits, and demand for CAD increases.

For traders, these commodity correlations have direct implications. Since CAD and oil prices are positively correlated, when oil prices rise, USD/CAD typically falls as the Canadian dollar strengthens against the USD.

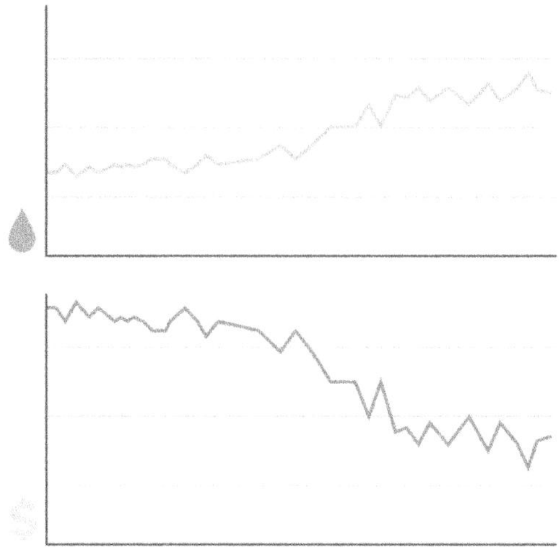

Similar commodity relationships exist with other currencies:

- AUD/USD often rises with gold prices (Australia is a major gold producer)
- NZD tends to move with dairy prices (New Zealand's key export)
- RUB often follows natural gas prices (Russia's major export)

These relationships aren't fixed but tend to hold over time.

Apply your correlation knowledge

Oil prices have just fallen 5% due to unexpected inventory data. As a trader, which move would make the most sense based on currency-commodity correlations? Remember the positive correlation between oil prices and the Canadian dollar.

- Buy AUD/USD (expecting AUD to strengthen)
- Buy USD/CAD (expecting CAD to weaken)
- Sell USD/CAD (expecting CAD to strengthen)
- No trade - oil prices don't affect currency markets

Answer: Buy USD/CAD (expecting CAD to weaken). The Canadian dollar tends to weaken when oil prices drop, because of its strong correlation with oil. That means USD/CAD is likely to rise. So, the trade that best reflects this relationship is buying USD/CAD to take advantage of the expected CAD weakness.

Moving to the risk management department, we learn how correlations affect portfolio risk. Multiple positions with high correlations can either amplify gains or multiply losses, depending on market direction. For example, if you go long on both EUR/USD and GBP/ USD, you're essentially doubling your exposure to USD weakness. If USD strengthens instead, both positions will likely lose simultaneously.

Spot the correlation risk

A trader has the following open positions: Long EUR/USD, Long GBP/USD, and Short USD/CHF. What risk is this trader primarily exposed to? Look for the common currency across all these pairs and consider how its movement would affect all positions.

- If the USD strengthens broadly, all positions could lose simultaneously
- The positions perfectly hedge each other, eliminating any risk
- If the EUR weakens, all positions would be affected
- This combination creates no correlation risk

Answer: If the USD strengthens broadly, all positions could lose simultaneously. All three positions (Long EUR/USD, Long GBP/USD, Short USD/CHF) would lose money if the USD strengthens broadly. This demonstrates correlation risk - when multiple positions are affected by the same market factor, potentially multiplying losses.

Let's recap what we've learned about currency correlations:

- Correlation measures how closely two variables move together, from +1 (same direction) to -1 (opposite direction)
- Currency pairs with the same base or quote currency often show strong correlations
- Many currencies correlate strongly with commodities - CAD with oil, AUD with gold
- Correlations create both trading opportunities and potential risks
- Understanding correlations helps traders make informed decisions and manage portfolio risk

Lesson 3: Pips and Lot Sizes

The language of Forex profits

We are back in London, where professional traders discuss their daily results. The numbers they mention sound small - "I made 50 pips on EUR/USD today" - but their smiles suggest significant profits.

To understand the language of Forex profits, we need to learn about two essential concepts: pips and lot sizes. These determine how price movements translate into actual profit or loss in your trading account.

Let's start with pips. A pip - percentage in point - is the standard unit for measuring price movement in Forex. For most currency pairs, it represents the fourth decimal place in the exchange rate.

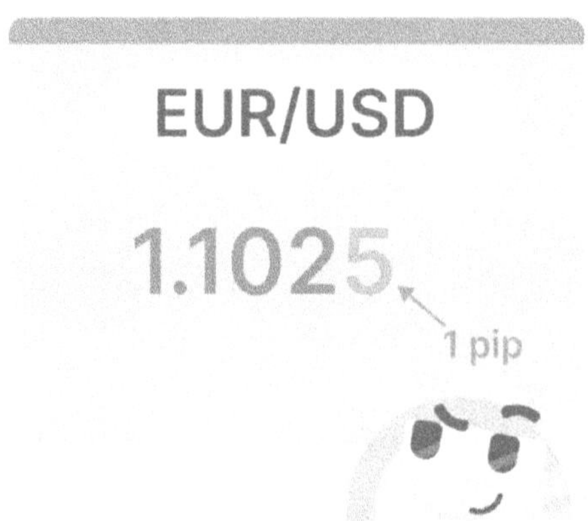

For example, if EUR/USD moves from 1.1025 to 1.1035, that's a 10-pip movement. Each pip represents 0.0001 of price change in these currency pairs. This standardization helps traders communicate precisely about market movements.

Japanese yen pairs are an exception. Since the yen has a much lower value per unit, these pairs are quoted with only two decimal places. For pairs like USD/JPY, one pip is the second decimal place (0.01).

Modern trading platforms often show a fifth decimal place (or third for JPY pairs). This smaller unit - 1/10th of a pip - is called a "pipette" or "fractional pip," allowing for even more precise pricing.

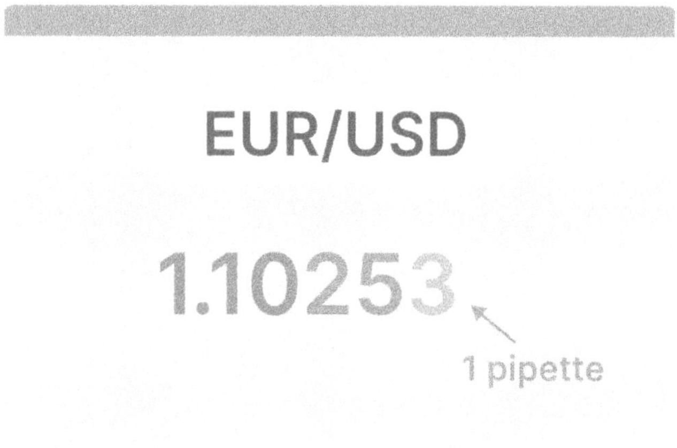

Find the pip value

Which price movement represents a 15-pip change in GBP/USD? Which is a 15-pip movement in GBP/USD? For GBP/USD, one pip is 0.0001, so calculate which option shows a change of 0.0015.

A. From 1.2450 to 1.2451
B. From 1.2450 to 1.2465
C. From 1.2450 to 1.2550
D. From 1.2450 to 1.2600

Answer: From 1.2450 to 1.2465 is a movement of 0.0015, which equals 15 pips. Since each pip is 0.0001 for GBP/USD, you multiply: 15 × 0.0001 = 0.0015.

Now, let's talk about lot sizes. A lot is the standardized trading volume in Forex. The standard lot size is 100,000 units of the base currency. This standardization helps maintain consistency across different brokers and trading platforms.

If you trade 1 standard lot of EUR/ USD, you're trading €100,000. If you trade 1 standard lot of USD/JPY, you're trading $100,000. The base currency (first in the pair) determines what currency the lot size refers to.

For greater flexibility, especially for traders with smaller accounts, the Forex market offers mini lots (10,000 units) and micro lots (1,000 units). Some brokers even offer nano lots (100 units) for beginners.

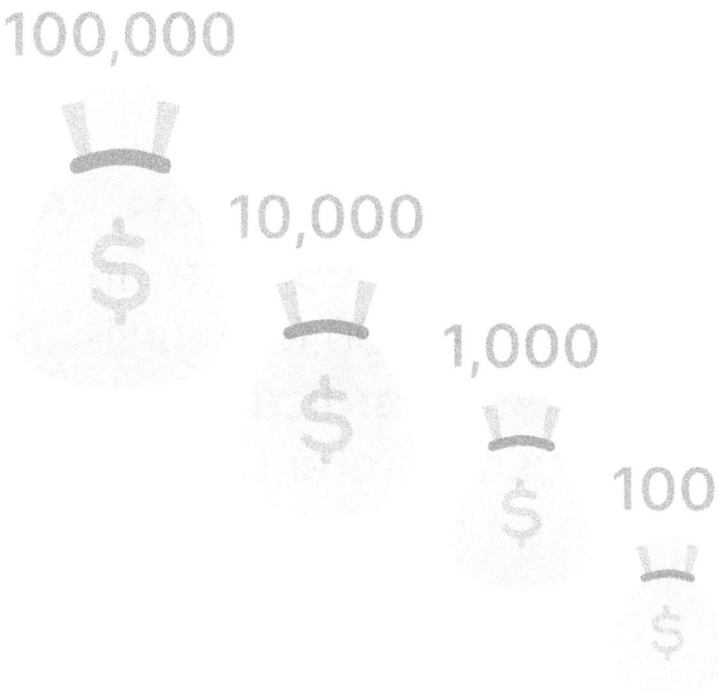

The relationship between pips and lot sizes determines the monetary value of each pip movement. This calculation is essential for understanding your potential profit or loss on each trade.

For major pairs where USD is the quote currency (second currency), the formula is simple:

- 1 pip with 1 standard lot = $10
- 1 pip with 1 mini lot = $1
- 1 pip with 1 micro lot = $0.10

This standardization makes calculating potential profits straightforward.

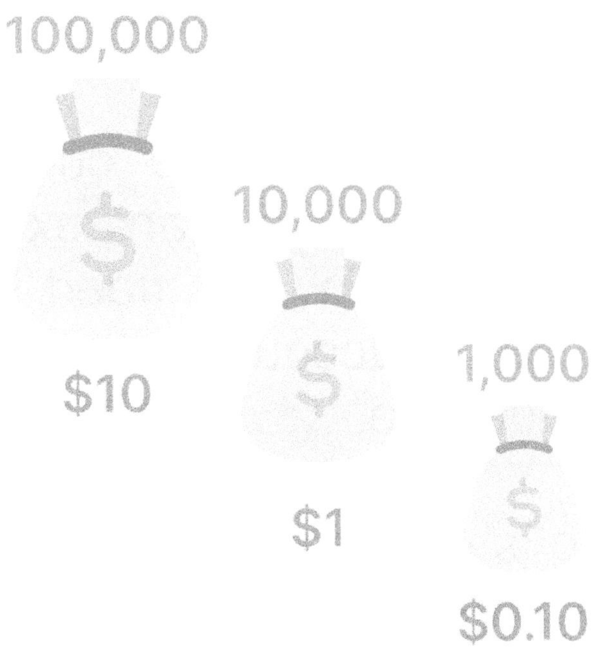

Calculate your profit

You buy 2 mini lots of EUR/USD at 1.1025 and sell at 1.1075. How much profit do you make? What is your profit on this trade? First, calculate the pip movement, then multiply by the pip value for mini lots.

- $100
- $10
- $5
- $500

Answer: $100. The price change is 50 pips, and with 2 mini lots, each pip is worth $2. That gives you a profit of $100. Double-check your pip value and lot size to calculate it correctly.

When USD is not the quote currency, the pip value calculation requires an extra step. For example, with GBP/JPY, you need to convert the pip value to your account currency using the current exchange rate.

Position sizing is where pip values become crucial for risk management. By knowing the pip value of your position, you can calculate exactly how much you stand to lose per pip and set your stop-loss accordingly.

Risk assessment

You have a $10,000 account and want to risk no more than 2% of account size on any trade. You're trading USD/CAD with a 50-pip stop-loss. What's the maximum standard lot size you should trade? Calculate your maximum risk amount in dollars, then divide by your potential loss in pips.

- 40 standard lots
- 4 standard lots
- 0.04 standard lots
- 0.4 standard lots

Answer: Your maximum risk is $200 (2% of $10,000). With a 50-pip stop-loss and knowing each pip is worth $10 per standard lot, you can calculate: $200 ÷ (50 pips × $10) = 0.4 standard lots.

Let's recap what we've learned about pips and lot sizes:

- A pip is the standard unit of price movement (usually the 4th decimal place)
- Standard lot = 100,000 units of base currency
- Mini lot = 10,000 units of base currency

- Micro lot = 1,000 units of base currency
- Understanding pip values and lot sizes is essential for calculating potential profit/loss and managing risk

Congratulations! You've completed this section and now have a solid understanding of how the Forex market operates, how brokers execute trades, and the fundamental math behind currency pairs, pips, and lot sizes. Take a moment to celebrate your progress - then, when you're ready, put your knowledge to the test!

QUIZ: Forex Trading Fundamentals

1. What is a pip in Forex trading?

A. The mandatory deposit required to open a Forex position
B. The commission charged by Forex brokers
C. The standard unit for measuring price movement, typically the fourth decimal place
D. The percentage of your account you should risk on each trade

2. Which of these currency pairs would be classified as a "minor pair"?

A. USD/MXN
B. USD/JPY
C. EUR/GBP
D. EUR/USD

3. If EUR/USD moves from 1.0520 to 1.0560, how many pips has it moved?

A. 0.40 pips

B. 40 pips
C. 400 pips
D. 4 pips

4. In the currency pair GBP/JPY, which is the base currency?

A. Neither is a base currency
B. JPY (Japanese Yen)
C. GBP (British Pound)
D. Both are base currencies

5. What is the value of 1 pip when trading 1 standard lot of EUR/USD?

A. $10
B. $1
C. $100
D. $0.10

6. When two currency pairs tend to move in opposite directions, what type of correlation do they have?

A. Zero correlation
B. Random correlation
C. Positive correlation

D. Negative correlation

7. Why is the Canadian dollar (CAD) typically positively correlated with oil prices?

A. Oil is priced exclusively in Canadian dollars
B. The Canadian government pegs its currency to oil prices
C. Canada is a major oil producer and exporter
D. Canadians consume more oil than other nations

8. If EUR/USD is quoted at 1.1050 and you want to buy €100,000, how many US dollars would you need (excluding any fees or spreads)?

A. $110,500
B. $100,000
C. $1,105
D. $90,497

9. If you want to risk no more than 2% of your $5,000 account on a trade with a 40-pip stop-loss, what is the maximum size you should trade in mini lots?

A. 25 mini lots
B. 0.25 mini lots
C. 2.5 mini lots
D. 250 mini lots

10. Which category of currency pairs typically has the widest spreads and highest volatility?

A. Exotic pairs
B. Major pairs
C. Minor pairs
D. Correlation pairs

Answer: 1. C; 2. C; 3. B; 4. C; 5. A; 6. D; 7. C; 8. A; 9. A; 10. A

Lesson 4: The Currency Game

Let's play a game!

Welcome to London's financial district! Are you ready to see what happens behind the scenes when you trade currencies?

How trading works

Let me show you how trading works with a simple game. Bucks will be our broker today, and I'll be the trader. Our game is about guessing whether the price of euros against dollars will go up or down.

The current price of euros is **1.2000 dollars**. This means 1 euro costs $1.20. Please add $20 as security to open the trade.

Round 1

I think this price will go up, so I want to place a trade.

Note, I never actually bought any euros. I'm simply making a prediction about the price direction. If I'm right, Bucks will pay me. If I'm wrong, I'll pay Bucks. This is how Forex trading typically works.

The first trade

Shortly after I place my trade predicting the euro price will rise, the price moves to 1.2020.

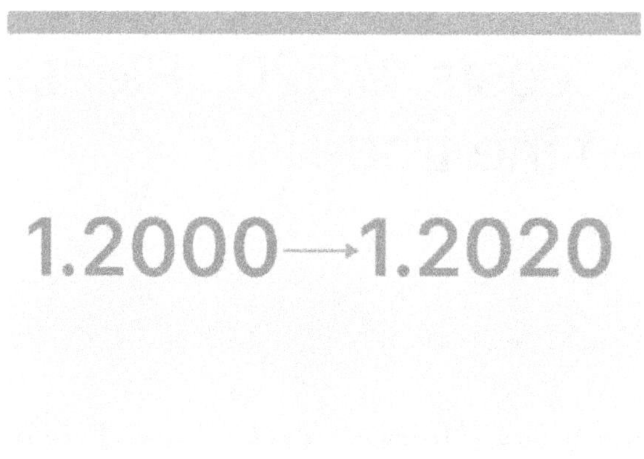

If 1 euro started at $1.2000 and moved to $1.2020, what's the result of my trade? Remember that I predicted the price would rise

- You need to pay more security money
- You are winning because the price went up as you predicted
- You are losing because the price went up

Answer: Since I predicted the price would go up and it did, my trade is currently profitable. The difference is $0.0020 per euro. In Forex, these seemingly small price movements can translate to significant percentage returns.

If you close your trade now, you'll make $2.

Wait, how is that possible? The price only moved by 20 pips (0.0020), which seems tiny in dollar terms!

This is where the broker's trade size comes in - they've applied a multiplier to my small deposit.

Instead of just betting on one euro, Bucks lets you control a trade size of 1,000 euros with your $20 deposit. So, the profit calculation is: 1,000 euros x

$0.0020 price increase = $2 profit. This is called leverage.

What would you do with this trade?

Alex is up $2 on his trade and needs to decide what to do next. Order these possible actions from lowest to highest risk. Locking in profits is usually the safest. The more passive or aggressive the action, the higher the risk.

- Take the $2 profit now while you're winning
- Ignore the trade and hope for the best
- Add more money to increase the trade size
- Wait to see if the price keeps rising

Answer:

- Take the $2 profit now while you're winning
- Wait to see if the price keeps rising
- Add more money to increase the trade size
- Ignore the trade and hope for the best

Round 1

I decide to close the trade and take my $2 profit. Broker Bucks returns my original $20 deposit plus the $2 profit. With just $20, I made a 10% return in a short time. Not bad! Let's try another trade.

The current price of euros is 1.2025 dollars. This means 1 euro costs $1.2025.

Round 2

I still think the price will go up, so I place another trade. This time, I give Broker Bucks all $22 as my security deposit.

Since you provided more money as security, I can increase your trade size. Now, instead of controlling 1,000 euros, you are controlling 1,100 euros. However, this means that small price movements will have even a bigger impact on your profits or losses.

Uh-oh - EUR drops!

Breaking news causes the euro to drop suddenly! The price falls to 1.2005. The price fell from 1.2025 to 1.2005, and my trade size is 1,100 euros. How much am I losing? Calculate the price difference and multiply by the trade size

- $20
- $0.22
- $2.20
- $22

Answer: The correct loss is based on the price drop of $0.0020 per euro, multiplied by the trade size of 1,100 euros. That gives a total loss of $2.20.

I'm feeling worried now. I've seen how quickly prices can move against me, causing unexpected losses. There must be something I can use to control this risk.

Help Alex!

Alex needs to think carefully about managing the risk. Which tool can help him avoid significant losses? It's a tool traders set to automatically close losing trades and limit risk.

- Profit multiplier
- Stop-loss orders
- More leverage
- Deposit bonus

Answer: A stop-loss order automatically closes my trade if the market moves too far against me, keeping losses manageable.

Ha! Forex might run 24/5, but my trading ends here for today. You still lost $2.20 - let me use that to buy myself some ice cream. Thanks for the treat!

And if you want to improve your chances next time, check out the next chapter of my book on Technical Analysis. It teaches you to predict market movements by analyzing charts, patterns, and indicators. See you then!

Chapter 3: Technical Analysis

Lesson 1: Types of Analysis

Ready to trade smarter?

You're making incredible progress! Each step brings you closer to trading like a pro. Today, we'll explore the different types of analysis that traders use to make informed decisions. Ready to dive in? Let's go!

Trading without analysis is like trying to solve a math problem without a formula. It helps traders avoid unnecessary risks and make strategic decisions instead of guessing.

Successful traders rely on market psychology to understand what drives price movements. To make informed decisions, they use two main strategies: **fundamental analysis** and **technical analysis**. You already have some knowledge of both - now it's time to explore them in more depth.

Fundamental analysis helps traders evaluate a company's financial strength by reviewing its earnings, assets, debts, and market position. It gives a clear picture of a company's value and long-term growth potential.

In fundamental analysis, traders first ask: Is the company increasing its revenue and profit? Consistent sales growth and rising profits attract investors and can lead to higher stock prices over time.

Next, traders check: What gives this company an edge over its competitors? Strong brands, innovative products, or market leadership help companies maintain growth and profitability, making them more attractive to traders.

Traders also assess whether economic conditions support this company's growth. High interest rates, inflation, or weak consumer demand may limit profits. A favorable economy, on the other hand, can fuel business expansion.

Now that you understand how traders evaluate a company, let's see what you've learned!

Key factors of fundamental analysis

Think like a trader! Match the key factors to fundamental analysis, but be careful - some options are sneaky and don't belong! Fundamental analysis focuses on a company's long-term value, financial health, and market position - not short-term price movements or emotions!

- Competitive advantage
- Price momentum shifts
- Chart patterns
- Trader sentiment
- Economic conditions
- Revenue and profit growth

Answer:

- Competitive advantage
- Economic conditions
- Revenue and profit growth

Great job! Now that you've learned how to analyze a company's value, let's move on to **technical analysis** - the key to understanding market trends and price movements.

Technical analysis focuses on price charts, trends, and patterns. Instead of financial reports, traders use this information to determine when to enter or exit trades based on market behavior.

Every price movement reflects changes in supply and demand. **Technical analysis** helps traders interpret these movements and forecast future price trends with greater confidence.

Let's sum up! You've just taken a big step forward - learning how traders evaluate both companies and markets.

- **Fundamental analysis** shows a company's value
- **Technical analysis** reveals price behavior

Next, we'll take it further by learning how to read charts and spot trends using technical analysis!

Lesson 2: The Core Principles

Let's explore technical analysis!

You've seen how important technical analysis is in understanding market behavior. Now, let's take a closer look at how it works. In this section, we'll explore the key principles behind technical analysis and how traders use them to navigate price movements with confidence!

Technical analysis as we know it today began with Charles Dow, a co-founder of the Dow Jones Industrial Average (DJIA) - one of the oldest stock market indexes. In the early 1900s, Dow introduced key ideas about how markets behave.

Dow believed that market prices are not random. Instead, they follow patterns and trends that repeat over time. His work laid the foundation for technical analysis, which helps traders study price movements to make better trading decisions.

Modern traders rely on three key principles to guide their decisions. Let's examine each one closely.

One of the core principles of technical analysis is that the market discounts everything. This means all available information - whether it's company news, earnings reports, economic data, or even trader sentiment - is already factored into a stock's price.

Imagine a major tech company announces a new product launch and is expected to boost profits. Before you even read the news, the stock price may have already jumped because thousands of traders reacted immediately.

That's how technical analysts view the price - as a reflection of all known information. You don't need to hunt down every headline. Focus on the price - it shows you the full picture.

In technical analysis, prices react instantly to news. Traders don't wait - any new information is quickly reflected in the price, which is why analysts focus on price movements, not reports.

Another core principle of technical analysis is that trends persist. This means that prices usually move in a certain direction - either upward, downward, or sideways - rather than randomly jumping around. Your job as a trader? Spot the trend early and trade with it, not against it!

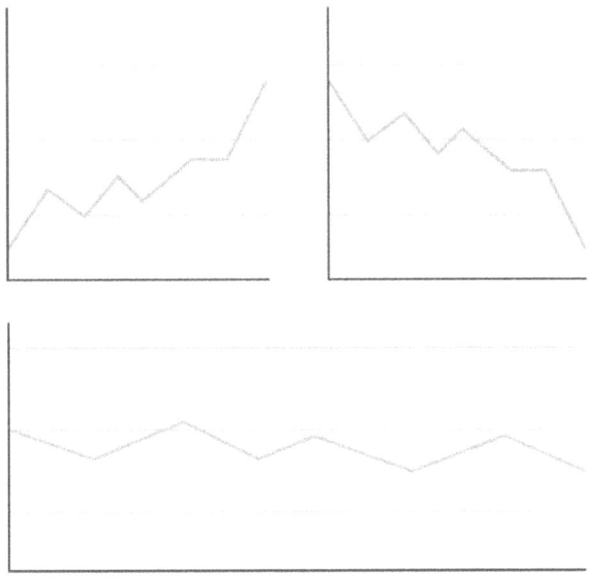

Once you've identified a trend, stay with it - until strong signals tell you it's over. This principle helps traders catch profits while avoiding premature exits.

If a stock price has been steadily climbing, the trends persist principle suggests that it will likely keep rising - unless clear signals show the trend is changing.

Last but not least, you must remember that history repeats itself in the market. Traders often react the same way to price movements - driven by emotions like fear and greed. That's why certain price patterns keep showing up. By recognizing these patterns, you can anticipate future moves.

One classic example is the double top pattern. It forms when the price rises to a peak, pulls back, and then rises again to the same level - only to fall afterward.

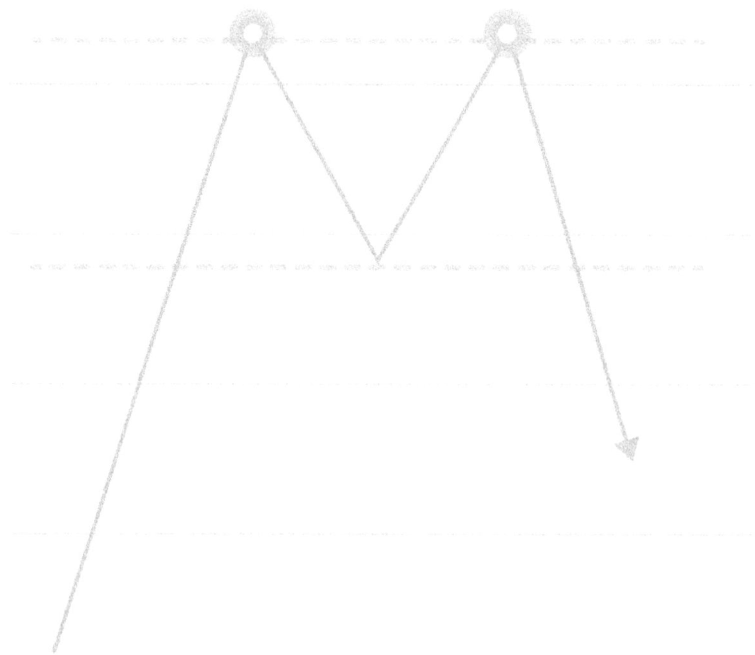

Why does this happen? Traders recognize the pattern, expect the price to drop after the second peak, and start selling - causing the price to fall.

Market patterns repeat because traders tend to react the same way to similar price movements. By studying past patterns, traders can better predict what might happen next.

Great work! You've just explored the foundation of technical analysis - how price reflects information, trends persist, and history repeats. These ideas help traders read charts with more confidence. Next, you'll learn how to use different chart types to apply what you've learned.

Lesson 3: Trading Charts Types

It's time to decode trading charts!

With the basics of technical analysis under your belt, it's time to dive into the charts. They will help you turn price movements into clear, actionable insights. By the end of this section, you'll know how to read different chart types, recognize patterns, and use them to trade smarter.

Let's begin with the most straightforward chart type: the line chart. It links data points - often closing prices - over time with straight lines, forming a continuous representation of an asset's price movement.

Line charts are fundamental tools in trading because they offer a clear and straightforward view of an asset's price movement over time.

In line charts, you can easily spot overall market directions - whether prices are moving up, down, or sideways. They also reduce market noise, allowing you to concentrate on essential information without distractions from intraday price fluctuations.

Let's take a closer look at line charts and how to read them. Once you know how to interpret them, you'll be able to quickly see patterns and market changes!

First, pay attention to the horizontal line at the bottom - it is called the X- axis. This axis typically represents time intervals - such as days, weeks, or months. It allows you to observe how the data evolves over these periods.

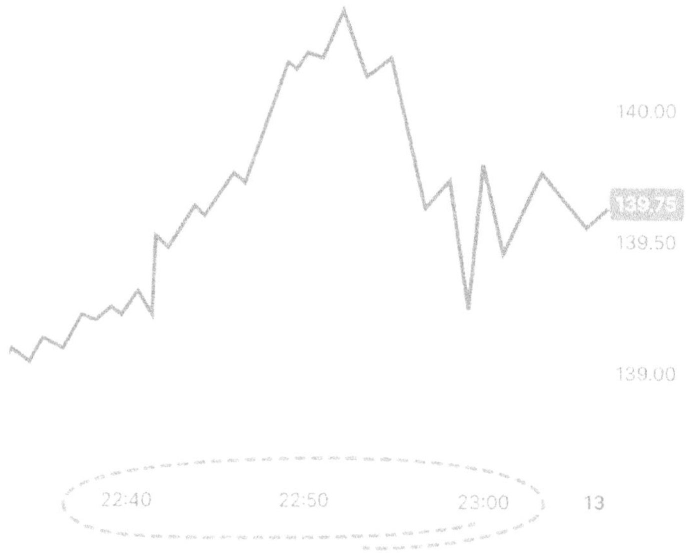

Now, let's move to the vertical line - the Y-axis. It shows the price levels of an asset. It helps you measure how much the price rises or falls.

Each dot on the chart is called a data point. These points show the price at a specific time.

Next, we connect the dots. Straight lines link each data point to the next, creating a continuous line. By looking at the direction of the line, you can spot price trends. This helps you decide when to trade.

Let's recap line charts!

Match elements of the line chart with what they represent! Focus on what the chart shows visually - the axes, dots, and lines. Ignore things like volume, colors, or extra information outside the chart structure!

- Y-axis - Price at a specific time
- X-axis - Price levels of the asset
- Data point - Time intervals (days, weeks)

Answer:

- Y-axis - Price levels of the asset
- X-axis - Time intervals (days, weeks)
- Data point - Price at a specific time

Excellent job! Now you know how to read line charts, you might ask why traders love line charts. First, they make it easy to spot trends. You can quickly see if the price is rising, falling, or staying the same.

Spot the trend!

You're analyzing the chart. Here's now the price has moved over the last several sessions:

Look at how the price bounces within a small range without consistently making higher highs or lower lows. What trend is shown in this chart?

- Downward trend
- Sideways trend
- Upward trend
- No trend

Answer: Sideways trend. In a sideways trend, the price stays within a range. No consistent higher highs or lower lows.

Line charts are also great for comparing. You can overlay multiple assets on one chart to see how they perform side by side. This will help you compare stocks, sectors, or currencies at a glance.

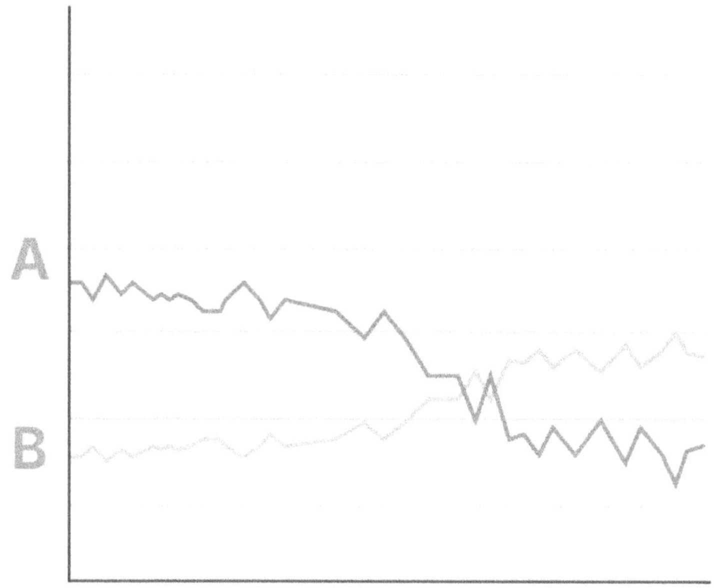

As you remember, history tends to repeat itself. Line charts help traders analyze historical price movements, showing how markets reacted to events or economic changes.

You now know how to read line charts and spot trends in line charts! But line charts are just one tool in a trader's toolkit. Sometimes, you need more detailed information - like how much the price moved within a single time period or how much trading volume occurred. That's where bar charts come in!

Bar charts give you even more information than line charts as they show not just price direction, but also the opening, high, low, and closing prices for each time period. They're not as popular among traders now, but they're a good foundation for understanding candlestick charts - which we'll look at further.

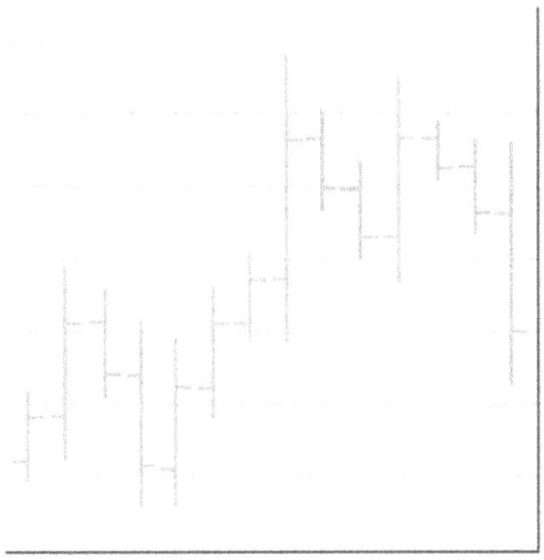

Each bar shows what happened to the price during one time period. The price always opens on the left side (1) of the bar, and it closes on the right side (2). The top of the bar shows the highest price reached (3), and the bottom shows the lowest price (4) traded during that time.

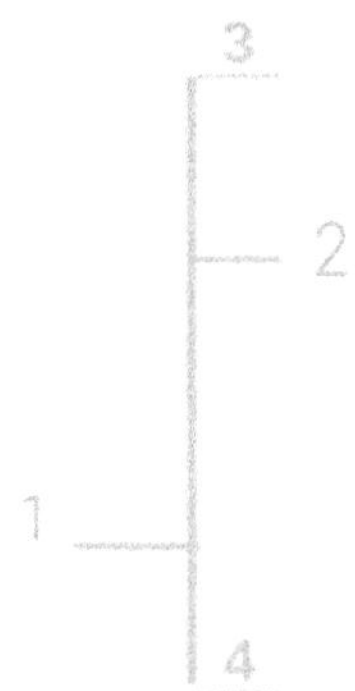

Each bar shows price movement for one specific time period - like one day, one hour, or one minute. When you put many bars together on a chart, you can see how the price changes over time.

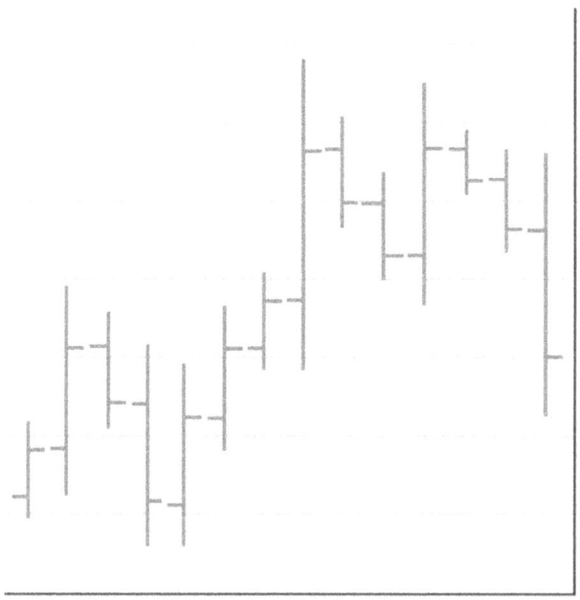

Let's read the bar together!

Take a close look at the bar in front of you. Can you figure out where the price opened, where it closed, and what the highest and lowest prices were? Don't worry if it feels tricky at first - just focus on the numbers!

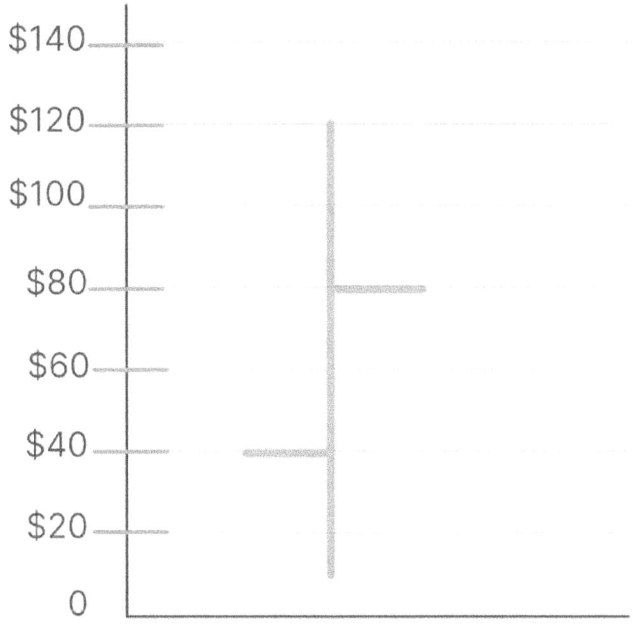

What are the opening, closing, highest, and lowest prices shown on this bar? Left = Open, Right = Close, Top = High, Bottom = Low. Focus on matching the numbers - you're almost there!

Answer: 0 - $40, C - $80, L - $10, H - $120

In short, bar charts give you a clear view of market direction and how active or risky the price movement is. In the next section, we'll explore a new chart type that presents this information even faster and more visually - candlestick charts. But first, let's take a quick quiz to review line and bar charts!

QUIZ: Charts

1. What does the X-axis on a line chart usually represent?

A. Price levels
B. Time intervals (days, weeks, months)
C. Highest price of the day
D. Trading volume

2. In a line chart, what does each data point show?

A. Moving average
B. Trading volume
C. Price at a specific time
D. Number of trades

3. What is the main purpose of a line chart?

A. To display opening and closing prices
B. To show trading volume
C. To highlight intraday price fluctuations
D. To show the overall price trend over time

4. How are data points connected in a line chart?

A. By straight lines
B. By candlesticks
C. By bars
D. By arrows

5. What can traders quickly identify using a line chart?

A. Whether prices are moving up, down, or sideways
B. Trading volume for each session
C. Detailed price range within a session
D. Opening and closing prices in one period

6. What extra information does a bar chart show compared to a line chart?

A. Stock ticker symbols
B. Only closing prices
C. Opening, high, low, and closing prices
D. Trading volume

7. What part of a bar chart shows the highest price during a time period?

A. The right notch
B. The top of the bar
C. The bottom of the bar
D. The left notch

8. What does the left notch on a bar chart represent?

A. Highest price
B. Closing price
C. Opening price
D. Trading volume

9. What does the right notch on a bar chart represent?

A. Closing price
B. Lowest price
C. Highest price
D. Opening price

10. Where do you find the closing price on a bar chart?

A. The top of the vertical bar
B. The bottom of the vertical bar
C. The small tick on the left side of the bar

D. The small tick on the right side of the bar

Answer: 1. B; 2. C; 3. D; 4. A; 5. A; 6. C; 7. B; 8. C; 9. A; 10. D

Lesson 4: Candlestick Charts 101

Let's explore candlestick charts!

You've learned how to read line and bar charts. Now, let's move to the most popular chart type - candlestick charts. By the end of this section, you'll know how to read candlesticks, interpret price action, and apply this skill to trading decisions. Let's go!

We will start by breaking down the structure of a candlestick. Just like bars, every candlestick consists of four key components:

- Opening price
- Closing price
- Highest price
- Lowest price

These components are displayed in two main parts. The body is the thick, rectangular part of the candle, representing the range between the opening and closing prices.

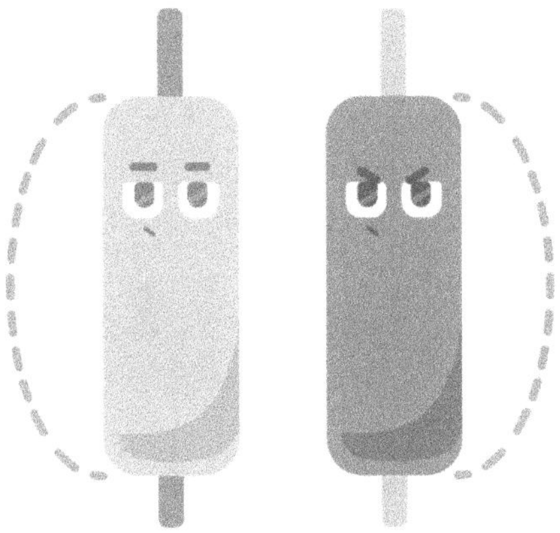

Candlestick charts use colors - green or red - to instantly show if the price increased or decreased during the period. If the close is higher than the open, the body is usually green. If the close is lower than the open, the body is red.

In other words, a green candlestick signals a bullish pattern, which indicates strong demand and buying pressure. A red candlestick shows a bearish pattern, signaling selling pressure and weaker demand.

The wicks, also called shadows, are the thin lines extending above and below the candlestick body. The upper wick shows the highest price reached during the time period. The lower wick shows the lowest price reached. Together, the wicks reveal how much the price moved beyond the opening and closing levels.

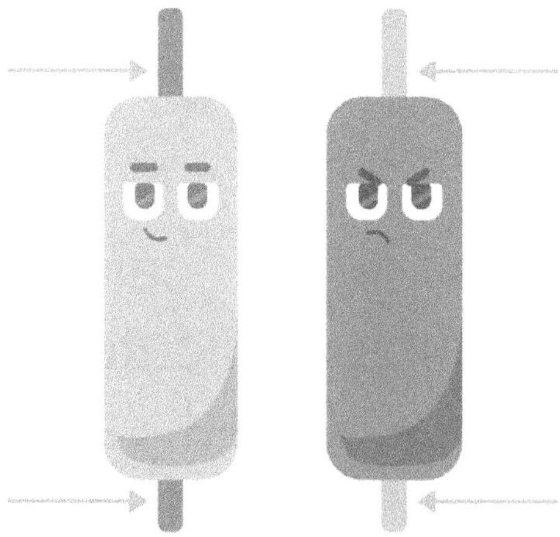

To illustrate this clearly, let's look at an example. In the candlestick below, you can see that the shares opened at $10 (1) at the start of the hour and closed at $20 (2) by the end of the hour, indicating a strong upward movement during that period.

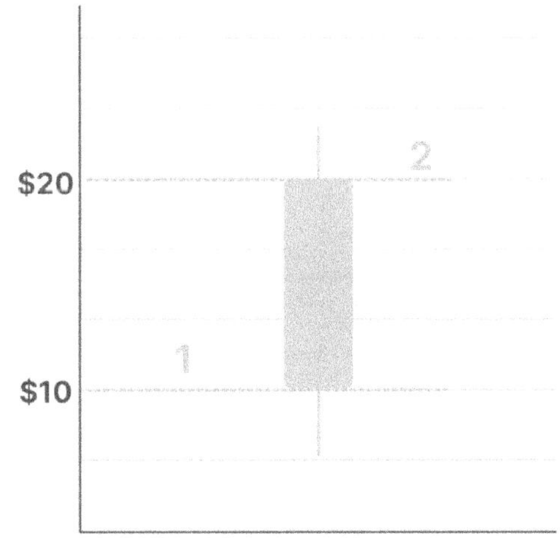

During the same period, the price also reached its highest point, reflecting the maximum level the market achieved (3), and its lowest point (4), showing how far the price dropped before the candle closed.

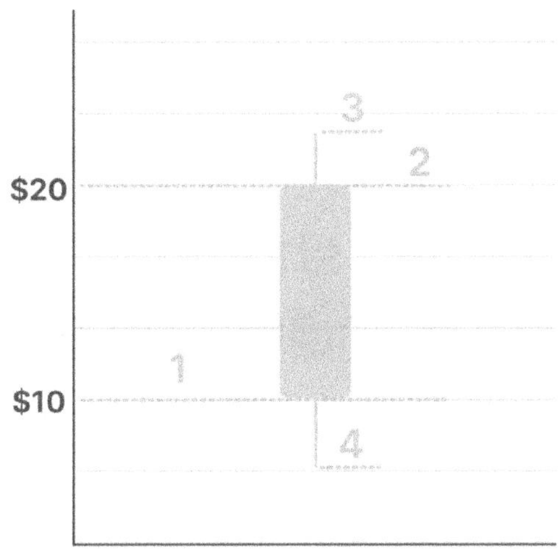

Guess the color!

Let's put that knowledge to the test. The closing price is $15 and the opening price is $10. Take a look at the relationship between the opening price and the closing price to answer the following question. Remember, the color depends on the relationship between the opening and closing prices.

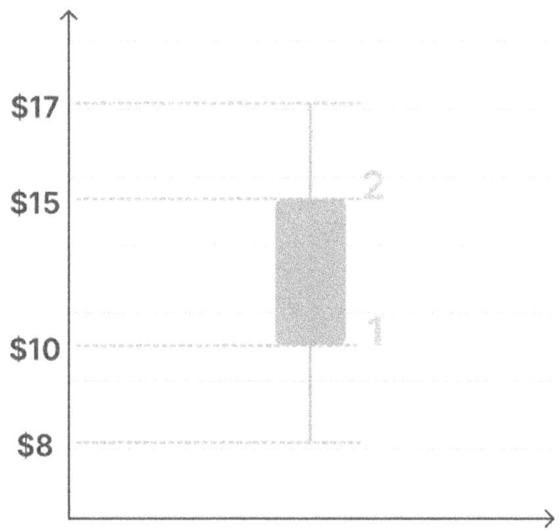

What color should the candlestick be?

- Green
- Red

Answer: This candle should be green. The closing price ($15) is higher than the opening price ($10), which indicates an upward price movement during this period. Green candles always show a closing price higher than the opening price.

Just like a green candlestick, a red candlestick shows the open (1), close (2), high (3), and low (4). The difference is that the close is below the open, meaning the price dropped. In the candlestick shown below, the price opened at $20 at the start of the hour and closed at $10 by the end of the hour, indicating a downward move.

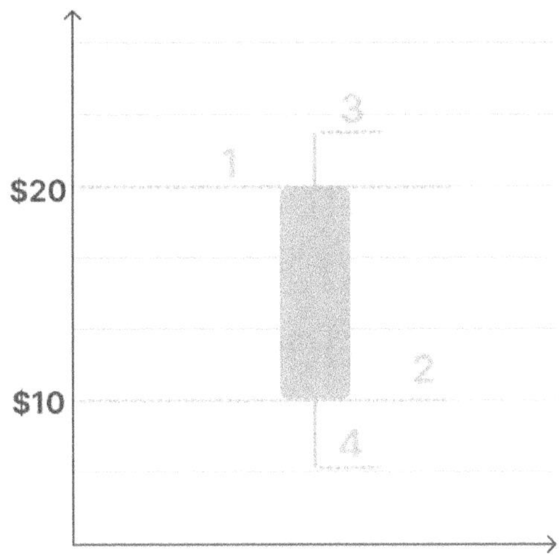

Each candlestick tells the story of price movement within a specific time period. A candlestick's color shows price direction: green for upward movement, red for downward movement. This reflects market sentiment - bullish or bearish.

Meanwhile, you can check the volatility by looking at the wicks. Long wicks indicate large price swings (high volatility), while short wicks show stable movement (low volatility). Candlesticks display the same information as bar charts but highlight direction and volatility more clearly, making it easier for traders to read market trends at a glance.

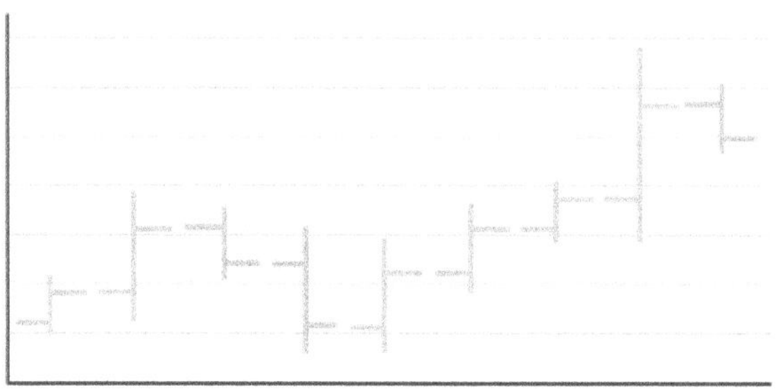

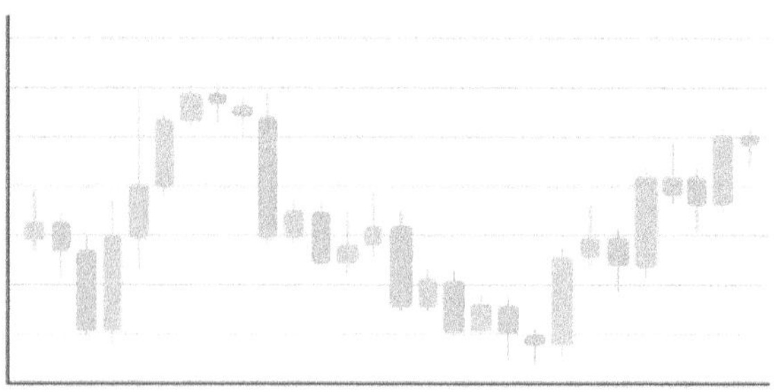

Interpreting the candle's story

Let's practice interpreting what a candlestick tells us about market activity. Consider the opening and closing prices, as well as the highs and lows.

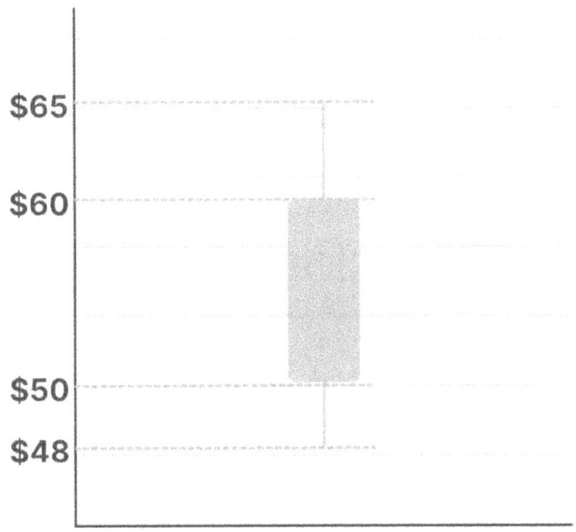

Based on this candlestick, which statement best describes what happened in the market during this period?

- The price opened and closed at the same level
- The market experienced strong buying pressure overall, despite some volatility
- There was consistent selling pressure throughout the period
- The market was stable with little price movement

Answer: This green candlestick indicates strong buying pressure with some volatility. It shows:

1) Upward movement (opened $50, closed $60)

2) Bullish momentum (high $65)

3) Some volatility (low $48)

4) Buyers prevailed (closed $10 higher)

A candlestick's color shows price direction: green for upward movement, red for downward movement. This reflects market sentiment - bullish or bearish. At the same time, you can assess the volatility by looking at the wicks. Long wicks indicate large price swings (high volatility), while short wicks show stable movement (low volatility).

But candlesticks don't stand alone - they connect and form a continuous story. Each candle's opening price often matches the closing price of the one before, creating a smooth, linked sequence of price movement.

In other words, to identify the candle color, you have to compare the opening and closing prices:

- If the close is higher than the open, the candle is green - buyers pushed the price up.
- If the close is lower than the open, the candle is red - sellers drove the price down.

Connecting the candles

Let's try to connect the candles to tell a broader story of price movement. Take a look at the relationship between the opening (1) and closing (2) prices for each candle. Remember, the color depends on whether the closing price is higher or lower than the opening price for each candle.
What is the correct sequence of colors for all four candlesticks, from left to right?

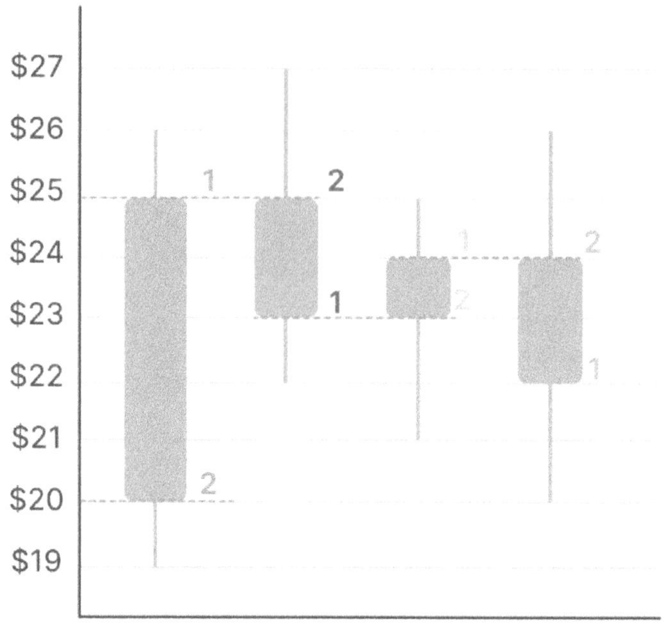

- Red, Green, Green, Red
- Green, Red, Red, Green
- Red, Green, Red, Green
- Green, Red, Green, Red

Answer: Red, Green, Red, Green. Remember, green means the closing price was higher than the opening price, while red means it was lower.

As I've mentioned, candlesticks connect to tell the story of price movement. But how that story unfolds depends on the timeframe you choose to view it.

You already know that most candlestick charts are time-based. Each candle forms after a specific period - like 1 minute, 1 hour, or 1 day. Popular timeframes include: 1-minute, 5-minute, 15-minute, 1-hour, 4-hour, daily, weekly, and monthly charts.

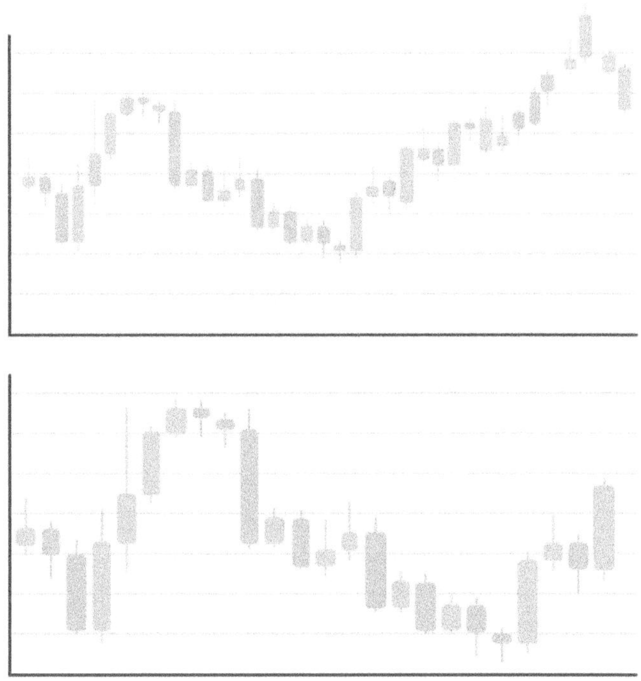

Why should you look at common timeframes? Because when most traders focus on the same timeframes - like 1-hour, 4-hour, or daily charts - it creates consistency in how market patterns are formed and interpreted. The collective decisions of many traders reacting to the same chart signals can strengthen and confirm trends, making patterns on common timeframes more meaningful, reliable, and impactful.

Uncommon timeframes don't give an advantage. Fewer traders watch them, so price patterns have less influence. Popular timeframes are stronger because more traders respond to the same signals.

Great job! You've mastered how to read candlestick charts and interpret price action. Next, we'll take things further. After a short quiz, we'll explore chart patterns - key techniques traders use to predict market moves and trade smarter.

QUIZ: Candlestick Charts

1. What does the body of a candlestick represent?

A. The range between the opening and closing prices
B. The highest price only
C. The total number of trades
D. The volume of the asset

2. If the closing price is higher than the opening price, what color is the candlestick usually?

A. Red
B. Blue
C. Yellow
D. Green

3. What do the wicks on a candlestick show?

A. The average price

B. The highest and lowest prices during the period
C. Timeframe duration
D. Trading volume

4. A red candlestick means:

A. The price stayed the same
B. The closing price is lower than the opening price
C. The price increased
D. No trades occurred

5. What is the main difference between bar charts and candlestick charts?

A. Bar charts are not used in trading
B. Candlestick charts only show closing prices
C. Bar charts show more price information
D. Candlestick charts use color to show price direction

6. What does a long wick on a candlestick usually indicate?

A. No price movement
B. Stable market

C. High price volatility
D. Low trading volume

7. What does a green candlestick typically signal?

A. Market was flat
B. No price changes occurred
C. Sellers pushed the price down
D. Buyers pushed the price up (bullish)

8. Why do traders prefer popular timeframes when reading candlestick charts?

A. More traders watch them, making patterns more reliable
B. They change the candlestick color
C. They display less data
D. They show larger price movements

9. What does a candlestick's direction help traders understand?

A. The total number of trades
B. The asset's market cap
C. The timeframe length

D. Whether price moved up or down during the period

10. Which four key prices do each candlestick display?

A. Open, Close, Volume, High
B. Volume, Close, Open, Average
C. Open, High, Low, Close
D. Trade count, High, Low, Close

Answer: 1. A; 2. D; 3. B; 4. B; 5. D; 6. C; 7. D; 8. A; 9. D; 10. C

SECTION 4: CANDLESTICK PATTERNS, MARKET TRENDS, AND SUPPORT & RESISTANCE

Chapter 1: Candlestick Patterns

Lesson 1: Hammer and Shooting Star

Let's explore new patterns!

Understanding patterns isn't just theory - it's a skill that shapes your trading strategy. You're now ready to recognize patterns like Hammer and Shooting Star, which can guide your decisions in real time. Let's dive in!

Let's start with a Hammer pattern. It is a bullish reversal candlestick pattern that appears after a downtrend. This pattern suggests that, despite selling pressure driving prices down, buyers stepped in to push prices back up, closing near the opening price.

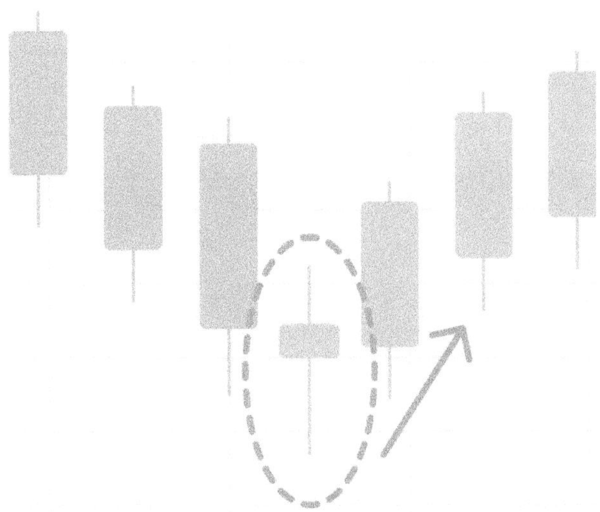

How can you recognize Hammer? It looks like a hammer with a handle and a small head. The candle has a small body and is located near the top of the trading range. This shows that although prices moved lower during the session, they recovered and closed near where they opened.

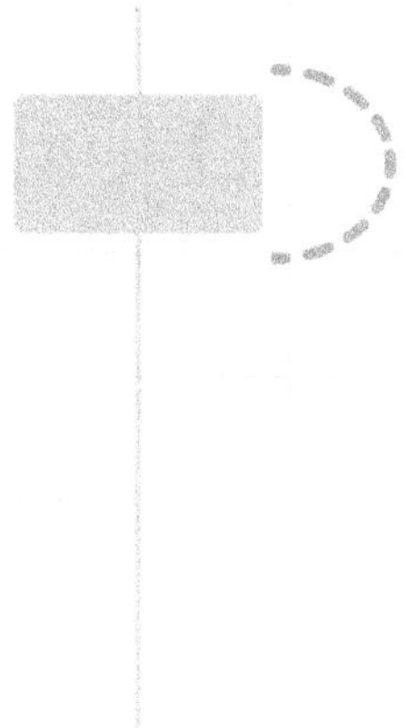

You can also see that the lower wick is at least twice the length of the body, showing that sellers drove the price significantly lower, but buyers pushed it back up before the close.

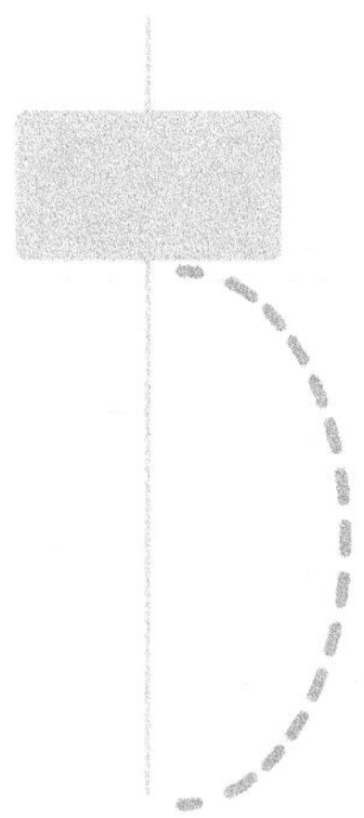

Hammer candlestick usually has little to no upper wick. This means there was minimal upward movement beyond the opening price.

Picture this: the market is in a strong downtrend. Sellers have been in control, driving prices down. But then, a Hammer candlestick forms, signaling a possible change. The price dropped as low as $45 but bounced back to close near $50. This suggests that buyers stepped in aggressively, absorbing selling pressure.

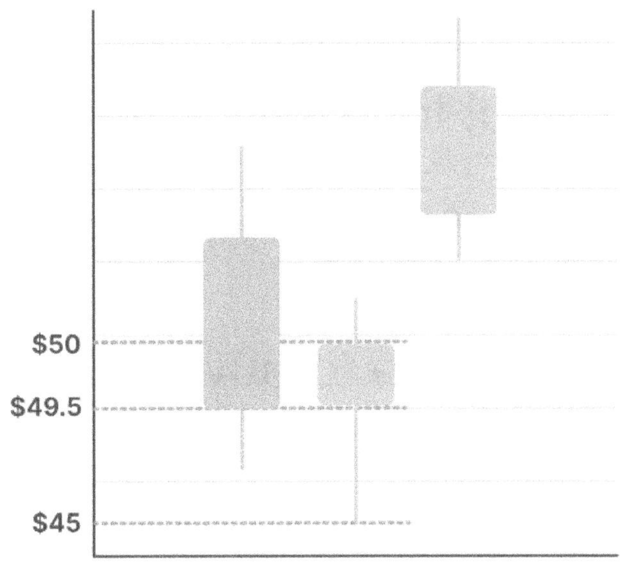

What does it mean for traders? This could mean the downtrend is weakening and the price might start going up soon. Many traders will wait for the next candle to close higher before deciding to buy - this confirmation helps reduce risk. Once confirmed, it's your chance to enter a trade and ride the potential uptrend.

Make a decision!

Based on the Hammer candlestick we just analyzed, what does this signal about market sentiment? What does this candlestick pattern typically suggest? Remember how the price movement throughout the session ended.

- The market is in perfect balance, no clear direction
- It could be a good time to buy, expecting prices to go up

- This pattern doesn't provide any useful information

Answer: This candlestick suggests prices might rise, so it could be a good time to buy. The long lower wick means prices dropped at first, but closing near the top shows buyers pushed the price back up. This indicates strong buying pressure that may continue.

We've just seen how the Hammer can signal the end of a downtrend and the start of a potential uptrend. Now, let's flip the script. There's a pattern that tells us the opposite - that an uptrend might be losing strength. It's called the Shooting star.

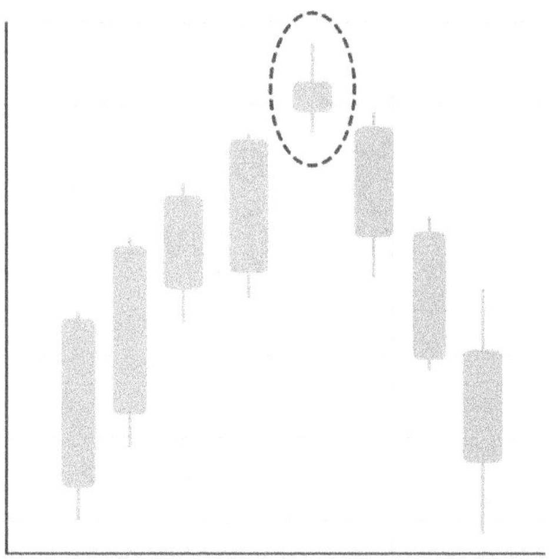

A Shooting Star forms after an uptrend and shows us that while buyers tried to push the price higher, sellers stepped in and forced the price back down before the session closed. It's like a warning light flashing: the market's upward momentum might be fading, and a reversal could be on the horizon.

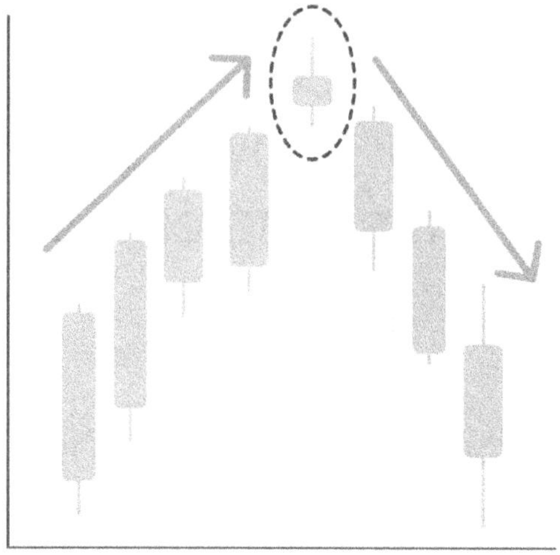

Visually, the Shooting Star mirrors the Hammer but in reverse. It has a small real body positioned at the lower end of the trading range and a long upper shadow, reflecting a failed attempt by buyers to sustain higher prices. There's usually no lower wick, making the signal even stronger.

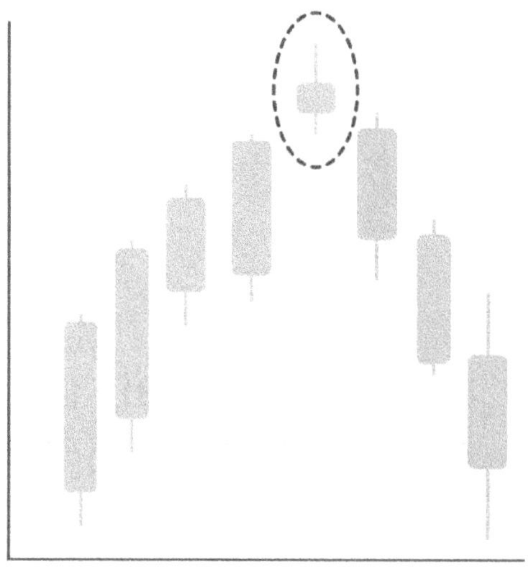

Imagine a stock that has been rising steadily over several days, moving from $80 to $95. On the day the Shooting Star forms. What happened? The price opened at $94, and surged up to $100 as buyers pushed higher, but couldn't hold. Sellers stepped in, driving the price back down to close near $95, just above the open.

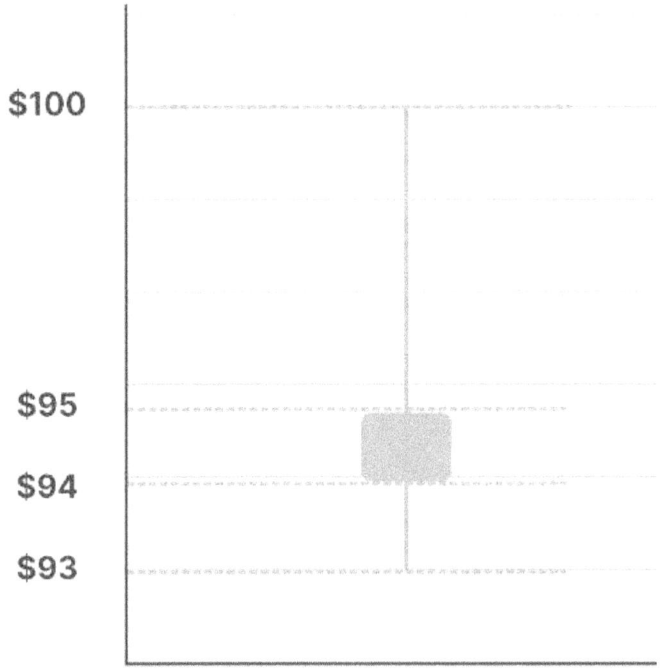

When you spot a Shooting Star at the top of an uptrend, it suggests that buying pressure might be weakening. But experienced traders don't react right away - they wait for confirmation, usually in the form of a red candle closing lower the next day. This confirmation shows that sellers are taking control.

Once the signal is confirmed, traders often respond by closing their long positions to lock in profits or by entering a sell trade to take advantage of the potential reversal.

Make a decision!

Based on the Shooting Star candlestick we just analyzed, what does this signal about market sentiment? What does this candlestick pattern typically suggest? Focus on how the price reacted after reaching a high during the session.

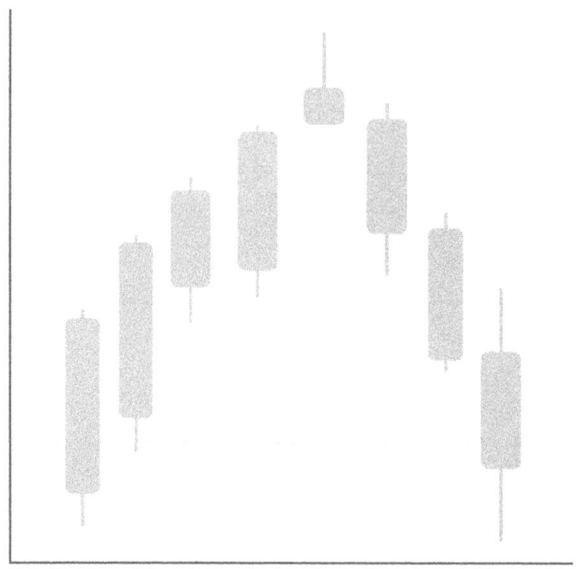

- The market is stable with no clear trend
- It's a strong buy signal, prices are likely to rise

- It could be a good time to sell, expecting prices to fall
- This pattern doesn't give any useful information

Answer: This candlestick suggests it could be a good time to sell, expecting prices to fall. The long upper wick shows buyers lost control, and the close near the session's low indicates sellers are gaining strength.

Great work! You now know how to spot both Hammer and Shooting Star patterns and more importantly, make smart trading decisions when you see them. You've added two powerful tools to your trading toolkit. Ready to take it further? Let's continue and explore even more candlestick patterns that can sharpen your strategy!

Lesson 2: Engulfing Patterns

Let's explore patterns!

You've learned how single candlesticks tell a story - now, let's take it further. In this section, we'll explore Engulfing patterns, where two candles together reveal powerful signals of potential trend reversals. Let's learn how to recognize them, confirm the setup, and confidently decide whether to buy or sell.

A Bullish Engulfing pattern is a powerful reversal signal that often appears at the end of a downtrend, indicating a potential shift from bearish to bullish sentiment.

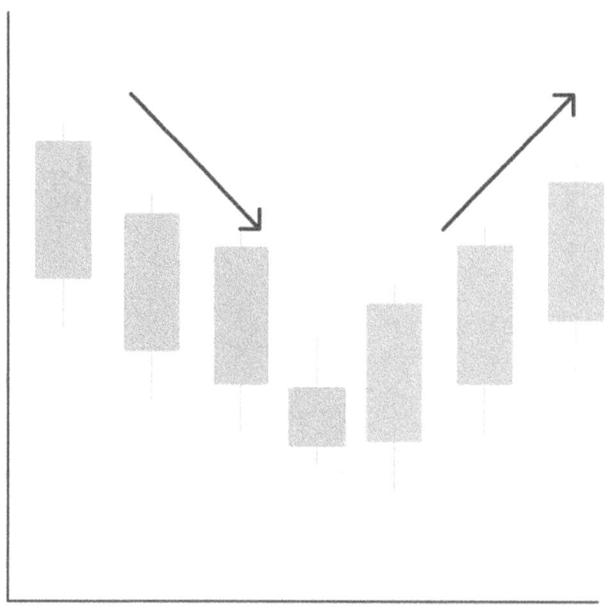

You are looking at Bullish Engulfing if you see a small red bearish candlestick that is followed by a larger green bullish candlestick that completely engulfs the body of the first candle.

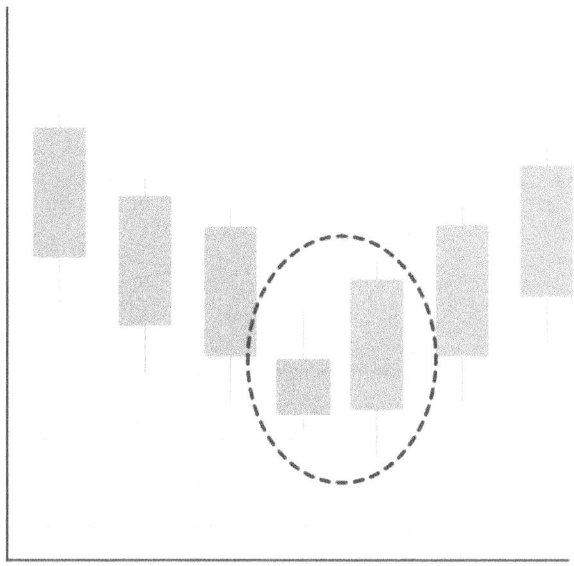

This pattern typically forms over two consecutive time periods - whether you're viewing a daily chart, hourly chart, or any other timeframe. What matters is that the second candle fully covers the first, signaling a potential shift in momentum.

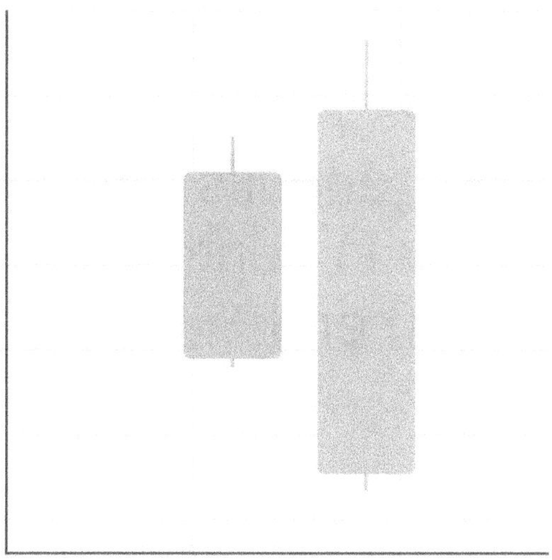

Here's what's unfolding: Sellers initially control the market, pressing prices lower. Then, strong buying momentum steps in, reversing the move and lifting the price above the prior session's open. This decisive shift hints at a possible bullish reversal.

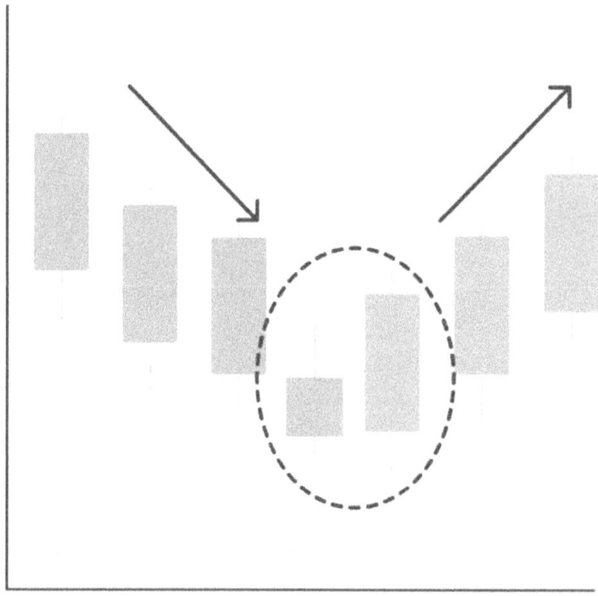

Let's visualize it: The stock's price has been sliding. On Day 1, it opens at $50 and closes at $48 - sellers are clearly in charge. But on Day 2, it opens at $47, rallies, and closes strong at $51. This bullish candle engulfs the first one, a sign that buyers are now in control and the downtrend may be coming to an end.

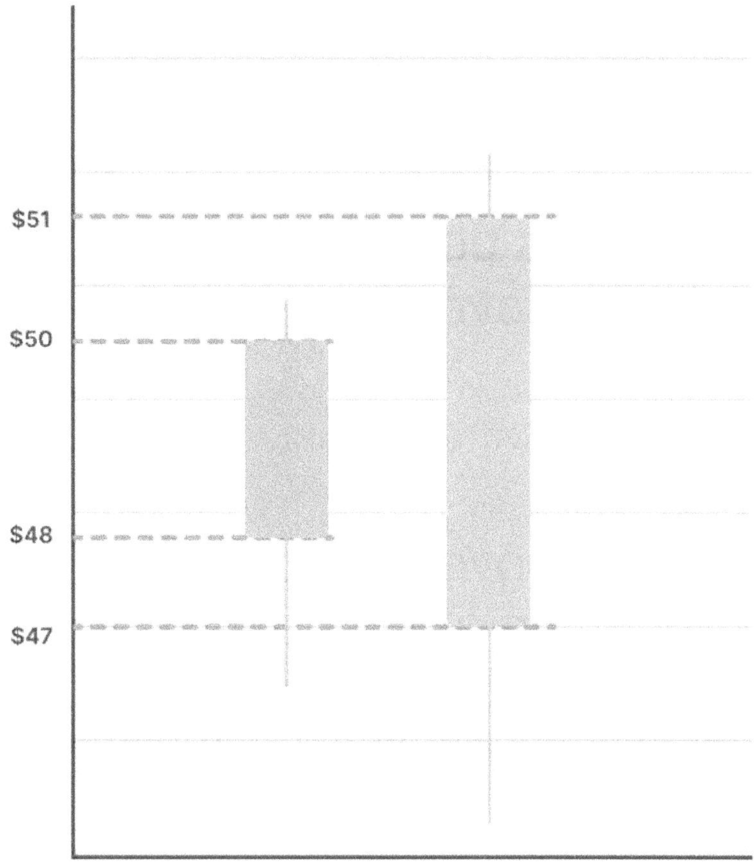

After spotting a Bullish Engulfing, traders typically wait for the next candle to close higher. This confirmation strengthens the signal. Once confirmed, they may enter a buy trade.

Make a trading decision!

You spot a Bullish Engulfing pattern on the chart. Day 1 closed at $48, and Day 2 closed at $51, fully engulfing Day 1. Rearrange the steps in the correct order to make a smart trading decision. Think about how confirmation and risk management should guide your action.

- Consider entering a buy trade
- Set a take-profit and monitor the trade
- Place a stop-loss below the low of Day 2
- Wait for close above $51 to confirm

Answer:

- Wait for close above $51 to confirm
- Consider entering a buy trade
- Place a stop-loss below the low of Day 2
- Set a take-profit and monitor the trade

Excellent! You've learned how to spot when buyers are stepping in. Now, let's flip the chart - time to learn how the Bearish Engulfing pattern can signal when sellers might be ready to take control.

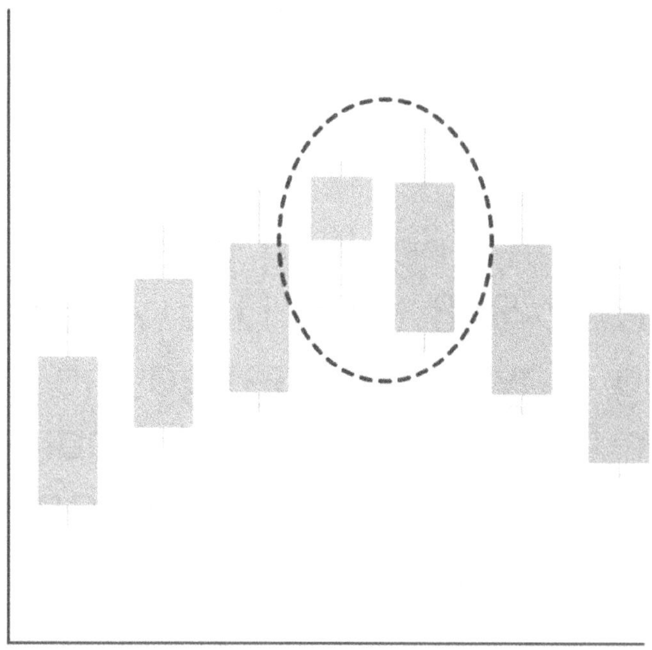

A Bearish Engulfing pattern is a strong reversal signal that typically appears at the end of an uptrend, indicating a potential shift from bullish to bearish sentiment.

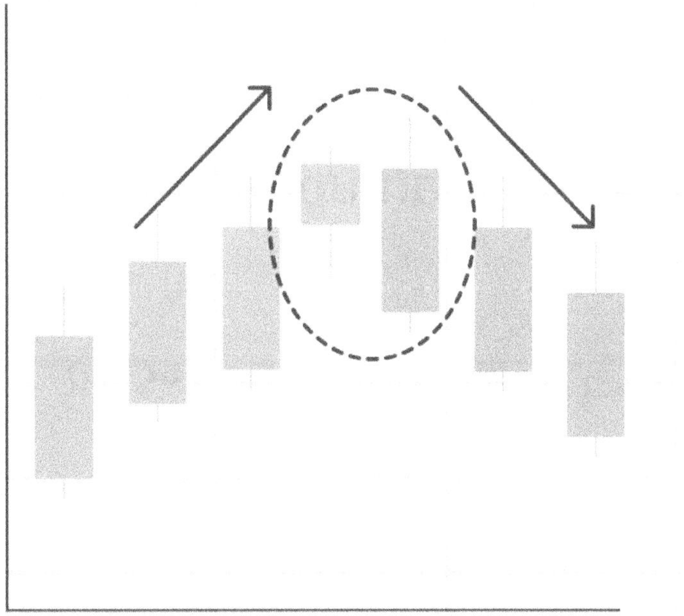

You are looking at a Bearish Engulfing pattern if you see a small green bullish candlestick, which is followed by a larger red candlestick that completely engulfs the body of the first candle, signaling strong selling interest.

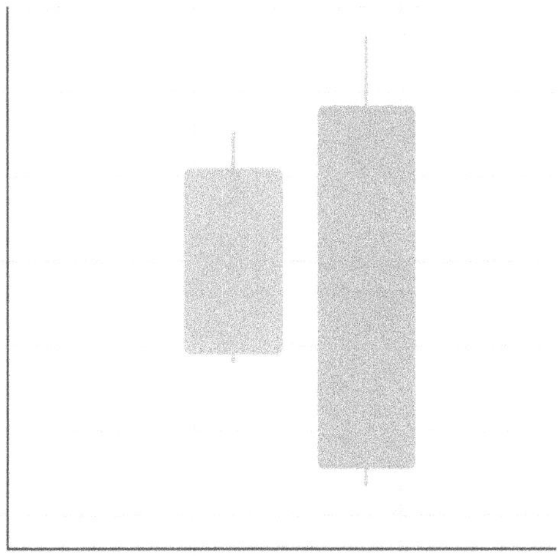

Here's how it plays out: Buyers are in control at first, steadily pushing prices higher. But then, sellers step in with force, driving the price back down and closing below the previous session's open. This strong shift signals a potential bearish reversal.

Consider a stock in an uptrend with the following candlesticks:

- Day 1: Opens at $100, closes at $102 (bullish candle)
- Day 2: Opens at $103, closes at $99 (bearish candle engulfing the previous day's body)

This pattern suggests that sellers have taken control, potentially reversing the prior uptrend.

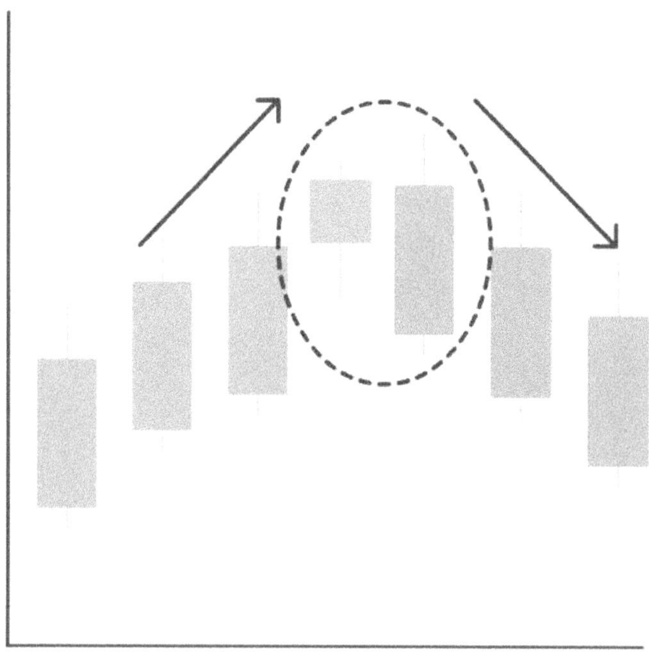

Just like with Bullish Engulfing, traders usually wait for confirmation before acting. If the next candle closes lower, it confirms sellers are in control. Once confirmed, many traders consider entering a short trade.

What's your next move?

You spot a Bearish Engulfing pattern after a strong uptrend.

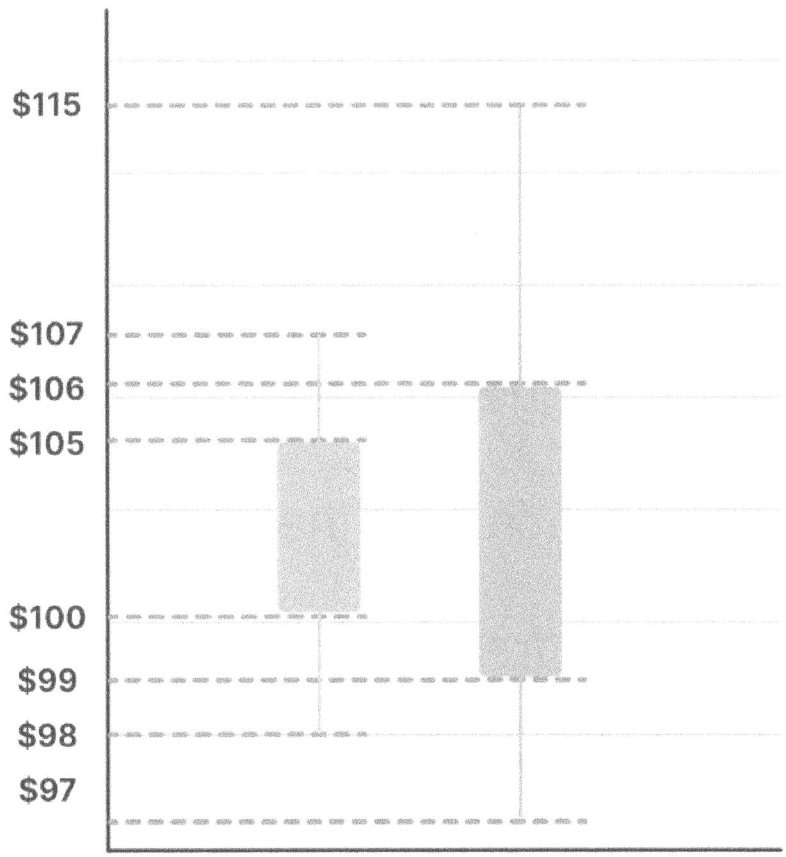

What should you do next? Think about how confirmation and risk management should guide your action.

- Ignore the pattern; it's not a strong signal
- Wait for the next candle to close lower, then consider entering a short trade
- Immediately buy, expecting the uptrend to continue

Answer: Wait for the next candle to close lower, then consider entering a short trade. Recognizing a Bearish Engulfing pattern is just the first step - waiting for confirmation helps reduce false signals and improves your risk management.

Not all Bullish and Bearish Engulfing patterns are equally strong. Stronger signals usually have:

- A larger second candle that fully engulfs the first
- A clear, extended trend before the pattern
- High trading volume during the engulfing candle

These details help you judge if the pattern is worth acting on - or if it's better to wait.

You've mastered Engulfing patterns and know how to recognize when buyers or sellers are taking control. Now, you're ready to apply this knowledge in real trading situations. Next, we'll explore another key pattern to sharpen your trading strategy even further.

Lesson 3: Doji Patterns

Reading market uncertainty - Doji patterns

You've seen how Engulfing patterns signal strong momentum shifts - Where buyers clearly overpower sellers, or the other way around. But what happens when neither side has the upper hand? That's where Doji patterns come into play. In this part, we'll break down three key Doji variations and show you how to recognize them to anticipate potential market reversals.

Let's start with the basics - what is a Doji? A Doji forms when the opening and closing prices are nearly identical, creating a candle with little or no body. This signals a balance between buyers and sellers during that session, showing market indecision.

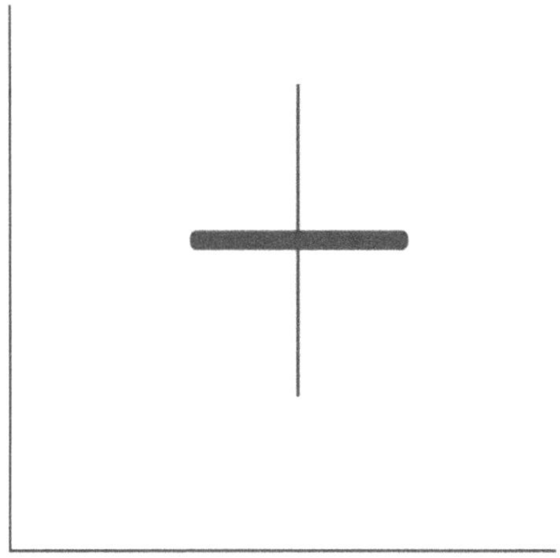

On a chart, a Doji appears as a cross or plus sign due to its minimal body. This shape reflects the market's indecision, as prices moved higher and lower during the session but closed at or near the opening price.

While Dojis can appear during any phase, they're most telling after a strong trend. Their presence hints at hesitation - maybe a reversal, maybe just a pause. Either way, it's a moment where smart traders take notice and prepare.

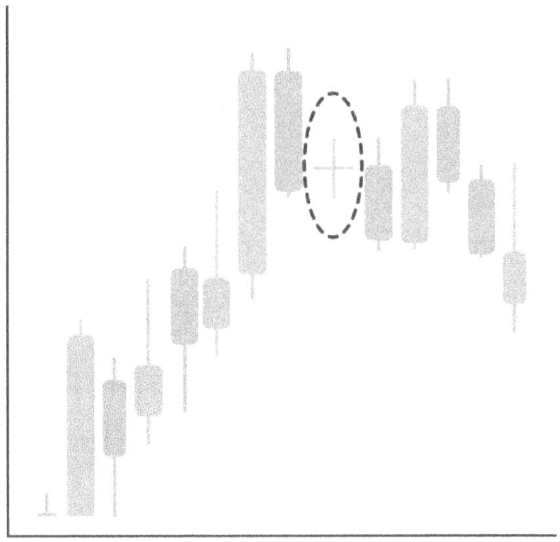

A Doji tells you the market is undecided. Your move? Stay patient. Watch what happens next - look for a strong candle to confirm if the trend continues or reverses. And if you're in a trade, consider tightening that stop-loss.

Doji in action

You're analyzing a stock that has been in a strong uptrend for the past month. Today, you notice a Doji pattern forming.

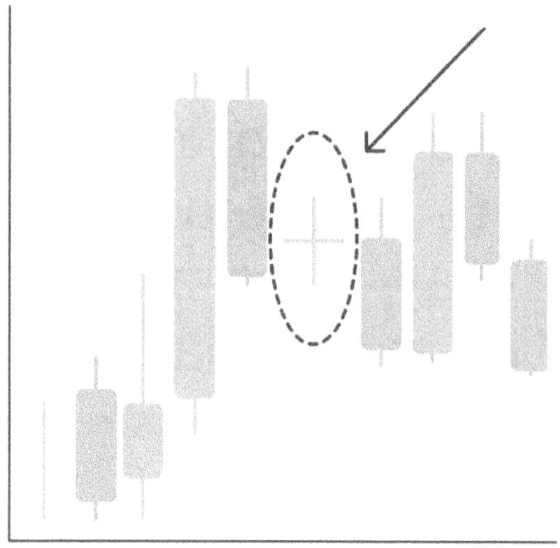

From this chart, what's the most logical next step? A Doji signals indecision in the market. Before acting, it's smart to wait for confirmation from the next candle to see if buyers or sellers take control.

- Ignore the Doji
- Buy more now
- Wait to see the next candle
- Sell immediately

Answer: Wait to see the next candle. Doji candles suggest uncertainty - waiting for the next candle helps confirm the market's direction before making a move.

Well done! Now you've seen how a Doji signals market indecision and how smart traders stay patient, waiting for confirmation before acting. Recognizing moments of hesitation in the market is just as important as spotting clear trends - it keeps you one step ahead.

Doji shows indecision. But sometimes, that indecision leans toward one side. Let's look at the Gravestone Doji, where buyers lose control and sellers step in.

The Gravestone Doji has a small or nonexistent body at the lower end, with a long upper wick. It tells us buyers pushed prices higher - but sellers stepped in and forced prices back down by the close.

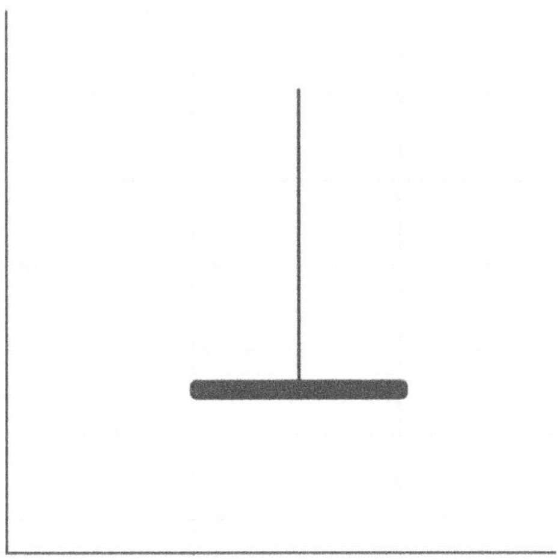

Visually, it resembles an inverted "T". This pattern is especially meaningful after an uptrend, hinting that buying pressure may be weakening.

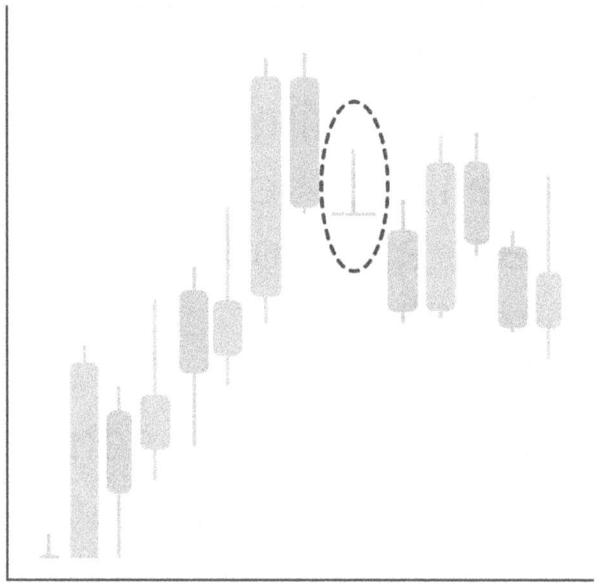

Like the standard Doji, the Gravestone has the open and close prices at the same level - typically near the session's low - while the long upper shadow reflects failed attempts by buyers to maintain higher prices.

This signals strong selling pressure overcoming buyers. Traders often see this as an early warning of a potential trend reversal, where sellers may start taking control.

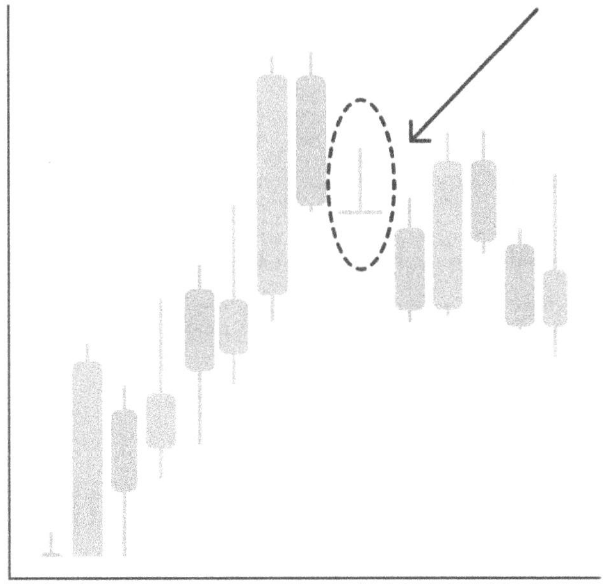

As with other patterns, confirmation is crucial when you spot a Gravestone Doji. Traders typically wait for the next candle to close lower, confirming that sellers are gaining strength. If confirmed, many will consider exiting long positions or preparing to enter a short trade. To manage risk, a stop-loss is usually placed above the high of the Gravestone.

Now, meet the Dragonfly Doji - the mirror image of the Gravestone Doji, carrying a different message.

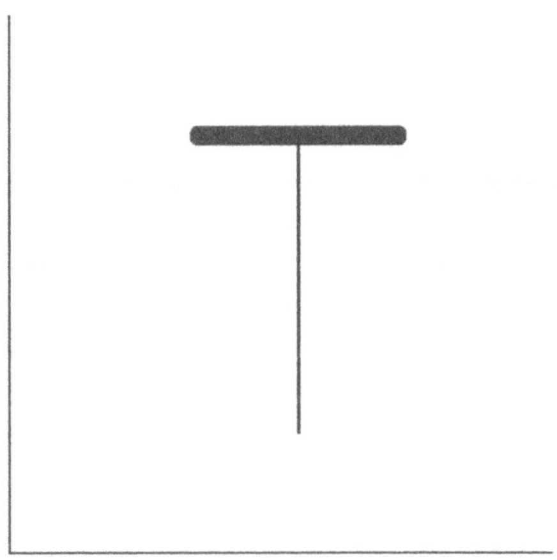

The Dragonfly Doji has a long lower wick and a small or no body at the top. This shows sellers drove prices down during the session, but buyers fought back, pushing the price back to the open by the close.

This pattern often forms at the bottom of downtrends, hinting at a possible uptrend reversal. It signals that buyers are stepping in at lower levels.

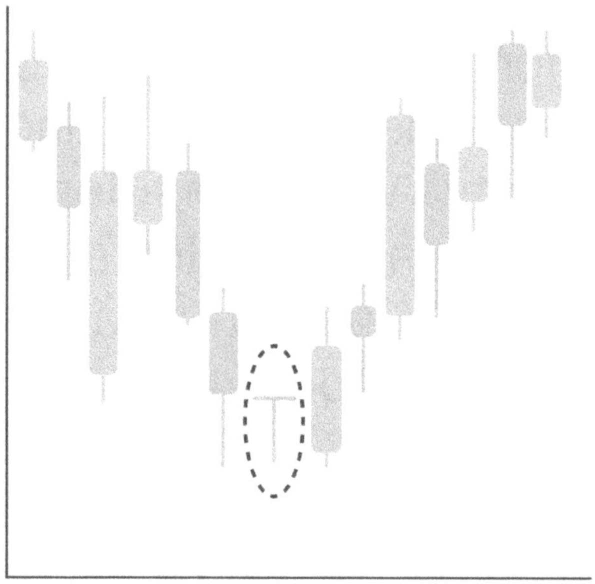

Like other Doji variations, the Dragonfly's open and close are at the same level, near the high of the session. Its long lower wick shows rejected lower prices - a clear sign of buying strength.

It's crucial to look for confirmation following a Dragonfly Doji, as it suggests a significant shift from selling to buying momentum that may lead to an upward trend.

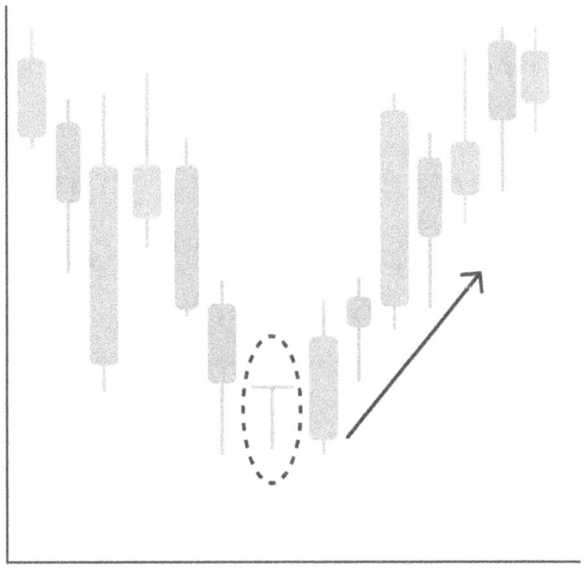

The Dragonfly Doji can signal that buying interest is strong and may outweigh selling pressure, leading to a potential uptrend.

Doji patterns are characterized by having the opening and closing prices at or very close to the same level, creating a minimal or nonexistent body.

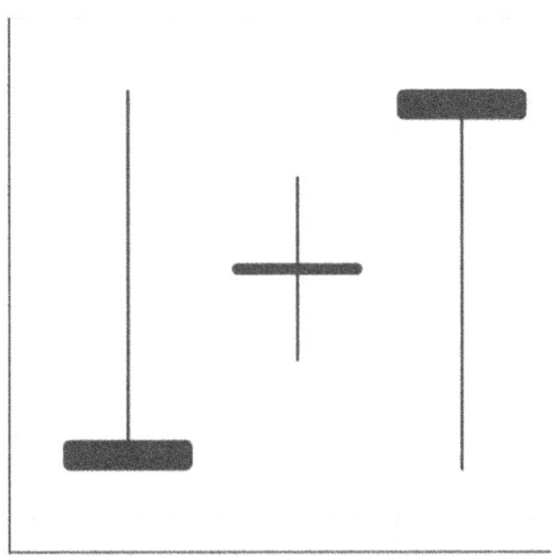

You're now familiar with the classic Doji, Gravestone Doji, and Dragonfly Doji. Let's practice spotting and understanding them in action.

Interpreting the Dragonfly

You're monitoring a stock that's been in a downtrend. You observe a Dragonfly Doji forming at a support level, followed by a strong bullish candle.

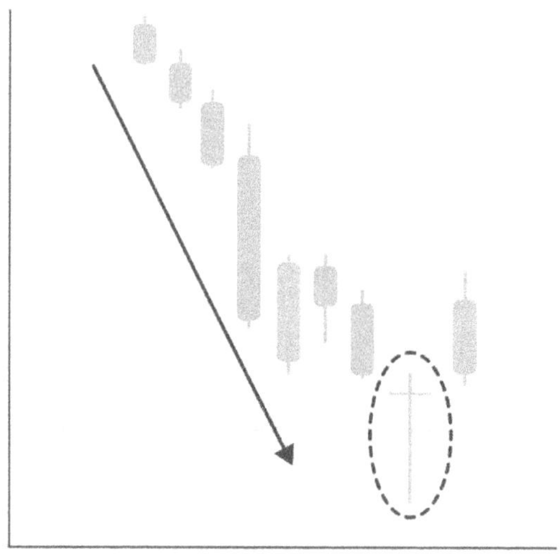

What does this pattern suggest about market dynamics, and what might be a prudent trading strategy? Think about what the Dragonfly Doji represents, especially at support levels, and the importance of the confirming bullish candle.

- It suggests a potential reversal; consider a small long position with a stop-loss below the Doji's low
- The pattern is irrelevant; stick to the downtrend and look for selling opportunities
- The pattern is bearish; increase short positions as the downtrend will likely continue
- It's a strong bullish reversal signal; immediately open a large long position

Answer: The Dragonfly Doji at support suggests a strong rejection of lower prices. The following bullish candle confirms buying pressure. A small long position with a stop-loss below the Doji's low balances the reversal opportunity with prudent risk management. Always consider the broader market context too.

The Doji and its variations offer a snapshot into moments of market equilibrium where neither sellers nor buyers have clear control. Recognizing these patterns can help traders anticipate significant shifts in market sentiment, thus aiding in making more informed trading decisions. As always, confirmation is key to validating these patterns before making any trades.

Great job! You can now confidently spot Doji patterns and understand what they reveal about market sentiment. Before moving on, let's put your knowledge to the test with a quick quiz!

QUIZ: Make A Decision

1. You're watching a stock in a downtrend. Price opens at $30, drops to $25, but rallies and closes at $29, forming a Hammer. What should you do next?

A. Ignore it; the downtrend is strong
B. Wait for a confirmation candle closing higher before considering a buy
C. Enter a short trade immediately
D. Buy right after the Hammer without confirmation

2. A stock has been in an uptrend. Opens at $80, pushes up to $90, but closes back at $81, forming a Shooting Star. Your move?

A. Buy right after the Shooting Star
B. Ignore the Shooting Star; trend is strong
C. Wait for a lower close next candle, then consider selling
D. Add more to your long position immediately

3. After a steady downtrend

A. Sell immediately
B. Wait for a confirmation candle closing above $52, then consider a long trade
C. Ignore the pattern and stick to the downtrend
D. Go short after Day 2 closes

4. In an uptrend

A. Add to long positions
B. Ignore the candle and hold long
C. Wait for a lower close the next day, then consider shorting
D. Immediately open a large buy order

5. After a long uptrend, you notice

A. Immediately sell all positions
B. Double down on long positions
C. Ignore the Doji - it doesn't matter
D. Wait for confirmation - watch if the next candle moves lower

6. Stock opens at $120, moves to $130, but closes back at $120, forming a Gravestone

Doji at the top of an uptrend. What should you do?

A. Ignore the pattern completely
B. Open a short trade without waiting
C. Wait for confirmation - look for a lower close before deciding
D. Add to your long trade immediately

7. A stock in a downtrend opens at $60, drops to $52, but closes at $60, forming a Dragonfly Doji. What's the best move?

A. Wait for confirmation with a bullish candle, then consider buying
B. Immediately open a short trade
C. Increase selling volume - downtrend is intact
D. Ignore the pattern

8. You're watching a stock at a key support level

A. Short the stock immediately
B. Watch for confirmation, then consider a long position with stop-loss below $40
C. Ignore the pattern - it's risky
D. Buy immediately without confirmation

9. A stock is approaching a known resistance level

A. Open a large long trade immediately
B. Ignore the pattern - it's not reliable
C. Wait for the next candle to confirm the reversal, then consider a short trade with a stop-loss above $99
D. Buy more, expecting the uptrend to continue

10. You're monitoring a strong uptrend. Today, you notice a Doji candle - price opens and closes at $120, with highs and lows showing significant movement. How should you react?

A. Close all positions without checking confirmation
B. Wait for the next candle to confirm if the trend will continue or reverse
C. Immediately sell, assuming a reversal is guaranteed
D. Ignore the Doji and add to your long position right away

Answer: 1. B; 2. C; 3. B; 4. C; 5. D; 6. C; 7. A; 8. B; 9. C; 10. B

Chapter 2: Market Trends and Support & Resistance

Lesson 1: Identifying Trends

Looking at the bigger picture!

Now that you've learned key candlestick patterns, it's time to step back and see the market's overall direction. Patterns show short-term moves. Trends reveal whether the market is climbing, falling, or shifting. Mastering trends helps you trade smarter let's dive in!

You may already know this - but let's make it clear: a trend is the overall direction the market is moving. - In an uptrend, prices are generally rising. - In a downtrend, prices are generally falling. Recognizing the trend helps you trade with the market, not against it.

In an uptrend, price forms a series of higher highs and higher lows. Each peak is higher than the last, and each pullback doesn't fall below the previous one. This shows buyers are in control, pushing prices higher over time. In an uptrend, traders look for buying opportunities, aiming to enter on pullbacks and ride the trend upward.

In an upward trend, you should keep an eye on swing highs, which happen when the price peaks and pulls back. It's a local maximum - Where buyers slow down and sellers start stepping in. Each new swing high is typically higher than the last, showing buyer strength. Spotting swing highs helps traders plan exits or spot weakening momentum.

When the trend is upward, traders use trend-following strategies to profit from the ongoing rise. They often buy during pullbacks, using tools like moving averages to confirm the trend's direction. To protect profits, they place trailing stop-losses, adjusting them as the price moves higher. The key is to stay with the trend until clear signs of reversal appear.

In a downtrend trend, the price forms a series of lower highs and lower lows. Each rally fails to reach the previous high, and prices continue to fall. This signals sellers are in control, steadily pushing prices lower. In a downtrend, traders look for selling opportunities - often entering after small rallies, aiming to follow the downward momentum.

Pay attention to swing lows that happen when the price drops to a low point, and then starts moving back up. In a downtrend, swing lows often get lower, showing sellers are in control. Knowing swing lows helps traders identify good entry points or when a trend might reverse.

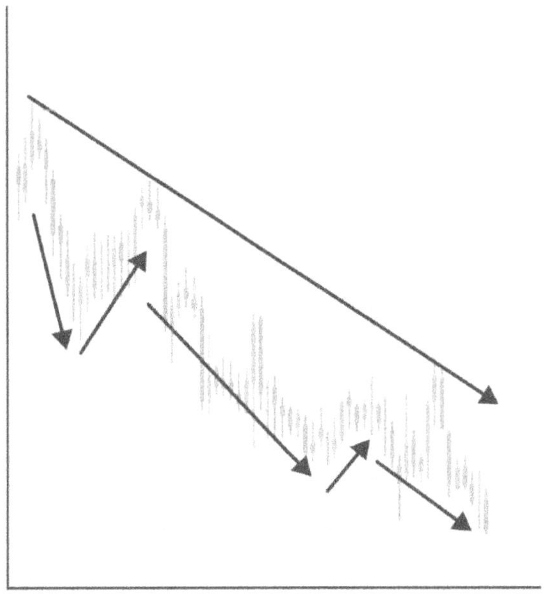

In a downtrend, traders also apply trend-following strategies to benefit from falling prices. They typically sell during small rallies, confirming the downtrend with indicators like moving averages. To manage risk, they set trailing stop-losses above recent highs, locking in profits as the trend continues downward. The goal is to follow the trend until signs of reversal appear.

Let's match trends!

Look closely at the charts. Are prices rising or falling?

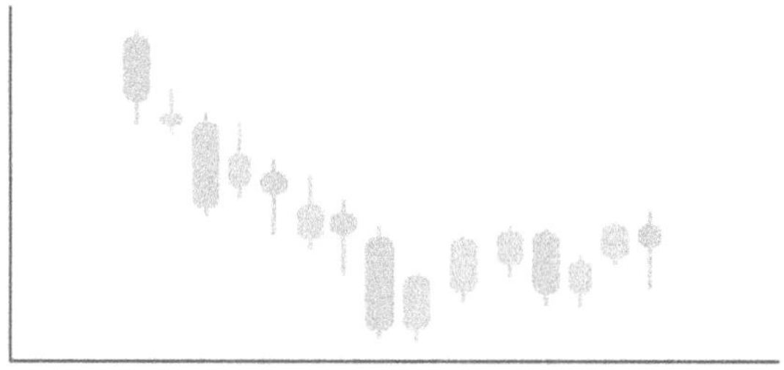

In an uptrend, prices form higher highs and higher lows. In a downtrend, they form lower highs and lower lows. Based on the pattern of highs and lows, select which one shows an upward trend or downtrend.

- 2 is an upward trend and 1 is a downward trend.
- 1 is an upward trend and 2 is a downward trend.

Answer: 1 is an upward trend and 2 is a downward trend. Spotting trends like this is key to understanding market momentum.

At first glance, spotting whether the market is bullish or bearish may seem easy. But predicting what happens next? That's where it gets tricky.

Market prices don't move randomly - they reflect the decisions of countless traders reacting to emotions, expectations, and news. Behind every price shift is a battle of supply and demand, driven by psychology. By spotting these patterns, you can better anticipate what might happen next.

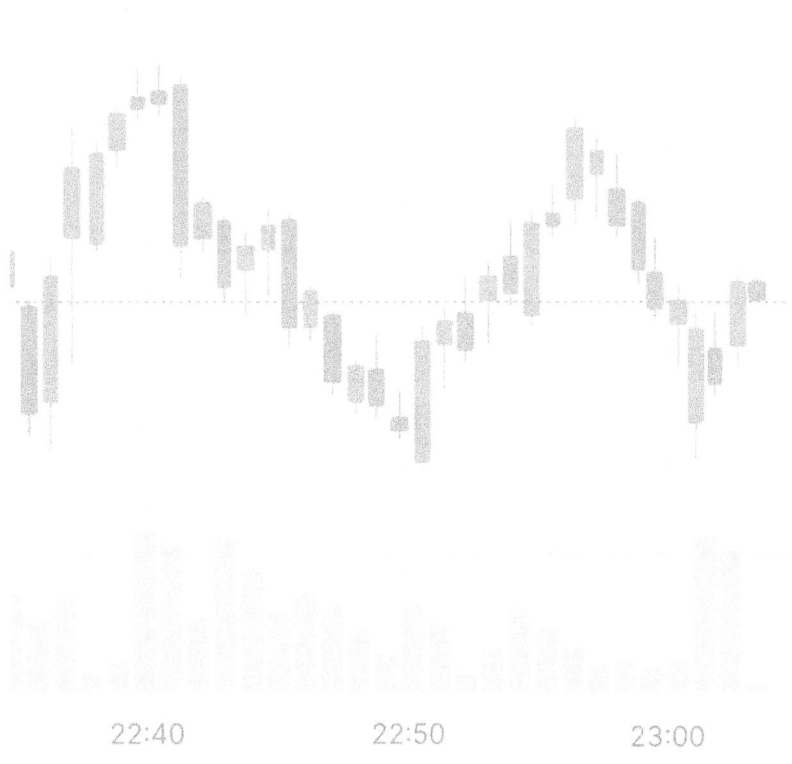

Imagine a stock priced at $100 suddenly falls to $90 due to disappointing earnings news. Traders fear more losses, quickly selling their positions. This selling pressure pushes the price even lower to $85 and then to $80, creating a bearish trend.

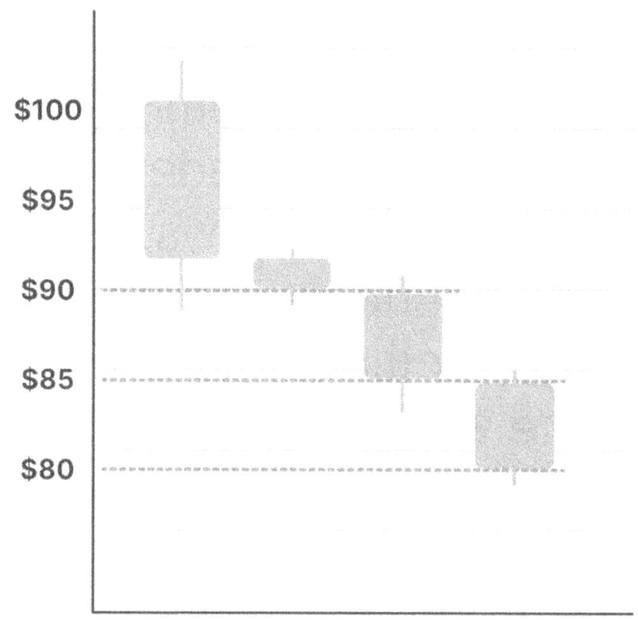

Now consider a stock that moves from $50 to $65 after news of a breakthrough product. Traders see potential easy profits, so they rush to buy. This spike in buying drives the price even higher, from $65 → $70 → $75, forming an uptrend due to increased demand.

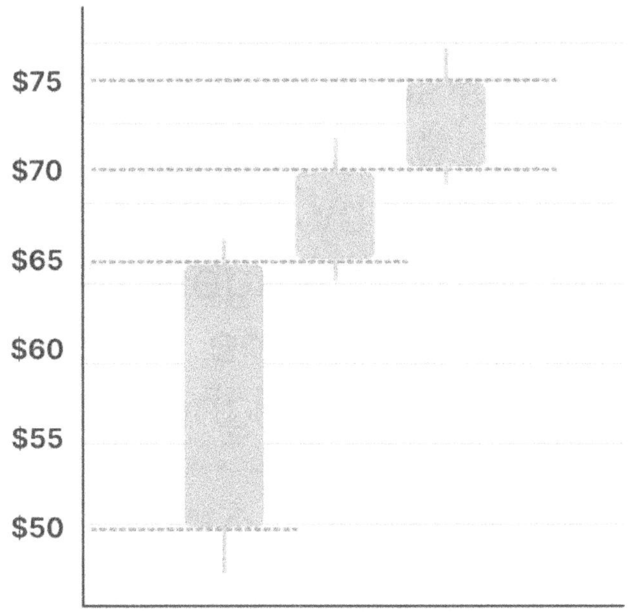

A strong trend is usually supported by good volume. For instance, during an uptrend from $100 to $120, increasing volume confirms buyer confidence. But if the price rises from $120 to $125 on low volume, it suggests weakening momentum and possible reversal ahead.

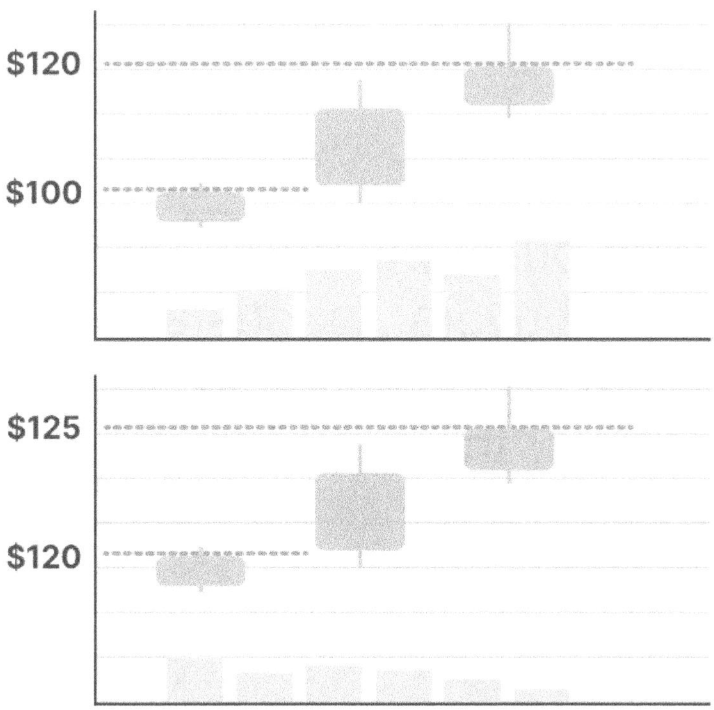

Now, let's look at this stock that has been climbing steadily - rising from $200 to $220, then to $240. Each move is supported by strong trading volume. But now, something changes. As the price approaches $245, the volume noticeably drops. The price struggles to push higher.

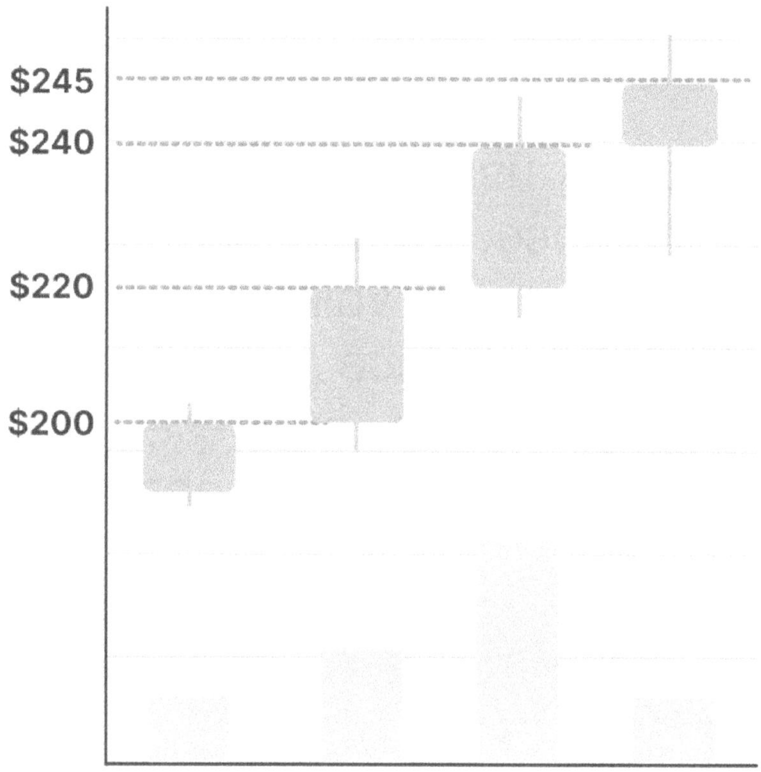

This signals that buying interest might be fading. Without enough buyers to sustain momentum, some traders may start locking in profits. If selling pressure increases, the uptrend could weaken or even reverse.

However, no trend continues endlessly. Even in the strongest trends, prices often pause or shift temporarily. These pauses are known as pullbacks - short-term moves against the trend.

For instance, after a stock rises steadily from $20 to $40, some traders close their positions to secure gains. This profit-taking temporarily drops the price to $35, creating a pullback before potentially resuming upward momentum.

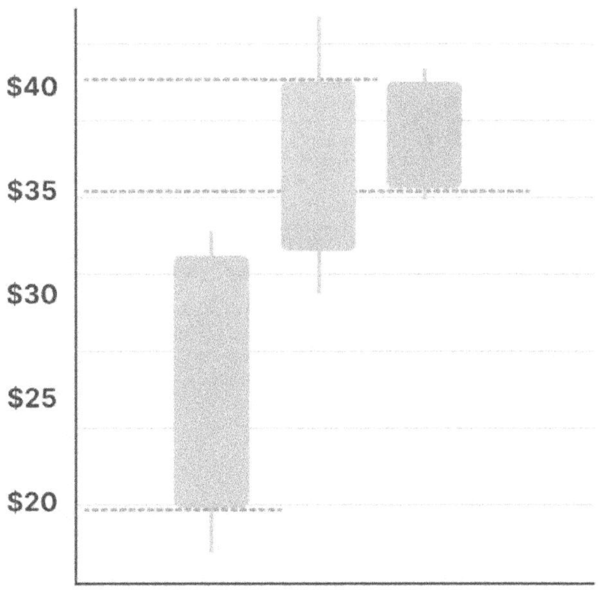

Pullbacks happen in downtrends too. Imagine a stock falling steadily from $80 to $60. Some traders might see this drop as a buying opportunity, briefly pushing the price up to $65. However, if selling pressure remains strong, the price soon resumes its downward move, continuing the downtrend to $55.

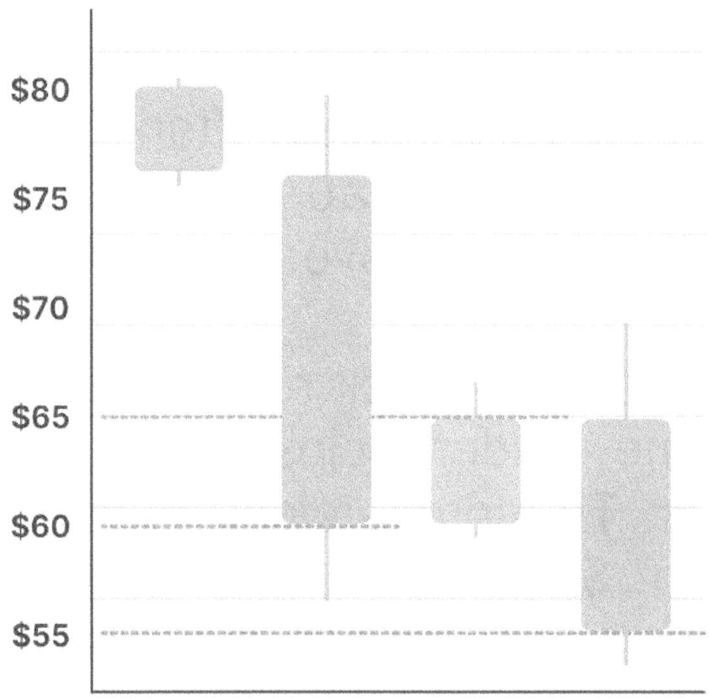

What's your move?

You're analyzing Stock ABC and here's what you see: The price steadily climbed from $150 → $165

→ $172. Recently, it pulled back to $168 and has been struggling to break above $172 for several sessions.

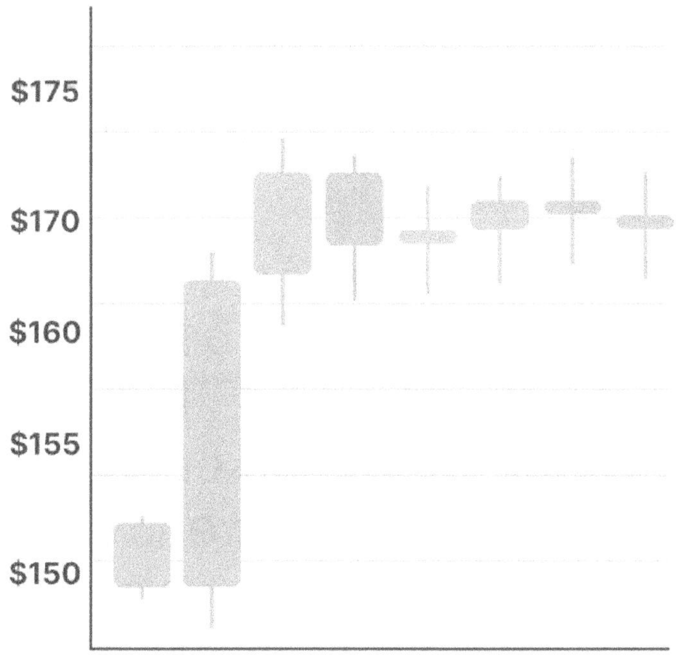

The price is showing resistance at $172 and struggling to break through. Watching how it behaves around this level can help you avoid jumping in too early or missing a reversal. What would you do next based on this price behavior?

- Wait and watch
- Ignore short-term moves
- Buy now
- Prepare to sell

Answer: Wait and watch. The price is testing a resistance level. Waiting for a clear breakout or breakdown helps reduce the risk of acting on indecision.

No matter which action you choose, you've seen how price behavior can hint at what's coming next.

A pullback is a small pause before the trend resumes. A reversal, however, flips the entire trend. It happens when the market shifts direction - uptrend to downtrend, or downtrend to uptrend.

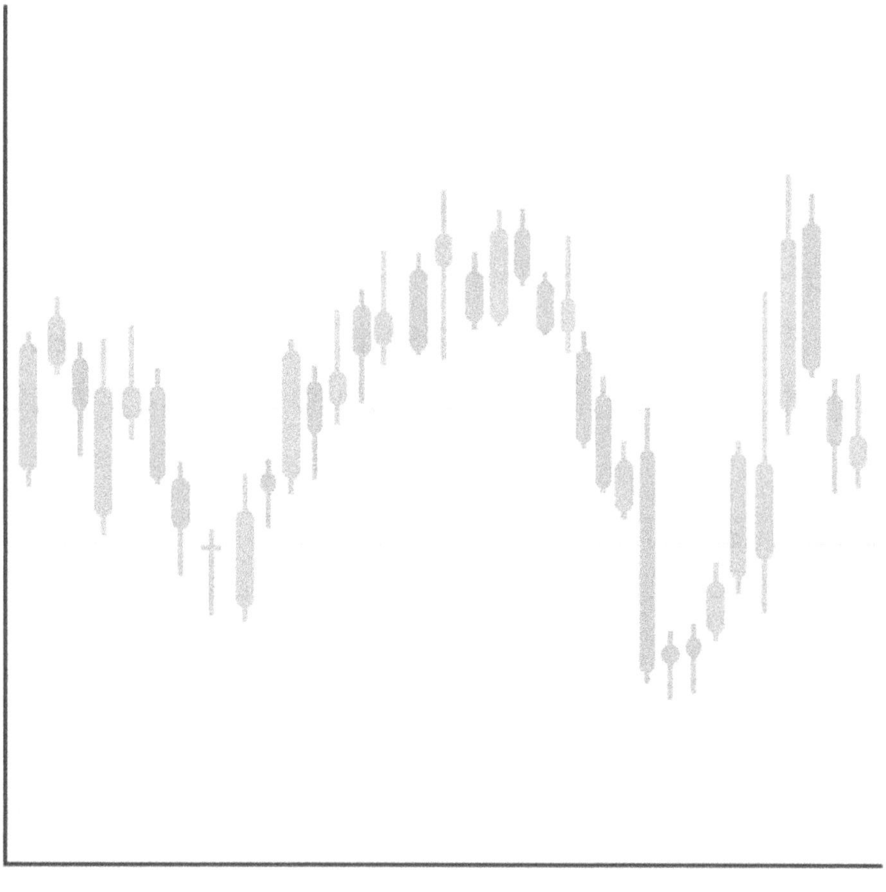

The patterns you've already learned - like Engulfing, Doji, Hammer, and Shooting Star - often signal these reversals before they fully unfold. Spot them early, and you'll be ready to adjust before the market moves.

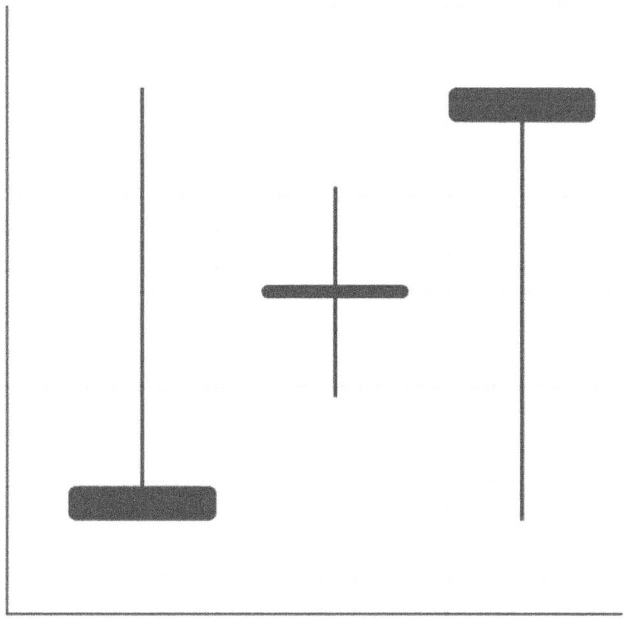

Great job! You can now confidently spot uptrends, downtrends, and reversals - all key skills for making smart trading decisions. But remember, trends don't move endlessly. They often pause or reverse at important price levels. Next, we'll explore how to identify those key price levels, so you can better predict where price might bounce, reverse, or breakthrough. Let's keep going!

Lesson 2: Support and Resistance

Spotting market support and resistance

Every trend faces key price levels where momentum pauses, reverses, or breaks through. In this section, I will show you how to spot support and resistance - and how to recognize powerful breakouts when they happen. Let's dive in!

Support and resistance are critical price levels where the market often pauses or reverses. Think of them as invisible barriers - support acts like a floor, while resistance acts like a ceiling - shaping price movement.

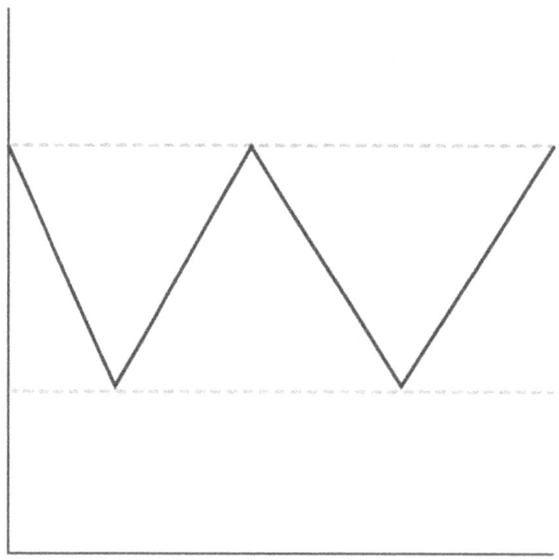

Let's look at resistance first. When the price reaches this level, selling pressure increases, and the price often stops rising - or even falls. Many traders use resistance to take profits or look for short (sell) opportunities.

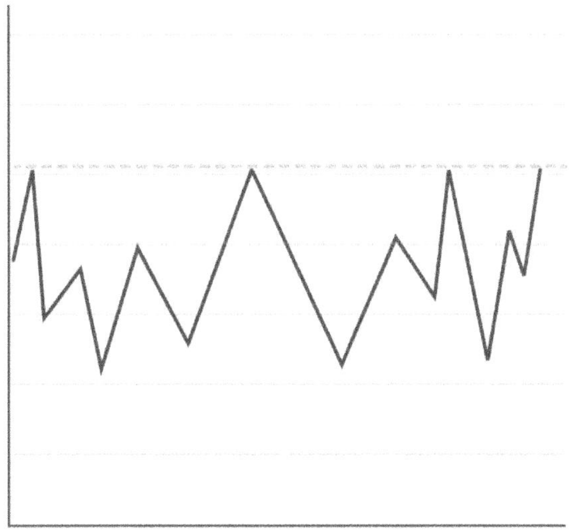

In a strong trend, old resistance can become new support. Once the price breaks above resistance, it may pull back - but that resistance level often becomes a new place where buyers step in. Spotting this helps you enter trades with the trend.

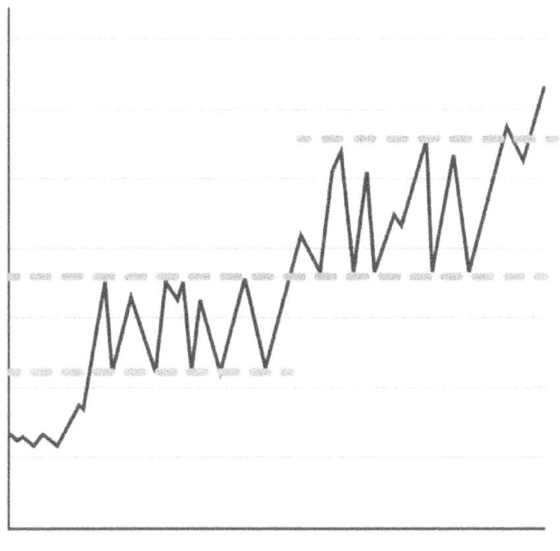

Now, let's look at support. When the price drops to this level, buying pressure increases, stopping the price from falling further. Traders use support to find buy opportunities or set stop-losses safely.

Let's look at a real example. In this bullish trend, can you see how the previous resistance level is now acting as support during the pullback?

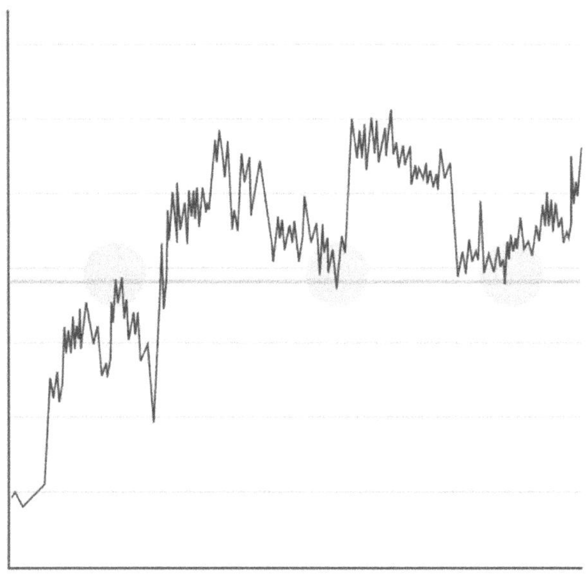

Identifying support and resistance

Now it's your turn. Look at this chart and identity the key support and resistance levels.

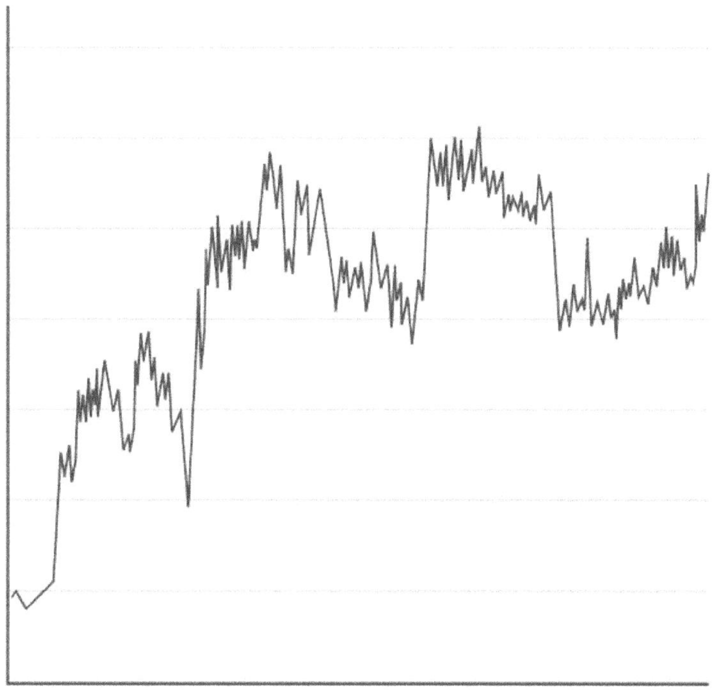

How many clear support or resistance levels can you identify? Look for levels where the price has reversed multiple times.

A. 1
B. 2
C. 4
D. 3

Answer: 1. Remember, support and resistance levels are areas where the price has reversed direction more than once. These are areas where price has consistently reversed, acting as barriers to price movement.

Knowing where support and resistance levels are is one thing - but how can you actually use them to profit? Let's break down how traders apply these levels to make smart entry, exit, and stop-loss decisions.

When price approaches resistance, it often struggles to move higher. Traders can:

- Take profits near resistance after a strong uptrend.
- Open short (sell) trades, expecting the price to reverse downward.
- Place stop-losses just above resistance to limit the risk if the price breaks through.

Applying support and resistance

Let's test your understanding. In this bearish trend, where would be a good potential entry point based on support and resistance? Think about where sellers are likely to step in during a rally.

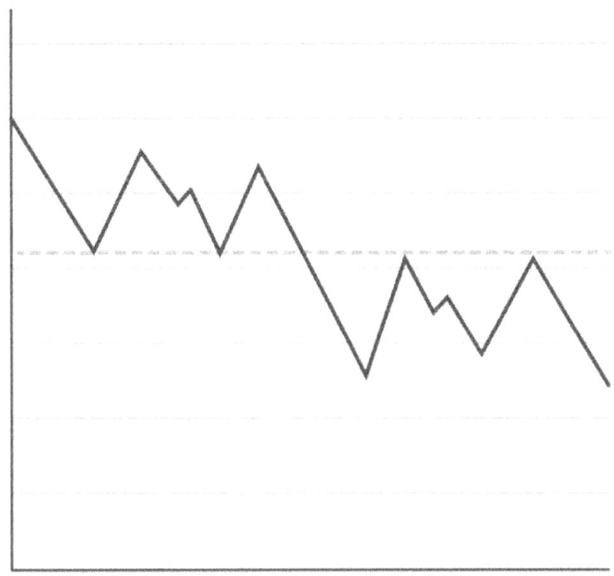

- Midway between support and the previous high
- At the current price
- At the resistance level
- At the support level

Answer: The resistance level is the most promising entry point in a bearish trend. In a bearish trend, traders look for selling opportunities at resistance levels during rallies. That's where sellers are likely to step back in, pushing prices lower.

In contrast, when price approaches support, buyers often step in. Traders can:

1. Enter buy trades near support, expecting the price to bounce upward.

2. Place stop-losses just below support to protect against breakdowns.

3. Add to positions if the price holds and moves higher from support.

Applying support and resistance

Let's test your understanding. In this bullish trend, where would be a good potential entry point based on support and resistance?

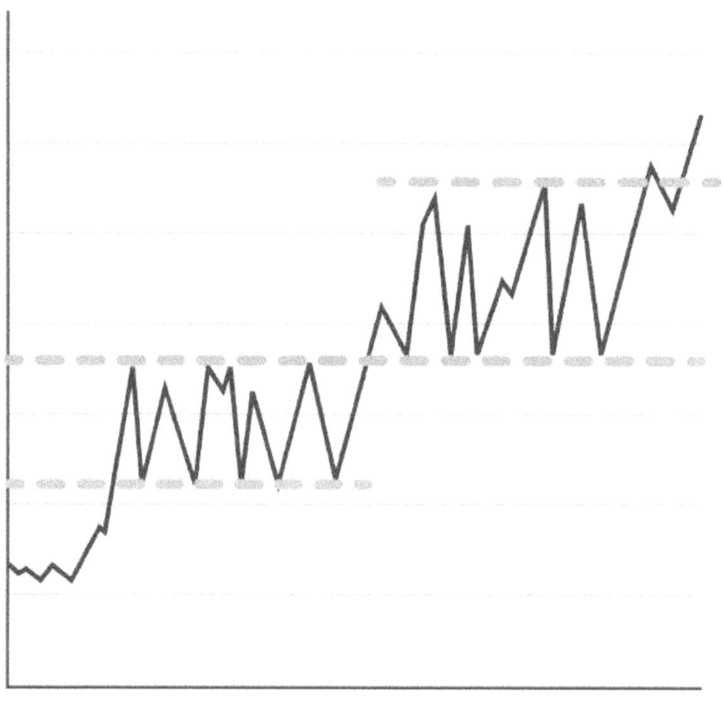

Where's the most promising entry point based on support and resistance? Think about where buyers are likely to step in during a pullback.

- Midway between support and the previous high
- At the support level
- At the resistance level
- At the current price

Answer: The support level is the most promising entry point. Consider where the price is likely to find support in a bullish trend during a pullback. It's where buyers are likely to step in, potentially ending the pullback and resuming the uptrend.

But price doesn't always bounce off these levels. Sometimes, momentum builds, and the price breaks straight through support or resistance. These moments are called breakouts - and they often lead to strong, fast price moves.

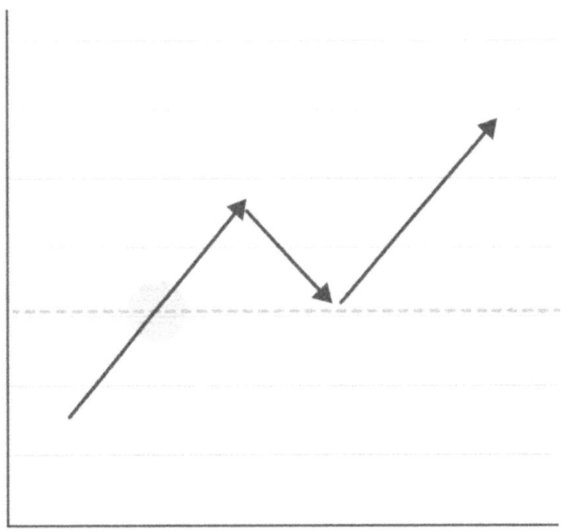

Breakouts occur when the price keeps testing a support or resistance level multiple times without fully breaking it. Over time, pressure builds. Eventually, either buyers gain enough strength to push the price above resistance, or sellers dominate enough to drive it below support. Sometimes, major news or events can speed up this process, causing prices to break through these key levels quickly.

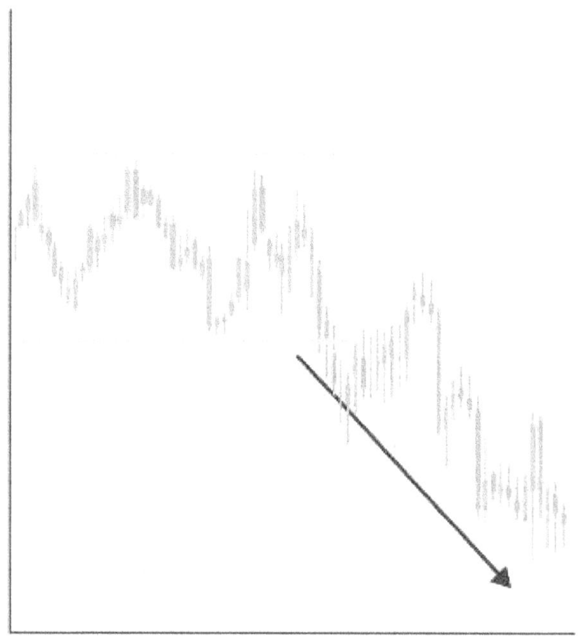

A bullish breakout happens when the price breaks above a resistance level. This shows strong buying pressure, and traders often buy, expecting the price to keep rising.

A bearish breakout occurs when the price breaks below a support level. This signals that sellers are in control, and traders may sell, expecting the price to fall further.

When trading breakouts, timing, and risk management are key. Traders typically enter a buy trade when the price breaks above resistance, or enter a sell trade when the price breaks below support.

To protect themselves, they place a stop-loss just outside the breakout level - below the breakout point for bullish trades, or above it for bearish trades - in case the breakout fails.

How will you respond to the breakout?

Take a look at Stock ABC, which has been trading between $50 (support) and $60 (resistance) for several weeks. Suddenly, the price breaks above the $60 resistance level and quickly rises to $63.

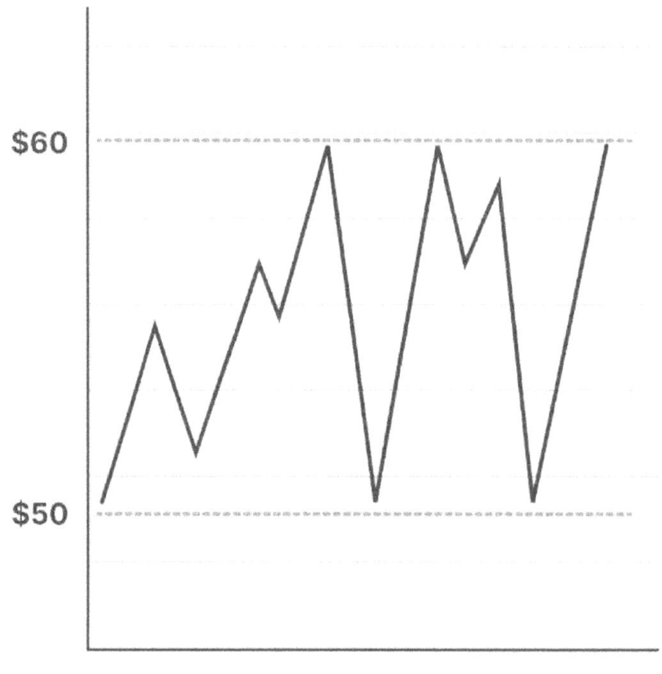

Based on this price movement, what action would you consider? Breaking above a strong resistance level can signal a bullish breakout. But smart traders still look for confirmation before jumping in.

- Avoid trading
- Sell
- Wait and watch
- Buy

Answer: Buy. A breakout above resistance often signals continued upward momentum. Buying after confirmation can be a strong move - just remember to manage risk. Breakout above a well-tested resistance level is often a bullish signal. Ignoring it or acting too cautiously might mean missing a potential opportunity.

No matter which option you choose, the key takeaway is this: breakouts offer exciting opportunities, but they require careful analysis. Strong momentum often continues - but breakouts might fail, trapping traders.

Watch out! Sometimes, the price pushes briefly beyond a support or resistance level but quickly reverses - this is known as a false breakout. It can catch traders off guard if they enter too soon.

To avoid this, traders wait for confirmation, such as a strong close beyond the level or a retest where price holds above or below the broken level. They also check for increased trading volume, which signals stronger momentum and makes the breakout more reliable.

Action plan

You're watching a stock test the $100 resistance multiple times. Finally, it breaks through and jumps to $105. Think like a trader - how would you plan your entry and exit? Reorder the steps to build a strong breakout strategy. A strong breakout strategy starts with spotting key levels, waiting for confirmation, and managing risk. Your goal is to enter with momentum - but protect yourself in case the breakout fails.

- Enter buy trade
- Place stop-loss below $100
- Spot breakout with strong momentum
- Identify resistance at $100
- Monitor for trend continuation or reversal

Answer:

- Identify resistance at $100
- Spot breakout with strong momentum
- Enter buy trade
- Place stop-loss at $100
- Monitor for trend continuation or reversal

You've now mastered how to use support, resistance, and breakouts to make smarter trading decisions. But here's the thing - markets don't always move in clear trends. Sometimes, the price moves sideways, stuck between key levels without a clear direction. Next, let's explore how to spot these sideways markets and adjust your strategy to profit from them.

Lesson 3: Market Ranges vs Trends

Market ranges vs trends

By now, you've learned how to recognize trends, reversals, and breakouts. But here's an important question every trader must ask: Is the market trending... or stuck in a range? Knowing the difference is crucial. In this section, you'll learn how to spot range-bound markets and adjust your trades to profit inside the range - or catch the breakout when the price escapes it.

A range-bound market occurs when prices oscillate between specific highs and lows, creating a horizontal channel. The upper boundary acts as resistance, while the lower boundary serves as support. In this environment, prices lack a clear directional trend and move sideways within a confined range.

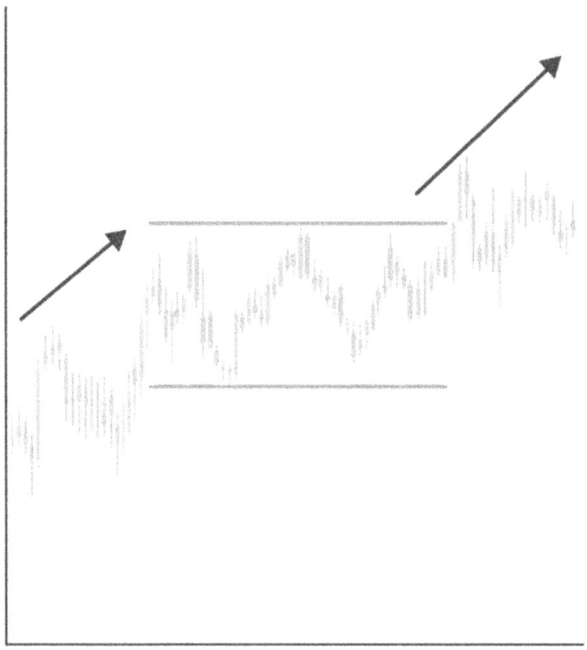

Imagine a stock fluctuating between $50 (support) and $60 (resistance) over several weeks. Traders observe that each time the price nears $50, it rebounds upward, and when it approaches $60, it retreats downward.

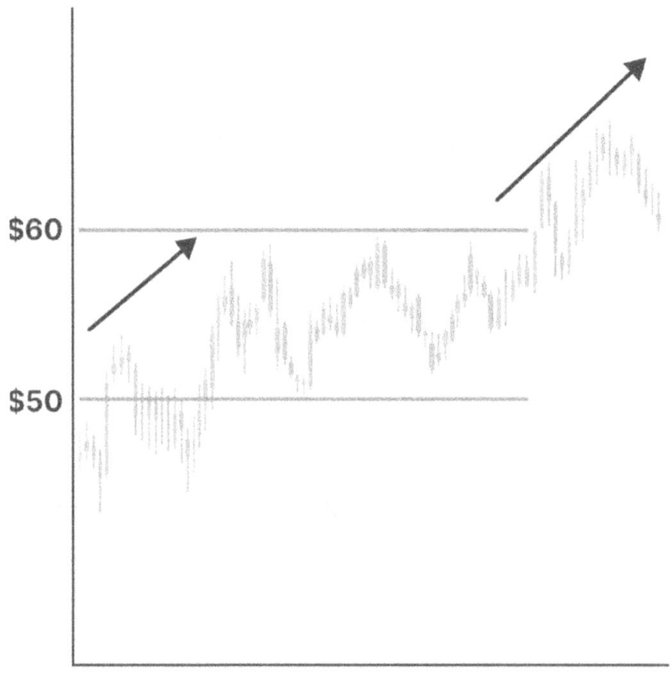

In this kind of market, traders take advantage of the predictable movement: - They buy near support ($50), expecting the price to bounce up. - They sell near resistance ($60), expecting the price to pull back down. This strategy is called range trading. It works best when the market shows no clear trend and keeps bouncing between the same levels.

But no range lasts forever. At some point, the price may break out of the range - either above resistance or below support - signaling the start of a new trend.

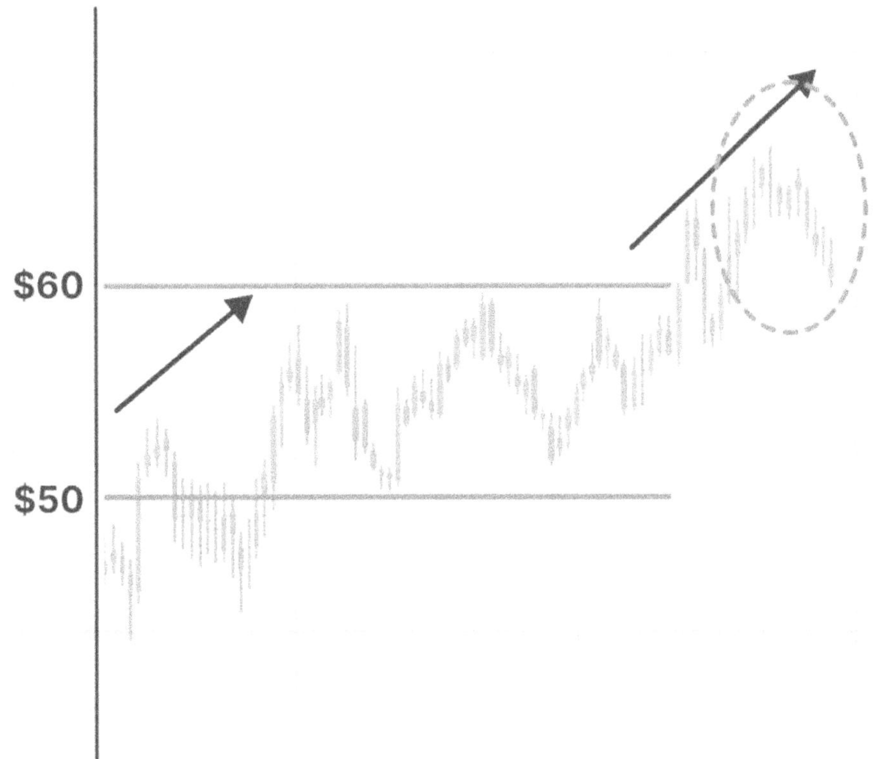

When a breakout happens:

- Buyers step in when the price breaks above resistance, expecting continued upward momentum.
- Sellers take control when the price breaks below support, expecting the price to fall further.
- Traders enter trades in the direction of the breakout, often setting stop-losses just outside the old range to manage risk.

Quick check!

The stock has now surged to $61, breaking above the previous $60 resistance with strong momentum and high volume.

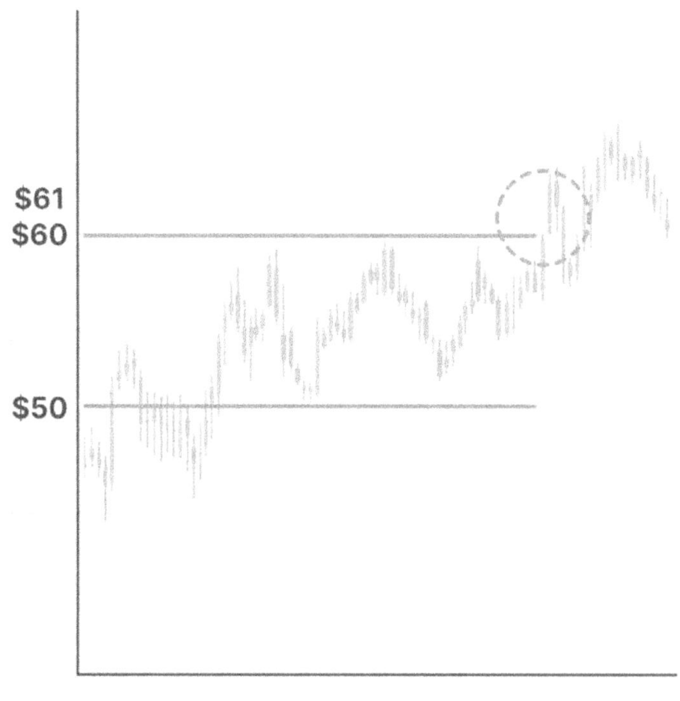

What does strong momentum and volume after breaking resistance usually signal? What should you do after spotting this breakout?

- Sell immediately - price will likely reverse
- Wait indefinitely to see if the price drops back to $50
- Enter a buy trade, expecting the trend to continue upward
- Avoid trading breakouts

Answer: Enter a buy trade, expecting the trend to continue upward. A breakout above resistance, especially with strong volume, is a signal to buy. Traders expect the price to continue rising.

Once the breakout holds, the market often shifts into a clear trend. This is the perfect time to use what you already know - trend-following strategies:

- Enter in the direction of the breakout
- Use trailing stop-losses to protect profits as the trend grows
- Stay in the trade until you spot clear signs of reversal

What are you going to do?

A stock is in a clear downtrend, forming lower highs and lower lows. After a brief rally, the price hits a resistance level and starts falling again.

Trend-followers trade in the direction of the prevailing trend - what's that here? What's the smart move using a trend-following strategy?

- Enter a sell trade as the price resumes falling
- Avoid trading; downtrends are too risky
- Wait for the price to move sideways
- Buy, expecting the rally to continue

Answer: Enter a sell trade as the price resumes falling. Selling after a small rally in a downtrend is classic trend-following.

Great job! You've built a strong foundation in technical analysis. You now understand how to recognize market trends, spot key levels like support and resistance, apply trend-following and range-trading strategies, and identify important candlestick patterns. These skills will allow you to read charts confidently and make well-informed trading decisions.

But this is just the beginning. The more you practice applying these concepts, the more effective and confident you'll become in real market conditions. Ready to take your skills to the next level? Let's continue!

SECTION 5: INDICATORS

Chapter 1: Technical Indicators

Lesson 1: What Are Technical Indicators?

Trade smarter with indicators!

You've already built a solid foundation in technical analysis. Now it's time to level up! In this lesson, you'll learn what indicators are, how to use them, and which types are best for spotting momentum. Let's start!

You've likely heard of indicators. Let's break them down. They're math-based tools that analyze price or volume to help you spot trends, momentum shifts, and key market signals.

They're designed to help traders understand what the market is doing right now - and what it might do next. They're not direct buy or sell signals, but tools to guide decisions by highlighting patterns and market behavior.

Every strategy needs the right tools. Trend indicators like Moving Averages show direction, while momentum tools like RSI or MACD spot shifts or reversals. This may sound complicated, but do not worry, I will guide you through every indicator in the upcoming lessons.

So the thing is - price charts show market movement, but not always the meaning. Indicators add context, confirming trends or questioning momentum, to reduce guesswork and improve your decisions.

Have you ever second-guessed a trade or acted on impulse? In volatile markets, emotions can quickly override logic. Technical indicators help remove that uncertainty by offering consistent, data-based signals. By relying on objective tools rather than gut feelings, you're more likely to follow your plan and make disciplined, well-timed decisions.

Consistency is another key to developing a sustainable trading approach. Indicators allow traders to apply the same logic across different trades, reducing variation in how decisions are made. With clear signals and repeatable rules, you can measure their performance more effectively, refine your strategies, and improve over time.

Lastly, the market is full of information, and not all of it is useful. Indicators act as filters, helping you focus on what matters most. They take the complexity of price movements and present it in a way that's easier to interpret and act on. That said, using too many indicators can be counterproductive. The goal is to find a small set of tools that support your strategy - tools that help clarify the market, not complicate it.

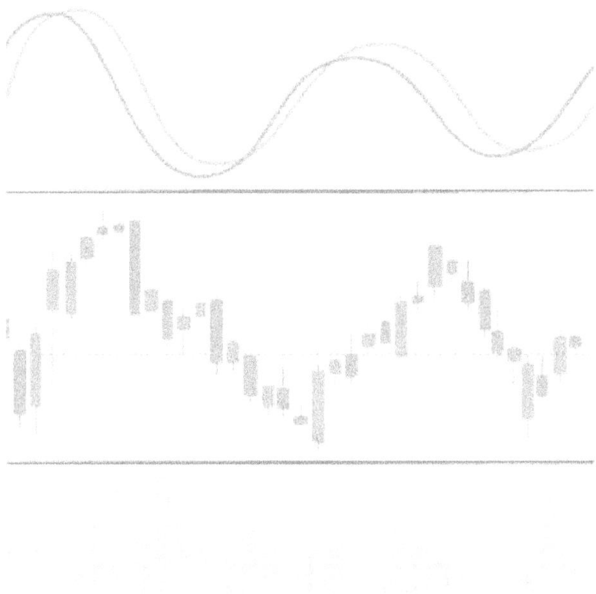

Why should you use indicators?

Let's put your knowledge to the test. Select the three main reasons traders use indicators. Think about how indicators support your trading process - they help you plan, confirm, and stay calm under pressure. Focus on the choices that involve decision-making, discipline, and clarity, not unrealistic promises or shortcuts.

- Spot entries and exits
- Guarantee profits
- Reduce emotional decisions
- Confirm market moves
- Predict exact timing
- Replace trading strategies

Answer:

- Spot entries and exits
- Reduce emotional decisions
- Confirm market moves

Excellent! Now that you understand why indicators are essential, it's time to look deeper. Not all technical indicators serve the same function - most fall into one of two main categories: leading and lagging. Let's take a closer look at each category.

Leading indicators are designed to anticipate future price movements. They analyze current market conditions to suggest where the price might go next. Traders often use them to identify early signs of reversals or shifts in momentum before the actual price move occurs.

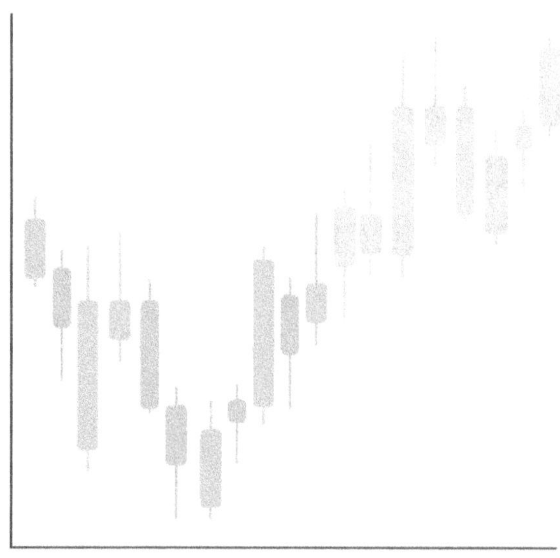

While leading indicators can offer earlier entry opportunities, they also carry a higher risk of false signals. They are most effective when used in combination with other forms of confirmation.

Lagging indicators are used to confirm what the market is already doing. Instead of predicting future movements, they validate trends that are currently in progress. These tools are often based on historical data and smooth out price action to reduce noise.

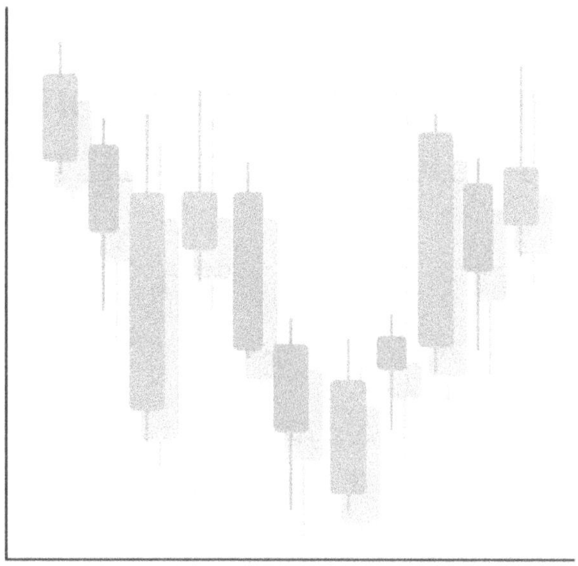

Because they react after a move has begun, lagging indicators can help traders avoid premature entries and stay aligned with broader market trends. They are especially useful in trend-following strategies where confirmation is more important than early entry.

Leading indicators are great for early in signals but need confirmation. Lagging indicators respond more slowly, but help validate what the market is already doing. Think preparation vs. confirmation.

Well done! You now know what technical indicators are, why traders use them, and the key difference between leading and lagging types. In the next lesson, we'll dive deeper into leading indicators. You'll learn how specific leading indicators work, what they reveal, and how to use them to identify potential market moves before they happen.

Lesson 2: Leading Indicators

How to spot a trend before it happens?

As you already know, successful trading isn't just about reacting - it's about anticipating. That's why traders use leading indicators. In this lesson, you'll learn what leading indicators are, how they work, and how to use some of the most popular ones in your own strategy.

Leading indicators are used to predict future price movements before a trend starts. They're meant to help traders anticipate what might happen next, not confirm what already occurred.

Leading indicators measure how the market is moving. A key focus is momentum - the strength or speed of a price move:

- Fast, strong moves = rising momentum (1)
- Slower moves = weakening momentum (2)

When momentum fades, it could mean the current trend is running out of steam.

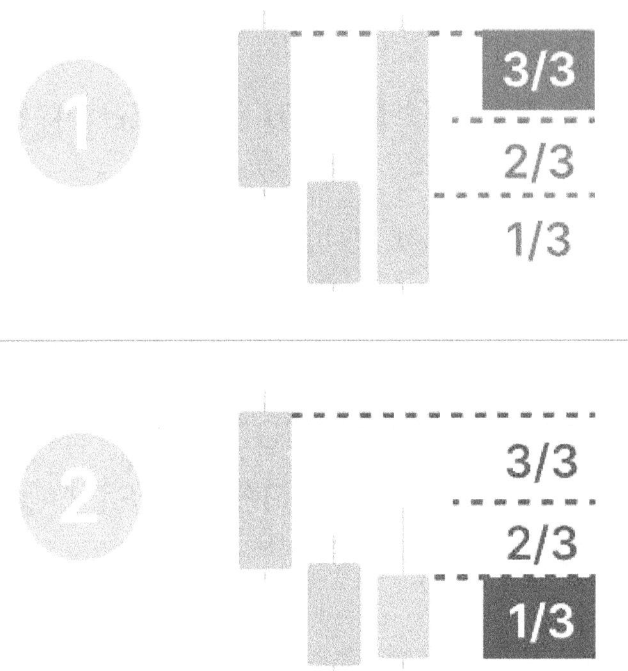

If momentum is rising, it's often a sign to ride the trend - enter trades in the direction of the move and stay in as long as momentum continues. When momentum slows, it may be time to prepare for a reversal or tighten your stop-loss to protect profits. By watching momentum closely, you can make better entries, exits and avoid getting caught in weak trends.

Choose the best entry point

You see a bullish market with three entry opportunities: Phase A, B, and C. Each phase reflects a different level of momentum behind the price movement. You're looking for a safe and efficient entry, not too early, not too late. Momentum is useful when it's building, not when it's exhausted or just beginning. Find the phase where the trend has formed but hasn't yet faded.

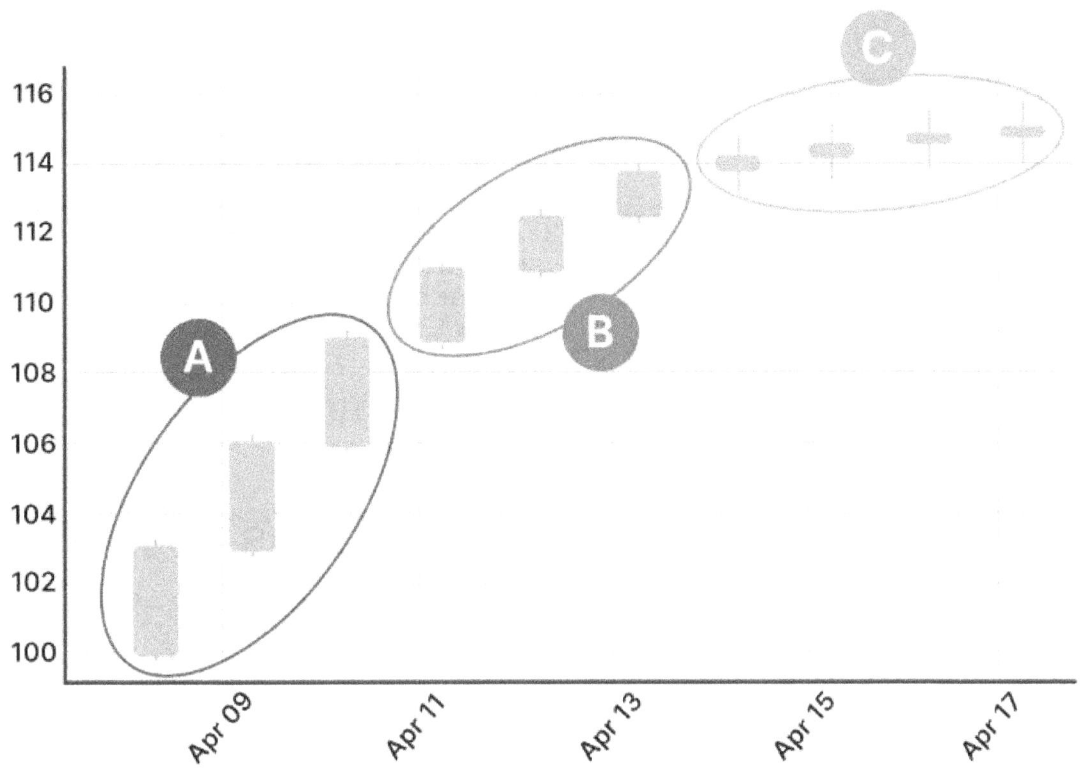

Answer: Phase A might be too early, and Phase C too unstable. Phase B hits the sweet spot - momentum is still strong, but price action is more stable.

Leading indicators help detect these shifts in pressure before the price actually reacts. Spotting changes in buying or selling pressure early gives traders the chance to prepare for trend reversals, breakouts, or breakdowns with stronger timing and better risk control.

Reacting to market pressure

Understanding who's in control - buyers, sellers, or neither - can help guide your next trading decision. If buyers or sellers are clearly in control, traders tend to follow them. But when the market is balanced, it's wise to hold off until a breakout confirms a new direction. Match each market pressure condition with the most suitable action.

- Sellers are in control - Avoid longs, consider going short
- Buyers and sellers are balanced - Looking for buying opportunities
- Buyers are in control - Wait for direction

Answer:

- Sellers are in control - Avoid longs, consider going short

- Buyers and sellers are balanced - Wait for direction
- Buyers are in control - Looking for buying opportunities

Tracking momentum and market pressure sounds complex, but you don't have to do it by hand. Leading indicators automatically analyze this for you, so you can spend less time guessing and more time making smart trades.

Now let's explore three of the most common leading indicators. The first one you'll learn about is the Relative Strength Index (RSI). It measures how strong recent price movements are and shows whether something might be overbought (too high) or oversold (too low).

The RSI gives you a number between 0 and 100, and that number can help you decide when to enter or exit a trade.

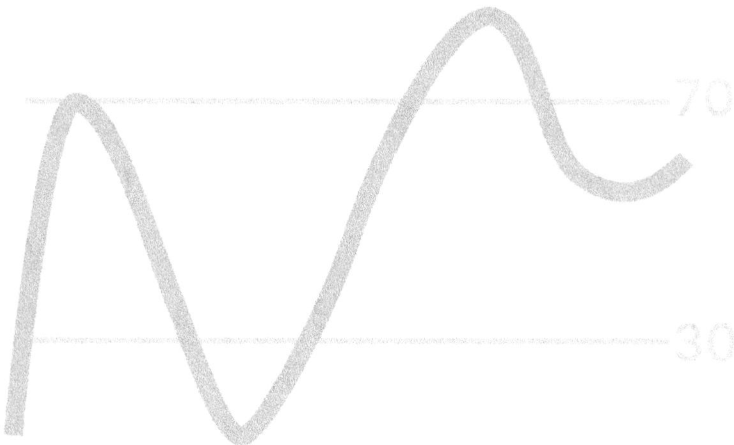

In other words, RSI can help you catch potential reversals - times when the market might change direction. Here's the simplest way to use it:

- RSI below 30: Market may be oversold - potential buy signal
- RSI around 50: Neutral zone - no strong signal
- RSI above 70: Market may be overbought - potential sell or take-profit signal

An RSI of above 70 means the market may be overbought. That's often a sign the price could pull back soon. Instead of buying, traders usually wait - or look to sell when RSI is above 70.

Now let's move on to another popular leading indicator: the Stochastic Oscillator. It helps traders spot momentum shifts by comparing the current price to its recent range. In other words, it shows whether the market is losing strength or ready to turn.

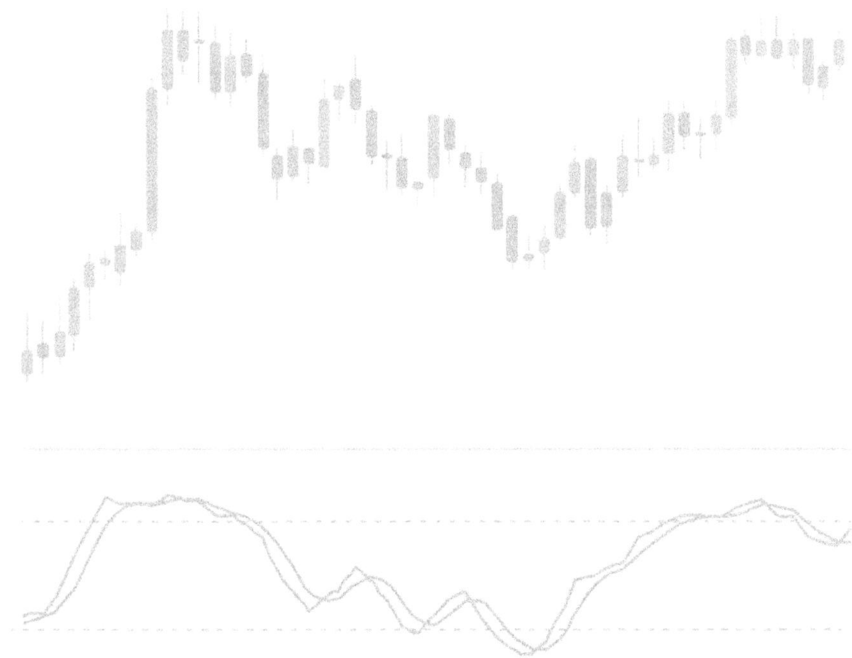

The Stochastic Oscillator gives you two lines that move between 0 and 100:

- The first line (called %K) shows the current momentum based on recent prices.
- The second line (called %D) is a smoothed version of that first line - it helps confirm the signal.

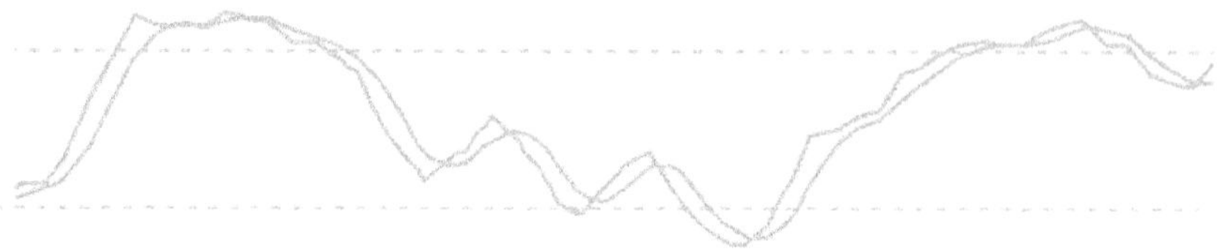

When the %K line crosses above the %D line from below the 20 level, it can be a buy signal. When %K crosses below %D from above the 80 level, it can be a sell signal. This crossover helps traders decide if the change in momentum is strong enough to act on.

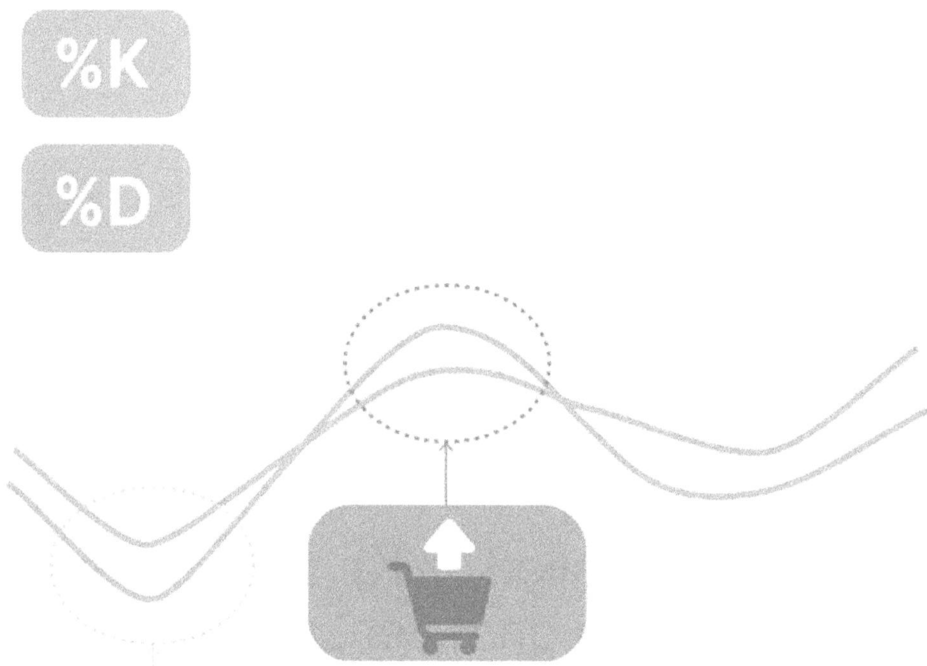

Matching the Stochastic behavior with the signal

The Stochastic Oscillator helps spot shifts in momentum, especially during overbought or oversold conditions. Match each behavior with what it likely means for your trading decision. Think about what it means when the market is oversold (under 20) or overbought (over 80). A crossover in those zones can signal that a shift is coming.

- %K crosses above %D below 20 - Possible buying signal
- %K and %D haven't crossed - Possible selling signal
- %K crosses below %D above 80 - Wait for confirmation

Answer:

- %K crosses above %D below 20 - Possible buying signal
- %K and %D haven't crossed - Wait for confirmation
- %K crosses below %D above 80 - Possible selling signal

Now let's explore another leading indicator: Fibonacci Retracement. It helps traders find potential pullback zones - places where the price might pause or reverse before continuing its trend.

Traders identify a significant price movement (either upward or downward) and apply the Fibonacci Retracement tool from the start to the end of that move. The tool then plots horizontal lines at key Fibonacci levels: 0.236 (23.6%), 0.382 (38.2%), 0.5 (50%), 0.618 (61.8%), 1.0 (100%).

Traders often treat Fibonacci levels as key decision zones during a pullback. When price reaches the 0.382 level, it's seen as a shallow Retracement - this suggests strong momentum, and traders may look for early opportunities to rejoin the trend.

The 0.5 level, although not a Fibonacci ratio, is widely recognized as a common pause point. At this level, traders typically wait for confirmation before entering or adding to a trade.

The 0.618 level, known as the golden ratio, is one of the most closely watched. It's often seen as a

strong potential reversal area, where traders may place entries, stop-losses, or take-profits depending on their strategy.

Fibonacci Retracement in action

Every great Fibonacci setup starts with a process. Can you arrange the steps in the right order to find key levels and plan your next move? Start by understanding where the market is going. Then look at the recent price move, apply the tool, and only react once you see how the price behaves.

- Identify the trend
- Draw Fibonacci retracement
- Watch price at key level
- Find high and low

Answer:

- Identify the trend
- Find high and low
- Draw Fibonacci retracement
- Watch price at key level

Excellent! You've just explored how leading indicators help traders anticipate what the market might do next, rather than simply reacting to price movements. You now understand how momentum and market pressure work, and how leading indicators can help you identify potential turning points, entry opportunities, and key reaction zones. But this is only part of the picture. In lesson 4, we'll focus on lagging indicators!

Lesson 3: Practice Leading Indicators

Are you ready?

Time to turn theory into action! In this lesson, you'll practice using three powerful leading indicators: RSI, Stochastic Oscillator, and Fibonacci Retracement. Don't worry if it feels tricky at first - practice makes perfect, and each task is here to help you improve step by step.

Let's practice using RSI

Apple's price just bounced off recent lows and is currently trading at $199.74. The RSI reads 45.92. There's no major breakout or breakdown yet. RSI around 45 suggests neutral momentum. It's not a clear buy or sell. Look for confirmation.

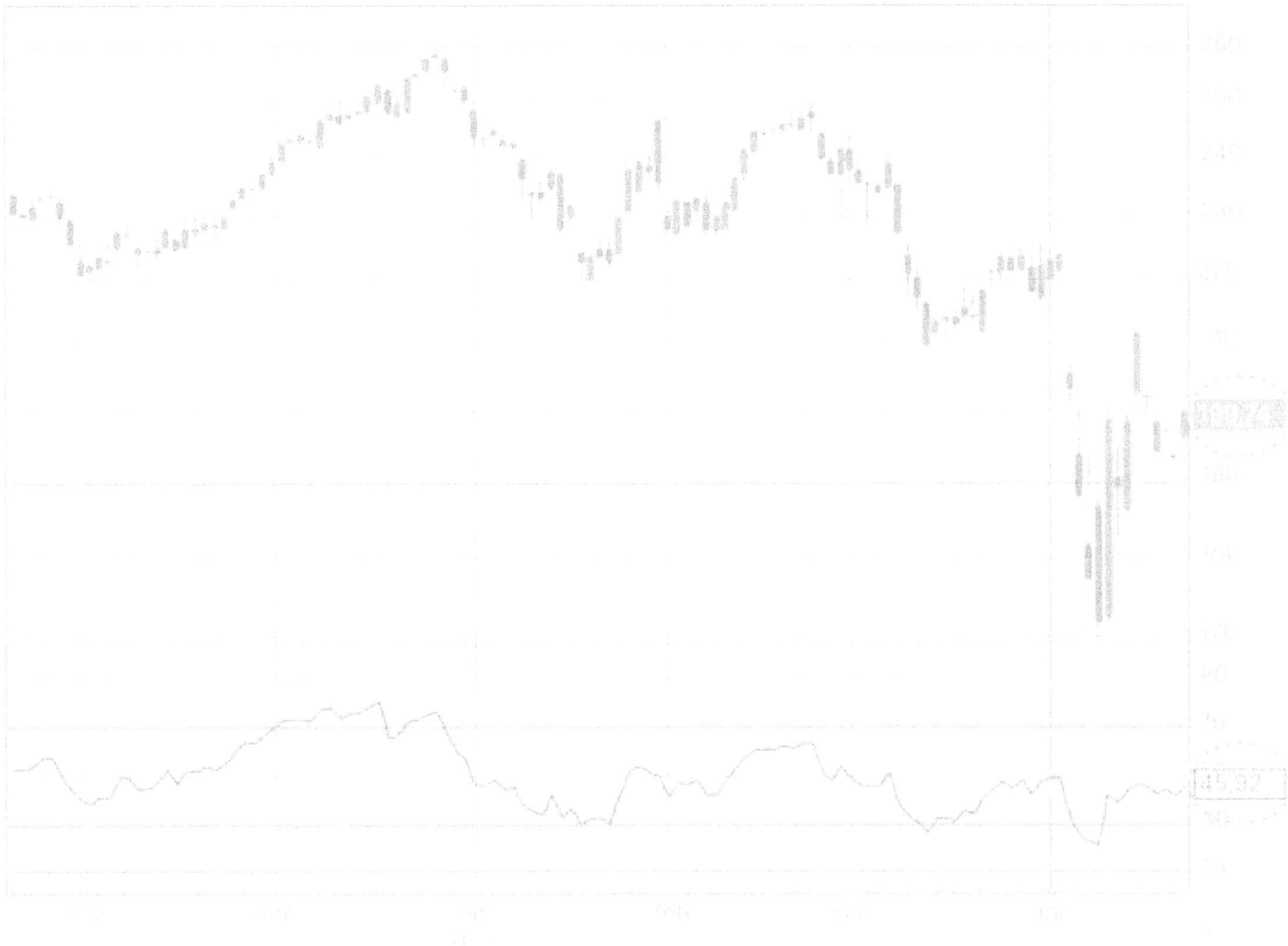

Based on this RSI level and the recent price action, what's the smartest move right now?

- Sell quickly, because the price will drop again
- Buy now, because momentum looks strong
- Wait for more confirmation before trading
- Short the stock, because RSI is too high

Answer: Wait for more confirmation before trading. RSI at 45.92 is neutral, meaning there's no strong buying or selling pressure. The price recently bounced, but without a clear breakout or RSI shift, it's smarter to wait and avoid guessing.

Make a decision

The EUR/USD price has spiked sharply, and the RSI is now above 84. Momentum is strong, but the price is far from recent support zones. RSI above 70 suggests overbought conditions. Think about whether this rally can realistically continue or if caution is wiser.

Based on the current RSI and price action, what's the most reasonable move?

- Do nothing and wait
- Sell or take profit
- Enter a new long trade
- Open a short trade immediately

Answer: Sell or take profit. The RSI is at an extreme level, suggesting the move may be overextended. It's a good time to lock in gains or wait for a better re-entry point.

Buy, sell, or wait?

Starbucks has recently shown a sharp drop followed by a strong green candle. The Stochastic Oscillator is in the oversold zone, and %K (1) has crossed above %D (2).

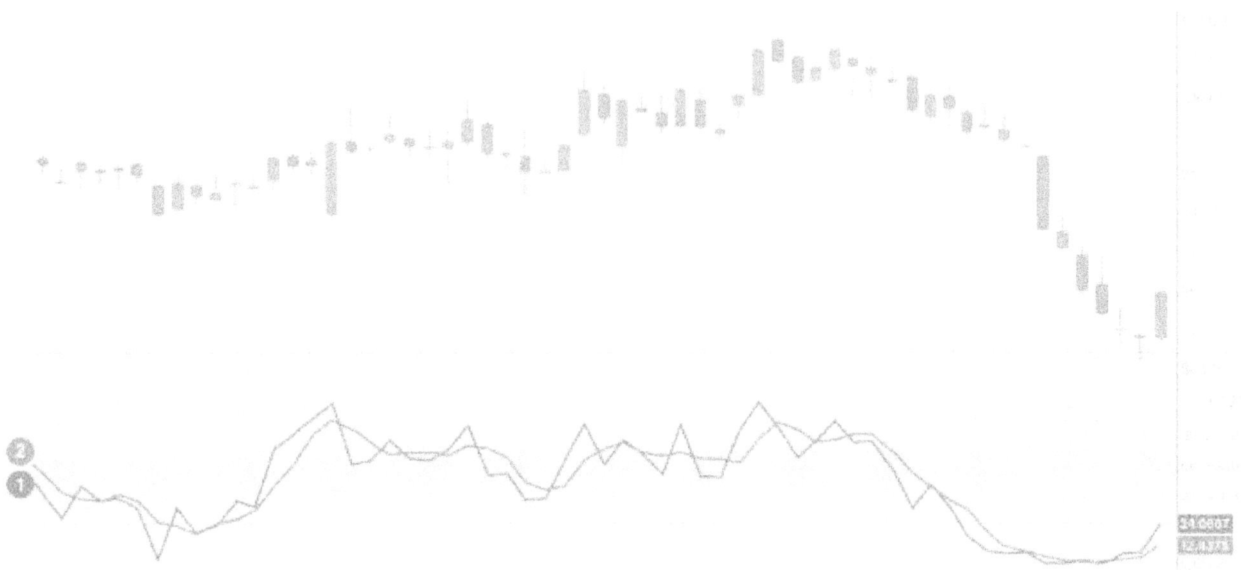

When the Stochastic Oscillator shows a crossover in the oversold zone, it's often an early sign that buyers are stepping in. Look for price confirmation like a strong green candle to support your decision. What would be the best action now?

- Do nothing
- Consider buying
- Wait
- Consider selling

Answer: Consider buying. The Stochastic crossover (%K above %D) in the oversold zone is a classic early signal of potential reversal. Combined with a strong green candle, it suggests growing bullish momentum.

Time to practice using Fibonacci retracement!

Tesla surged from $239 to $486. Now trading near $479, you expect a pullback and use Fibonacci Retracement to spot potential support. The 0.382 Fibonacci level is often viewed as the first meaningful support in a healthy pullback after a strong uptrend.

What level might offer a strong support and buy opportunity based on historical Fibonacci logic?

- Around $391 (0.382 level)
- Around $291 (0.786 level)
- Around $427 (0.236 level)
- Around $486 (recent high)

Answer: Around $391 (0.382 level). If a pullback starts, Fibonacci levels like 0.382 or 0.5 often act as support, giving traders potential buy zones during a retracement.

Make a decision!

After bouncing off the 0.618 level, Netflix couldn't hold gains and has fallen through multiple retracement levels. It's now nearing the 1.0 level. The 100% Fibonacci level often acts as a key support. If price nears this level after breaking several retracements, it may signal weakness, not a guaranteed bounce.

If you're already holding a long position, what should you do?

- Hedge with options but keep the position open

- Tighten your stop or exit to minimize loss
- Double down and add more to your position
- Ignore the drop - retracements always bounce back

Answer: Tighten your stop or exit to minimize loss. Remember that falling below key Fibonacci levels signals fading momentum. Nearing the 1.0 level means the full rally is gone. With no strong support left, protecting your position is the smart move.

Nice job using RSI, Stochastic, and Fibonacci! These tools help you spot momentum and turning points. Keep practicing - consistency comes with experience. You're on the right track!

Lesson 4: Lagging Indicators

Let's explore lagging indicators!

You don't always need to catch the first move. Sometimes, the real opportunity is staying with the trend once it's confirmed. In this lesson, you'll explore what makes lagging indicators different, how they work, and how to use them to stay aligned with market trends.

Lagging indicators help traders confirm trend direction, filter out short-term price noise, and avoid acting on false signals. They're especially useful in trending markets, where the goal is to stay in the move as long as it lasts - even if you miss the very beginning.

Instead of reacting to each new price movement instantly, lagging indicators look at patterns in past price data over a set number of periods. They calculate averages, trends, or changes based on that data to reveal what direction the market is moving in overall.

Because they wait for confirmation, lagging indicators are often slower to respond than leading indicators. They don't try to catch the start of a move - they wait until the move is real. The delay makes lagging indicators more reliable in spotting true trends - and in filtering out fake moves.

Now that you know how lagging indicators work, let's see how they help traders confirm that a trend is real. Each one uses price data a little differently, but they all aim to filter out the noise and show you whether the market is truly trending or just bouncing around.

One of the most popular lagging indicators is the Moving Average (MA). It calculates the average of past prices over a set period to create a smooth line on your chart. This line filters out daily fluctuations and shows the general market direction, making it easier to stay focused on the trend.

If the price consistently stays above the MA, it's a sign of an uptrend. If it remains below, it often confirms a downtrend. MAs don't predict what's coming next, but they give traders confidence that the trend they're seeing is real and worth following.

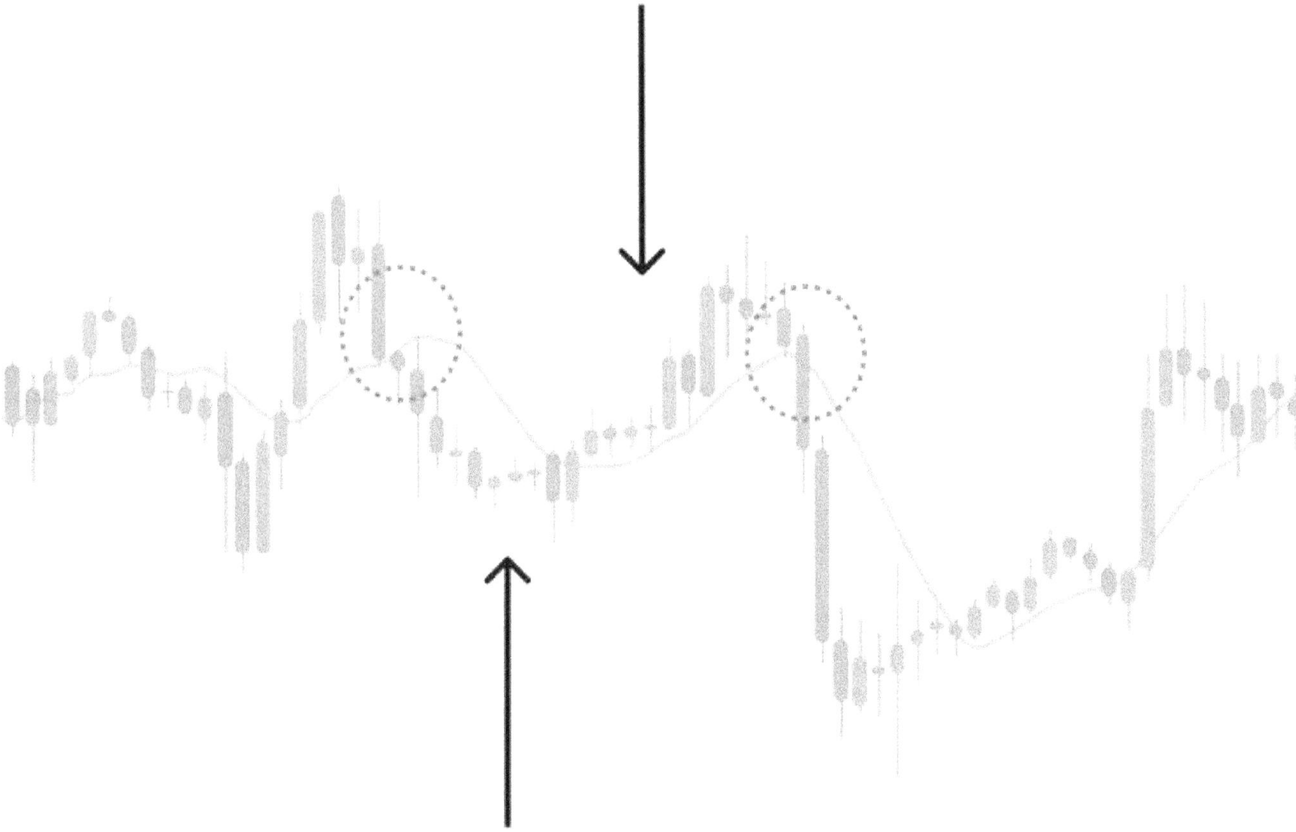

Use the indicator to make a decision!

The price has just broken above the moving average and stayed there for the last few candles. The moving average is starting to slope upward. Think about how the moving average behaves: it's like a trail showing where the market has been. If price stays above a rising trail, the market is likely gaining strength.

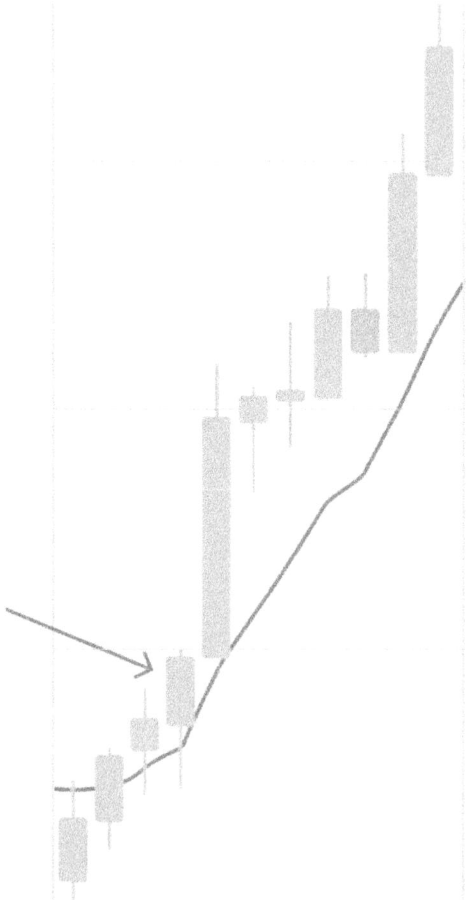

What does this most likely indicate?

- A confirmed uptrend and possible long entry
- A sideways market - no action needed
- A false breakout - better to avoid
- An overbought signal - prepare to sell

Answer: A confirmed uptrend and possible long entry. A break and hold above a rising moving average is a strong sign of a developing uptrend. Many traders see this as confirmation to enter long.

You've seen how MAs can smooth out price and confirm trend direction. But what if you want more insights? That's where MACD comes in, which stands for Moving Average Convergence Divergence.

MACD compares two moving averages to show whether momentum is building or fading. It is made up of three components.

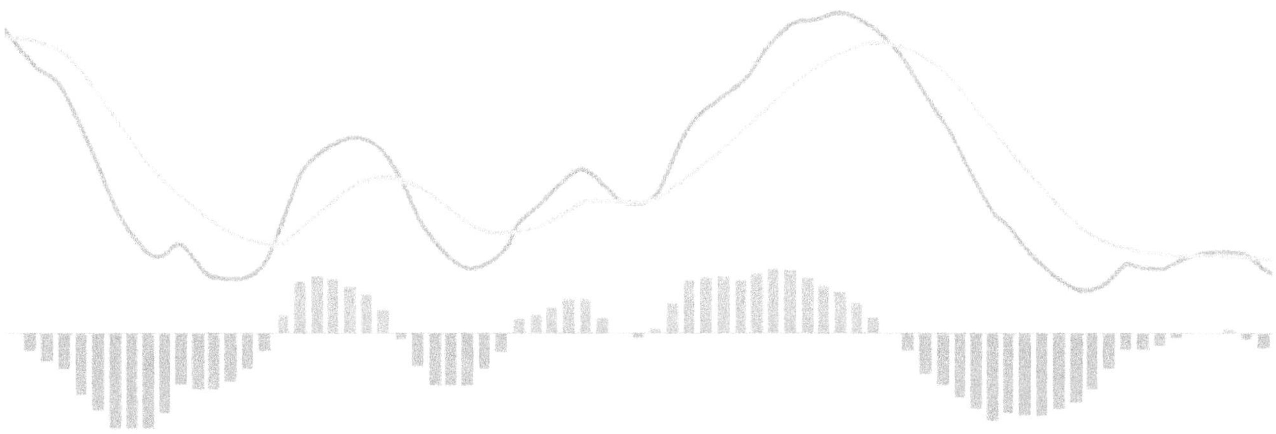

The first element is the MACD Line, which shows the difference between two moving averages (usually 12 and 26 periods). When the line rises, momentum is strengthening. When it falls, momentum may be fading.

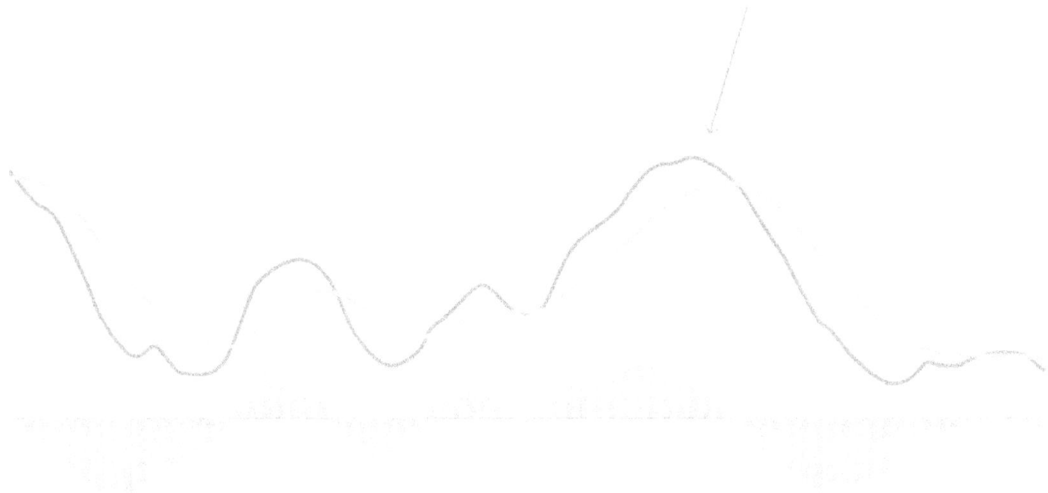

There is also the Signal Line - a moving average of the MACD line. It acts as a smoother, giving clearer entry and exit signals when the MACD Line crosses above or below it.

You can also see a histogram. It is a visual bar chart showing the distance between the MACD Line and the Signal Line. A histogram helps traders see at a glance whether momentum is strengthening or weakening. Bigger bars mean stronger moves; shrinking bars suggest momentum is fading.

Elements of MACD

Each part of the MACD plays a specific role in helping traders understand momentum and confirm trends. Think of the MACD line as the core movement, the Signal line as a filter, and the Histogram as your visual momentum meter. Can you match them correctly?

- MACD Line - Compares two averages

- Histogram - Smoothes entry signals
- Signal Line - Shows momentum strength

Answer:

- MACD Line - Compares two averages
- Histogram - Shows momentum strength
- Signal Line - Smoothes entry signals

Nice work! Now that you understand how MACD helps confirm momentum and trend strength, let's explore another powerful tool: Bollinger Bands. This indicator doesn't just confirm direction - it shows you how volatile the market is and where the price might be overextended.

Bollinger Bands consist of three lines plotted directly on your price chart. A middle band (1) is a simple moving average (usually 20 periods). An upper band (2) is placed two standard deviations above the moving average. A lower band (3) is placed two standard deviations below the moving average.

How to interpret these bands? If price touches or moves along the upper band (1), it often confirms an uptrend. If price hugs the lower band (2), it may confirm a downtrend. If price moves outside the bands (3), it could signal a reversal or pullback - but only if supported by other signals.

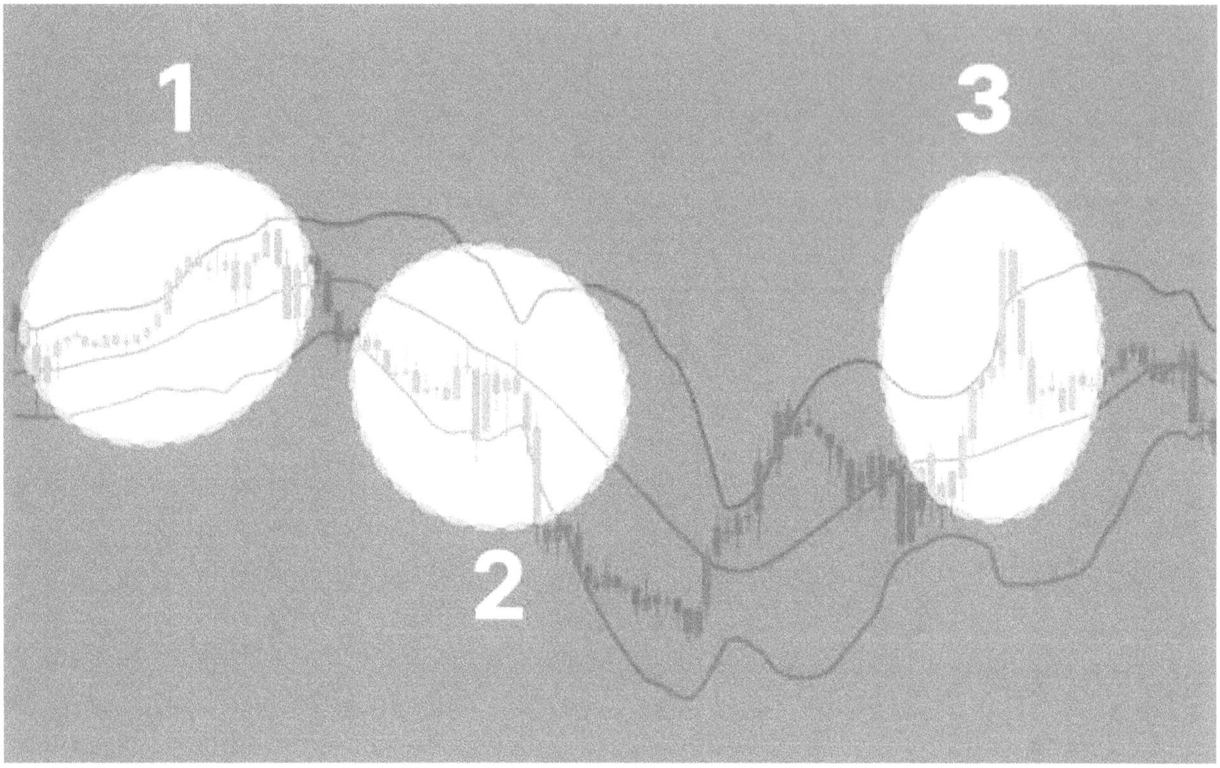

Bollinger Bands help traders understand not just direction, but how strong or risky a move might be. They're especially useful for spotting potential breakouts, measuring trend strength, and identifying overbought or oversold conditions.

How well can you read Bollinger Bands?

You're watching the market, and the price starts dancing near the bands. What does it mean? Think of the bands as flexible boundaries. If price rides along one, it's usually confirming the trend.

But when it breaks outside, it might be warning you of a change. Match each behavior to the most likely market condition.

- Price breaks outside the band - Trend is strong upward
- Price hugs the lower band - Downtrend may continue
- Price moves along the upper band - Watch for reversal

Answer:

- Price breaks outside the band - Watch for reversal
- Price hugs the lower band - Downtrend may continue
- Price moves along the upper band - Trend is strong upward

You've just learned how lagging indicators help confirm trends, filter noise, and guide better decisions. Now you know the basics of Moving Averages, MACD, and Bollinger Bands. Next up - a quick practice session to help you review and lock in what you've learned about lagging indicators. Let's go!

Lesson 5: Practice Lagging Indicators

Are you ready?

Let's put your knowledge to the test! In this lesson, you'll work with key lagging indicators - Moving Averages, MACD, and Bollinger Bands. It's okay if it feels challenging at first. With practice, you'll gain the confidence to read trends and signals more clearly.

Make a decision!

Netflix has been in a strong uptrend, riding above the 9-day moving average. But recently, price action has flattened, and candles are hovering around the moving average, showing hesitation. When price flattens near a moving average, it could mean trend exhaustion or a pause before continuation. Confirmation matters.

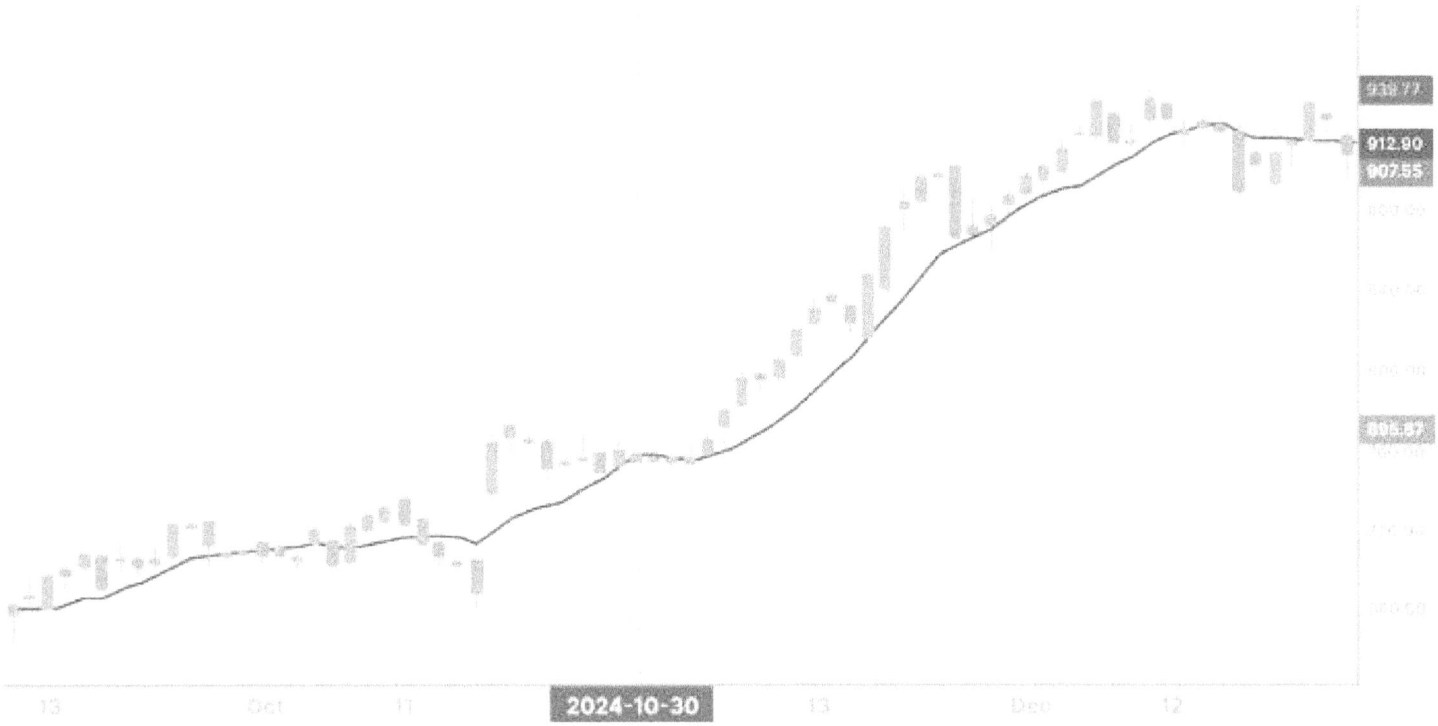

You're holding a long position. What should you do based on this price behavior?

- Exit now
- Short it
- Add more
- Stay in

Answer: Stay in. Although momentum has slowed, price hasn't closed decisively below the MA. Without a strong breakdown or reversal signal, exiting now may be premature. Holding allows you to stay with the trend while watching for confirmation.

What would you do?

Meta was in a strong uptrend, supported by the 30-day MA. Recently, the price has broken below the MA with several red candles. A break below the MA after a strong uptrend could signal a trend reversal. Watch for confirmation before reacting.

You're holding a long position. Based on the price action relative to the MA, what's your move?

- Buy more
- Set a stop-loss just below support and monitor
- Exit the position
- Hold tight

Answer: Set a stop-loss just below support and monitor. While the price has broken below the MA, a full reversal isn't confirmed yet. Placing a stop-loss gives you protection in case the decline continues, while still giving the trade room to recover if this is just a pullback.

What's your move?

You've been watching Amazon and waiting for a potential entry. The MACD line (blue) has recently crossed above the signal line (red). At the same time, price action is trending higher with strong green candles. A MACD bullish crossover paired with rising price action can indicate a strong upward trend, especially if supported by momentum.

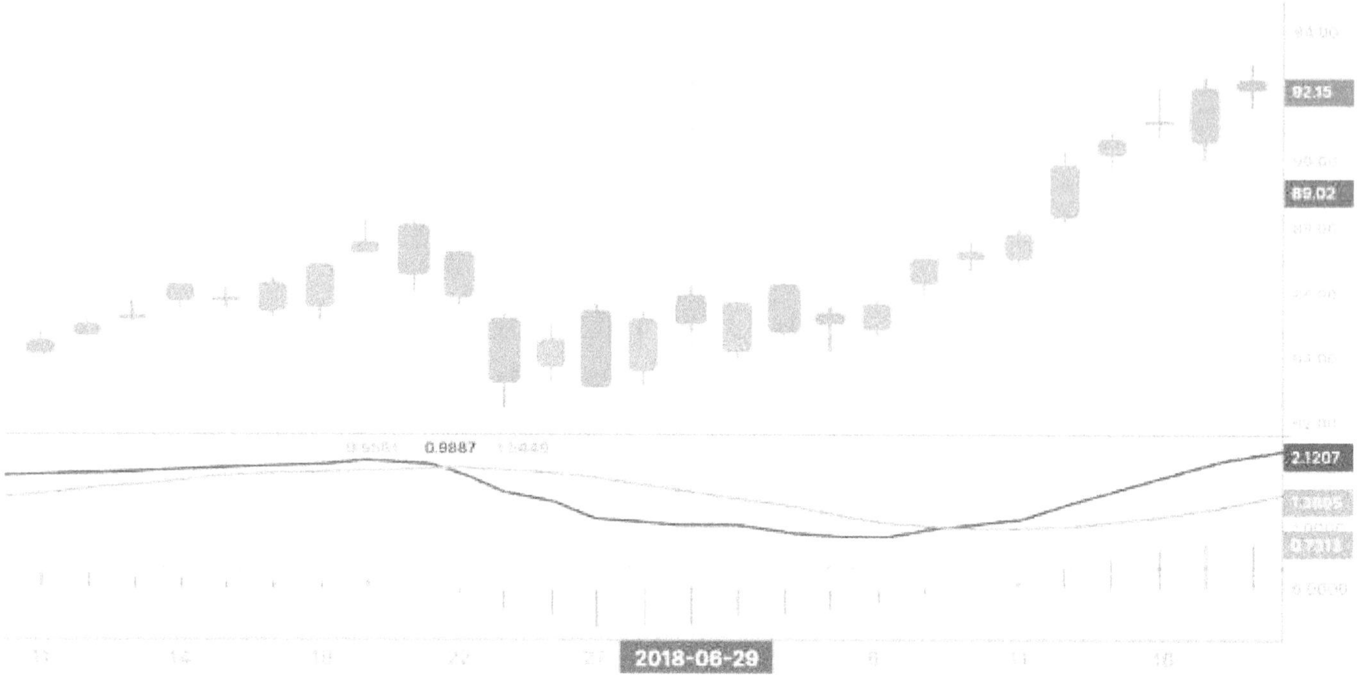

Based on the MACD and recent price action, what would be a reasonable move?

- Ignore it
- Wait for a pullback
- Enter a long trade
- Short the stock

Answer: Enter a long trade. When the MACD line crosses above the signal line, it indicates increasing bullish momentum. In this chart, the crossover aligns with strong green candles and a consistent upward trend, making it a logical point for a long entry.

Make a decision!

GBP/USD has just pushed above the upper Bollinger Band with a strong sequence of green candles. But the price is now outside the volatility envelope. When price closes above the upper Bollinger Band, it signals strong momentum but also potential overextension. Context matters!

What would be the most reasonable action to take at this stage?

- Enter a long trade now
- Open a short position immediately
- Take profits or tighten your stop
- Do nothing and wait for the price to return to the mid-band

Answer: Take profits or tighten your stop. A push above the upper Bollinger Band shows bullish momentum, but prices outside the band often revert to the mean (mid-band). This is a good moment to manage risk, either locking in gains or tightening stops in case of a pullback. It's not necessarily a reversal signal, but it's not ideal for fresh entries without confirmation.

Congratulations! You've practiced using key indicators - Moving Averages, MACD and Bollinger Bands - to make smart trading decisions. Up next: a quick quiz to test what you've learned.

QUIZ: Indicators

1. What is the main purpose of technical indicators?

A. To replace trading strategies
B. To guarantee profits
C. To help traders make informed decisions
D. To remove all market risk

2. What do leading indicators aim to do?

A. Predict future price movement
B. Highlight volume spikes
C. Show real-time news
D. Confirm past price movement

3. What does RSI measure?

A. Whether a market is overbought or oversold
B. Price volatility
C. Volume strength
D. Trend reversals

4. When does RSI typically suggest a buy signal?

A. When RSI falls to or below 30
B. When RSI hits 50
C. When RSI equals 100
D. When RSI rises above 70

5. What does MACD help confirm?

A. Volatility range
B. Exact price levels
C. Economic news impact
D. Momentum and trend direction

6. What does the histogram in MACD represent?

A. The distance between the MACD and the Signal Line
B. Volume traded
C. Current price
D. Price range

7. What does a price moving along the upper Bollinger Band usually indicate?

A. No clear trend
B. A false breakout
C. A strong uptrend
D. An oversold market

8. Which indicator is best for confirming an existing trend?

A. Moving Average
B. Stochastic Oscillator
C. Fibonacci Retracement
D. RSI

9. What kind of data do lagging indicators rely on?

A. Economic forecasts
B. Social sentiment
C. Historical price data
D. News headlines

10. What is the 61.8% Fibonacci level often seen as?

A. A moving average
B. The start of a trend
C. A strong reversal zone

D. A guaranteed entry

Answer: 1. C; 2. A; 3. A; 4. A; 5. D; 6. A; 7. C; 8. A; 9. C; 10. C

Chapter 2: Moving Averages

Lesson 1: Simple Moving Averages

It's time to explore Simple Moving Averages!

Ready to take your chart-reading skills to the next level? This lesson breaks down how Simple Moving Averages are calculated, how they help identify trends, and when to trust them or take them with caution.

You already know that moving averages help smooth out price data. Unlike other types of moving averages, a Simple Moving Average (SMA) gives equal weight to each closing price in the period, creating a steady line that shows the market's overall direction.

To calculate an SMA, you add up the closing prices (A) over a specific number of periods, then divide that total by the number of periods:

- SMA = (A1 + A2 + A3.. + An) / n

Now that you understand how SMA is calculated, here's the next question: What if you used 10 or even 50 periods instead? The number of periods you choose directly affects how the SMA behaves.

Shorter-period SMAs (like 5 or 10) follow price closely. They (1) react quickly and can help spot short-term reversals, but they may also generate false signals during volatility.

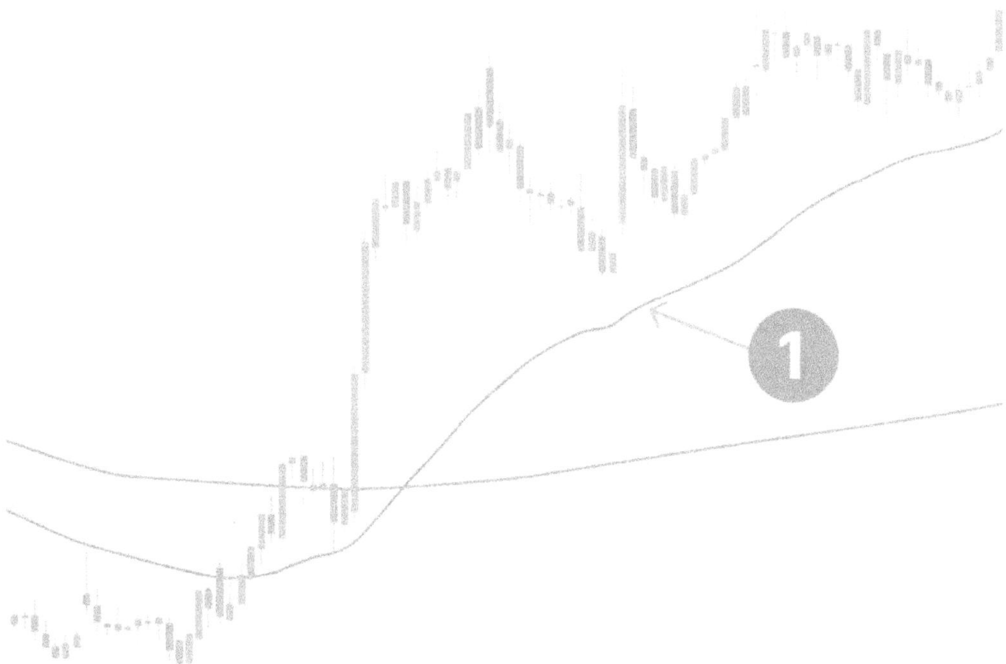

Longer-period SMAs (like 50 or 200) respond more slowly. They (2) smooth out noise and help confirm stronger, more stable trends, but they might delay entry or exit points.

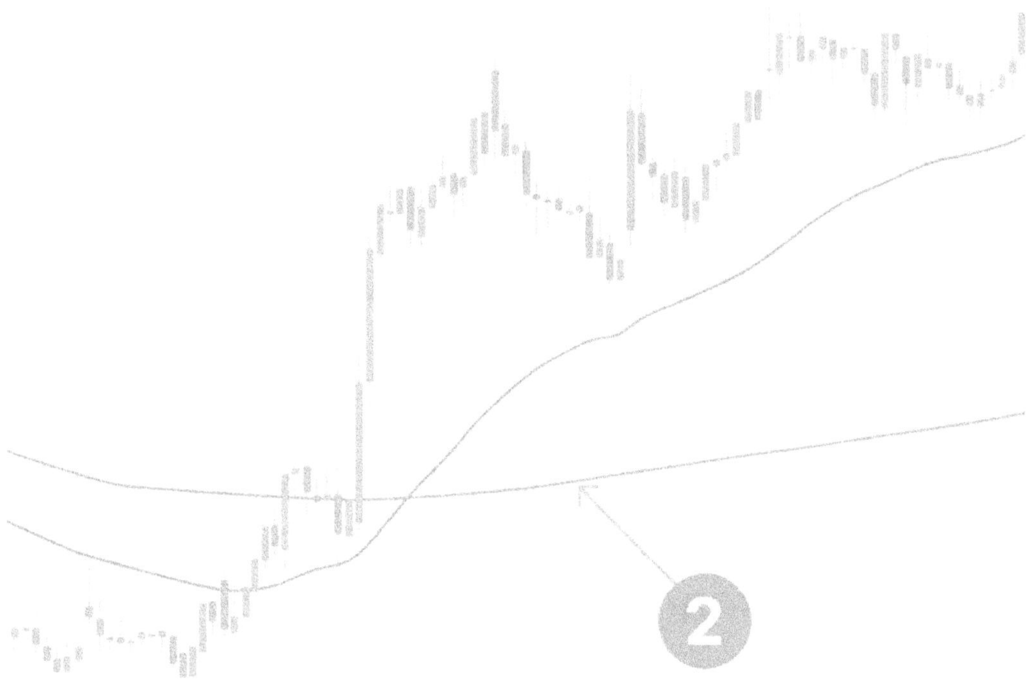

The length of the indicator you use should match how you trade. If you're a short-term trader - like a day trader or scalper - you'll need to react quickly. Shorter SMAs respond faster to price changes and help you spot quick shifts in direction.

If you're a long-term trader - like a swing or position trader - you're more interested in spotting the overall trend. Longer SMAs help smooth out short-term noise and reveal the bigger picture. Remember that there's no "best" setting - just the best one for your strategy.

Meet Alex: The short-term trader

Alex is a day trader who enters and exits trades within minutes or hours. He needs to react fast to small price movements and identify quick trend changes. Short-term traders need indicators that respond quickly to price changes. Which Simple Moving Average period is most suitable for Alex's trading style?

- 10
- 50
- 100
- 200

Answer: A 10-period SMA gives Alex fast feedback, which suits his day trading strategy.

Meet Jane: The long-term trader

Jane is a swing trader who holds positions for several days or weeks. She wants to filter out market noise and follow the broader trend. Longer holding periods call for smoother signals that filter out short-term noise. Which SMA period is most suitable for Jane's strategy?

A. 100
B. 5
C. 10
D. 20

Answer: A 100-period SMA helps Jane focus on the bigger picture and avoid reacting to minor fluctuations.

Choosing the right period is just step one. SMAs work best in clear, trending markets, where price moves steadily up or down. In these conditions, they help confirm direction and support confident trading decisions.

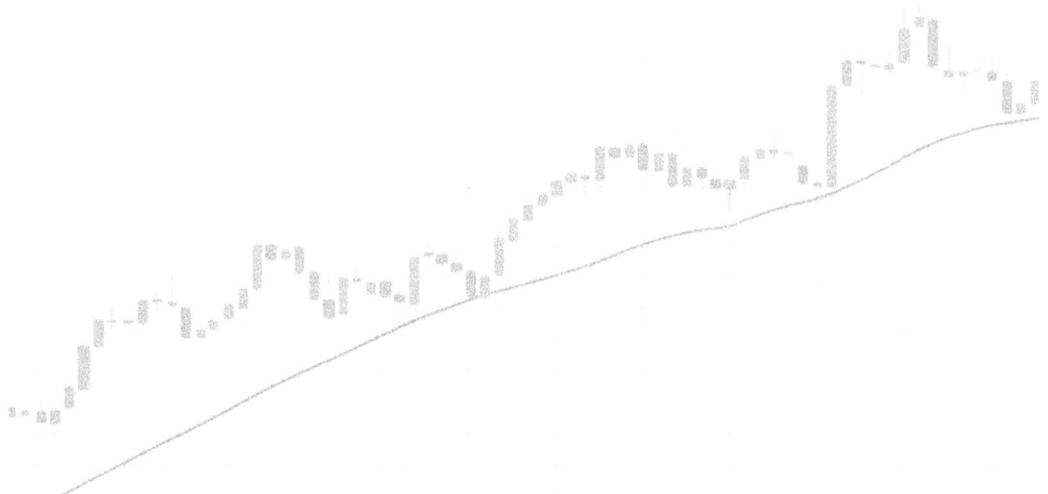

But in sideways or choppy markets, the SMAs tend to flatten out. This can lead to false signals that trigger early entries or exits. That's why context is key - before acting on a SMA signal, always assess whether the market is trending or just moving sideways.

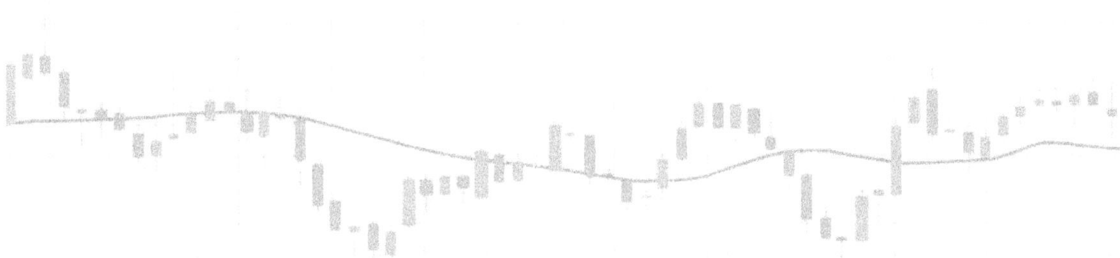

SMAs can also act as dynamic support or resistance. If price bounces off an SMA from above, the line acts as support (1). If the price is below and struggles to break through, it acts as resistance (2).

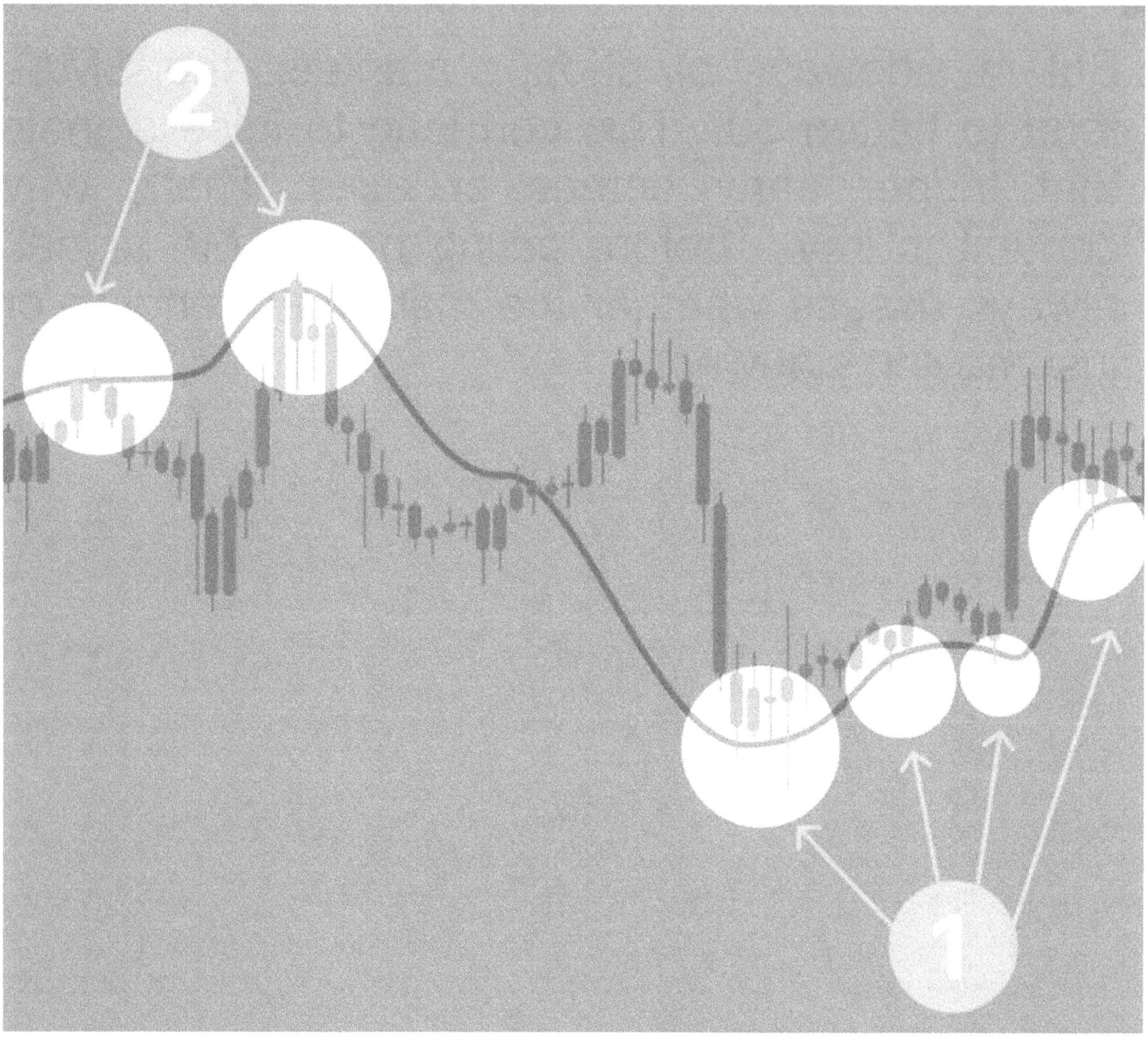

Signals are stronger when the SMA aligns with other key levels, like support, resistance, or trendlines, creating confluence that boosts trader confidence.

What does the Simple Moving Average tell you?

Think about what each SMA signal suggests - momentum building, fading, or pausing. Match the behavior to what a trader would likely do next. Match the Simple Moving Average behavior to the action it might suggest. Each clue helps you decide whether to enter, stay, or wait.

- The Indicator acts as resistance - Watch for price bounce
- The Indicator aligns with trendline - Confluence, act with care
- The Indicator holds as support - Wait

Answer:

- The Indicator acts as resistance - Wait
- The Indicator aligns with trendline - Confluence, act with care
- The Indicator holds as support - Watch for price bounce

In short, SMAs smooth price action, highlight trends, and act as dynamic support or resistance. But they lag behind price and can give false signals in choppy or sideways conditions. For best results, use them with confirmation from other tools.

Well done! You've just completed one of the core concepts in technical analysis: the Simple Moving Average. You've learned how to calculate it, when to apply it, and how it helps spot trends. Up next: the Exponential Moving Average, a more reactive tool that helps you catch market moves earlier. Let's keep going!

Lesson 2: Exponential Moving Average

Let's explore Exponential Moving Averages!

Now that you've got a solid grip on Simple Moving Averages, it's time to level up. In this lesson, we'll dive into the Exponential Moving Average. You'll learn how it's calculated, how it compares to an SMA, and how to use it to spot both short-term and long-term trends.

The Exponential Moving Average (EMA) (1) is a moving average that puts more weight on recent price data. It reacts quicker to price changes than Simple Moving Average (2), making it useful for short-term trading or fast-moving markets.

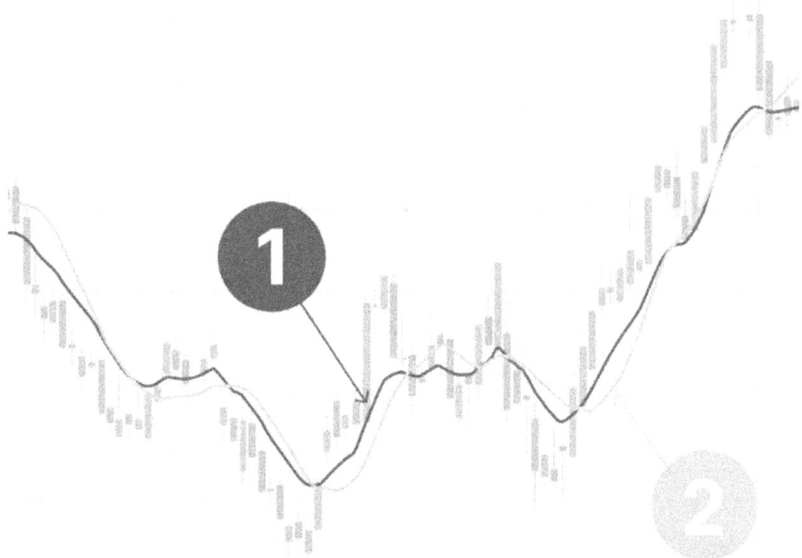

EMA is designed to respond faster to recent price changes than a SMA. Instead of averaging all prices equally, the EMA applies a weighting multiplier to give more influence to the most recent price and less to older prices.

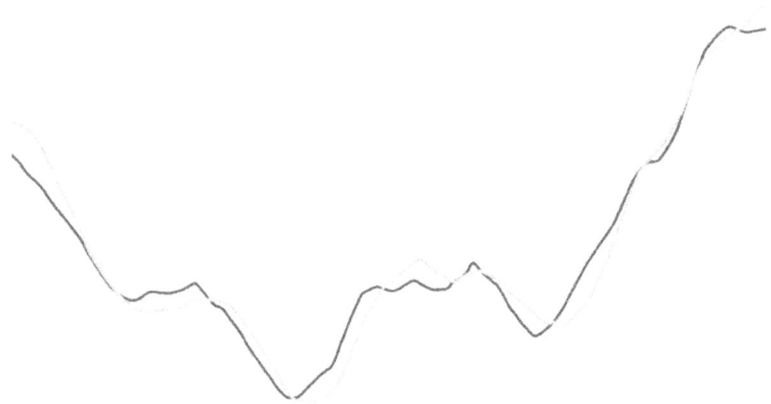

Looks complicated? Don't worry about the math - your platform will calculate it. However, understanding how EMA gives more importance to recent prices will help you trust its signals.

Now let's see how it stacks up against the SMA. They both smooth out the price. However, the EMA (1) is quicker to react to recent moves, while the SMA (2) stays calm and steady.

EMA is more responsive. Because it gives priority to the latest price data, it adjusts quickly when the price changes direction. This makes it useful in fast-moving markets, where early entry or exit matters. But this speed comes at a cost - it may give false signals during sideways or volatile markets.

Let's say a stock suddenly jumps. The EMA will rise quickly to reflect that move, helping you jump in sooner. But if that spike is short-lived, it might "overreact" and lead you into a losing trade.

The SMA moves slowly because it treats all prices equally. This makes it more stable and less likely to be fooled by short-term volatility. It is useful when you prefer confirmation over speed. For example, when you're following longer-term trends or avoiding whipsaws in noisy markets.

Imagine a market that keeps bouncing up and down. The EMA might react to every small move, while the SMA stays more stable, helping you ignore the noise and focus on the bigger trend.

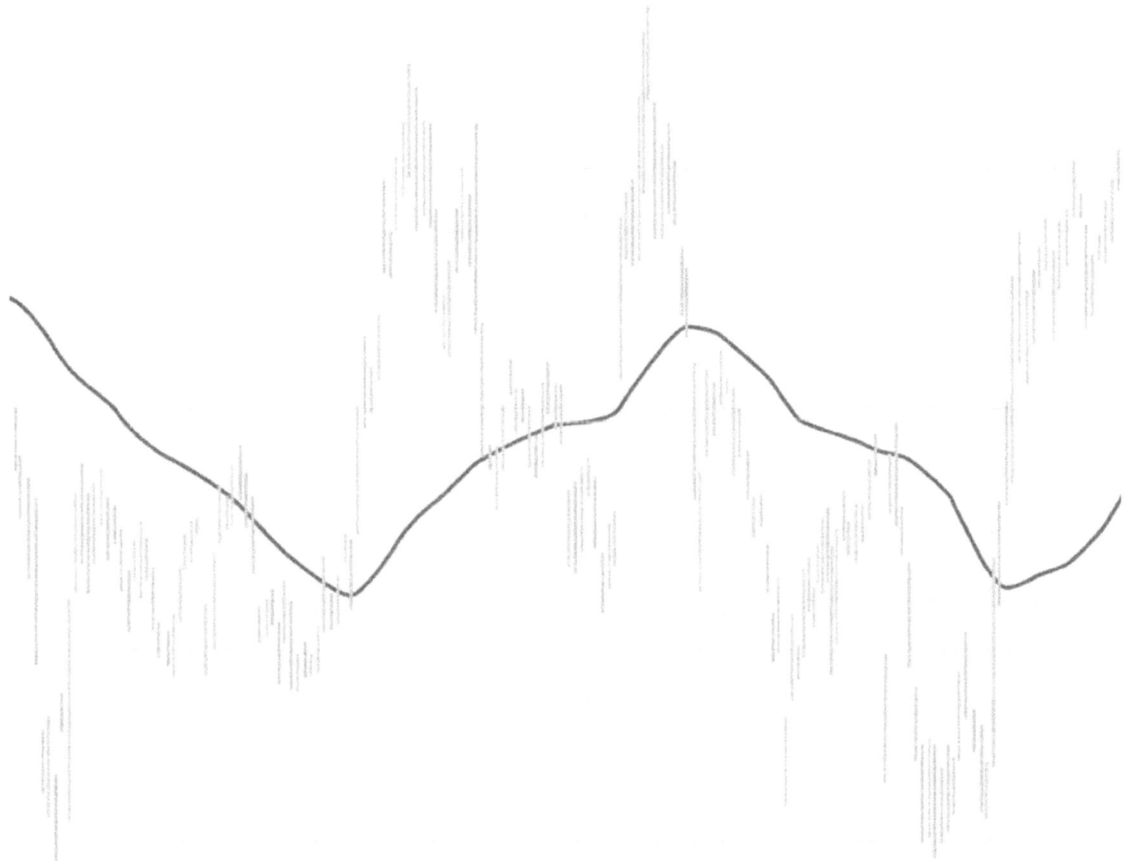

Now that you understand how both the Simple and Exponential Moving Averages work, you might be wondering: Which one is better for your strategy? The answer depends on how you trade.

Traders use the Exponential Moving Average when they need faster signals - perfect for short-term trading where speed matters more than precision. Meanwhile, traders choose the Simple Moving Average when they're focused on longer-term trends, prefer smoother signals, and can afford to wait for confirmation.

Spot Exponential Moving Average

Exponential Moving Averages respond faster than Simple Moving Averages because they give more importance to recent prices. Think about speed and sensitivity. Test your knowledge! Pick the three facts that best describe Exponential Moving Average.

- Best for long-term view
- Equal weight to all days
- Reacts quickly to price
- Great for short-term trends
- Smoother than other averages
- More weight on recent data

Answer:

- Reacts quickly to price
- Great for short-term trends
- More weight on recent data

Not all Exponential Moving Averages work the same way. Just as with Simple Moving Averages, what matters is the period you choose. Shorter EMAs (1), like 9 or 12, react faster and are great for short-term trades. Longer EMAs (2), like 50 or 200, move more slowly and are better for spotting big-picture trends.

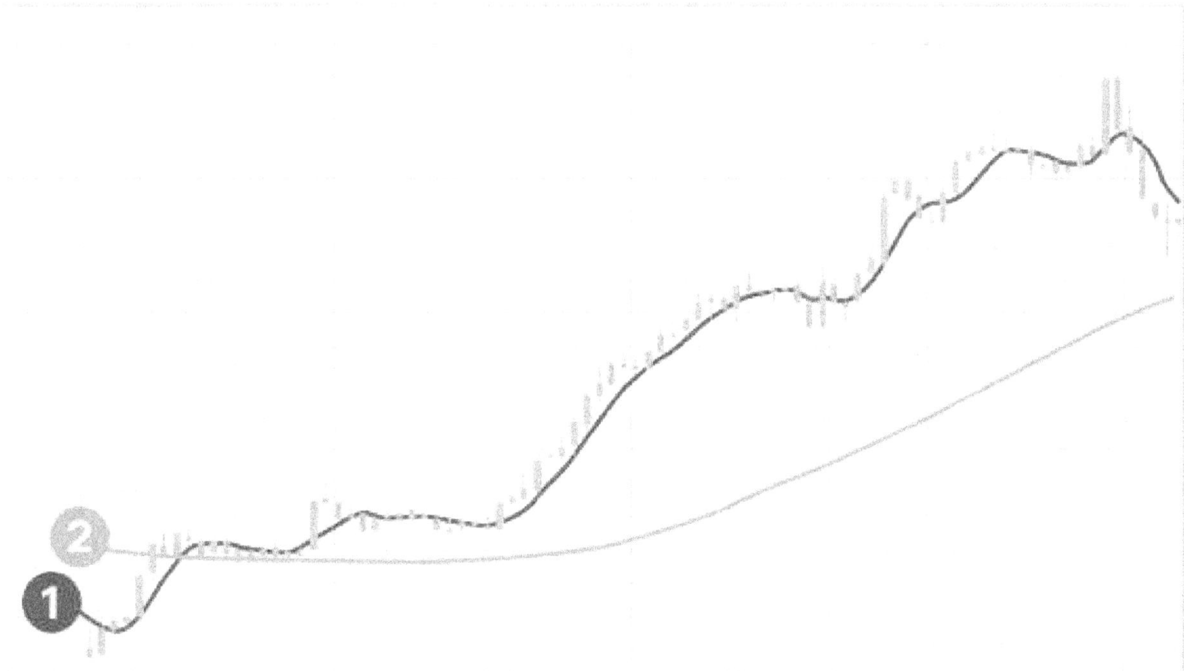

What does the Exponential Moving Average period tell us?

Different EMA periods reveal different insights. The shorter the EMA, the faster it reacts. Longer EMAs give slower, steadier trend signals - great for confirmation, not for timing snap entries. Can you match each EMA length to what it typically helps a trader understand?

- 21-period EMA - Tracks quick momentum shifts
- 50-period EMA - Balances short- and mid-term trends
- 9-period EMA - Helps confirm overall trend direction

Answer:

- 21-period EMA - Balances short- and mid-term trends
- 50-period EMA - Helps confirm overall trend direction
- 9-period EMA - Tracks quick momentum shifts

You've now mastered the Exponential Moving Average - how it works, why it reacts faster, and when to use it. Next, we'll explore crossover strategies to help you time your trades more effectively. Let's go!

Lesson 3: Crossover Strategies

It's time to explore crossover strategies!

Now that you know how Simple and Exponential Moving Averages work, it's time to combine them. In this lesson, we'll explore crossover strategies, powerful tools for spotting trend shifts and confirmations. Let's get started!

Using a single MA can give you a general sense of direction, but what if you want more detail? That's where combining two MAs comes in. By comparing a short-term average (1) with a long-term one (2), traders get a clearer picture of momentum shifts and possible trend changes.

When the short SMA crosses above the long one, it's often called a Golden Cross (1) - a bullish signal suggesting a strong upward trend may follow. When the short SMA crosses below the long SMA, it's known as a Death Cross (2) - a bearish signal that could indicate a downtrend.

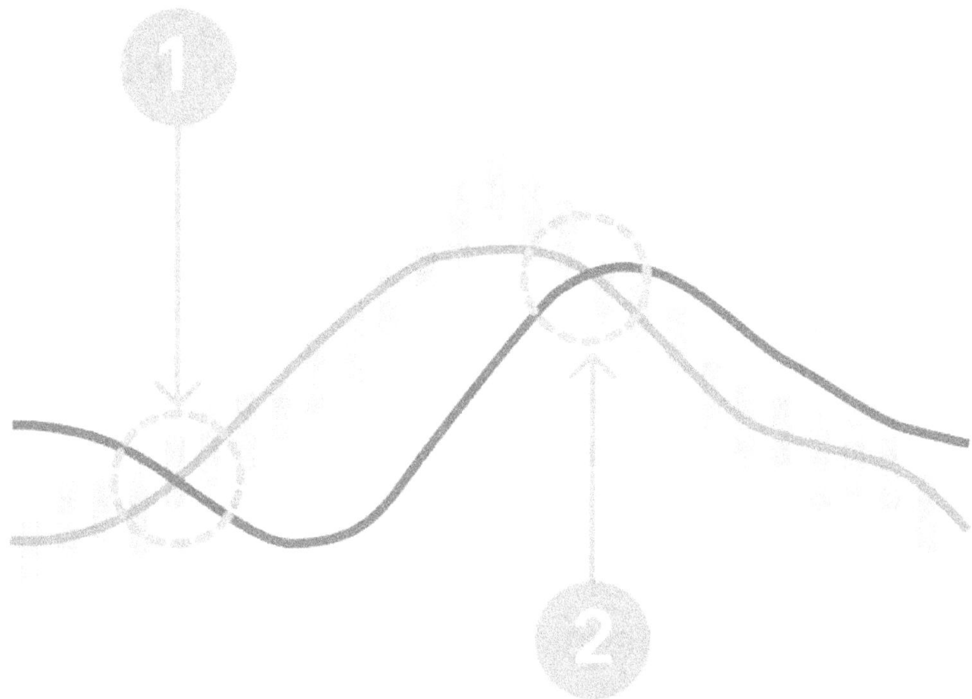

In an uptrend, a Golden Cross signals rising momentum. Traders often use this to:

- Enter long trades
- Add to existing positions
- Hold through small pullbacks, trusting the trend

In downtrends, a Death Cross warns of weakness. Traders use it to:

- Close or reduce long positions
- Enter short trades
- Avoid buying dips until the trend changes

But remember: these signals work best in trending markets, not sideways ones.

Golden and Death Cross signals can be used with both Simple and Exponential Moving Averages. The classic setup uses SMA 50 and SMA 200, but many traders prefer using EMA 9 and EMA 21 for faster, short-term signals. It all depends on your trading style - SMA gives smoother, long-term confirmation, while EMA reacts quicker for earlier entries.

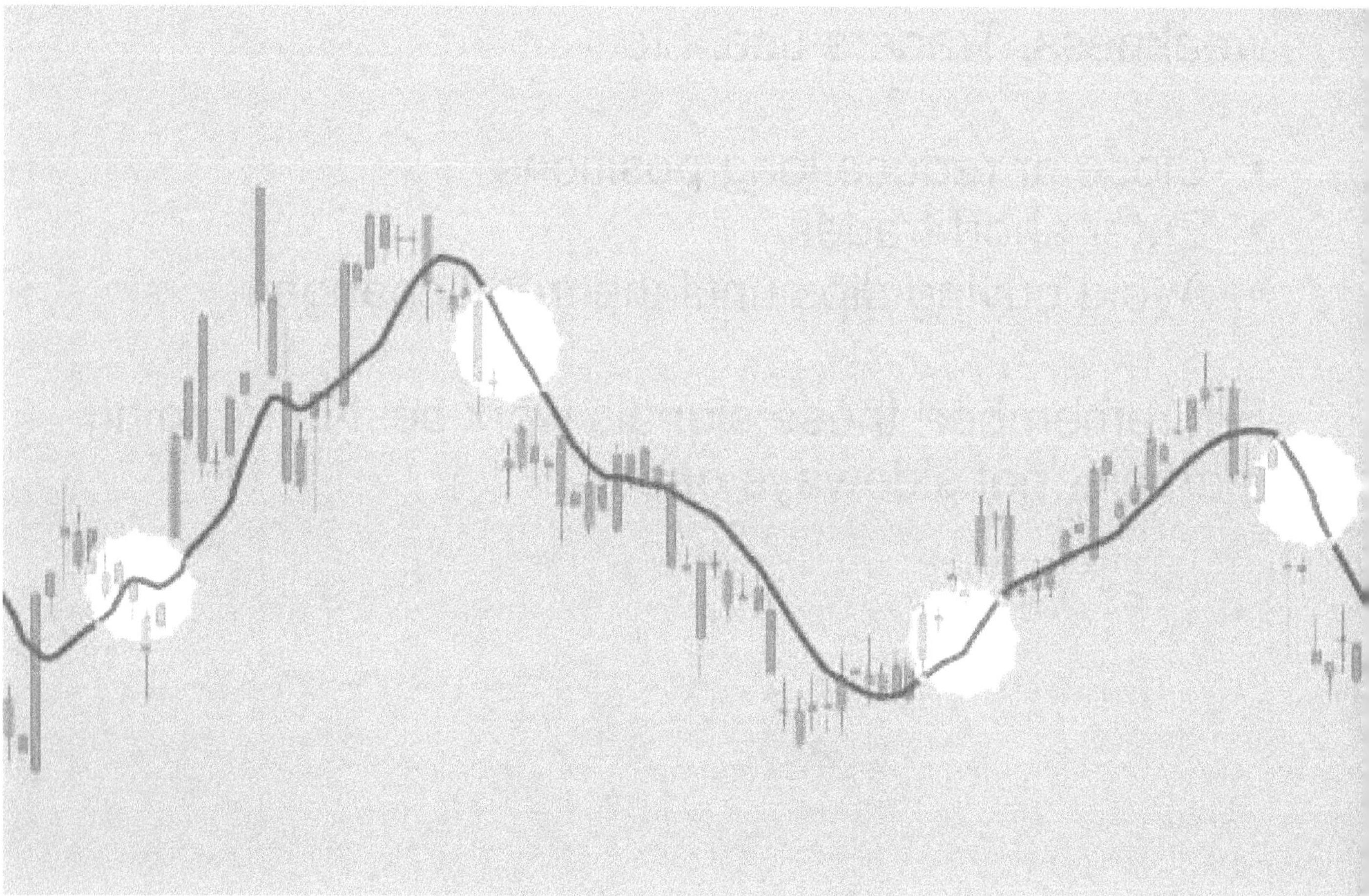

What's your next move?

You're analyzing a stock using the 50-period and 200-period Simple Moving Averages. The 50-SMA just crossed above the 200-SMA after a long downtrend. A Golden Cross signals bullish momentum. Think about confirmation and timing before jumping in.

How would you respond to this potential Golden Cross setup?

- Do nothing - it's just noise
- Enter a long trade (Buy)
- Short the stock (Sell)
- Wait for price confirmation

Answer: Enter a long trade (Buy). The Golden Cross often signals a strong entry point for trend-following traders.

Now you know what a crossover is, but did you know you can also combine different types of MAs to enhance your strategy? Using both the EMA and SMA together can help you balance speed and stability, giving you sharper signals and stronger confirmation in any market condition.

As you know, SMA helps confirm the bigger picture while EMA gives you faster signals. When used together, they balance each other out, helping you stay in trades longer while still reacting to momentum shifts.

The periods you choose affect how your EMA and SMA behave. Let me introduce you to a strategy that does just that: The Multi-period Moving Average Crossover Momentum Strategy. It helps you spot when short-term momentum breaks through longer-term trends, so you can ride big moves with confidence.

This strategy combines a 9-period EMA (1), a 30-period SMA (2), and a 50-period SMA (3). The 9

EMA responds quickly to price, while the 30 and 50 SMAs show the broader market trend.

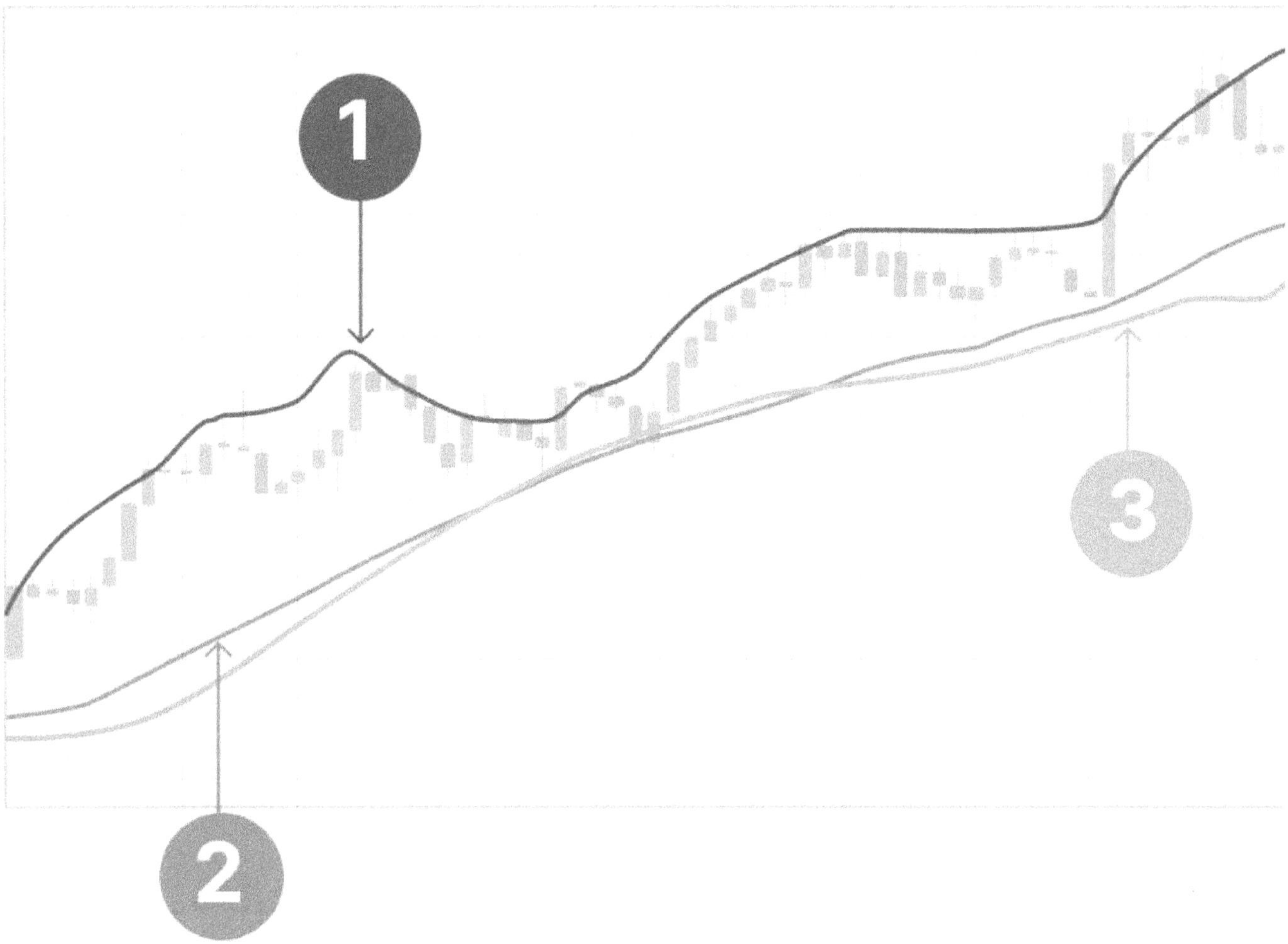

You're looking for crossovers between the 9 EMA and the slower SMAs. When the 9 EMA crosses over or under the 30 and 50 SMAs, it gives clues about momentum and direction.

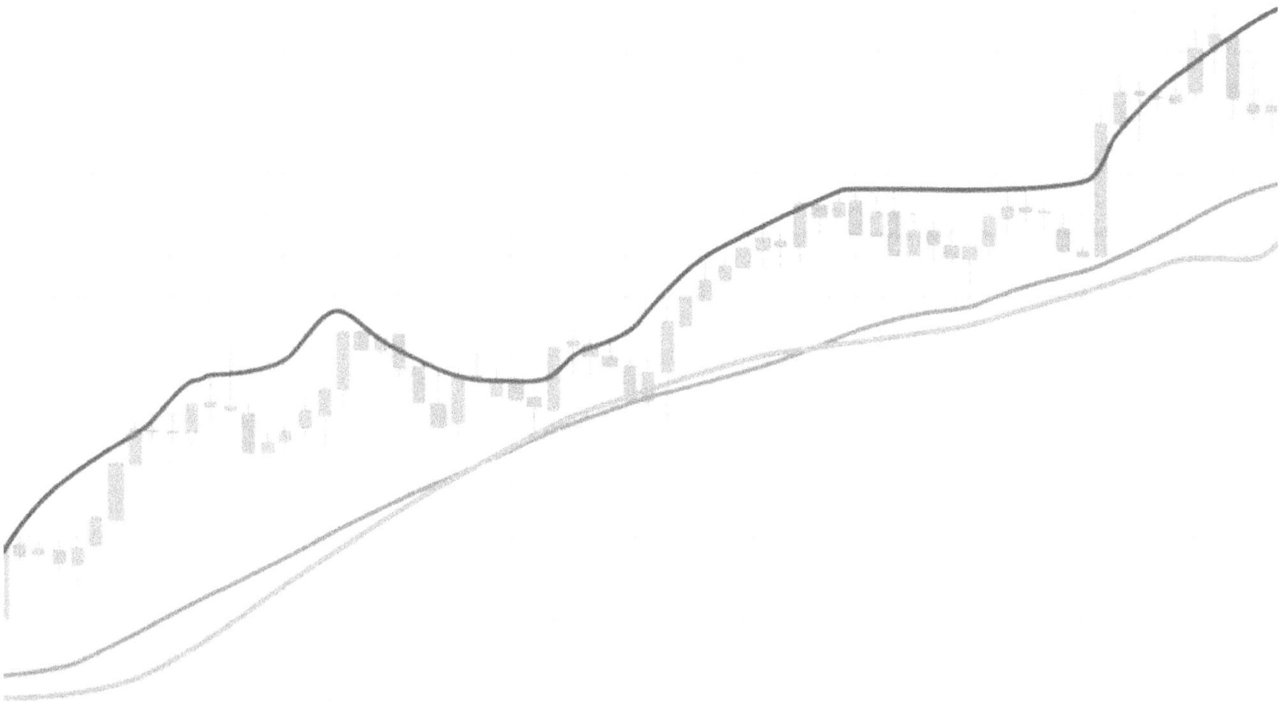

When the 9 EMA crosses above both the 30 and 50 SMAs, it shows strong upward momentum. This is often a signal to:

- Enter a long trade
- Add to an existing position

When the 9 EMA crosses below both the 30 and 50 SMAs, it may suggest the start of a downtrend. Traders may:

- Enter a short trade
- Exit or reduce long positions

- Tighten stop-losses

If the 9 EMA keeps crossing above and below the 30 and 50 SMAs, the market might lack direction. In this case, it's often better to:

- Stay out of trades
- Wait for a clearer signal
- Use range-bound strategies instead

Match the market signal to the action

The 9 EMA is interacting with the 30 and 50 SMAs in different ways. If the fast EMA rises above the slower SMAs, think momentum is picking up. If it drops below, think downside risk. If it can't decide - maybe you shouldn't either. Can you match each signal with the action a trader might take?

- 9 EMA crosses below both SMAs - Enter or add to long position
- 9 EMA crosses above both SMAs - Wait for clarity or trade ranges
- 9 EMA moves back and forth - Exit long or consider short trade

Answer:

- 9 EMA crosses below both SMAs - Exit long or consider short trade
- 9 EMA crosses above both SMAs - Enter or add to long position
- 9 EMA moves back and forth - Wait for clarity or trade ranges

Excellent! Remember that technical tools are flexible. The same EMA/ SMA combo that works for one trader might not suit another. Don't stop at one strategy - tweak the periods, try confirmations, and build a method that gives you confidence in your trades!

Congratulations! You've now mastered crossover strategies using both SMA and EMA. You've seen how to spot momentum shifts, identify trend changes, and respond in different market conditions. Now it's time to put your knowledge to the test with a quick quiz to reinforce what you've learned!

QUIZ: Moving Averages

1. What is the key characteristic of a Simple Moving Average?

A. It only uses recent data
B. It gives equal weight to all prices
C. It's only used for long-term trading
D. It reacts faster to price changes

2. Which of the following describes the Exponential Moving Average?

A. It is slower than Simple Moving Average
B. It places more weight on recent prices
C. It only works on daily charts
D. It gives equal weight to all prices

3. What does a shorter-period moving average (like a 5-SMA or 9-EMA) typically do?

A. It reacts quickly to price changes
B. It filters out more noise
C. It provides stronger long-term trends

D. It moves more slowly than long SMAs

4. Which moving average is better suited for short-term trades?

A. Simple Moving Average (SMA)
B. Exponential Moving Average
C. Moving Average Convergence
D. Divergence (MACD)
E. Bollinger Bands

5. What does a Golden Cross signal?

A. A short-term dip is coming
B. A bullish trend may be starting
C. The market is in consolidation
D. A bearish reversal has occurred

6. What does a Death Cross usually indicate?

A. A strong resistance breakout
B. A sideways market
C. High volatility
D. A potential downtrend

7. In the Multi-period Moving Average Crossover strategy, which line reacts the fastest?

A. 200 SMA
B. 50 SMA
C. 9 EMA
D. 30 SMA

8. When the 9 EMA crosses below both the 30 and 50 SMAs, what is it often a signal of?

A. Price stabilization
B. Bullish confirmation
C. Downward momentum
D. Range-bound entry

9. What should you do if the 9 EMA keeps crossing back and forth through the SMAs?

A. Wait for cleaner signals
B. Short the stock
C. Buy on every cross
D. Add to your position

10. Why do traders combine SMA and EMA in a strategy?

A. To avoid using indicators
B. To balance speed with stability
C. To track fundamentals
D. To only trade in sideways markets

Answer: 1. B; 2. B; 3. A; 4. B; 5. B; 6. D; 7. C; 8. C; 9. A; 10. B

Chapter 3: RSI Insights

Lesson 1: RSI Basics

Let's explore RSI!

In this lesson, we'll take a closer look at the Relative Strength Index (RSI). You'll learn what RSI is, how it's calculated, and how to interpret its values on a 0-100 scale. By the end, you'll understand how RSI can help you gauge market strength and spot potential turning points.

RSI doesn't measure volume. It measures price momentum by comparing average gains and losses over a specific number of periods.

Now that you know RSI measures price momentum, let's look at how it's actually calculated. You won't need to do the math manually, but knowing the formula helps you trust what RSI tells you.

The RSI compares average gains and losses over a set period to measure momentum. If gains are stronger, RSI rises. If losses outweigh gains, RSI falls. The result is a number from 0 to 100 that shows whether the market is strong (closer to 100) or weak (closer to 0).

RSI values and their meanings

- 0: The market is extremely oversold
- 30: This is an oversold zone
- 50: This is a neutral zone
- 70: This is an overbought zone
- 100: The market is extremely overbought

RSI signal

You're watching a stock, and its RSI just dropped to 28. Think about what it means when RSI falls below 30. It's usually related to oversold conditions.

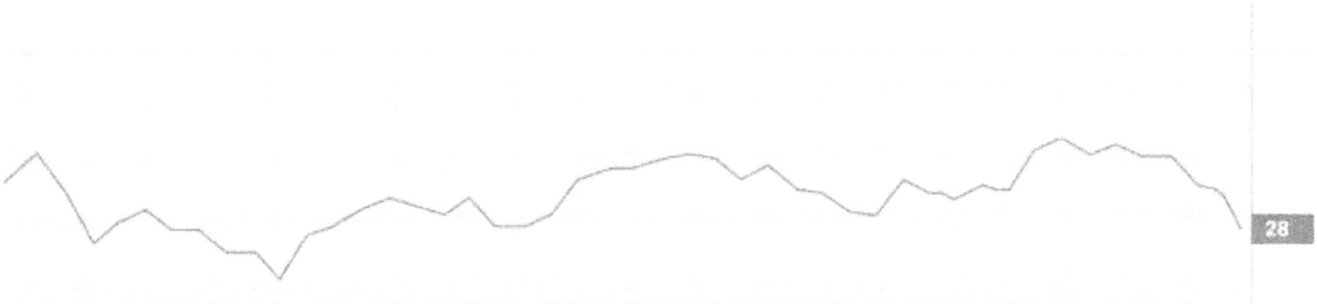

What does this typically signal?

- A strong sell signal
- No signal at all
- A potential buy signal
- The trend is accelerating upward

Answer: A potential buy signal. An RSI below 30 doesn't suggest strong momentum or an uptrend. It points to an oversold condition. Selling now might mean missing a bounce.

You've learned how RSI is calculated and what its values mean. Next, we'll explore how RSI behaves in different market conditions and how that changes the way traders interpret signals.

Lesson 2: Overbought and Oversold Conditions

Spotting overbought & oversold conditions

It's time to explore two of its most useful features: identifying overbought and oversold conditions. In this lesson, you'll learn how to recognize when the market might be stretched too far in one direction and how traders use this to prepare for possible reversals or pullbacks.

As you already know, RSI highlights overbought and oversold zones. But how do these levels actually work in different market conditions?

When RSI moves above 70, the asset is considered overbought, meaning it's experienced strong recent gains and may be due for a pullback. But overbought doesn't always mean "sell" right away. In strong uptrends, RSI can stay high for a while.

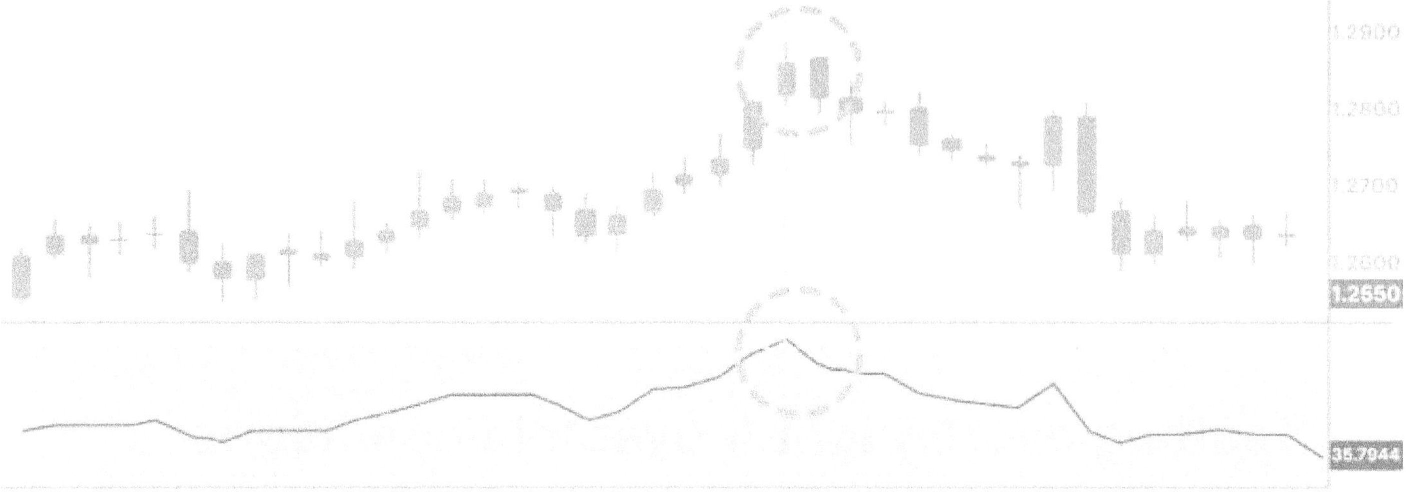

When RSI drops below 30, the asset is considered oversold, meaning it's seen significant losses and might bounce soon. Just like with overbought conditions, a low RSI isn't an automatic "buy" signal. It depends on the broader trend.

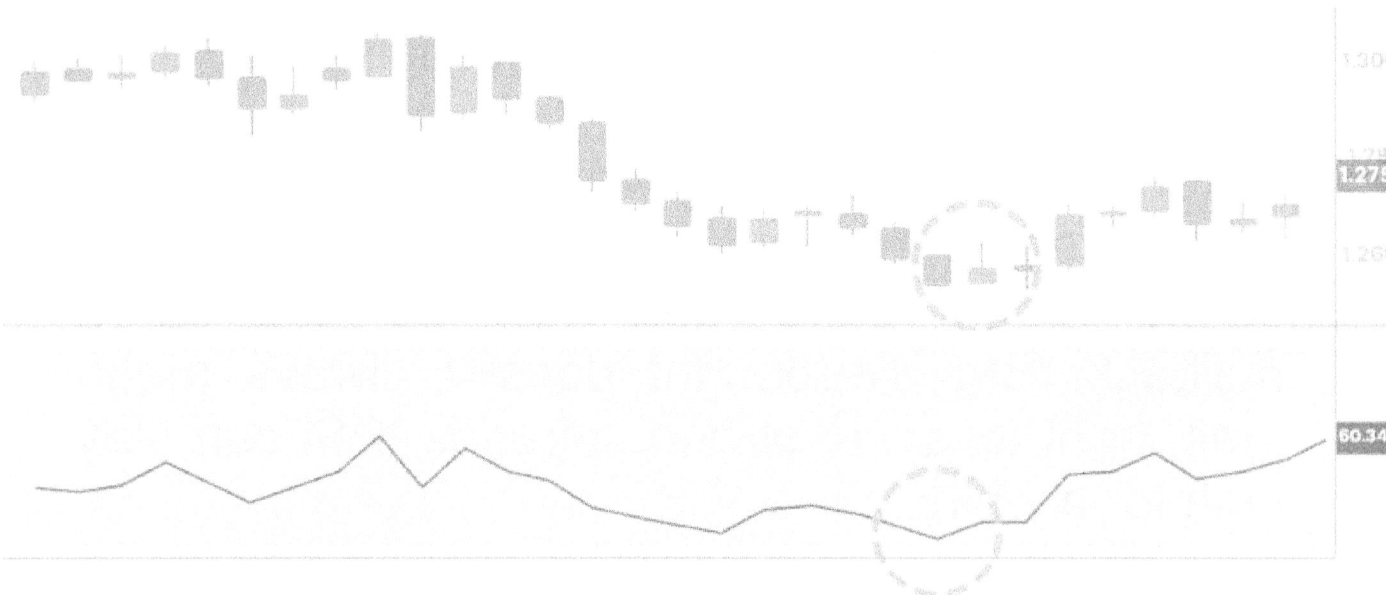

Overbought and oversold zones work well in trending markets, where there's a clear upward or downward direction. But not all markets are so straightforward. In some conditions, RSI may give misleading signals or whipsaw frequently.

In highly volatile markets, price moves fast, and RSI can whipsaw between extremes. These shifts often happen too quickly to act on and can lead to false signals. In such an environment, use support/ resistance or trend filters to confirm trades.

Additionally, when momentum is strong, like during a breakout, RSI can stay in overbought or oversold territory much longer than expected. This doesn't mean reversal - it shows momentum.

Understanding RSI

RSI is most useful in trending markets and is based on average gains and losses. It can give misleading signals in sideways conditions and shouldn't be used in isolation. Pick the 3 facts that best describe how RSI behaves in different types of market conditions.

- Unreliable in flat markets
- Settings don’t affect zones
- Always means reversal
- Confirms trend momentum

- Use avg gain/loss
- Works best alone

Answer:
- Unreliable in flat markets
- Confirms trend momentum
- Use avg gain/loss

There's one more factor that affects how RSI behaves - the setting you use. Those oversold and overbought zones can shift depending on your RSI setting. A shorter setting gives quicker signals, while a longer setting reacts more slowly.

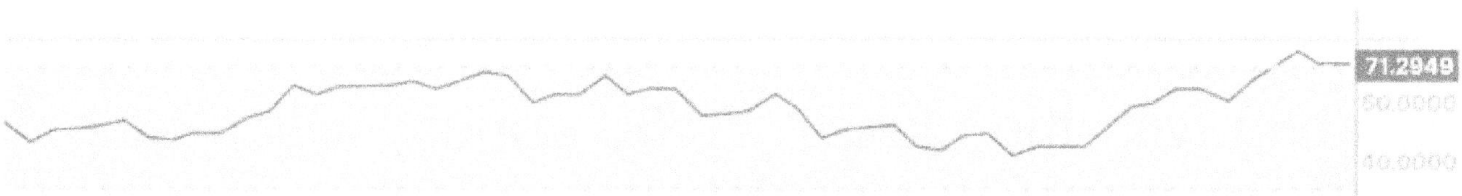

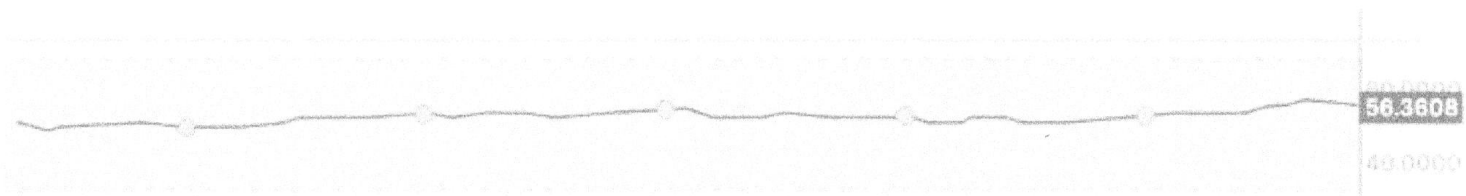

How should you choose your RSI setting? It depends on your trading style. If you prefer short-term trading or scalping, you should use settings like 5 or 7, where 90 might signal overbought and 10 oversold. It is great for speed, but creates more noise.

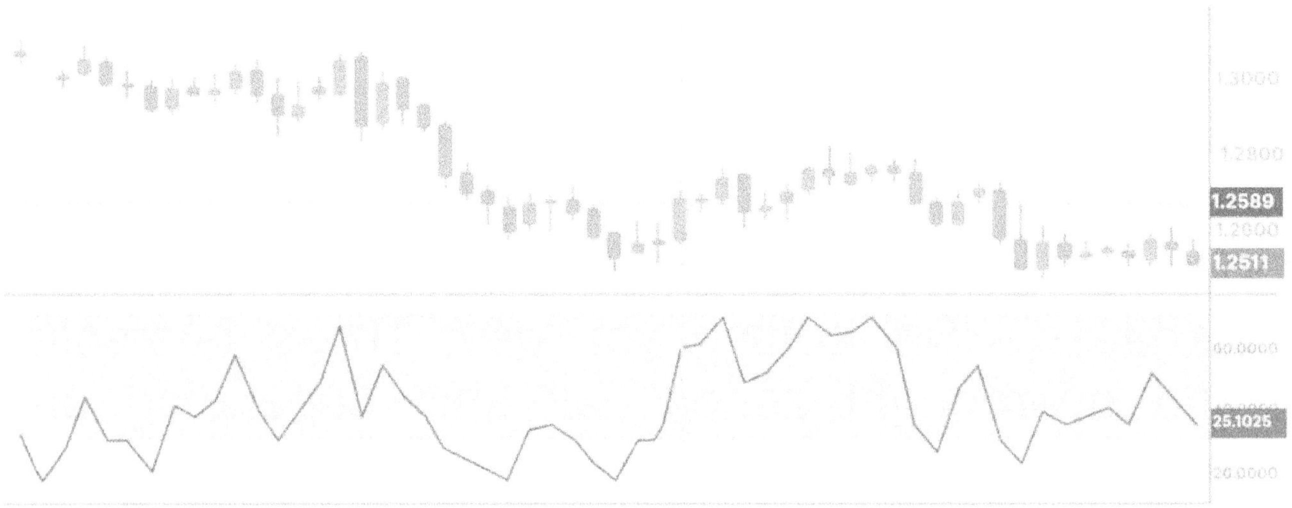

Swing traders often use the default 14-period setting with the classic 70/30 zones, which helps balance reactivity and stability.

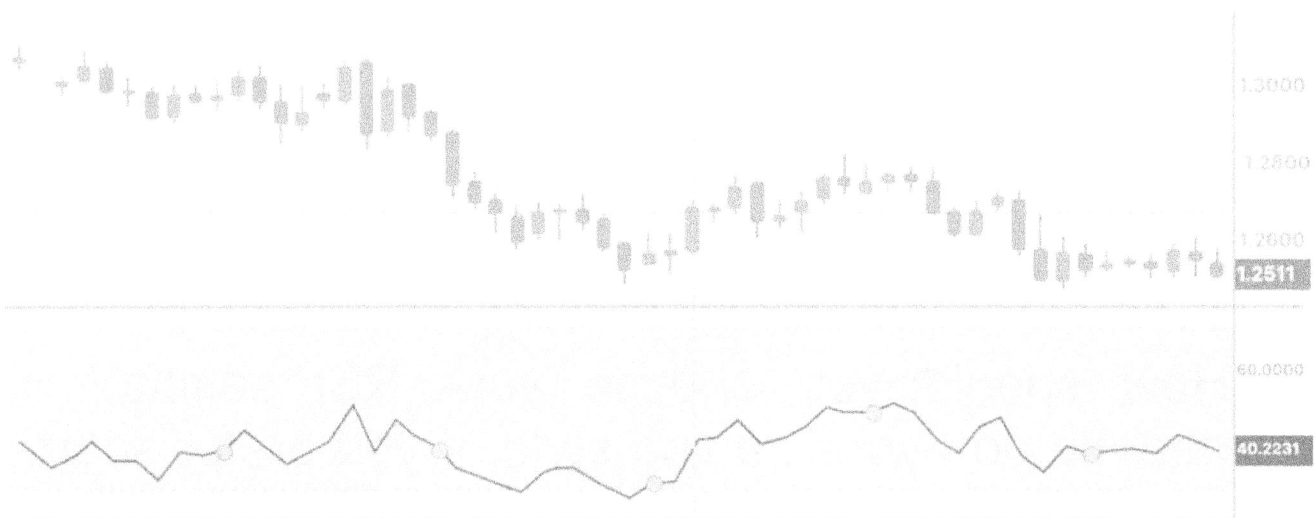

Longer-term traders might use 21 or more, focusing on broader moves, where 60/40 might be more relevant.

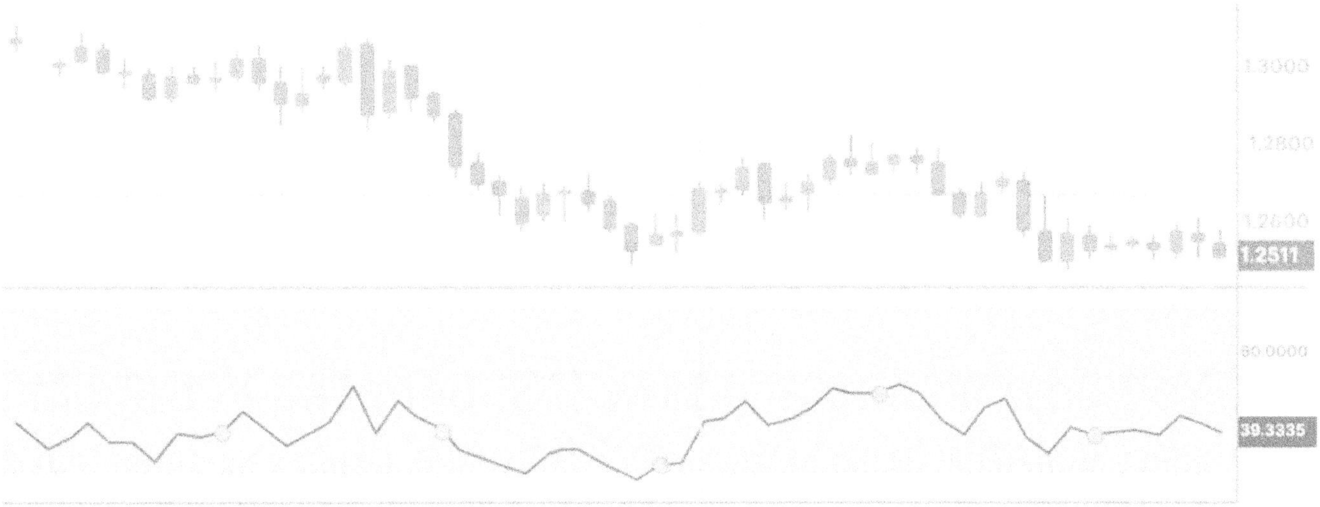

Remember that your RSI setting changes what the signal means. Shorter settings = quicker signals but more false alarms. Longer settings = slower but more reliable confirmation.

The right RSI setting

Different traders use different RSI periods and thresholds based on their strategies. Shorter timeframes need more sensitive RSI levels. Match each trading style with the most common RSI setting.

- Scalping - RSI 14 | 70/30 levels
- Swing trading - RSI 5/7 | 90/10 levels
- Day trading - RSI 10-14 | 80/20 levels

Answer:

- Scalping - RSI 5/7 | 90/10 levels
- Swing trading - RSI 14 | 70/30 levels
- Day trading - RSI 10-14 | 80/20 levels

You now understand how RSI behaves in trending and volatile markets, and how to choose the right settings for your style. Next, we'll explore divergence, a powerful tool to help you stay ahead of trend changes.

Lesson 3: RSI Divergence

Spot reversals with RSI divergence

In this lesson, we're digging deeper into RSI by focusing on divergence, a key concept that helps traders predict potential reversals before they happen. You'll learn the difference between regular and hidden divergence and how to use each one in real trading scenarios.

Remember, RSI works best as a confirmation tool, not a standalone signal. One powerful confirmation method is spotting divergence, when RSI and price move in opposite directions. This can be an early warning sign that the current trend may be about to reverse.

Not all divergence is the same. You can see the Bullish Divergence when the price goes down (making lower lows), but RSI goes up (making higher lows). This suggests the downtrend may be weakening, and a price rise could be coming.

Even though bullish divergence hints at a possible reversal, it's not a guaranteed signal to buy right away. Smart traders wait for confirmation, like a breakout, a bullish candle pattern, or RSI crossing above 30, before entering a trade. Confirmation helps reduce the risk of false signals.

On the other hand, the Bearish Divergence can be detected when the price goes up (making higher highs), but RSI goes down (making lower highs). This may signal that the uptrend is losing strength, and a price drop could follow.

Bearish divergence can signal that momentum is fading. Bearish divergence often suggests a weakening uptrend. It's not a guaranteed reversal, but a sign to watch for confirmation and prepare for a potential sell.

Remember that Regular divergence happens when price and RSI move in opposite directions at key extremes and often signals a possible trend reversal.

Let's practice using RSI divergence

Take a look at this EUR/GBP 4-hour chart. Price is making higher highs, but RSI is making lower highs. This is a classic RSI divergence setup. Divergence is an early warning, not a guaranteed reversal. Wait for confirmation like a bearish candlestick pattern or a break of support before acting.

You spot this divergence after the third push higher. What action would you consider?

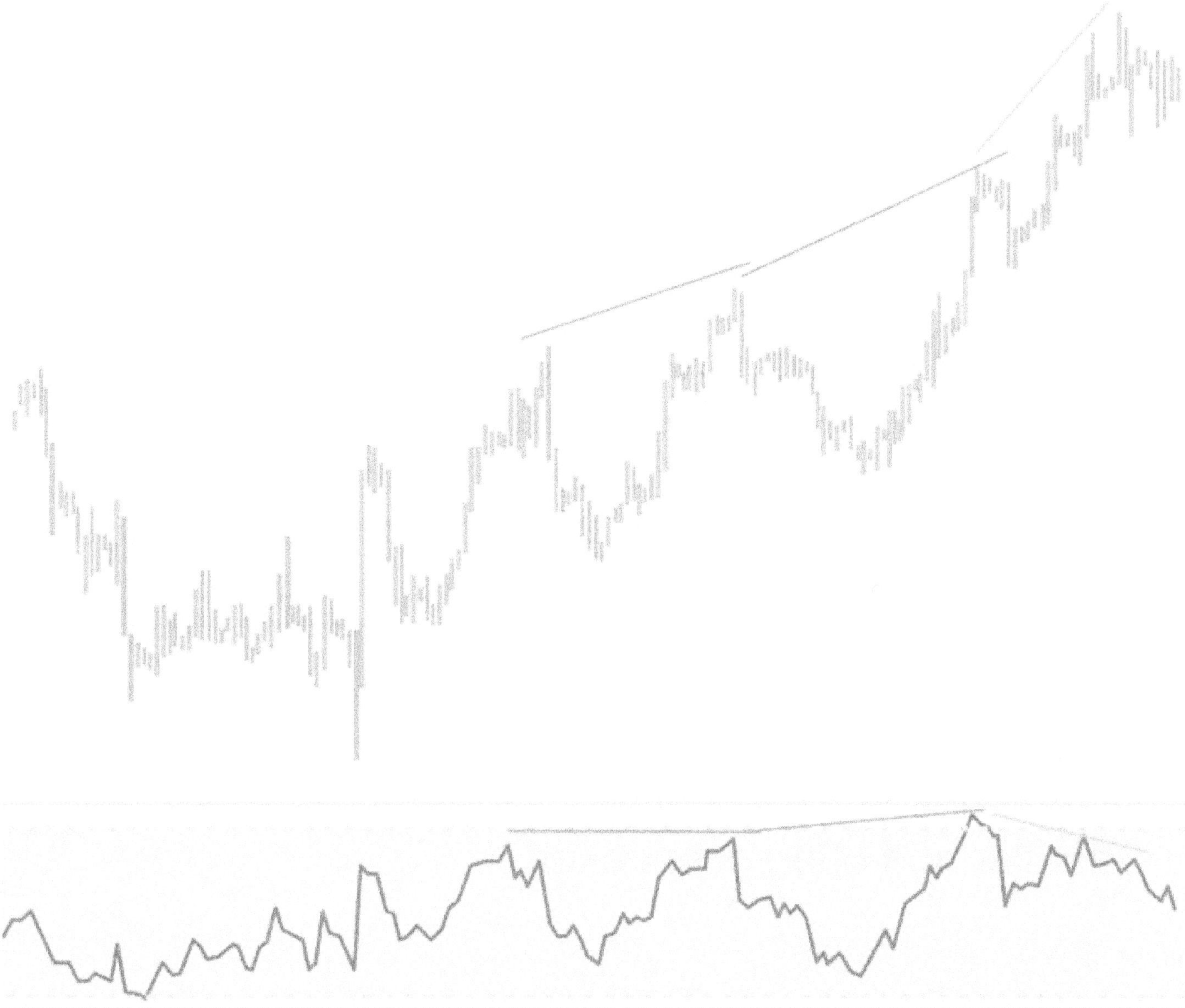

- Immediately short the market at the peak
- Enter a long trade - the trend is still up
- Ignore the RSI - it's lagging and not reliable
- Wait for price confirmation before entering a short

Answer: Wait for price confirmation before entering a short. While RSI divergence signals that the uptrend might be losing momentum, it doesn't guarantee a reversal. Waiting for price confirmation, like a bearish candle pattern or a break below support, helps you avoid false signals and improves trade timing.

Although spotting divergence is powerful, it's best not to rely on it alone. Always confirm with price action or other tools. For example, wait for a lower high in price, a break of a support level, or a bearish candlestick pattern before taking action.

While regular divergence signals potential trend reversals, hidden divergence indicates trend continuation. It's called "hidden" because it's subtler and often overlooked.

A Bullish Hidden Divergence occurs when price forms higher lows, but RSI forms lower lows. It suggests that the uptrend will continue.

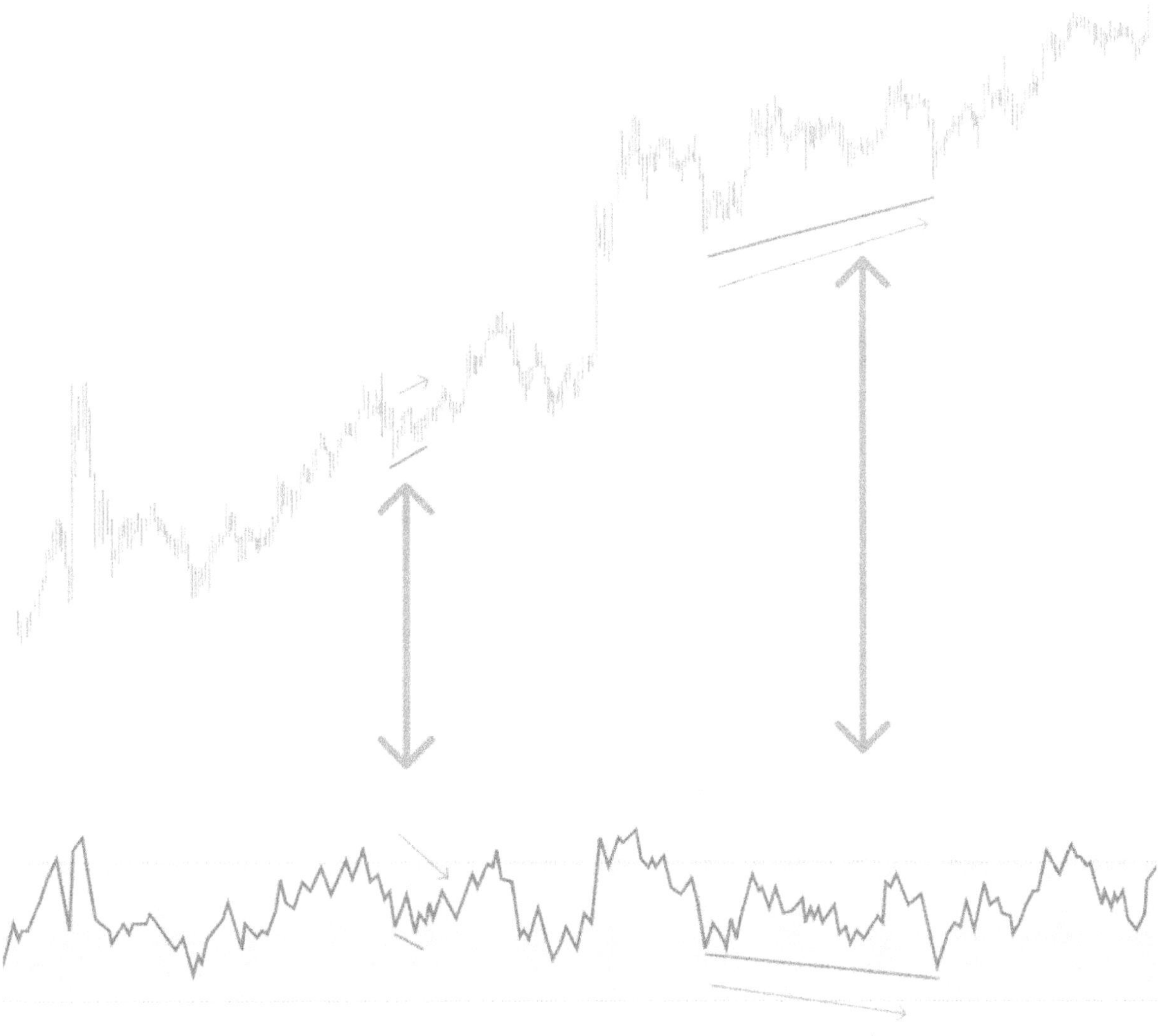

Bearish Hidden Divergence occurs when price forms lower highs, but RSI forms higher highs. It indicates the downtrend may persist.

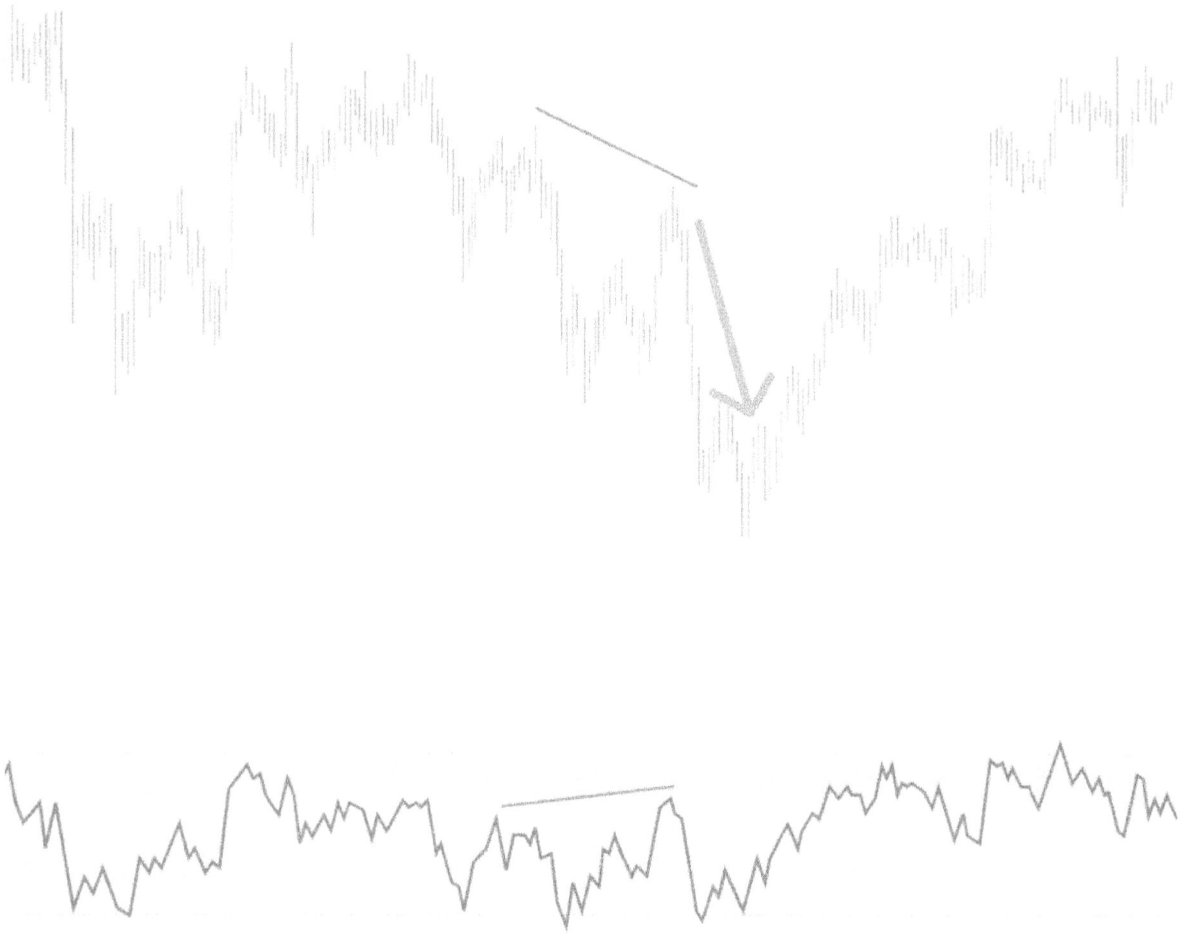

Regular or hidden divergence?

You're analyzing a stock in an uptrend. After a dip, the price forms a higher low, but RSI shows a lower low, signaling weaker momentum. Price is still trending upward, but RSI is showing weakness. Think about which type of divergence signals trend continuation when momentum

temporarily fades. What kind of divergence does this show, and what could happen next?

- No clear divergence; RSI doesn't help here
- Hidden Bearish Divergence; Downtrend continuation
- Hidden Bullish Divergence; Uptrend likely to continue
- Regular Bearish Divergence; Trend reversal expected

Answer: Hidden Bullish Divergence; Uptrend likely to continue. This is Hidden Bullish divergence. The price is forming higher lows, which confirms the uptrend. RSI making lower lows suggests a loss of short-term momentum, but in this case, it usually means the trend will continue, not reverse. Remember: regular divergence signals reversal, while hidden divergence supports the current trend. Price made a higher low (still in an uptrend), so this isn't bearish; it's a sign the uptrend might resume soon.

You've explored how RSI divergence reveals potential turning points and how hidden divergence can tip you off to trend continuation. Now, let's test what you've learned with a quick quiz!

QUIZ: RSI Insights

1. What does RSI primarily measure?

A. The strength of candlestick patterns
B. Trading volume over time
C. Price momentum based on average gains and losses
D. Support and resistance levels

2. What does an RSI value below 30 typically indicate?

A. Volume is increasing
B. The asset may be oversold
C. The asset is overbought
D. A breakout is occurring

3. What does a bullish divergence show?

A. RSI is above 70, signaling momentum
B. Price is making lower lows, but RSI is making higher lows

C. Price is making higher highs, and RSI confirms it
D. Price is below the moving average

4. In a volatile market, RSI can...

A. Provide highly accurate reversal points
B. Whipsaw and give false signals
C. Stay flat
D. Show consistent breakouts

5. Which RSI setting is best for scalping?

A. RSI 5-7 with 90/10 thresholds
B. RSI 21 with 60/40 thresholds
C. RSI 14 with 70/30 thresholds
D. RSI 14 with 50/50 thresholds

6. Which of these best defines a hidden bullish divergence?

A. Price makes lower lows, RSI makes higher lows
B. Price makes higher lows, RSI makes lower lows
C. Price and RSI both trend down
D. RSI crosses above 50

7. Why shouldn't you act immediately on bullish divergence?

A. Bullish divergence means sell
B. Volume has dropped
C. RSI always lags price
D. It's a potential signal, not a confirmation

8. What is the purpose of using RSI with other indicators?

A. To confirm signals and reduce false entries
B. To remove the need for price analysis
C. To make RSI calculations easier
D. To find overbought conditions quicker

9. What does an RSI above 70 usually suggest?

A. A bullish breakout is starting
B. The market may be overbought
C. The asset is undervalued
D. Bearish divergence is confirmed

10. What type of divergence suggests trend continuation?

A. Directional RSI
B. Hidden divergence
C. Regular divergence
D. Triple divergence

Answer: 1. C; 2. B; 3. B; 4. B; 5. A; 6. B; 7. D; 8. A; 9. B; 10. B

Chapter 4: Pattern Recognition

Lesson 1: Why Price Action Matters

Reading charts with indicators

In this part, we'll see how indicators can enhance your ability to read chart behavior. We'll explore how traders combine price action with tools like RSI and Moving Averages to confirm setups, filter out noise, and make more confident decisions.

Before jumping in, let's review our knowledge about RSI and Moving Averages!

RSI measures momentum, indicating overbought (above 70) or oversold (below 30) conditions, while Moving Averages smooth out price data to identify trend direction.

MA trends - focus on the price's position relative to the moving average and the slope of the MA line:

- Price above rising MA - Uptrend

- Price below falling MA - Downtrend
- Price near flat MA - Sideways or range-bound

RSI values and their meanings:

- 0: The market is extremely oversold
- 30: This is an oversold zone
- 50: This is a neutral zone
- 70: This is an overbought zone
- 100: The market is extremely overbought

Great job reviewing the basics! Now let's see how combining RSI with Moving Averages can help you spot trend strength, confirm reversals, and avoid false signals.

To use the Moving Average + RSI crossover strategy effectively, you need to set up two indicators on your chart. First, you need to set up two Moving Averages: A fast MA (e.g., 10-period) to track short-term price movements and a slow MA (e.g., 50-period) to represent the longer-term trend.

Next, add the Relative Strength Index: Use a default 14-period RSI.

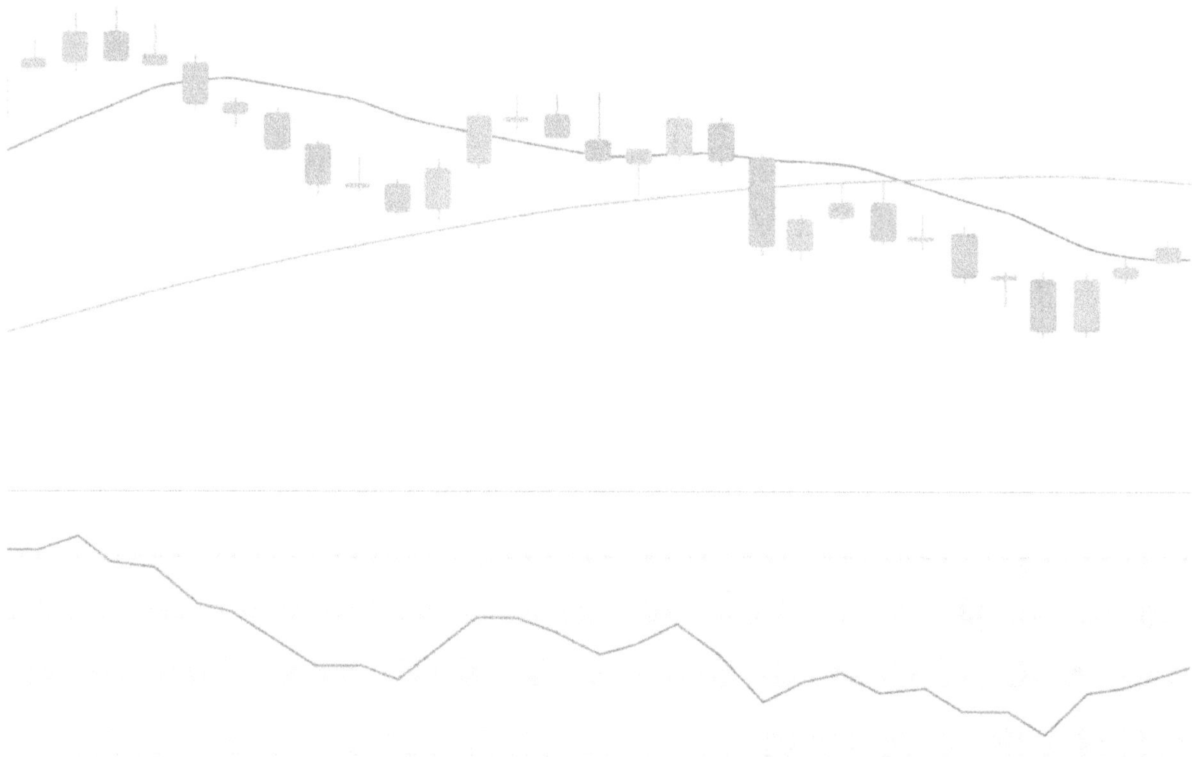

Depending on your trading style, you'll need to adjust your Moving Averages and RSI settings:

- Short-term traders (e.g., scalping): Use 5 and 20 MA + RSI 7 on 5 - 15 minute charts
- Swing traders: Use 10 and 50 MA + RSI 14 on 1 - 4 hour charts
- Long-term traders: Use 50 and 200 MA + RSI 21 on dally or weekly charts

This strategy combines two key ideas: trend confirmation and momentum reversal. The MA crossover shows a change in trend, while the RSI confirms whether the market is stretched in one direction. When both agree, you get a more reliable entry signal.

Let's explore how MA and RSI work together. A fast MA (1) crossing above a slow MA (2) signals growing bullish momentum. To confirm this move, the RSI should also cross above the 50 level. This suggests that the buyers are gaining control, and the market has underlying strength behind the breakout.

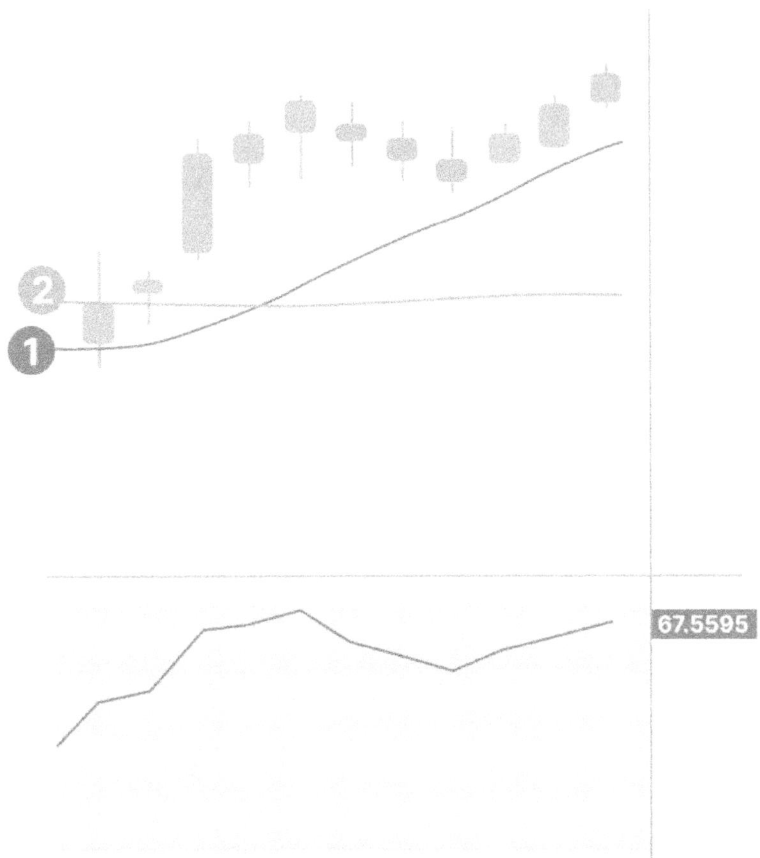

You spot the fast MA crossing above the slow MA, and RSI is currently at 67.55. Entering a buy trade now would be supported by both trend and momentum. True or false?

Answer: True. The fast MA crossing above the slow MA shows a potential uptrend. RSI at 67 confirms bullish momentum. Together, they support a strong buy signal.

A sell signal occurs when the fast MA (1) crosses below the slow MA (2), suggesting the short-term trend is weakening and may be reversing. For confirmation, the RSI should also move below the 50 line, showing bearish momentum. This combination increases the probability that the downtrend will continue.

Even with powerful tools like MAs and RSI, false signals can still happen, especially in choppy or uncertain markets. That's why, don't trade immediately after a crossover. Make sure the RSI supports the direction - above 50 for buys, below 50 for sells. If RSI lags or disagrees, skip the trade.

Indicators don't work in isolation. Check where the price is relative to support/ resistance. A buy signal at strong resistance is riskier than one after a breakout. Use horizontal zones or recent highs/ lows to filter noise.

Don't forget that MAs and RSI give better signals in trending markets. In sideways or volatile ranges, they can whipsaw. Look for smooth price movement and clear direction before relying on crossovers.

Now you know how to combine Moving Averages and RSI to read chart behavior more clearly. Up next, we'll zoom in on price consolidation patterns - like triangles, flags, and rectangles - and show you how they signal breakouts and market direction.

Lesson 2: Consolidation Patterns

What if the trend isn't clear?

You've learned how to use indicators in trending markets. But when price moves sideways or stalls, things get trickier. Let's explore how patterns like triangles, flags, and rectangles - and your indicators - can guide you through uncertainty.

Consolidation occurs when the market pauses, moving sideways within a range. It's a period of indecision where traders accumulate or distribute positions before the next significant move.

There are several common consolidation patterns that traders watch closely. These patterns don't last forever, because sooner or later, price breaks out. Let's break down three key patterns!

One of the most common consolidation patterns is the triangle. As price moves sideways with lower highs and higher lows, it forms a tightening range. This signals that the market is coiling, building pressure before a breakout.

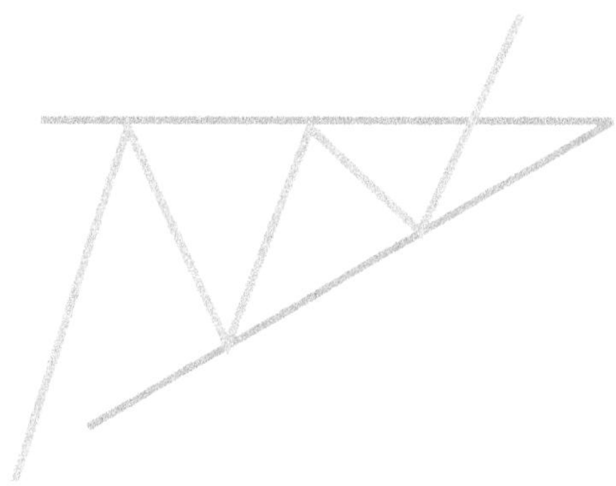

An ascending triangle is a bullish pattern that usually appears during an uptrend. It forms when the price keeps making higher lows, but struggles to break through a horizontal resistance level. The price usually bounces between a flat upper resistance (1) line and a rising lower support (2).

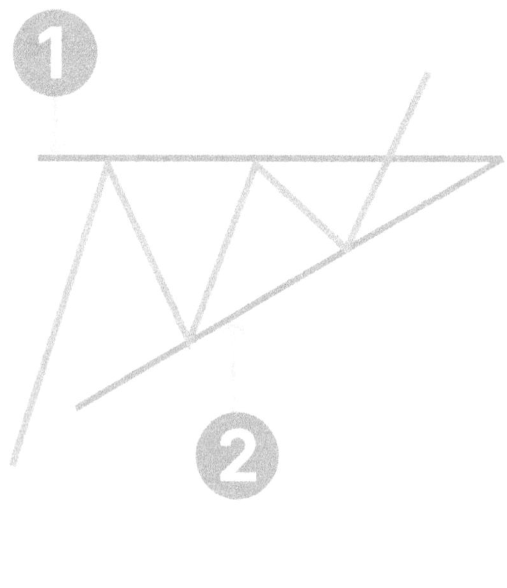

An ascending triangle shows that buyers are becoming more aggressive over time. When the price finally breaks above that resistance - especially with strong volume - it can signal that the uptrend is ready to continue.

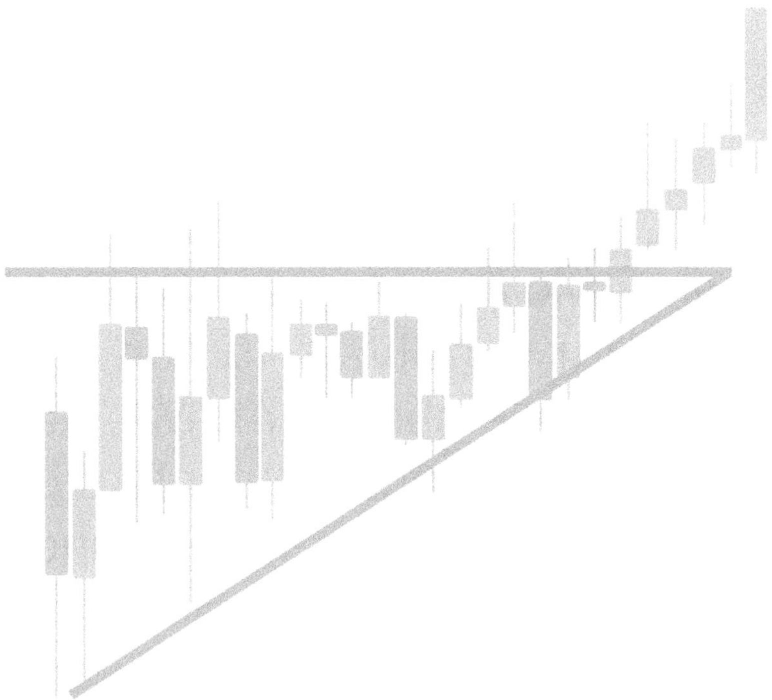

Traders may enter a buy trade at that breakout point. To manage risk, they often place a stop loss just below the most recent low inside the triangle. For the target, they measure the height of the triangle and project it upward from the breakout area to estimate how far the price might go.

Indicators like Moving Averages and RSI can strengthen your analysis when trading an ascending triangle. A short-term MA staying close to the price suggests tight momentum building up. If the price holds above both short- and long-term MAs, it often signals underlying bullish strength.

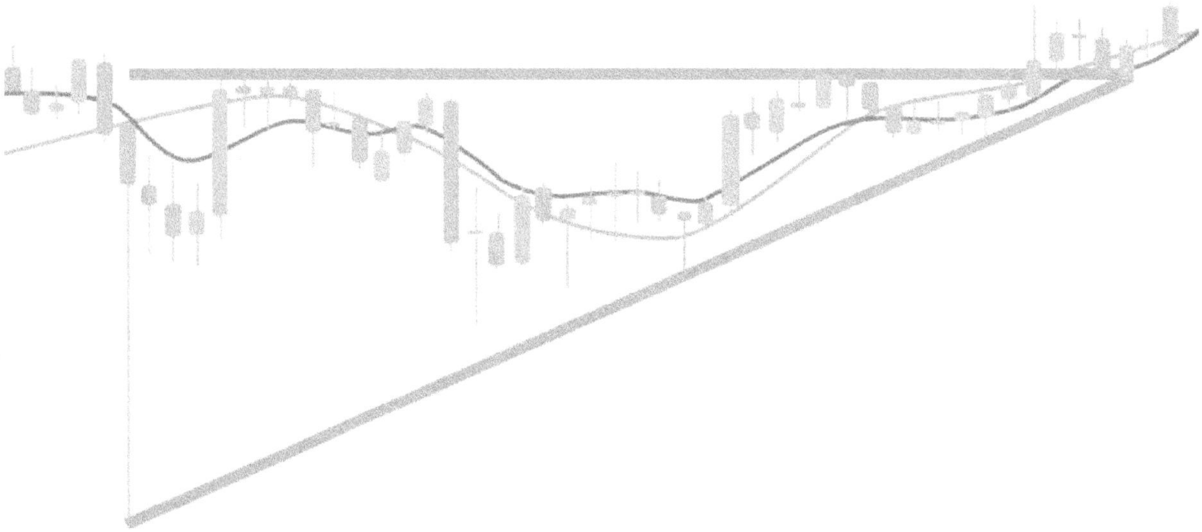

At the same time, if the RSI rises and holds above the 50 level, it indicates momentum is shifting in favor of buyers. If price breaks above resistance with these confirmations, traders may consider entering with stronger confidence.

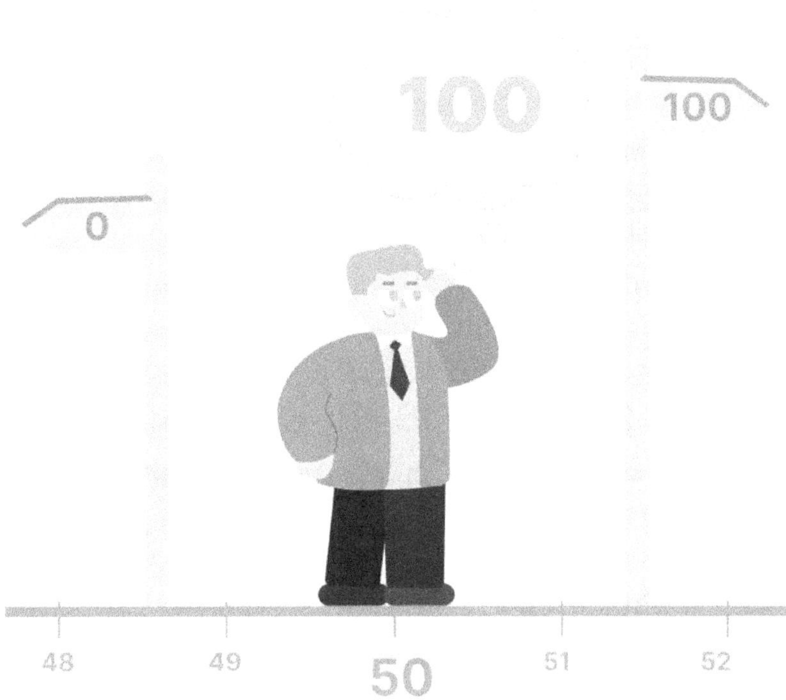

Confirming an ascending triangle breakout

Choose 3 indicator signs that support a bullish breakout after an ascending triangle pattern. Look for signs of rising momentum and price strength to support a bullish continuation.

- RSI holds above 50
- Price above both MAs
- MA crossover down
- Price below long MA
- Short MA rising steadily
- RSI below 30

Answer:

- RSI holds above 50
- Price above both MAs
- Short MA rising steadily

A descending triangle is a bearish chart pattern that often forms during a downtrend and suggests that sellers are gaining strength. It's characterized by a flat support line and a series of lower highs. Traders usually watch for a breakdown below the support level to confirm the pattern.

To trade a descending triangle, traders often wait for a breakout below support and enter short positions. A stop loss is placed above the last lower high, and the target is set by projecting the triangle's height downward.

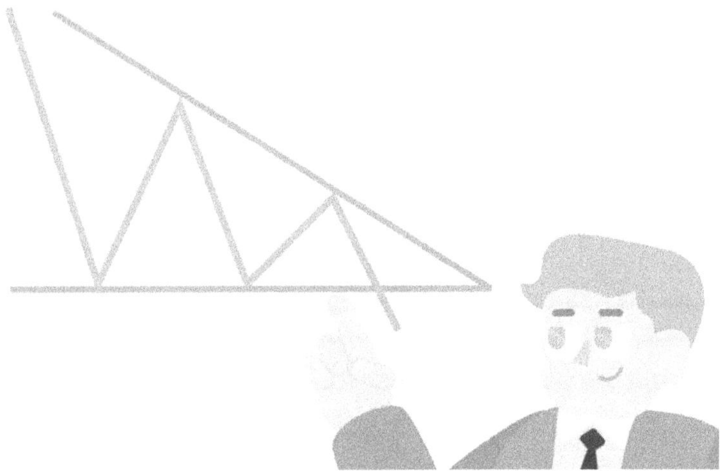

Moving Averages and RSI can help confirm the setup. A falling short-term MA, staying above the price, supports the idea of downward pressure. If both short- and long-term MAs are sloping down, it further confirms the bearish trend.

RSI holding below 50, or especially dipping near 30, shows bearish momentum and adds confidence to a potential breakdown.

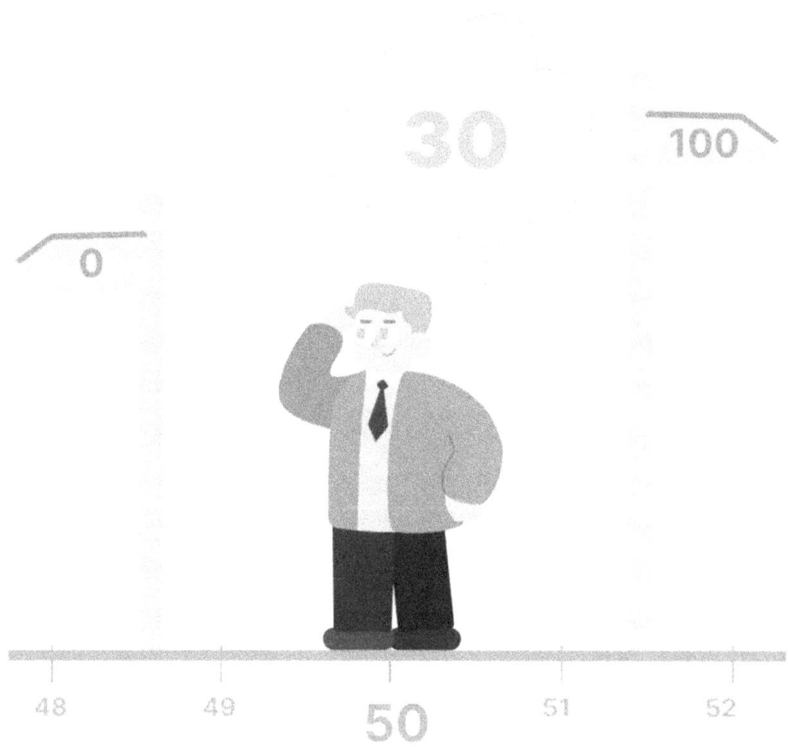

A descending triangle with downward-sloping MAs and an RSI below 50 suggests a stronger chance of a bearish breakout. True or false?

Answer: True. When both the short- and long-term MAs are trending down and RSI holds below 50, these indicators confirm weakening momentum. In the context of a descending triangle, this alignment strengthens the case for a potential breakdown below support.

A symmetrical triangle forms when the price moves between converging support and resistance lines, creating a series of lower highs and higher lows. This pattern shows indecision - neither buyers nor sellers are in control. It can break out in either direction.

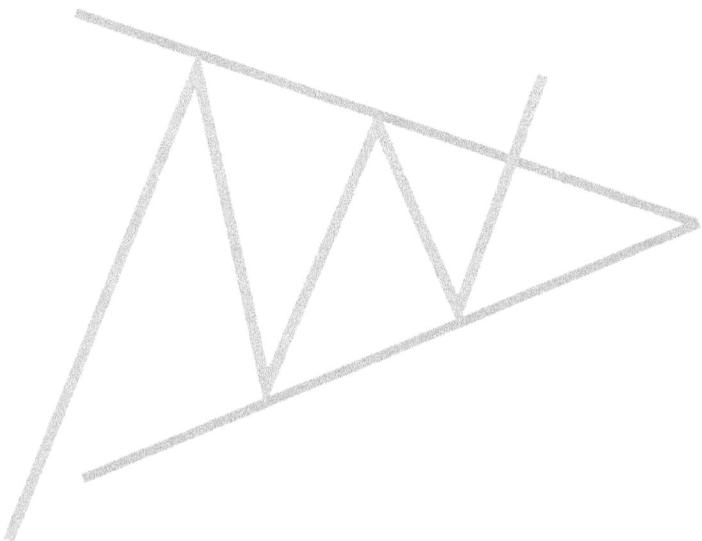

Traders typically wait for a decisive breakout above or below the triangle with increased volume before acting. A breakout to the upside may signal the start of a new uptrend, while a break below suggests continued weakness.

Moving Averages and RSI can help confirm the direction of a symmetrical triangle breakout. If the price crosses above both moving averages and they are sloping upward, it supports a bullish breakout.

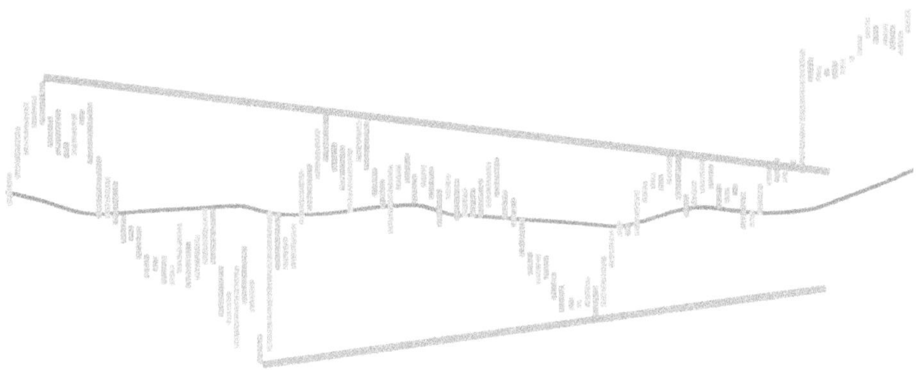

On the other hand, if the price stays below both MAs and they are sloping downward, it signals a possible bearish move. RSI can further strengthen the signal - if it rises above 50, it adds confidence to an upward breakout; if it drops below 50, it supports a downside break.

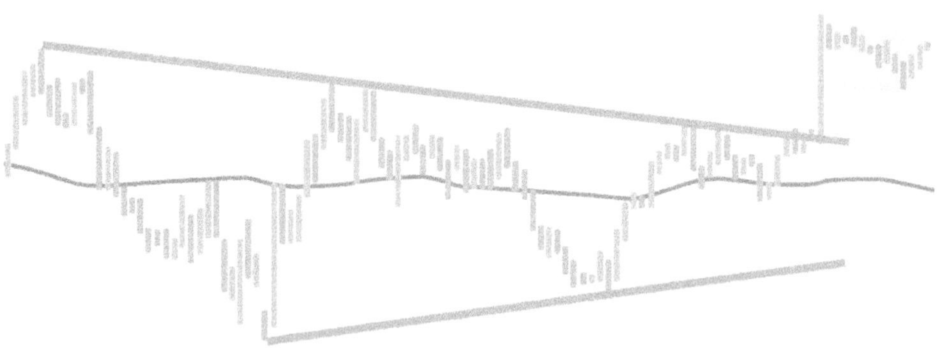

Symmetrical triangle breakout

You spot a symmetrical triangle. Price is squeezing between converging trendlines. The moving averages are flat, but RSI just crossed above 50 and price is testing the upper boundary of the triangle. When RSI rises above 50 and price presses against resistance, it may signal growing bullish pressure inside a symmetrical triangle.

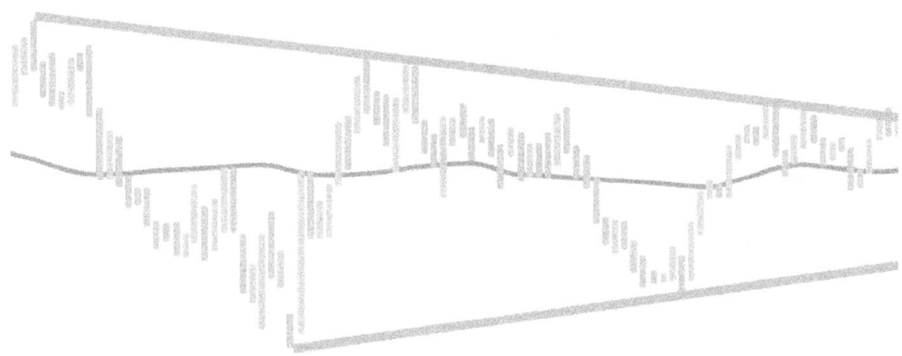

Based on this setup, what's the most likely direction of the breakout?

- Sideways
- Upward breakout
- Downward breakout
- No clear signal

Answer: Upward breakout. RSI above 50 suggests bullish momentum, and price testing the upper trendline signals pressure building from buyers. Together, these are strong signs of a potential upward breakout from the symmetrical triangle.

A flag pattern signals a brief consolidation before the prevailing trend resumes. It comprises two main components: the flagpole (1), representing a sharp price movement, and the flag (2), a rectangular or parallelogram-shaped consolidation that slopes against the trend.

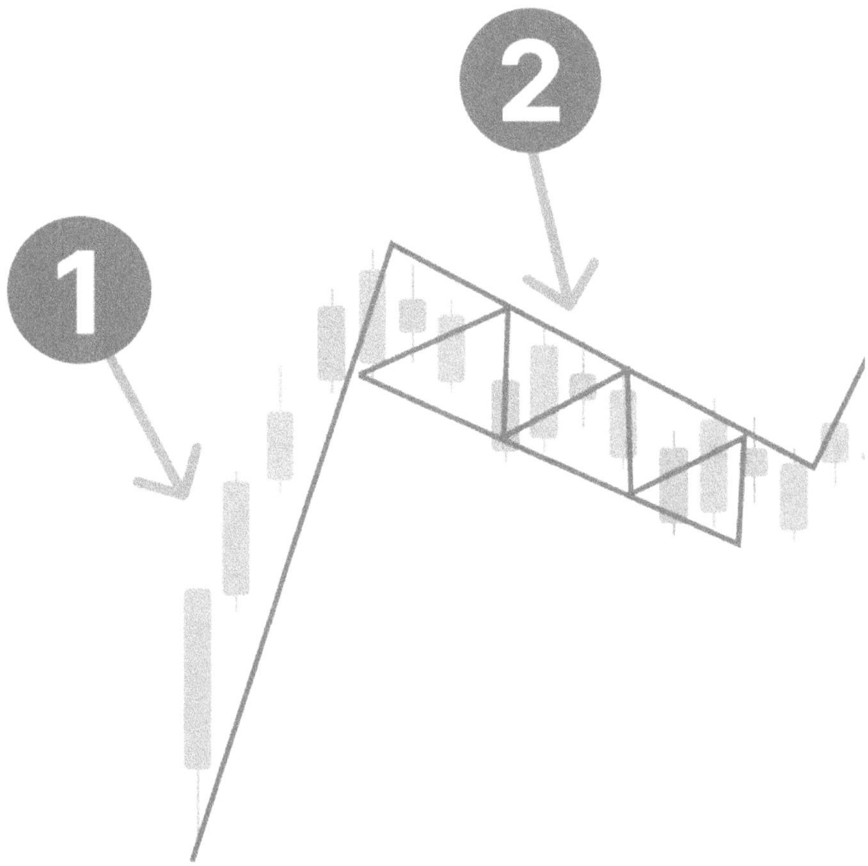

This pattern indicates a temporary pause in the market, often leading to a breakout in the direction of the initial trend.

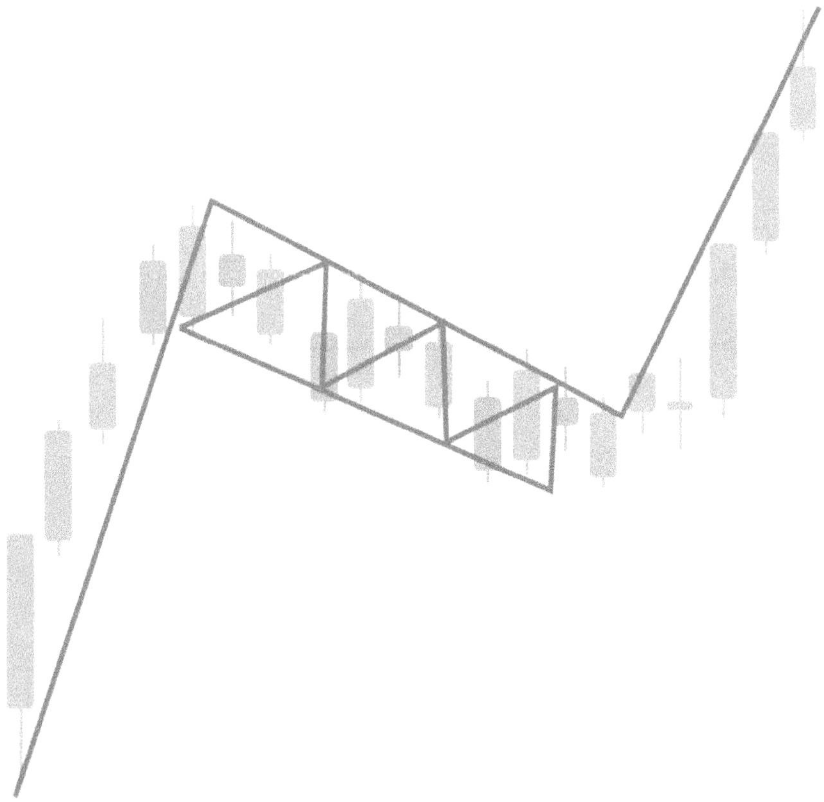

There are bullish and bearish flag patterns. A bullish flag (1) follows a strong uptrend with a slight pullback, while a bearish flag (2) forms after a downtrend with a brief upward consolidation. Both suggest that the market is likely to continue in the direction of the preceding trend upon breakout.

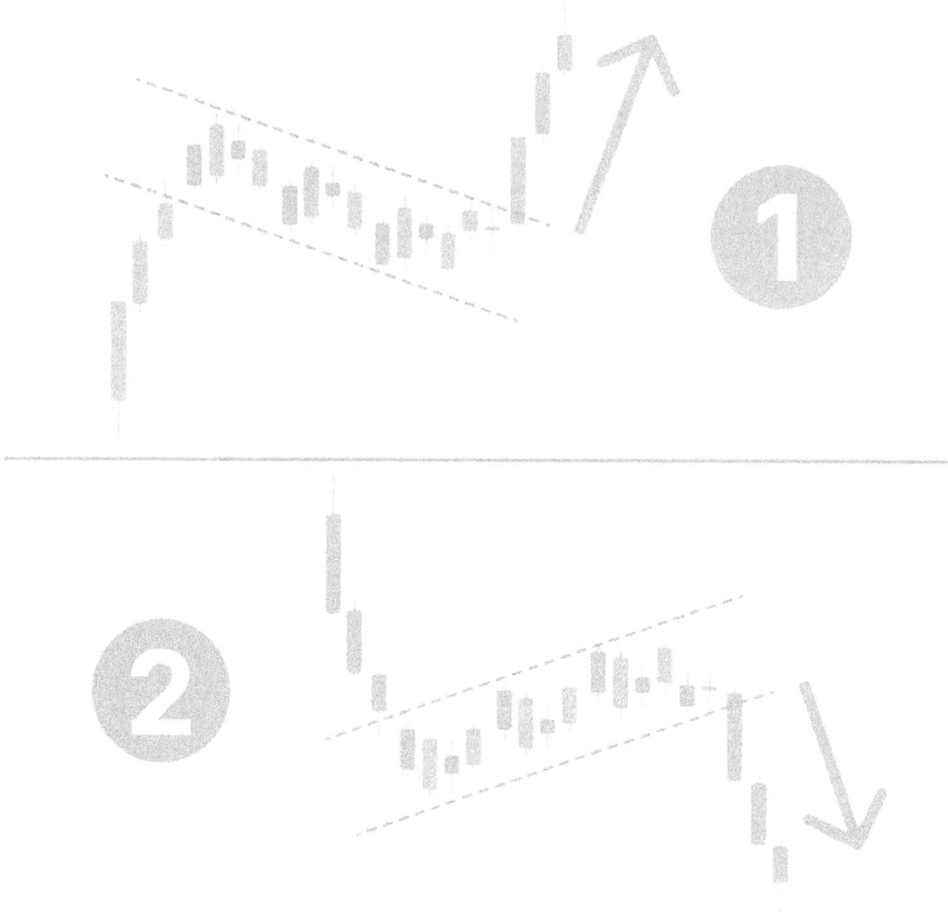

To trade this pattern, traders often enter positions in the direction of the breakout, set stop-loss orders just outside the flag's boundaries, and project the flagpole's length from the breakout point to estimate potential price targets.

Indicators can strengthen flag pattern analysis. In bullish flags, price stays above rising MAs and RSI holds above 50; in bearish flags, price stays below falling MAs and RSI stays below 50.

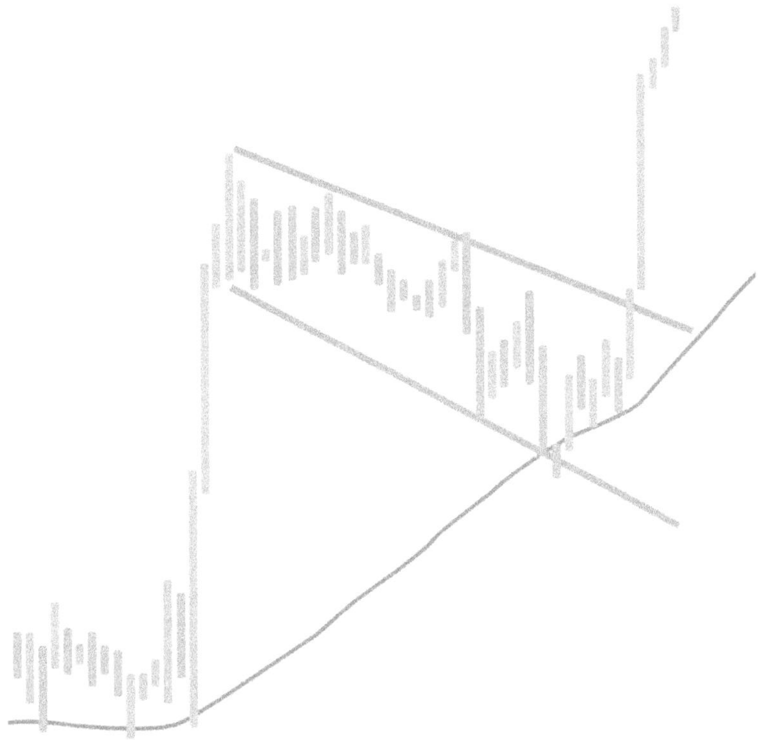

Matching signals to flag types

Match each signal to the correct flag pattern it supports. Look at how RSI and MA behavior confirm the direction of the breakout from each flag pattern.

- Bearish flag - Price above rising MA
- Bullish flag - RSI above 50
- Bullish flag - Price below falling MA

Answer:

- Bearish flag - Price below falling MA
- Bullish flag - RSI above 50
- Bullish flag - Price above rising MA

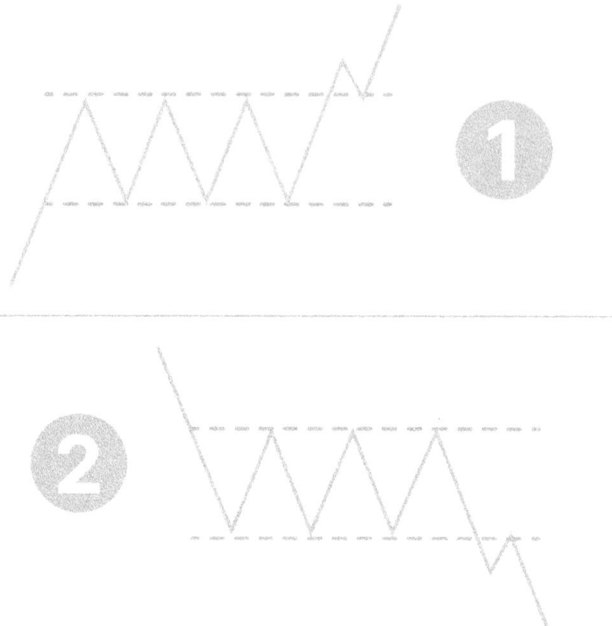

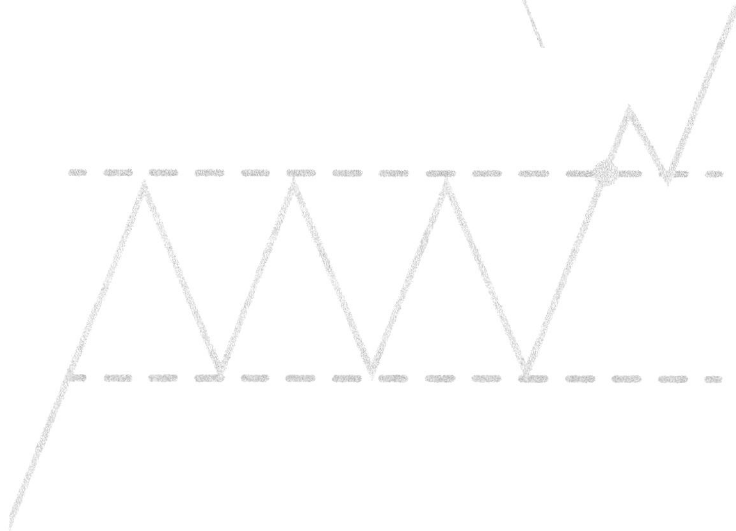

A rectangle pattern forms when an asset's price moves within a defined range, bouncing between a horizontal support level and a horizontal resistance level. This creates a visual "box" on the chart, signaling a pause in the current trend as buyers and sellers remain in relative balance.

There are two types of rectangle patterns: bullish and bearish. A bullish rectangle (1) occurs during an uptrend and usually results in a breakout to the upside, while a bearish rectangle (2) develops in a downtrend and often breaks lower.

Traders spot rectangles when price bounces at least twice between clear support and resistance levels. This signals consolidation. A breakout beyond the range often resumes the prior trend, and traders enter once the price closes outside the box with strong momentum.
Moving Averages and RSI help confirm rectangle

breakouts. In bullish rectangles, price often stays

above a rising MA; in bearish ones, it stays below a falling MA. RSI near 50 shows indecision, but a move above or below 50 on breakout adds confirmation.

If price breaks out of a rectangle pattern while RSI remains near 50 and both moving averages are flat, it strongly confirms the breakout. True or false?

Answer: False. RSI near 50 and flat moving averages suggest indecision and lack of momentum. For a breakout to be confirmed, traders look for RSI to move above 50 (in bullish breakouts) or below 50 (in bearish ones), along with sloping MAs to support the direction.

You've just learned how to identify and trade triangles, flags, and rectangles, and how indicators can help confirm your setups. Next up: we'll dive into continuation and reversal patterns - key tools for spotting turning points and confirming new trends.

Lesson 3: Continuation and Reversal Patterns

Time to spot the market's turning points!

In this lesson, we'll dive into continuation and reversal patterns - key formations that signal whether the trend is about to continue or change. You'll explore Head & Shoulders, Wedges, and Double Tops/Bottoms, and see how indicators like RSI and Moving Averages can strengthen your decisions.

Let's start with reversal patterns. These signal the end of a trend and often appear after long uptrends or downtrends, hinting that the market may be ready to reverse direction.

A Head & Shoulders pattern signals a potential trend reversal. It features a left shoulder (1), a head (2), and a right shoulder (3), followed by a break below the neckline (4).

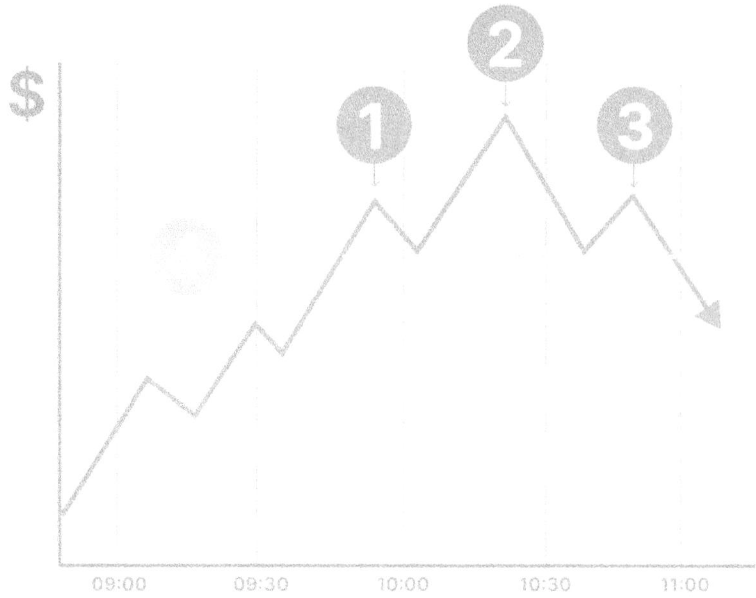

This pattern shows weakening buyer strength. Price makes a high, then a higher high, but fails to push higher a third time. Buyers lose momentum. When price breaks below the neckline (support between the two lows), it confirms a possible reversal from an uptrend to a downtrend.

Indicators can give early warning signs during a Head & Shoulders pattern. If RSI shows lower highs while price is forming the right shoulder, it means momentum is fading - buyers are losing strength. At the same time, Moving Averages may flatten or start to cross downward, hinting that the uptrend is running out of steam.

Make a decision!

You're analyzing a chart and notice a Head & Shoulders pattern forming. RSI is showing lower highs, and the price just broke below the neckline. When a Head & Shoulders completes with a neckline break and RSI confirms weakening momentum, it often signals a trend reversal.

What's the most informed decision based on this setup?

- Ignore the pattern
- Wait for RSI to rise above 70
- Enter a short position
- Buy now

Answer: Enter a short position. The price breaking below the neckline, confirmed by bearish RSI divergence, suggests the uptrend is losing steam. A short entry here aligns with the reversal signal.

Now let's move on to the Double Top and Bottom patterns. A Double Top (1) signals a bearish reversal after two peaks. A Double Bottom (2) suggests a bullish reversal after two dips. Breakout through the neckline confirms the setup.

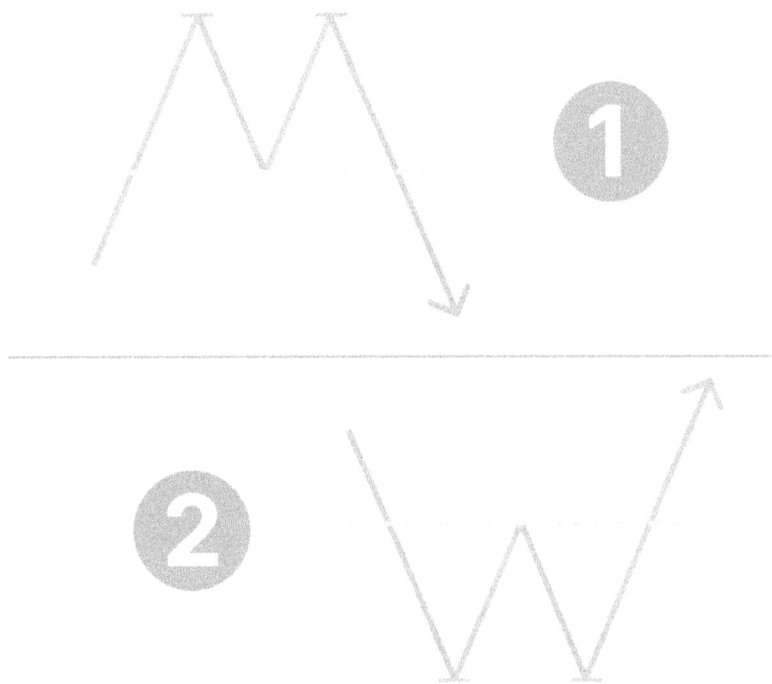

A Double Top signals buyer weakness, confirmed when price breaks below the neckline. RSI often shows bearish divergence (price makes a higher high while RSI makes a lower high), indicating fading momentum. Moving Averages may flatten or slope down, confirming a potential reversal.

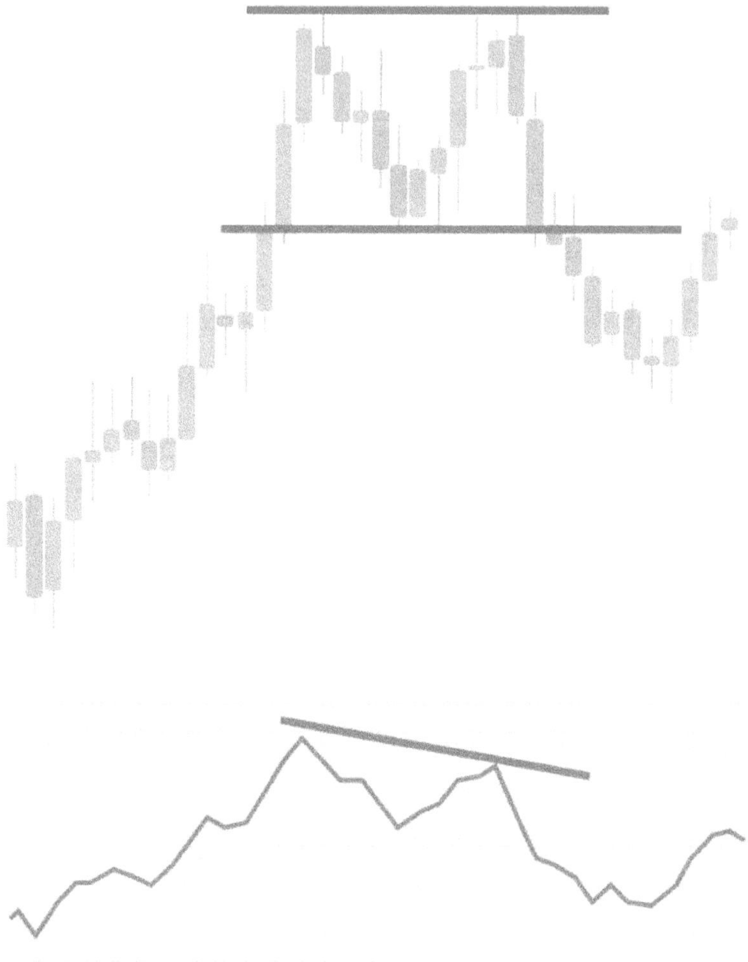

When traders spot a Double Top, they usually wait for the price to break below the neckline before entering a short position, often placing a stop-loss above the second peak and setting a target equal to the height of the pattern.

A Double Bottom forms after a downtrend, when price tests the same low twice without breaking lower, signaling weakening seller control. A breakout above the neckline confirms a reversal.

Bullish RSI divergence and upward-sloping MAs strengthen the case for a move higher.

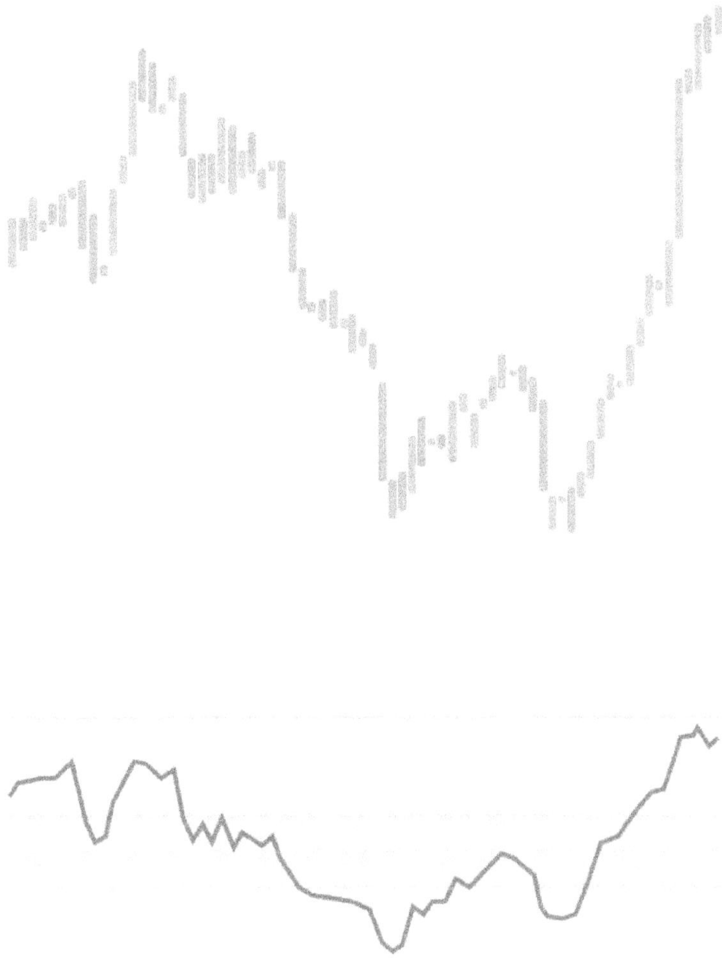

For a Double Bottom, traders wait for a break above the neckline (resistance between the lows) to enter a long trade, placing a stop-loss below the second bottom and targeting a move equal to the pattern's height. This helps manage risk and confirm the reversal before committing.

Match pattern with trader's decision

Which actions match each pattern setup? Drag the right decision to the pattern it supports. Both patterns form after strong trends. Think about what traders do once the price breaks key support or resistance. Which one leads to a long entry, and which one signals a chance to go short?

- Double Bottom - Short after neckline breaks
- Double Top - Buy after neckline breaks

Answer:

- Double Bottom - Buy after neckline breaks
- Double Top - Short after neckline breaks

Lastly, Wedges are powerful patterns that can signal reversals or continuations. A Falling Wedge (1) during a downtrend often breaks upward. A Rising Wedge (2) in an uptrend may break lower.

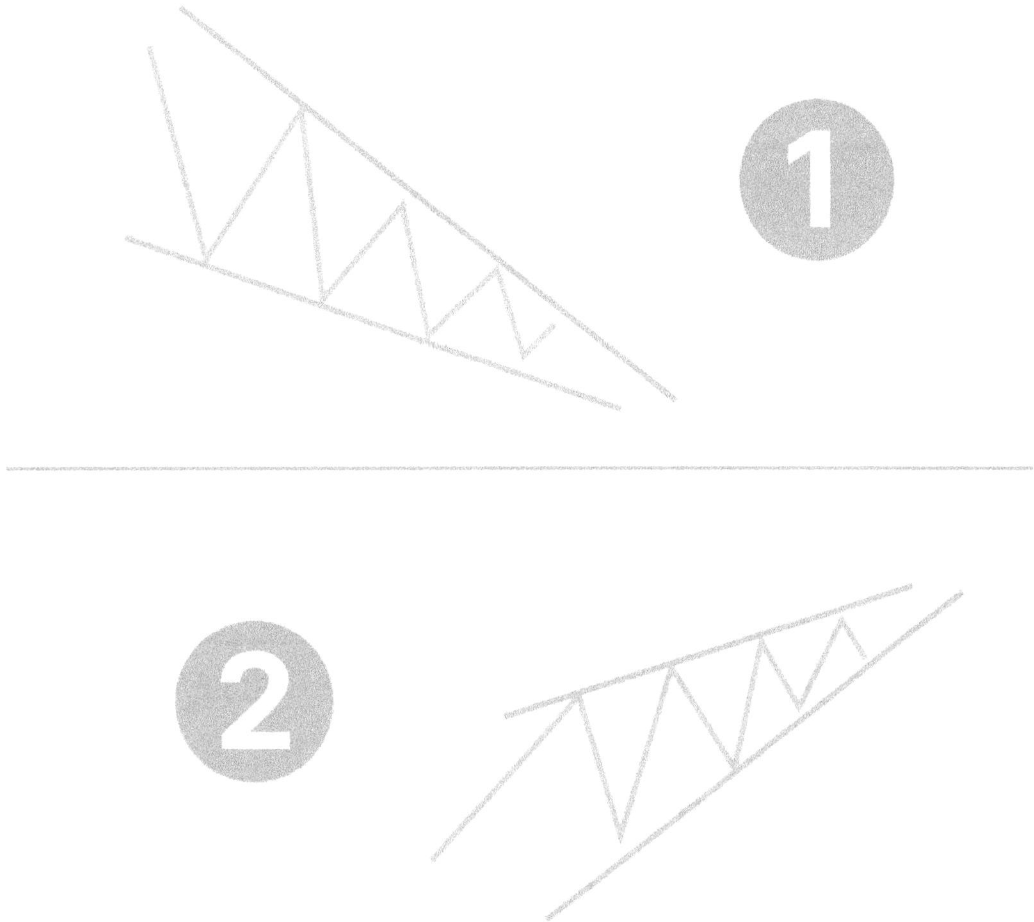

Rising Wedge forms during an uptrend and signals a potential bearish reversal. Price makes higher highs and higher lows, but with weakening momentum. Bearish divergence on RSI and downward-sloping MAs can confirm fading strength. A break below the wedge often triggers short entries.

Falling Wedge appears after a downtrend and signals a bullish reversal. Price forms lower highs and lows, but selling pressure weakens. Bullish RSI divergence and rising MAs help confirm the setup. A breakout above the wedge may signal a long opportunity.

When traders see a rising wedge, they wait for a breakdown below support to go short. For a falling wedge, they watch for a breakout above resistance to go long. RSI or MA confirmation strengthens the signal. Stop-losses are set just outside the wedge.

It a Falling Wedge forms during an uptrend and breaks upward, or a Rising Wedge forms in a downtrend and breaks lower, the trend may resume.

To detect this, traders look at the bigger context, volume behavior, and confirmation from RSI and Moving Averages. An RSI holding above 50 in a falling wedge or below 50 in a rising wedge can suggest trend continuation.

How do traders analyze wedge patterns?

Put the steps in the correct order to analyze a wedge pattern and decide whether it signals a reversal or continuation. The wedge shape alone isn't enough - context, breakout, and indicators complete the picture.

- Check trend direction
- Confine with RSI and MAs
- Look for breakout direction
- Identify if it’s a Falling or Rising

Answer:

- Identify if it’s a Falling or Rising
- Check trend direction
- Look for breakout direction

Excellent! Now you know how to recognize powerful reversal patterns and how indicators like RSI and Moving Averages can confirm them. These tools help you avoid false signals and trade with confidence when trends shift. In the next lesson, we'll explore how Moving Averages act as more than just trend indicators.

Lesson 4: Support and Resistance with MAs

Dynamic support & resistance

You saw how price reacts to patterns like triangles, flags, and wedges. But what if you could spot key bounce or breakout zones even without a clear pattern? In this lesson, you'll learn how Moving Averages act as dynamic support and resistance to help you make smarter entries and exits in real time.

Unlike static horizontal lines, MAs adjust with price, providing dynamic zones of interest. Traders often watch these lines for potential bounce or break opportunities.

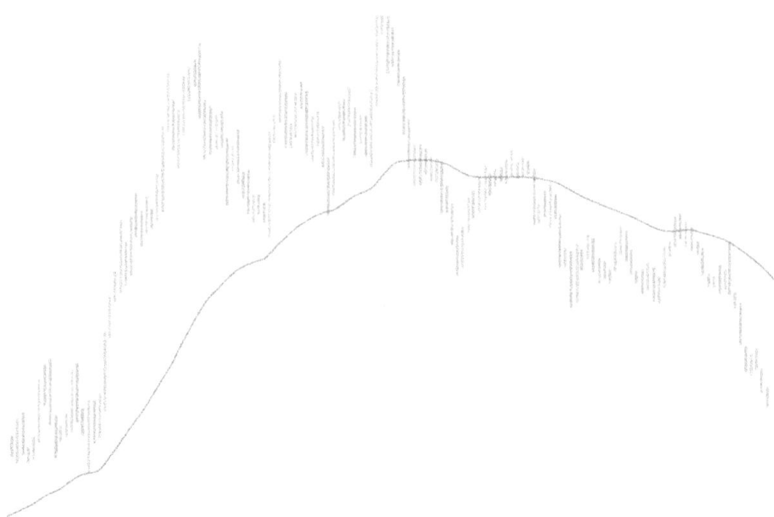

When the price approaches a rising MA from above, it may act as support (1). Conversely, a falling MA can serve as resistance (2) when the price approaches from below.

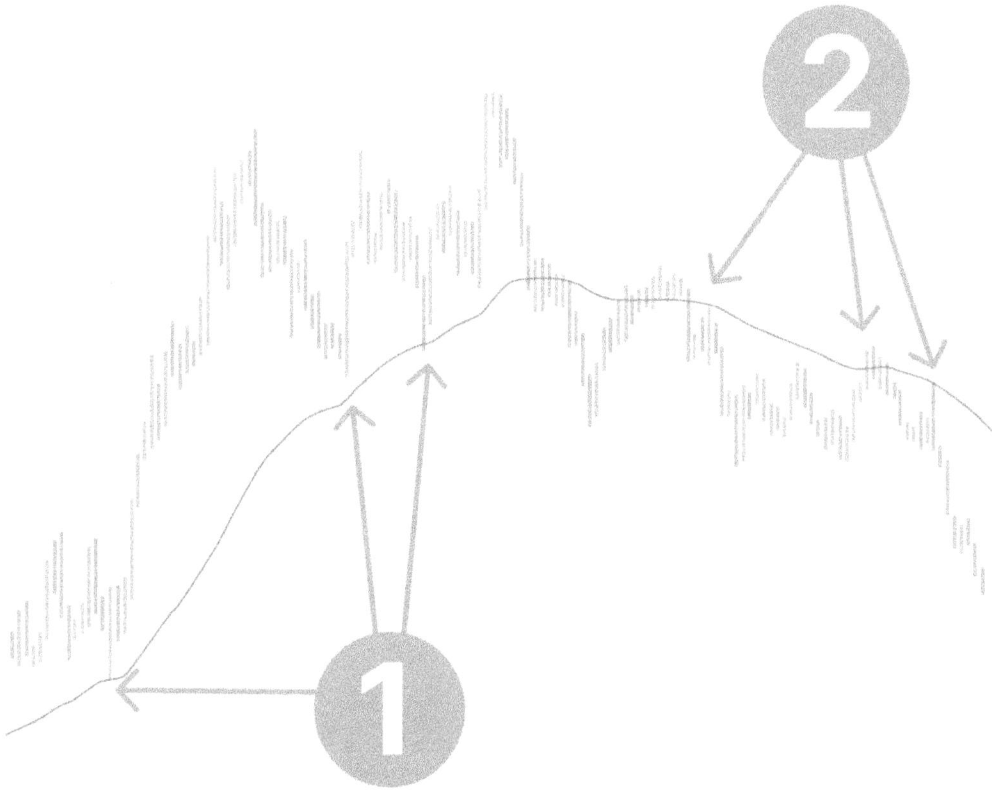

A rising MA acts as support when the price approaches it from above. A falling MA acts as resistance when the price approaches from below.

Traders often use multiple MAs to create a zone. For instance, the area between the 10 EMA and

20 EMA can act as a dynamic support or resistance zone.

This zone acts as a flexible area where the price may bounce or reverse. If price pulls back into the zone, it can signal a good entry with the trend. A strong break below or above may suggest a trend shift. Watch how the price reacts inside the zone to decide your next move.

Make a decision!

You're watching X's chart. Price has pulled back into the zone between the 10 MA and 20 MA, then formed a strong bullish candle bouncing upward. Both MAs are still sloping up. When price pulls back into a rising MA zone and holds, it often signals a continuation of the trend.

What would be the most strategic trading decision at this point?

- Close all positions, because the trend is unclear
- Do nothing, wait for MAs to cross downward
- Enter a long trade, because the MAs acted as support and the price bounced
- Enter a short trade, because the bounce is likely a trap

Answer: Enter a long trade, because the MAs acted as support and the price bounced. The price bounced off the rising MAs, which often act as support during an uptrend. Entering short or waiting too long could mean missing the continuation move. Always check the slope and reaction around the MAs. Price pulled back into the dynamic support zone created by the 10 and 20 MAs, then bounced upward with a strong candle. Both MAs are still rising, confirming bullish momentum - a classic continuation setup.

Remember, MAs are not foolproof. Price may overshoot or undershoot these lines. To make smarter trading decisions, traders often combine MAs with RSI for momentum, candlestick patterns for confirmation, and support/ resistance zones for context. This helps filter false signals and improves timing.

What's your move?

You notice the price is consistently above both the 10 and 20 MA, and RSI is at 66.33. The trend is clearly upward with higher lows and strong momentum. Being near overbought doesn't always mean reversal - check trend context and wait for smart entry. What's the most logical decision?

- Wait for RSI to hit 70 before buying
- Enter a long trade immediately
- Look for a pullback to the MAs for entry
- Sell now because RSI is high

Answer: Look for a pullback to the MAs for entry. While the trend is strong and momentum is bullish, jumping in after multiple green candles and near-overbought RSI can be risky. Waiting for a minor pullback to the dynamic support zone (10-20 MA) offers a safer, lower-risk entry in the direction of the trend.

You've just learned how MAs can act as dynamic support and resistance, offering flexible zones for smarter trade entries and exits. Ready to test your knowledge? Let's dive into a quick quiz before we move on.

QUIZ: Pattern Recognition

1. What does it mean when the fast Moving Average crosses above the slow Moving Average, and RSI is above 50?

A. A bearish crossover signal
B. A sign to stay out of the market
C. A potential bullish signal confirmed by momentum
D. RSI is likely to reverse soon

2. In an ascending triangle, what usually signals a strong bullish breakout?

A. Price breaks above resistance with RSI holding above 50
B. RSI drops below 30
C. Price makes a lower low
D. Moving Averages are flat

3. Which of the following confirms a descending triangle breakdown?

A. RSI rises above 70
B. Price stays above support
C. RSI drops below 50, and price breaks support
D. MA crossover to the upside

4. How do traders typically react to a confirmed Head & Shoulders pattern with RSI showing lower highs?

A. Ignore the signal and hold
B. Enter a short trade after the neckline breaks
C. Buy at the neckline
D. Wait for RSI to rise above 70

5. What signals a strong bullish confirmation in a bullish flag pattern?

A. MA crossover to the downside
B. RSI near 30 and price below MAs
C. Sideways movement with flat MAs
D. Price above rising MAs and RSI above 50

6. Which indicator combination weakens a rectangle breakout signal?

A. RSI above 50 and upward-sloping MAs
B. RSI below 30 and falling MAs

C. RSI near 50 and flat MAs
D. Price and RSI breaking above resistance

7. What usually happens after a double bottom pattern forms and breaks the neckline?

A. A bullish reversal
B. A continuation of the downtrend
C. Traders enter short positions
D. Market stays range-bound

8. In a falling wedge, which signal confirms a potential long entry?

A. Price forms lower highs and lower lows with no breakout
B. Breakout above the wedge with RSI above 50
C. RSI below 30 and MAs sloping down
D. MAs flatten and RSI stays near 40

9. The price just bounced upward from the 10 and 20 MA zone, and both MAs are pointing up. What does this usually mean?

A. It's unclear - better to wait
B. The trend is ending - time to sell
C. It's a good time to consider buying

D. RSI is too high to trade

10. Which sign shows that an uptrend is still healthy?

A. Price is above rising moving averages and RSI stays above 50
B. Moving averages are flat and RSI is near 50
C. Price is below both moving averages and RSI is falling
D. Price is bouncing between support and resistance with no clear trend

Answer: 1. C; 2. A; 3. C; 4. B; 5. D; 6. C; 7. A; 8. B; 9. C; 10. A

Chapter 5: MACD Mastery

Lesson 1: MACD Basics

Let's explore the MACD indicator!

This lesson will guide you through the fundamentals of the MACD indicator. You'll see why MACD is more than just a crossover tool; it's a dynamic way to read the strength behind price action. By the end of this lesson, you'll know how to read and apply it.

Understanding MACD starts with strong basics. Let's review our knowledge of MACD components!

- MACD Line: Difference between two EMAs
- Signal Line: Smoothed average of the MACD Line
- MACD histogram: Gap between MACD and Signal Line

Those are the key parts of the MACD. Now, let's break them down one by one and see how they work together in real trading.

As you know, MACD stands for Moving Average Convergence Divergence. It tracks momentum and trend changes based on moving averages.

Let's start with the MACD Line. It measures the difference between two moving averages - a fast one (12 periods) and a slow one (26 periods).

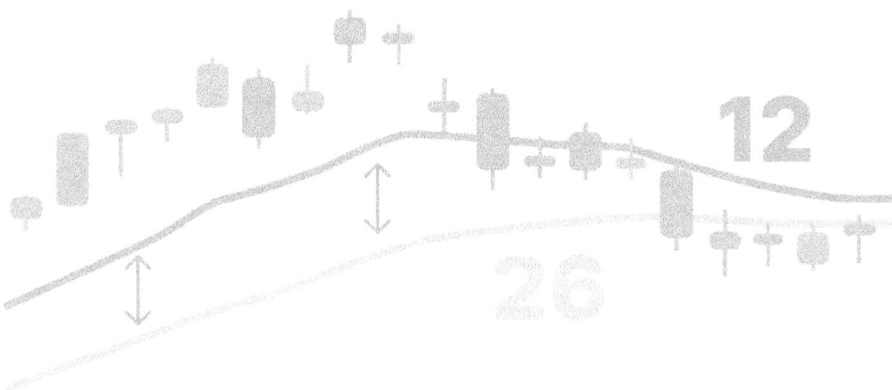

When the MACD Line rises, it means the faster-moving price is pulling away from the slower one, showing stronger upward momentum. When it falls, it means downward momentum is building.

The Signal Line (1) is a slower, smoother version of the MACD Line (2). It's a moving average (9-period EMA) of the MACD Line itself. It doesn't react as fast, but it filters out false signals and gives you a second opinion.

Do you remember?

In the last lesson, we learned about MACD crossovers.

If the MACD Line crosses above the Signal Line, what does it usually signal? Remember, crossing above means buyers are gaining strength!

- No change
- Increase in volatility
- Sell opportunity
- Buy opportunity

Answer: Buy opportunity. When the MACD Line crosses above the Signal Line, it usually means bullish momentum is building and often points to a buy setup.

The Histogram shows the distance between the MACD and the Signal Line. If the Histogram is above the zero line, it shows bullish momentum. If it's below the zero line, it shows bearish momentum. Bigger bars mean stronger momentum; smaller bars mean weakening momentum.

When the MACD Histogram bars expand upward, it indicates that bullish momentum is strengthening. The bigger the bars, the more powerful the ongoing trend. Traders often see this as a sign to stay with the trend or look for continuation setups.

Traders don't solely rely on just one part of the MACD. They analyze the MACD Line, the Signal Line, and the Histogram together to fully understand market momentum, trend strength, and potential reversals. So, let's practice using MACD!

Can you read the full MACD story?

Look carefully at the MACD chart around late November to early December.

Watch if the MACD Line crosses above or below the Signal Line, check if the Histogram is growing or shrinking, and notice whether it's above or below the zero line. Using the MACD Line (1), Signal Line (2), and Histogram together, what is the best interpretation of the market situation?

- A bearish crossover has occurred, momentum is weakening, and caution is needed
- Momentum is strong, the bullish trend is accelerating, and the MACD supports further upside
- There is no clear signal from the MACD; the market is neutral
- A bullish crossover just happened, and momentum is strengthening

Answer: A bearish crossover has occurred, momentum is weakening, and caution is needed. Always use all three elements together. Momentum is actually fading. The MACD Line has crossed below the Signal Line, the Histogram is shrinking and moving below zero - all signs of weakening momentum and a possible trend reversal.

Great job! Now that you can confidently read MACD signals, here is one more thing. Before you act on a signal, make sure the MACD Line moves clearly up or down. Check that a real crossover between the MACD Line and Signal Line has happened, not just small noise.

Look at the Histogram - if it's growing, the trend is getting stronger; if it's shrinking, momentum is slowing down. See where the Histogram is compared to the zero line - above means bullish strength, below means bearish pressure.

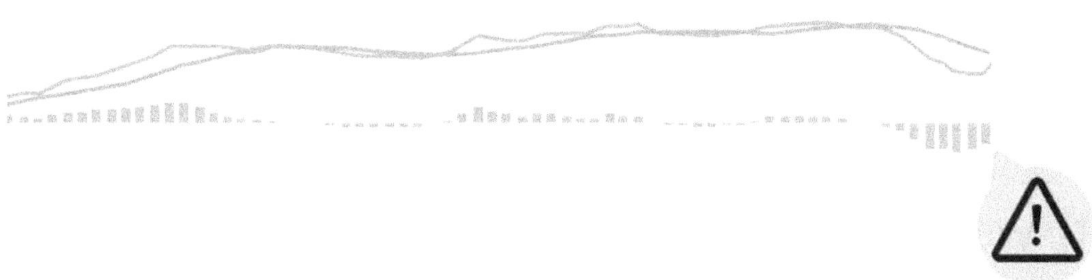

MACD signals checklist

Which 3 checks should you always make before acting on a MACD signal? Always check the MACD Line direction, the crossover, the Histogram strength, and confirm with real price action before making a trade.

- Trade only if price is flat
- MACD Line rising or falling
- Zero line doesn't matter
- Histogram supports trend
- Meaningful crossover happened
- Ignore price action signals

Answer:

- MACD Line rising or falling
- Histogram supports trend
- Meaningful crossover happened

You now know how to read the MACD Line, Signal Line, and Histogram together to spot momentum shifts and confirm trading signals. Next, we'll dive deeper into the MACD Histogram and learn how it reveals real market momentum.

Lesson 2: MACD Histogram & Momentum

Understanding market momentum with the MACD histogram

Now that you have a solid understanding of how the MACD works, let's focus on one of its most powerful parts: the histogram. By the end of this lesson, you'll know how to read the histogram, recognize momentum changes, and use them to make smarter trading decisions.

Momentum is not simply about whether prices are rising or falling - it tells you how much energy is behind those moves. Strong momentum means a price move is powerful and likely to continue. Weak momentum suggests a move may be slowing down or losing strength, even if the price is still going in the same direction.

The MACD histogram visualizes momentum changes in the market. When the histogram bars expand, it means momentum is increasing, suggesting that the current trend is gaining strength. When the histogram bars contract, it signals that momentum is weakening, showing that the trend is losing power.

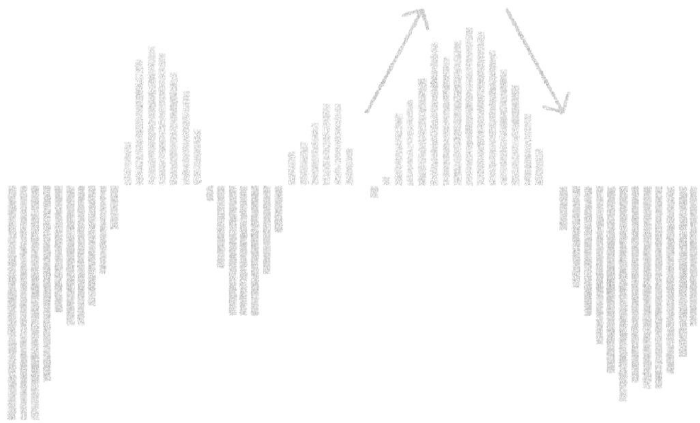

The position of the histogram relative to the zero line also matters. When the histogram is above zero (1), it shows bullish momentum; when it is below zero (2), it shows bearish momentum.

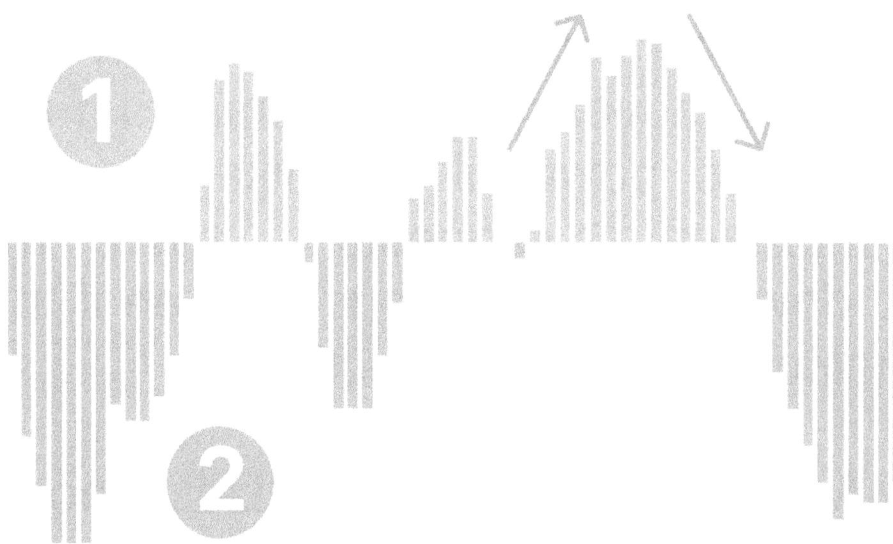

Match the signals

Match each behavior to what it tells you about momentum. Expanding bars show strengthening moves, contracting bars warn of fading strength, and the zero line shows bullish or bearish bias.

- Contracting bars - Momentum increasing
- Expanding bars - Momentum weakening

Answer:

- Contracting bars - Momentum weakening
- Expanding bars - Momentum increasing

Match the signals

Match each behavior to what it tells you about trend bias. Expanding bars show strengthening moves, contracting bars warn of fading strength, and the zero line shows bullish or bearish bias.

- Above zero line - Bearish momentum
- Below zero line - Bullish momentum

Answer:

- Above zero line - Bullish momentum
- Below zero line - Bearish momentum

Traders use the MACD histogram to spot potential trend reversals and price swings. By reading changes in momentum, they can anticipate when a move might slow down, reverse, or strengthen.

Good job! Now, let's break down how the MACD histogram shows momentum changes in real trading. When the histogram crosses the zero line, it often marks important signal moments.

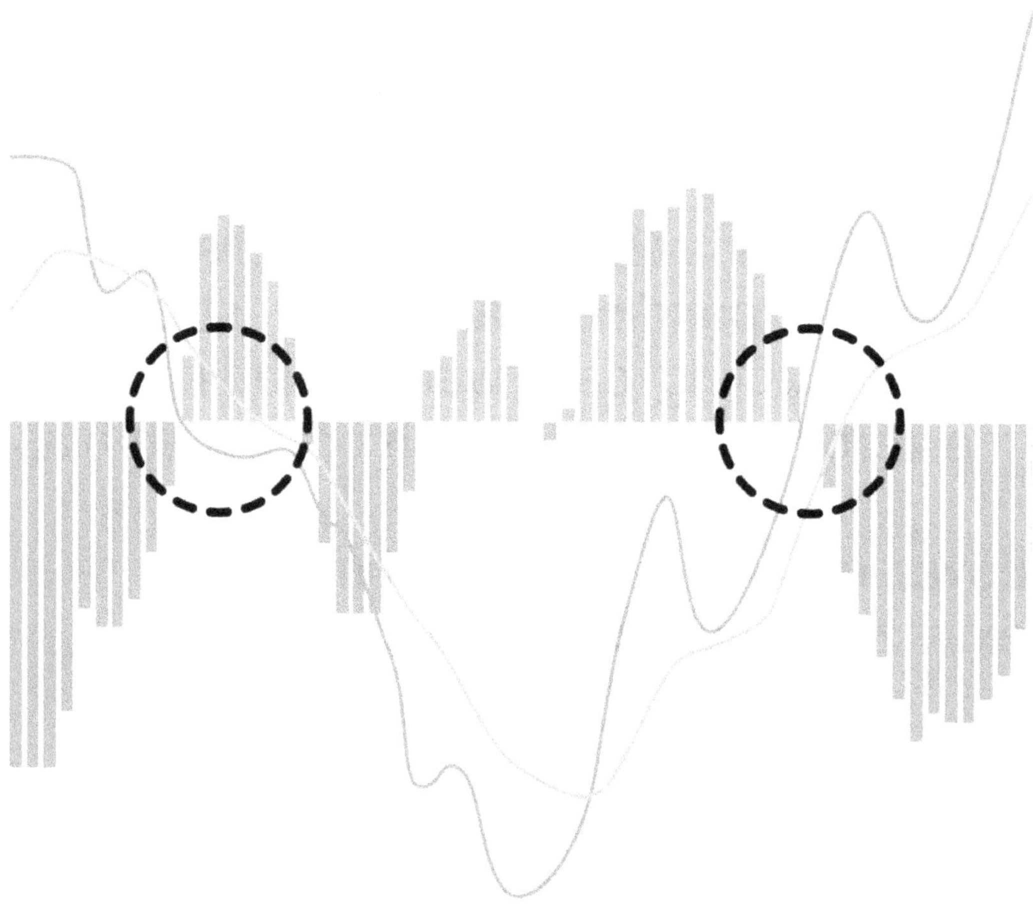

If the histogram crosses above zero, it usually means the MACD Line has crossed above the Signal Line - a classic buy signal. Meanwhile, if the histogram crosses below zero, it usually means the MACD Line has crossed below the Signal Line, often seen as a sell signal.

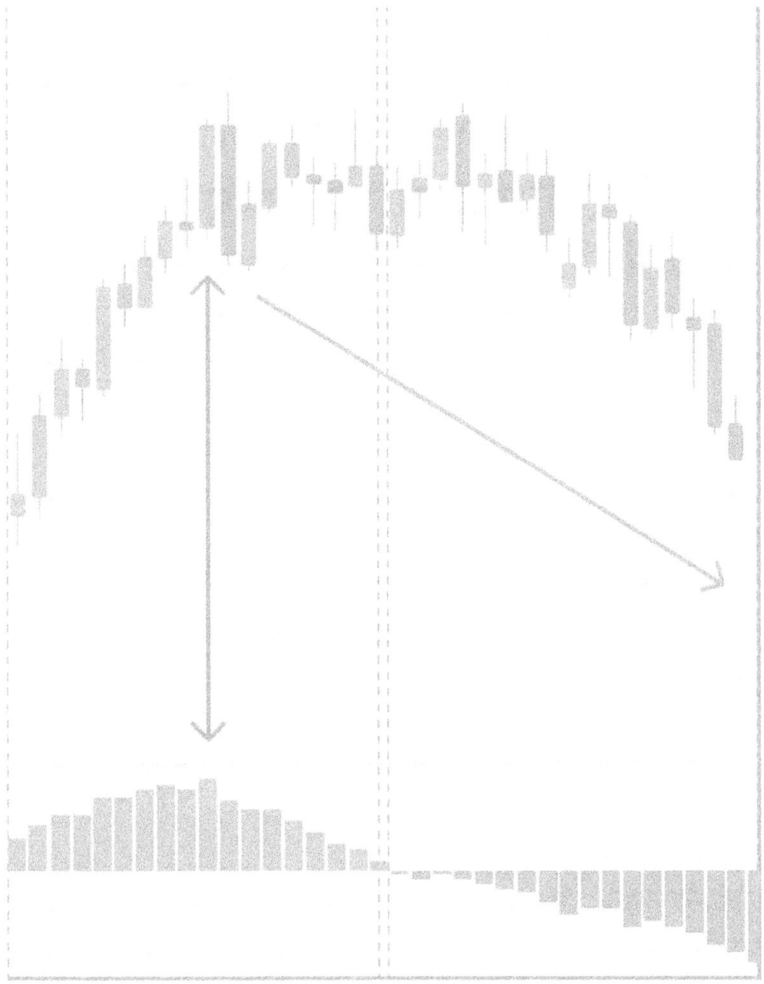

Zero crossings show that momentum has shifted enough to change the relationship between fast and slow trends. Many traders watch these moments closely, but smart traders confirm them with other evidence.

What's your move?

You notice that the Histogram bars are shrinking upward, and the MACD Line is getting closer to the Signal Line. You are currently not in a position. Shrinking bearish momentum and converging lines suggest a potential change, but smart traders always wait for confirmation before acting.

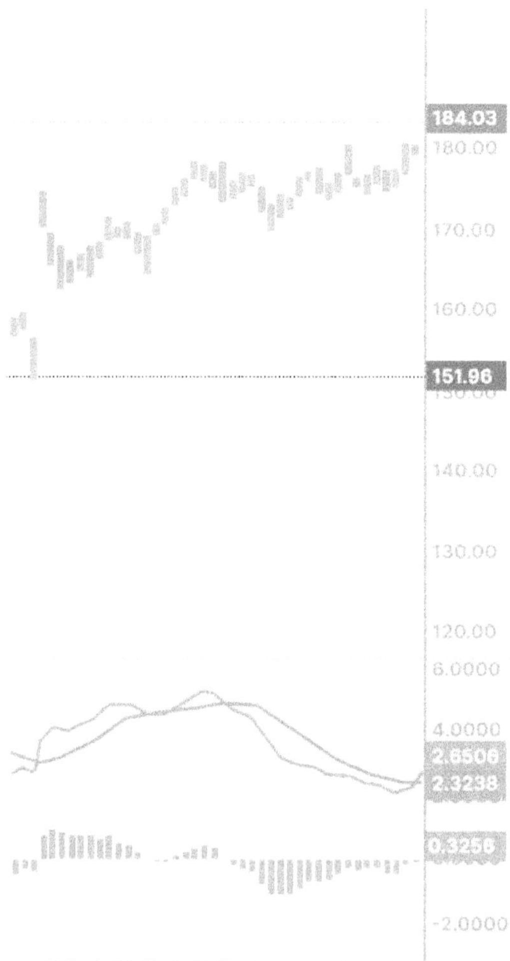

What would be the most logical action?

- Stay out of the market because momentum is still bearish
- Short the market, expecting bearish momentum to continue
- Start preparing for a potential bullish entry if further confirmation appears
- Immediately enter a long position without waiting for confirmation

Answer: Start preparing for a potential bullish entry if further confirmation appears. Shrinking bearish momentum is a warning that the trend might change, but acting too soon without confirmation can lead to false signals. The histogram and MACD behavior hint at a weakening bearish trend, but confirmation, like a crossover or bullish price pattern, is needed before entering.

Additionally, peaks and troughs in the MACD histogram can be early warnings that a trend is losing strength. A peak happens when bullish momentum is strong, but now starts weakening. A trough happens when bearish momentum is strong but now begins to fade.

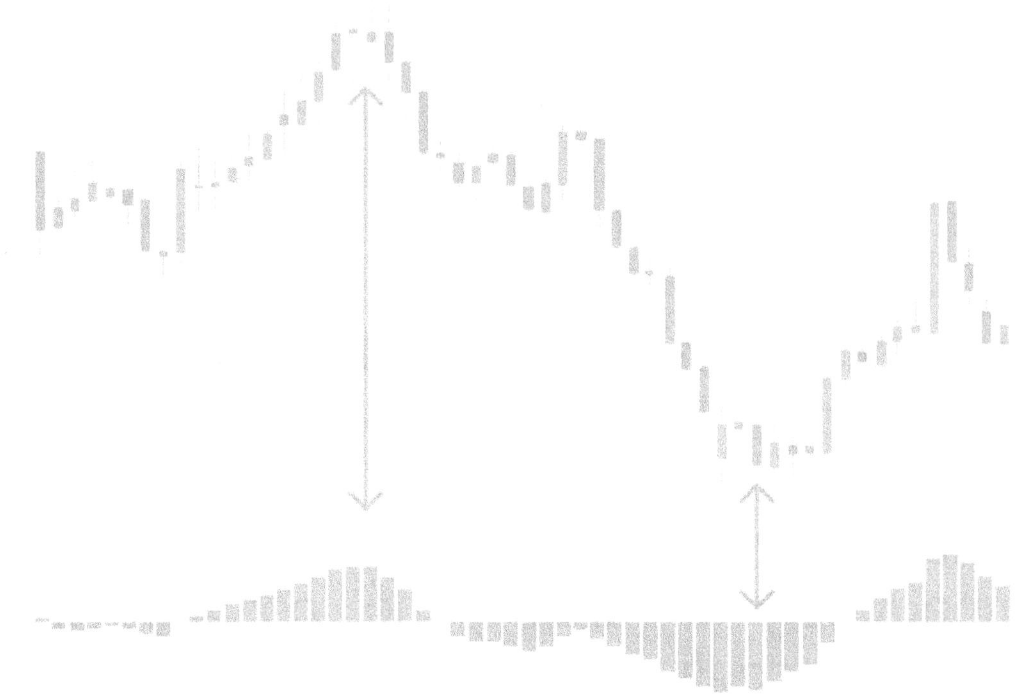

When the histogram forms a peak or trough and then shrinks back toward the zero line, it often means the trend could slow down, consolidate, or even reverse. However, just like shrinking bars, peaks and troughs alone do not guarantee a reversal. They are signals to pay attention and look for confirmation in price action.

What happens next?

You notice the MACD histogram has peaked and is now shrinking back toward the zero line. The MACD Line is still above the Signal Line, but momentum is clearly slowing down. A shrinking Histogram after a peak signals momentum loss. It doesn't guarantee an immediate reversal, but warns of possible slowdown or change.

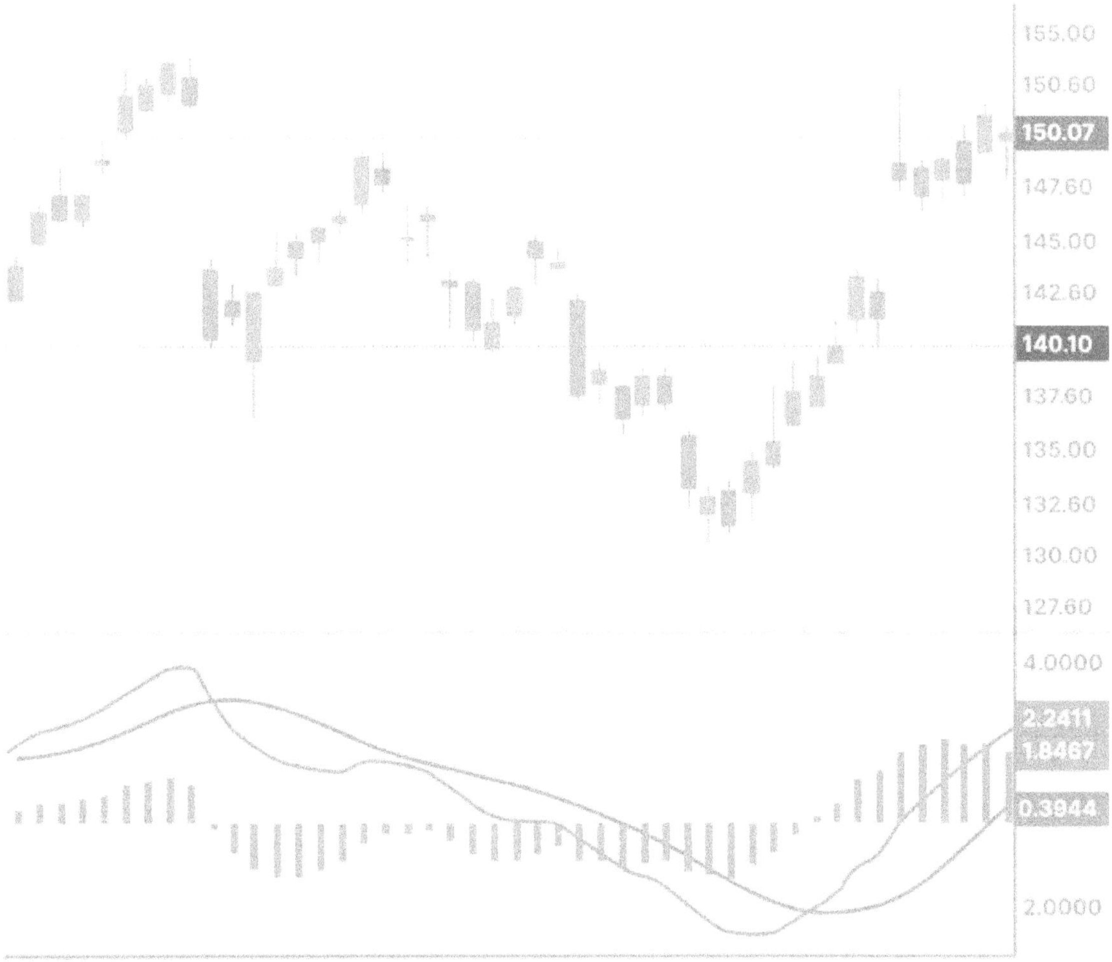

What is the most likely scenario to watch for?

- Momentum will recover sharply without any warning
- The market might pause, consolidate, or prepare for a possible reversal

- The trend might continue strongly without any slowdown
- A strong bearish breakdown is certain and immediate

Answer: The market might pause, consolidate, or prepare for a possible reversal. Shrinking after a peak shows that strength is fading. This often leads to consolidation or hesitation before a new move develops.

You now know how to use the MACD histogram to spot momentum shifts, peaks, and slowdowns! In the next lesson, we'll learn how to combine MACD with trend direction and price patterns to make even better trading decisions.

Lesson 3: MACD Divergence Use

Combining MACD with trends and price patterns

Now that you know how to read the MACD Histogram, it's time to take your skills further by combining MACD signals with trend direction and price patterns. By the end of this lesson, you'll know how to confirm MACD setups using the overall trend and important price action.

When the MACD and price charts move together, they confirm the strength of the current trend. Rising prices with a rising MACD, or falling prices with a falling MACD, show that momentum supports the direction of the move.

What's the market showing?

Look at the price and the MACD chart. When both price and MACD move upward together, it shows healthy momentum supporting the trend. Prices are rising, but what does the MACD tell you about the strength behind the move?

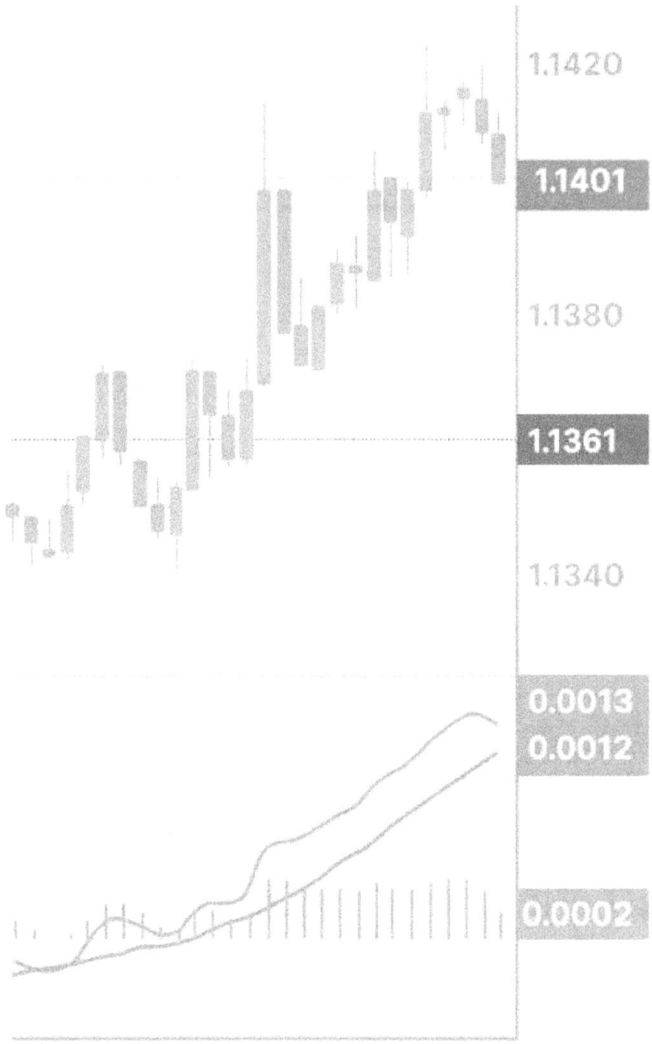

- The price is rising, and the MACD is also rising, confirming strong bullish momentum
- The price is rising, but the MACD is falling, suggesting a bearish divergence
- The price is rising, but the MACD Histogram is deeply negative, warning of a possible crash
- The price is rising, but the MACD is flat, warning of weakening momentum

Answer: The price is rising, and the MACD is also rising, confirming strong bullish momentum. Remember, when MACD rises with price, it confirms that the trend is supported by healthy momentum. Watch for divergence signs if momentum starts to weaken. A strong alignment between price action and MACD indicates that bullish momentum is still under control.

However, when the MACD (1) and price start (2) moving in opposite directions - a situation called divergence - it signals that momentum may be weakening. This often serves as an early warning that the current trend could slow down, lose strength, or even reverse.

Bullish divergence happens when the price makes lower lows, but the MACD forms higher lows. This suggests that bearish momentum is weakening, even if sellers are still active. It can signal a potential reversal where buyers may soon regain control, but confirmation is needed before trading.

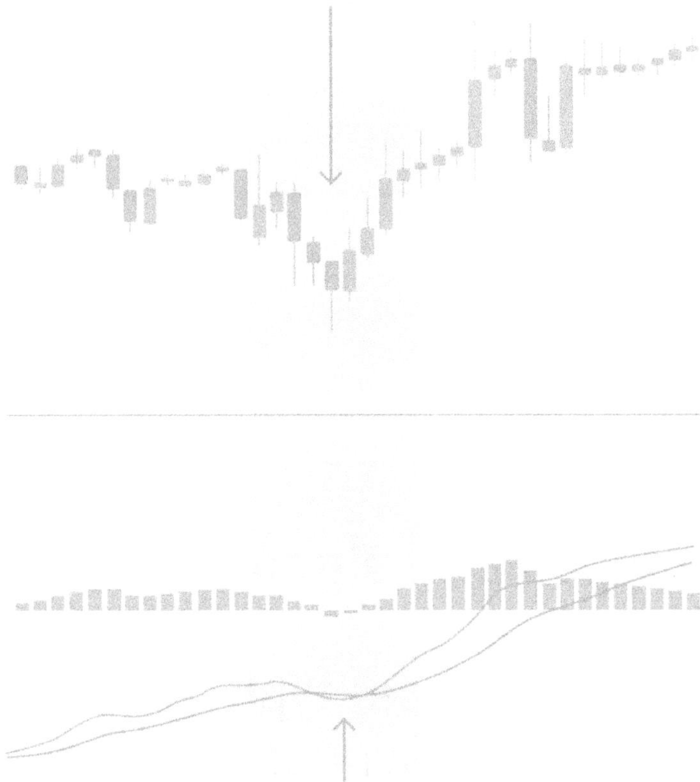

In bearish divergence, the price keeps pushing higher, but the MACD cannot keep up, suggesting that buyers are losing strength. This can be an early warning of a slowdown or a possible bearish reversal, but as always, further price action confirmation strengthens the setup.

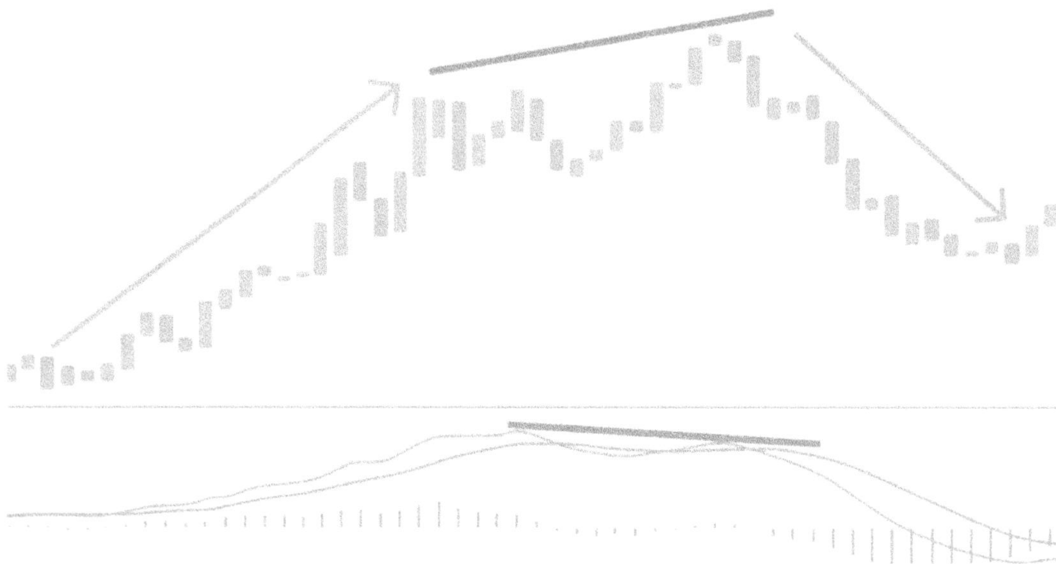

Divergence types and signals

Match each divergence type to the price and MACD behavior it describes. Bullish divergence happens when the price keeps falling but the MACD starts rising. Bearish divergence happens when the price keeps rising but the MACD weakens. No divergence means they move in the same direction.

- Bullish divergence - Price and MACD are the same

- Bearish divergence - Price is down, MACD is up
- No divergence - Price is up, MACD is down

Answer:

- Bullish divergence - Price is down, MACD is up
- Bearish divergence - Price is up, MACD is down
- No divergence - Price and MACD are the same

When spotting bullish or bearish divergence with the MACD, make sure there is enough space between the first and second highs or lows, usually at least ten price bars apart. Markets move in waves, and a full wave between points gives a more reliable signal.

If the highs or lows are too close together, it could mean that the current wave is still developing and the market has not yet completed its move.

The divergence should also be obvious. A clear lower high or higher low on the MACD compared to price action shows a stronger momentum shift. The clearer and more separated the divergence, the more trustworthy the signal becomes.

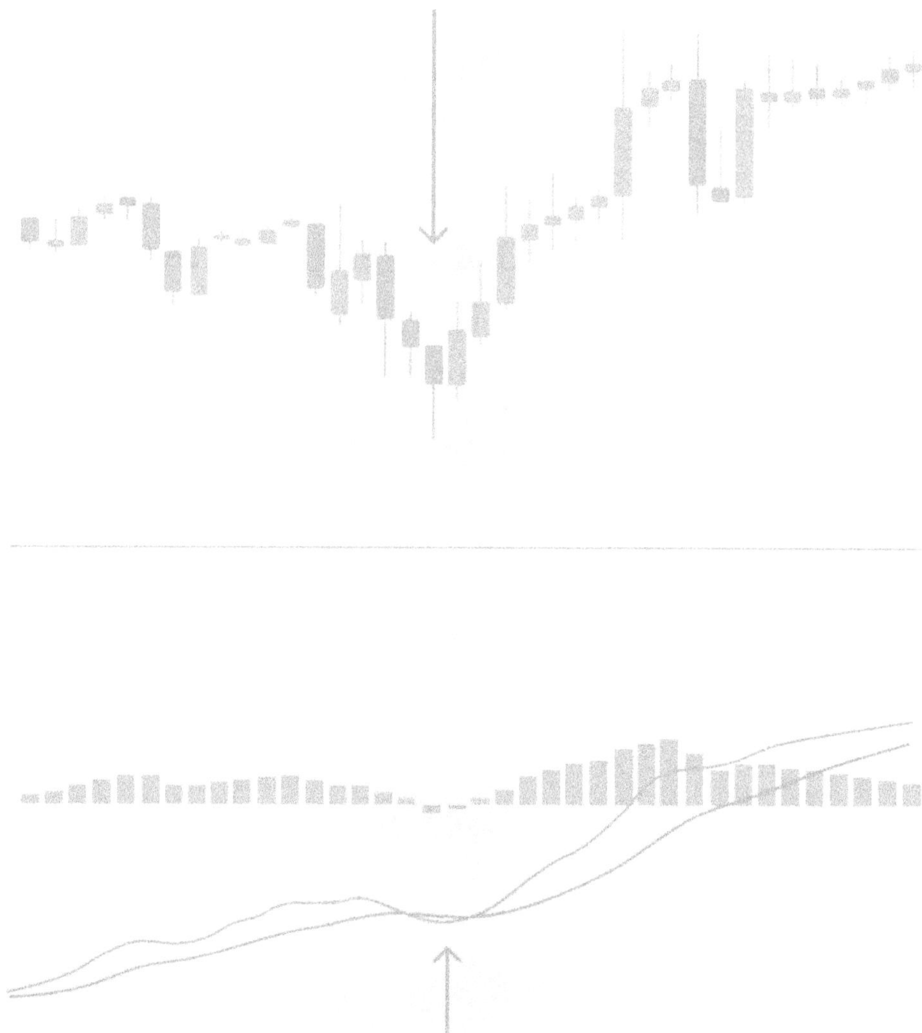

Time to practice!

You notice the price has made lower lows, while the MACD has formed higher lows, creating a clear bullish divergence. The price is now starting to rise after the divergence appears. Bullish divergence suggests a potential reversal upward, but smart traders always confirm the move with price action before entering. What is the smartest action to take?

- Wait for the MACD to cross below the Signal Line before making any decision
- Stay out of the market because divergence means nothing
- Immediately open a short position because the price is falling
- Prepare to buy, but wait for confirmation, like a breakout or bullish candle

Answer: Prepare to buy, but wait for confirmation, like a breakout or bullish candle. Divergence gives early warning, but you still need to confirm the move with price action before trading. Bullish divergence shows weakening selling pressure, but waiting for price confirmation improves your chances of entering at the right time.

What's your move?

You see the price making a lower low, but the MACD is making a higher low. Price has not yet reversed strongly - momentum is just starting to shift. Bullish divergence warns that selling pressure is weakening, but price confirmation is still needed before entering a trade.

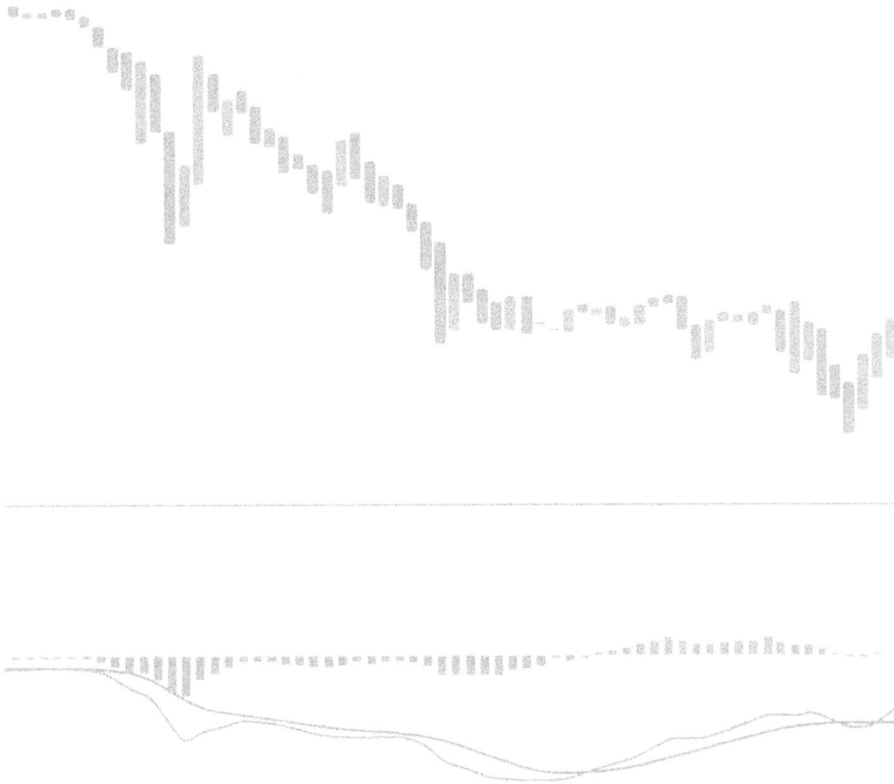

What is the smartest action to take now?

- Watch closely for bullish confirmation, like a breakout or strong bullish candle
- Open a short position expecting another price drop
- Immediately open a large long position
- Ignore the divergence because the market is still bearish

Answer: Watch closely for bullish confirmation, like a breakout or strong bullish candle. Divergence shows weakening selling pressure, but it's safer to wait for confirmation before making a trade decision. Divergence is an early signal that momentum may change. Waiting for price confirmation helps you avoid false entries.

Excellent! You've learned how to spot divergence, recognize momentum shifts, and understand when price and MACD agree or disagree. Up next, we'll have a short quiz to review everything you've learned and make sure you're ready to apply these skills confidently.

QUIZ: MACD Mastery

1. What does the MACD Line represent?

A. The distance from the zero line
B. The difference between the two EMAs (typically 12 and 26 periods)
C. A moving average of the Signal Line
D. The difference between price and volume

2. When the MACD Line crosses above the Signal Line, what does it usually indicate?

A. A buy opportunity due to bullish momentum
B. A strong sell signal
C. An increase in volatility
D. That price will stay flat

3. What does the MACD Histogram show?

A. The total volume of trades
B. The actual price trend

C. The distance between the MACD Line and the Signal Line
D. The size of candlesticks

4. What does it mean when the MACD Histogram bars are shrinking?

A. A reversal is guaranteed
B. Momentum is weakening
C. Momentum is accelerating
D. A sideways market has begun

5. What does bullish divergence look like on the chart?

A. Price and MACD both make higher highs
B. Price and MACD move exactly together
C. Price makes lower lows while the MACD makes higher lows
D. MACD makes lower lows while the price is flat

6. What should you do if you spot bullish divergence?

A. Ignore the divergence because the price is falling
B. Open a long position immediately

C. Prepare to buy, but wait for confirmation from the price
D. Open a short position because the momentum is low

7. What confirms a reliable MACD signal?

A. Only a crossover
B. A sharp move without checking the lines
C. Just the Histogram shape
D. MACD Line direction, meaningful crossover, and Histogram strength

8. If the MACD Histogram crosses above the zero line, what does it typically mean?

A. The trend is ending
B. The market is oversold
C. Volume is increasing
D. MACD Line has crossed above the Signal Line

9. What does bearish divergence suggest?

A. Price is falling, and MACD is also falling
B. Price is rising, but momentum is fading, warning of a possible reversal

C. The Signal Line is unreliable
D. Momentum is strengthening

10. When should a trader act on a MACD signal?

A. As soon as one line moves
B. Without checking the trend
C. When the Histogram touches zero
D. After confirming the crossover, Histogram direction, and price action

Answer: 1. B; 2. A; 3. C; 4. B; 5. C; 6. C; 7. D; 8. D; 9. B; 10. D

Chapter 6: Bollinger Band Tactic

Lesson 1: Bollinger Band Structure

Understanding Bollinger Bands

Bollinger Bands are a popular technical analysis tool used to visualize price volatility and potential turning points in the market. In this lesson, you'll learn how these bands form a dynamic range around price and what their movement reveals about market conditions.

Bollinger Bands help traders measure market volatility and spot price reversals. By visualizing the price range, they assess if an asset is overbought or oversold, aiding trading decisions. Before we dive in, let's quickly recap the key components of Bollinger Bands!

Bollinger Bands components

Match each component of Bollinger Bands with what it represents! Remember, the middle line is the SMA, while the upper and lower bands help define overbought and oversold conditions based on standard deviations.

- Lower band - 20-day simple moving average
- Middle line - Two standard deviations below
- Upper band - Two standard deviations above

Answer:

- Lower band - Two standard deviations below
- Middle line - 20-day simple moving average
- Upper band - Two standard deviations above

Now that we've reviewed the key components, let's explore how Bollinger Bands help traders make informed decisions!

Traders choose a 20-day SMA because it matches a typical month of trading, which allows traders to capture a short-term trend without being overly reactive to daily volatility. The 20-day SMA reflects the near-term trend, acting as a baseline for price movement.

The SMA serves as the "center line" around which the upper and lower bands are drawn. The upper and lower bands are placed two standard deviations above and below it, respectively. Standard deviations help identify the range of typical price fluctuations based on the recent price history.

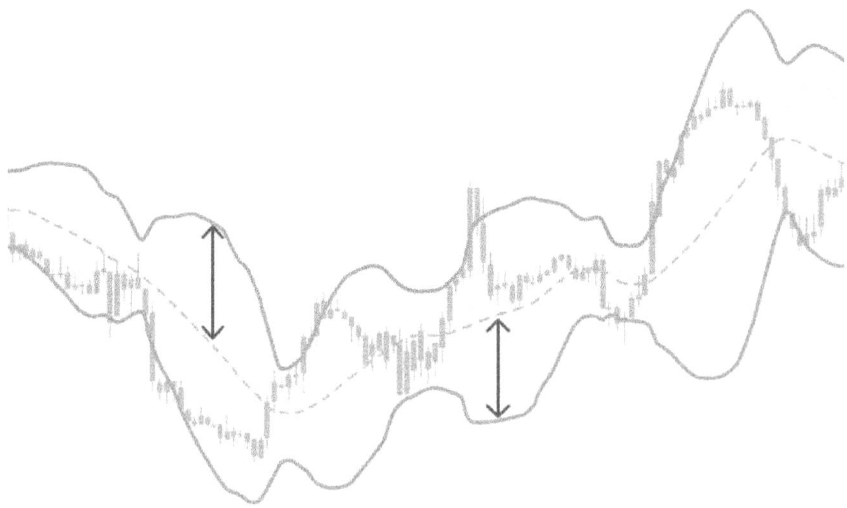

When the price nears the upper band, it could signal an overbought market, suggesting a potential pullback. On the other hand, when the price approaches the lower band, it may indicate an oversold condition, presenting a potential buying opportunity.

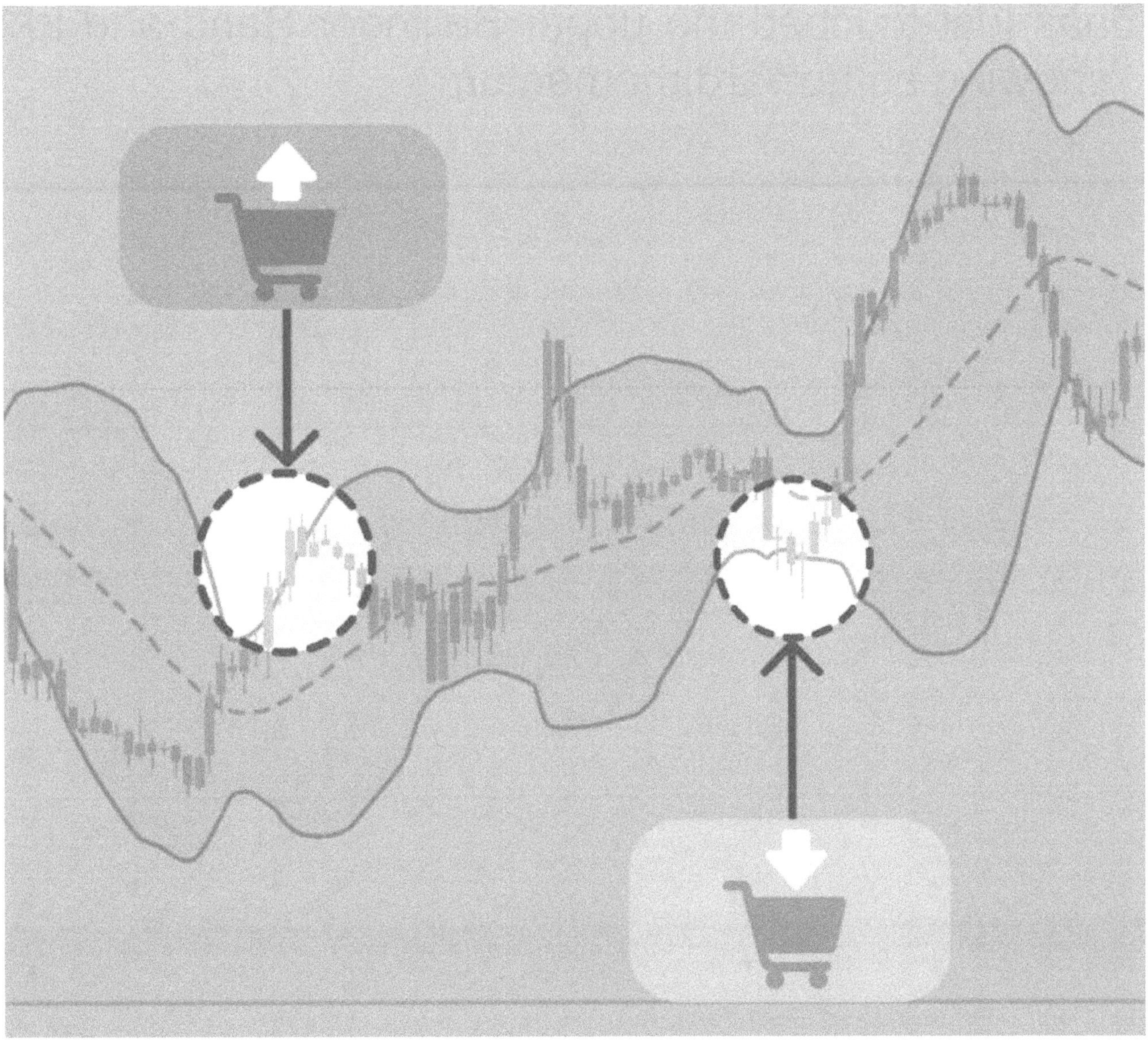

When the price is near the 20-day SMA, it suggests a neutral market. In this case, traders typically wait for confirmation of a breakout.

Trading decision based on Bollinger Bands

Look at the chart for the USD/JPY pair. The price has just touched the upper Bollinger Band and is showing an upward momentum.

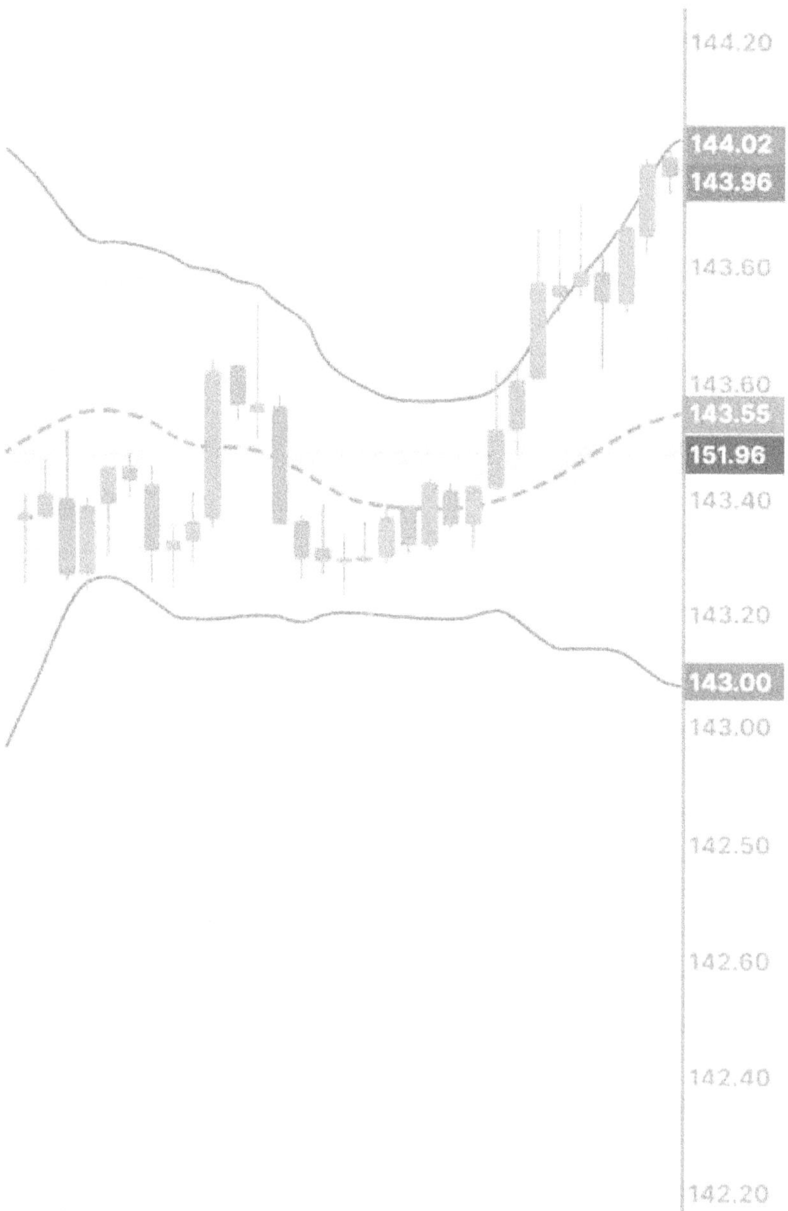

Strong momentum near the upper Bollinger Band suggests the market may be overbought. Consider selling to capture profits, as a pullback is often expected. Always look for confirmation from other indicators before acting. Based on this chart, what is the best course of action?

- Enter a buy position, expecting the price to continue rising
- Sell, expecting a pullback as the price may be overbought
- Hold the position, waiting for confirmation of a breakout
- Enter a short position, expecting a sharp reversal

Answer: Sell, expecting a pullback as the price may be overbought. The price touching the upper Bollinger Band suggests an overbought condition, making it a good opportunity to sell or take profits, anticipating a short-term pullback. Always confirm with other indicators for a more reliable decision.

Nevertheless, keep in mind that Bollinger Bands are secondary indicators, meaning they should not be used in isolation. While they measure volatility and identify potential reversals, combining them with primary indicators like trend lines, RSI, or MACD helps confirm signals and improve accuracy.

For example, combining Bollinger Bands with the Relative Strength Index (RSI) provides a powerful confirmation tool. If the price touches the lower Bollinger Band and the RSI shows oversold conditions (below 30), it signals a potential buying opportunity.

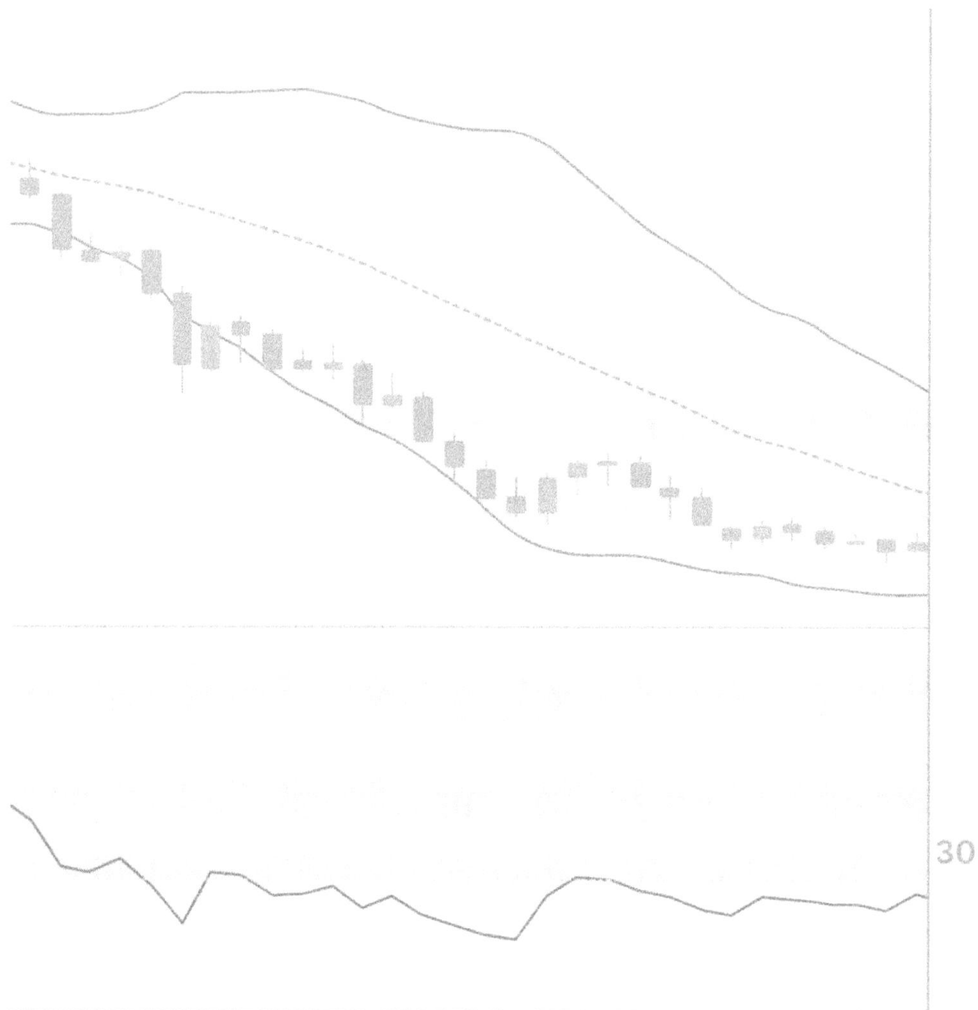

Conversely, if the price reaches the upper band and the RSI indicates overbought conditions (above 70), it suggests a possible selling point.

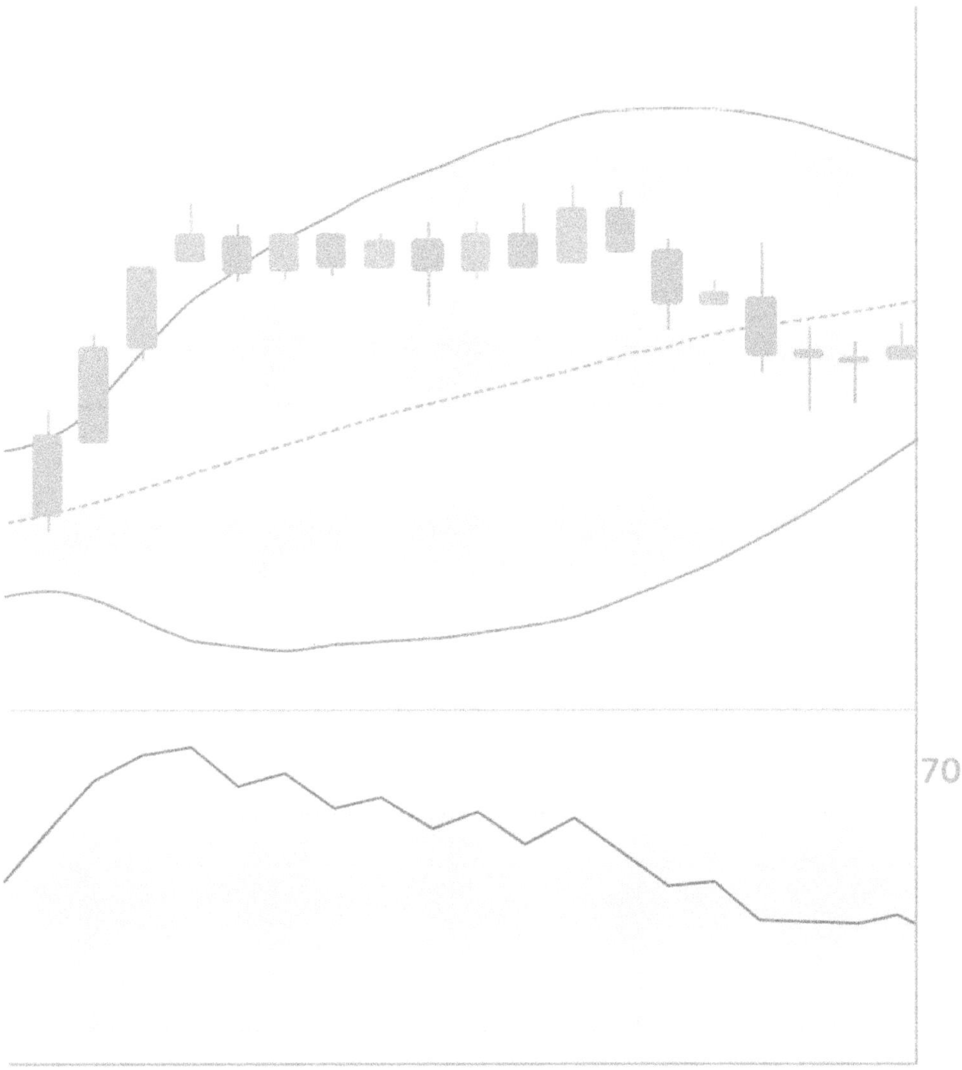

What's your move?

Look at the chart for the USD/EUR pair. The price is approaching the upper Bollinger Band, and the

RSI is approaching the overbought level. When the price touches the upper Bollinger Band and RSI is above 70, it suggests an overbought market, often signaling a potential reversal or pullback.

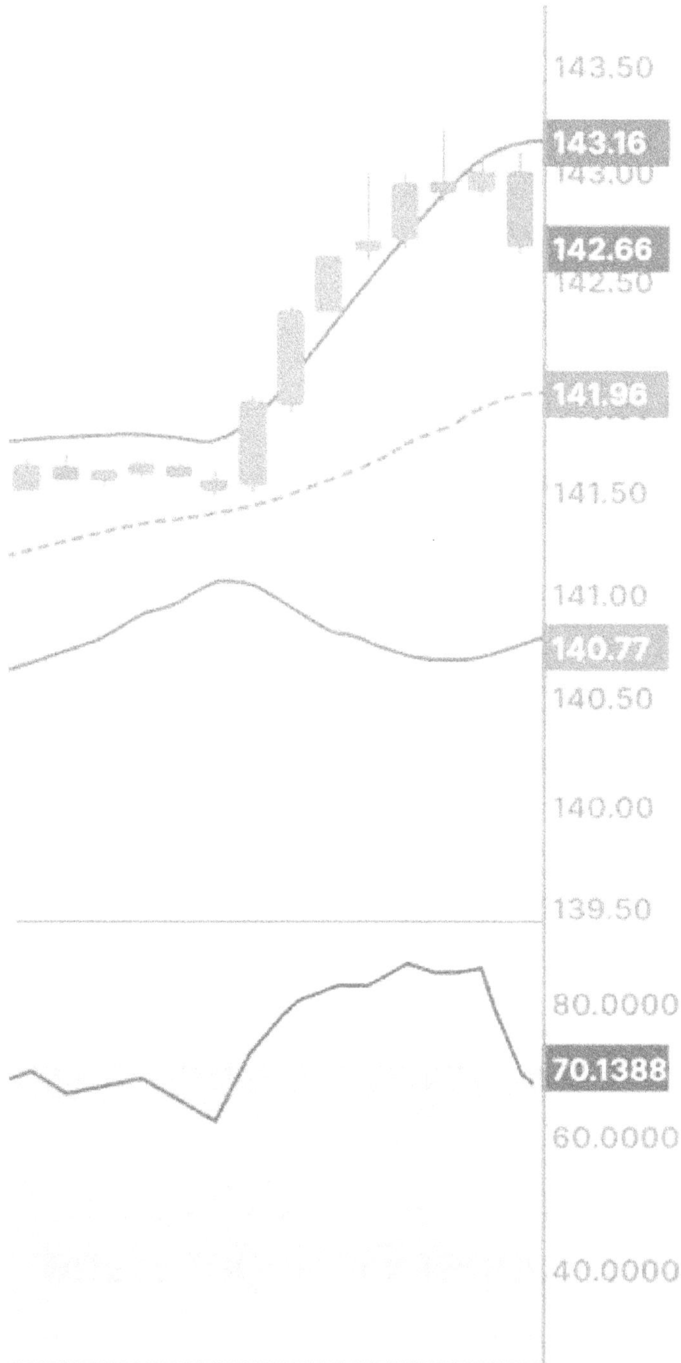

Based on this chart, what should you consider doing?

- Hold, waiting for confirmation of the trend
- Sell, anticipating a price pullback or reversal
- Buy, expecting the price to continue rising
- Enter a short position, expecting a sharp drop

Answer: Sell, anticipating a price pullback or reversal. When the price touches the upper Bollinger Band and the RSI is above 70, it indicates an overbought condition, suggesting that the market may be due for a pullback or reversal. This is a common signal for traders to sell or take profits, anticipating a short-term correction before the trend continues.

We've covered the basics of Bollinger Bands, how to use them to identify overbought and oversold conditions, and how combining them with indicators like RSI can enhance trading decisions. Next, we'll explore squeeze patterns and breakouts, focusing on identifying low volatility and breakout opportunities.

Lesson 2: Squeeze Patterns & Breakouts

Let's learn more about Bollinger Bands!

In this lesson, you'll uncover how Bollinger Bands can help you spot Squeeze Patterns, signaling upcoming breakouts. By the end, you'll be able to identify these key moments when the market is about to make a big move, and trade with confidence.

Let's focus on the Squeeze Pattern, which occurs when the Bollinger Bands tighten, meaning the distance between the upper and lower bands contracts.

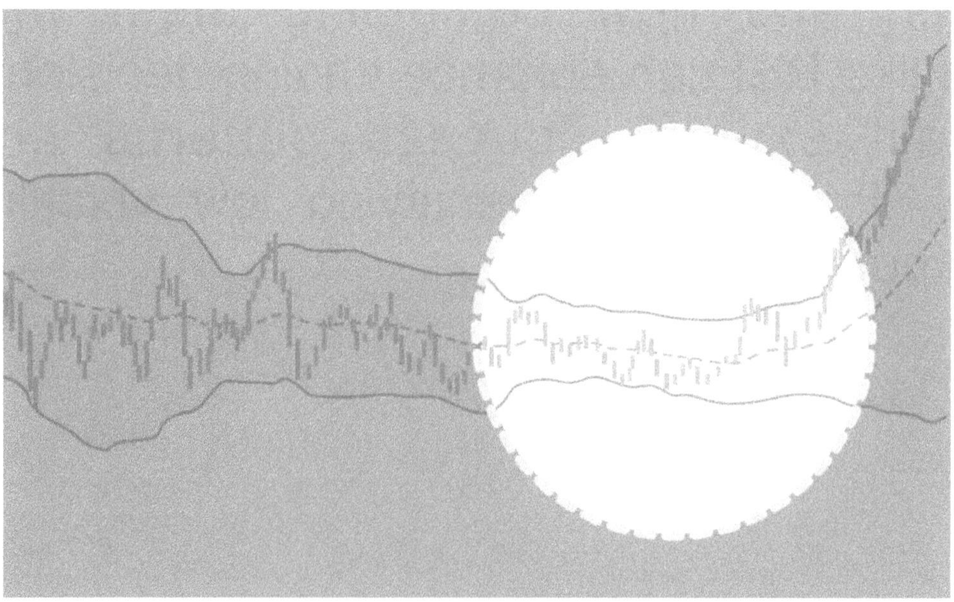

This narrowing happens when price volatility decreases, signaling that the market is in a period of consolidation. The price action tends to slow down, moving within a relatively tight range, as neither buyers nor sellers are dominating the market.

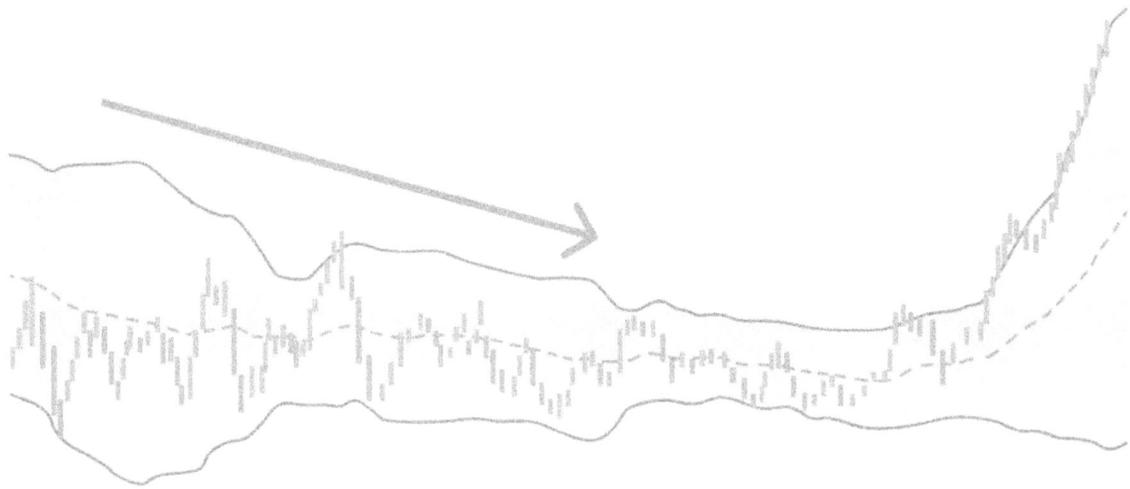

In this phase, market participants are uncertain about the direction of the price, and the volatility typically drops to its lowest point.

The contraction of the Bollinger Bands indicates reduced market movement. This often signals a period of low volatility. It can happen after a strong price move, as the market takes a breather. It may also occur when traders are waiting for important news or economic data.

Traders often see this as a sign that the market is "building pressure." This pressure often results in a breakout once the market picks a direction, which could be either up or down.

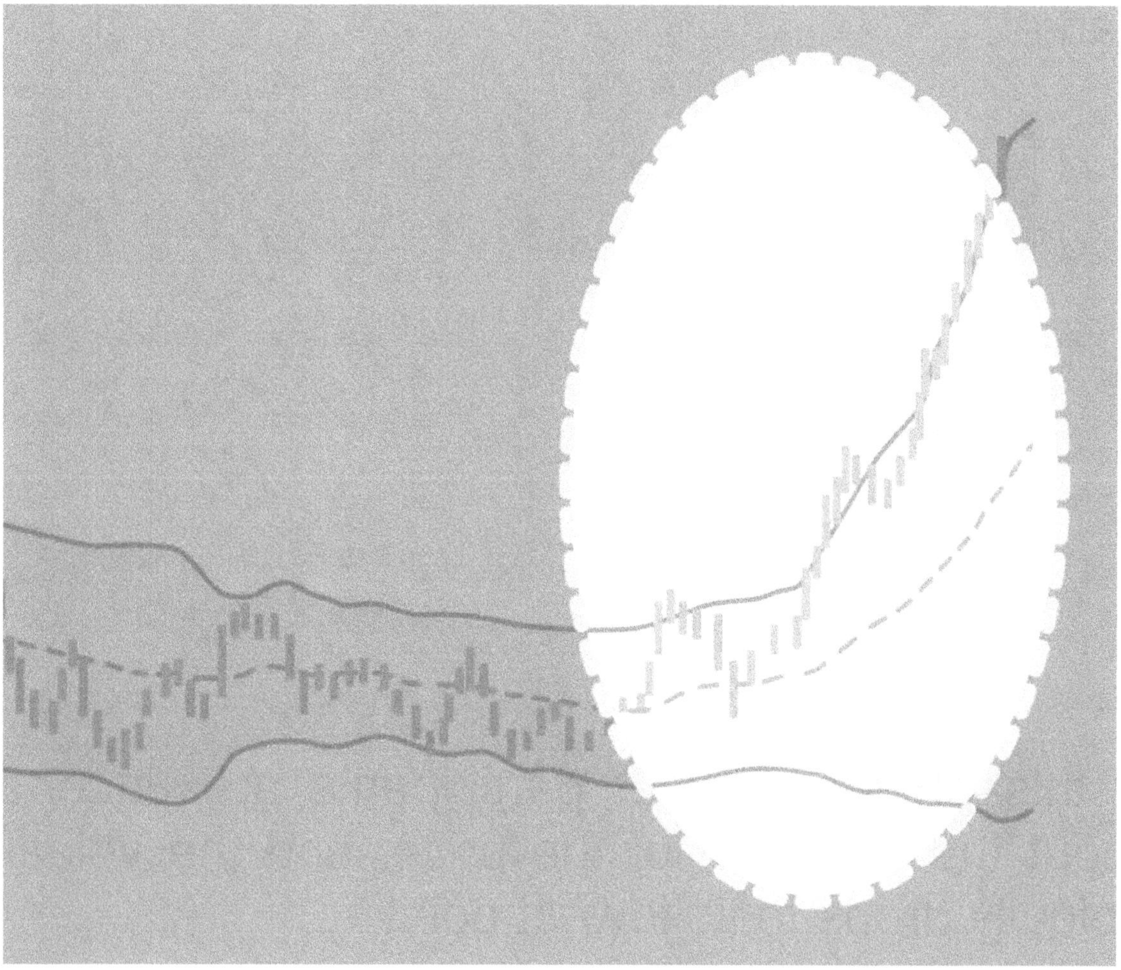

A squeeze pattern should not be ignored! It often signals a buildup of pressure and is typically followed by a significant price move, either up or down.

The breakout direction often follows the prior trend. If the market was rising before the squeeze, an upward breakout is more likely. If it was falling, a downward breakout is more probable.

Traders also pay attention to key support and resistance levels. A squeeze near resistance might result in an upward breakout, while a squeeze near support could signal a downward breakout.

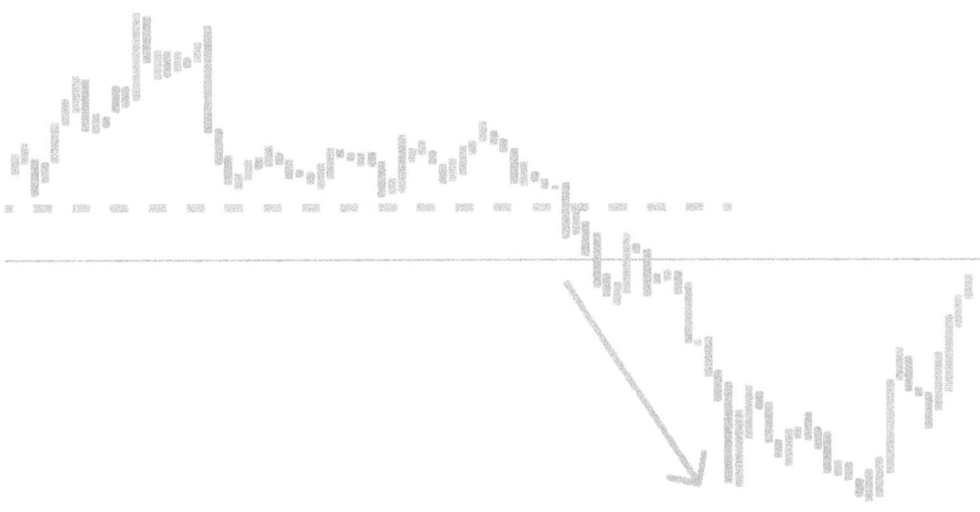

Volume also matters. A breakout with high volume shows strong market interest and is more likely to continue. A breakout with low volume may lack support, increasing the risk of a false move.

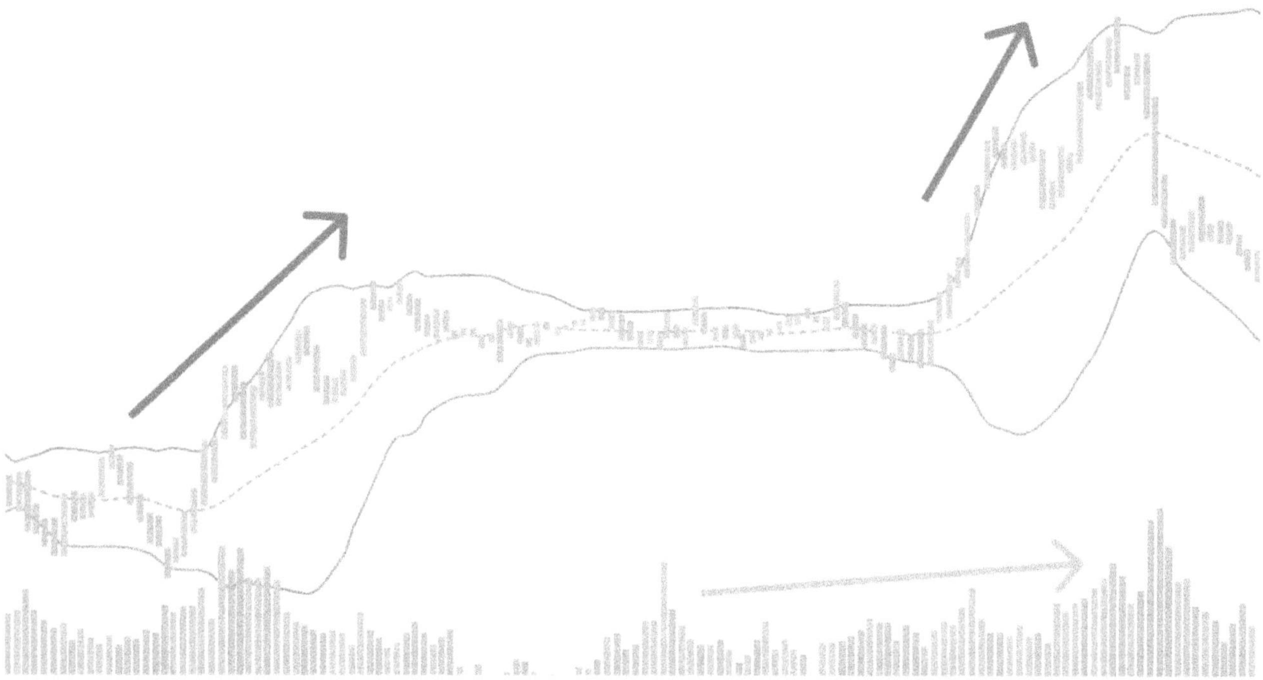

Additional indicators like the RSI can help confirm the direction. An RSI above 70 suggests an overbought market, potentially indicating a downward breakout, while an RSI below 30 signals an oversold market, suggesting an upward breakout.

Identify signals of a bearish breakout

Select the 3 signs that suggest a bearish breakout. A bearish breakout is more likely when the market is in a downtrend, the squeeze is near resistance, RSI shows overbought conditions, and volume confirms strength in the breakout.

- RSI below 30
- Price near support
- Squeeze near resistance
- Low volume breakout
- Breakout with volume surge
- RSI above 70

Answer:

- Squeeze near resistance
- Breakout with volume surge
- RSI above 70

Remember that traders usually enter (1) a trade once a breakout is confirmed by volume and additional indicators, like RSI or MACD. They exit when the breakout fails or if the price begins to reverse after the initial move (2).

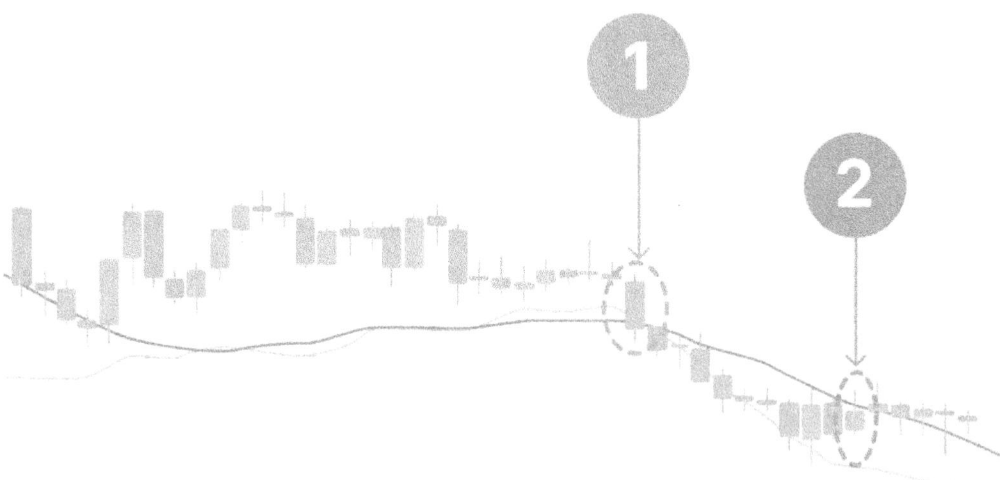

But be careful! False breakouts can be spotted when the price moves beyond key levels (support, resistance, or Bollinger Bands) but fails to sustain the move. Common signs include weak volume, quick price reversal, or no confirmation from other indicators like RSI or MACD.

To manage the risk of false breakouts, use stop-loss orders just outside the breakout level. This helps protect your position in case the price reverses. It's also important to wait for additional confirmation (such as volume or other indicators) before entering the trade.

Make a decision

Look at the chart for Starbucks. The price is approaching the lower Bollinger Band, and the RSI is below 30. When the price touches the lower Bollinger Band and the RSI is below 30, it often indicates an oversold condition, signaling a potential buying opportunity. Always confirm with other indicators before making a decision.

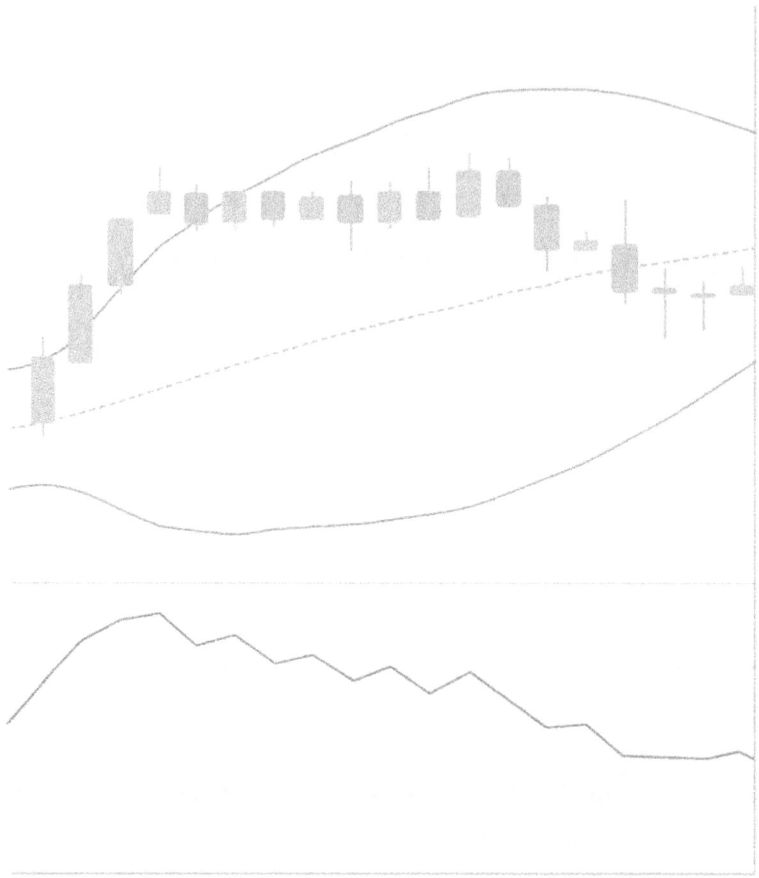

What should you consider doing in this situation?

- Buy, expecting the price to reverse and move upward
- Enter a short position, expecting a sharp drop
- Hold the position, waiting for confirmation of the trend
- Sell, expecting further downward movement

Answer: Buy, expecting the price to reverse and move upward. When the price touches the lower Bollinger Band and the RSI is below 30, it indicates an oversold market, suggesting a potential buying opportunity. The price may reverse toward the middle band, but always confirm with additional indicators to avoid false signals.

In this lesson, we covered how Bollinger Bands help identify Squeeze Patterns and breakouts.. Next, we'll explore how Bollinger Bands can be used in Different Markets, focusing on range-bound vs. trending market applications.

Lesson 3: Using Bollinger Bands in Different Markets

Bollinger Bands in different markets

In this lesson, you will learn how to apply Bollinger Bands in different market conditions, specifically in range-bound markets and trending markets. By the end of the lesson, you'll understand how to adapt your trading strategy to each market type, using the Bollinger Bands to identify key opportunities for entry and exit.

A ranging market is characterized by the price bouncing between support and resistance levels, moving sideways, and not forming a clear trend.

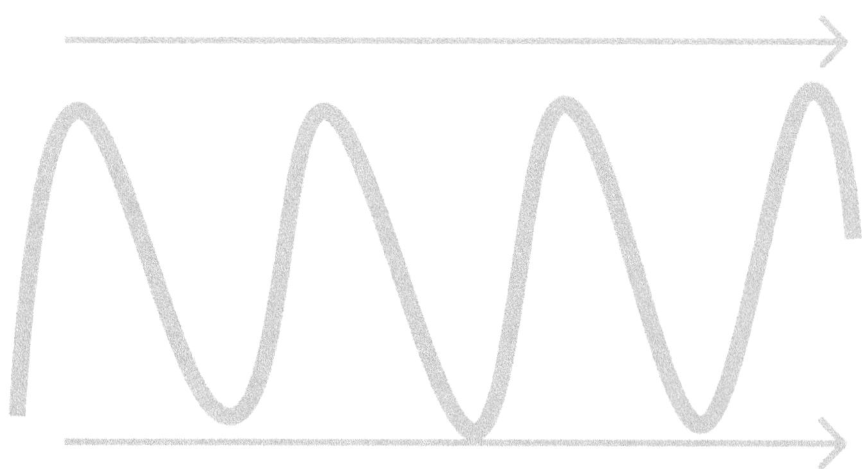

A range-bound market moves between support and resistance without a clear trend. Bollinger Bands help in these conditions by acting as dynamic support and resistance levels.

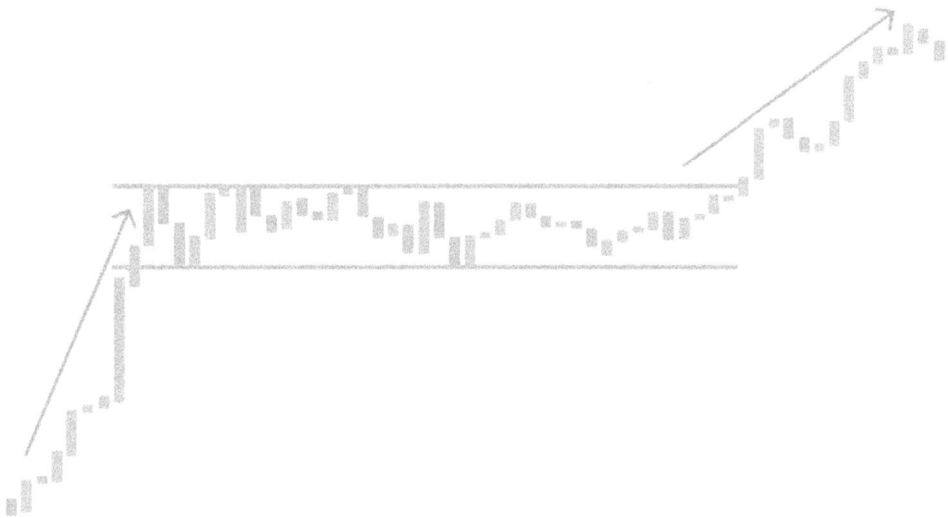

Because the bands expand and contract with volatility, they naturally wrap around price action, mirroring the support and resistance levels.

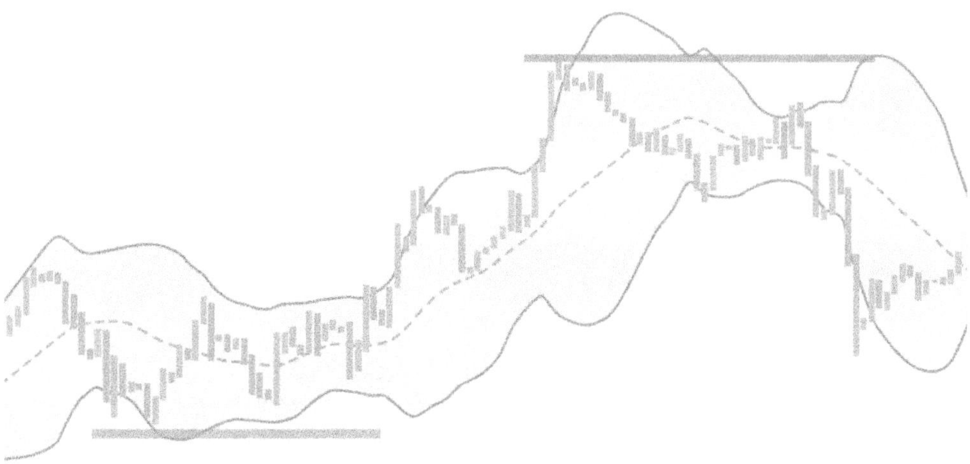

When the price reaches or nears the upper band, it acts like a resistance line. It may be considered overbought, and traders expect it might soon fall.

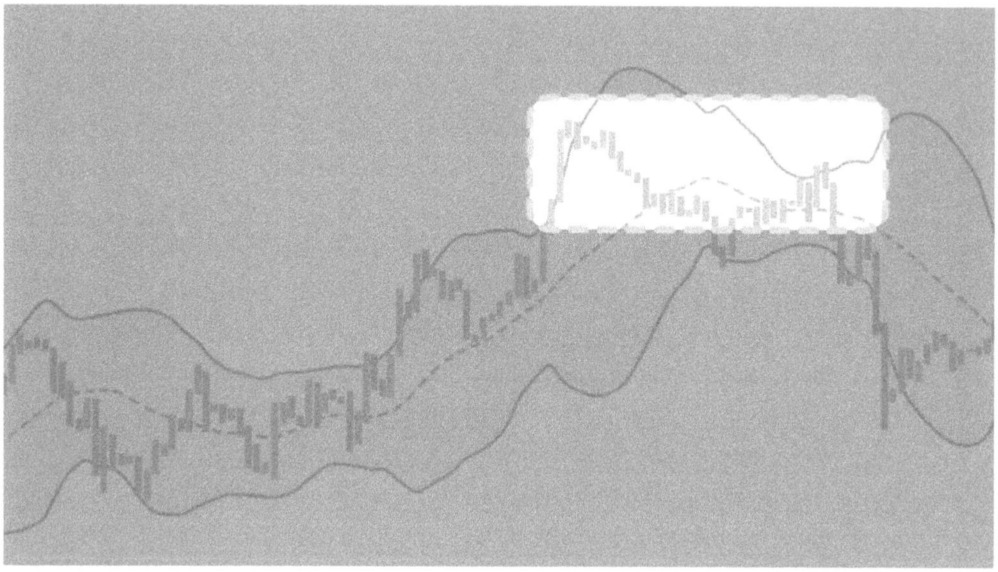

When the price touches or nears the lower band, it acts like a support line. The market may be oversold, and a price bounce upward is likely.

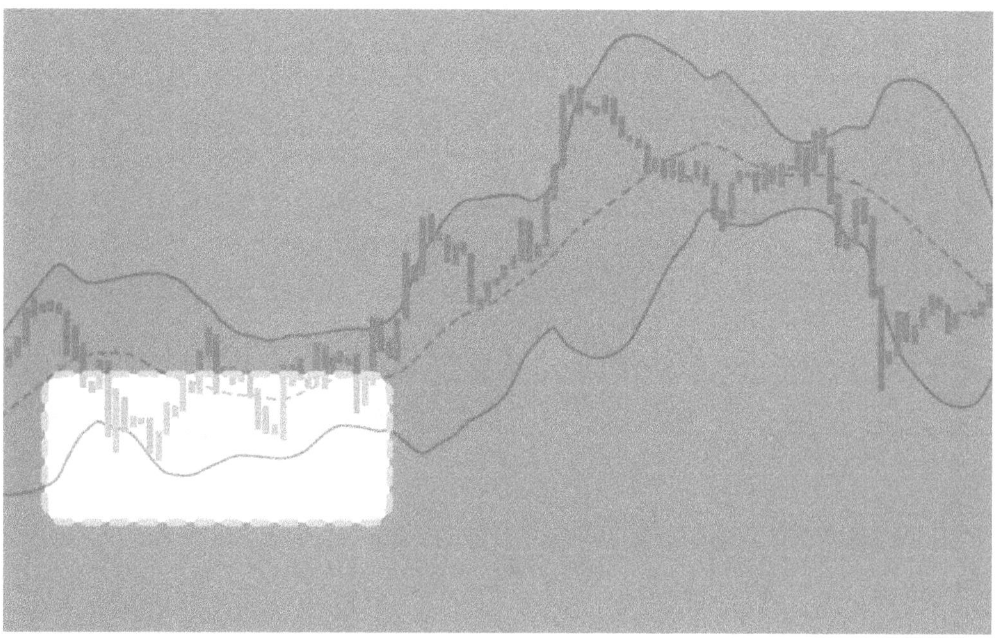

Traders take advantage of this predictable behavior by either buying near the lower band, expecting the price to rise, or selling near the upper band, expecting the price to fall.

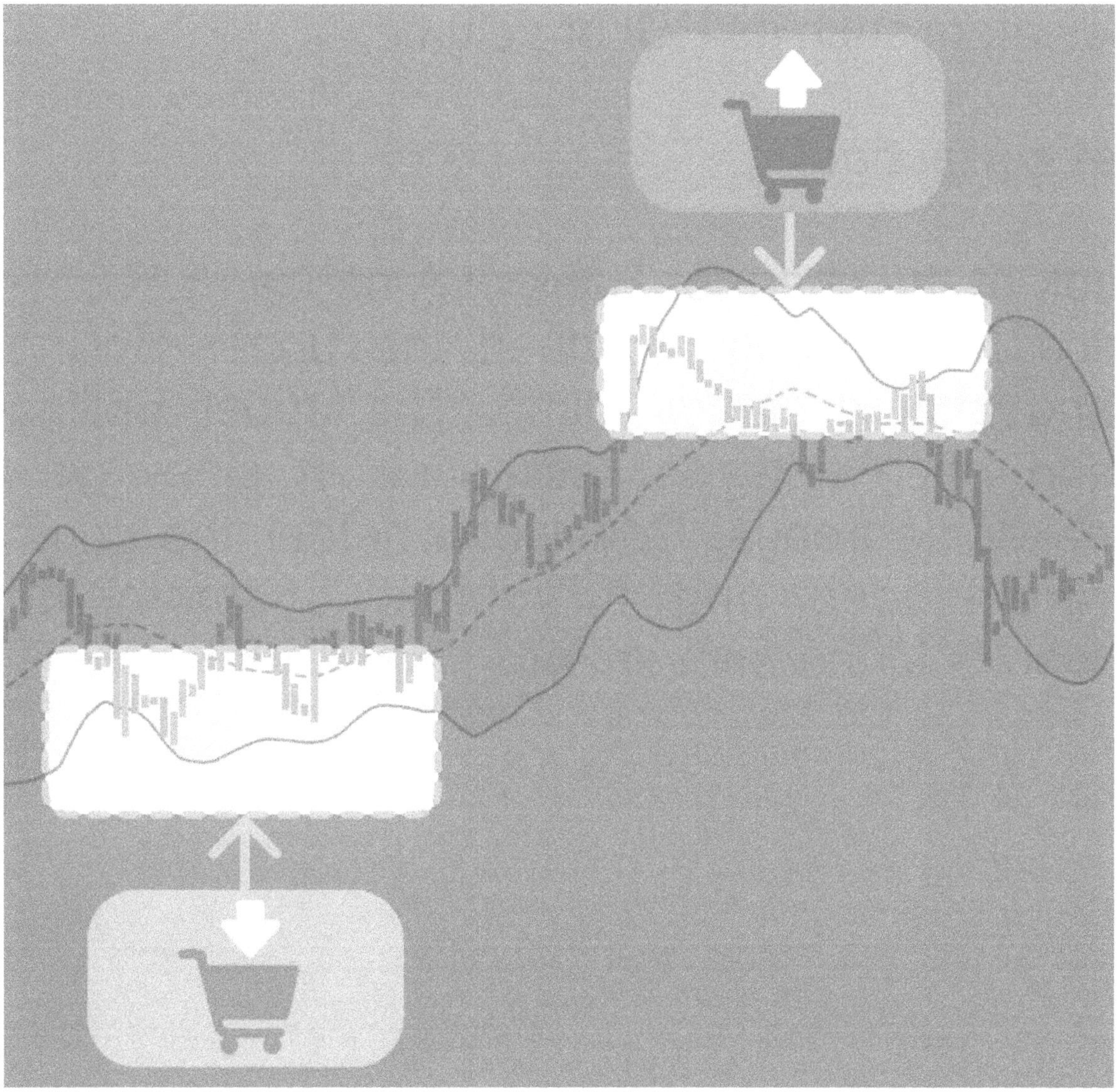

Remember, this strategy works best in non-trending markets. Always confirm that the market is range-bound. Otherwise, you risk entering just before a breakout, when the price starts trending strongly in one direction.

To reduce false signals, many traders also combine Bollinger Bands with confirmation indicators such as RSI or volume.

Let's practice!

Look at the chart for Bank of America (BAC). The price has recently touched the upper Bollinger Band after a steady climb. The upper Bollinger Band often acts as resistance in sideways or weakening trends. Consider whether the price is overextended and if volume or momentum supports further movement.

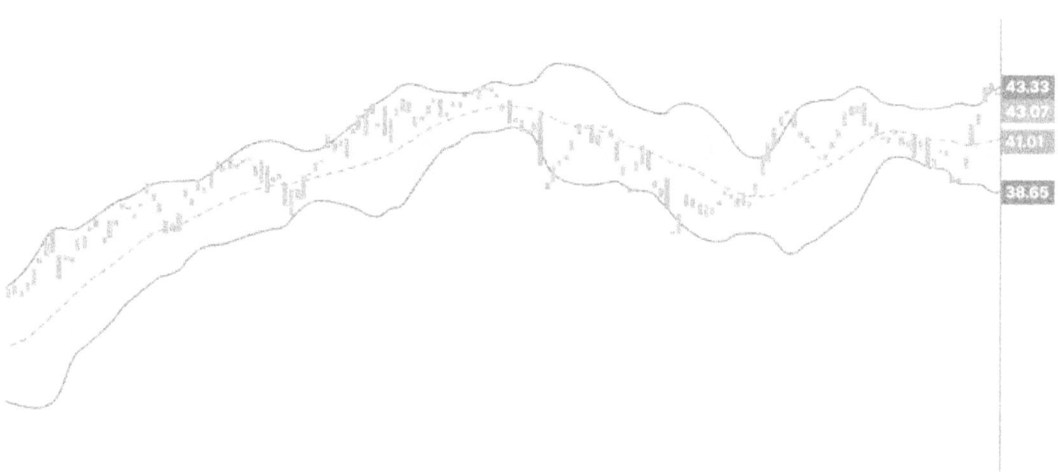

Based on this chart and the position near the upper Bollinger Band, what would be a reasonable next step?

- Buy, expecting a strong breakout to continue upward
- Hold the position and wait for confirmation from RSI or volume
- Sell, expecting the price to pull back from resistance
- Enter a short position immediately, expecting a sharp reversal

Answer: Sell, expecting the price to pull back from resistance. The price is testing the upper Bollinger Band, which often acts as dynamic resistance. Unless confirmed by strong momentum or a breakout pattern, this may be a signal to take profits or prepare for a potential pullback. Always confirm with other indicators before committing.

While you can trade the highs and lows of the range, the market won't stay there forever. A breakout eventually ends the range and starts a trend.

How can you predict if a breakout is coming? You already know the answer - watch for the signs of a squeeze! When the Bollinger Bands tighten and the market quiets down, it's often a signal that a big move is on the way.

In a trending market, the price consistently moves in one direction - either upward (uptrend) or downward (downtrend) - without returning to previous levels.

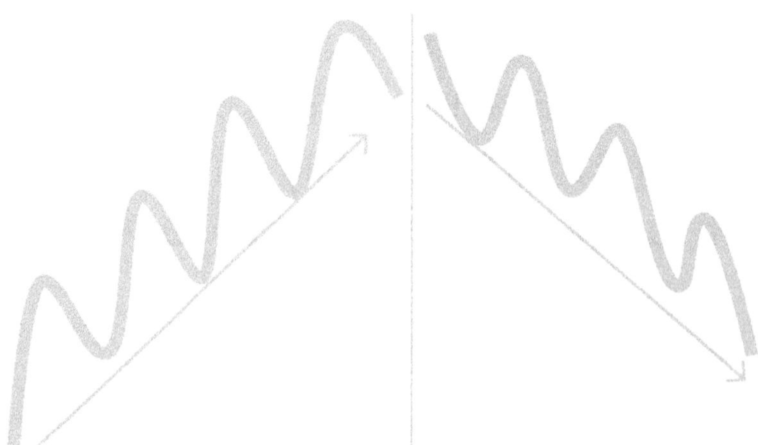

Bollinger Bands are particularly helpful in trending markets because they expand with volatility and adapt to the price movement, giving traders real-time guidance on trend strength and potential pullbacks.

In an uptrend, the price often rides along the upper Bollinger Band, showing strength and momentum. Traders look for buying opportunities near the middle band or lower band, expecting the trend to resume.

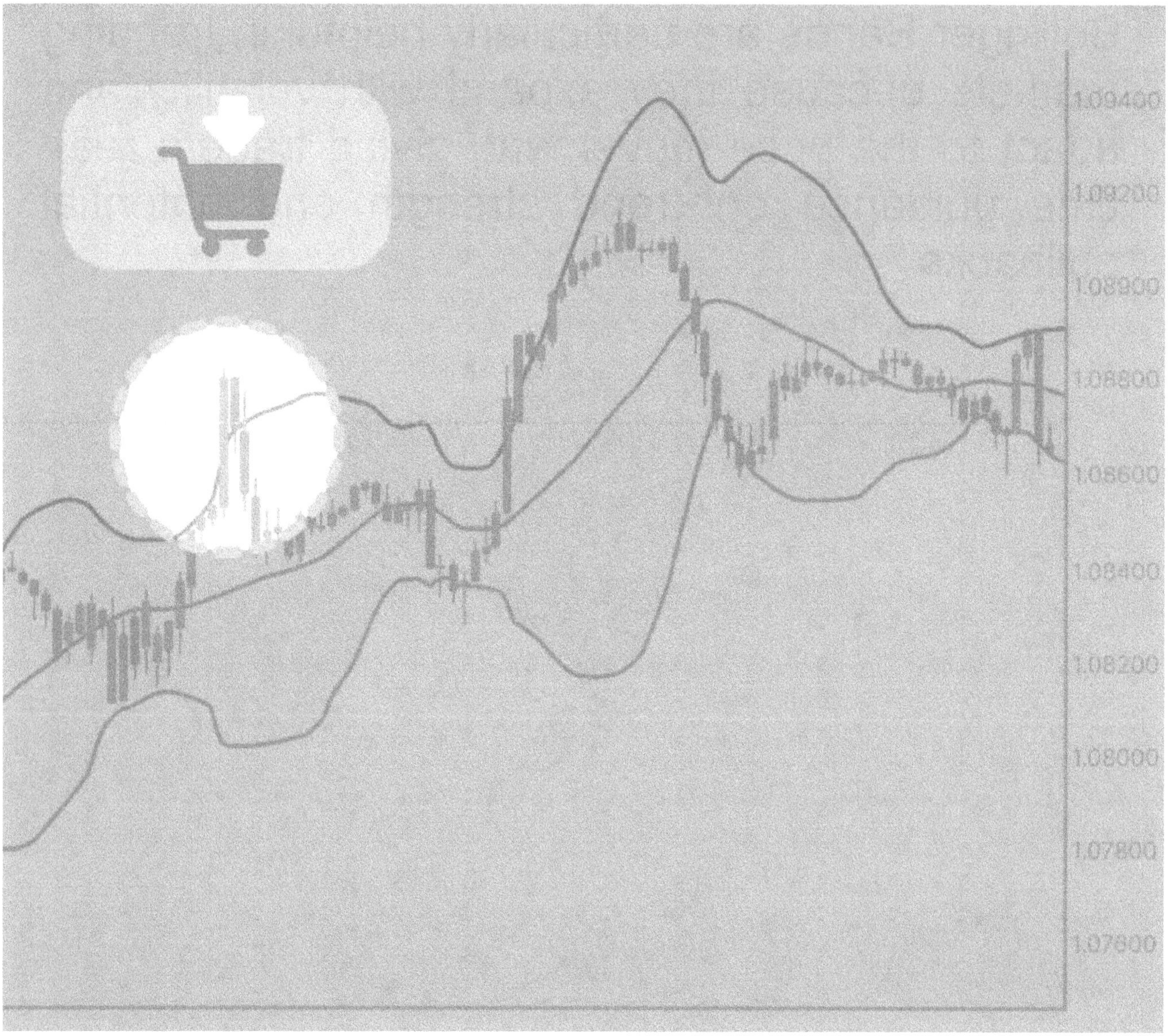

In a downtrend, the price tends to hug the lower Bollinger Band, signaling sustained selling pressure. Traders look to sell when the price pulls back to the upper or middle band, anticipating a continuation downward.

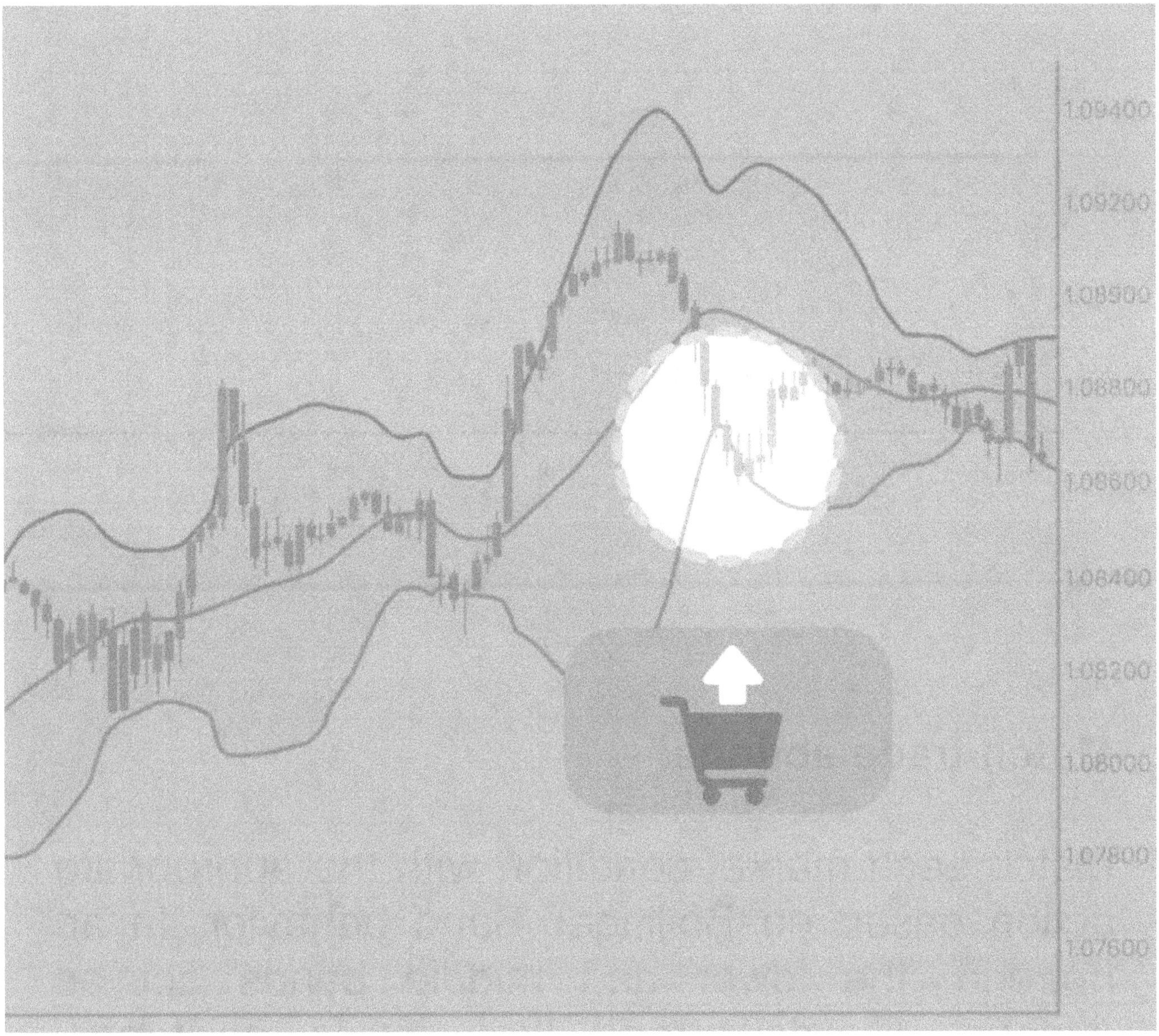

In an uptrend, the lower and middle bands act as support, while in a downtrend, they become resistance. Traders use these pullbacks to enter in the direction of the trend.

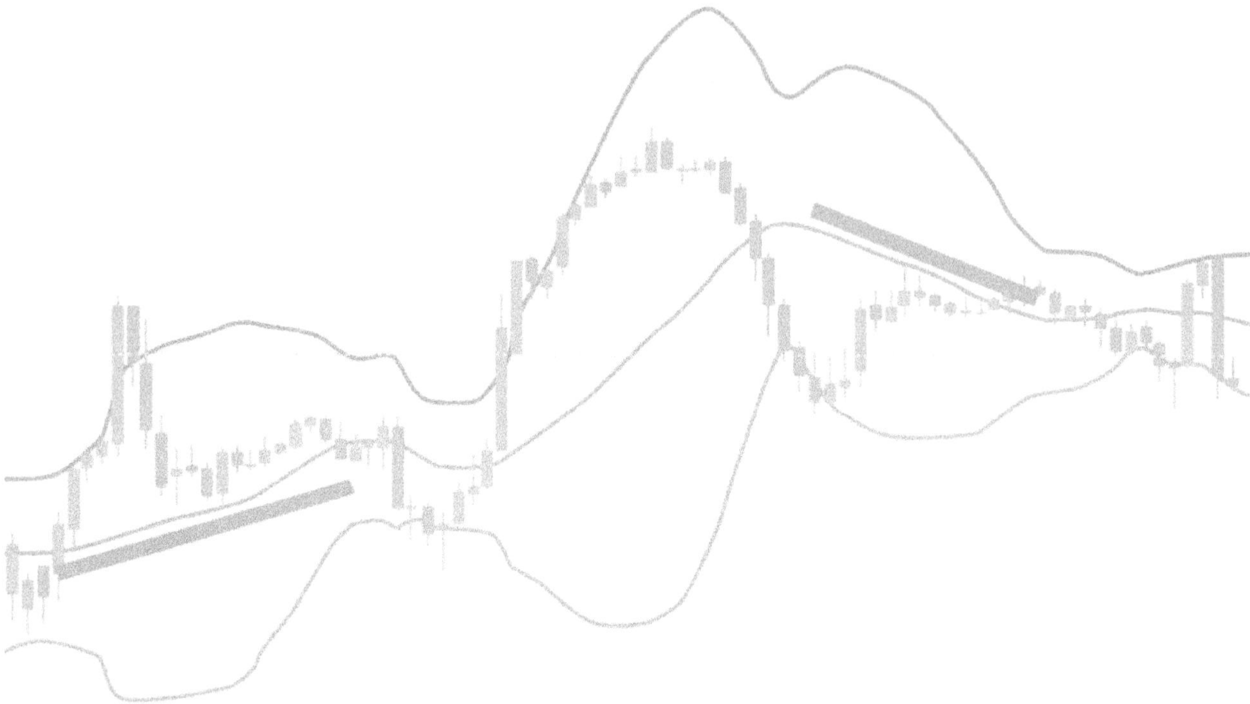

Match trade actions!

Match each market condition with the appropriate action based on Bollinger Band behavior. In an uptrend, the lower and middle bands act as support. In a downtrend, they act as resistance. Use band pullbacks for trend-following entries.

- Downtrend - Buy in the middle/lower band
- Uptrend - Sell at the upper/middle band

Answer:

- Downtrend - Sell at the upper/middle band

- Uptrend - Buy in the middle/lower band

Bollinger Bands work even better when combined with momentum indicators like RSI or MACD. These tools help filter out false signals and confirm the strength of a trend.

Whether you're trading in a range or a trend, proper risk management is essential. Breakouts can fail, trends can reverse, and ranges can expand. That's why setting stop-loss orders just outside key Bollinger Band levels is a smart way to protect your capital.

What's your move?

Look at this Bank of America chart. The price has recently moved above the middle Bollinger Band, volume has increased, and RSI is nearing 55. The middle band has been broken, volume is rising, and RSI is above neutral. For a stronger signal, traders often wait for a close above the upper band with higher momentum. Based on the Bollinger Bands, volume, and RSI, what would be the most reasonable trading decision right now?

-

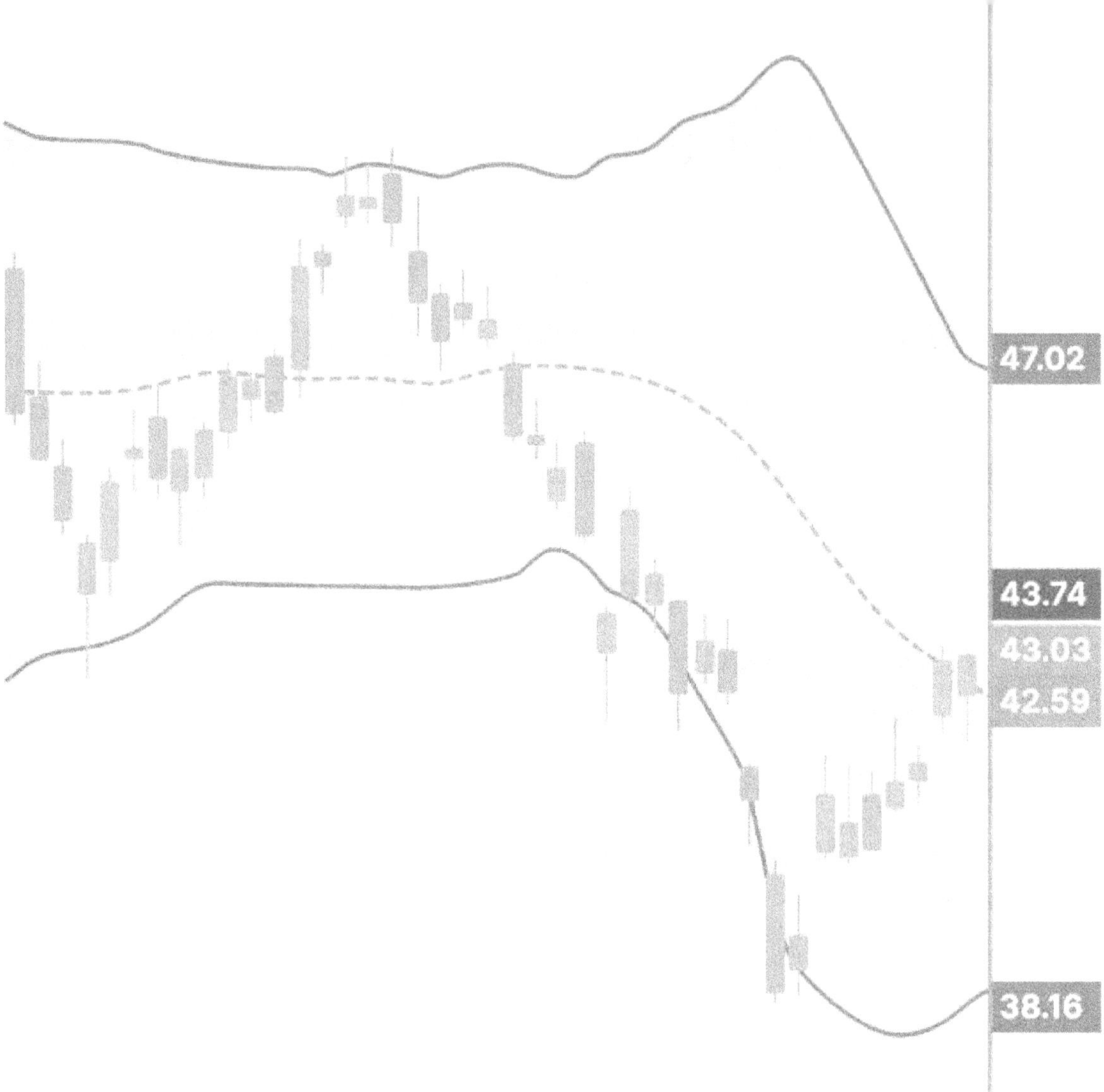

- Enter a buy trade, expecting the breakout to continue
- Wait for the price to close above the upper Bollinger Band with higher volume
- Sell immediately, expecting a reversal from resistance
- Short the market based on the RSI being near 55.

Answer: Wait for the price to close above the upper Bollinger Band with higher volume. While the move above the middle band with rising volume and RSI near 55 is promising, it's safer to wait for a confirmed breakout above the upper band. Entering too early could lead to a false signal.

In this lesson, you've learned how to apply Bollinger Bands effectively in both range-bound and trending markets, identify entry points, confirm breakouts, and manage risk. You're now ready to put your knowledge to the test. Next is a short quiz to reinforce what you've learned!

QUIZ: Bollinger Band Tactic

1. What does it mean when the price touches the upper Bollinger Band in a range-bound market?

A. It means the price will stay flat
B. It suggests that volatility is decreasing
C. It confirms a strong breakout is starting
D. It may signal overbought conditions and a possible pullback

2. What is the best tactic when the price touches the lower Bollinger Band and RSI is below 30?

A. Look for a potential buy signal, confirming with other indicators
B. Avoid trading until the RSI reaches 70
C. Sell to exit before a breakdown
D. Enter a short position immediately

3. What does a Bollinger Band "squeeze" indicate?

A. That the price will reverse sharply
B. That RSI is overbought
C. An immediate trend continuation
D. A buildup of pressure that often leads to a breakout

4. In a squeeze scenario, what makes a breakout more reliable?

A. A contraction of RSI
B. A histogram crossover
C. A volume surge accompanying the breakout
D. Flat movement along the middle band

5. What combination suggests a strong bearish breakout?

A. Price bouncing at support, RSI below 30
B. RSI above 70, squeeze near resistance, and breakout with volume
C. Histogram shrinking and RSI at 50
D. Middle band breakout with no volume

6. When price rides the upper band in a strong uptrend, what tactic is recommended?

A. Wait for a complete squeeze

B. Buy on pullbacks to the middle or lower band
C. Sell immediately when the price touches the upper band
D. Trade only if RSI drops below 30

7. What does a range-bound Bollinger Band setup suggest to a trader?

A. Always wait for the MACD to cross
B. Buy near the lower band, sell near the upper band
C. Avoid all trades until RSI reaches 50
D. Trade in the direction of the last breakout

8. What's a smart move when Bollinger Bands contract and the price nears a key resistance level?

A. Ignore Bollinger Bands in resistance zones
B. Sell before volume rises
C. Immediately enter a short position
D. Watch for a potential breakout to the upside, but wait for confirmation

9. What should a trader do to manage risk during breakout trading with Bollinger Bands?

A. Use stop-loss orders just outside the breakout level
B. Ignore volume confirmation
C. Only rely on Bollinger Bands without confirmation
D. Enter with full capital during the squeeze

10. What role does the middle Bollinger Band play in both uptrends and downtrends?

A. It replaces the need for volume analysis
B. It often acts as a support in uptrends and resistance in downtrends
C. It signals trend exhaustion
D. It triggers entry without confirmation

Answer: 1. D; 2. A; 3. D; 4. C; 5. B; 6. B; 7. B; 8. D; 9. A; 10. B

Chapter 7: Fibonacci Scenarios

Lesson 1: Key Fibonacci Levels

It's time to recall Fibonacci levels!

In this lesson, you'll explore the most important Fibonacci retracement levels used by traders. You'll learn how these levels help identify potential reversal zones, gauge correction depth, and build more strategic entry and exit plans. Let's start!

Three percentages commonly used in Fibonacci retracement are:

- 38.2%
- 61.8%
- 78.6%

But you might be wondering - why 38.2%, 61.8%, or 78.6%? These percentages aren't random. They're based on a special number sequence found in nature, art, and even human behavior.

Fibonacci levels come from a number sequence where each number is the sum of the two before it: 0, 1, 1, 2, 3, 5, 8, 13, 21, 34, ... When you divide one number by the next, or by others in the sequence, you get ratios like:

- 61.8% (for example, 21 ÷ 34)
- 38.2% (for example, 21 ÷ 55)
- 23.6% (for example, 13 ÷ 55)

Fibonacci levels work because prices move in waves, not straight lines. After a big move, traders expect a pullback. Since many watch levels like 38.2%, 50%, and 61.8%, they often trigger real buying or selling reactions.

Hence, here are the key levels traders use: 0.236 - 0.382 - 0,5 - 0.618 - 0.786. Even though 0.5 isn't from the Fibonacci sequence, it's widely used because markets often retrace about half of a previous move before continuing.

Traders use Fibonacci levels to spot potential reversal points after a price move. They draw the levels from a recent high to low (in a downtrend) or low to high (in an uptrend).

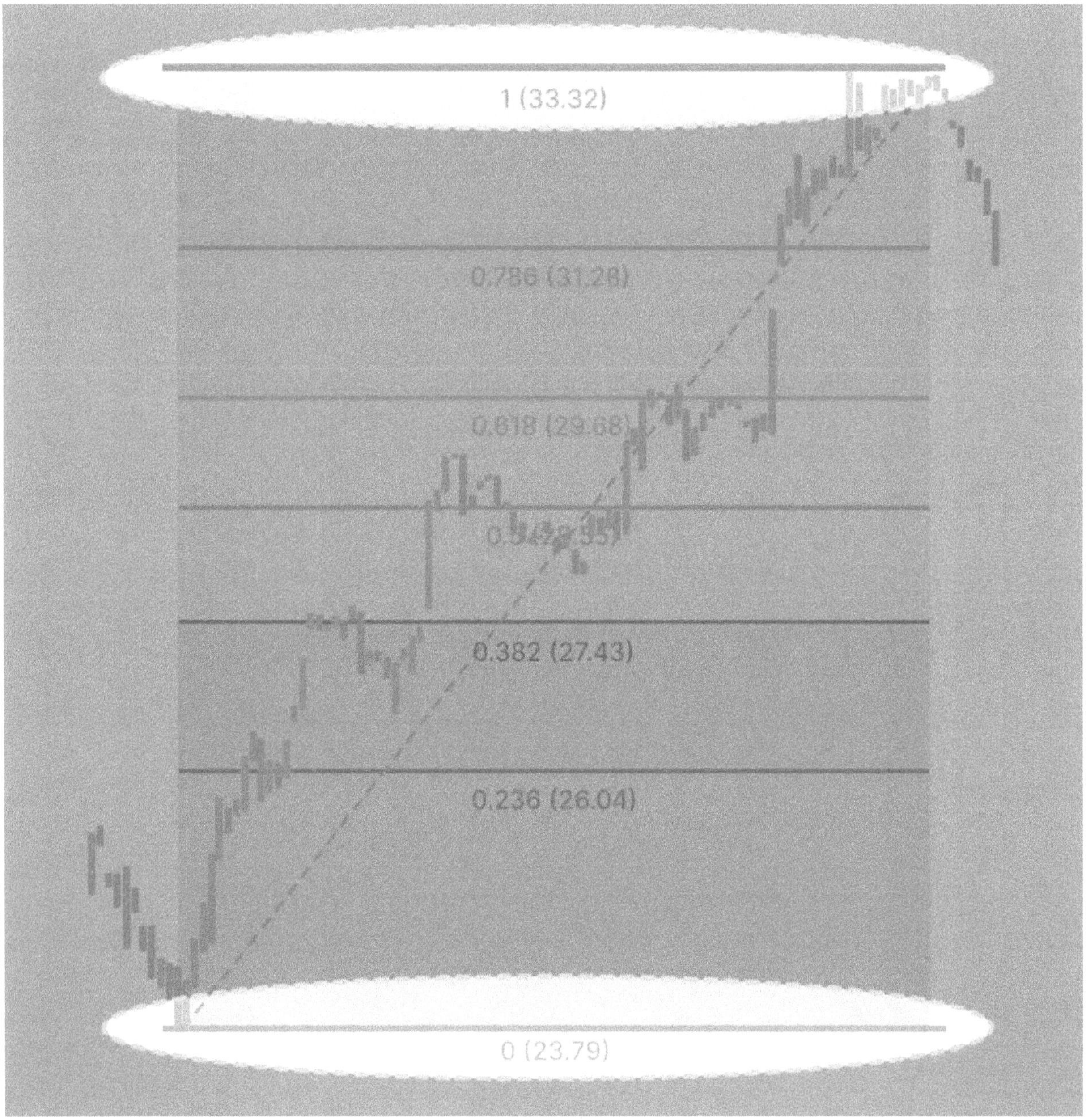

These levels act like guideposts showing where price might pause, bounce, or reverse. In an uptrend, traders look to buy when the price pulls back to levels like 0,382 or 0,5.

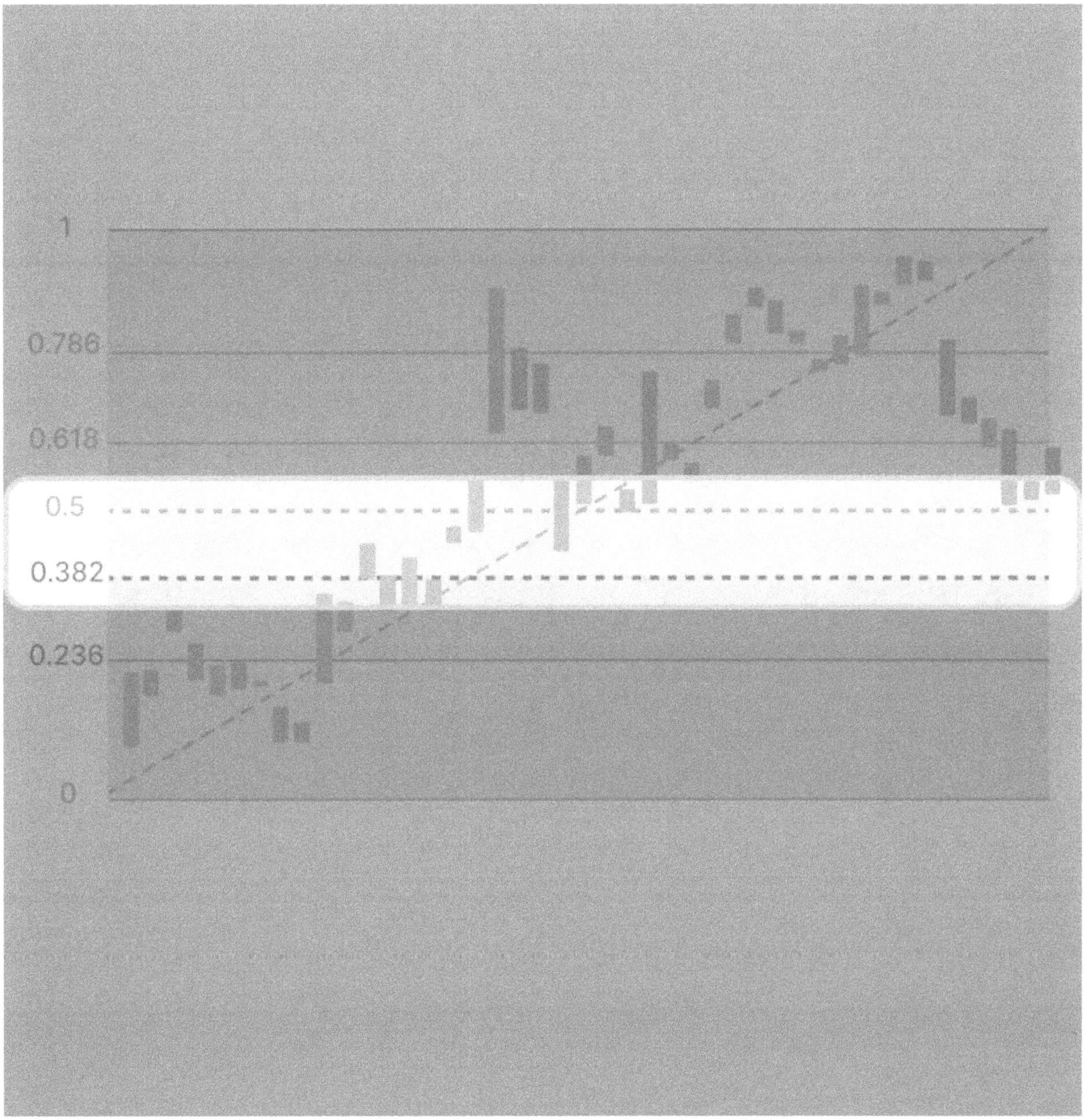

In a downtrend, they may sell if the price retraces to 0,618 or 0,786. This helps them plan smart entry points, place stop-losses, and choose profit targets.

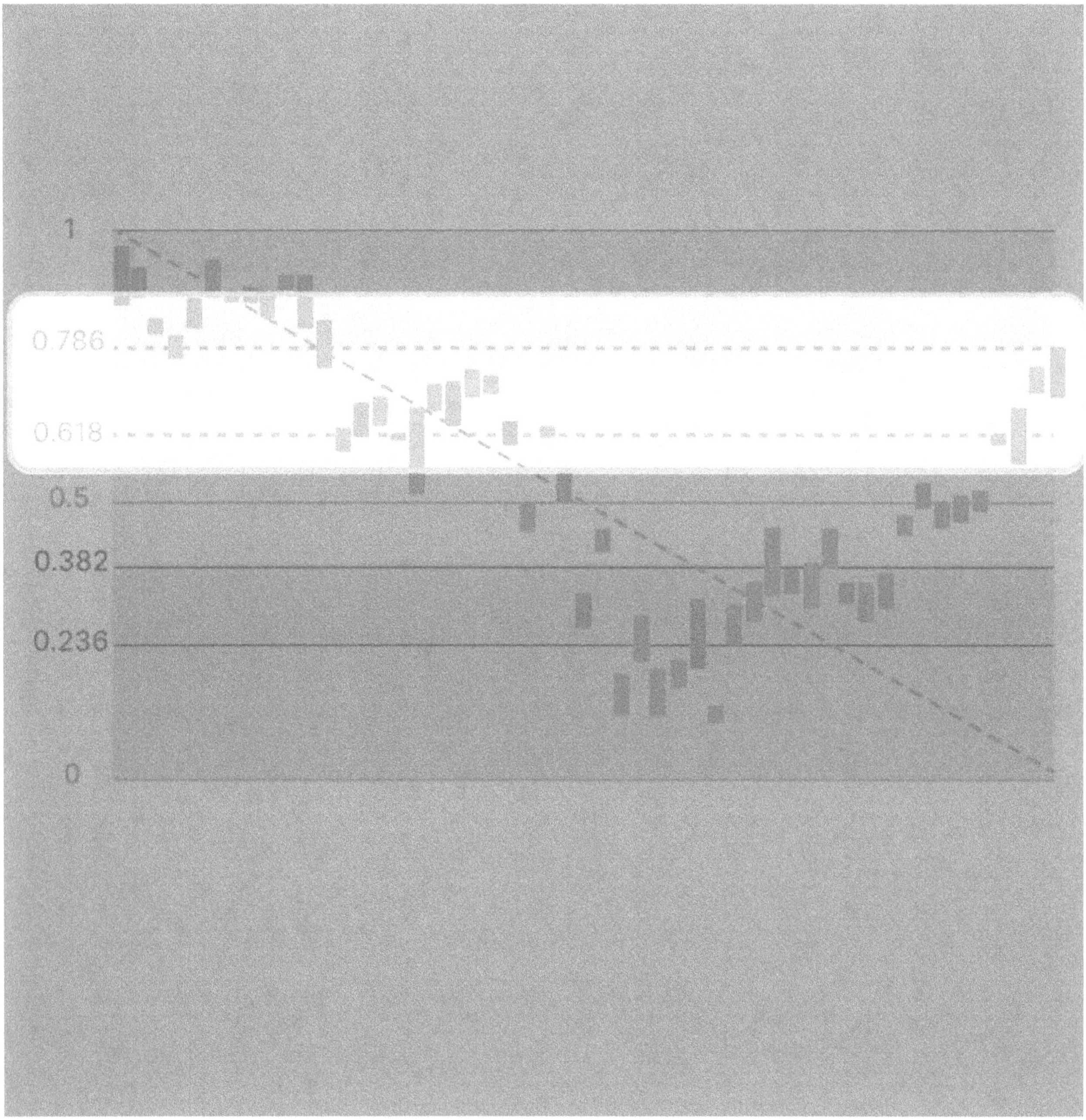

Let's recall the Fibonacci trade steps

Arrange the steps in the correct order to plan a Fibonacci-based trade. Start with the trend, then draw levels, wait for price action, and finally take action with a plan.

- Spot swing high and low, then draw Fibonacci level
- Wait for price pullback to enter the trade
- Identify the trend
- Set stop-loss and target

Answer:

- Identify the trend
- Spot swing high and low, then draw Fibonacci level
- Wait for price pullback to enter the trade
- Set stop-loss and target

Great! Now that you know the basics of Fibonacci retracement and how traders use it to plan their moves, it's time to put your knowledge into action.

Make a decision!

BABA has pulled back to the 61.8% Fibonacci retracement level after a strong upward move. 61.8% is a key Fibonacci level where many traders look for long setups after a retracement in an uptrend.

What action would you take based on this setup?

- Buy - enter long expecting a continuation of the uptrend

- Wait - monitor for more confirmation above the 50% level
- Sell - expect a breakdown below the 61.8% level
- Avoid trading - too much uncertainty in the move

Answer: Buy - enter long expecting a continuation of the uptrend. 0,618 is often seen as a high-probability reversal zone in trending markets.

You've now mastered the basics of Fibonacci retracement - what the levels mean, where they come from, and how traders use them in real trading decisions. Next, we'll explore how another Fibonacci tool is used - not for finding pullbacks, but for projecting future price targets.

Lesson 2: Retracement vs Extension

Fibonacci Retracement vs. extension

In this lesson, you'll discover the difference between Fibonacci Retracement and Extension. By the end of this lesson, you'll understand how to apply each tool to real setups and use both to build a complete trade plan.

As you already know, traders use Fibonacci Retracement levels to predict where the price might pause or reverse before continuing. There is also a tool called Fibonacci Extension, which helps traders estimate how far the price might go after the trend resumes.

While retracement levels focus on pullbacks within a trend, Fibonacci Extension is used after the pullback ends to project how far the price might move in the direction of the trend. It helps traders set realistic profit targets based on previous price action.

Let's see how it works and how to set it up! Before using Fibonacci Extension, you need to spot a clear move in the market. In an uptrend, look for a price swing from a low (Point 2) to a high (Point 1), and the end of the retracement (Point 3).

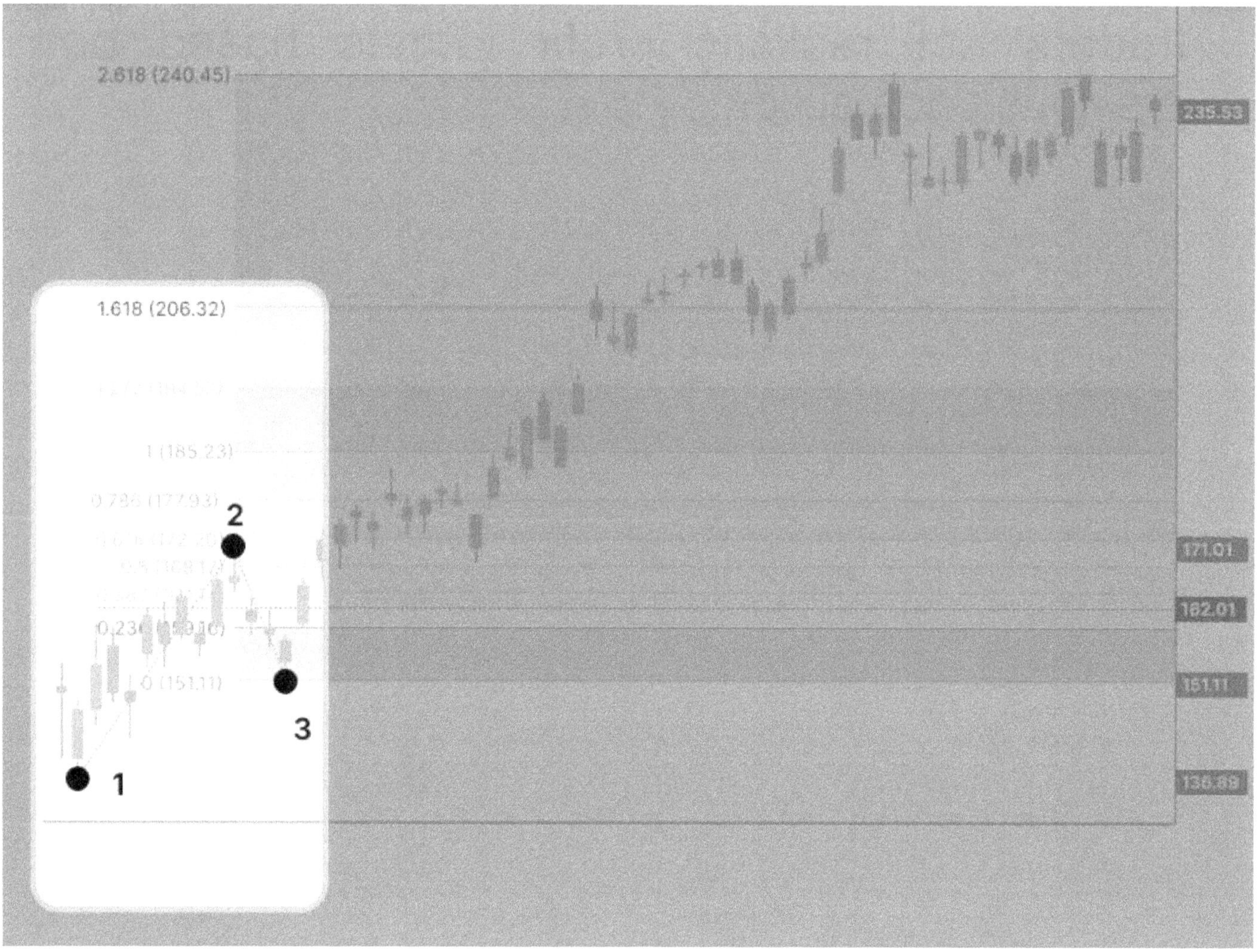

In a downtrend, look for a swing from a high (Point 1) to a low (Point 2), and the end of the retracement (Point 3).

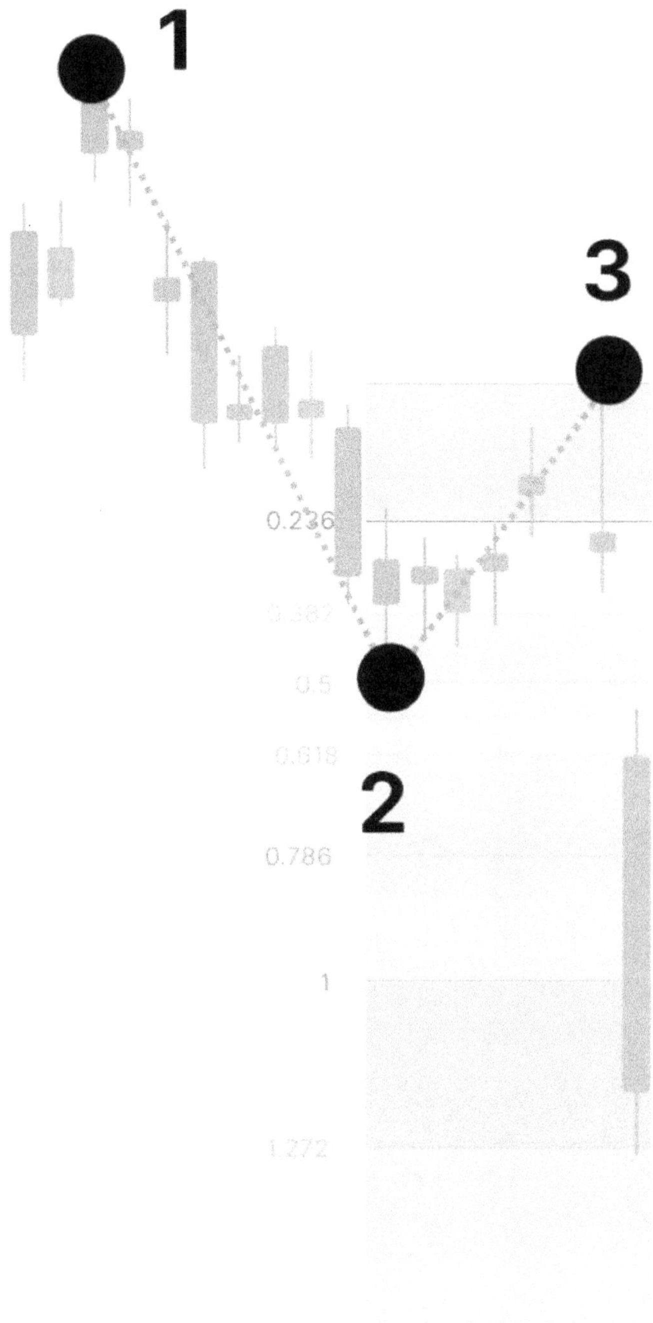

After a strong price movement and a retracement, traders often want to know how far the price might continue in the original direction. Fibonacci extension levels offer zones where the price may reach before losing momentum.

In an uptrend, once the price finds support at Point 3 and starts rising again, traders may enter a long trade. Fibonacci extensions like 1.272 and 1.618 serve as common take-profit targets, while a stop-loss is placed just below Point 3 to manage risk.

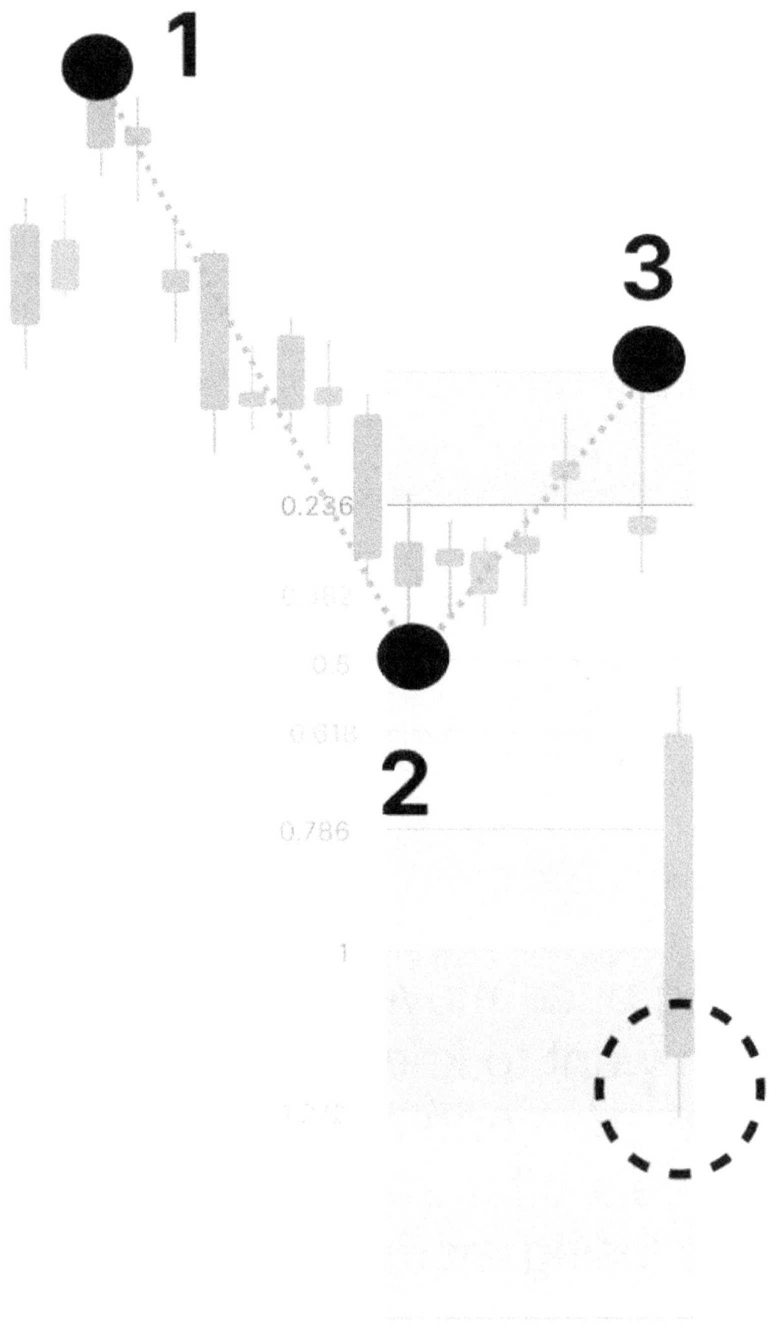

In a downtrend, traders use Fibonacci Extension to project targets below the previous low, typically at 1.272 or 1.618. They go short after the retracement ends at Point 3 and place a stop-loss just above that point.

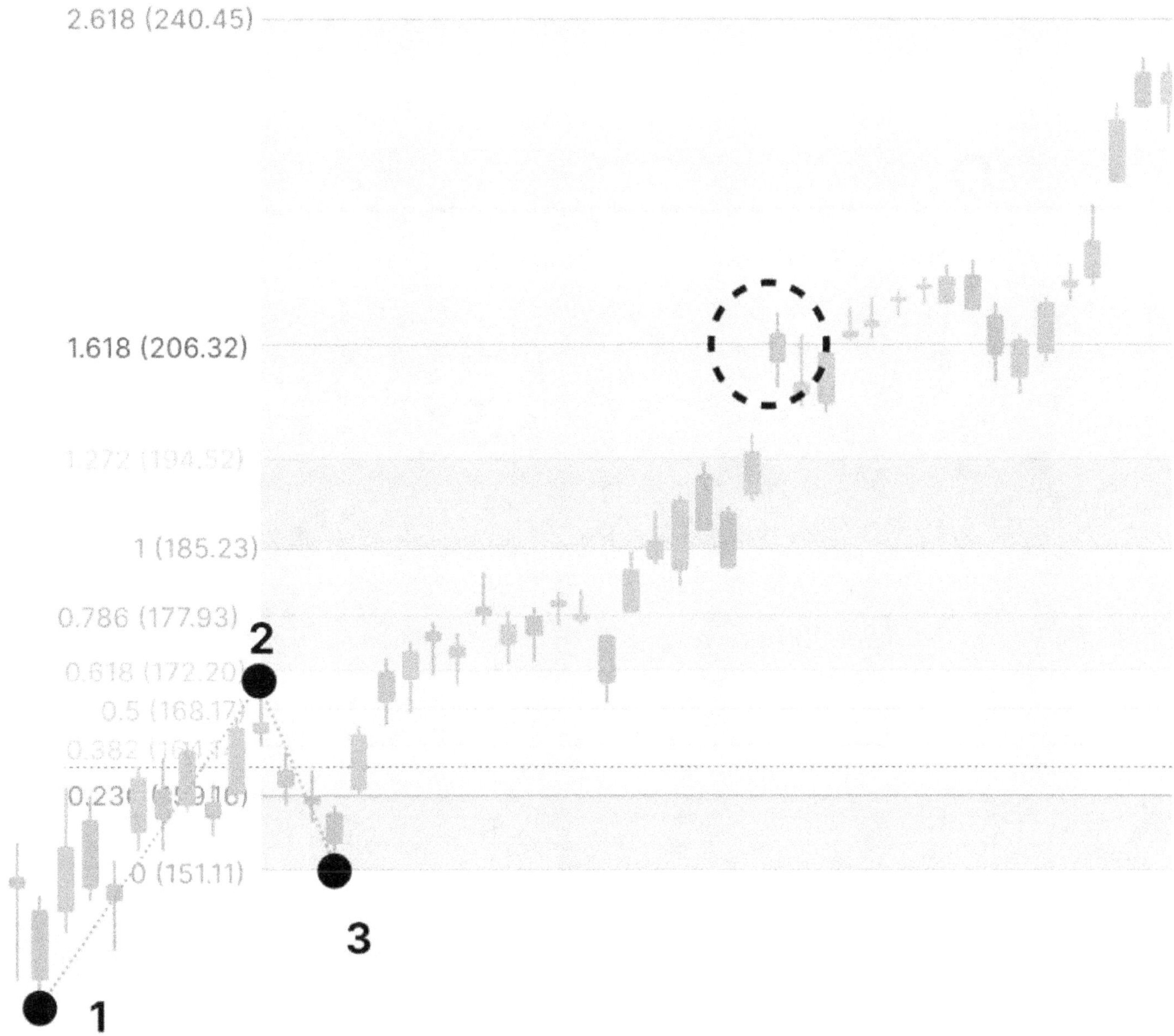

Fibonacci Extension is a useful guide, but not always exact. That's why traders combine it with tools like support/ resistance, trendlines, moving averages, RSI, or MACD to confirm stronger trade setups.

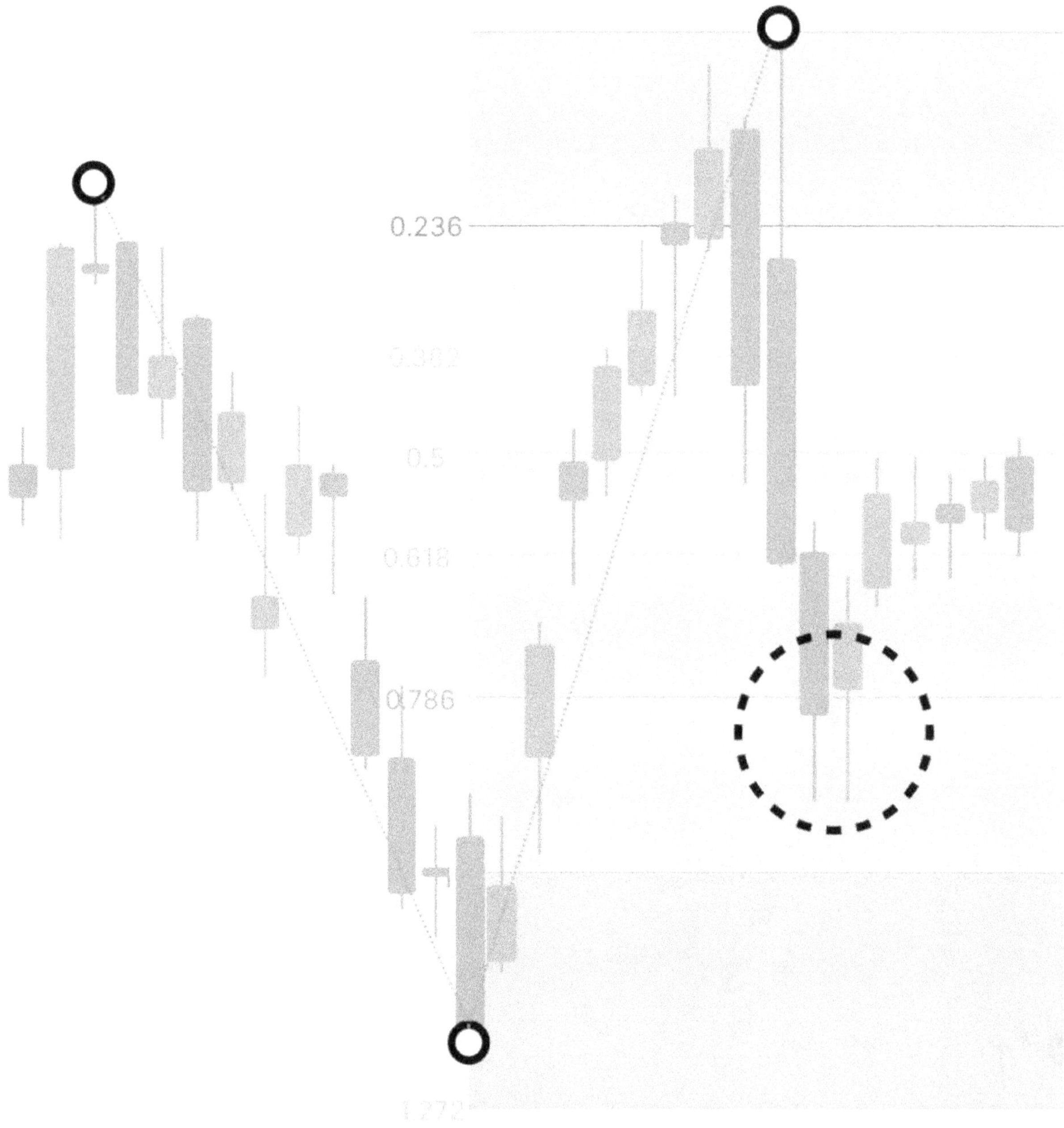

Now that you know how Fibonacci Extensions work and how to apply them in real trading situations, it's time to put your knowledge into action.

Make a decision!

Price has broken below the 1.272 Fibonacci Extension level after continuing the downtrend. Momentum remains strong, and no clear reversal signs are visible. A clean break below the 1.272 extension with strong momentum often signals continuation, but it's important to assess volume and other confirmations.

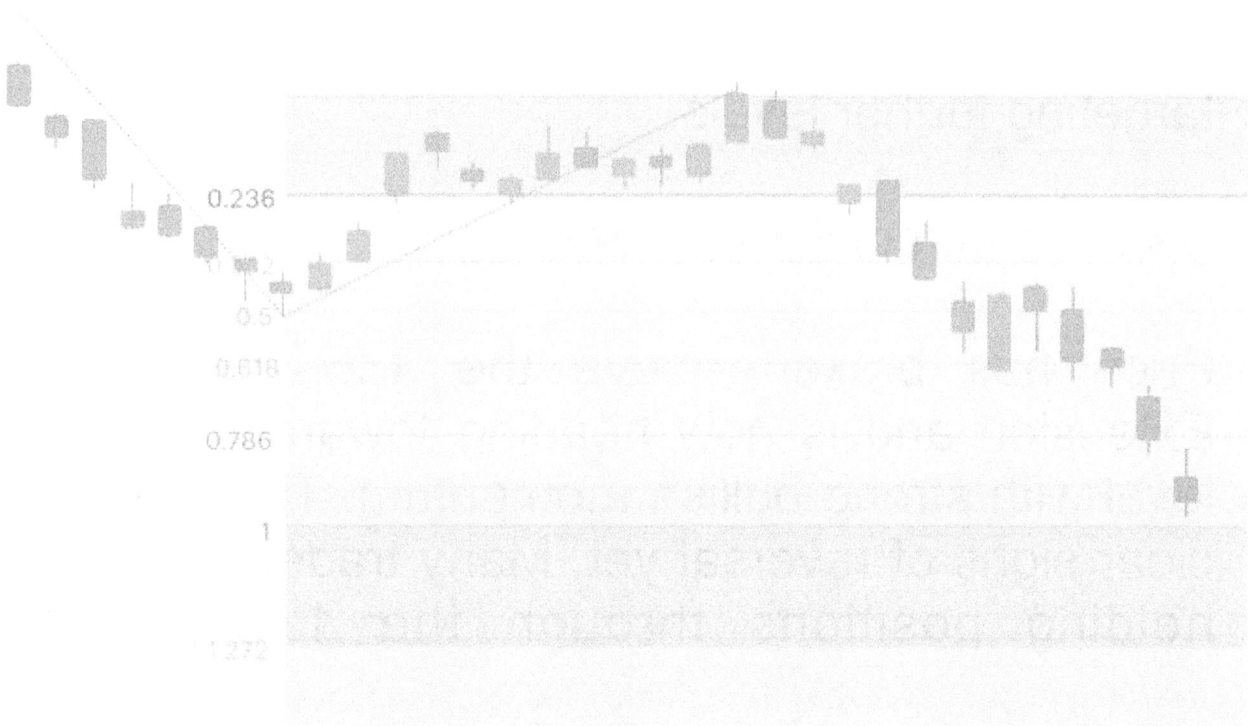

What action would you consider in this situation?

- Close all trades - avoid any further risk at this stage
- Go short - the break below 1.272 suggests strong bearish momentum
- Go long - the price has dropped too far and might reverse soon
- Wait - monitor for signs of exhaustion or reversal before entering

Answer: Go short - the break below 1.272 suggests strong bearish momentum. Without a strong reversal signal, going long or closing early may miss the ongoing trend opportunity. Breaking below 1.272 often suggests the trend is still strong, and many traders continue short positions targeting further levels.

Use Fibonacci Extension!

Price has broken above the 1.272 Fibonacci Extension and is now heading toward the 1.618 level with strong bullish momentum. There are no clear signs of reversal yet. Many traders continue holding positions through the 1.272 level, targeting 1.618 or higher, especially in strong uptrends.

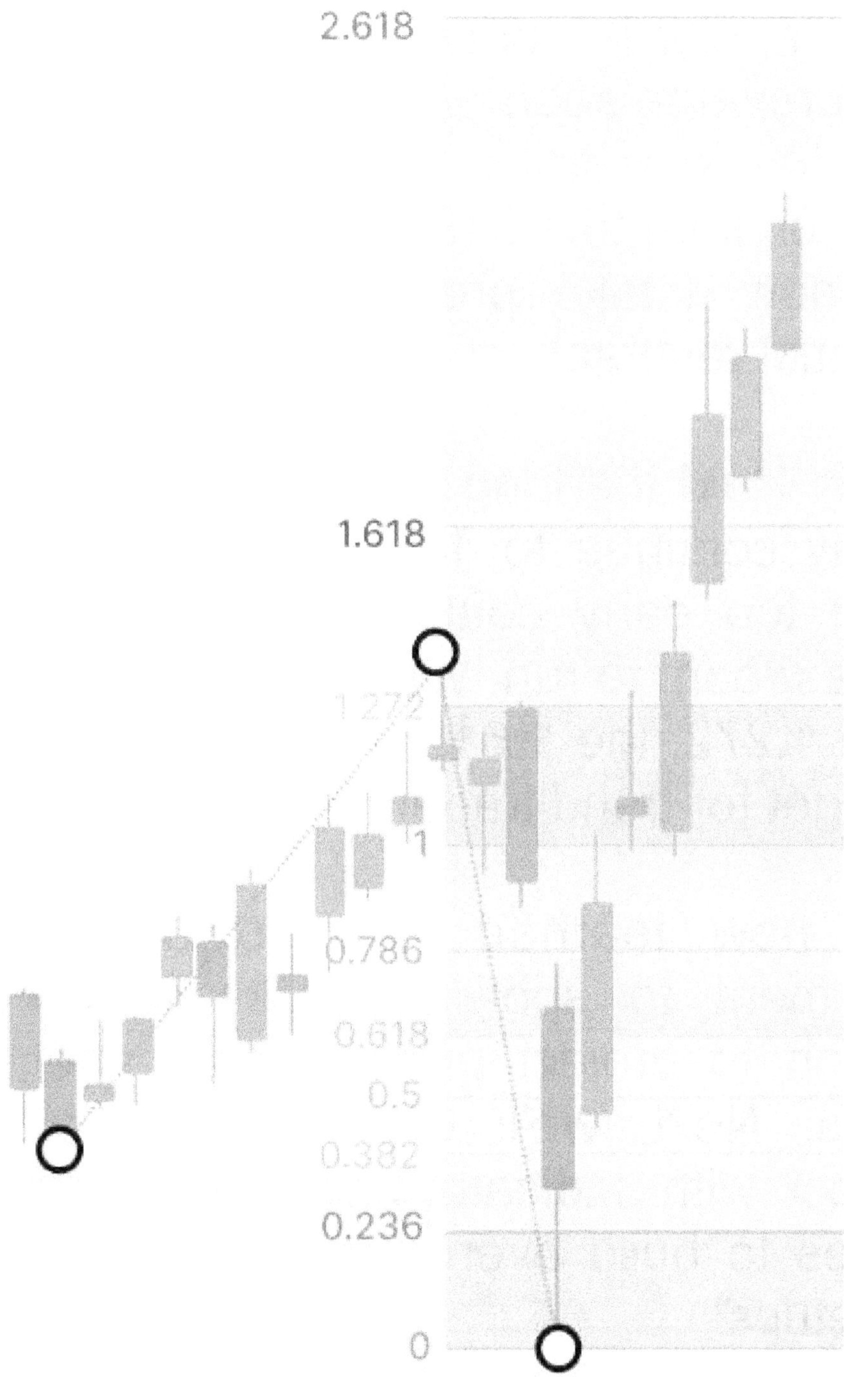

How would you manage your position in this situation?

- Avoid trading - wait for the price to settle before making a move
- Open a short - price is near resistance and might reverse soon
- Hold the long trade - the trend is strong and may continue to 1.618 or higher
- Exit now - take profits at 1.272 to avoid a potential reversal

Answer: Hold the long trade - the trend is strong and may continue to 1.618 or higher. Exiting or shorting too early could cut profits short if the trend has room to run. When price moves strongly through 1.272, the 1.618 level becomes a natural next target for trend traders.

You've now learned how to use Fibonacci Retracement to spot pullbacks and Fibonacci Extension to project price targets after a trend resumes. Next, we'll explore how to combine Fibonacci with indicators like RSI and Moving Averages to build even stronger, more confident trade setups!

Lesson 3: Confluence with Indicators

It's time to combine indicators!

In this lesson, you'll learn how to enhance your trading decisions by combining Fibonacci retracement and extension levels with the Relative Strength Index (RSI) and Moving Averages (MA). By the end, you'll understand how these tools work together to identify high-probability trade setups.

Let's review each indicator with what it helps you see in the market.

- Fibonacci Levels: Key price reaction zones (price structure)
- Moving Average: Trend direction (trend strength)
- RSI: Overbought or oversold momentum (momentum)

You now remember what each indicator tells you. Now let's go a step further and see what happens when they all line up at the same price area.

A confluence happens when two or more technical tools point to the same area on the chart. This overlap gives that price level more importance and makes it more likely to trigger a strong reaction.

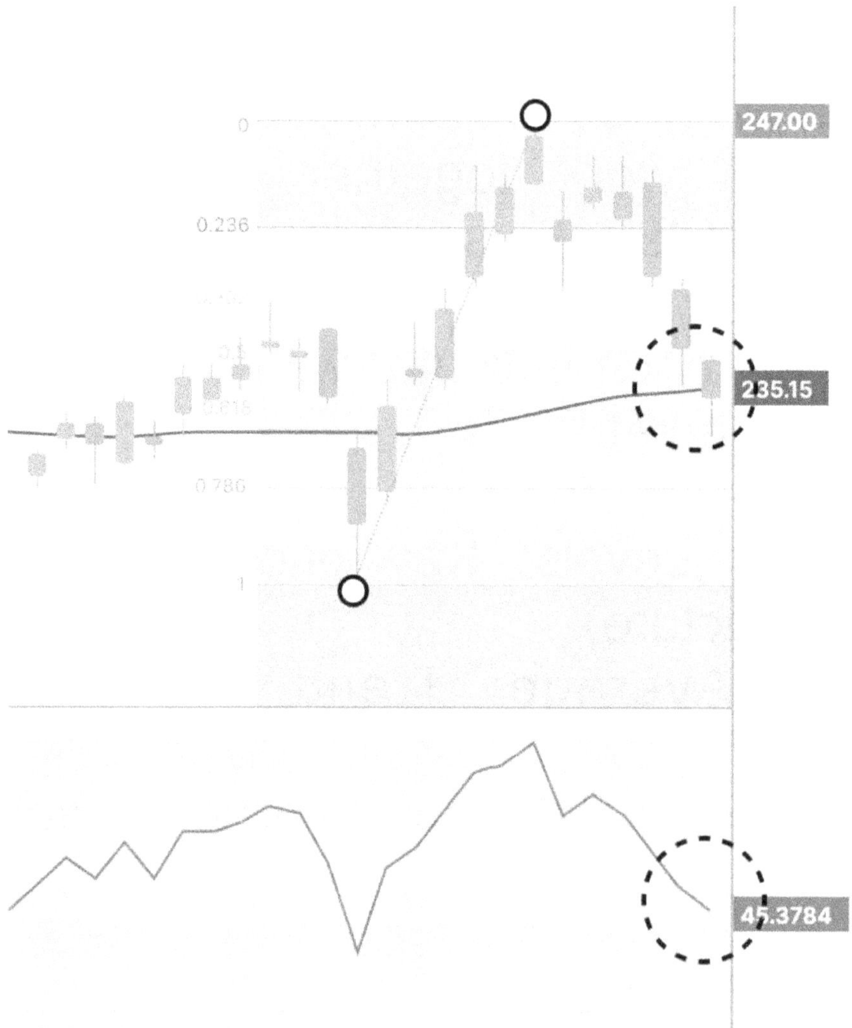

For example, imagine the price is pulling back in an uptrend and reaches the 61.8% Fibonacci level. At the same time, the 50-period Moving Average is right around that zone, and RS is near 45, showing fading momentum. Together, these signals create a confluence zone where a bounce is more likely.

When price reaches a confluence zone (for example, a Fibonacci level that aligns with a Moving Average and confirmation from RSI), it signals a potential reaction area.

That reaction could be:

- A bounce in an uptrend (where traders look to go long)
- A rejection in a downtrend (where traders look to go short)

Confluence or not?

Price has retraced to the 61.8% Fibonacci level while also touching the 50-period Moving Average. RSI is near 56 and rising. Confluence doesn't require extreme RSI levels - alignment of multiple tools near the same level can be enough.

Based on this setup, would you consider this a confluence zone?

- Not sure - need more time to evaluate price action
- Yes - multiple indicators align at the same price zone

- No - RSI isn't low enough to confirm a reversal
- No - only Fibonacci is relevant here

Answer: Yes - multiple indicators align at the same price zone. Even without an oversold RSI, the alignment of multiple tools still strengthens the setup. The 61.8% Fib, the MA, and supportive RSI together form a strong confluence signal.

What if there is no confluence? In such a case, it's usually best for a trader to stay cautious. Without multiple indicators aligning, the setup is considered weaker and carries more risk. In these situations, traders often wait for stronger confirmation, such as a clear candlestick pattern or shift in momentum, before taking action.

Confluence or not?

Price is reacting near the 61.8% Fibonacci level. The Moving Average is slightly below, and RSI is around 57. True confluence requires multiple indicators confirming the same zone, not just one tool reacting.

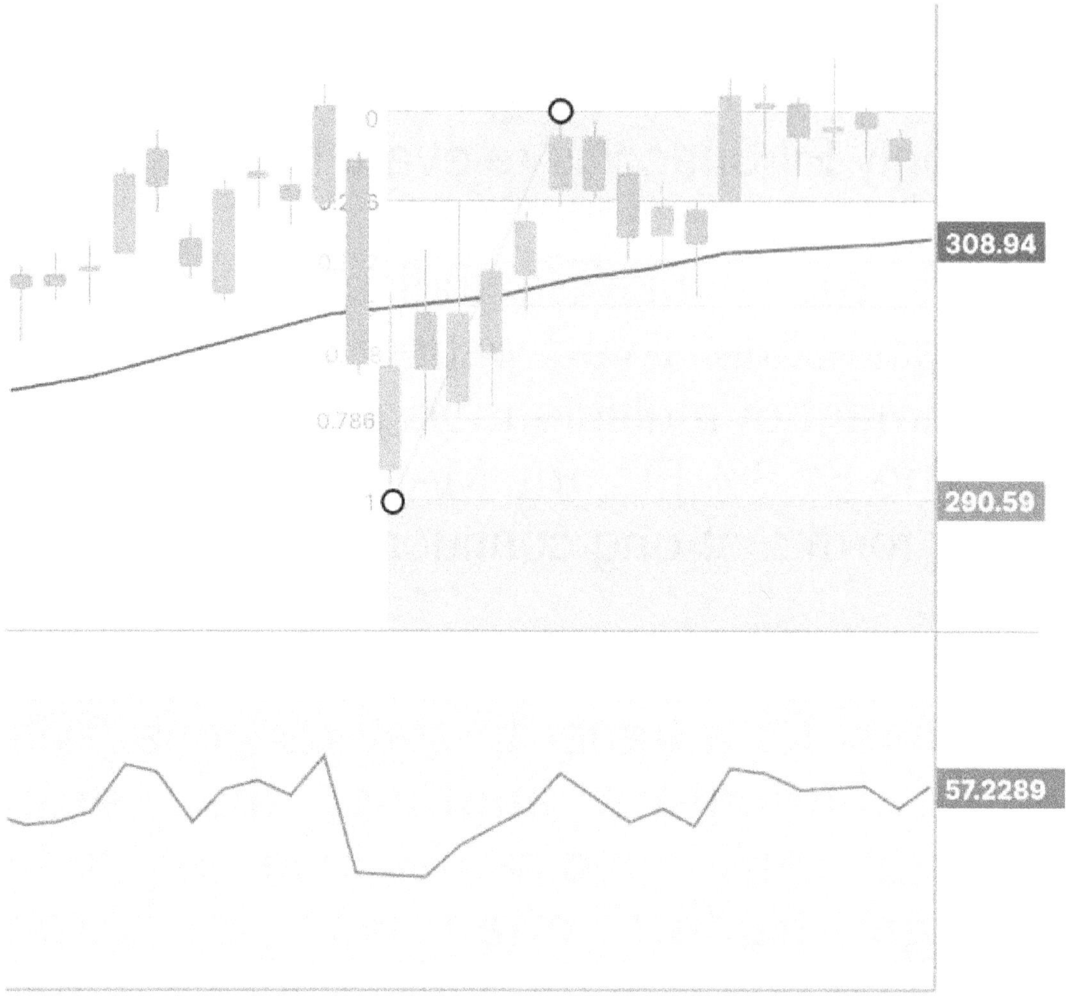

Based on what you see, would you consider this a valid confluence?

- No, the indicators aren't clearly aligned
- Yes, all tools point to the same area
- Yes, price bounced near the Fib level
- Maybe, RSI confirms, but MA is too far

Answer: No, the indicators aren't clearly aligned. One indicator reacting is helpful, but confluence needs at least two or more indicators pointing to the same zone. Without clear alignment between Fibonacci, MA, and RSI, this isn't a strong confluence setup.

Now that you know how to use Fibonacci levels, RSI, and Moving Averages together to spot confluence, it's time to apply what you've learned. Let's put your skills to the test with real chart scenarios.

Make a decision

Price is approaching the 0.382 Fibonacci retracement level while the RSI is recovering toward 50. However, the 200-period Moving Average is still above and trending downward. Strong setups usually involve multiple indicators confirming the same zone. Without that, it may be wise to stay cautious.

How would you approach this setup?

- Buy, price is recovering, and RSI is rising
- Wait, there's no strong confluence yet
- Sell, price is near resistance with weak trend
- Enter long, the Fib level alone is enough

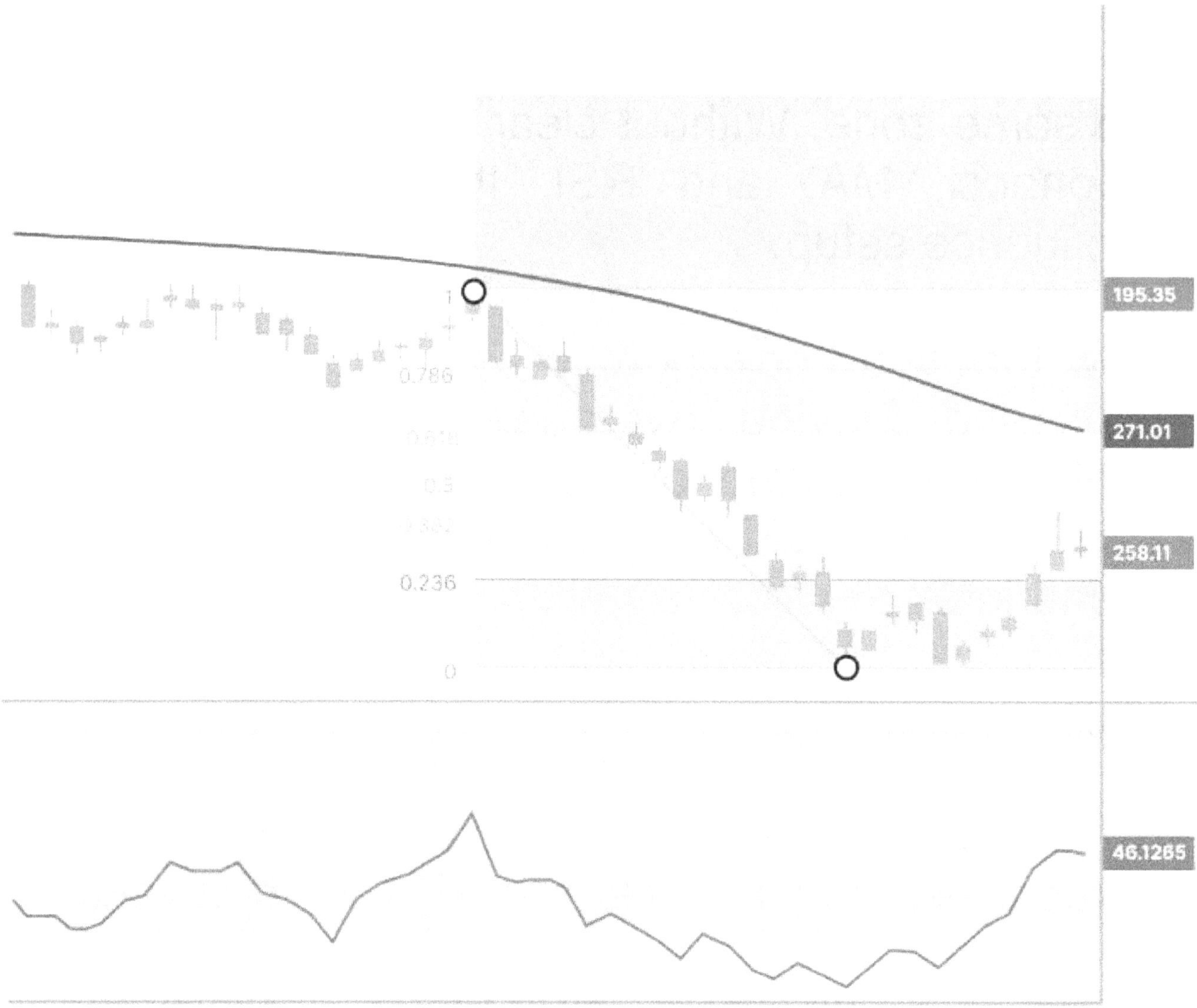

Answer: Wait, there's no strong confluence yet. Without full confluence, relying on just one or two signals increases the risk of a false move. With no strong alignment between MA, Fib, and RSI, it's better to wait for more confirmation.

What will you do?

Price is pushing into the 0.618 Fibonacci retracement level while the Moving Average is also nearby. RSI is rising and is currently near 57.

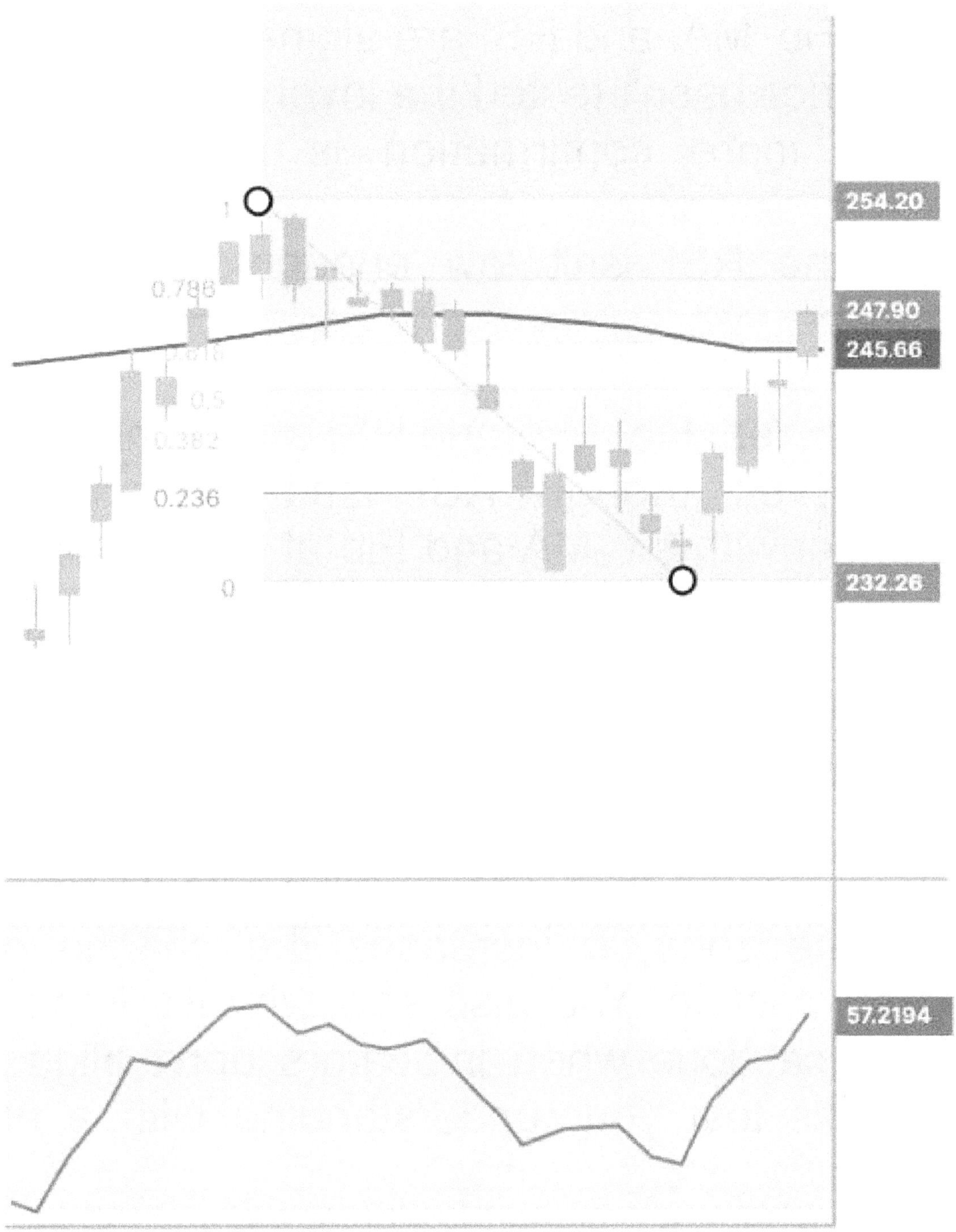

Strong setups often appear when multiple tools agree at the same level, even if RSI isn't in the oversold zone. Would you consider this a strong confluence zone for a potential long entry?

- Yes, Fib, MA, and RSI are aligned at this level
- No, price hasn't tested the level clearly
- Wait, more confirmation is needed before acting
- No, the RSI isn't low enough to confirm a bounce

Answer: Yes, Fib, MA, and RSI are aligned at this level. Even though RSI isn't oversold, the alignment with the MA and Fib at 0.618 still gives this setup strength. This is a solid confluence setup - price meets the 0.618 Fibonacci level, aligns with the MA, and RSI momentum is supportive.

Now you know that when multiple tools point to the same zone, it increases the chance of a market reaction. You also saw why it's important to stay cautious when indicators don't align. Up next: let's test your understanding with a quick quiz!

QUIZ: Fibonacci Scenarios

1. Price has retraced to the 61.8% Fibonacci level in an uptrend. RSI is stable, and a bounce is forming. What would many traders do?

A. Buy, expecting the uptrend to resume from this key level
B. Sell, assuming the price will break lower
C. Short, expecting a deep retracement
D. Wait, avoid action without RSI in oversold

2. You're planning a Fibonacci-based trade. What's the first step?

A. Enter the trade
B. Identify the trend
C. Draw Fibonacci levels
D. Wait for a price pullback

3. You draw a Fibonacci Extension after a retracement. Price breaks above the 1.272

level with strong momentum. What should you consider?

A. Hold your long trade, price may continue toward 1.618
B. Go short, the price is extended
C. Stay out, this is unpredictable
D. Exit the trade immediately

4. The price has broken below the 1.272 Fibonacci Extension in a downtrend with strong momentum. What might a trader do?

A. Go long - the price might bounce soon
B. Go short - the bearish move may continue
C. Hold - RSI is neutral
D. Close all trades - the trend is unclear

5. Price pulls back to the 0.382 Fibonacci retracement level. RSI is near 50 and recovering. The 200-period MA is still above and sloping down. What's the best action?

A. Wait - no strong confluence at this point
B. Sell - price might fail at 0.382
C. Buy - RSI is turning up
D. Enter long - Fibonacci level is enough

6. Price touches the 0.618 Fibonacci level. The 50-period MA is nearby, and RSI is at 57. What does this suggest?

A. Market is bearish - avoid trading
B. No signal - RSI isn't oversold
C. Confluence is weak - not valid
D. A strong confluence zone for a potential long entry

7. What is the main purpose of Fibonacci Extension levels?

A. To project future price targets after a retracement
B. To identify oversold conditions
C. To replace RSI and Moving Averages
D. To set stop-loss points only

8. Price touches the 61.8% Fib level and also aligns with a Moving Average. RSI is near 56. What is this called?

A. Extension failure
B. Trend reversal
C. Pullback zone - ignore other indicators
D. Confluence zone

9. Why do traders combine Fibonacci with RSI or Moving Averages?

A. To avoid drawing Fibonacci levels
B. To remove emotion from all trades
C. To only follow RSI signals
D. To strengthen their setups with multiple confirmations

10. If price reacts only to the Fibonacci level, but MA and RSI do not align, what should a trader do?

A. Ignore the other indicators
B. Use Fibonacci alone without confirmation
C. Enter the trade confidently
D. Be cautious

Answer: 1. A; 2. B; 3. A; 4. B; 5. A; 6. D; 7. A; 8. D; 9. D; 10. D

Chapter 8: Divergence In Action

Lesson 1: Divergence As A Strategic Signal

Let's explore divergence!

You already know that divergence can signal a potential shift in momentum, but today, we'll look deeper. We'll explore why divergence is best used as a supporting tool rather than a primary trigger, and how combining it with other indicators can lead to smarter, more reliable trade decisions.

Divergence occurs when the price and an indicator move in opposite directions, which may signal a potential reversal or shift in momentum.

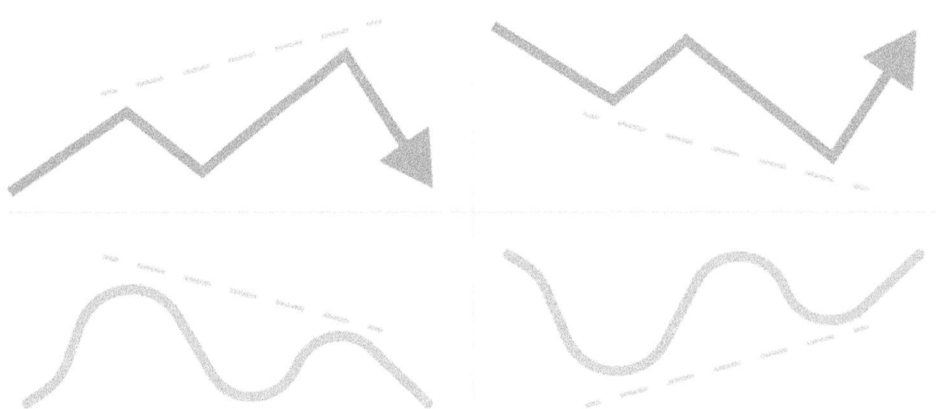

Now that you recalled what divergence is, let's look at the two most common types. Bullish divergence happens when price makes lower lows but the indicator makes higher lows, suggesting that selling pressure is weakening.

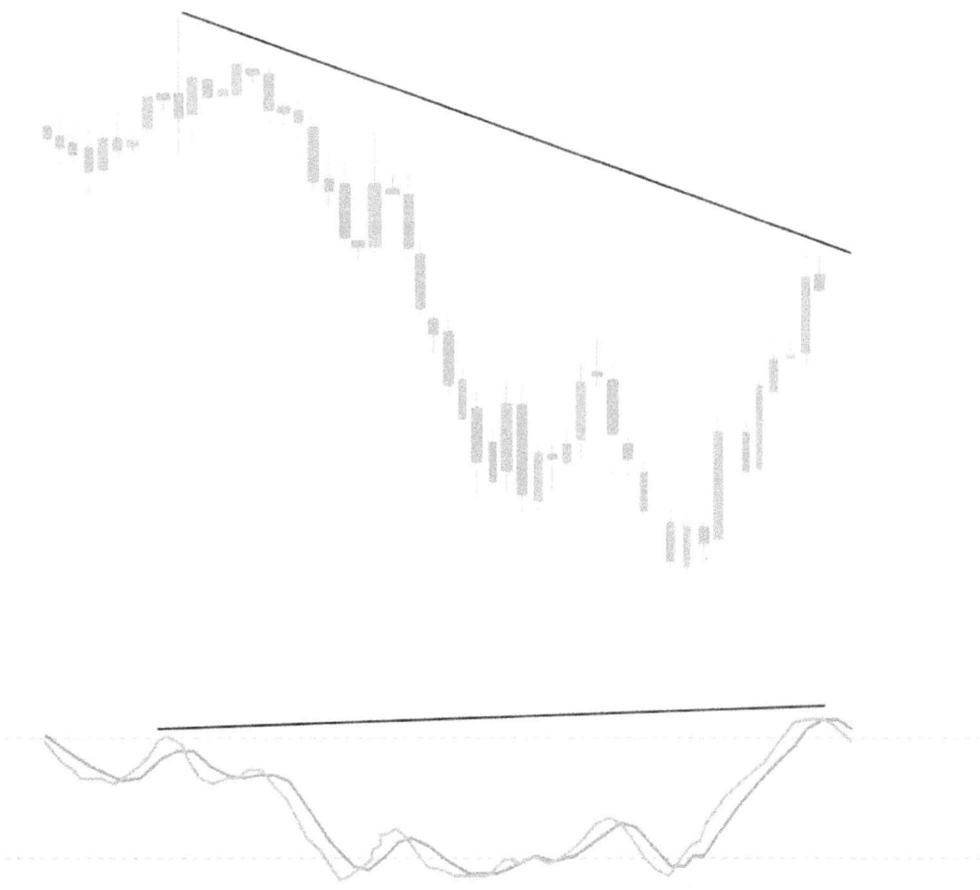

Bearish divergence is the opposite: price makes higher highs while the indicator makes lower highs, hinting that buying momentum is slowing down.

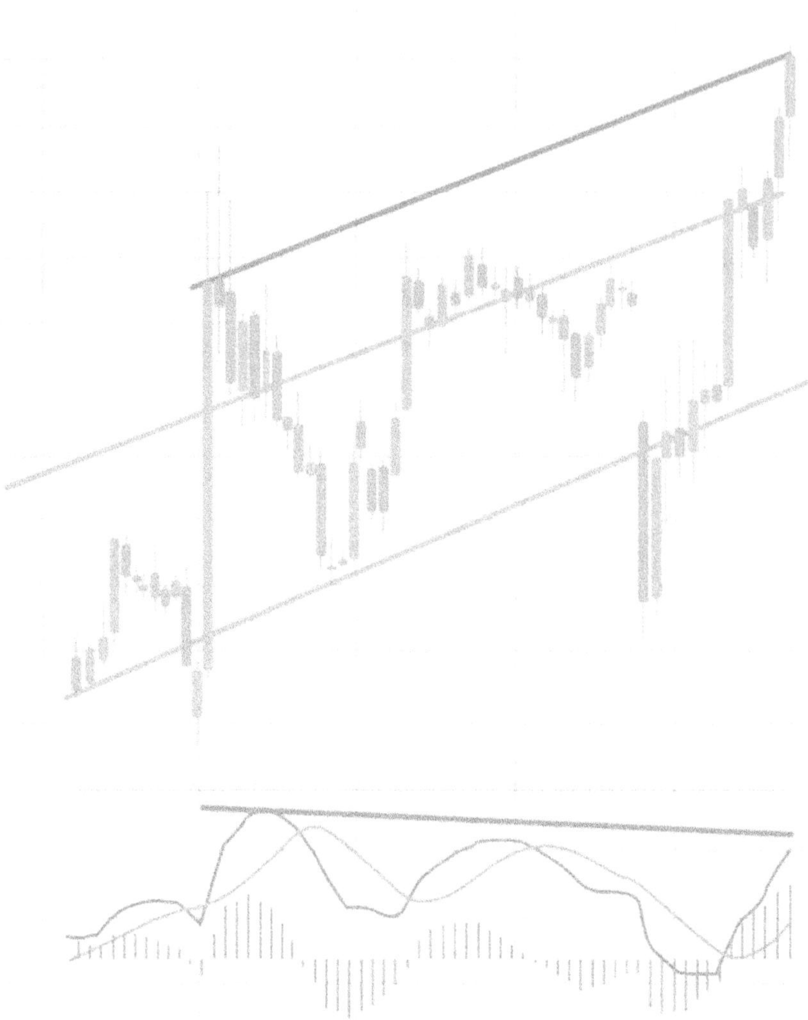

Divergence signals that a trend may be losing strength - it's an early clue, not a guarantee. Smart traders don't act on it alone; they wait for confirmation from support/resistance, trendlines, candlestick patterns, or volume before making a move.

How do they get confirmation? They study candlestick patterns. Reversal signals like a doji, hammer, or engulfing candle near the divergence area give traders extra confidence that a shift in direction could be forming.

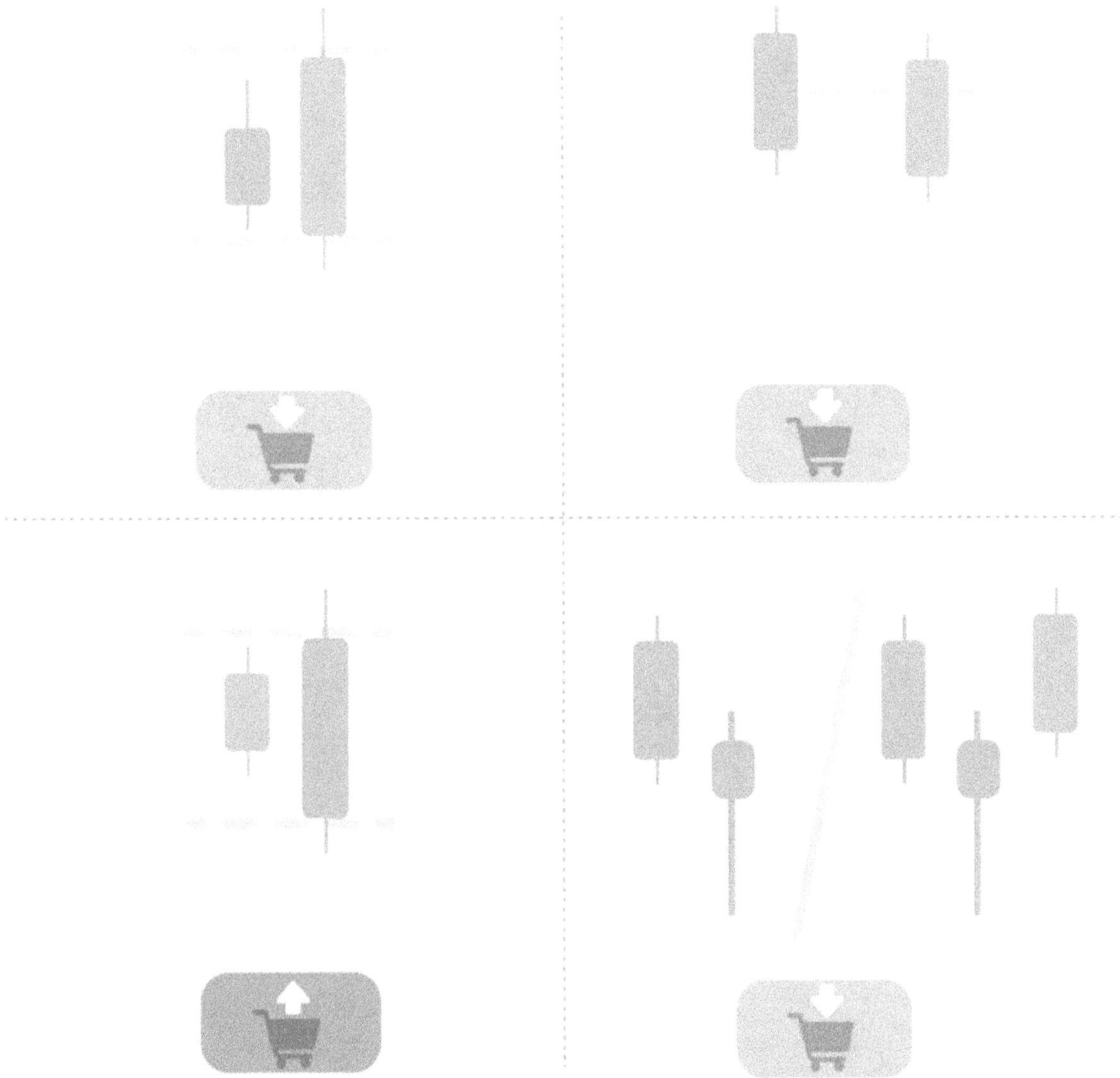

They also check support and resistance levels. If divergence occurs near a key support (for bullish divergence) or resistance (for bearish divergence), it adds weight to the setup because the price is reacting at a meaningful level on the chart.

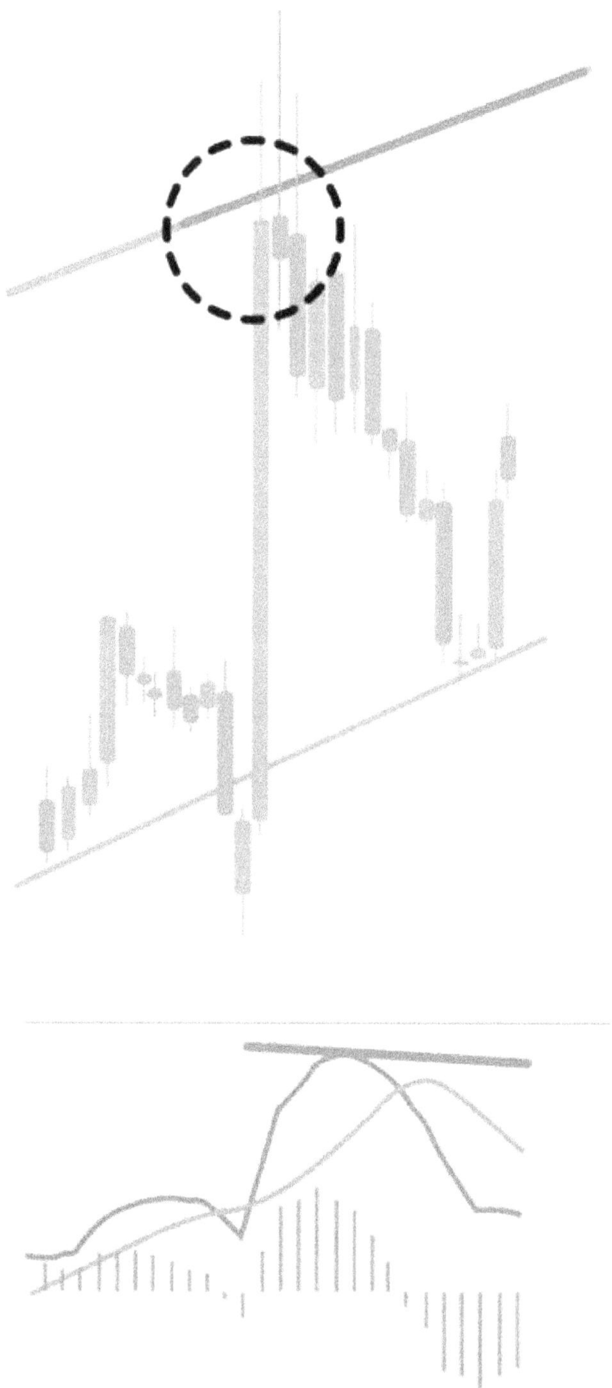

Finally, traders look at volume. A spike in volume during a breakout or during a confirming candle strengthens the signal. Rising volume means more market participants are stepping in, which helps validate the direction suggested by divergence.

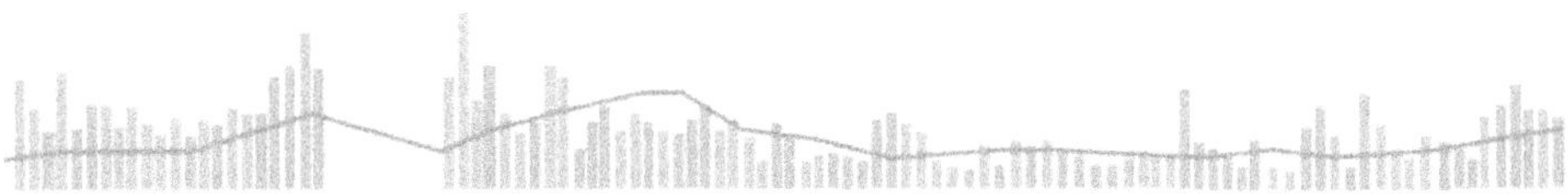

In case of confirmation in a bullish divergence, traders might enter a buy position. To manage risk, they place a stop loss (1) just below the most recent swing low - the lowest point of the last downward move. This way, if the price continues to drop instead of reversing, the loss is limited.

If bearish divergence is confirmed, traders may enter a sell position. To manage risk, they place a stop loss (1) just above the most recent swing high, which is the highest point of the last upward move. This helps limit losses if the price unexpectedly continues rising.

Let's practice!

You're analyzing this daily chart of the Dow Jones Industrial Average. Price recently made a lower low, but the MACD histogram and MACD line seem to be forming a higher low. Think about what makes divergence useful but risky. Is it strong enough to act on alone, or do smart traders wait for something more?

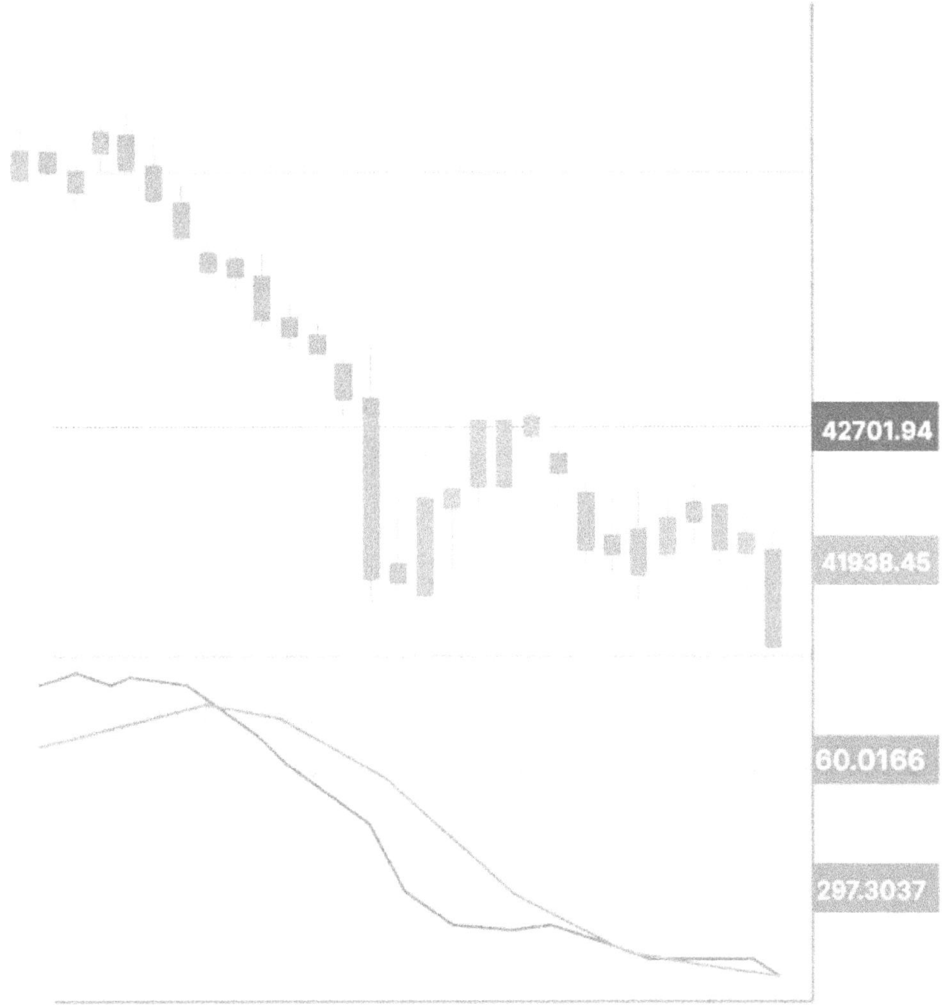

Based on this setup, what would be your next move?

- Enter a short position, because this is just a temporary bounce in a downtrend.
- Ignore the MACD, because price is still in a downtrend, and divergence is unreliable.
- Enter a buy trade immediately, because this is a clear bullish divergence.
- Wait for a bullish confirmation candle and a break above recent highs before entering.

Answer: Wait for a bullish confirmation candle and a break above recent highs before entering. Divergence signals a possible momentum shift, but without confirmation, it could fail. A bullish candlestick or a break above resistance adds evidence and reduces the risk of a false signal.

Now you've seen how divergence can signal a shift in momentum and why it's best used as a supporting tool. Next, you'll learn how both RSI and MACD reveal different types of divergence and how to apply them with even more precision.

Lesson 2: Regular vs Hidden Divergence Review

Let's explore regular and hidden divergence!

In this lesson, you'll learn more about regular and hidden divergence, and how they help traders spot either a potential reversal or a continuation of the trend. We'll explore how to identify them using RSI and MACD. By the end of this lesson, you'll be confidently reading momentum shifts and trend strength.

Regular vs. hidden divergence

We'd previously discussed regular and hidden divergence. One divergence helps spot turning points; the other confirms the trend is still continuing. Can you match each type with what it signals?

- Hidden Divergence - Signals a possible reversal

- Regular Divergence - Signals trend continuation

Answer:

- Hidden Divergence - Signals trend continuation
- Regular Divergence - Signals a possible reversal

Excellent! Don't forget that regular divergence (1) signals a possible trend reversal. It shows that momentum is weakening, and a change in direction could be coming. But hidden divergence (2) suggests the existing trend is still strong, even if the price is pulling back.

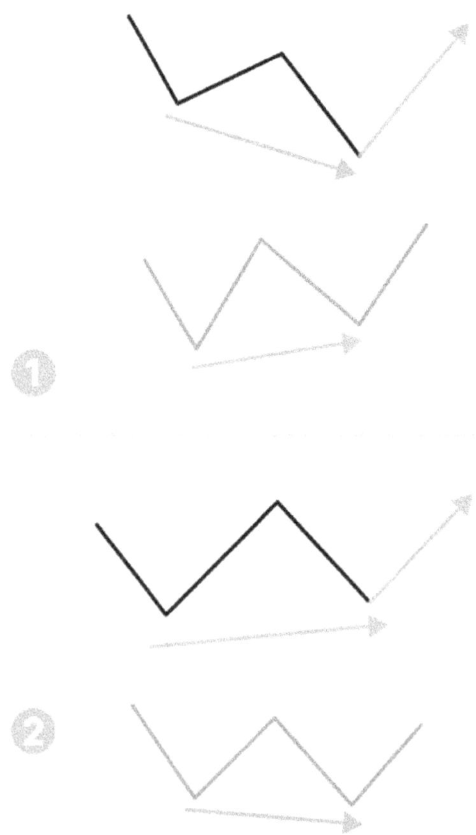

Hidden divergence usually appears during a pullback or correction within an ongoing trend. It helps traders spot opportunities to rejoin a trend, not escape it. Understanding it helps you decide whether to expect a reversal or trust the continuation.

In a bullish hidden divergence, the price makes higher lows, while the indicator makes lower lows, showing that the uptrend is still supported by momentum.

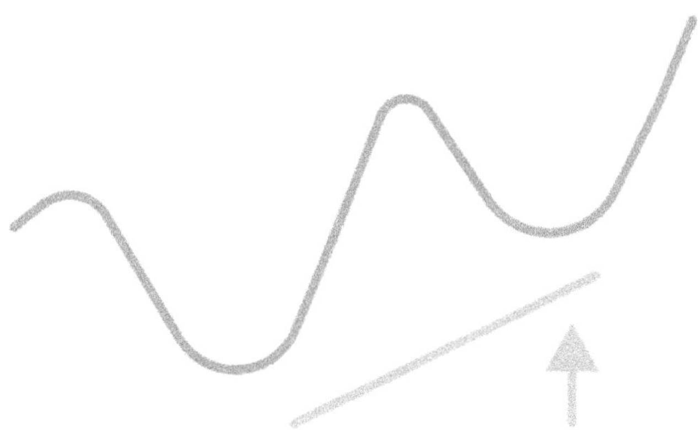

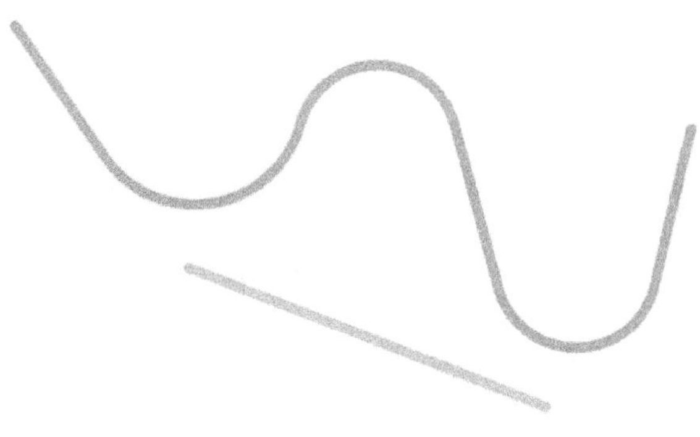

When traders notice bullish hidden divergence, they understand that the current uptrend is likely to continue. They don't enter immediately. Instead, they look for confirmation, such as a bounce from a trendline or support level, or the appearance of a bullish candlestick pattern.

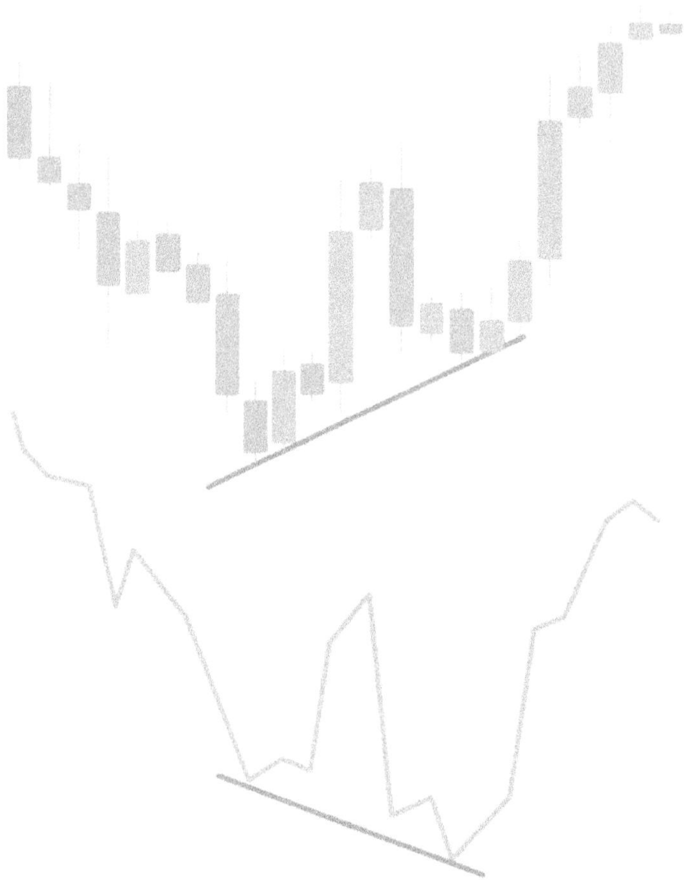

Once the setup is confirmed, they enter a buy trade, placing a stop loss just below the recent higher low to manage risk. Their take-profit target is often set at the next resistance level or based on a favorable risk-reward ratio.

In a bearish hidden divergence, price makes lower highs, but the indicator shows higher highs, signaling that the downtrend is likely to resume.

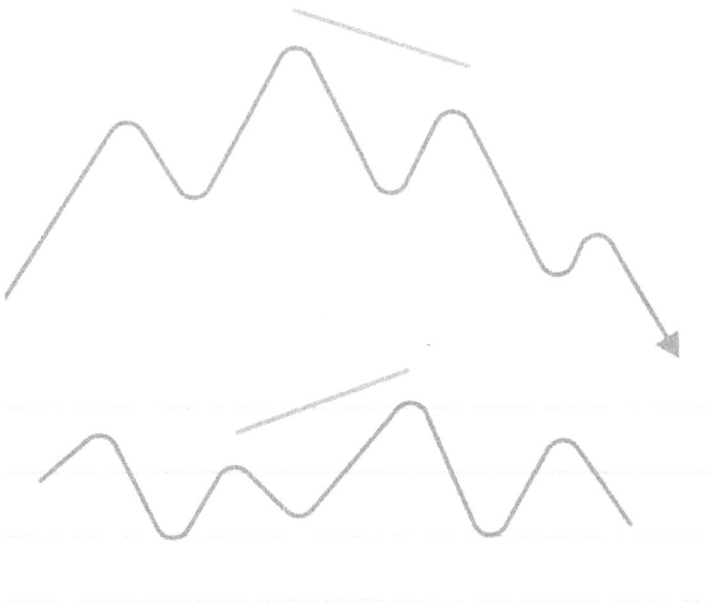

In the case of bearish hidden divergence, traders interpret it as a signal that the existing downtrend is likely to resume after a short-term upward correction. They wait for confirmation, such as a rejection from a resistance level or a bearish candlestick formation, before entering a sell trade.

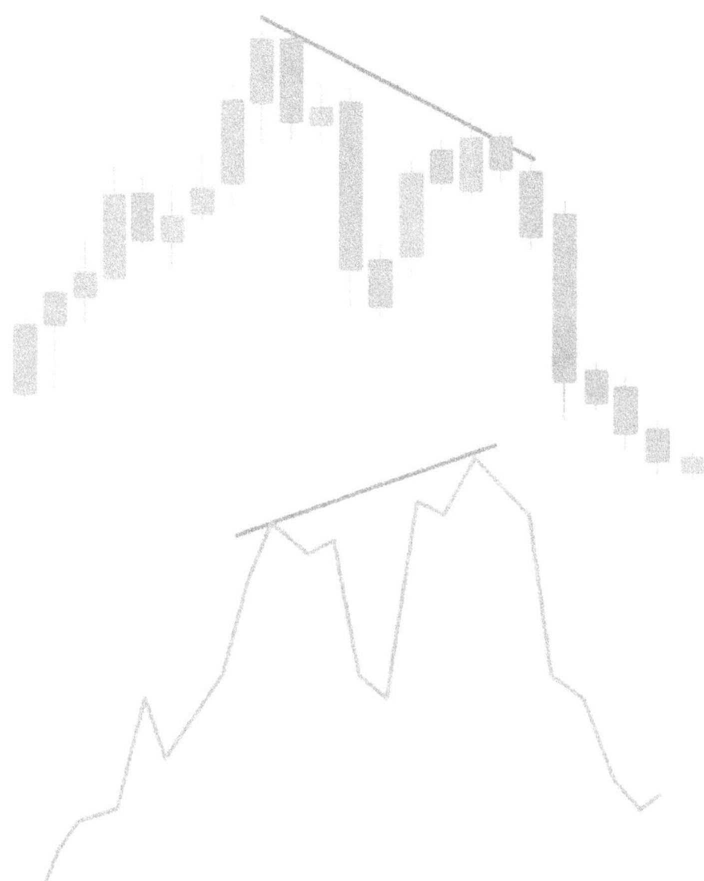

To protect their position, they place a stop loss above the recent lower high and aim to take profit near the next support level or according to a predefined risk-reward setup. Hidden divergence helps them stay aligned with the dominant trend while timing their entry more effectively.

Can you spot the divergence type?

Look at the chart carefully. The price is making higher lows, while the indicator is making lower lows. Think about whether the price is continuing in the same direction or reversing. Also, focus on whether the price or indicator is making higher or lower highs/lows.

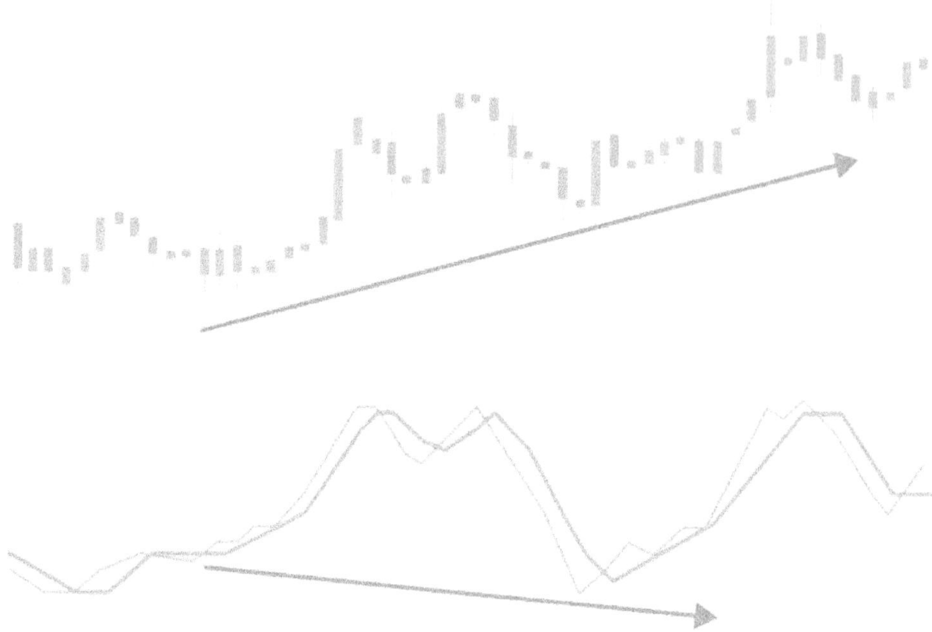

What kind of divergence is shown in this chart?

- Regular Bullish Divergence
- Hidden Bearish Divergence
- Regular Bearish Divergence
- Hidden Bullish Divergence

Answer: Hidden Bullish Divergence. Price is making higher lows (uptrend continues), while the indicator is making lower lows. This setup confirms hidden bullish divergence, which signals trend continuation upward.

Practice making decisions with RSI!

You're looking at a chart showing price making higher lows, while RSI is making lower lows. Think about what hidden divergence typically signals: reversal or continuation? Also, what confirms that the trend is ready to resume?

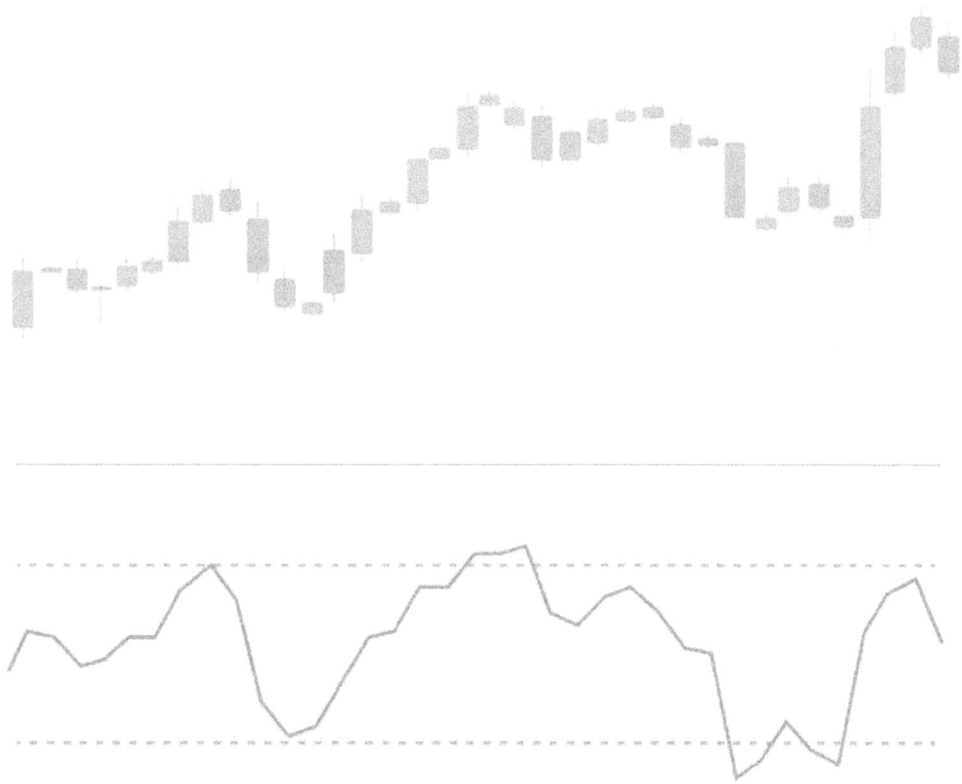

What does this setup suggest, and would you respond?

- Enter a buy trade if there's confirmation from price action

- Enter a sell trade now, expecting a trend reversal
- Do nothing - RSI divergence isn't reliable
- Wait for the RSI to drop below 30 before entering any trade

Answer: Enter a buy trade if there's confirmation from price action. This is a case of hidden bullish divergence, which signals potential trend continuation. If confirmed by bullish price action, it's an opportunity to rejoin the uptrend.

On the other hand, MACD, with its moving averages and histogram, shows momentum shifts and trend strength more smoothly over time. Together, they help traders see when momentum supports a trend, even if price appears to stall, making them especially useful for confirming trend continuation setups.

Practice making decisions with MACD!

You're analyzing this uptrend on AUDI USD. The price is making higher lows, while the MACD line and histogram are making lower lows. Hidden divergence in an uptrend often signals that the trend is still strong. Confirmation matters, so look for a bullish candle or trendline bounce.

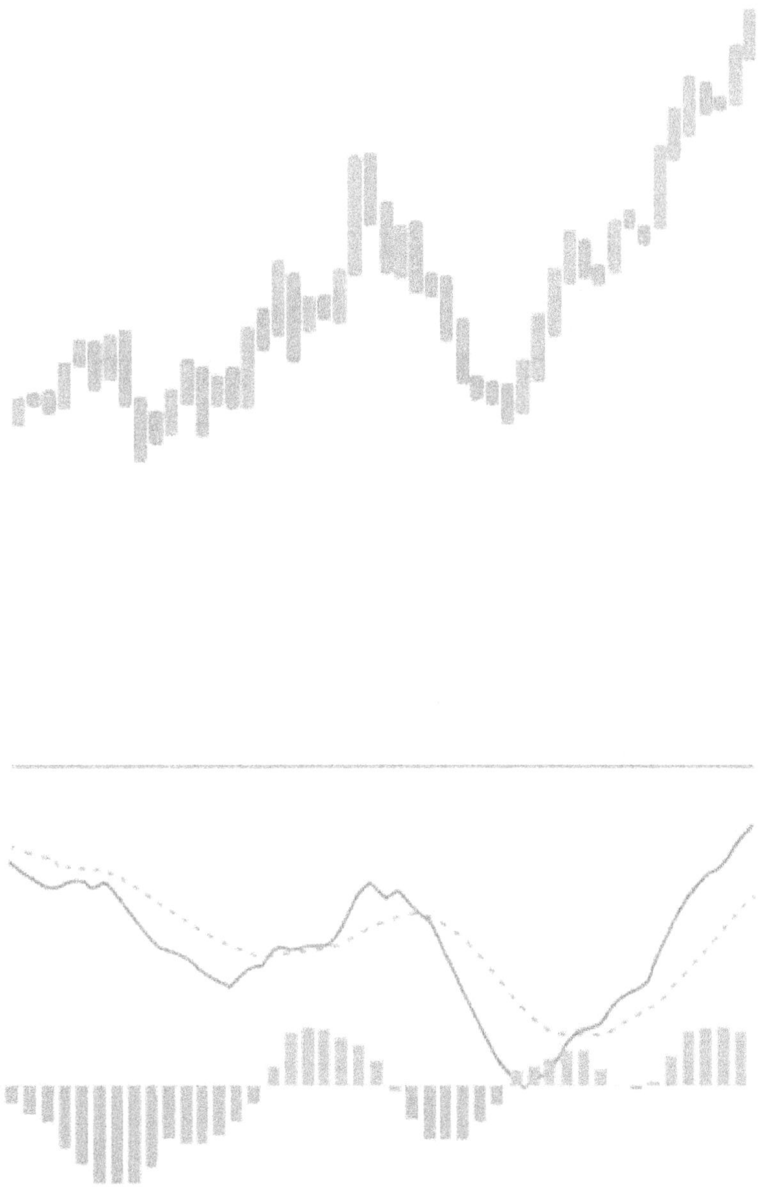

Based on this setup, what would you do next?

- Enter a buy trade near the confirmation candle, placing a stop loss below the recent swing low
- Enter a sell trade expecting the trend to reverse
- Wait for the MACD to cross the zero line before doing anything
- Avoid trading because the divergence signal is unclear

Answer: Enter a buy trade near the confirmation candle, placing a stop loss below the recent swing low. Hidden bullish MACD divergence suggests trend continuation, and the confirmation candle supports a buying decision with managed risk.

Excellent job! You've learned how to recognize both regular and hidden divergence using RSI and MACD, and how to respond based on trend strength and momentum. Up next, we'll explore how divergence can improve your risk management.

Lesson 3: Risk Management with Divergence

How to manage risks with divergence?

In this lesson, you'll learn how divergence goes beyond spotting entries - it's a powerful tool for managing risk. By the end, you'll know how traders use it to place strategic stop-losses, time their exits more effectively, and better understand the market context.

Let's start with regular divergence. Since it signals a possible trend reversal, traders must be cautious with risk management. In the case of a regular bullish divergence, traders wait for confirmation, such as a bullish candlestick or a break above resistance, before entering a buy trade.

Traders place a stop-loss (1) just below the recent swing low to limit losses if the reversal fails. They go long (2) after confirmation, and aim for take-profit (3) at the next resistance level, usually using a 1:2 risk-reward ratio to ensure the potential profit is twice the risk.

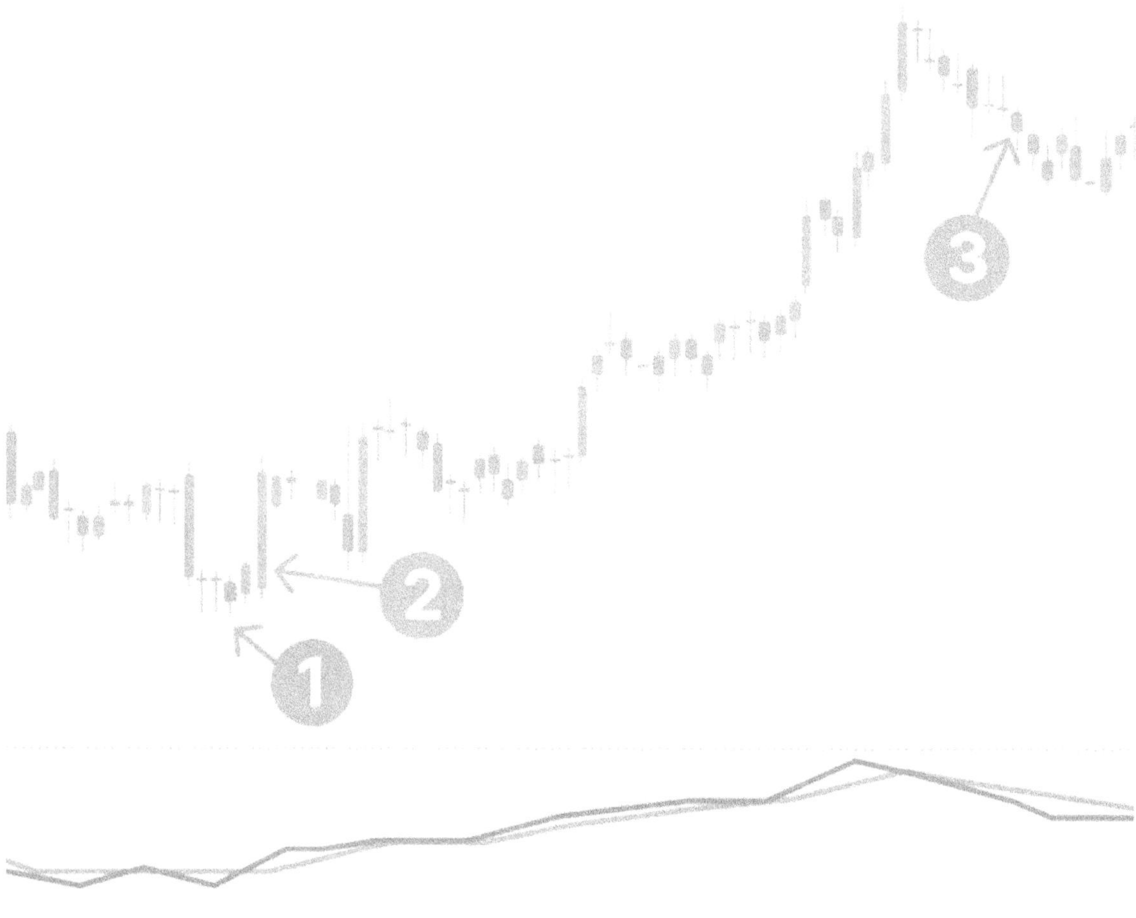

A 1:2 risk-reward ratio means risking 1 unit to gain 2. For example, if the stop-loss (1) is 50 pips below the entry, the take-profit (2) would be 100 pips above. This ensures that even with some losing trades, consistent risk-reward planning can still lead to long-term profitability.

In regular bearish divergence, traders confirm through a bearish pattern or a support break before entering a sell trade. A stop-loss (1) is set just above the recent swing high, the short entry is made (2), and the take-profit (3) is placed near the next support level, targeting a 1:2 risk-reward.

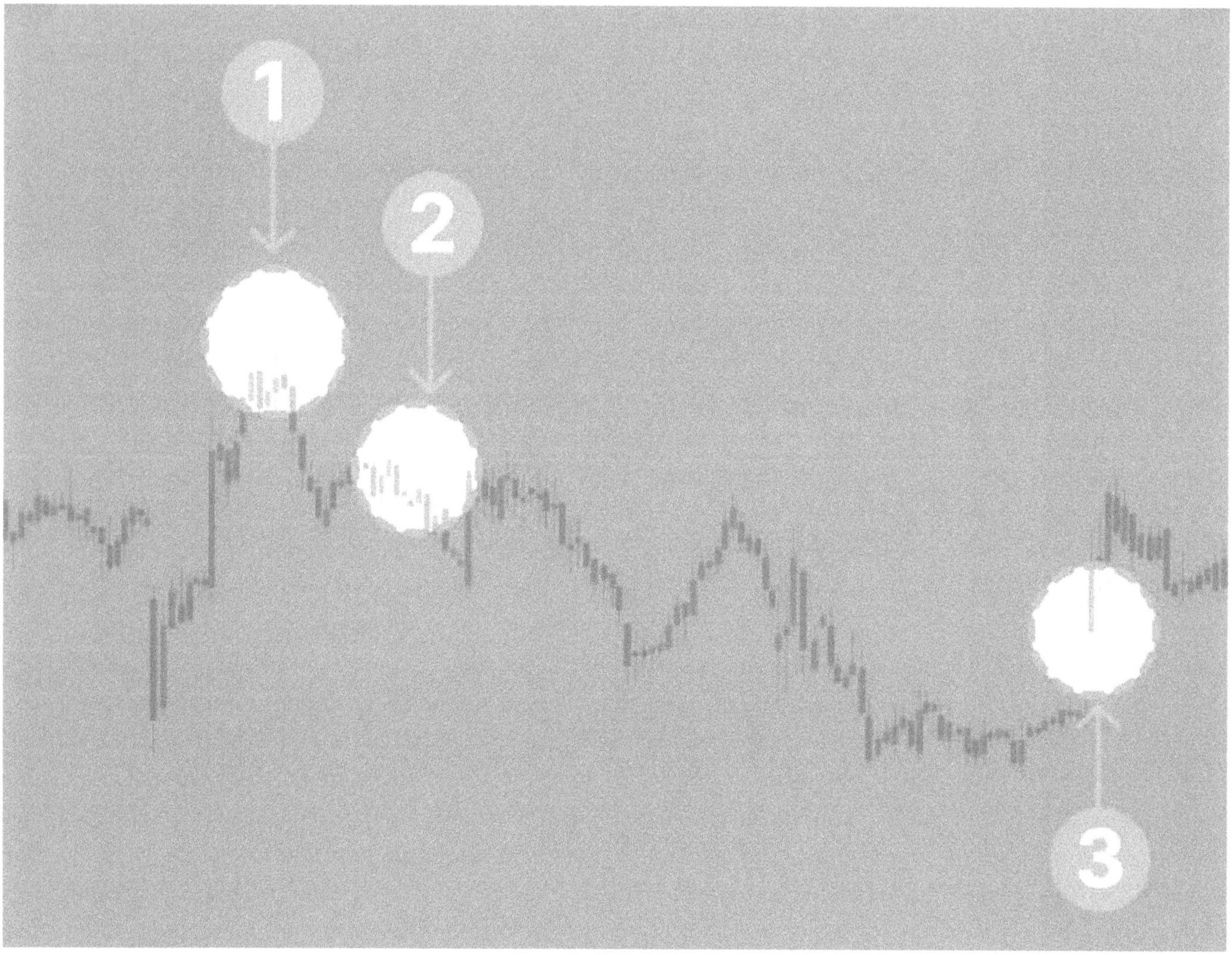

Match stop-loss and trade action to each setup

You're comparing regular bullish and bearish divergence. If the market is expected to reverse up, traders buy and place their stop just below the last low. If it's reversing down, they sell and protect the position above the last high. Can you match each scenario with the correct stop-loss and trade action?

- Bullish Stop-Loss - Buy after confirmation
- Bearish Divergence - Sell after confirmation
- Bullish Divergence - Below the recent swing low

Answer:

- Bullish Stop-Loss - Below the recent swing low
- Bearish Divergence - Sell after confirmation
- Bullish Divergence - Buy after confirmation

In hidden bullish divergence, traders wait for confirmation, like a trendline bounce or bullish candle, before entering a long position. They place a stop-loss (1) below the recent higher low and set a take-profit (2) at the next resistance or using a 1:2 risk-reward ratio.

In hidden bearish divergence, traders wait for confirmation, like a resistance rejection or bearish candle, before entering a short trade. They place a stop-loss (1) above the recent lower high and set a take-profit (2) near the next support, often using a 1:2 risk-reward ratio.

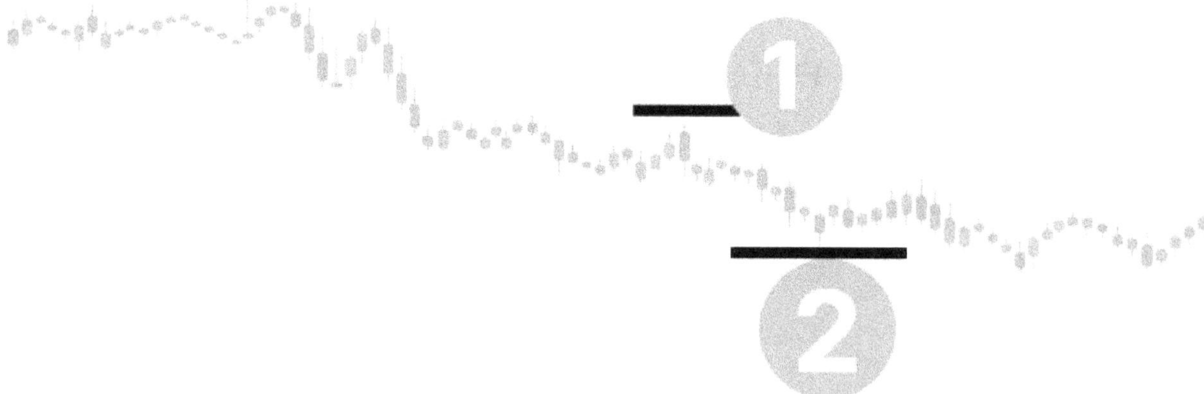

A quick check!

You've spotted hidden bullish divergence on the chart. After confirmation from a bullish candle, you decide to enter a long trade. A good stop-loss protects your trade if the trend fails. A smart take-profit targets a logical resistance area, ideally with a 1:2 risk-reward ratio.

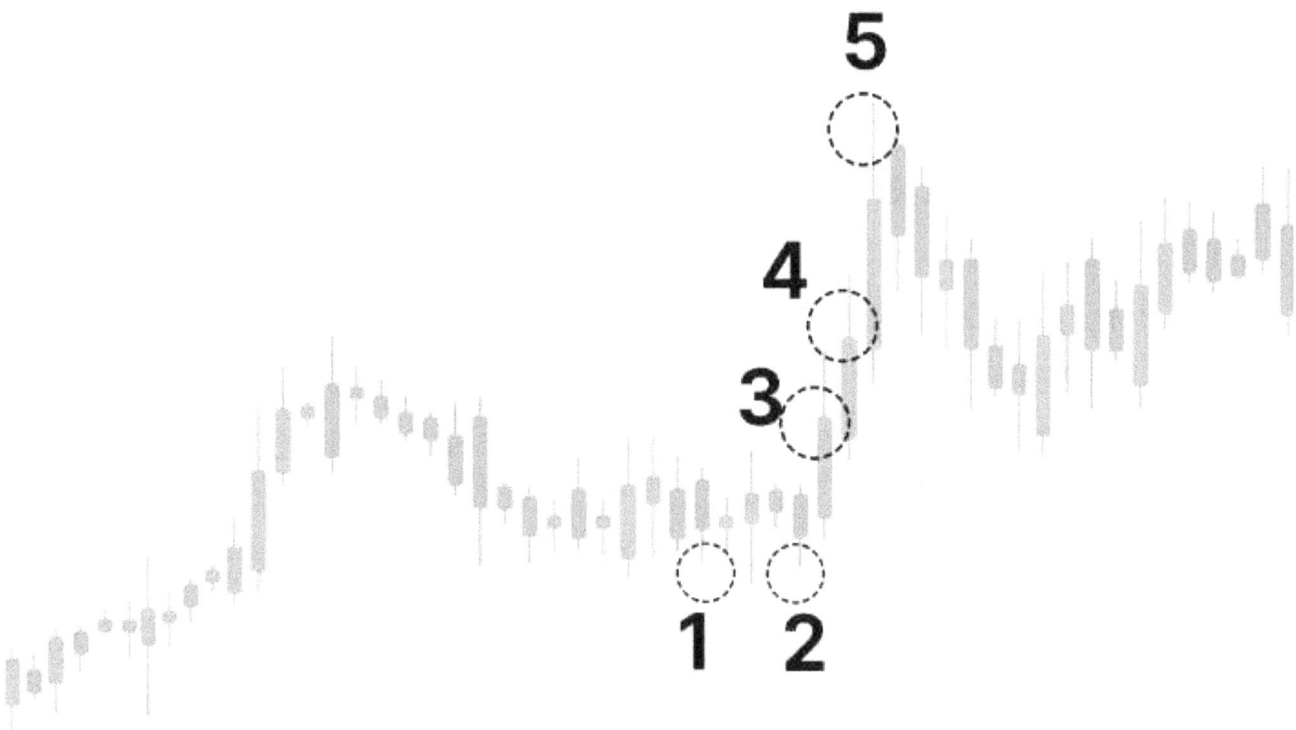

Look at the 5 points marked on the chart and choose the best stop-loss and take-profit positions for this setup.

- 3 - stop-loss; 4 - take-profit
- 1 - stop-loss; 5 - take-profit
- 2 - stop-loss; 5 - take-profit
- 3 - stop-loss; 5 - take-profit

Answer: 1 - stop-loss; 5 - take-profit. Point 1 is the ideal stop-loss because it's placed just below the recent higher low, protecting the trade if the trend fails to continue. Point 5 is a strong take-profit target, aligned with the previous major high and offering a good risk-reward ratio.

Markets don't always move at the same pace. In high-volatility conditions, tight stop-losses often get hit before price moves in your favor. That's why smart traders adapt their stop-loss distance based on volatility, not just price structure.

When volatility is high, price moves are fast, and candles are large. If you set your stop-loss too close to the entry, you risk being taken out by normal fluctuations. You can use indicators like the Bollinger Bands or Moving Averages to guide placement.

For example, in a bullish setup, you can place your stop-loss just outside the lower Bollinger

Band or below a rising moving average like the 20 EMA to allow for natural price swings.

In a bearish setup, place your stop-loss just above the upper Bollinger Band or slightly above a falling moving average like the 20 EMA to give the trade room during a pullback without exiting too early.

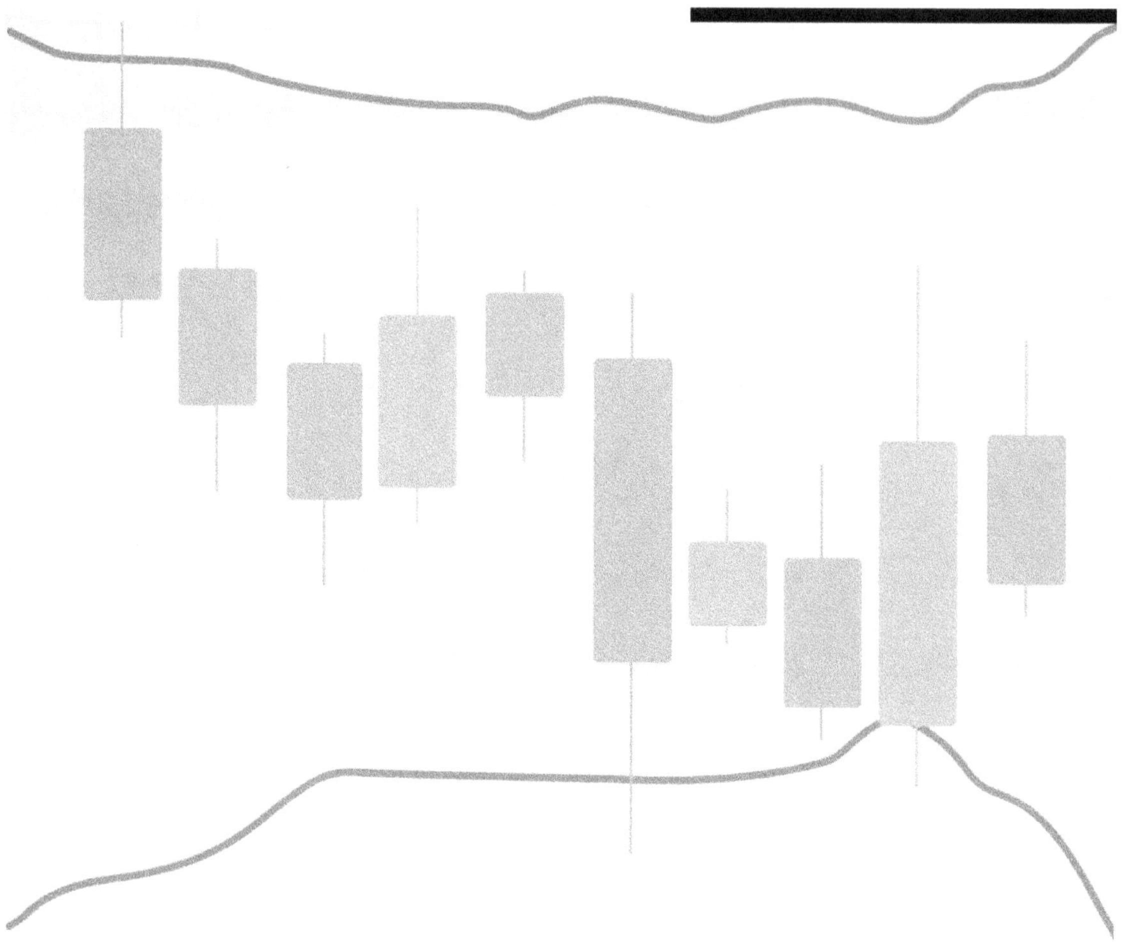

When volatility is low, price is more stable and compressed within narrow ranges. In this environment, large moves are less likely, so tighter stops are more efficient.

In low-volatility bullish setups, traders use indicators like RSI or MACD for confirmation. If RSI holds above 50 or MACD stays above the signal line, a stop-loss just below support limits risk without overreacting to minor price moves.

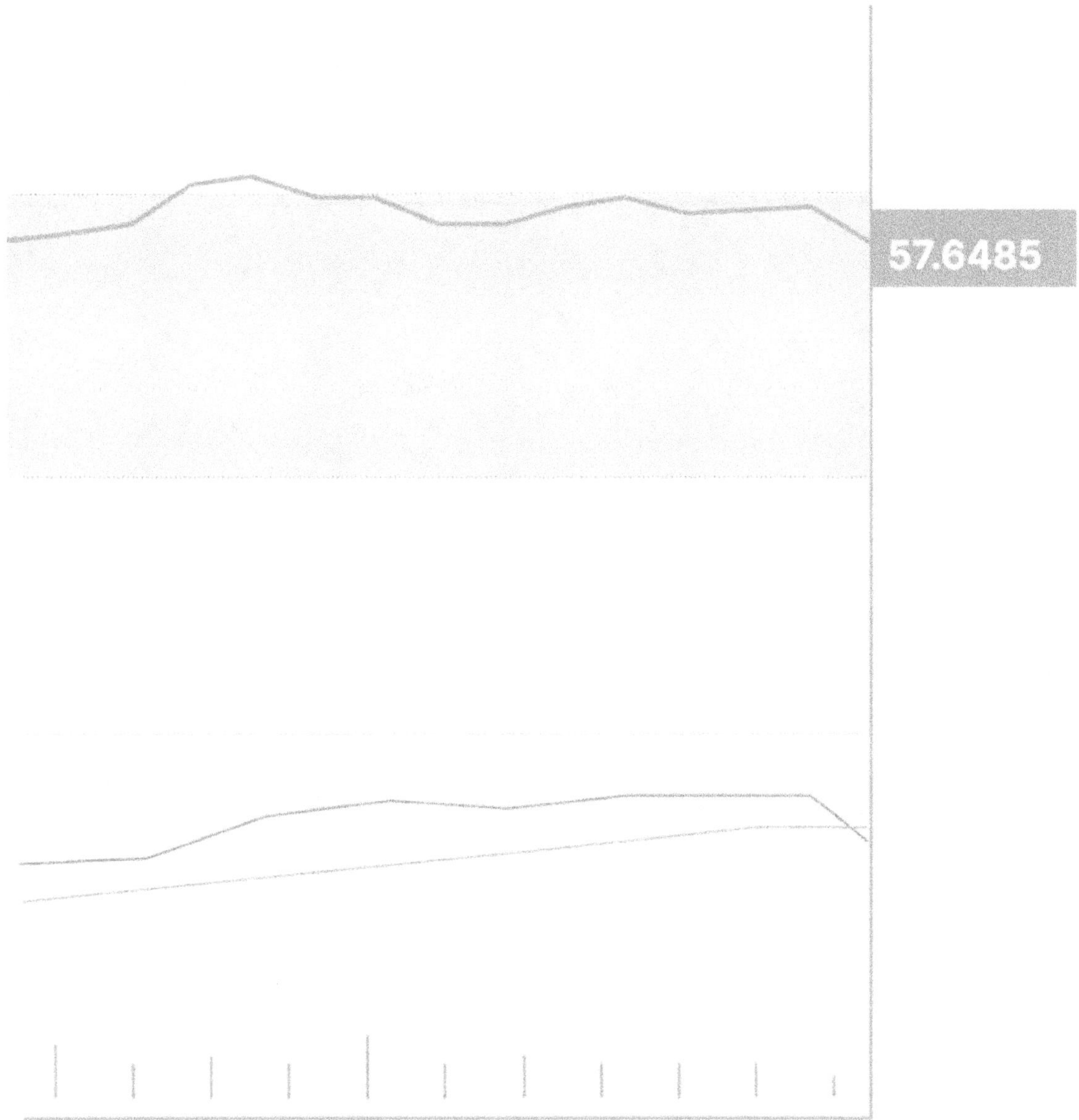

In a bearish low-volatility scenario, if RSI stays below 50 or MACD is below the signal line, a stop-loss placed just above that resistance is appropriate. It's tight enough to protect capital if the trend fails, but gives the trade room to play out without being overly exposed.

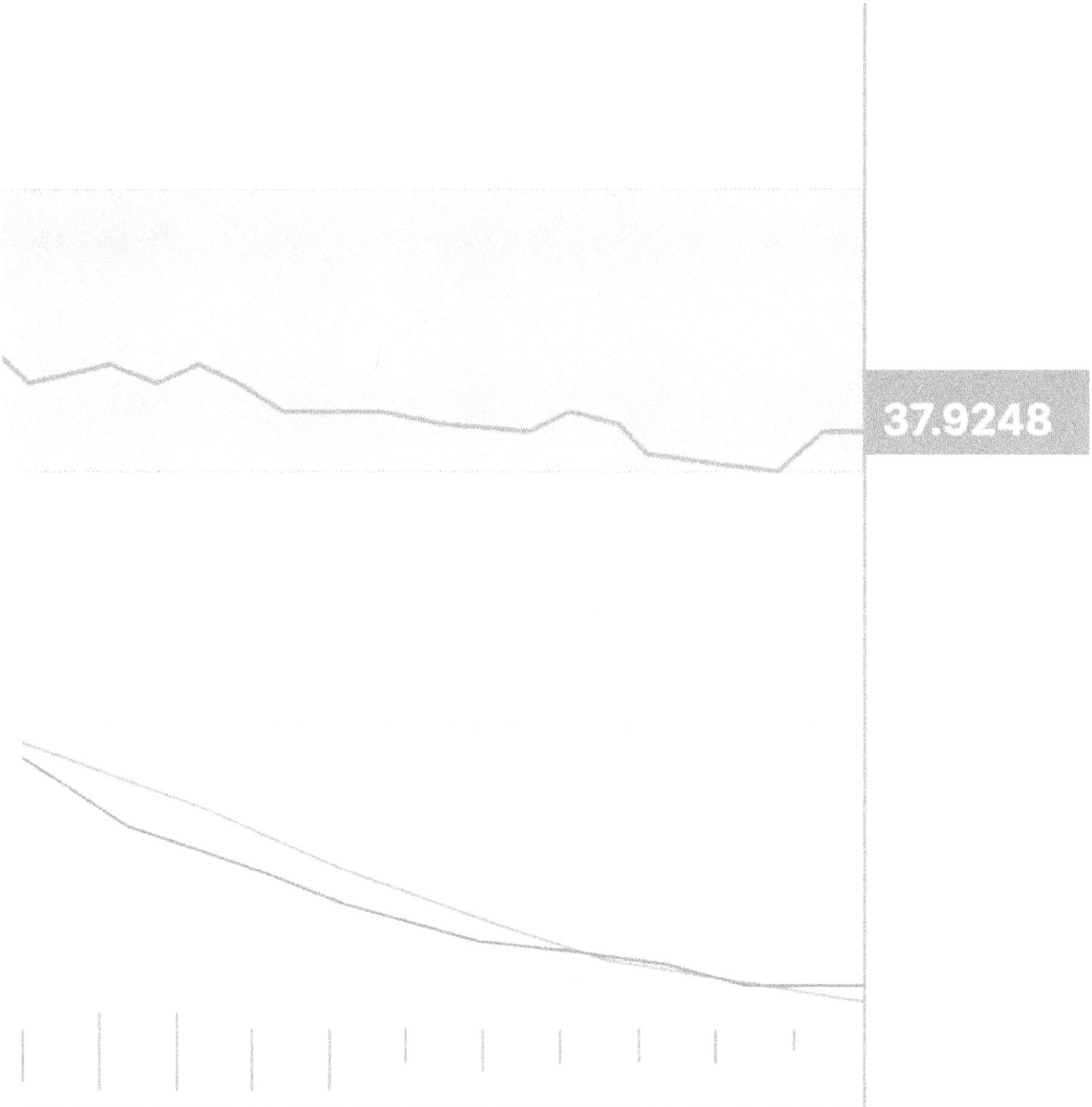

Match the setup with the correct stop-loss and signal

In calm markets, indicators help confirm subtle trend strength. In volatile markets, traders give their stops more room, placing them beyond dynamic levels like bands or moving averages. Match each scenario with the appropriate stop-loss position and indicator behavior.

- Bearish Low Volatility - Stop below Bollinger Band or EMA
- Bullish High Volatility - RSI above 50, stop below support
- Bullish Low Volatility - RSI below 50, stop above resistance

Answer:

- Bearish Low Volatility - RSI below 50, stop above resistance
- Bullish High Volatility - Stop below Bollinger Band or EMA
- Bullish Low Volatility - RSI above 50, stop below support

You've now seen how divergence isn't just for spotting entries - it's a key part of risk management. Up next: let's test what you've learned in a short quiz to check your knowledge.

QUIZ: Divergence In Action

1. What does regular divergence typically signal?

A. A breakout confirmation
B. A potential trend reversal
C. A continuation of the trend
D. A strong trend with volume

2. Which of the following best describes bullish regular divergence?

A. Price makes higher highs, the indicator makes higher highs
B. Price makes lower lows, the indicator makes higher lows
C. Price makes lower highs, the indicator makes lower highs
D. Price and indicator both make lower lows

3. When does hidden bullish divergence occur?

A. Price makes lower highs, the indicator makes higher highs
B. The indicator makes higher lows, price makes lower lows
C. Price and indicator both make higher highs
D. Price makes higher lows, the indicator makes lower lows

4. What is the main reason traders wait for confirmation before trading divergence?

A. Divergence alone may give false signals
B. Price always follows RSI immediately
C. It helps avoid overbought/ oversold zones
D. Indicators are never reliable

5. In bearish hidden divergence, what does the price do?

A. Makes higher highs
B. Makes equal highs
C. Makes lower highs
D. Stays in a range

6. Where should traders usually place a stop-loss in a confirmed bullish divergence setup?

A. Just below the most recent swing low
B. Above the resistance level
C. Far below the last trendline
D. At the highest point of the last candle

7. What's the benefit of using MACD and RSI together to confirm divergence?

A. They avoid the use of candlestick confirmation
B. They show both momentum and trend shifts
C. They give the same signals
D. They remove the need for price action

8. Which situation reflects a high-volatility bullish setup for setting stop-losses?

A. Place a stop-loss above the last high
B. Place a stop-loss below RSI
C. Place a stop-loss below the lower Bollinger Band or 20 EMA
D. Use a fixed pip amount every time

9. In low-volatility bearish setups, where should traders generally place their stop-loss?

A. Just above resistance
B. At the midpoint between last highs

C. Above the upper Bollinger Band
D. Far below the last support

10. You're analyzing a chart where price makes higher lows and MACD makes lower lows. What type of divergence is this, and what's the likely trade?

A. Hidden bullish divergence - buy after confirmation
B. Regular bearish divergence - short immediately
C. Regular bullish divergence - sell after rejection
D. Hidden bearish divergence - sell at support

Answers: 1. B; 2. B; 3. D; 4. A; 5. C; 6. A; 7. B; 8. C; 9. A; 10. A

SECTION 6: FUNDAMENTAL ANALYSIS

Chapter 1: Fundamental Analysis Basics

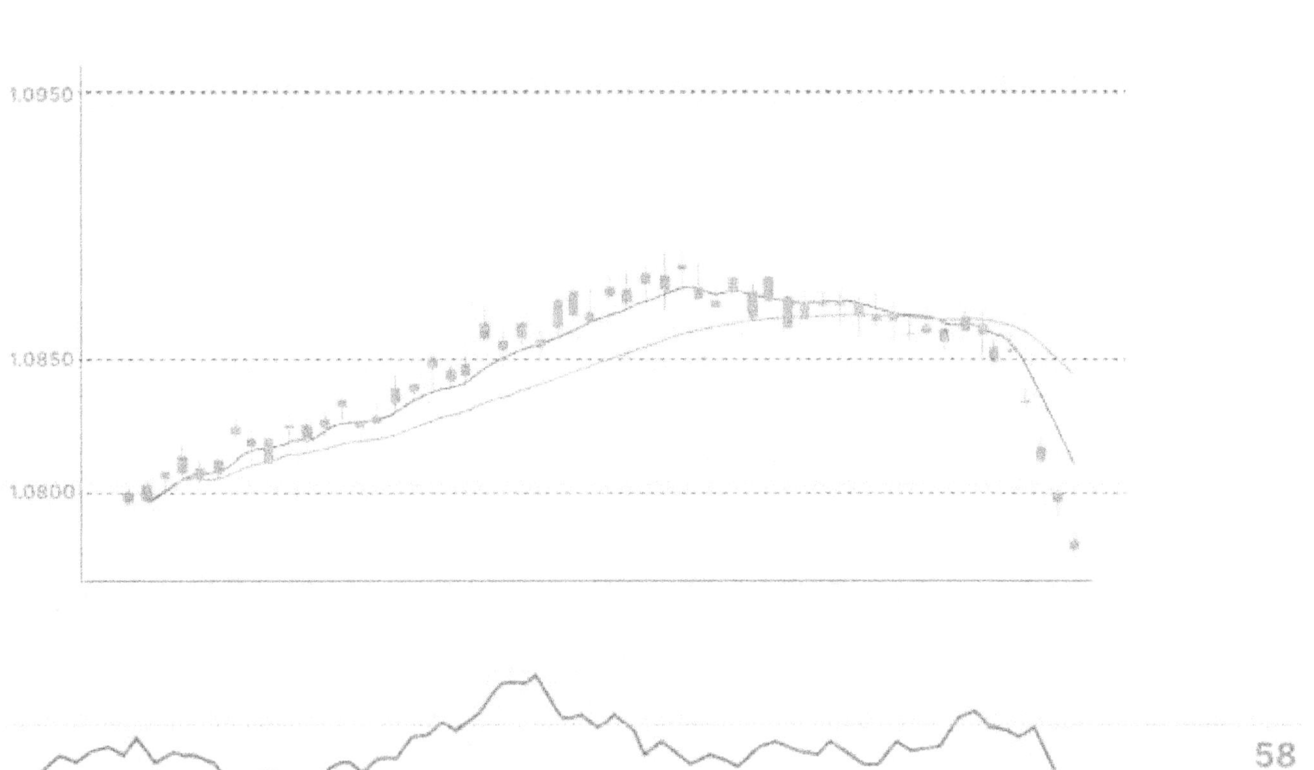

Lesson 1: Why Look Beyond Charts

Charts tell half the story

Technical setups may fail. Perfect patterns break the wrong way. Price ignores support and resistance. Time to discover what actually drives those candles and indicators you've mastered.

Charts reveal the market's footprints. Fundamental analysis shows what created those footprints. Every significant price movement has a catalyst - rarely random, usually rooted in economic reality. Mastering these catalysts gives you an edge that pure technical traders lack.

Let me show you a setup I journaled recently. EUR/USD formed what looked like a textbook bull flag: price above the 50 and 200 EMAs, RSI near 58, and tight consolidation after a rally.

I entered long at 1.0850 with a stop at 1.0800 and target at 1.0950. Technically, it looked solid. But, within hours, the European Central Bank (ECB) President made unexpected comments suggesting interest rates would remain lower than markets anticipated.

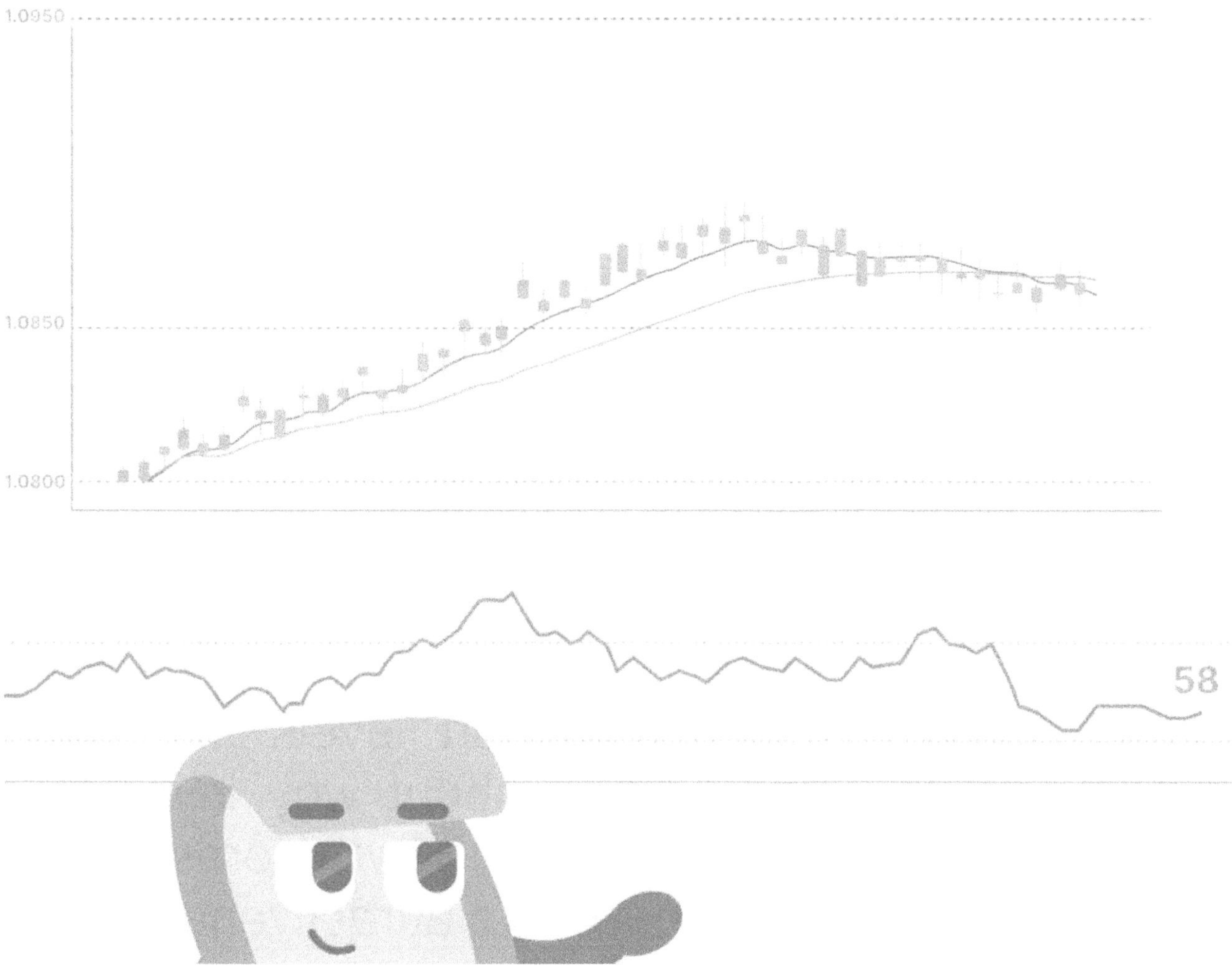

EUR/USD immediately crashed through my stop loss. This wasn't a failure of technical analysis - it was a lesson about market priorities.

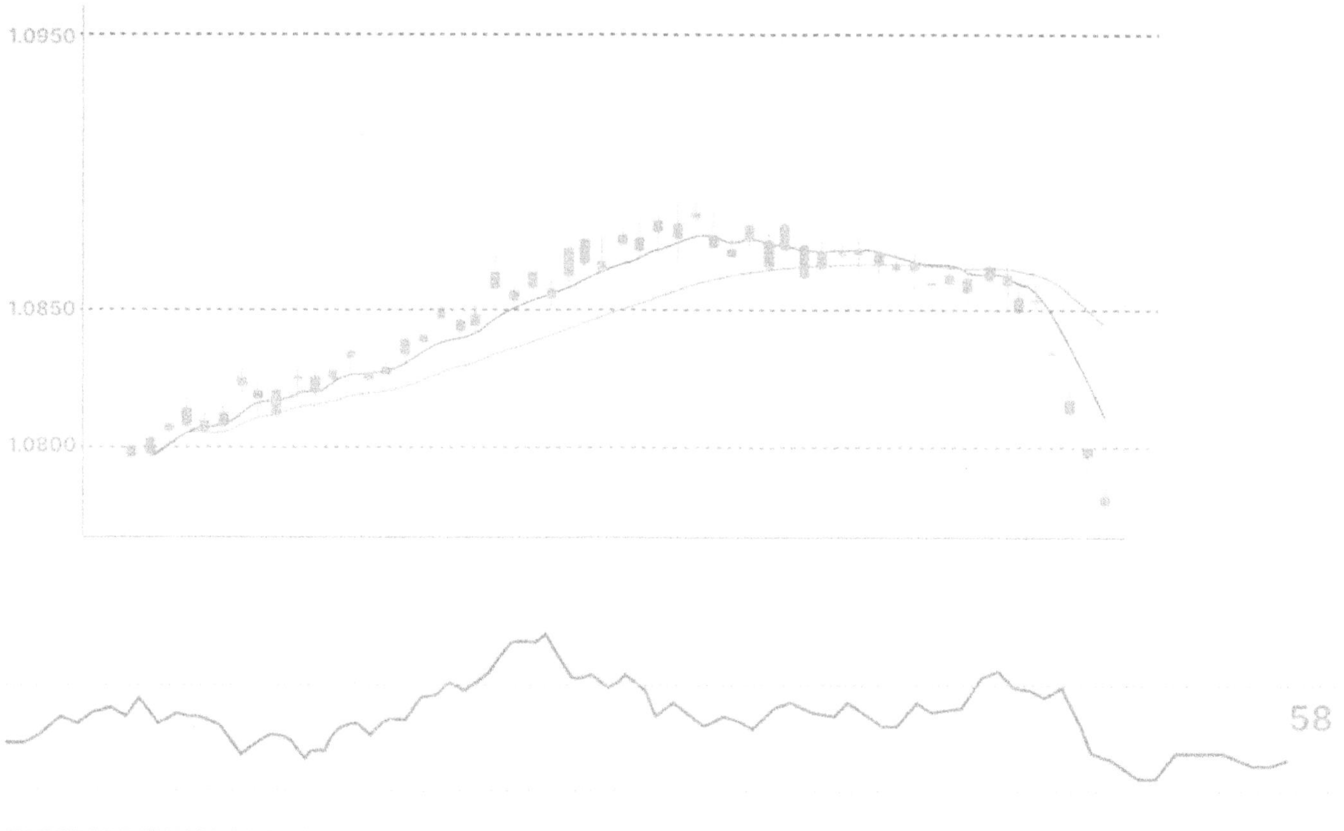

ECB announcement

Looking at the EUR/USD chart, a sharp decline broke through multiple support levels after the ECB announcement. Think about why investors buy or sell currencies, and how interest rate expectations affect a currency's attractiveness.

What likely caused this technical breakdown?

- Trading volume was too light to sustain the uptrend

- The moving averages hadn't confirmed the bull pattern
- Lower interest rate expectations reduced demand for euros
- The bull flag pattern was incorrectly identified from the start

Answer: Lower interest rate expectations reduced demand for euros. While technical factors like pattern identification, volume, and indicator confirmation are important, they don't explain the immediate sharp reaction to the ECB announcement. The fundamental change in interest rate expectations created a much stronger force in the market. When the ECB signaled lower interest rates than expected, it immediately made the euro less attractive to investors seeking yield. This fundamental shift in supply and demand dynamics overwhelmed the bullish technical pattern. No technical indicator alone could have predicted this catalyst.

So, what exactly is fundamental analysis? It's the study of economic, financial, and other external factors that affect asset prices. While technical analysis studies the price movement itself, fundamental analysis examines the underlying forces that cause those movements.

Fundamental analysis focuses on different factors depending on the market. If you trade currencies, you pay most attention to interest rates and central banks. For stocks, it's all about company earnings and growth. And for commodities, prices move with supply and demand.

Match markets with their key drivers

Different markets respond to different fundamental factors. Think about what specifically creates buying or selling pressure in each of these different markets. Match each market type with one of its primary price drivers.

- Commodities - Production and inventory levels
- Currency - Quarterly earning reports
- Stocks - Interest rate decisions

Answer:

- Commodities - Production and inventory levels
- Currency - Interest rate decisions
- Stocks - Quarterly earning reports

Trading with only technical analysis is like driving while looking only in the rearview mirror. You can see where you've been, but not what's ahead. Fundamental analysis lets you look through the windshield to spot upcoming bends in the road - giving you time to adjust your strategy accordingly.

Blending technicals and fundamentals

You're analyzing a stock that shows a bullish technical pattern. The company is scheduled to release quarterly earnings tomorrow. Consider the potential impact of a scheduled announcement on your technical setup. How might you approach this situation?

- Research analyst expectations for the earnings
- Trade based only on the technical pattern
- Wait until after earnings before making a trading decision
- Focus on other trading opportunities instead

Answer: Wait until after earnings before making a trading decision. Trading based only on technical patterns before a high-impact event like earnings can be risky. Earnings announcements frequently cause significant price movements that can override existing technical setups, potentially leading to unexpected losses. Earnings announcements often create significant volatility that can invalidate technical patterns. By waiting until after the announcement, you can see how the market reacts to the fundamental information, then apply your technical analysis to find better entry points with the trend rather than against it.

My results improved dramatically when I started integrating fundamental awareness into my technical trading. For example, I now avoid trading around major economic announcements for my day trades. For multi-week positions, I ensure the fundamental outlook aligns with my technical entry points.

Technical analysis gives you the what - patterns, levels, and potential entry points. Fundamental analysis gives you the why - the underlying forces driving those patterns. Whether you trade stocks, crypto, or forex, these principles apply across the board. In our next lesson, we'll explore the core principles that make fundamental analysis truly effective. Get ready to see the markets with new eyes.

Lesson 2: Principles of Fundamental Analysis

Three principles that matter

All markets - forex, stocks, crypto, commodities - follow three basic rules of fundamental analysis. Understanding these rules helps you trade more successfully.

- Principle 1: Every price move has a reason. Prices never move randomly. Every significant trend, reversal, or breakout has a real-world cause driving it. Our job is to find these causes.

Bitcoin surge

Bitcoin jumped from $10,000 to $60,000 in 2020-2021. Several factors contributed to this rise - let's try to identify one of them. Think about real-world events that created actual buying demand for Bitcoin during this period.

Which of the following is a fundamental factor that likely contributed to the surge?

- Bitcoin's moving averages crossing bullishly
- A perfect technical chart pattern forming
- Major institutions buying Bitcoin as an investment
- Trading volume increasing on exchanges

Answer: Major institutions buying Bitcoin as an investment. Technical signals like chart patterns and volume help spot price moves, but they don't explain why prices rise. Bitcoin's 2020-2021 surge was driven by major institutions - like Tesla, Square, and investment funds - buying in. That real-world demand, along with inflation fears and growing use in payments, pushed prices up. The chart patterns just reflected what was already happening.

- Principle 2: Market reactions are predictable. Markets tend to react in consistent ways to repeated events. That's why it's possible to predict how certain fundamental factors - like interest rate changes or political shocks - will likely affect asset prices.

For example, one well-known market pattern is how prices react to data compared to expectations. It's not just the number that matters, but whether it surprises. When results exceed expectations, prices often rise. When they disappoint, prices tend to fall.

UK unemployment data

UK unemployment drops to 4.1% from last month's 4.3%. However, economists had expected a bigger drop to 3.9%. Markets often react not to whether data improved or worsened, but to whether it met expectations. How is the British pound likely to react to this worse-than-expected result?

- Stays flat with no significant move
- Follows only its technical chart pattern

- Rises, because unemployment decreased
- Falls, despite improvement from last month

Answer: Falls, despite improvement from last month. The fact that unemployment improved from last month isn't what moves markets. Even though unemployment improved from 4.3% to 4.1%, it came in worse than the expected 3.9%. Markets react to the gap between expectations and reality. Markets focus on whether the actual number beat or missed expectations. When data disappoints compared to forecasts, currency values typically decline, regardless of improvement from previous readings.

- Principle 3: Some factors can't be predicted. Economic reports and elections follow schedules. But wars, natural disasters, and surprise policy changes happen without warning. These unpredictable events often move markets most dramatically.

Market in shock

A pipeline explosion disrupts oil supply in a major region. The market wasn't expecting it. Unpredictable shocks require you to pause, gather context, and adjust with care. What is the best first step for a trader in this scenario?

- Assume the market will bounce back
- Ignore the event and stick to the plan
- Buy more oil stocks immediately
- Reassess exposure and volatility before reacting

Answer: Reassess exposure and volatility before reacting. Jumping into new trades or ignoring the event completely can both backfire. Unplanned shocks like this pipeline explosion create volatility and uncertainty. The best response is to pause, assess your risk, and act only after understanding how the situation is unfolding. When an unpredictable shock hits the market, your first move should be to pause and reassess. Sudden events often bring volatility, so reviewing exposure and managing risk gives you clarity before taking action. Acting with information - not emotion - is key.

These three principles work together in all markets: identify what's causing price moves, understand how markets typically react to events, and manage risk for unpredictable events.

Match principles to scenarios

Match each trading scenario with the fundamental principle it best demonstrates. Think about which principle each scenario most clearly illustrates.

- Gold rises after inflation report beats forecast - Some factors can't be predicted
- Currency strengthens after rate hike - Every price move has a reason
- Stock crashes on surprise CEO resignation - Market reactions are predictable

Answer:

- Gold rises after inflation report beats forecast - Market reactions are predictable
- Currency strengthens after rate hike - Every price move has a reason
- Stock crashes on surprise CEO resignation - Some factors can't be predicted

You've now mastered the three core principles of fundamental analysis:

1. Price moves always have reasons,

2. Market reactions follow predictable patterns based on expectations

3. Some events can't be forecast.

In the next lesson, we'll explore exactly what moves forex, stocks, and commodities. You'll learn which specific fundamental factors to watch for each market you trade.

Lesson 3: Forces That Move Markets

What moves your market?

Different assets respond to different fundamental forces. Knowing which factors impact your specific trading instrument helps you focus on the right information at the right time.

Markets respond to different types of fundamental forces: macroeconomic (affecting entire economies), microeconomic (affecting specific sectors or companies), and supply/ demand factors (affecting availability and consumption).

Let's explore what drives each major market. For different assets, some factors matter more than others. Can you guess which fundamental factors have the strongest impact on each market type?

Fed raises rates

The Federal Reserve just increased US interest rates by 0.25%, higher than the expected 0.15% hike. The same day, several US companies report strong earnings. Think about which factor most directly affects capital flow between currencies. What will impact USD/JPY more?

- The interest rate increase
- Both equally important
- Neither - technicals matter more
- US company earnings reports

Answer: The interest rate increase. Interest rate decisions are the primary driver for currency pairs. When the Fed raises rates more than expected, the dollar becomes more attractive to investors seeking yield. This creates direct buying pressure on USD/JPY as investors buy dollars and sell yen to capture the higher interest rate.

For forex traders, these factors matter most in this order:

1. Interest rate decisions and expectations

2. Inflation data (affects future rates)

3. Economic growth indicators (GDP, employment)

4. Trade balances and government policy

5. Market risk sentiment

Always check the economic calendar for these high-impact events before trading currencies.

Earnings release day

A company reports quarterly results: revenue up 8% (analysts expected 10%), profit margins improved to 42% (above 40% expectation), and strong growth in services. The Fed also cut rates today. For individual stocks, which factor most directly reflects the company's actual business performance? What will drive the stock price?

- The Fed rate cut
- Both equally important
- Overall market sentiment
- The mixed earnings results

Answer: The mixed earnings results. While broader market factors like Fed decisions affect the entire market, they typically don't override company-specific results on earnings day. For individual stocks, company-specific earnings results typically drive the largest price reactions, especially on the actual earnings day. The mixed results (revenue miss but margin beat) will likely be the primary focus for Apple investors, with the broader market impact from the Fed decision playing a secondary role.

Individual stocks respond most strongly to company-specific factors. Earnings results, revenue growth, profit margins, product launches, and management changes drive the biggest price moves for most stocks.

Bitcoin breaks out

Bitcoin suddenly jumps 15%. On the same day, a major payment processor announces Bitcoin integration, the Federal Reserve raises interest rates, and stock markets fall. Which event most directly affects Bitcoin's utility and potential user base? Which likely caused Bitcoin's surge?

- Fed interest rate increase
- Stock market decline

- Purely technical breakout
- Payment processor adoption news

Answer: Payment processor adoption news. Major adoption announcements like payment processor integration typically drive the strongest crypto price movements. This directly expands Bitcoin's utility and potential user base. While monetary policy and broader markets can influence crypto, institutional and commercial adoption milestones create the most powerful fundamental catalysts.

Cryptocurrencies respond to a unique set of drivers. While they share some similarities with traditional assets, factors like adoption news, regulatory developments, and technological updates often create the most significant price moves.

For cryptocurrency traders, these factors typically matter most:

1. Adoption milestones (institutional buyers, payment integration)

2. Regulatory news (government policies, SEC decisions)

3. Technological developments (upgrades, forks)

4. Market sentiment and liquidity flows

5. Macroeconomic factors (inflation, risk appetite)

Monitoring crypto-specific news sources is essential for staying ahead of these catalysts.

OPEC (Organization of the Petroleum Exporting Countries) announcement

OPEC+ announces a surprise 1 million barrel per day oil production cut. The same day brings weak global economic data and a stock market decline. There is a factor that directly changes the physical availability of oil in the market. What will impact oil prices most?

- Weak economic data
- The OPEC+ production cut
- Technical support levels
- Stock market decline

Answer: The OPEC+ production cut. While economic data and market sentiment affect oil demand expectations over time, immediate changes to physical supply typically create the strongest short-term price reactions. Supply reductions of this magnitude typically outweigh other factors in the short term, as they directly change the physical oil available in the market. The OPEC+ production cut directly reduces oil supply by 1 million barrels per day, creating an immediate fundamental imbalance. Commodity traders focus primarily on these supply-demand shifts.

Commodities respond most directly to supply and demand fundamentals. Production changes, inventory levels, weather patterns, and consumption trends drive prices for oil, metals, and agricultural products.

Match assets to their primary drivers

Different assets respond most strongly to different fundamental factors. Match each asset with its most important price driver - the specific type of news that typically causes its largest immediate price moves.

- EUR/USD - Quarterly earnings vs expectations
- Tech stocks - Production cuts and inventory levels
- Crude oil - Central bank interest rate decisions

Answer:

- EUR/USD - Central bank interest rate decisions
- Tech stocks - Quarterly earnings vs expectations
- Crude oil - Production cuts and inventory levels

You now know what drives each major market. While all assets respond to multiple factors, focusing on the most relevant drivers for your specific instrument will make your fundamental analysis more effective. Apply this knowledge to any market you trade.

QUIZ: Fundamental Analysis Basics

1. What is the primary purpose of fundamental analysis in trading?

A. Track historical price movements only
B. Create complex chart patterns
C. Study economic factors that affect asset prices
D. Find support and resistance levels

2. What principle explains why the EUR/USD might fall when

A. ECB signals lower rates?
B. Random market fluctuations occur daily
C. Chart indicators determine all movements
D. Technical patterns always prevail
E. Every price move has a reason

3. What relationship best describes fundamental and technical analysis?

A. Fundamentals explain why, technicals show what
B. Neither approach provides trading value
C. Fundamentals replace the need for technicals
D. Technical patterns predict fundamental news

4. How do markets typically react when data comes in worse than expectations?

A. Only technical factors matter
B. Asset prices usually fall
C. Asset prices always rise
D. Markets show no reaction

5. What is the best response when an unpredictable event shocks the market?

A. Ignore the event completely
B. Immediately enter new positions
C. Reassess exposure before reacting
D. Follow only technical signals

6. Which asset is most directly affected by production cuts and inventory levels?

A. Commodities like crude oil
B. Government bonds

C. Technology stocks
D. Currency pairs

7. For individual stocks, what typically drives the largest price reactions?

A. Company-specific earnings results
B. Federal Reserve decisions
C. Commodity price changes
D. Currency fluctuations

8. What most powerfully impacts cryptocurrency prices?

A. Interest rate changes
B. Employment reports
C. Adoption and regulatory developments
D. Manufacturing data

9. Which principle explains why markets react similarly to recurring events?

A. Some factors cannot be predicted
B. All price moves are random
C. Every chart pattern has meaning
D. Market reactions are predictable

10. What does combining technical and fundamental analysis help traders achieve?

A. Trading exclusively on breaking news
B. Understanding both what happens and why
C. Ignoring market fundamentals entirely
D. Creating more complex chart patterns

Answer: 1. C; 2. D; 3. A; 4. B; 5. C; 6. A; 7. A; 8. C; 9. D; 10. B

Chapter 2: Economic Indicators

Lesson 1: Employment and Growth Data

Understanding growth and jobs

Let's explore the economic indicators that move markets. Employment and growth data tell us if economies are expanding or contracting and how many people have jobs. These numbers drive central bank decisions and market movements.

Why do traders care about these numbers? Simple - they move markets predictably. Strong growth and employment typically lead to higher interest rates, strengthening currencies and pressuring bond prices. Weak numbers often cause the opposite reaction.

Let's start with GDP - Gross Domestic Product. This measures the total value of all goods and services a country produces, showing if an economy is growing or shrinking. It's usually reported quarterly as a percentage change from the previous period.

GDP growth meaning

A country reports that its GDP grew by 2.5% last quarter. GDP measures the total economic output of a country. What does this tell traders about the economy? What does 2.5% GDP growth indicate?

- Prices increased by 2.5%
- The economy shrank by 2.5%
- Unemployment rose by 2.5%
- The economy expanded by 2.5% since last quarter

Answer: GDP growth has a specific meaning in economic reports that differs from other economic metrics. 2.5% GDP growth means the economy expanded by that percentage since the previous quarter. This positive growth indicates the economy is producing more goods and services, typically creating a favorable environment for businesses. Traders often see sustained GDP growth as positive for stocks and the country's currency.

GDP comes in three versions: advance (first estimate), preliminary (second estimate), and final. Markets usually react most to the advance release since it's the first look at growth. Later revisions still matter if they significantly change the growth picture.

Now let's turn to employment data. The monthly jobs report shows how many new jobs the economy created. This number directly reflects economic health - more jobs typically mean more spending, driving further growth and potentially higher interest rates.

Jobs report impact

A country's monthly jobs report shows 50,000 more jobs created than economists expected.How do better-than-expected job numbers typically affect interest rate expectations? How would markets typically react?

- No significant market movement
- Stock markets decline sharply
- The country's currency strengthens
- The country's currency weakens

Answer: Better-than-expected job creation has a typical pattern of market impact, particularly on a country's currency. When job creation exceeds expectations, it signals economic strength. Markets typically expect the central bank may raise interest rates sooner or higher to prevent the economy from overheating. Higher interest rates attract foreign capital seeking better returns, causing the country's currency to strengthen against others.

The unemployment rate shows the percentage of the labor force without jobs. It's calculated by dividing unemployed people by the total labor force. Lower rates suggest economic strength, while rising unemployment often signals economic troubles.

Interpreting unemployment

Country A's unemployment rate drops from 8% to 7%, but its workforce participation also declines. What happens to the unemployment rate when people leave the workforce entirely? What does this suggest about job market health? What does this combination mean?

- Unemployment drop confirms strong job growth
- Job market might be weaker than the lower unemployment suggests
- Both metrics show equally positive news
- Neither metric provides useful trading information

Answer: The combination of falling unemployment and falling participation creates a specific interpretation for traders. When unemployment falls but participation also declines, it suggests people are leaving the workforce rather than finding jobs. This indicates a potentially weaker job market than the headline unemployment figure suggests. Traders often look past initial positive reactions to falling unemployment when participation is also dropping, as it signals underlying economic weakness.

Employment and GDP data affect all markets, but in different ways:

- Currencies: Stronger data typically strengthens a country's currency
- Stocks: Often rise on good data, but may fall if interest rate increases seem likely

- Bonds: Usually fall in price (yields rise) on strong economic data
- Commodities: Industrial commodities often rise on strong growth expectations

Growth and employment data from major economies shape markets around the world. One key release is the U.S. Non-Farm Payrolls (NFP) report, published monthly. It includes job creation, the unemployment rate, and wage growth - all of which can move not just the U.S. dollar, but also global stocks, commodities, and emerging market currencies. Similarly, China's GDP data affects trade-sensitive assets worldwide.

How markets react to NFP

Speed and surprise define the first reaction; analysis follows. Put in order what typically happens when the NFP report is released.

- Forex, equity, and bond markets react
- Report is released at 8:30 a.m. ET
- Analysts interpret the data in depth
- Traders compare numbers to forecasts

Answer:

- Report is released at 8:30 a.m. ET
- Traders compare numbers to forecasts
- Forex, equity, and bond markets react
- Analysts interpret the data in depth

Regions and countries release these indicators at different times, creating a calendar of market-moving events. US jobs data comes out on the first Friday of each month. GDP figures typically appear quarterly. Understanding this schedule helps traders prepare for potential market moves.

Let's recap what we've learned:

- GDP measures total economic output, showing if an economy is growing or contracting.
- Employment data reveals job market health through new jobs created, the unemployment rate, and wage growth.
- These indicators drive markets because they directly influence central bank interest rate decisions and provide the clearest picture of economic strength or weakness.

Lesson 2: Inflation and Prices

The power of price changes

After exploring employment and growth data, let's examine another critical economic indicator: inflation. Central banks pay extremely close attention to inflation, making it one of the most powerful market movers across all financial instruments.

Inflation measures how much prices for goods and services rise over time. When prices increase rapidly, each unit of currency buys fewer goods. This erodes purchasing power and creates economic pressures that central banks try to control through interest rate changes.

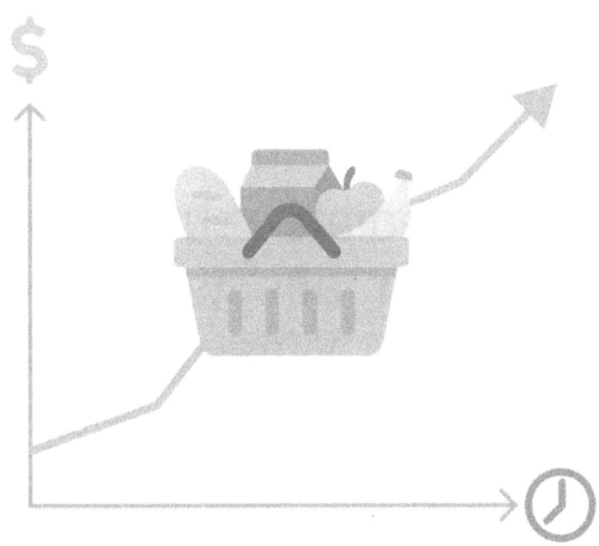

Why does inflation matter for markets? Central banks in most countries target moderate inflation (usually around 2%). When inflation rises too high, they typically raise interest rates to cool the economy. When inflation falls too low, they may cut rates to stimulate growth.

Inflation surprise

A country reports inflation at 4.2%, significantly above the expected 3.5% and the central bank's 2% target. Think about how unexpected high inflation affects central bank interest rate expectations. How would this likely affect the country's currency in the short term?

- Weakens despite the high inflation reading
- Initially rises, then completely reverses
- Strengthens as higher rates become more likely
- No significant movement

Answer: Strengthens as higher rates become more likely. Surprisingly high inflation doesn't typically cause immediate currency weakness. Consider how inflation affects a central bank's likely next policy move. When inflation comes in much higher than expected (4.2% vs 3.5%), it signals the central bank may need to raise interest rates sooner or more aggressively to bring price increases under control. Higher interest rates make the currency more attractive to investors seeking better returns, causing it to strengthen against other currencies in the short term.

The Consumer Price Index (CPI) is the most widely watched inflation measure. It tracks the average price of a basket of consumer goods and services over time. Most countries release CPI monthly, and markets react strongly to unexpected changes in these readings.

Beyond the headline CPI number, markets pay close attention to "core inflation," which excludes volatile food and energy prices. Core inflation better reveals underlying price trends and is often seen as a more reliable indicator of long-term inflation pressures.

Headline vs. core

Monthly CPI data shows headline inflation at 5.1% (expected 5.0%), while core inflation drops to 3.2% (expected 3.6%). Which measure better indicates the underlying inflation trend that influences long-term central bank policy? What's the market interpretation?

- Focus on core - inflation pressures easing
- Impossible to determine from these figures
- Focus on headline - inflation pressures rising
- Equal weight to both - neutral overall

Answer: Focus on core - inflation pressures easing. Markets don't give equal weight to headline and core inflation, especially when they send conflicting signals about price pressures. Markets typically place more importance on core inflation for gauging underlying price trends. The significant drop in core inflation to 3.2% (below the expected 3.6%) suggests easing price pressures despite the slightly higher headline number. This could reduce expectations for aggressive rate hikes, potentially weakening the currency and boosting stocks as markets anticipate a less restrictive monetary policy.

The Producer Price Index (PPI) measures inflation from the perspective of sellers rather than consumers. It tracks price changes for raw materials, intermediate goods, and finished products before they reach consumers. PPI often serves as an early indicator of future CPI movements.

Why watch both CP| and PPI? Changes in producer prices often pass through to consumer prices with a delay. Rising PPI may signal future consumer inflation, while falling PPI can indicate upcoming consumer price relief. This relationship helps traders anticipate future inflation trends.

CPI (prices paid by households) is what consumers feel; PPI (prices charged by producers) is what businesses charge.

Inflation expectations are another crucial factor that affects markets. Central banks monitor not just current inflation but what businesses and consumers expect future inflation to be. These expectations can become self-fulfilling as people adjust their behavior based on anticipated price changes.

Different markets react differently to inflation surprises:

- Currencies: Higher inflation expectations typically strengthen currencies in the short term (due to rate hike expectations)
- Bonds: Rising inflation usually pushes bond prices down (yields up)
- Stocks: Often fall on high inflation, but some sectors (commodities, energy) may benefit
- Gold: Traditionally rises during periods of high inflation

Inflation sources matter

Two countries both report 4% inflation. Country A's inflation comes from strong consumer demand and economic growth. Country B's comes from supply shortages and rising input costs. Consider which type of inflation typically accompanies a healthier economy with better investment prospects. Try to guess: Which economy would investors LIKELY favor?

- Both equally attractive
- Country A (demand-driven inflation)
- Neither attractive with 4% inflation
- Country B (supply-driven inflation)

Answer: Country A (demand-driven inflation). Investors would typically favor Country A with demand-driven inflation. This type of inflation results from strong economic growth and consumer spending power - positive signs for corporate profits and investment returns. Supply-driven inflation (Country B) often indicates economic problems like resource shortages or supply chain disruptions, which can hurt growth and corporate profits despite similar headline inflation numbers.

Trading inflation data effectively requires:

- Knowing both the previous reading and market expectations
- Distinguishing between headline and core inflation measures
- Understanding the central bank's inflation target and recent communications
- Monitoring related indicators like PPI for early signals
- Being alert to changes in inflation expectations

Inflation indicators rank among the most powerful market movers because they directly influence central bank policy decisions. By understanding how different inflation measures affect interest rate expectations, you can better anticipate market reactions across currencies, bonds, stocks, and commodities when price data surprises the market. See you in the next lesson!

Lesson 3: Business and Trade Health

The business indicators

Let's turn our attention to indicators that reveal business and trade conditions. These reports often provide early warnings about economic direction before they show up in broader GDP or employment figures.

The Purchasing Managers' Index (PMI) is one of the most important business indicators. This monthly survey asks business managers if key activities like production, new orders, and employment are improving or worsening. The responses create a single number that instantly shows business conditions.

PMI readings work on a simple scale: numbers above 50 indicate business expansion, while readings below 50 signal contraction. The further from 50, the stronger the trend. A reading of 55 shows solid growth, while 45 indicates significant contraction.

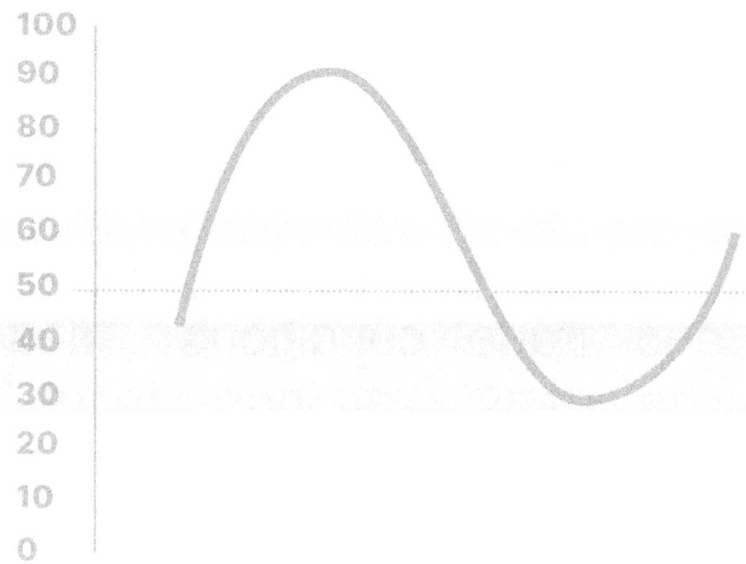

Imagine you're analyzing market conditions. Employment data looks strong, but you notice manufacturing activity has declined for three straight months. This contradictory signal might warn of future economic weakness not yet visible in headline figures.

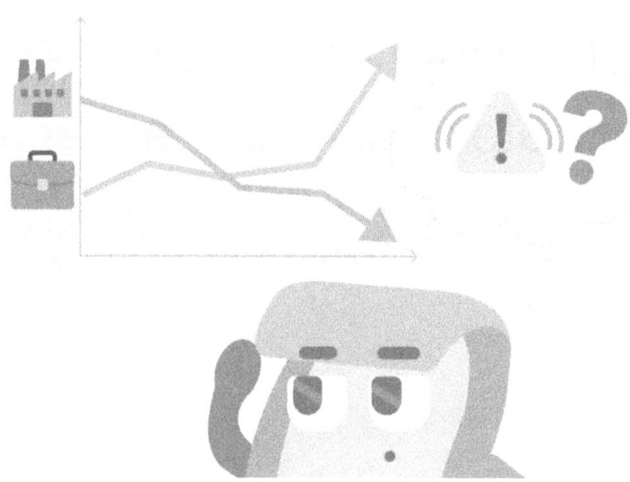

Manufacturing signals

The 50.0 mark on PMI reports acts as a dividing line between expansion and contraction. The Purchasing Managers' Index (PMI) for a country drops from 53.2 to 48.6. What does this suggest about the country's manufacturing sector and overall economic direction? What does this PMI change mean?

- Manufacturing is now contracting
- Manufacturing is still expanding
- No significant change in conditions
- The data is insufficient to interpret

Answer: Manufacturing is now contracting. PMI readings have a specific interpretation threshold that helps determine whether business activity is expanding or contracting. The drop from 53.2 to 48.6 shows manufacturing shifting from expansion to contraction. Any PMI reading above 50 indicates expansion, while readings below 50 signal contraction. This significant drop below the critical 50 level suggests manufacturing activity is now shrinking, potentially warning of broader economic weakness ahead.

Markets typically react to PMI reports in these ways:

- Strong PMI readings boost the country's currency and stock market while pressuring bonds.
- Weak PMI readings typically pressure the currency and stocks while supporting bonds through expectations of potential rate cuts.

Sector importance

A country reports Manufacturing PMI at 48.0 (contracting) but Services PMI at 53.5 (expanding). Services represent 75% of this economy. Consider the relative size of each sector and its current performance. What's the likely overall economic direction?

- Already in recession
- Still growing despite manufacturing weakness
- Heading into recession
- Impossible to determine from these numbers

Answer: Still growing despite manufacturing weakness. When evaluating mixed economic signals, the relative size of different sectors significantly affects the overall economic picture. With services (75% of the economy) expanding at 53.5 while manufacturing (a smaller portion) contracts at 48.0, the overall economy is likely still growing. The much larger services sector's expansion outweighs manufacturing weakness. Traders often focus on the services PMI in developed economies precisely because it covers a larger portion of economic activity.

Next, trade balance reports show the difference between a country's exports and imports. A surplus means a country exports more than it imports, while a deficit indicates the opposite. These reports reveal both domestic demand and foreign appetite for the country's products.

What drives trade balances matters as much as the headline number. A surplus from strong exports suggests economic strength, while a surplus from collapsing imports often indicates domestic weakness. Similarly, deficits from strong imports (high domestic demand) differ from deficits caused by weak exports.

Trade balance analysis

A country's trade deficit suddenly shrinks by 50%. Looking deeper, exports remained flat while imports fell sharply. Consider what would cause imports to drop significantly while exports remain unchanged. What does this pattern indicate?

- Improving export competitiveness
- Domestic economy likely weakening
- Strong economic growth
- Balanced economic expansion

Answer: Domestic economy likely weakening. The composition of trade balance changes provides important clues about underlying economic conditions beyond the headline figure. A shrinking trade deficit caused by falling imports rather than rising exports typically indicates domestic economic weakness. Sharp import declines often reflect reduced consumer and business spending power within the country. Although the smaller deficit might seem positive at first glance, traders recognize this pattern as a warning sign about deteriorating internal demand.

Finally, retail sales data shows consumer spending at stores and online. Since consumers drive roughly 70% of developed economies, this monthly report provides crucial insight into economic health. Strong retail sales typically support economic growth, while weak consumer spending often precedes broader economic problems.

Consumer spending clues

Monthly retail sales unexpectedly fall 1.2% overall, but excluding automobiles, sales rose 0.4%. Consider whether the spending weakness appears widespread or concentrated in a specific segment. What does this pattern suggest?

- Statistical error in the data collection
- Beginning of consumer-led recession
- Specific weakness in auto sector rather than broader consumer pullback
- Consumers shifting from physical stores to online shopping

Answer: Specific weakness in auto sector rather than broader consumer pullback. When retail sales data shows significant variation between categories, it offers specific insights about consumer behavior patterns. When overall retail sales fall but rise excluding autos, it typically indicates specific issues in the automotive sector rather than a broader consumer spending pullback. This pattern suggests consumers continue spending in most categories (positive sign) while car sales face sector-specific challenges. Traders would likely view this as less concerning than broad-based spending declines across multiple categories.

Putting it all together: Business and trade indicators provide valuable early signals about economic direction, often warning of changes before they appear in GDP or employment data. By monitoring PMI reports, industrial production, trade balances, and retail sales, you can spot potential turning points that create trading opportunities across multiple markets.

QUIZ: Economic Indicators

1. What does GDP primarily measure in an economy?

A. Unemployment rate across different sectors
B. Consumer spending habits only
C. Currency strength against other nations
D. Total value of goods and services produced

2. When inflation comes in higher than expected, how does this typically affect a country's currency in the short term?

A. Strengthens as higher interest rates become likely
B. Remains unchanged regardless of the reading
C. Falls sharply then quickly rebounds
D. Weakens as economic stability decreases

3. What does a PMI reading below 50 indicate about business conditions?

A. No change in business conditions

B. Data is insufficient to draw conclusions
C. Business activity is contracting
D. Business activity is expanding

4. What is the main difference between CPI and PPI?

A. CPI is less important to traders than PPI
B. CPI measures consumer prices, PPI measures producer prices
C. CPI is released monthly, PPI quarterly
D. CP| includes services, PPI excludes services

5. Why do traders often focus more on core inflation than headline inflation?

A. Updates more frequently than headline figures
B. Includes more product categories
C. Better reveals underlying price trends
D. Always shows higher percentage increases

6. What typically causes a country's trade deficit to shrink when exports remain flat?

A. Declining imports suggesting domestic weakness

B. Currency strengthening against trading partners
C. Reduced trade barriers with partner nations
D. Improving export quality boosting prices

7. How do markets typically react to strong PMI readings?

A. Strengthen currency and stocks, pressure bonds
B. Weaken currency and strengthen bonds
C. Reduce volatility across all asset classes
D. Have no predictable effect on markets

8. What makes U.S. Non-Farm Payrolls (NFP) significant for global markets?

A. Never causes significant market volatility
B. Only matters for U.S. domestic traders
C. Affects not just USD but global assets
D. Only released once yearly

9. What does it suggest when unemployment falls but workforce participation also declines?

A. Job market might be weaker than numbers suggest

B. Imminent recession regardless of other indicators
C. Technical error in data collection methods
D. Unambiguously positive economic conditions

10. Which type of inflation do investors typically view more favorably?

A. Neither type is relevant to investment decisions
B. Demand-driven from economic growth
C. Both types are viewed identically
D. Supply-driven from resource shortages

Answer: 1. D; 2. A; 3. C; 4. B; 5. C; 6. A; 7. A; 8. C; 9. A; 10. B

Lesson 4: Reading and Reacting to Scheduled Events

Fundamental tools

Economic releases happen on a regular schedule, creating predictable opportunities for prepared traders.

To track scheduled economic events and indicators, traders use economic calendars. These essential online tools show upcoming market-moving events across all countries and markets in one organized view.

The most important part of using an economic calendar is knowing how the data compares to expectations. It's not just when the data comes out - but whether it surprises the market.

What information do economic calendars provide? They typically show the date, time, event name, affected country/currency, previous result, forecast, and importance level for each upcoming release.

Economic calendar components

Each component helps traders prepare in a specific way. Match each economic calendar component with its purpose for traders.

- Forecast - Potential market impact magnitude
- Important level - What markets have already priced in
- Previous result - Baseline for measuring surprise factor

Answer:

- Forecast - What markets have already priced in
- Important level - Potential market impact magnitude
- Previous result - Baseline for measuring surprise factor

Importance level indicates the potential market impact of each release. Calendars use different systems to mark this - stars (1-3), colors (green, yellow, red), or explicit labels (low, medium, high).

- High-impact events can change market direction and create significant volatility.
- Medium-impact news can create temporary volatility and short-term opportunities. These might cause market reactions but rarely change established trends or create lasting momentum.
- Low-impact releases usually cause little to no price reaction and offer limited trading value.

High-impact events (3 stars/red) have the greatest potential to move markets. These include central bank decisions, employment reports, inflation data, and GDP releases.

Medium-impact events (2 stars/yellow) may create some market movement but typically have less dramatic effects. These include retail sales, manufacturing indices, and trade balance figures.

Low-impact events (1 star/green) rarely cause significant market reactions. These include minor regional data, low-tier surveys, and secondary economic indicators.

Sort by importance

Arrange these economic events from highest market impact (1) to lowest market impact (4). Consider which events typically receive the most media attention and create the largest price movements.

- Minor construction permits data
- Central bank interest rate decision
- Monthly employment report
- Regional manufacturing survey

Answer:

- Central bank interest rate decision
- Monthly employment report

- Regional manufacturing survey
- Minor construction permits data

Economic calendars also display the "Actual" result once data is released. This field remains empty until the official announcement, then updates with the real figure, often color-coded to show if it beat, met, or missed expectations.

Direction check

Inflation was expected to fall by 0.3%, but the actual report showed a rise of 0.2%. Going from a negative forecast to a positive actual result signals a full reversal in price direction. What does this change in sign imply?

- Prices fell less than expected
- Prices rose instead of falling
- Inflation met expectations

Answer: Prices rose instead of falling. This wasn't just a minor miss - it was a change in direction. The forecast expected prices to fall, but the actual result showed they rose. That kind of reversal often catches the market off guard. The market expected deflation - a drop in prices - but the actual result showed inflation instead. Even though the difference may seem small, this kind of reversal can lead to a sharp shift in sentiment or policy expectations.

Let's recap: Economic calendars are essential tools that organize upcoming data releases by date, time, and importance. They provide key information including event name, country/ currency, previous results, and market forecasts. Traders can filter calendars to focus on high-impact events relevant to their markets and use them to prepare for scheduled volatility.

Lesson 5: Context Is King

From analysis to action

We've learned to understand economic calendars. Now comes the crucial question: How do we actually execute trades around these fundamental events while managing the unique risks they present?

The biggest challenge with fundamental event trading is timing. Consider this scenario: A jobs report is about to be released. You have a strong view on its potential outcome and market impact. But using a market order at the exact moment of release is extremely risky.

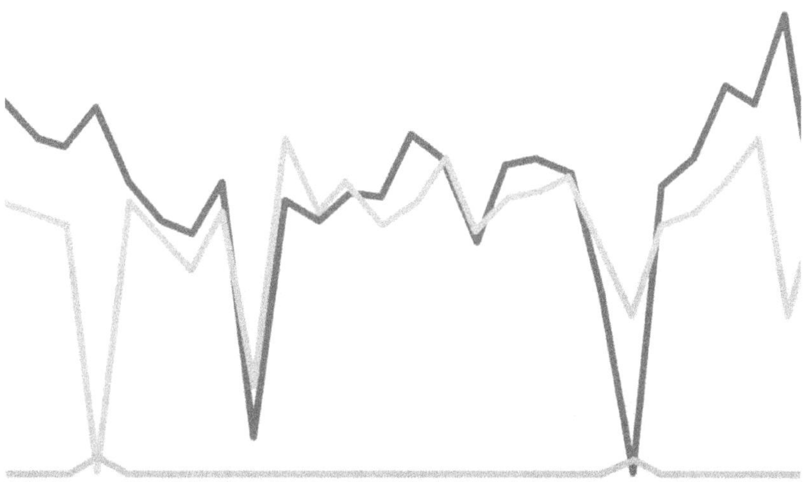

Market orders during news releases often result in poor execution prices due to widening spreads and price gaps. Many traders address this execution challenge by using pending orders placed at technical levels before the news release. These orders allow traders to specify exact entry prices and avoid making split-second decisions during maximum volatility.

Solving execution problems

You want to trade a stock's earnings announcement but are concerned about execution quality during the volatility spike. Which method allows you to specify your exact entry price without requiring split-second decisions? How to solve this problem?

- Place multiple small market orders
- Use market orders the moment headlines appear
- Place pending orders at key levels before the release
- Call your broker during the announcement

Answer: Place pending orders at key levels before the release. Market orders and rapid manual execution during announcements frequently result in slippage and poor fills due to widening spreads and rapidly changing prices. This approach typically creates inconsistent execution results. Pending orders placed at technical levels before announcements often provide more consistent execution. By identifying key price levels in advance and placing limit or stop orders, traders can specify their exact entry prices without needing to make split-second decisions when volatility and spreads are at their highest.

The second major challenge with event trading is premature stop-loss triggers. Normal volatility expands dramatically during fundamental events. A stop loss that works perfectly during regular trading will almost certainly be triggered by normal announcement volatility rather than a true trend reversal.

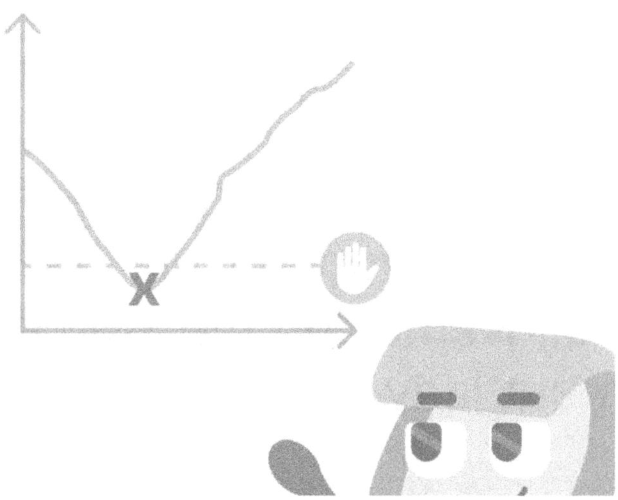

For example, when crude oil inventory reports are released, price typically moves 2-3% within minutes - often in both directions before establishing a trend. A standard 1% stop loss virtually guarantees being stopped out even if your directional view proves correct.

Surviving volatility spikes

You're trading gold during an inflation report that typically creates 2% price swings within minutes. Your normal stop loss is 0.7%. How can you accommodate the expected volatility while maintaining protection? What adjustment would help avoid premature stop triggers?

- Widen your stop to at least 2-3%
- Keep your standard 0.7% stop
- Move your stop closer to entry
- Use no stop loss at all

Answer: Widen your stop to at least 2-3%. A stop loss set at 0.7% or moved even closer is too tight for an event that regularly causes 2% swings - you're likely to get stopped out before the move even plays out. Removing the stop entirely avoids that problem but leaves you exposed to unlimited loss. To stay protected while allowing room for the price to move, you need a stop that reflects expected volatility. When trading during high-volatility events, your stop loss should be wide enough to withstand normal price fluctuations. Setting it near the average swing range - 2 to 3% in this case - gives your trade room to breathe while still limiting risk if the move goes against you.

However, wider stops present a new consideration: increased risk per trade. When stop distances expand, the potential loss per position also increases if the trade moves unfavorably.

Managing risk with wider stops

You normally trade with a 1% stop and a position size of $9,000, risking $90 per trade. A key event now requires a 3% stop to avoid noise. To keep total risk constant, reduce position size when your stop widens. What position size would keep your risk per trade at $90?

- $3,000
- $6,000

- $9,000
- $1,000

Answer: $3000. Keeping the same $9,000 position size while tripling your stop means your risk per trade also triples - up to $270. Choosing $6,000 or $1,000 might reduce risk, but not in proportion to the stop size. The only way to maintain the original $90 risk is to reduce your position size to one-third, or $3,000 x 3% = $90, which matches your normal risk level. This is how position sizing and stop distance work together to control risk.

Position sizing can be adjusted proportionally to stop distance. For instance, if an event requires a stop three times wider than normal, reducing position size to one-third of the standard amount maintains the same total risk. This mathematical relationship helps balance the need for wider stops with prudent risk management.

This method acknowledges that fundamental events can drive price significantly in either direction. Rather than predicting the outcome, you prepare for both possibilities, entering only when price confirms direction by breaking a key technical level. This combines fundamental catalysts with technical confirmation.

Some traders find that even pending orders don't solve execution issues. Instead of trading the immediate reaction, wait for the initial volatility to subside (typically 15-30 minutes), then enter when price establishes a clear direction.

Retail trader considerations

A trader using a standard online brokerage platform frequently experiences slippage when trading announcements. Which method acknowledges execution limitations while still providing trading opportunities? Which approach might best address this limitation?

- Place pending orders very close to current price
- Try to enter market orders more quickly
- Wait for post-event confirmation before entering
- Use multiple smaller market orders

Answer: Wait for post-event confirmation before entering. Attempting faster market order execution or placing orders very close to current price typically doesn't solve fundamental execution challenges during high volatility. These approaches still expose traders to slippage and poor fills. Waiting for post-event confirmation often provides a more reliable approach for traders with standard execution capabilities. By allowing the initial volatility explosion to subside before entering, traders can operate in more normalized market conditions with tighter spreads and clearer directional signals, even though they miss the initial price movement.

This method trades reliability for some initial movement. By allowing the market to digest the news and establish direction, traders gain clearer signals at the expense of missing the first portion of the move. This approach may be particularly suitable for those without institutional-grade execution capabilities.

These solutions work across all trading instruments. Whether you trade stocks around earnings, currencies around economic data, commodities around inventory reports, or cryptocurrencies around regulatory news, the same principles apply: pending orders for execution quality, wider stops for volatility, and adjusted position sizing for risk management.

Congratulations on completing the fundamental analysis section! You've now learned how economic data drives markets, how narratives shape price action, and how to combine fundamental catalysts with technical execution. These skills provide a solid foundation for more informed trading decisions across any market you choose to trade.

SECTION 7: TRADING STRATEGY

Chapter 1: Building and Testing Your Trading Strategy

Lesson 1: How To Build A Strategy

Let's build your first trading strategy

Every pro trader follows a plan. No guessing. No chasing. In this lesson, you'll learn what a trading strategy really is and how to create one that fits your style, risk appetite, and market goals. Let's start!

A trading strategy is your rulebook for the market. It gives structure by answering four essential questions. It defines what you'll trade, like stocks, forex, or crypto, based on what fits your style.

It also tells you when to enter, using specific setups and signals, not guesswork. It shows when to exit, whether for profit or loss, so you're never stuck wondering what to do.

And it controls how much to risk, keeping your losses small and your capital protected. With these rules, you trade with purpose, not emotion.

Don't worry, we'll explore entry, exit, and risk management in detail in the next lessons.

Once your strategy has rules for what, when, and how much to trade, the next step is knowing if it actually works. That's where performance metrics come in. They help you measure your results and see if your strategy has a real, repeatable edge.

A good strategy has a solid win rate, meaning it succeeds often enough to stay consistent. If you take 10 trades and win 5, your win rate is 50%. It helps you understand how frequently your setup works.

But just winning isn't enough - you also need strong risk-reward, where your winners are bigger than your losers. For example, if you risk $100 and aim for $200, that's a 1:2 risk-reward ratio.

Your edge is what makes your strategy profitable over time. It's the combination of win rate and risk-reward that, when repeated, puts the odds in your favor, not just by luck, but by design.

Match the metric to its purpose

Each metric plays a key role in measuring your strategy. Match them with what they reveal about your trading system. A strong edge needs more than just a high win rate.

- Win rate - Long-term trading advantage
- Risk-reward ratio - % of trades that win
- Strategy edge - Profit vs risk per trade

Answer:

- Win rate - % of trades that win
- Risk-reward ratio - Profit vs risk per trade
- Strategy edge - Long-term trading advantage

Now that you understand win rate, risk-reward, and edge. Let's see how they work together in a real trade. Here's a simple strategy example using an Apple chart that brings these metrics to life with clear entry, stop, and target levels.

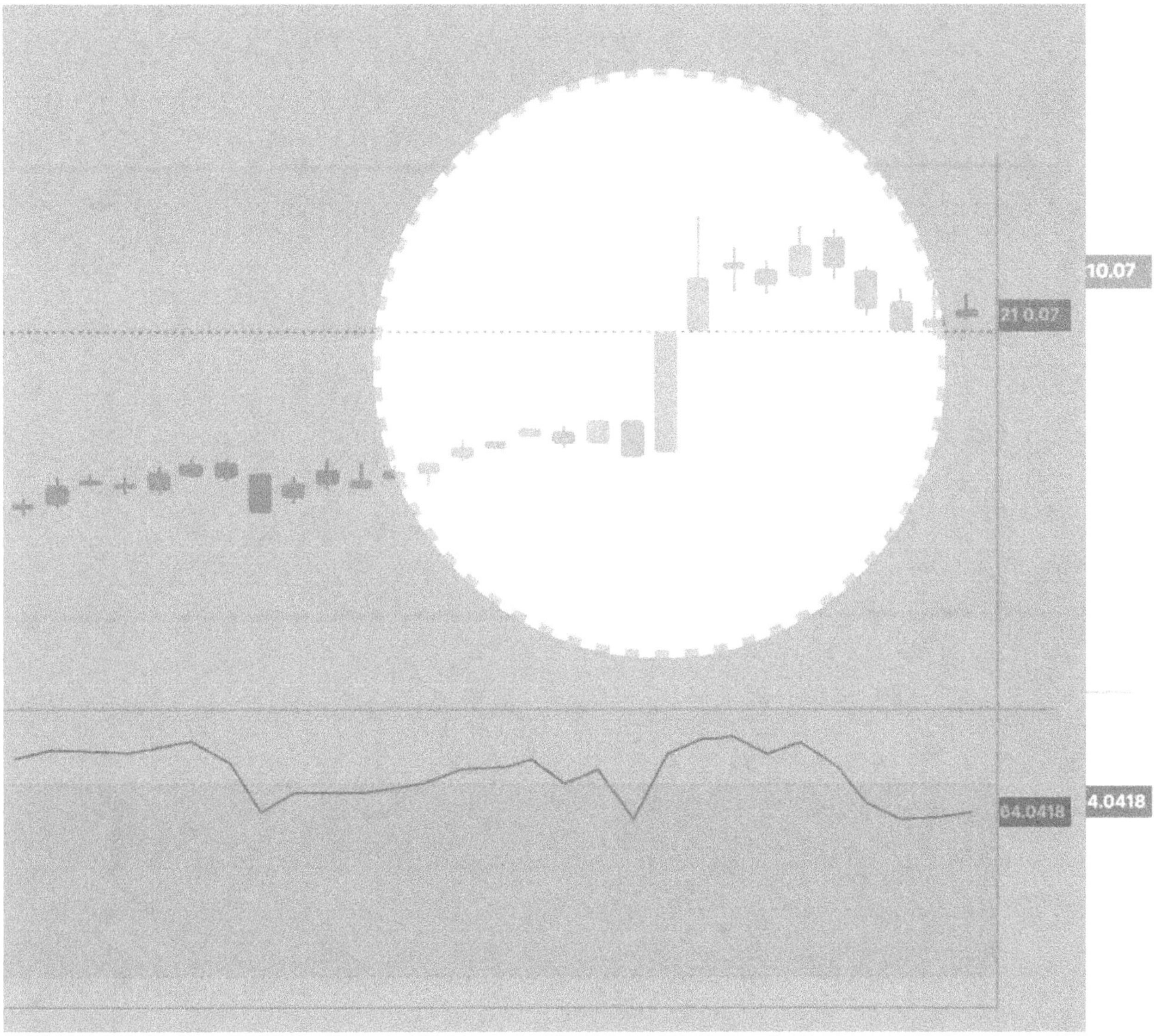

This Apple daily chart shows a strong breakout around mid-June. After a period of sideways movement with small candles, a large bullish candle forms, closing well above the previous range. This candle has a significant volume spike, signaling strong buying interest.

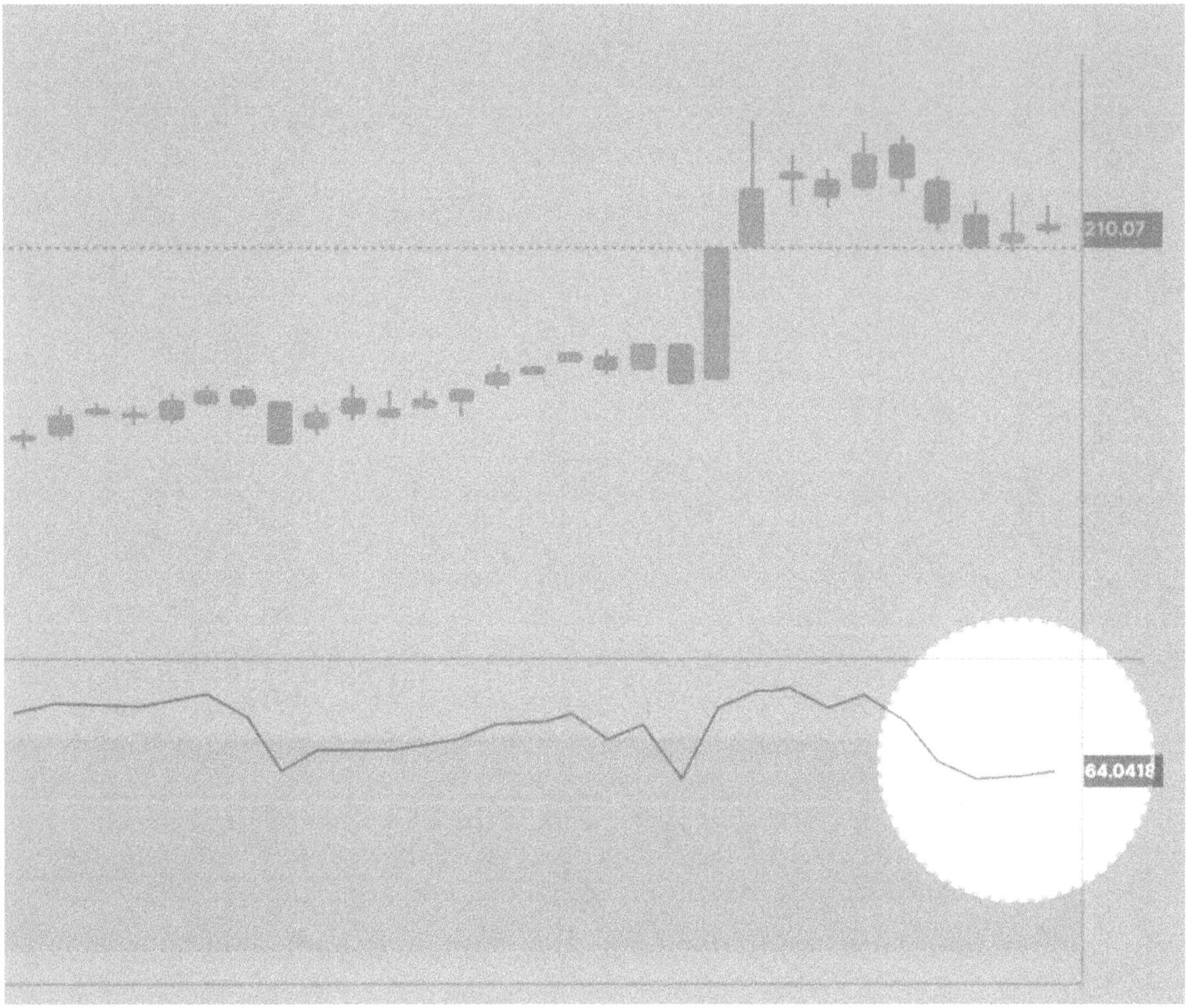

At the same time, the RSI climbs above 50, confirming bullish momentum. A trader using this setup might enter at the close of that breakout candle.

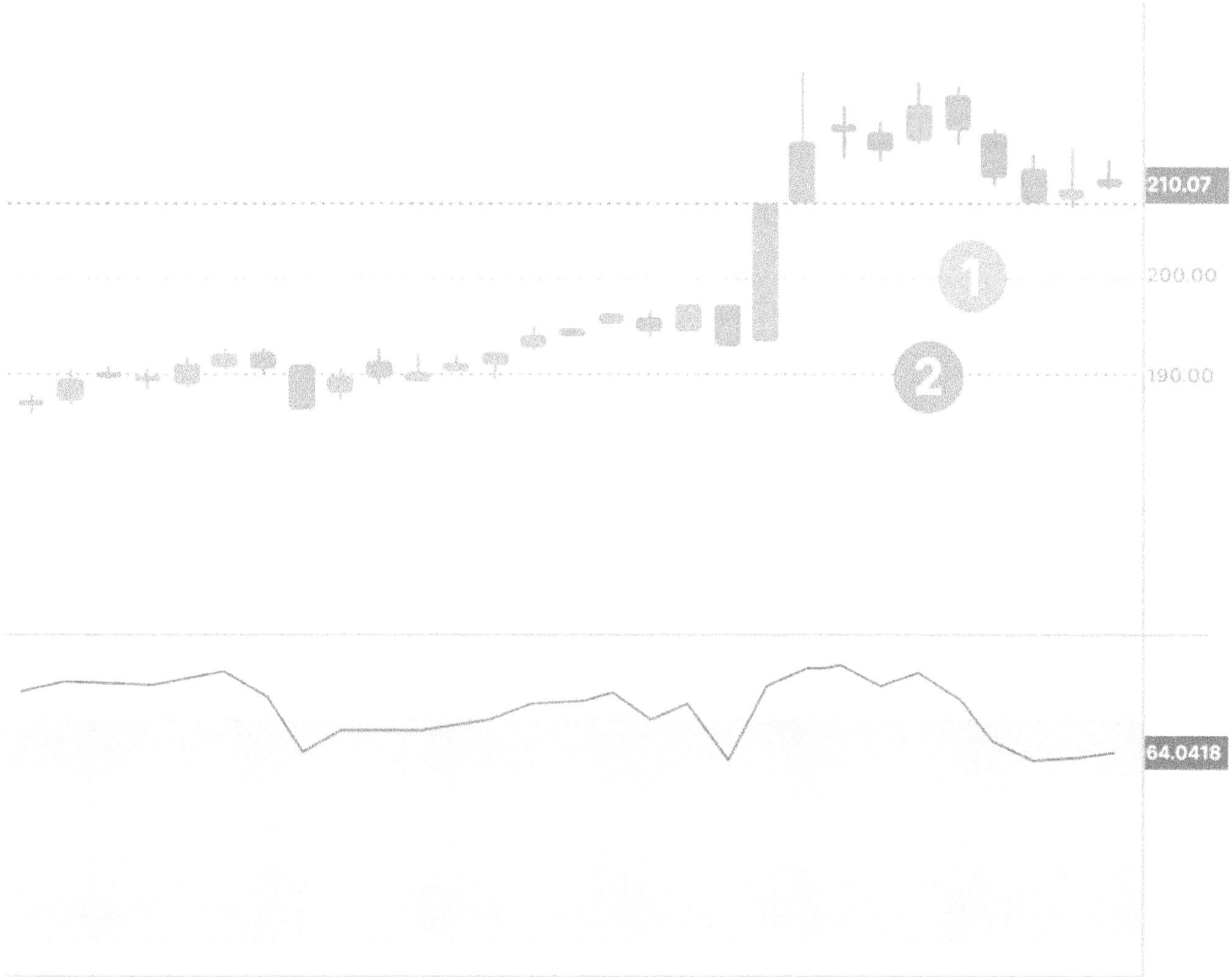

To manage risk, they could place a stop-loss just below the low of that same candle. For example, if the entry (1) is near $200 and the candle's low is around $190, the stop-loss (2) would be set $10 below the entry.

With a 2:1 risk-reward target, the take-profit (3) would be placed $20 above the entry price - around $220. This creates a clear, logical trade plan based on price action, volume confirmation, and momentum - all key elements of a solid strategy.

A trading strategy might feel like a lot to build, but you won't do it all at once. You'll use a simple checklist to build it step by step. It includes your asset, entry signal, stop-loss, target, and risk amount. In the next lessons, we'll walk through each part together. So by the end, you'll have your own complete strategy ready to go.

Excellent! You've just taken your first step toward building a real trading strategy. You now understand what a strategy is, how it's structured, and why performance metrics matter. In the next lesson, we'll zoom in on two of the most important parts - how to enter and exit trades with precision.

Lesson 2: Entry and Exit Rules

From setup to system

You know the setup. Now let's turn it into a system. In this lesson, you'll learn how to define precise entry and exit rules so every trade follows a plan, not emotion.

Every trading strategy needs two anchors: when to enter and when to exit. Without them, you're reacting instead of executing. Great traders predefine the exact conditions that trigger action.

Let's start with entries. The goal is to catch high-probability setups, not just random moves. That means the conditions should align in your favor, like a clear trend, a strong indicator signal, or a reliable chart pattern.

You also need confirmation - a trigger that tells you it's time to act. It could be a breakout candle, a volume surge, a bullish pattern, or an indicator crossover. A trigger adds timing and confidence to your setup, not just a guess.

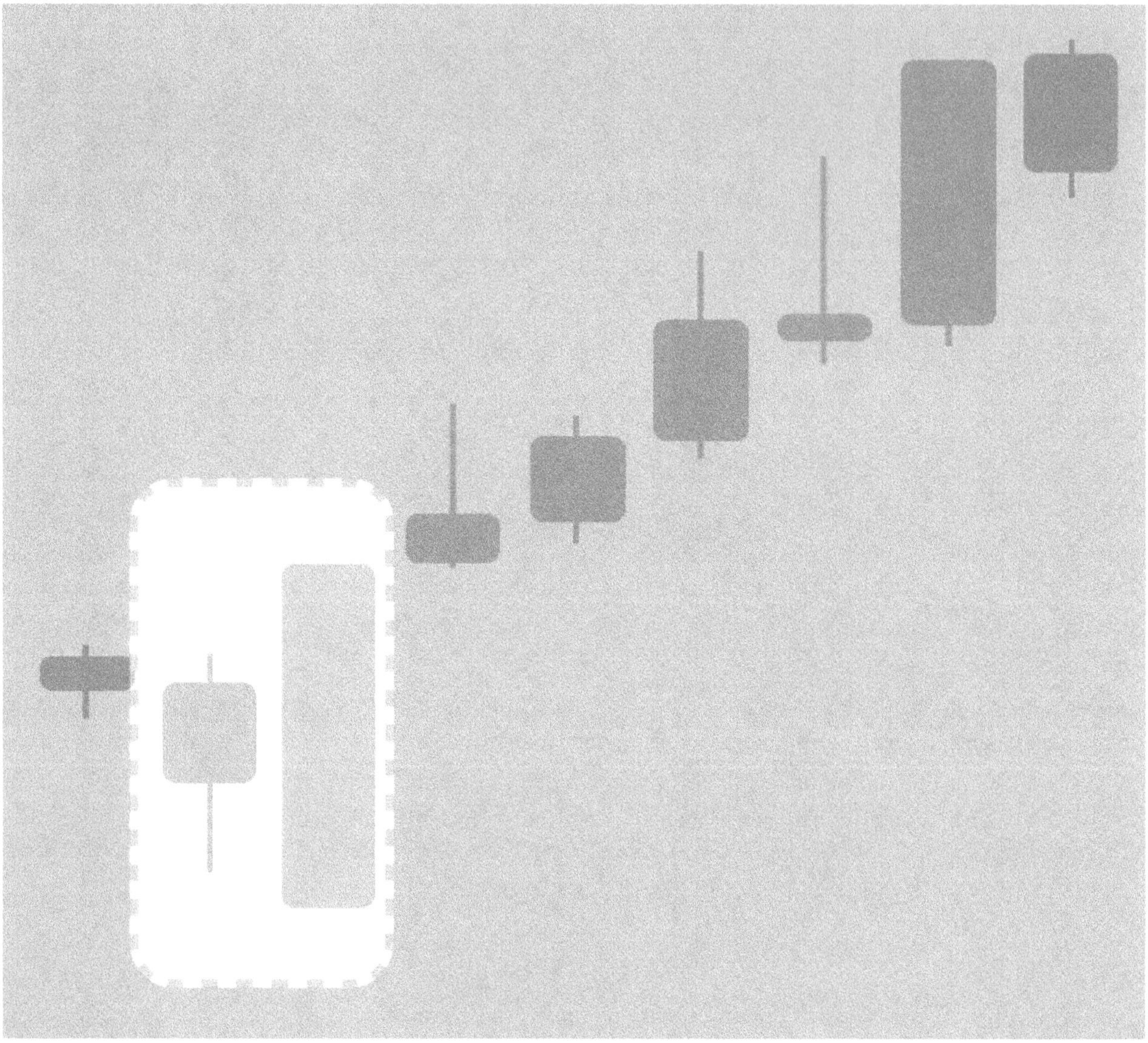

What makes a good entry?

Pick 3 signs that confirm a strong entry setup. Look for signs that support momentum and confirm that the setup is active, not just forming.

- Market is quiet and flat
- Breakout candle
- Clear market trend
- Watching RSI at 50 flat
- No trend direction
- Volume spike

Answer:

- Breakout candle
- Clear market trend
- Volume spike

Good traders plan the risk before they place a trade. That means setting a stop-loss level and deciding how much of your capital you're willing to risk. You should always know where you'll exit if the trade goes wrong, and how much that loss would cost.

Start by identifying a logical place for your stop-loss - this could be below the most recent swing low in an uptrend, or above a swing high in a downtrend. That stop-loss level marks the price where your trade idea is no longer valid.

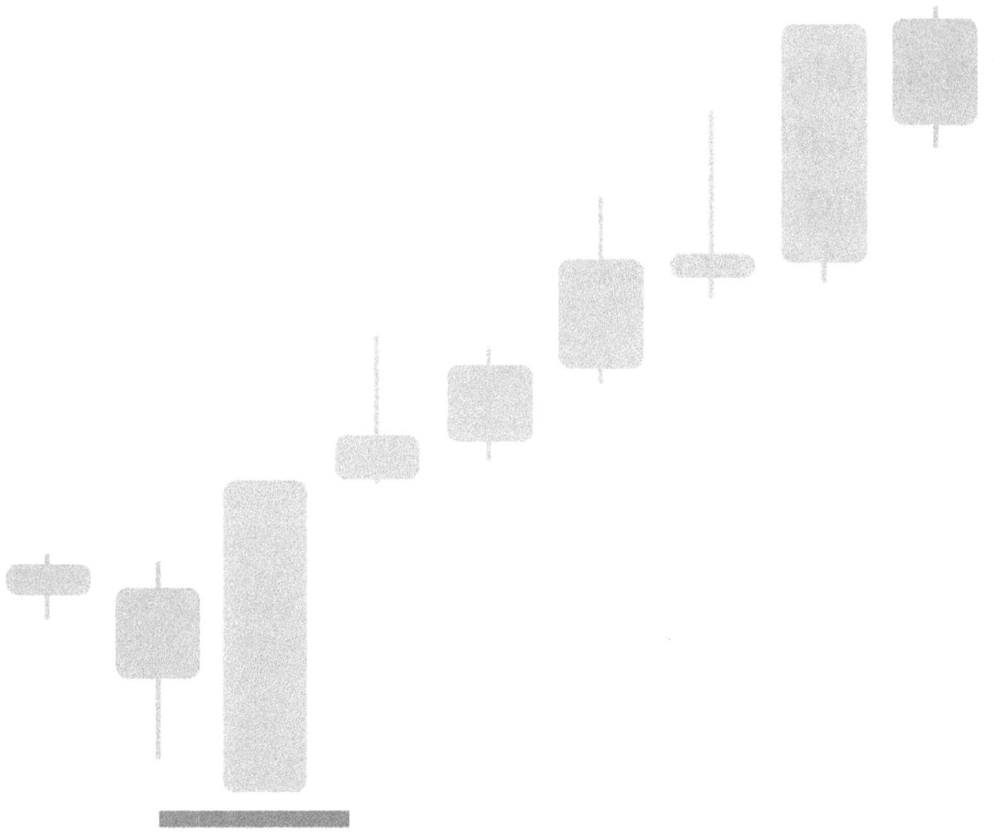

Next, decide how much you want to risk. A common rule is to risk no more than 1-2% of your total account balance on a single trade. For example, if your account is $5000 and you risk

1%, that means you're willing to lose up to $50 on that trade.

Then calculate position size. If your entry is $200 and stop-loss is $190, that's $10 risk per share. If you're risking $50 total, divide $50 by $10 - you can buy 5 shares. This keeps your loss within the plan. This is just one basic example. We'll explore more risk management methods in future lessons.

Where's the entry?

Look at the META chart. Price recently dropped and started bouncing near $420. The RSI is climbing from near oversold levels. A good entry trigger should confirm that buyers are stepping in. Look for a strong bullish candle that breaks above recent price action, not just any bounce.

Which candle gives the strongest entry signal based on confirmation?

- A strong green candle that closes above recent highs near $440
- A red candle with a long lower wick, just before the breakout
- A red Doji candle at the bottom of the pullback

- A small green candle inside the consolidation range near $430

Answer: A strong green candle that closes above recent highs near $440. A strong green candle closes above recent highs with strong bullish momentum. It confirms that buyers are stepping in, especially as RSI is rising from oversold levels.

Now let's talk about exits. Every trade needs a clear plan before you enter. A take-profit is often set near resistance (or support in a downtrend) or by using a reward-to-risk ratio, like 2:1, where your target is twice the size of your stop.

Equally important is your stop-loss. It protects your capital if the trade fails and should be placed where your setup no longer makes sense, like

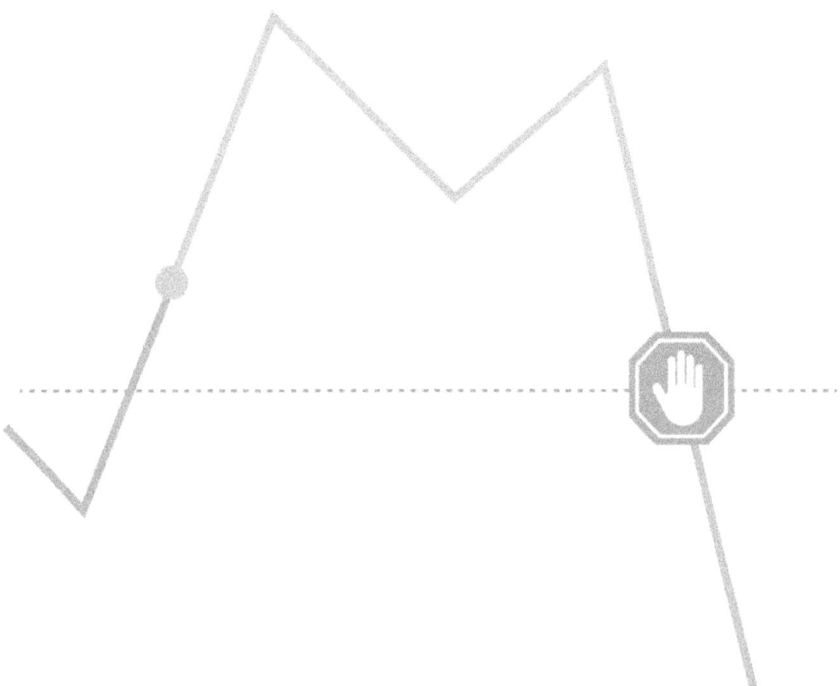

below a swing low in a buy trade or above a swing high in a sell trade.

Let's look at the two most popular exit strategies - fixed targets and trailing stops - using the META chart. With a fixed target, you choose a price level in advance to take profit. In this case, a logical target (1) would be the previous support area near $480-$490, which now acts as resistance.

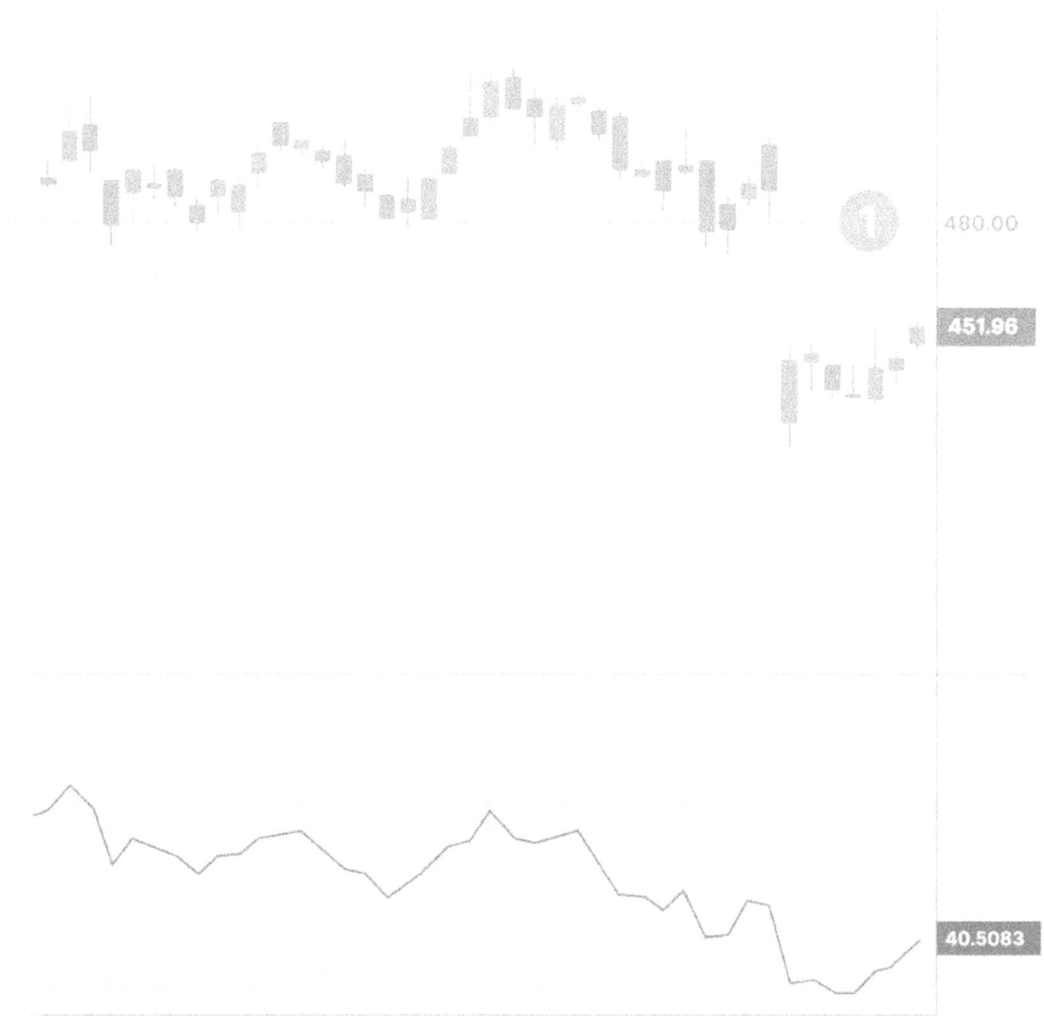

This gives the trade room to move while aiming for a 2:1 reward-to-risk ratio. With a stop-loss at $420, you're risking $20 to gain $40. Once the target is hit, the trade is closed - no need to adjust it further.

Fixed targets are simple and help with discipline by setting exits in advance. They support consistent reward-to-risk planning, ideal for hands-off trading. But they may limit profits if the market keeps moving after your target is hit, especially in strong trends.

That's where trailing stops come in - they let you capture more from strong trends. You start with the same entry (1) at $440 and an initial stop-loss (2) around $420. But instead of setting a fixed target, you follow the price by adjusting your stop as the trade moves up.

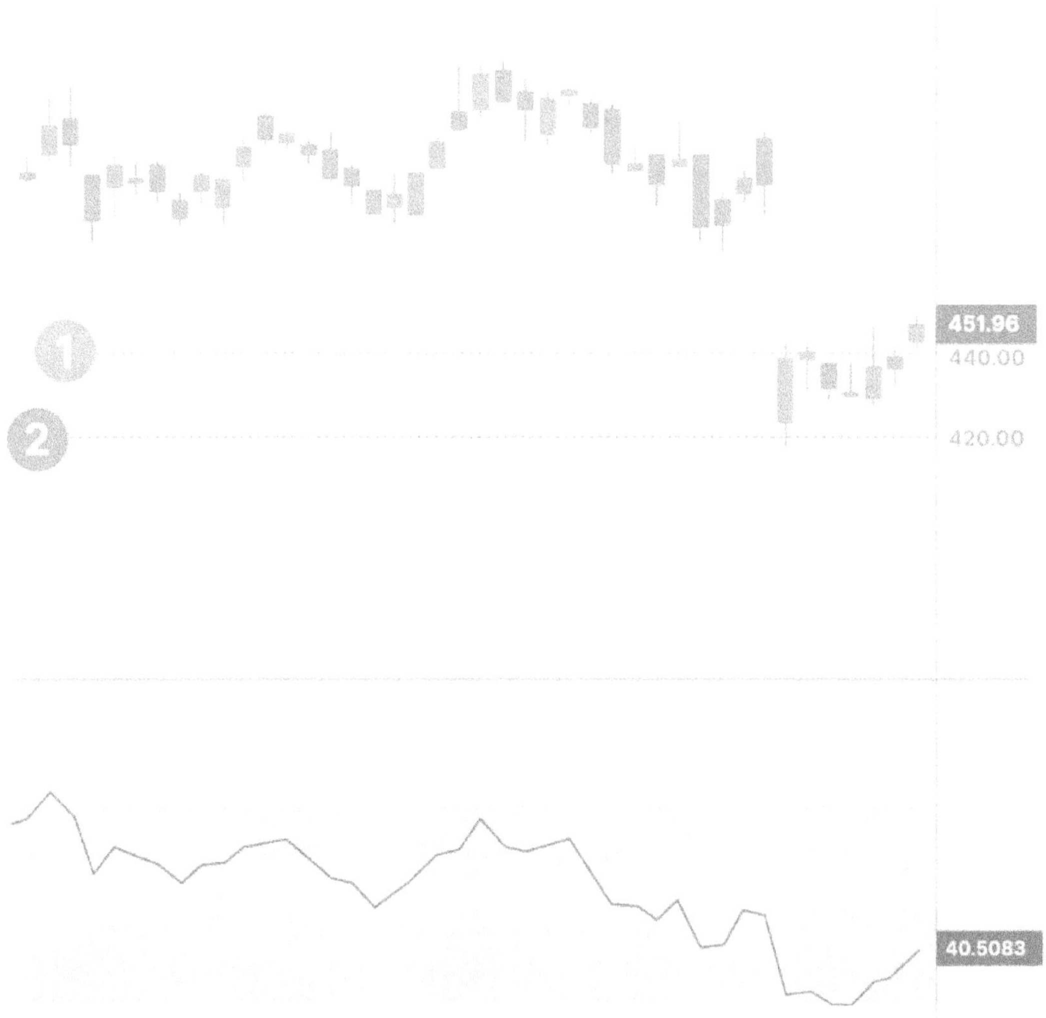

For example, after price breaks $460, you might move your stop to just below that level, such as $445. If the price keeps rising, you continue trailing the stop just below each new swing low. You stay in the trade until the price hits your stop, maximizing gains while managing risk.

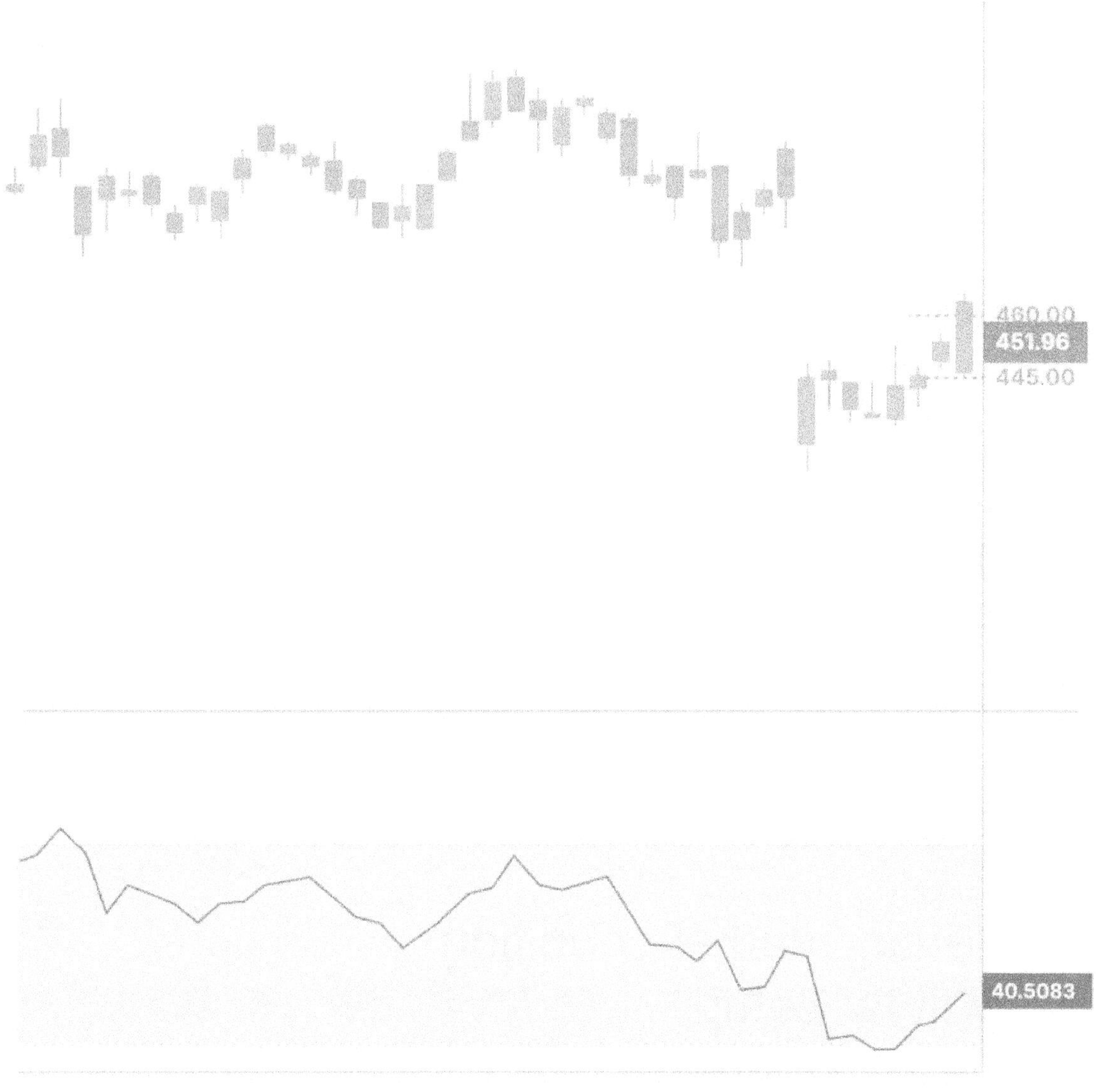

Trailing stops let you stay in a trade as long as the price moves in your favor, helping capture more profit in trends. They lock in gains as the price rises, but may exit early on pullbacks and require more management. They're flexible but less predictable than fixed targets.

Entry plan checklist

Now you know the essentials of both entry and exit rules, let's review what you've learned. Your checklist should always flow from context → trigger → risk. Put the steps of a solid entry rule in the correct order.

- Confirm trigger
- Identify market condition
- Define risk
- Wait for setup

Answer:

- Identify market condition
- Wait for setup
- Confirm trigger
- Define risk

You've now learned how to build clear entry and exit rules - what to trade, when to act, and how to manage risk. Next, we'll explore how to optimize your strategy by adjusting key parameters and testing performance across different scenarios.

Lesson 3: Strategy Optimization

It's time to optimize your strategy!

You've built a trading strategy. But is it the best version of itself? In this lesson, you'll learn how to improve your strategy's performance by adjusting its components, avoiding overfitting, and testing across different scenarios.

Optimization means tweaking your strategy's variables to improve performance, without changing the core idea. You're not guessing; you're testing different inputs, like entry setups, stop-loss size, or reward-to-risk ratios, to find what works best.

A small change, like adjusting your stop-loss or take-profit, can impact results. For example, testing a 1:2 reward-to-risk ratio may lead to fewer wins, but switching to 1:3 could improve your win rate and make the strategy more consistent.

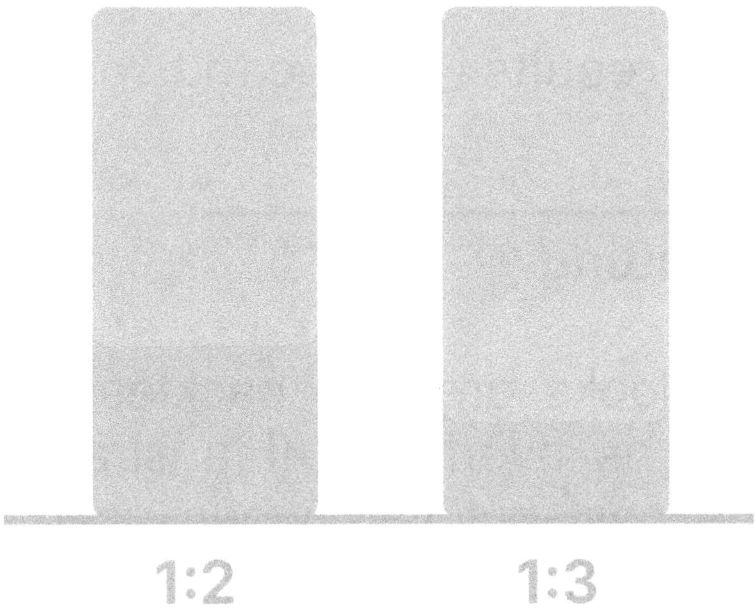

Similarly, you might run your setup on both the 1-hour and 4-hour charts. By comparing the outcomes, such as win rate, average profit, and drawdown, you might see that the 4-hour version performs more steadily or avoids false signals.

This process is called forward testing or backtesting, and it's how traders discover what combinations give better, more reliable results. We'll cover how to apply both methods step by step as we move forward.

But beware: if you adjust too much, you may create a strategy that looks great in past data but fails in real trades. This is called overfitting. It happens when a strategy is too tailored to one set of historical results and can't handle live conditions.

Signs of overfitting

Your strategy looks great in backtests, but you suspect that it is overfitted. If a strategy looks perfect in the past but fails when used live, it's likely too customized to old data and not flexible enough for real market changes. What is a clear sign that your trading strategy might be overfitted?

- It shows strong results during live trading
- It uses simple, rule-based logic
- It performs well across multiple assets and timeframes
- It has very high backtest performance, but fails in real conditions

Answer: It has very high backtest performance, but fails in real conditions. Overfitting happens when a strategy is too perfectly tuned to past data. It may look great in backtests, but it doesn't generalize to live markets.

To avoid it, keep your strategy simple and logical. Avoid adding too many filters or over-optimizing every detail just to improve backtest performance. A solid strategy should work across different market conditions, not just one stock or timeframe.

And be cautious of strategies that show perfect results with no drawdowns; real trading always includes some losses. The goal isn't perfection - it's consistency across changing markets.

That's where scenario testing comes in. It helps you move beyond backtest results and see how your strategy holds up in different real-world situations. It means checking how your strategy performs in various market environments.

For example, during strong trends, sideways consolidations, high volatility news events, and calm, slow-moving periods. You can also test it on different timeframes or with other assets. The goal is to make sure your strategy isn't just working by chance or under ideal conditions.

If your results fall apart in other scenarios, the strategy needs more work. A reliable strategy should adapt, not collapse, when the market changes. Scenario testing helps you find those weaknesses early, before risking real money.

What is scenario testing?

Select the market types where a strategy should be tested. A strong strategy should work across different trends, volatility levels, and timeframes - not just during ideal setups.

- Highest profit trades only
- Sideways markets
- Bull/Bear markets
- Trending markets
- Only best trade examples
- One week of data

Answer:

- Sideways markets
- Bull/Bear markets
- Trending markets

Now that you understand the importance of testing across different market conditions, let's look at what you can actually adjust inside your strategy to improve performance.

Here are key parameters you might test:

- Entry timing (e.g., candle close vs. confirmation)
- Stop-loss distance (tight vs. wide)
- Risk per trade (1% vs. 2%)
- Reward-to-risk ratio
- Timeframe (1H vs. 4H)
- Indicator settings (e.g,. 9 EMA vs 20 EMA)

Test one change at a time so you know what's working.

When you test changes, track performance using consistent metrics like:

- Win rate Average: the percentage of trades that end in profit.
- Average R multiple: how much you earn per trade relative to your risk.
- Profit factor: total profit divided by total loss.
- Drawdown: the largest drop from a peak to a low in your account balance.

They help you spot whether the strategy is improving or just looking better on the surface.

It might feel like a lot to test and track, but don't worry. In the next lessons, we'll walk you through each type of testing step by step, and you'll get to practice applying them to your own strategy.

Great work! In this lesson, you learned how to optimize your strategy by adjusting key parameters, avoiding overfitting, and testing across different market conditions. Next, we'll take it further with backtesting - you'll learn how to apply your strategy to historical data, measure its edge, and practice using demo platforms to build real trading confidence.

Lesson 4: Backtesting

Let's backtest strategies!

Now that you know the theory behind building a strategy, it's time to see how testing really works. In this lesson, you'll learn how to apply your setup to historical data, track real results, and find out if your strategy truly has an edge. Let's dive in.

Backtesting is applying your strategy to past market data to see how it would have performed. It lets you test your rules without risking real money. The goal is to find a statistical edge - a repeatable advantage that leads to more wins than losses over time.

A good backtest answers one key question: "If I followed these rules in the past, would I have made money consistently?" If yes, the strategy may be worth using in real time.

To backtest well, you need clear rules - entry, exit, stop-loss, take-profit, and position size. Vague strategies give weak results. You can test manually by scrolling charts and logging trades, or use software for automation. Manual helps you learn, software helps you scale.

To explain it better, let's walk through a real example. We scroll the Alibaba chart for lower highs and lows, wait for a pullback to resistance, and once a bearish candle appears, we log the entry.

We enter (1) after a pullback to resistance, and a bearish candle forms. The stop-loss (2) goes just above the pullback high. The take-profit (3) is set at twice that distance, giving a clean 2:1 reward-to-risk setup.

Now we wait and see what happens next on the chart. If the price hits the target before the stop, we mark it as a win. If it hits the stop first, it's a loss. We log the outcome, date, price, and R-multiple in our tracker.

After completing 20-30 backtested trades, analyze your data to see how the strategy performs overall. Start by checking your win rate (the percentage of trades that were profitable), your average R (how much you made relative to how much you risked), and how well your losses were controlled.

A positive average R (above +1.0), a win rate around 45-60%, and drawdowns smaller than 5R suggest your strategy may have a real edge. But if drawdowns exceed 10R, the win rate is below 40%, or setups feel unclear and inconsistent, that's a red flag.

To get reliable results, test honestly - don't skip ahead or pick only strong setups. Take every valid trade, even if it looks boring. This mirrors real trading and shows how your strategy performs over time, not just in ideal cases.

Let's practice backtesting together!

Look at the current 4-hour chart of GOOGL. The chart shows a market in a clear uptrend with regular pullbacks. The chart shows a strong uptrend with clear pullbacks to support - trade with the trend, not against it.

Which setup would be the best for backtesting?

- Buy mid-range, tight stop, take-profit at recent high
- Buy after pullback, stop below swing low, take-profit at 2x stop-loss distance
- Sell after spike, stop above high, take-profit at 1:1

- Short near top, stop above resistance, take-profit mid-range

Answer: Buy after pullback, stop below swing low, take-profit at 2x stop-loss distance. You buy after a pullback in an uptrend when a bullish candle confirms support. The stop-loss is placed just below the recent swing low to limit risk if the trend fails. The take-profit is set at twice the stop distance, aiming for a 2:1 reward-to-risk ratio.

Now that you've identified the strategy, you need to test it on multiple trades to see if it really works. Backtesting your strategy 20-30 times is enough to know if it works in the long run.

Analyze the backtest results

A good strategy doesn't need a high win rate if the average R is strong and losses are controlled. You've backtested the pullback continuation strategy over 25 trades. Win rate: 52%. Average R per trade: +1.3. Max drawdown: -3R. Based on these metrics, is the strategy showing a real edge?

- The strategy is promising and shows a positive edge
- The number of trades is too high to trust the results
- The drawdown is too large to continue testing
- The win rate is too low; the strategy should be discarded

Answer: The strategy is promising and shows a positive edge. The strategy has a solid win rate, strong average R, and low drawdown. With 25 trades tested, it shows consistency and a real edge.

Your backtest isn't the end - it's just the beginning of refining your strategy. Once you've reviewed the results, use what you've learned to improve your rules. If you notice your stop-loss is too tight or your entry trigger isn't reliable, make a small adjustment.

But don't change too much at once - tweak one variable at a time, then run the backtest again. This helps you understand exactly what's making the strategy better, or worse. Over time, these small adjustments can turn a decent setup into a strong, reliable trading system.

You now know how to apply a strategy to historical data, track results, and analyze performance with real metrics. Backtesting helps you build trust in your system before risking real capital. But this is just the beginning. Next, we'll take it further with forward testing - applying your strategy in real-time conditions to see how it holds up in live markets.

Lesson 5: Forward Testing

Let's learn about forward testing!

You've backtested your strategy - now it's time to test it live. In this lesson, you'll learn how to forward test your system in real-time using demo platforms, track results honestly, and gain the confidence to go live when you're ready.

Unlike backtesting, which uses past data, forward testing happens in the present. You wait for real candles to form and make decisions as if you were trading live, but with no financial risk. It's the final step before trading with real funds, and it shows how your system performs in real time.

To begin forward testing, first open a demo trading account on a platform that lets you place real-time simulated trades (FOREX.com, eToro.com, or ig.com is highly recommended). Set up your chart with the indicators and timeframes used in your strategy - this keeps everything consistent.

Then, wait for a valid setup to appear based on your strategy rules. Don't rush. Watch the market like you would if real money were on the line. When your entry signal is triggered, place the trade on your demo account, using the same stop-loss and take-profit rules from your backtest.

After placing the trade, log the details immediately. Include the date, instrument, entry price, stop-loss, take-profit level, result (win or loss), and R-multiple. You can use a spreadsheet, journal app, or even a notebook - just keep it consistent and detailed.

Repeat this for at least 20-30 trades to build enough data. You'll start to see which setups work, where you hesitate, and how your system performs in real-time. This process mirrors live trading but without the pressure of real capital.

Remember the strategy we developed while backtesting before? It involved buying after a pullback, stopping below the swing low, and setting a take-profit at 2x stop-loss distance. Now, we'll apply that exact setup to Google's current 4-hour chart for forward testing.

Is this strategy reliable?

You forward-tested your GOOGL pullback strategy over 20 trades. Here are the results: win rate: 35%; average R per trade: +0.4; max drawdown: -8R. A low win rate, weak average R, and high drawdown suggest the system isn't performing well enough yet.

Do these results suggest that the strategy has a reliable edge?

- The results show weak performance - it's likely the strategy needs adjustment or simplification
- The drawdown is low enough to continue testing confidently
- The win rate is fine because the average R is positive
- The strategy is working as expected and is ready for live trading

Answer: The results show weak performance - it's likely the strategy needs adjustment or simplification. A 35% win rate with an average R of just +0.4 and a drawdown of -8R suggests the strategy is underperforming. It may lack a clear edge or need better-defined entry and exit rules. Before moving forward, it's best to pause, review your trades, and refine the weak points.

If your forward testing results are weak, don't scrap the strategy - refine it. Start by reviewing your trade journal. Were the entries too early? Stops too tight? Signals unclear? Tweak one element at a time. Then re-test for another 10-20 trades.

Forward testing helps you build not just a strategy, but trading confidence. Every good system needs proof in real conditions, and that's what this step gives you. Once your strategy proves itself in forward testing, you're closer to going live.

Steps of Forward Testing

Forward testing mirrors live trading - stick to your rules, track trades as they happen, and review your results after a full sample size.

1. Backtest your strategy on historical data
2. Place a demo trade in real-time
3. Record the trade details in your tracker
4. Analyze results after 20-30 trades

To improve accuracy, always forward test using the same setup as in backtesting. That means the same entry signals, stop-loss levels, position sizing, and reward-to-risk ratios. If you change the rules mid-test, your results won't reflect reality.

Forward testing also helps you track your behavior. Do you hesitate to enter? Close early? Ignore your stop? These insights are just as important as the win rate. Your mindset and discipline shape your results as much as your strategy.

Once forward testing shows consistent results, you can start small-scale live trading. Trade with minimum risk - just enough to get used to real money emotions. This is where confidence and caution meet.

Great job! You now know how to test your strategy in real-time using a demo account. You learned how to follow your rules, track trades, measure results, and recognize when your strategy needs refinement. Next, you'll learn how to organize your trade data, review outcomes, and refine your system using real insights - not just gut feelings.

Lesson 6: Documenting Strategy Performance

How to keep records?

Every good trader keeps records. In this lesson, you'll learn how to track your results, review your trades, and improve your strategy over time, step by step.

Why document your performance? Because memory fades, but data doesn't. Writing things down helps you stay objective, spot patterns, and make better decisions.

A strong trade journal tracks exact trade details, not emotions or outside opinions. Focus on data you can measure and review. The 3 key items that should always be recorded to track your trade performance effectively are:

- Date and time
- Entry and exit price
- Stop-loss and take-profit

Now, add your reasoning. This is where your journal becomes powerful. Write down why you took the trade, what setup you saw, and whether it followed your rules. This helps you stay accountable and spot patterns in your decision-making.

Here's what a simple trade log might look like:

- Instrument: GOOGL
- Entry: $198
- Stop-loss: $195
- Take-profit: $204
- Result: +2R
- Reason: Pullback with confirmation
- Followed plan: Yes

After every 10-20 trades, take a moment to review your performance. Check your win rate to see how often your trades are profitable. Look at your average R to understand how much you're making relative to what you risk. Most importantly, ask yourself - are you consistently following your own rules?

Use visual cues - green for wins, red for losses - to spot streaks and mistakes. Look for patterns:

Are your entries too early? Are you cutting profits short or letting losses run? Your journal helps you recognize which setups work and where your strategy needs work.

The steps of documenting strategy performance

Logging comes first, adjustment comes last:

1. Lodge trades consistently

2. Analyze metrics like win rate

3. Identify setup or execution issues

4. Adjust strategy if needed

Don't just log the wins - record every trade, even the losses and mistakes. This builds discipline and gives you a complete picture of your strategy's strengths and weaknesses.

Use tags or categories to group your trades and uncover deeper patterns. For example:

- Strategy A vs. Strategy B: Which one performs better?
- Trending vs. range-bound market: Does your setup work in both conditions?
- Clean vs. messy setups: Are clearer patterns producing better results?

Tagging helps you filter trades later, compare outcomes, and refine specific parts of your system with precision. The more detail you capture now, the smarter your improvements will be later.

Eventually, your trade journal becomes more than just a record - it becomes a feedback loop:

Strategy → Trade → Log → Review → Adjust → Repeat.

This loop is how great traders stay sharp and evolve.

Real improvement comes from your own tracked experience. Improvement in trading comes from experience and tracking it. A trade log helps you spot what works, what doesn't, and why. Reviewing it regularly lets you make informed adjustments instead of guessing or chasing trends.

You've learned how to document trades, review performance, and refine your strategy using clear data, not guesswork. Trade journals help you spot what's working, fix what's not, and grow as a trader. Up next: let's review everything you've learned with a quick quiz to lock it in!

QUIZ: Building and Testing Your Trading Strategy

1. You're building your first trading strategy. What's the most important first step?

- Choose a random entry signal and optimize later
- Watch the market and copy others' trades
- Decide your exact take-profit level
- Define what asset you'll trade and why it fits your style

2. You just created a strategy that wins 40% of the time, but each win is 3 times larger than your losses. What does this suggest?

- You may have a strong risk-reward edge
- The win rate is too low to trade
- The strategy is only luck-based
- You need to increase position size immediately

3. You backtested a breakout strategy over 30 trades. It shows a 50% win rate and average R of +1.5. What's your next move?

- Discard the strategy due to average performance
- Try adding 10 new indicators to increase accuracy
- Consider forward testing in demo with confidence
- Use real money immediately without testing

4. You're evaluating your system's win rate. Out of 20 trades, 12 were profitable. What's your win rate?

- 12%
- 40%
- 20%
- 60%

5. You have a $5000 account and want to risk 1% per trade. The distance between your entry and stop-loss is $10. How many shares can you buy?

- 10

- 100
- 50
- 5

6. You notice that your setup looks great in backtests but fails repeatedly in live demo trading. What's the likely issue?

- The RSI isn't accurate enough
- Your strategy may be overfitted to past data
- You haven't optimized for 15-minute charts
- You need more indicators

7. You're reviewing performance data. Which combination suggests your strategy has a real edge?

- No losses, but only tested 3 trades
- Win rate 30%, drawdown 12R, no defined exit
- Win rate around 55%, average R above 1.2, drawdown under 5R
- All wins are over +3R, but the total profit is break-even

8. What's a red flag that a strategy may not be reliable?

- It shows a 45% win rate with strong reward-to-risk
- It's tested on at least 20 trades
- It has simple entry and exit rules
- It performs well only on one stock or timeframe

9. You adjust your stop-loss and re-test the strategy. What should you do next?

- Adjust three components at once to save time
- Change one variable at a time and measure results
- Skip backtesting and test it live immediately
- Use only 5 trades to confirm if it works

10. After analyzing your metrics, you notice your average R has dropped after a strategy tweak. What's the best response?

- Revert the change or try another single adjustment
- Ignore it and focus on the win rate only
- Remove all stop-losses for higher gains
- Add more trades quickly to mask the result

Answer: 1. D; 2. A; 3. C; 4. D; 5. D; 6. B; 7. C; 8. D; 9. B; 10. A

Chapter 2: Mastering Risk Management

Lesson 1: Risk Management Fundamentals

Let's explore risk management!

In this lesson, we'll explore the building blocks of risk management. By the end, you'll understand how to manage risk per trade, use risk-reward ratios, calculate expected value, and control your trading outcomes with more confidence.

As you already know, risk management is the backbone of successful trading. It ensures that losses are controlled and capital is preserved, allowing traders to stay in the game long enough to realize profits.

But how much should you risk on a single trade? That's where the concept of risk per trade comes in. It is the maximum amount you're willing to lose on one trade. Most traders risk only 1-2% of their capital per trade. This keeps individual losses small while allowing for long-term growth.

To calculate your risk per trade, start with your account size, for example, \$10,000. Then choose the percentage you're willing to risk, such as 2%. Multiply the account size by the risk percentage: \$10,000 × 0.02 = \$200. This means you'll risk no more than \$200 on that trade.

$$\$10,000 \times 0,02 = \$200$$

Traders typically risk 1-2% per trade to protect their capital and stay in the game long term. Knowing your risk per trade helps you limit losses, stay consistent, and protect your account from major drawdowns. But managing risk isn't just about limiting losses - it's also about aiming for smart gains. That's where the risk-reward ratio comes in.

The risk-reward ratio shows how much you could gain for every dollar you risk. A 1:2 ratio means risking \$1 to make \$2. The risk-reward ratio helps you avoid low-quality trades and build long-term profit, even with a modest win rate.

1:2

There are several common types of risk-reward ratio setups traders use, depending on their strategy and goals:

- 1:1 risk-reward ratio - You risk and aim to gain the same amount. This requires a high win rate (over 50%) to stay profitable. It's often used in fast-moving markets or for scalping.
- 1:2 risk-reward ratio - You risk $1 to gain $2. A popular setup that allows profitability even if you win only 40% of the time. It balances risk-reward well.
- 1:3 or higher risk-reward ratio - You aim to gain much more than you risk. These setups can be highly profitable with even lower win rates (around 30%), but they require patience and precision. Often used by trend-following traders.

- Less than 1:1 - You risk more than you stand to gain. This is usually avoided, unless part of a high-probability scalping strategy. It demands a very high win rate to be sustainable.

Different trading styles suit different risk-reward setups. Think about how long trades are held and how often setups work out - a higher risk-reward ratio often means fewer but bigger wins.

- Trend-following or longer holds - 1:3 risk-reward ratio
- Balanced swing or day trading - 1:2 risk-reward ratio
- Scalping or fast trades - 1:1 risk-reward ratio

You've seen how different risk-reward ratio setups suit different trading styles. Now let's apply this to real numbers. Imagine you put a stop-loss (1) at $50. If your take-profit (2) is $100, then your risk-reward ratio is 1:2. This means for every $1 you risk, you aim to make $2. Even if only half of your trades win, you're still ahead because your winners are larger than your losers. This is why setting the right risk-reward ratio helps you stay profitable even with a modest win rate.

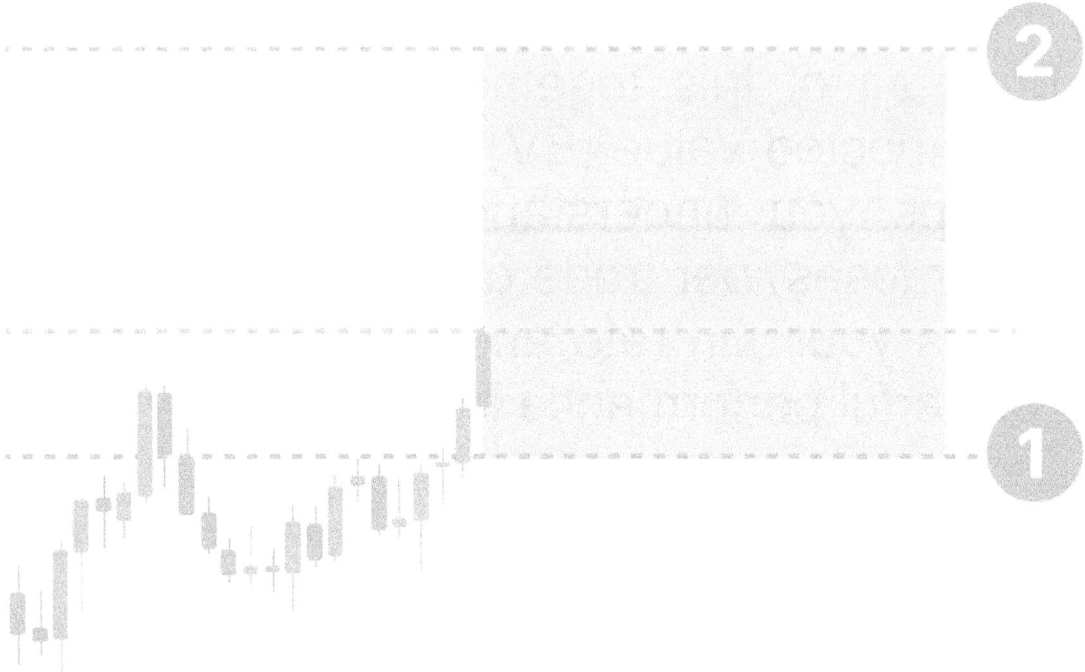

But risk-reward ratio is only half the equation. The other part is win rate - the percentage of trades that end in profit. For example, if you take 100 trades and win 60 of them, your win rate is 60%. Together, win rate and risk-reward ratio tell you whether a strategy is truly profitable.

You don't need to win all the time to be profitable. A strategy with a 40% win rate and a 1:3 risk-reward ratio can still beat one with a 70% win rate and a 1:1 risk-reward ratio. The key is balance. Do your big wins outweigh your small losses? This is what creates a positive trading edge.

To bring all of this together, we use a concept called Expected Value (EV). EV is a statistical tool that helps you understand what your strategy earns (or loses) per trade on average over time. It combines your win rate and risk-reward ratio into one powerful performance measure.

Here's how you calculate it:

EV = (Win Rate × Average Win) - (Loss Rate x Average Loss)

Let's say you win 50% of your trades, each winning $100, and lose 50%, each losing $50:

EV = (0.5 × $100) - (0.5 × $50) = $25

This means, on average, you can expect to make $25 per trade.

If your expected value is positive, it means your system makes money over time, even if individual trades vary. Positive EV is the sign of a healthy strategy. This is what allows professionals to trust their edge and stick with their plan through losing streaks. However, a negative EV means that your strategy is losing money on average and needs to be re-evaluated.

Even a strategy with positive EV can fail without risk control. To avoid it, manage your risk per trade and protect your capital from losing streaks.

Now you've learned the key parts of risk management - risk per trade, risk-reward ratio, win rate, and expected value. Next, we'll cover position sizing - the final piece that ties it all together in live trades.

Lesson 2: Position Sizing

Position sizing essentials

Winning strategies might fail without proper sizing. That's why, in this lesson, you'll learn how to calculate the right number of shares to trade. We'll explore fixed percentage, fixed dollar, and volatility-based sizing methods to help you manage risk with precision.

Position sizing is about determining how much of an asset to trade so your loss stays within your risk tolerance. It ensures that no single trade can cause major damage to your account.

The most common method is fixed percentage sizing. You risk a set % of your capital per trade, like 1% or 2%. Traders choose it because it scales naturally with performance, but it does require recalculating the position for every trade.

To calculate it:

1. Choose your risk %
2. Multiply it by your account size
3. Divide by the $ amount between your entry and stop-loss

Let's calculate a fixed percentage sizing!

You have a $12,000 trading account and want to risk 2% on a trade. Your entry price is $60, and your stop-loss is at $58. First, calculate your dollar risk. Then divide that by your risk per share. What is the correct position size based on fixed percentage risk?

- 120 shares
- 100 shares
- 240 shares
- 60 shares

Answer: 120 shares. You're risking 2% of a $12,000 account, which is $240. Your stop-loss is $2 per share ($60 entry - $58 stop), so: $240 ÷ $2 = 120 shares.

Fixed dollar sizing, on the other hand, involves risking the same dollar amount every time, like $100 per trade. It's simple to apply, which appeals to part-time traders or beginners. But, it doesn't adapt to changes in account size, and you might risk too much or too little.

Volatility-based sizing adjusts your position according to market volatility. The more volatile the asset, the smaller your position. This protects you from wild price swings.

To measure volatility, traders often use the Average True Range (ATR). It shows the average price movement over a set number of periods (usually 14). For example, if the ATR is $5, it means the price moves about $5 per period.

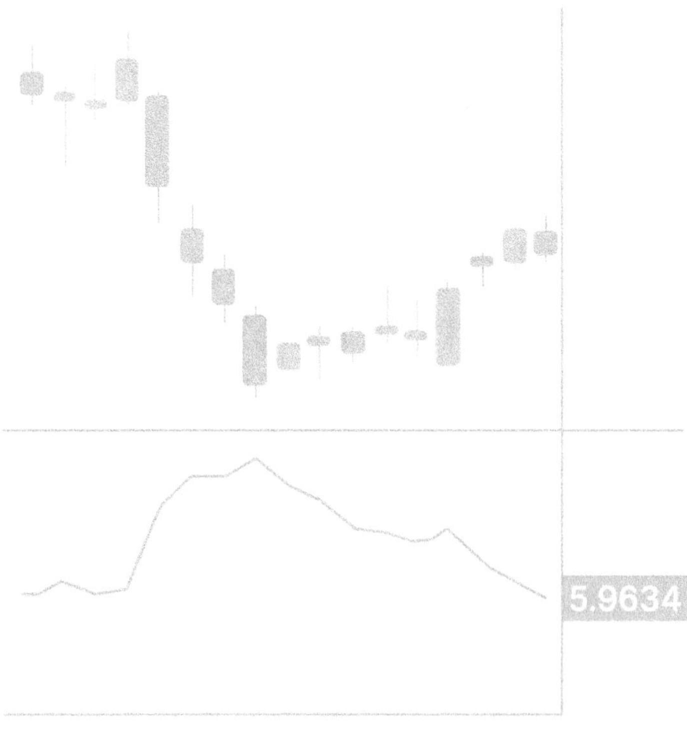

Here's how it works:

- You decide how much money you're willing to risk ($100).
- You divide that risk by the ATR ($100 ÷ $5).
- That gives you your position size: 20 shares.

This method helps you avoid oversized positions in volatile markets and underexposed ones in calm markets. It adapts your trade size to market conditions, making your risk control smarter and more stable.

It's time to calculate volatility-based sizing

You want to risk $200 on a trade. The ATR is $4. Divide your risk ($200) by the ATR ($4) to find the correct position size. Based on volatility-based sizing, how many shares should you buy?

- 40 shares
- 50 shares
- 80 shares
- 25 shares

Answer: 50 shares. You're risking $200, and the average price movement (ATR) is $4. $200 ÷ $4 =

50 shares. This keeps your risk aligned with market volatility.

Sizing methods and their features

Think about how flexible or scalable each sizing method is - some are dynamic, while others stay the same regardless of market or account size.

- Volatility-based sizing - Adapts to market changes
- Fixed dollar sizing - Simple and consistent
- Fixed percentage sizing - Grows with account

Combining position sizing methods allows you to adapt more intelligently to account growth and changing market conditions.

For example, you might start with fixed percentage sizing, risking 2% of your account per trade. But instead of applying it blindly, you add a volatility filter using ATR.

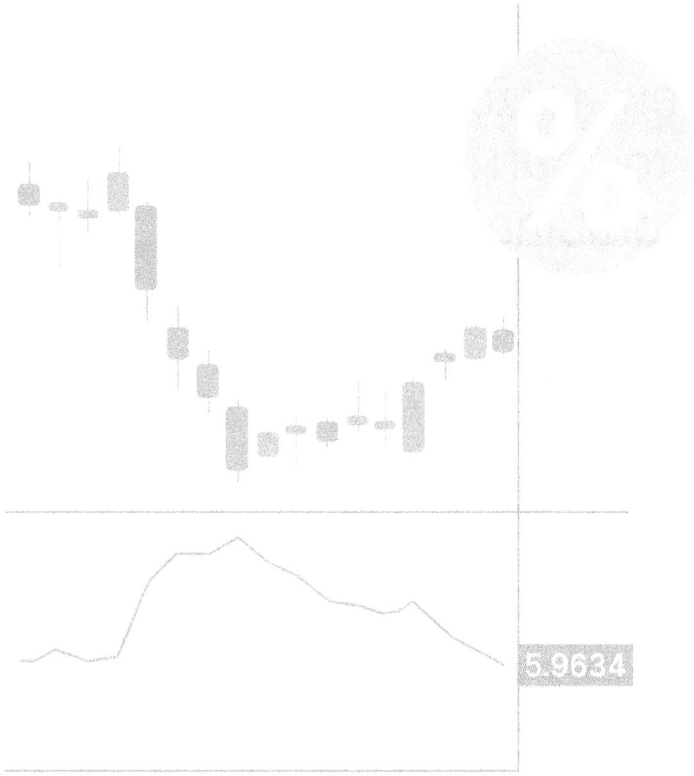

If the ATR shows low volatility, you can proceed with your full position size. If the market is highly volatile, you reduce the size or skip the trade to avoid being shaken out. This approach protects your capital during choppy conditions while allowing you to scale up when the market is stable.

Combine sizing methods

You have a $10,000 account. The ATR of the asset is $2. You want to risk 2% of your account, but only if volatility allows it. First, calculate how many shares you can buy with your chosen risk amount. Then, factor in the ATR to size the trade according to current volatility. Which option reflects a combination of fixed percentage and volatility-based sizing?

- Buy 20 shares - ATR is $10, so a smaller position for safety
- Buy 50 shares - based on $100 risk and $2 ATR
- Buy 200 shares - fixed dollar sizing, $200 per trade
- Buy 100 shares - based on 2% fixed risk, ignoring ATR

Answer: Buy 50 shares - based on $100 risk and $2 ATR. You're risking 2% of a $10,000 account, which is $200. But you want to trade only when volatility is reasonable. With an ATR of $2 and a more cautious risk limit of $100, divide $100 by $2 = 50 shares. This reflects a combined approach using both fixed % and volatility-based sizing.

Great job! In this lesson, you learned how position sizing helps control risk and protect your account. Next, we'll dive into stop-loss orders and learn how to set them effectively to safeguard your trades.

Lesson 3: Stop-loss Orders

Let's explore stop-losses!

Even the best trades can go wrong. That's why every smart trader uses a stop-loss. In this lesson, you'll learn how to set different types of stop-losses to protect your capital and stay in control, no matter what the market does.

A stop-loss is a predefined price level where your trade is automatically closed to limit your loss. Without a stop-loss, you risk holding losing trades too long, hoping they'll recover. This can drain your account. With a stop, you define the maximum you're willing to lose before you even enter the trade.

One of the simplest and most commonly used tools is the fixed stop-loss. It stays at one price level and doesn't move. For example, if you buy at $100 and place a stop at $95, the trade will close if the price hits $95, locking in a $5 loss per share.

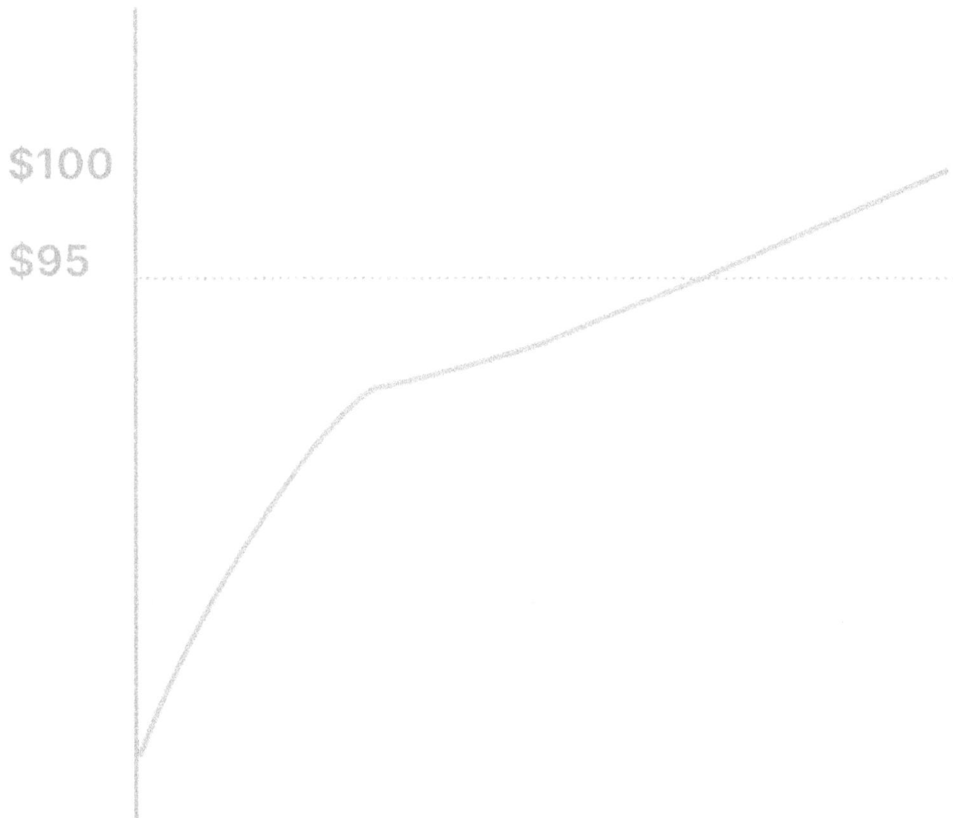

Where to place your stop-Loss

Setting your stop-loss in the right place is crucial. A fixed stop should be based on market structure. Think about where your trade idea becomes invalid. Stops should go just beyond structure, not inside the noise.

- Range breakout - Below/above breakout level
- Long trade - Below recent swing low
- Short trade - Above recent swing high

Fixed stop-losses are great for structure and discipline, but they don't adapt to new information. That's where trailing stops come in. A trailing stop moves with the price.

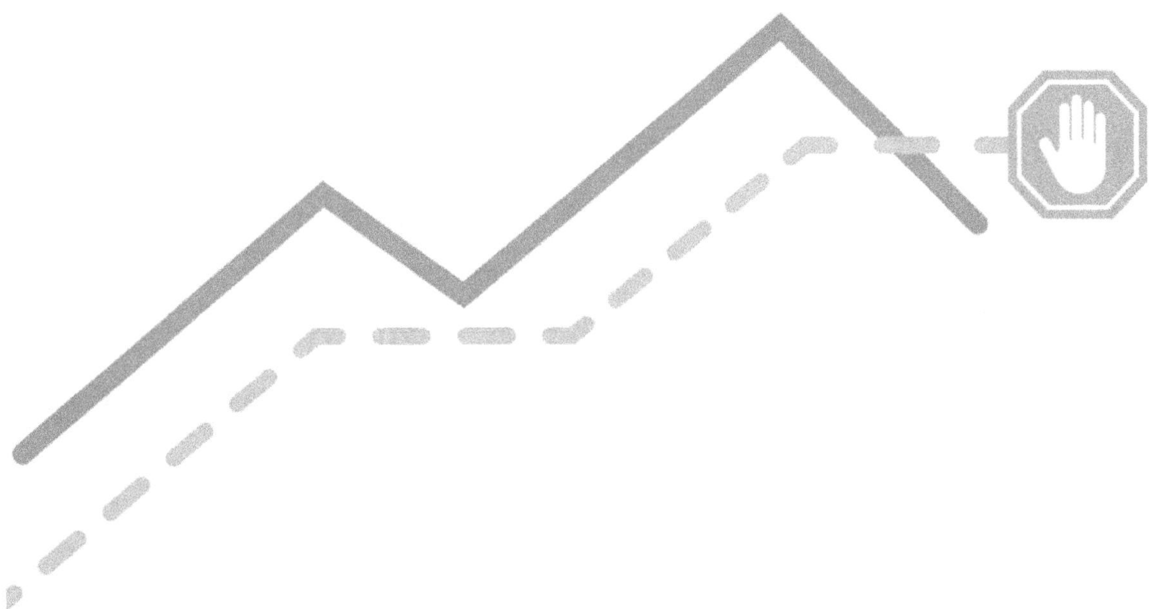

For example, if your stop is $5 below your entry and price moves up $10, your stop moves up too, still $5 below. You lock in profits as the trend continues.

Trailing stops can be set manually, but many platforms allow you to automate them, so they adjust without intervention. They are particularly useful in trending markets, where you want to stay in the trade as long as the trend is strong, but still protect your gains in case of a reversal.

However, they require careful calibration: setting the stop too tight can result in getting stopped out on normal pullbacks, while setting it too wide might give up too much of your profit.

Where should your trailing stop be?

You entered a long position on Twitter at $36.00. The price has now reached $42.50. You're using a $2 trailing stop-loss. A trailing stop-loss moves up with the market. Subtract the trailing amount from the highest price reached since entry. Based on a $2 trailing stop, what is the correct stop-loss level now that the price is at $42.50?

- $44.50
- $40.50
- $36.00
- $42.00

Answer: $40.50. With a trailing stop-loss of $2 and the current price at $42.50, your stop should now be at $40.50. It trails behind the price, locking in gains while allowing room for the trade to grow.

Another approach is a time-based stop-loss. It is a strategy where a trader exits a trade after a set period of time, regardless of whether the price has hit the stop-loss or take-profit level.

This stop is useful for momentum-based trades. If the price hasn't moved in your favor within a set time, like 3 days for a swing trade or 30 minutes for a day trade, it likely means the setup is failing or momentum is fading.

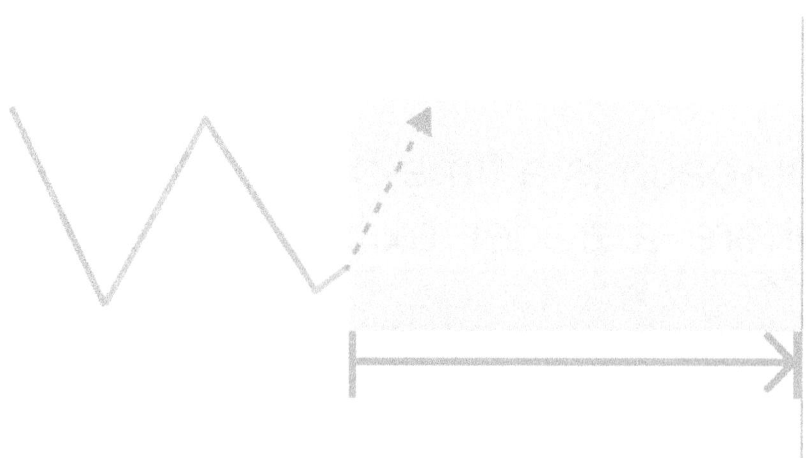

Exiting based on time helps avoid capital being tied up in trades that are stagnating, reducing opportunity cost, and protecting against slow, grinding reversals. It adds structure, especially in markets that move sideways or lack clear direction.

To choose the right time for a time-based stop-loss, align it with your trading style and the trade's expected duration:

- Day traders: Set a stop at 15 to 60 minutes if the price doesn't move in your favor.
- Swing traders: Use a window of 2-5 days for the setup to play out.

So, how do you choose the right stop-loss? It depends on your trading style, volatility, and setup. Trend-followers might use trailing stops. Range traders may prefer fixed stops below support.

Over time, your stop strategy should evolve. Track which stop types work best in your setups. Review how often you're stopped out and how tight is too tight.

What's a smart stop-loss order?

Never place stops based on gut feeling.

- Define entry setup
- Identify invalidation point
- Choose stop-loss method
- Size the position

Great job! You now understand fixed, trailing, and time-based stop-losses - and how to set them smartly. Next, we'll move on to drawdown management - you'll learn what drawdowns are, how to keep them within safe limits, and how to recover when your trading hits a rough patch.

Lesson 4: Drawdown Management

How to manage drawdown?

Losses are part of trading, but how you handle them defines your long-term success. In this lesson, you'll learn what drawdowns are, why they matter, and how to manage them without losing control of your strategy or emotions.

A drawdown is the decline in your account from a peak to a low point before it recovers. For example, if your account drops from $10,000 to $8,500, that's a $1,500 or 15% drawdown. It measures how much your account pulls back during losing streaks.

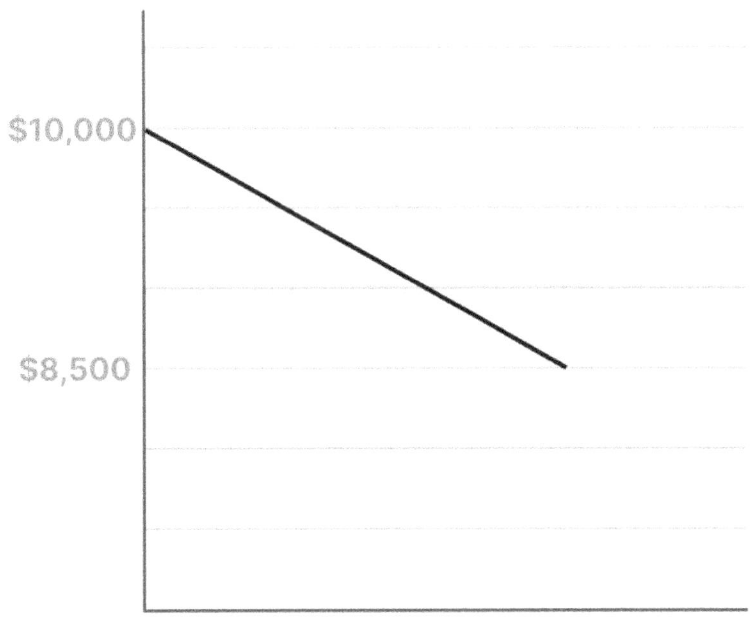

Drawdowns are normal. Even great strategies go through losing streaks. But if your drawdowns are too deep or happen too often, it may be a sign that your risk is too high or your system needs refinement.

There are two types of drawdowns:

- Absolute drawdown: The amount your account has fallen below its starting balance.
- Maximum drawdown: The biggest drop from any peak to a low point during a given period. This is the key risk metric traders watch.

For example, if your account started at $10,000 and dropped to $9,200 before rising again, your absolute drawdown is $800 (1). If your account grew to $12,000 before falling to $9,200, your maximum drawdown is $2,800 (2).

Drawdowns are more than just numbers - they show how much recovery effort you'll need to get back to where you started. What makes them dangerous is that the deeper the loss, the harder the recovery becomes - not in a linear way, but exponentially.

Let's break it down. If your account drops 10%, you only need an 11.1% gain to get back to the original balance. That's manageable. But if your account drops 50%, you now need a 100% gain - you have to double your account, just to recover that loss.

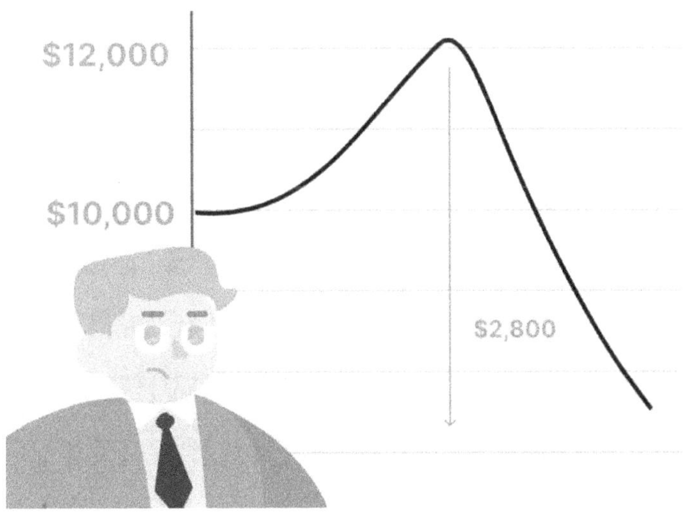

Smaller drawdowns are easier to recover from. Large ones can destroy confidence and capital. Aim to keep drawdowns under control.

Acceptable drawdown levels vary, but here's a rough guide to summarize:

- Less than 10%: Excellent risk control
- 10-20%: Acceptable for aggressive strategies
- Over 30%: Dangerous territory

To minimize drawdown, control your risk per trade. If you consistently risk 1% per trade, a 5-trade losing streak means only a 5% drawdown. If you risk 5% per trade, the same streak cuts your account by over 20%.

Avoid over-leveraging. Using too much margin or large position sizes increases the size of every loss. That makes drawdowns deeper and harder to recover from.

Keep your win rate (1) and risk-reward ratio (2) in balance. A high win rate with a poor risk-reward setup can lead to deep drawdowns when a few losses hit. A balanced edge with consistent R-multiples helps smooth the equity curve.

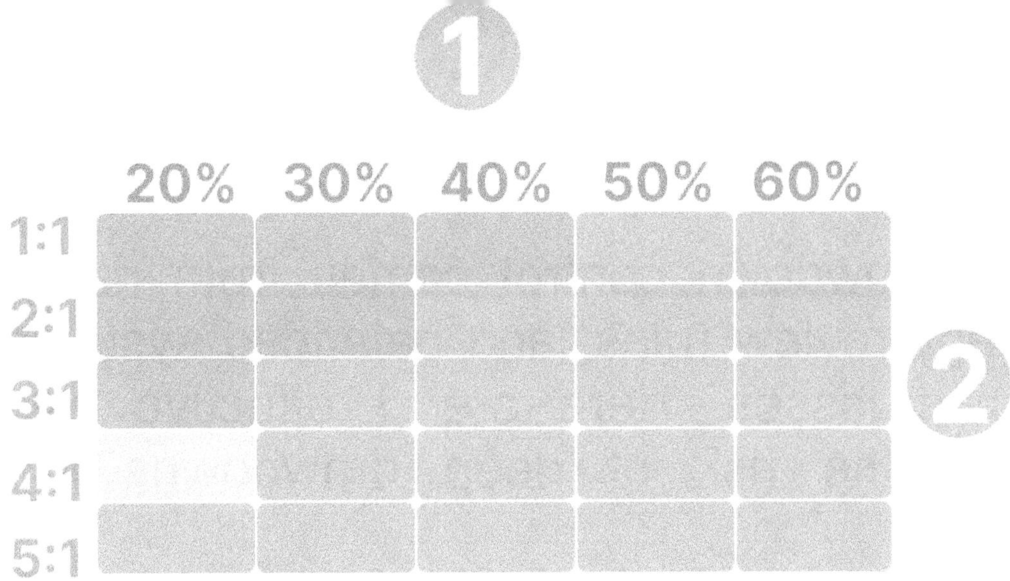

Set a personal max drawdown rule. For example, if your drawdown hits 15%, you pause trading. This gives you time to review your trades, re-center emotionally, and protect your capital from further damage.

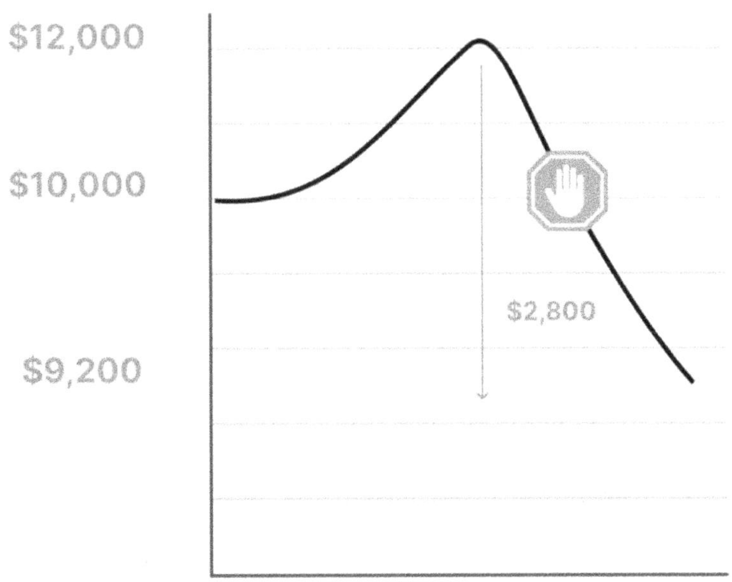

Avoiding Deep Drawdowns

Good drawdown control comes from risk limits, strategy review rules, and balanced systems, not chasing losses. Here are 3 effective ways to reduce the risk of deep drawdowns in your trading:

- Risk 1% per trade
- Balance risk/reward and win rate
- Set a max drawdown rule

To recover from drawdowns, avoid revenge trading. Don't rush to make back losses with oversized trades. Stay calm, reduce size, and focus on clean setups. The goal is stability, not urgency.

Sometimes, a drawdown tells you it's time to adapt, not quit. Consider small adjustments to your stop-loss placement, trade frequency, or filtering out low-quality setups if drawdowns repeat.

Use a journal to track how you felt during drawdowns. Include notes like:

- Mistakes you made
- When you exited early or held too long

This helps you separate emotional patterns from strategy flaws.

Spot the Risky Behavior

A trader with a $20,000 account is down 15% after a losing streak. They plan to double their next position size to "make it back faster." Increasing risk after losses is a common mistake. The smart move is to reduce risk, not amplify it. What's the best response to this situation?

- It's normal to take bigger risks after a losing streak
- This is emotional trading. They should pause and reassess before continuing
- Doubling the position is smart - it shows confidence in their system
- They should continue trading but risk 5% per trade to recover losses

Answer: This is emotional trading. They should pause and reassess before continuing. The trader is overreacting to a drawdown by increasing risk.

Instead, they should pause, review their strategy, and return with discipline. Chasing losses often leads to bigger drawdowns.

Now you know what drawdowns are, now to manage them, and how to bounce back wisely. Remember - losses don't destroy traders, poor risk habits do. Up next, we'll explore essential risk management formulas to calculate your maximum allowable loss thresholds.

Lesson 5: Risk Management Formulas

Get ready to explore risk management formulas

In this lesson, you'll explore powerful formulas that help traders decide how much to risk and how to protect their capital. We'll cover max loss thresholds, the Kelly Criterion, and more - step by step.

Risk formulas turn gut feeling into data. They show how much to risk per trade, how to avoid account blowups, and how to grow steadily. You'll learn how to apply them practically, even if you're not a math expert.

Let's start with the most basic: Maximum loss threshold. This tells you when to stop trading. Common rule: don't let your total loss exceed 20% of your account. If you hit that, pause and reassess your strategy.

Calculate your maximum loss threshold

You're using a 20% max loss threshold. Your account is $10,000. 20% of $10,000 = $2,000. Once that's lost, it's time to pause, reassess, and protect your capital. Based on your max loss limit, when should you stop trading?

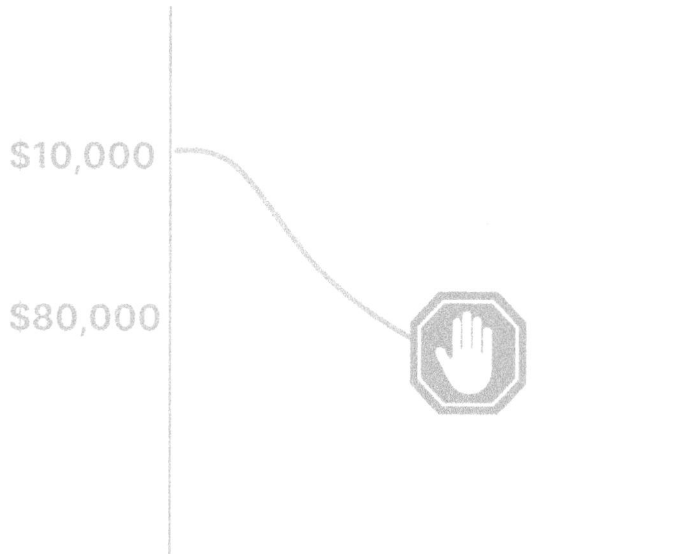

- After losing $1,000
- After losing $500
- After losing $5,000
- After losing $2,000

Answer: After losing $2,000. If your max loss threshold is 20% on a $10,000 account, you're allowed to lose up to $2,000. Stopping sooner is cautious, but not aligned with your plan. 20% of $10,000 equals $2,000. That's your maximum acceptable loss before stopping trading. This rule helps prevent emotional decisions and protects your capital from further drawdown.

Now let's explore the Kelly Criterion. It's a formula used to find the optimal percentage of capital to risk based on your win rate and risk-reward ratio.

The formula: **Kelly% = Win rate - (Loss rate / risk-reward ratio)**

For example, you have a 60% win rate and a 1.5 risk-reward ratio. Kelly% = 0.6 - (0.4 / 1.5) = 33%. That means risk 33% of capital if you want to maximize growth, BUT it assumes perfect conditions.

$$K\% = 0.6 - \left(\frac{0.4}{1.5}\right) = 33\%$$

Apply the Kelly criterion

Your win rate is 50%, and your risk-reward ratio is 2:1. What is your Kelly%?

- 5%
- 20%
- 25%
- 10%

Answer: K% = 0.5 - (0.5/2) = 0.25 = 25%

In real trading, traders rarely use the full Kelly value because it assumes perfect conditions and no emotional error. Instead, many traders use:

- 1/2 Kelly (half Kelly) - to reduce volatility and risk
- 1/4 Kelly (quarter Kelly) - for very conservative growth

That would be about 16.5% or 8,25% risk in our example.

Here's how to interpret Kelly:

- A higher Kelly percentage suggests your edge is strong and you can afford to risk more.

- A lower Kelly percentage means your edge is weaker, and risking too much could lead to large drawdowns.
- If Kelly = 0 or negative, your system likely has no edge, and you should avoid trading it until it's improved.

Smart traders combine formulas like Kelly, fixed percentage risk, and max loss thresholds into one solid plan.

- First, they backtest and calculate Kelly to estimate their edge.
- Then, they use a reduced risk (like 2%) to size trades consistently.
- They also set a personal max loss limit to pause and adjust if things go wrong.

This formula-driven approach builds confidence, protects capital, and ensures their system stays adaptable, not emotional.

Make a decision based on Kelly%

You've calculated a Kelly percentage of 6%. Your current strategy has a 50% win rate and a 1:2 risk-reward ratio. You're about to place your next trade. Kelly% gives an optimal ceiling, not a minimum. Smart traders often risk less to reduce volatility. What's the most appropriate action based on this Kelly percentage?

- Risk more than 6% since the edge is positive
- Avoid trading entirely - Kelly suggests there's no edge
- Risk less than 6% to stay conservative and manage drawdowns
- Risk the full 6% on every trade, no matter the contexts

Answer: Risk less than 6% to stay conservative and manage drawdowns. The Kelly percentage is the maximum, not the target. Going above it increases risk and volatility, and using all of it may be too aggressive in real markets. Most traders risk less than that to control volatility and avoid large swings.

Well done! You now understand how to apply formulas to manage risk wisely. Next, we'll shift to practical risk management, where you will apply everything you learned in a quiz!

QUIZ: Mastering Risk Management

1. Your account is $10,000, and you're testing a new strategy. What is the smartest amount to risk per trade?

A. $500 (5%)
B. $300 (3%)
C. $100 (1%)
D. $1,000 (10%)

2. You want to risk $200 on a trade and the ATR of the asset is $4. What is your maximum position size?

A. 25 shares
B. 50 shares
C. 80 shares
D. 40 shares

3. Your $20,000 account has dropped to $17,800 after 10 trades. You're risking 2% per trade. What should you do?

A. Keep going as planned
B. Increase the risk to 4% to recover
C. Add more trades to recover faster
D. Pause and review your strategy

4. Your Kelly% calculation says 4%. How much should you risk per trade?

A. 4% (full Kelly)
B. 0.5% (ultra conservative)
C. 2% (half Kelly)
D. 6% (above Kelly)

5. You win 35% of trades and use a 1:3 risk-reward ratio

A. Yes, the risk-reward ratio
B. compensates for the low win rate
C. Only with high leverage
D. No, 35% is too low to succeed
E. Only with time-based exits

6. You calculate your expected value to be -$10 per trade. What should you do?

A. Add more trades to smooth results
B. Increase position size

C. Ignore it - it's not reliable
D. Stop trading and revise your strategy

7. You have a $12,000 account and want to risk 2% on a trade. Entry

A. 100 shares
B. 120 shares
C. 240 shares
D. 60 shares

8. Your account is $10,000, and your max loss threshold is 20%. At what point should you stop trading and reassess?

A. After a $2,000 loss
B. After a $1,000 loss
C. After a $5,000 loss
D. After a $500 loss

9. You're trading with a $10,000 account and use a 1% risk per trade rule. What is the maximum loss you should allow on a single trade?

A. $100
B. $50

C. $200
D. $500

10. Which of the following best helps prevent large drawdowns?

A. Keeping risk per trade under 2%
B. Risking 5% per trade to grow faster
C. Using leverage during losing streaks
D. Doubling position size after each loss

Answer: 1. C; 2. B; 3. D; 4. C; 5. A; 6. D; 7. B; 8. A; 9. A; 10. A

Chapter 3: Additional Must-Know Trading Insights

Lesson 1: Understanding Slippage

Let's uncover the real cost of slippage

Slippage might look like a minor issue on the surface, but over time, it can chip away at your strategy's performance. In this lesson, you'll learn what causes slippage, how to measure it, and how to adapt your system to stay consistent.

Slippage is the difference between the price you expected and the price you actually get. It often occurs during fast price moves or in thin markets where order books lack depth. Even if unnoticed in the moment, slippage consistently impacts your long-term returns.

For example, imagine you plan to buy at $100, but get filled at $102. That $2 difference is slippage. If your stop-loss was set at $95, your intended risk was $5 - now it's $7. That reduces your expected reward-to-risk ratio. If instead, you were filled at $99, that's positive slippage. It increases your edge - but happens far less frequently.

There are three common types of slippage:

- Negative slippage means your fill is worse than expected.
- Positive slippage means you're filled better.
- Hidden slippage comes from repeated small differences - not always obvious - but consistent enough to reduce performance over time.

But what drives the slippage? In most cases its volatility and liquidity. During news events or market opens, price moves fast, and spreads widen - leading to worse fills. Illiquid assets or large order sizes may struggle to find matching trades, resulting in slippage across price levels.

So, the market orders are highly prone to slippage - they execute at the best available price, which might not be ideal. Limit orders give you control, but you risk missing the trade if price never reaches your level. Your choice depends on the strategy: speed vs. price precision.

Slippage tracking is a must for serious traders. Use this formula:

Actual Fill - Planned Entry = Slippage.

Then divide it by your planned risk to see how it affects your reward-to-risk. Over time, you'll discover how much of your edge is lost at execution.

Say you win 50% of trades with a 2:1 reward-to-risk - great in theory. But if every trade slips 1%, your real R:R may be closer to 1.6:1, and profitability drops fast. This is why many strategies that backtest well fail in real execution.

Many brokers don't show slippage clearly - so track it yourself. Logging wins and losses isn't enough; you need to understand what caused them. Add notes like "slippage," "partial fill," or "limit missed" in your journal.

If your platform lets you set a max deviation - called "slippage tolerance" - use it. It prevents trades from filling beyond your set limit (like 0.3%), which is especially useful during news, breakouts, or high-volume sessions.

Slippage tolerance helps block bad fills during fast moves - but it can also mean missed trades.

- Tighter filters = more control, fewer entries
- Looser filters = more fills, less precision

Every strategy has a tipping point - where too much slippage breaks your edge. Scalping needs tight precision. Swing trading allows a bit more room.

These steps help you include slippage into your strategy decisions:

- Log in fill price vs. planned price
- Measure slippage in % per trade
- Adjust your reward-to-risk model
- Refine entry method or order type

You're doing great building slippage awareness. But remember - slippage can't always be avoided. It can be managed. When backtesting, adjust your entry price 0.2-0.5% worse than ideal to simulate real-world conditions. If your strategy still performs well, it's more likely to hold up in live markets.

Now you know what slippage is, why it happens, and how to manage it. Let's sum up:

- You don't need to eliminate slippage - just plan for it.
- Design your entries, stops, and position sizes with real execution in mind.

In the next lesson, you'll dive deeper into the market and limit orders.

Lesson 2: Market Orders vs. Limit Orders

Choose the right order for your strategy

Great strategies need precise execution. In this lesson, you'll learn how market and limit orders impact your results - and how to choose the right one for your setup, risk control, and trade logic.

A market order executes immediately at the best available price. It's useful during breakouts or fast-moving setups where speed matters more than entry precision - but you risk slippage. If the price is moving quickly and you wait for confirmation or hesitate even a few seconds, the price can jump significantly. That means you may end up buying at a much worse price than you planned - reducing your reward-to-risk ratio.

A limit order sets the maximum price you're willing to pay (for a buy) or the minimum you're willing to accept (for a sell). It's ideal for planned entries - like pullbacks, reversals, or entries at support zones. Limit orders give you price control and keep your execution aligned with your strategy's logic. But they don't guarantee a fill - the market must reach your price for the order to execute.

Choosing the right order type isn't just about preference - it's about fit. Some strategies need speed, others need structure. If you treat all entries the same, you risk chasing bad prices or missing good ones. Your order logic should follow your setup, not override it.

What order fits this MSFT setup?

MSFT is pulling back toward $310. A bullish engulfing candle appears after the decline - signaling a potential reversal. You don't want to enter too early. Instead, you're waiting for price to break just above the confirmation candle before getting in. The setup requires confirmation and price control. What order type would best fit this trade?

- Limit order above confirmation candle
- Market order at candle close

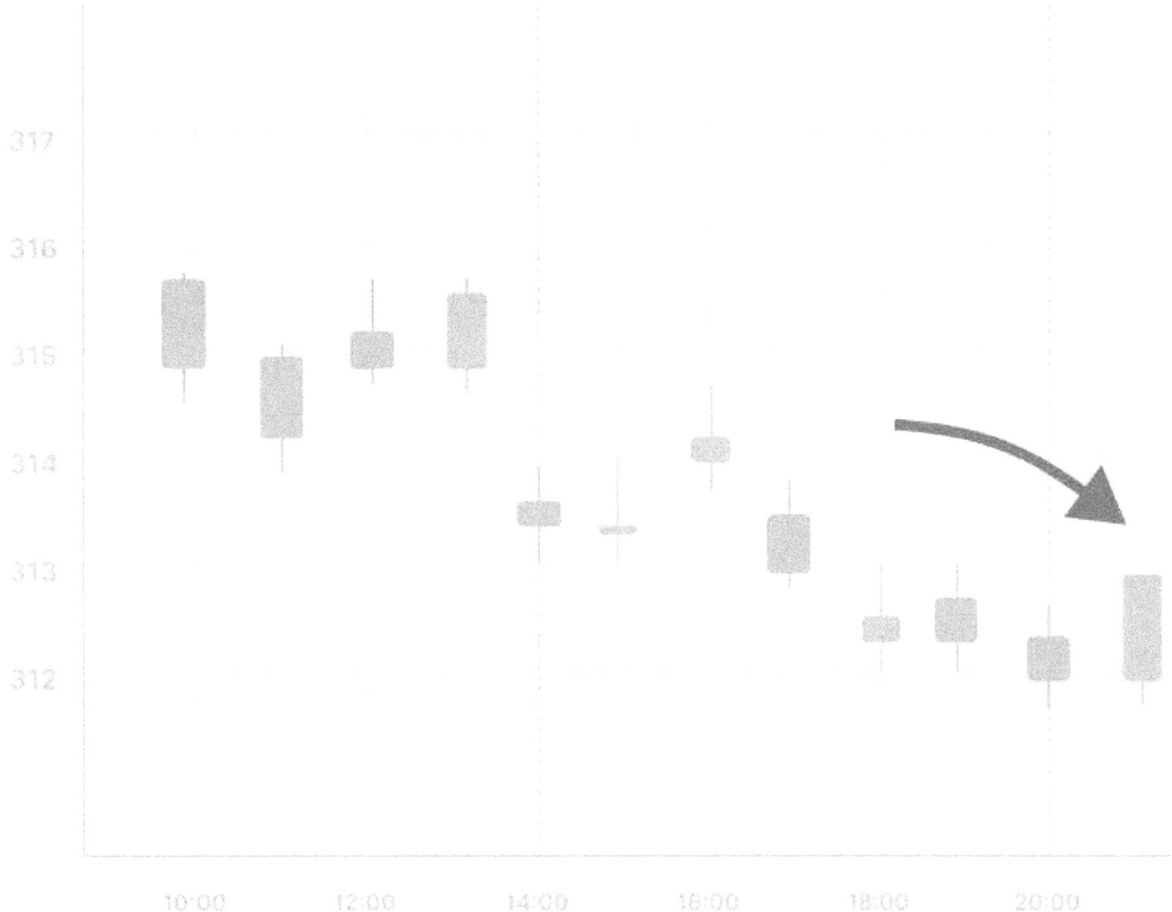

Answer: Limit order above confirmation candle. A market order might get you in too early - before the breakout confirms - or fill at a price that weakens your reward-to-risk setup. A limit order above the confirmation candle gives you both control and clarity. You're only entering if the market confirms your setup by pushing above the engulfing candle - showing real buying interest.

Great! Let's break down another example - this time, a breakout setup.

NVDA has been consolidating tightly near $980. You're watching for a breakout. Suddenly, a strong green candle closes clearly above the resistance zone - with increased volume. This is a classic breakout signal - but what matters most now is how you enter.

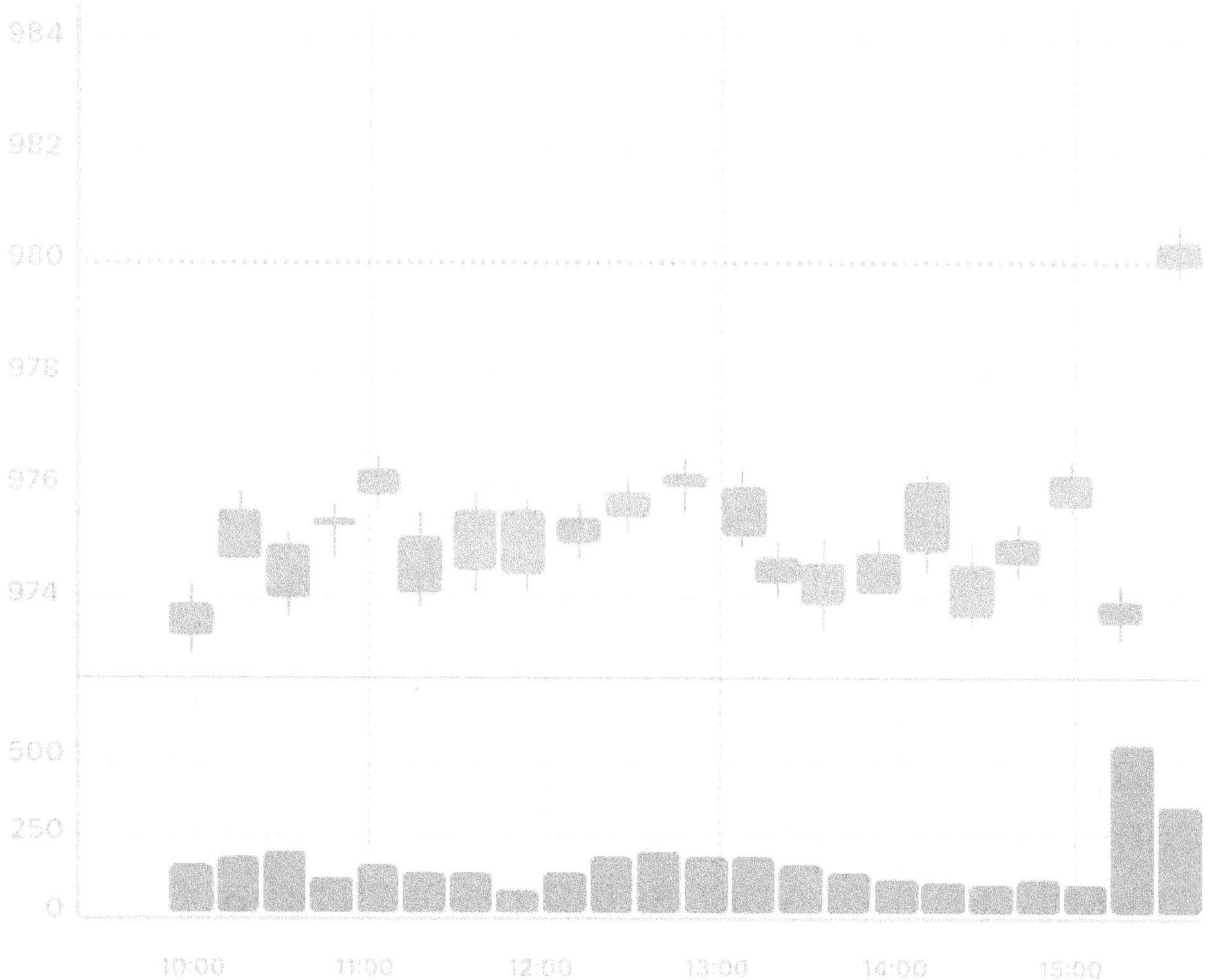

Best order type for this breakout?

NVDA just broke out of a consolidation range with a clean, high-volume green candle. Price is accelerating. You don't want to chase, but you also don't want to miss the move. Speed matters more than perfect price here. How do you enter?

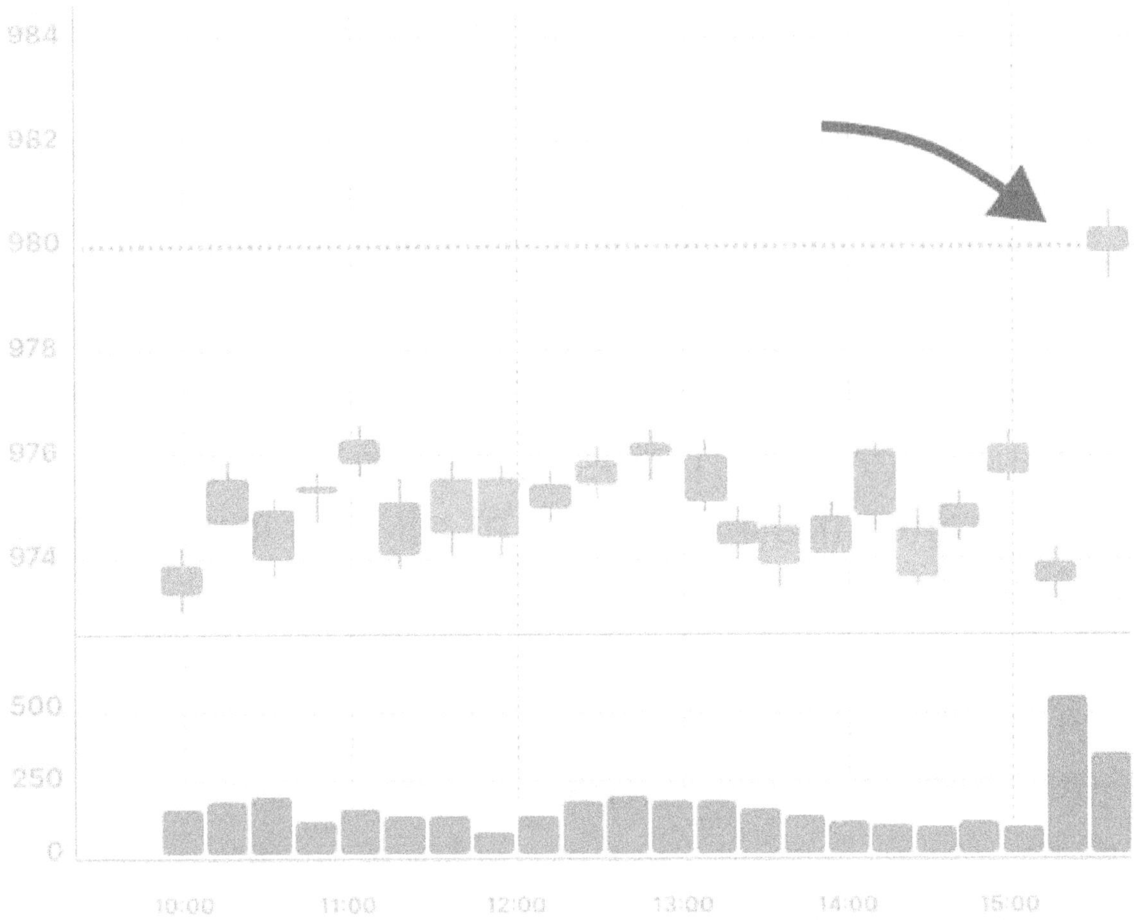

- Market order at candle close
- Limit order at breakout level

Answer: Market order at candle close. A limit order gives you price control, but in fast breakout setups, that control comes at a cost. When price breaks out strongly with momentum, it rarely pulls back right away. If you set a limit order near the breakout level, there's a high chance it won't get filled - and the move could run without you. You'd miss the opportunity because you were waiting for the perfect price instead of prioritizing entry during momentum. In a breakout, a market order helps you catch the momentum as it happens. You're prioritizing speed over precision. If you wait for price to come back to your level, you risk missing the entire move. In this case, a slightly worse entry is better than no entry at all - as long as your stop-loss and target are already planned.

As you can see, market orders fit momentum-based strategies. Use them when:

- Volume is strong
- A breakout candle closes above key resistance

Missing the move is riskier than entering with slight slippage. But remember - you sacrifice price control. The market might jump past your plan.

Limit orders on the other hand fit structure-based strategies. Use them when:

- You want to buy off support
- You're entering after a candle pattern confirmation
- You're trading pullbacks in a trend

Limit orders give you control - but they can leave you behind in fast markets.

Match the order to the setup

Match your order type to what the chart is actually telling you. The right order depends on the setup structure and execution logic.

- Market order - Clean structure + confirmation
- Limit order - Range-bound or unclear setup
- Wait or skip - Strong candle breakout

Answer:

- Market order - Strong candle breakout
- Limit order - Clean structure + confirmation
- Wait or skip - Range-bound or unclear setup

Great work. Both order types belong in your trading system. Smart traders don't commit to one - they adapt. It's not about always being fast or always being patient. It's about choosing what fits the current trade - and executing it without hesitation or fear.

Your logic should drive your execution style - not the other way around. Here is how to choose the right order type - step by step:

- Identify trade setup
- Check market condition
- Choose priority
- Select appropriate order type

Well done! You now know how to choose between market and limit orders based on structure, speed, and setup quality. Next, we'll look at how news events can disrupt execution - and how to protect your strategy when volatility surges.

Lesson 3: Improving Execution Speed

Let's upgrade your trade speed

Fast execution can make or break your strategy. In this lesson, you'll learn how to reduce slippage, choose the right tools, and build faster setups - so your trades hit when they're supposed to.

Even a great setup falls apart if the execution is late. When price is moving fast - like during breakouts - a delay of even 1-2 seconds can ruin your entry or shrink your reward-to-risk. Speed isn't just a bonus - it's part of your edge.

Execution speed is how quickly your trade reaches the market and gets filled. It depends on your broker, your internet, your platform, and the tools you use. VPS, hotkeys, templates - all of it matters.

Let's define the tools that boost your speed:

- Hotkeys let you place trades instantly - without opening menus or using your mouse. Perfect for breakout traders who need fast reaction.
- Pre-set Order Templates let you predefine your entry size, stop-loss, and target - no typing, no hesitation. Just one click and it's sent.
- VPS (Virtual Private Server) keeps your trading terminal close to the broker's servers - so your orders don't waste time traveling across the internet.
- DMA (Direct Market Access) gives you cleaner, faster fills by letting your order reach the market directly - without internal broker routing delays.

Market orders need speed the most. A late market entry on a breakout can mean entering after the move is over - or with too much slippage. Every second counts. Limit orders rely less on speed - but even they can lag if your platform is slow or you react late.

Execution tools should reduce delay - not rely on reactions. Improve your execution speed by using these 3 tools which boost real-time execution:

- Choose low-latency broker
- Trade on fast internet

- Use hotkeys for orders

Platforms with faster interfaces - fewer confirmation popups, clean one-click buttons - lead to better results. Slow UI leads to hesitation, re-checking, and worse fills. Test your tools before going live.

VPS and DMA can both reduce execution delay. VPS hosts your terminal closer to the broker's servers - so even during spikes, your order gets priority delivery. DMA cuts out extra routing, improving how clean and fast your fills are - especially in volatile markets.

Execution tools and their purposes

Each of the following tools speeds up a part of your execution flow:

- Order templates - Predefine size and stop-loss
- VPS - Faster connection to exchange
- Hotkeys - Send orders instantly

Execution strategy should be part of your system. Ask:

- Will you use manual or automated entries?
- Will you wait for confirmation or act preemptively?
- Is speed more important - or price precision?

Plan this before you click.

Strategy-ready execution checklist

The right tools + feedback loop = sharp execution. Use this checklist to improve your execution system:

- Choose a fast broker and platform
- Use hotkeys or order templates
- Test execution delay and refine
- Track fills and adjust plan

Well done! Now you understand how to speed up your trades - and how it helps your edge show up in real results. In the next lesson you will put your execution to the test with real market scenarios.

Lesson 4: Hands-on Execution Analysis

Let's break down your executions

You've come a long way. By now, you've learned how to build a setup, manage slippage, and execute with speed. This final lesson is about sharpening the last piece: reviewing how well you actually performed. Because great strategies don't just rely on entries - they rely on consistency. Let's see how clean your execution really is.

Execution analysis means comparing what you planned vs. what actually happened. Did your trade trigger fire too late? Did you exit early? This review improves your edge.
Common problems include:

- Late entry after confirmation
- Slippage on market order
- Missed limit fill
- Emotion-based early exit

Start by logging every trade. Include your entry/ exit price, method (market or limit), slippage, and the reason for the exit. Your journal is your source of truth. It shows what really happened, not just what you wanted to happen.

Good entry = timing + logic. Did your entry happen on your signal? Or did hesitation, platform delay, or self-doubt push you off-plan? Once you start spotting patterns in your delays, you can fix them.

What makes a quality entry?

A good entry is timely, planned, and risk-defined. Here are the 3 signs of a well-executed trade entry:

- Timed at confirmation
- Controlled risk in place
- Matches strategy setup

Review exits too. Ask yourself: was it based on plan, emotion, or reaction? Exiting too early kills your reward-to-risk. Too late, and the win might vanish. A strategy is only as good as its exits.

Track your metrics:

- Average slippage per trade
- Entry delay (in seconds or candles)
- How many exits matched your plan
- Win rate of market vs. limit orders

Let's say you planned to buy after a breakout. But you placed the order 3 candles later. Entry happened 1.2% worse than planned. That small delay shrank your reward-to-risk - and maybe turned a win into a break-even. Time matters.

You need data from both wins and losses to find patterns. Only full journaling shows whether your strategy actually works - or just worked once.

Use screenshots or screen recordings. What were you seeing when you clicked? Reviewing your actual actions reveals hesitation, lag, or confirmation bias. This is where you'll spot what needs work.

Metrics and their insights

Each execution stat tells you something. Use your stats to sharpen your strategy. Here are the metrics and their meanings:

- Exit timing - Aligned or emotional exit
- Entry delay - Hesitation or execution lag
- Slippage - Difference from planned fill

Once you've reviewed your trades, look for patterns:

- Are you always late on entries?
- Do your market orders slip too much?
- Are your exits mostly emotional?

Now, make one change to improve. That's how pros grow - one layer at a time.

Trade execution review steps

Reviewing leads to refining - and that sharpens your edge. Here are the steps to review your trade execution process:

- Log entry, exit, order type, and reasoning
- Compare execution with your plan
- Identify patterns or mistakes
- Adjust and test improvements

You did it - this was your final lesson in my book. You now know how to plan a setup, pick right order, reduce execution errors, and review your trades with precision. Most traders don't lose because of bad ideas - they lose because they don't track what actually happens. But you're different now. You're ready to trade like a strategist.

Afterword

As we bring this book to a close, I want to thank you—the reader—for taking this journey through the essential principles, analyses, and strategies that make up the foundation of smart trading. Whether you're just beginning or already deep in the markets, your commitment to learning is what separates you from the crowd.

Markets will always be unpredictable. Trends will rise and fall. Strategies will evolve. But one thing that never changes is the importance of knowledge, discipline, and emotional control. If there's a single idea I hope you take with you, it's this: success in trading is not a matter of luck—it's the result of preparation, patience, and persistence.

This book was written not just as a guide, but as a companion—a trusted reference you can return to whenever markets challenge your confidence or demand a fresh perspective. I wrote it with the lessons I've learned, the mistakes I've made, and the strategies that helped me push through.

No one can predict the market with certainty, but with the right tools and mindset, you can navigate it wisely. I encourage you to continue sharpening your skills, questioning your assumptions, and most importantly, never stop learning.

Thank you for allowing me to be a small part of your trading journey. Stay smart. Trade with purpose.

— Andy Hai Dinh
Author, Educator, Trader

OTHER BOOKS BY THIS AUTHOR

•Acrylic and Dipping Powder - Product Knowledge and Applications (Published: 2023)

•The Nail technician's Career Guide (Published: 2023)

•A Beginner's Guide to Trading - Stock and Forex Technical
Analysis (Published: 2025)

•WIN MORE, TRADE BETTER - A Practical Guide to Trading and Investing (Published: 2025)

•Modern Vietnamese Cuisine: The Best Home-Cooking Recipes (Published: 2025)

•Modern Vietnamese Cuisine 2: Family Meals For All Occasions (Published: 2025)

•Modern Vietnamese Cuisine 3: Delicious Street Food (Published 2025)

Watch for more at https://pensight.com/x/lona.

www.ingramcontent.com/pod-product-compliance
Lightning Source LLC
LaVergne TN
LVHW081958200926
848481LV00010B/2764